Zulu Newspaper Reader

Derek F. Gowlett

Dunwoody Press's Bantu Language Series

- Intermediate Swahili Newspaper Reader (1984)
  John B. K. Rutayuga, John D. Murphy
- Elementary Swahili Newspaper Reader (1985)
  Agnes Musyoki, John D. Murphy
- Lingala-English Dictionary (1995)
  Lumana Pashi, Alan Turnbull
- Sotho Newspaper Reader, Reference Grammar and
  Lexicon (1998)
  R. David Zorc, Paul Mokabe
- Kiswahili Language & Culture: A Textbook (1999)
  Lioba J. Moshi
- Lingala Parallel Texts (2002)
  David R. Woods
- Rwanda-Rundi Newspaper Reader (2002)
  Louise Nibagwire, R. David Zorc
- Xhosa Newspaper Reader and Lexicon (2002)
  Julian Lloyd, Linda Murphy-Marshall;
  R. David Zorc, Series Editor since 1998
- Shona Newspaper Reader and Reference Grammar (2003)
  Aquilina M. Mawadza
- Zulu Newspaper Reader (2004)
  Derek F. Gowlett; Edited by R. David Zorc

Zulu Newspaper Reader

Derek F. Gowlett

2004
Dunwoody Press

Zulu Newspaper Reader

All inquiries should be directed to:
Dunwoody Press
6564 Loisdale Ct., Suite 800
Springfield, VA 22150, USA

ISBN: 1-931546-01-0
Library of Congress Control Number: 2004100501
Printed and bound in the United States of America

Table of Contents

Foreword i

Acknowledgments iii

Preface v

Using the Vocabularies and Glossary vii

Introduction ix

Abbreviations x

Symbols xi

Sources of Readings xii

Resources xiii

Recommended Readings xvi

Grammar Sketch xix

1. Terminological Differences between This Reader and the Poulos-
Msimang Grammar xix

2. Analytical Differences between This Reader and the Poulos-
Msimang Grammar xix

2.1. The Noun Classes xix

2.2. Tenses xxi

2.3. Additional Material on Conjunctions xxii

3. Tables of Nominal Prefixes and Concords xliv

Frequency List l

Selections

Selection 1: Ama-Orange Citrus Cakes 3

Selection 2: Bayabonga kwaMpanza 8

Selection 3: Luphi Ubisi Noju? 12

Selection 4: Izinkanyezi 15

Selection 5: Abantu Manje Abavotele Imfundo 20

Selection 6: Sikhala Ngogesi Nje 29

Selection 7: Yekani Umuntu Omdala Aziphumulele Kade Ayidonsa
Indima 34

Selection 8: Ezomame kwelamaQiniso Eziphuma ebhodweni loMhleli
zishisa 37

Selection 9: Izingane Ezihlala Ezitaladini 45

Selection 10: Isandla esiqinile kubakhokhi-ntela 59

Selection 11: Ingaphinda izenzele kalula iKwaShaka kwiSoccer
Festival? 66

Selection 12: Inhlangano yomame esemkhankasweni wokusungula
izimboni ezincane zomphakathi...................................73

Selection 13: Abafundi batelekele ukungafiki kwezincwadi zokubhalela
ePM Burg..79

Selection 14: USebata – Indoda Engazenyezi Ngokungaboni
Kwayo!...88

Selection 15: Izinhlamvu zesitho sangasese ezincane..........................100

Selection 16: Uzethembe Uphephisa Abantu Ekufeni 103

Selection 17: Ifu elimnyama eMtata! 114

Selection 18: Olawula ukuhamba kwamabhanoyi.................................125

Selection 19: Abesimame abenza imisebenzi okwakungeyabesilisa....134

Selection 20: Zivikele Kumalaleveva 143

Selection 21: Ayazenzela amaphoyisa endaweni yaseNkume.............158

Selection 22: Ngifuna Usisi Oyisingili Nonomoya Ophansi................164

Selection 23: Amadoda Adlwengula Amanye..167

Selection 24: Ukuhlomula Komphakathi Wasemakhaya.....................187

Selection 25: Ukukhishwa kwezisu kuqubule izinkulumo eziningi 193

Selection 26: Kugwetshwa umabulalephindelela 202

Selection 27: Umvuzo wokusebenza ngokuzikhandla 210

Selection 28: Ngabe uxakwe yizikweleti? Likhona ikhambi. 223

Translations

Selection 1: Orange Citrus Cupcakes..233

Selection 2: The Mpanzas Are Grateful..233

Selection 3: Where Are the Milk and Honey?.......................................234

Selection 4: The Stars [Horoscope]...234

Selection 5: People Should Vote for Education Now............................234

Selection 6: We Need Electricity 236

Selection 7: Let the Old Man Enjoy His Retirement after His Long
Period of Labor...237

Selection 8: True Stories for Women from the Editor's Hot Pot..........237

Selection 9: Children Who Live on the Streets.....................................238

Selection 10: A Firm Hand with Taxpayers...241

Selection 11: Can the KwaShaka Soccer Team Do It Again at the
Soccer Festival?..242

Selection 12: Womens' Organization Involved in Setting up Small Community Industries 243

Selection 13: Student Boycott in Maritzburg over Failed Delivery of Stationery 244

Selection 14: Sebata: A Man Who Does Not Let His Blindness Get Him Down! 246

Selection 15: Small Testicles...248

Selection 16: Zethembe Is a Lifesaver 248

Selection 17: Dark Clouds over Umtata! 250

Selection 18: The Air-Traffic Controller 252

Selection 19: Women Who Do Jobs That Were for Men.....................254

Selection 20: Protect Yourself against Malaria 255

Selection 21: The Police Go Berserk in Nkume 258

Selection 22: Looking for a Single, Soft-Spoken Young Lady............260

Selection 23: Men Who Rape Men 260

Selection 24: Coexistence with a Rural Community............................264

Selection 25: Abortion: A Major Point of Debate 265

Selection 26: Serial Killer Sentenced...267

Selection 27: The Rewards of Hard Work 268

Selection 28: Are You Troubled by Debt? There Is a Solution 271

Glossary **273**

FOREWORD

This *Zulu Newspaper Reader* fills a gap in the literature of an otherwise well-documented and well-studied Southern (Nguni) Bantu language. While there are several textbooks, courses, grammars, and bilingual dictionaries available, the real-world forays of the Zulu press had escaped careful scrutiny. Derek Gowlett has, with thoroughness and dedication, here provided a marvelous survey of a wide variety of the genres and styles extant in the South African press.

Zulu enjoys a certain notoriety in that it is one of the very few African languages the name of which might be recognized by the average American. Perhaps only Swahili is more well known. Even so, of the hundreds of other African languages encompassing four distinct language families, both Swahili and Zulu are in the Bantu subfamily.

Zulu is not an easy language. It presents many challenges to both learners and teachers. The difficulties within the sound system (e.g., clicks) can be heard in the accompanying recording. Meanwhile, Zulu's grammatical complexities have met their match in Gowlett's clear, consistent, and insightful elucidation. He has patiently peeled each layer of each word, clarifying its root and complex affix structure. Drawing upon his lengthy experience as a teacher and lecturer in the Department of African Languages, University of Cape Town, he has made this book student-friendly throughout.

Rather than proceed on his own, the author has tied his grammatical explanations to the recently-published Poulos and Msimang *A Linguistic Analysis of Zulu* (1998), so that the student can have a singular point of reference. Nevertheless, in some instances, Gowlett has forged ahead by incorporating his insights into a few noun subclasses, a subsystem of perfect tense forms, and the complex usage of conjunctions, all of which are treated in the front matter.

We at the Language Research Center and Dunwoody Press are both pleased and grateful that Derek Gowlett took on this task and produced a study worthy of admiration and emulation.

R. David Zorc
Senior Linguist
McNeil Technologies, Inc.

i

Ackowledgments

The author would like to express his deepest gratitude to the following, whose invaluable assistance has made this book a reality:

Mrs. Dudu Luthuli — for her guidance on problematic matters of translation and idiom, and for her great patience during the recording of the readings, of which she is the sole voice.

Ms. Thandiwe Nxumalo — for her insightful responses to our questions about Zulu grammar.

Dr. R. David Zorc — for his multi-faceted wisdom, and above all for his constant encouragement which enabled me to complete this project in spite of health problems.

To all at McNeil Technologies, Inc. for their assistance, and especially their patience in putting up with my tardiness.

Derek F. Gowlett
Cape Town, South Africa
February 2004

PREFACE

This book provides an advanced beginner or intermediate student of Zulu with a variety of newspaper selections, complete with all grammatical and lexical information to decipher them. It is intended for self-study, but could as well be used in a classroom situation.

Altogether there are four sections:

Frontmatter: including the table of contents, acknowledgments, this preface, a list of abbreviations, the sources of the articles, and certain information regarding analytical and terminological differences found in the recommended Zulu grammar and this publication.

Part 1: the 28 reading selections
Part 2: English translations of the selections
Part 3: Zulu glossary (a composite for all the selections including grammatical information of every form or pattern that occurred).

The 28 articles have been taken from the following Zulu periodicals published between 1999 and 2001: *UMAFRIKA* and *Bona Zulu*. A full list of citations is presented later on in this introduction. The subject matter reflects a range and diversity of topics, genres and styles encountered in the Zulu press: a recipe (S1), an obituary (S2), political issues and opinions (S3, S5, S6, S7), education (S5, S13), a horoscope (S4), social issues – including Black and women's empowerment (S8, S9, S12, S14, S18, S19, S23, S25), justice and crime (S10, S21, S26), sports (S11), local news (S13), careers (S14, S16, S18, S27), medical or health issues (S15, S20, S25), natural disaster (S17), personal ad (S22), conservation and society (S24), farming (S27), and financial advice (S28).

Most articles are within the range of Level 2 of the ILR (Interagency Language Roundtable, formerly FSI or Foreign Service Institute) scale, except for selections S23, S25, S26, and S28, which go into L3. The articles start out short and simple, and get progressively more complex.

Every effort has been made to make this reader as self-contained as possible. All lexical and grammatical information is presented in the order of occurrence (i.e., not in alphabetical order). In each vocabulary, the immediately relevant (usually literal) translation of each full word (or phrase) is on the margin. Underneath this, indented, can be found additional information about root words or affixes. The student who wishes only basic information should stick to that presented on the left. Those who wish more details can use or study the indented material.

Once a word is introduced, it is not re-glossed unless it has a significant change in meaning. However, if a (root) word occurs in a derived form or compound, it will be re-glossed at its individual appearance. Each word and affix can be looked up in the overall Glossary, where one can review its meaning.

Part 2 consists of English translations for those who study without the benefit of a teacher. Since literal translations of words and phrases are supplied in the individual vocabularies, the translations tend to be free: the way similar concepts would be rendered in the American press. Every element of the original language is accounted for, but in terms of English order and idiom. For example, in S10, the phrase *izincwadi zokuthi baboshwe* 'warrants of arrest' literally means 'letters of that they should be arrested.' In S17 *Ukubakhona kukaMongameli* is rendered 'The president's presence' although it literally reads 'To be there of the president.' If one is jolted by such renditions, go back to the original to see how such a translation is justified.

Part 3 is a Zulu-English Glossary. It includes definitions for all the words, roots and affixes used in the readings, cross-referenced to the first reading in which each occurred. The presentation of entries in the form in which they actually occur is in line with the need for a beginner's dictionary, since a learner-friendly dictionary does not yet exist.

There are several problems in the use of existing Zulu dictionaries for the beginner. The main one is that an item may be 'buried' within a much larger word. For instance, the word *wayengakayidli* '(s)he had not yet eaten it' will not be found in any dictionary, and it takes considerable grammatical knowledge to know that the root of the word is -*dl*- 'eat,' which is where it should be looked up in a dictionary. In many instances the form of a word or root changes in particular environments, which again leads to problems in locating the item in a dictionary. Thus, for a beginner it would not be easy to recognize the noun *uju* 'honey' in *noju* 'and honey,' let alone *nasojwini* 'and in (or from) honey.' One would not know that the noun *izinti* 'sticks' should be looked up under *-thi* or *uthi* 'stick' depending upon the dictionary consulted, or that *-lunyw-* 'be bitten' derives from *-lum-* 'bite,' *-khishw-* 'be taken out' from *-khiph-* 'take out,' and *-vez-* 'bring out' from *-vel-* 'come from.'

Using the Vocabularies and Glossary

The vocabularies that appear at the end of each reading are given in the order in which they appear in the text, and not alphabetically (The Glossary, on the other hand, is given alphabetically.). In longer readings the text is divided into sections with each section preceded by a number, «x», that is repeated in the vocabulary to facilitate location of an item. Any item that has already appeared previously in a vocabulary is not repeated. If the reader is not familiar with a form in a particular reading, and cannot find it in the vocabulary concerned, then one should check the overall Glossary (p. 275).

Another reason that a particular item may not be found in a vocabulary, even though it has not appeared before, is that it should be easily deduced from previous knowledge. Thus, for example, if the noun **izicelo** 'requests' were to occur in a reading, it would not be given in the vocabulary if the singular, **isicelo**, has appeared previously, since a knowledge of the noun prefixes and noun class system should tell one unambiguously what the singular form would be. However, we have made sure that the singulars of *all* nouns are given in the Glossary.

The vocabularies and the overall Glossary have the following structure:

ABC def, ghi (jk) [L; M; N] {P} Sx, Sy

where **ABC** is the Zulu form (morpheme, word or phrase), which is given in alphabetical order. This is followed by 'def, ghi' which are one or more English glosses of the Zulu. Extra information about the meaning, such as the literal meaning of a phrase, or some explanation is sometimes given in (jk). Grammatical information, such as part of speech, noun class, singular or plural forms, tense, mood and aspect are given in [L; M; N]. Useful information such as the fact that a conjunction or auxiliary verb may require a particular mood to follow it is also given in the square brackets. Here too, information about the derivation of an item may be included, with more detail sometimes being given in the Glossary than in the individual vocabularies. The part of speech is not included for verbs, and is frequently omitted for phrases or clauses, which have been included in the vocabularies. In some cases, dialectal variants (preceded by 'var') are also included within the square brackets. {P} indicates that the Zulu words are adopted from a specific foreign language. The last item Sx, Sy appears only in the overall Glossary, and it indicates the particular reading(s) in which an item appears.

Examples of such entries are:

amantombazane young girl (up to puberty) [n. Cl. 6; sg **intombazane** Cl. 9] S08
ihhotela hotel [n. Cl. 5] {Eng or Afr *hotel*} S17
-khathaz-a tire; worry, disturb, bother, pester [v-caus; < **-khathal-** + **-Y-**; l + **Y** > **z**] S05

A comparison of the entries **amantombazane** and **ihhotela** reveals the convention that where the singular or plural of a noun is regularly predictable, it is not included in the grammatical information (cf. **ihhotela**). Thus, all Cl. 5 singulars would have plurals in Cl. 6, but Cl. 6 plurals are not necessarily in Cl. 5, but are fairly commonly in Cl. 9a, and by way of exception also Cl. 9 and Cl. 1. Where it is not predictable, for whatever reason, then the requisite information is provided. The entry for **-khathaz-a** exemplifies not only derivation from a simpler form, but one in which the derivation involves certain morphophonemic changes (loosely, changes in sound that result from the juxtaposition of two forms).

In the case of verbs and other predicative forms, if the mood or aspect is not stated, then it can be assumed that they are in the indicative mood, and are unspecified for aspect. Positive forms are unspecified, while negative ones are indicated by *neg*. Only in cases where there is some irregularity, or the structure is not transparent, do we give information about basic present tense forms. Other tenses, moods, and particular aspects are specified: e.g.

ngiyacela I am requesting [pres, disjoint] S08
angiboni I do not see [pres, neg] S14
ngangivame I was accustomed [rem past stative, conjunc] S18

The first two items are clearly in the present tense, positive and negative, respectively. The last item is in the remote past stative tense, conjunctive form.

INTRODUCTION

Zulu, known as *isiZulu* by its speakers, who call themselves *amaZulu* (sg. *umZulu*), is one of South Africa's eleven official languages. It is dominant in the province KwaZulu-Natal, where there are over 7,500,000 speakers of the language. Overall in South Africa, with over 10 million speakers, it is the language with the largest number of speakers, constituting 23.8% of the population.

It is to a large extent mutually understandable with Xhosa (found mainly in the Western Cape and Eastern Cape provinces), and Swati (found mainly in the Mpumalanga and Limpopo provinces – as well as being the major language of neighboring Swaziland), and with Zimbabwean Ndebele, which is one of the two major languages of that country. These four languages, with several minor dialects, make up the language cluster known as Nguni. The combined total of speakers of the Nguni languages in South Africa number some 20 million representing ±45% of the population.

Zulu is a member of the large Bantu family of ±600 languages which are spoken south of the so-called 'Bantu line,' which runs from Nigeria, across the Central African Republic, the Democratic Republic of Congo, Uganda and Kenya to southern Somalia. Not all languages spoken south of this line are Bantu or even related to Bantu. North of this line a large number of languages are spoken, which are related to Bantu, in many cases very distantly, and which, together with Bantu, constitute the Niger-Congo language family.

ABBREVIATIONS

1 p pl	1st person plural	exist cop	existential copulative
1 p sg	1st person singular	ext	extension
2 p pl	2nd person plural	fut	future
2 p sg	2nd person singular	hort	hortative
abs pron	absolute pronoun	ident cop	identificative copulative
adj	adjective		
adj conc	adjective concord	imper	imperative
adv	adverb	inch	inchoative
adv phr	adverb phrase	ind rel	indirect relative
adv rel	adverbial relationship	init vowel	initial vowel of noun prefix
Afr	(adopted from) Afrikaans	instr adv	instrumental adverb
agent adv	agentive adverb	intens	intensive (extension)
appl	applied or applicative (extension)	lit.	literally
		loc	locative
		loc cop	locational copulative
		loc n	locative noun
assoc	associative	loc pref	locative prefix
assoc adv	associative adverb	loc rel	locative relationship
assoc cop	associative copulative	n	noun
aux	auxiliary (verb)	narr	narrative aspect
bec	become	neg	negative
C	(a single) consonant (a single may be represented by two or three letters, e.g. mb, zw, tsh)	neut	neuter (extension)
		nom suff	nominalizing suffix
		NP	noun prefix
		obj	object
		obj rel	objectival relationship
caus	causative (extension)	OC	object concord
Cl.	Class	partic	participial aspect
compar	comparative	pass	passive (extension)
conc	concord	phr	phrase
conj	conjunction	P-M	Poulos-Msimang
cop	copulative	pos	position (deictic)
dem	demonstrative	poss	possessive
descr cop	descriptive copulative	poss conc	possessive concord
		poss pron	possessive pronoun
dimin	diminutive	pref	prefix
Eng	(adopted from) English	pres	present
		quant	quantitative
enum	enumerative	rec	recent
euph	euphemism	recip	reciprocal (extension)

x

rec past	recent past		transitive and intransitive
redup	reduplicative		
refl	reflexive	v.inch	inchoative verb
rel	relative; relationship	v-appl	verb with applied extension
rel conc	relative concord		
rel suff	relative suffix	v-caus	verb with causative extension
rem past	remote past		
SAJAL	South African Journal of African Languages	v-intens	verb with intensive extension
		vn	verbal noun
SC	subject concord	v-neut	verb with neuter extension
subjunc	subjunctive (mood)		
suff	suffix	v-pass	verb with passive extension
v	verb, verbal		
var	variant	v-recip	verb with reciprocal extension
VC	vowel + consonant		
v.i.	intransitive verb	v.t.	transitive verb
v.i. & t.	verb which is both	v.tt.	distransitive verb

SYMBOLS

<	derives from
>	produces, yields, results in
Ø-	a zero prefix, i.e. a theoretical prefix that has no actual realization in speech
VERB	represents any verb
-Y-	causative suffix which is apparent only in the effect it has on a preceding consonant, i.e.,

k + -Y- > s

l + -Y- > z

Sources of Readings

01   *Bona Zulu* February 1999, p.95

02   *UMAFRIKA* Vol. 86 #4976, March 9-13, 1999

03   *Bona Zulu* March 1999, p.8

04   *Bona Zulu* February 1999, p.122

05   *UMAFRIKA* Vol. 86 #4981, April 13-17, 1999

06   *UMAFRIKA* Vol. 86 #4979, March 30-April 3, 1999

07   *UMAFRIKA* Vol. 86 #4979, March 30-April 3, 1999

08   *UMAFRIKA* Vol. 86 #4982, April 20-24, 1999

09   *Bona Zulu* March 1999, p.24-25

10   *UMAFRIKA* Vol. 86 #4975 March 2-6, 1999, p.4

11   *UMAFRIKA* VOL. 86 #4981, April 13-17, 1999

12   *UMAFRIKA* Vol. 86 #4975 March 2-6,1999, p.5

13   *UMAFRIKA* Vol. 86 #4975 March 2-6, 1999, p. ??

14   *Bona Zulu* February 1999, p.16-17

15   *Bona Zulu* March 1999, p.115

16   *Bona Zulu* February 1999, p.56-57

17   *Bona Zulu* March 1999, p.20-21

18   *Bona Zulu* February 1999, p.74-75

19   *Bona Zulu* February 1999, p.62-63

20   *Bona Zulu* March 1999, pp 88-89

21   *UMAFRIKA* Vol. 86 #4979 March 30-April 3, 1999

22   *UMAFRIKA* Vol. 86 #4981 April 13-17, 1999

23   *Bona Zulu* July 1996, p.18-19

24   *Bona Zulu* March 1999, p.48-49

25   *Bona Zulu* February 1999, p.22-23

26   *UMAFRIKA* April 6-10, 1999, p.5

27   *Bona Zulu* March 1999, p.46-47

28   *Bona Zulu* February 1999, p.124

RESOURCES

The companion grammar to this reader is:

Poulos, George and Christian T. Msimang. 1998. *A Linguistic Analysis of Zulu*. Cape Town: Via Afrika.

Other useful linguistic and lexicographical sources for Zulu are:

Berglund, Axel-Ivar. 1989. *Zulu Thought Patterns and Symbolism*. Bloomington: Indiana University Press.

Beuchat, P-D. 1966. *The Verb in Zulu*. Johannesburg: Witwatersrand University Press.

Bosch, Sonja E. 1986. Subject agreement with denominal copulatives in Zulu. *SAJAL* 6: 57-61.

— 1988. Aspects of subject conjunction in Zulu. *SAJAL* 8: 70-74.

Canonici, Noverino N. 1990. Subclasses of Zulu nouns. *SAJAL* 10: 52-57.

— 1995. *Elements of Zulu Morpho-syntax*. Durban: Zulu Language and Literature, University of Natal, Durban. Revised ed.

Cope, Anthony T. 1963. Nomino-verbal constructions in Zulu. *African Language Studies* 4:69-97.

— 1984. *Zulu. ZULU A Comprehensive Course in the Zulu Language*. Durban: Department of Zulu Language and Literature, University of Natal, Durban. Revised ed.

Davey, A. S. 1984. Adjectives and Relatives in Zulu. *SAJAL* 4: 125-138.

De Kadt, Elizabeth. 1994. Towards a model for the study of politeness in Zulu. *SAJAL* 14: 103-112.

Dekker, A. M. and J. H. Ries 1958. *Woordeboek Afrikaans-Zoeloe Zoeloe-Afrikaans. Isichazimazwi IsiBhunu - IsiZulu IsiZulu-IsiBhunu*. N.p.: Afrikaanse Pers-Boekhandel.

Dent, George Robinson & C. L. S. Nyembezi. 1985. *Scholar's Zulu Dictionary*. Pietermaritzburg: Shuter and Shooter.

Doke, C. M. 1973. *Textbook of Zulu Grammar*. Cape Town: Longmans.

Doke, C. M. et al. 1990. *English-Zulu Zulu-English Dictionary*. Johannesburg: Witwatersrand University Press.

Engelbrecht, J. A. 1957. Notes on the Imperative in Zulu. *African Studies* 16: 102-107.

Fourie, D. J. 1990. Die hulpwerkwoord in Zulu. *SAJAL* 10: 118-124.

Goslin, B. du P. 1986. *Conversational Zulu for Beginners.* Pietermaritzburg: Shuter & Shooter.

Gowlett, Derek F. et al. 1999. *Speak Zulu with Us. Beginner's Course.* Cape Town: Mother Tongues Multimedia Development cc. [A multimedia course, with CD-ROM]

— 2001. *Speak Zulu with Us. Advanced Course.* Cape Town: Mother Tongues Multimedia Development cc. [CD-ROM course]

Hermanson, Eric A. and J. A. du Plessis 1997. The conceptual metaphor 'People are Animals' in Zulu. *SAJAL* 17: 49-56.

Hlongwane, J. B. 1995. Growth of the Zulu language and its structural changes. *SAJAL* 15: 60-64.

— 1996. The narrative tense in Zulu. *SAJAL* 16: 46-51.

Khumalo, J. S. M. 1989. 'Leftward ho!' in Zulu tonology. *SAJAL* 9: 59-69.

Koopman, A. 1979. Male and female names in Zulu. *African Studies* 38: 153-166.

— 1982. Zulu and English adoptives: Morphological and phonological interference. *SAJAL* 12 (Supp 1): 105-115.

— 1984. Zulu compound nouns — towards a preliminary analysis. *SAJAL* 4: 94-105.

Louw, J. A. 1954. The syntactical nature of the deficient verb and its complement in Zulu. *African Studies* 13: 147-152.

— 1962. On the segmental phonemes of Zulu. *Afrika und Übersee* 46: 43-92.

Malcolm, Daniel McK. and D. N. Bang. 1966. *A new Zulu manual.* Cape Town: Longmans.

Mathonsi, N. N. 1999. Semantic variation and change in the Greater Durban area. *SAJAL* 19: 227-236.

Mdontswa, Pumla V. and Mary C. Bill. 1996. The comparative function in Zulu. *SAJAL* 16: 18-25.

Moolman, M. M. K. 1984. The defective verbs -*thi* and -*sho* in Zulu. *SAJAL* Supp. 1: 135-144.

Munnik, Anne and Vivienne Roos 1996. *Learn Zulu Today.* Pietermaritzburg: Shuter & Shooter.

Mzolo, D. 1968. The Zulu noun with the initial vowel. *African Studies* 27: 195-210.

Naidoo, Shamile. 2001. Distinctive feature theory: from the linear to the nonlinear. An application to Isizulu. *SAJAL* 21: 80-88.

Nkabinde, A. C. 1982. *Isichazamazwi.* Pietermaritzburg: Shuter and Shooter. [monolingual dictionary]

Nyembezi, C. L. Sibusiso. 1990. *Learn Zulu*. Pietermaritzburg: Shuter and Shooter. Revised ed.

Posthumus, L. C. 1982. A review of the so-called -Be/-Ba Past tenses of Zulu. *SAJAL* 2: 94-108.

— 1990. Time reference in Zulu. *SAJAL* 10: 22-27.

— 1991. Past subjunctive or consecutive mood?. *SAJAL* 11: 91-95.

— 1993. The hierarchy of the essential verb categories in Zulu. *SAJAL* 13: 95-102.

Rycroft, David K. 1963. Tone in Zulu nouns. *African Language Studies* 4: 43-68.

Taljaard, P. C. & S. E. Bosch. 1993. *Handbook of IsiZulu*. Pretoria: Van Schaik. 2nd ed.

Van Rooyen, C. S. 1984. The reassessment of the moods in Zulu. *SAJAL* Supp. 1: 70-83.

Von Staden, P. M. S. 1973. The initial vowel of the noun in Zulu. *African Studies* 32: 163-181.

— 1982. Aspects of affective meaning in Zulu. *SAJAL* 2: 68-90.

Wilkes, Arnett. 1987. Comments on the function of the abbreviated absolute pronouns in Zulu grammar. *SAJAL* 7: 137-142.

— 1989. Unmarked possessives: Fact or fiction in Zulu grammar. *SAJAL* 9: 87-94.

— 1990. Comments on the so-called indefinite copulative relatives in Zulu. *SAJAL* 10: 34-39.

— 1991. Laying to rest certain myths concerning the subjunctive past tense in Zulu. *SAJAL* 11: 61-65.

Wilkes, Arnett & Nicholias Nkosi. 1966. *Teach yourself Zulu*. Chicago: NTC Publishing Group.

Ziervogel, D. et al. 1976. *A Handbook of the Zulu Language*. Pretoria: Van Schaik.

RECOMMENDED READINGS

We include the following historical and anthropological references, with two highly recommended items being given first:

E. A. Ritter. 1965. *Shaka Zulu.* London: Longman's Green.

Morris, Donald R. and Mangosuthu Chief Buthelezi 1998. *The Washing of the Spears: The Rise and Fall of the the Zulu Nation.* New York: Simon and Schuster.

Bryant, A. T. 1929. *Olden Times in Zululand and Natal; Containing Earlier Political History of the Eastern-Nguni Clans.* London: Longmans Green. [Facsimile reprint: 1965. Cape Town: Struik]

Cope, Nicholas. 1993. *To Bind the Nation: Solomon Ka Dinuzulu and Zulu Nationalism, 1913-1933.* Pieter-maritzburg: University of Natal Press.

Elliott, Aubrey. 1991. *Zulu: Heritage of a Nation.* Cape Town: Struik.

Guy, Jeff. 1982. *The Destruction of the Zulu Kingdom.* Johannesburg: Ravan Press.

Knight, Ian. 1994. *Zulu: The Study of a Nation Built on War.* New York: Sterling.

Krige, Eileen J. 1957. *The Social System of the Zulus.* Pieter-maritzburg: Shuter and Shooter. 3rd ed.

Lugg, H. C. *Life Under a Zulu Shield.* Pietermaritzburg: Shuter and Shooter.

Stanley, Diane & Peter Vennema. 1994. *Shaka: King of the Zulus.* New York: Mulberry Books.

Taylor, Stephen. 1994. *Shaka's Children: A History of the Zulu People.* London: Harper Collins.

The following are a few references for Zulu literature:

Canonici, N. N. 1993. *Izinganekwane — An Anthology of Zulu Folktales.* Durban: University of Natal, Durban.

—— 1998. Elements of Conflict and Protest in Zulu Literature. *SAJAL* 18: 57-64

Gérard, Albert S. 1971. *Four African literatures: Xhosa, Sotho, Zulu, Amharic.* Berkeley: University of California Press.

Gunner, Liz. 1991. *Musho! Zulu popular praises.* East Lansing: Michigan State University.

Kunene, Mazisi. 1970. *Zulu poems.*

— 1979. *Emperor Shaka the Great.* London: Heinemann.

Nxumalo, O. E. H. M. 1965. *Ikhwezi.* Cape Town: OUP.

Nyembezi, C. L. S. 1954. *Zulu proverbs.* Johannesburg: Witwatersrand University Press. US edition: 1990. Kinderhook, NY: International Book Distributors.]

— 1982. *Ubudoda abukhulelwa.* Pietermaritzburg: Shuter and Shooter. 3rd ed.

Rycroft, David K. and A. B. Ngcobo (eds.) 1988. *The praises of Dingana : Izibongo zikaDingana.* Durban: Killie Campbell Africana Library.

Stuart, James. 1968. *Izibongo: Zulu praise-poems.* Oxford University Press.

Vilakazi, B. Wallet. 1980. *Amal'ezulu.* Johannesburg: Witwatersradn University Press.

GRAMMAR SKETCH

1. Terminological Differences between This Reader and the Poulos-Msimang Grammar

There are certain cases where our grammatical analysis is the same as that of Poulos and Msimang (henceforth P-M), but where we use different terminology from them. The following is a list of these cases:

P-M	Gowlett
long form (of certain tenses)	disjoint (form)
short form (of certain tenses)	conjoint (form)
infinitive	verbal noun
past (tense)	remote past (tense)
past + present	remote past present
past + future	remote past future
past + potential	remote past pres, potential
perfect + present	past present
perfect + future	past future
principal	---[1]
consecutive/narrative	narrative
(aspect) prefix *-sa-*	persistive aspect prefix
(aspect) prefix *-se-*	exclusive aspect prefix
(aspect) prefix *-ka-*	negative exclusive aspect prefix
potential	present potential
identifying	identificative
demonstrative copulative	presentative demonstrative

2. Analytical Differences between This Reader and the Poulos-Msimang Grammar

2.1. The Noun Classes

Our treatment of the noun classes is essentially the same as that of Poulos-Msimang, but we recognize certain additional sub-classes. These are:

---

[1] We do not actually use the term 'principal' here, but in the absence of the indication of subjunctive mood or participial aspect, it can be assumed that the verb in question is in the default 'principal' form.

2.1.1. Cl. 3a: **uØ-**

P-M recognize a "variant form ***u-*** which is very rare in the grammar" and give the examples ***unyaka*** 'year' and ***unyezi*** 'moonlight.' Historically these derive from palatalization of ***mw*** in the original ****umwaka*** and ****umwezi***. In addition, our readings provide ***ugwayi*** 'tobacco.' There are also a number of adoptive nouns that also lack the **-m(u)-** element of the noun prefix, e.g.:

sg	*pl*
ufulawa flour	**ofulawa** (rare)
umese knife	**imimese/omese**
ugesi electricity	---

Since the singular forms take Cl. 3 concords in the speech of most people, it seems preferable to consider them as a sub-class of Cl. 3, i.e. Cl. 3a, just as Cl. 1a is a sub-class of Cl. 1a, with the noun prefix being ***uØ-***. If a person were to use Cl. 1 concords referring to these nouns, then obviously, they should be labeled as Cl. 1a, even if the plurals are in Cl. 4. Thus:

the color of the tobacco:	**umbala wogwayi** = Cl. 3a	
	umbala kagwayi = Cl. 1a	
the tobacco is not nice:	**ugwayi awumnandi** = Cl. 3a	
	ugwayi akamnandi = Cl. 1a	
if the knife is not blunt:	**uma umese ungebuthuntu** = Cl. 3a	
	uma umese engebuthuntu = Cl. 1a	

2.1.2. Cls. 9a & 10a: **iØ-** and **iziØ-**

The argument for the adoption of these sub-classes is set out by P-M on pp.61-62 of their grammar, though they do not mention two additional instances of Cl. 10a: nouns beginning with *l, h* and *hh*, at least in the speech of most speakers, e.g.:

sg	*pl*
ulwandle sea	**izilwandle**
uhabhu harp	**izihabhu**
uhhide convoy	**izihhide**

2.2. Tenses

2.2.1. Perfect Tense

P–M (p.266) give the following patterns for the formation of what they call the perfect tense:

pos. long form: **SC – R – ile**
short form: **SC – R – e**
neg.:   **(k)a – SC – R – anga**

In a footnote they say: "Later in this discussion it will be noted that -*ile* may be used in the negative, with inchoative roots to express a present *state*." What is *not* stated here is that the two different negative forms have different meanings, and thus should not be ascribed to the same tense, e.g.:

A: **isangoma asifanga** the diviner did not die
B: **isangoma asifile** the diviner is not dead
A: **idamu aligcwalanga** the dam did not fill up
B: **idamu aligcwele** the dam is not full
A: **asilalanga** we did not go to sleep
B: **asilele** we are not asleep

In our analysis, the A forms are labeled 'past tense,' while the B forms are named 'stative tense.'

With regard to inchoative verbs ending in **-al-, -alal-, -am-, -ath-** and **-as-**, they say: "What is even more peculiar is that while these roots accept the perfect marker **-e** and **-ile** in the normal way, in the stative form the **-a-** changes to **-e-** so that the endings become respectively; **-el-; -alel-; -em-; -eth-;** and **-es-**." Once again P-M, like most other Zulu grammarians, fail to note the fact that there is a clear difference between the various forms, e.g.:

A: **idamu ligcwalile** the dam filled up/became full
B: **idamu ligcwale kakhulu** the dam became very full
C: **idamu ligcwele** the dam is full
C: **idamu ligcwele kakhulu** the dam is very full
A: **uyifumbathile** (s)he took hold of it (in his/her fist)
B: **uyifumbathe ngamandla** (s)he took firm hold of it (in his/her fist)
C: **uyifumbethe** (s)he is holding it (in his/her fist)
C: **uyifumbethe ngamandla** (s)he is holding it firmly (in his/her fist)

A comparison of the above forms reveals that the A and B forms belong to one tense – the one we call 'past tense, disjoint and conjoint[2],' respectively – while the C forms belong to another – the one that we call 'stative,' in which there is no distinction between disjoint and conjoint forms.

2.2.2. Past + Perfect/Stative

In line with the discussion above, and our use of the term 'remote past' for P-M's 'past,' we make a distinction between a 'remote past past' and a 'remote past stative.'

2.2.3. Perfect + Perfect/Stative

In line with our analysis of the "perfect/stative," we label these 'past past' and 'past stative.'

2.2.4. Past Tense Negative

P-M say (p.271): "Two formatives are used to indicate the negative past tense and these are the very ones which are used for the negative perfect." In other words, there *is* no case for making a distinction between two different tenses. The fact of the matter is that in the positive, Zulu distinguishes a remote from a recent past, while in the negative, it does not. We thus label the negatives of both tenses as past negative.

2.3. Additional Material on Conjunctions

The use of conjunctions in Zulu can be fairly complex for non-native learners of the language. This is partially because of their varying significances and partially because of the way they affect (or do not affect) a following verb or copulative. Differences in the structure of Zulu and the structure of English can be problematic too. The conjunction may be embedded within a larger structure in which it is less easily recognizable. In some cases, there is an additional problem in that the conjunction is identical to another form from which it derives, which is *not* a conjunction. Cope (1984) is a useful reference for conjunctions.

---

[2] Loosely, *disjoint* forms are those where the verb is not syntactically closely linked to what follows, or where nothing follows, whereas *conjoint* forms are those in which the verb forms a syntactic unit with what follows.

2.3.1. ukuba

Context should normally sort out whether *ukuba* is being used as a copula, 'to become, to be,' or a conjunction, 'that.' As a copula, it has to be followed by: (a) an identificative copulative, which would generally begin with the prefixes *ng-* or *y-*; (b) by an associative form beginning with *na-*; or (c) by a locative.

2.3.1.1. ukuba in copulatives

(a) The following are examples of *ukuba* in identificative copulatives:

ngabhalisela ukufundela <u>ukuba</u> <u>ng</u>umlawuli[3] 'I registered to become a controller/marshal'

ibivame ukukhetha <u>ukuba</u> <u>ng</u>odokotela 'they used to choose to become doctors'

Okunye futhi okugcina ng<u>okuba</u> <u>yi</u>mbangela 'Something else that eventually became a cause (lit. that ended up by becoming …)'

wathola isitifiketi s<u>okuba</u> <u>yi</u>-switchboard operator '(s)he obtained a certificate to become a (lit. of to become it is a …) switchboard operator)'

kufanele uqale ng<u>okuba</u> <u>yi</u>lungu lombutho wamaphoyisa 'you must begin by becoming a member of the police force'

In the last three examples, *ukuba* is disguised by coalescence between the *a* of *nga-* or *sa-* and the first *u* of *ukuba*.

In some cases other identificative copulative prefixes may occur: **Uzimisele ng<u>okuba</u> <u>w</u>usizo** 'You should be prepared to be (of) assistance'

(b) The following are examples of *ukuba* in associative copulatives:

abenothando l<u>okuba</u> <u>ne</u>kwakhe elihle '(s)he should have a desire to have a beautiful home (lit. should be with a desire of becoming with a home …)'

---

[3] In the examples, we have underlined the particular structures under discussion, as also, where appropriate, the elements in the sentence that require their occurrence.

Ukuba nogazi 'having charm (lit. to become with charm)'

(c) The following are examples of **ukuba** in locative adverbs:

Ukubakhona kukaMongameli 'The presence (lit. the being there) of the president'

zama ukuba sendlini 'try to be indoors (lit. to be in the house)'

2.3.1.2. **ukuba** as a conjunction

As a conjunction, **ukuba** may be followed by various moods or aspects depending on the particular significance and context. In several contexts, the conjunctions **ukuba** and **ukuthi** may be used interchangeably. Note that *ukube* occurs as a dialectal variant to **ukuba** when it is used as a conjunction.

(a) + *subjunc:* "so that, in order that, that, to"
(in clauses of purpose or desire; often, though not necessarily, after verbs of desire, intention, instructing, requesting, ordering, preventing, causing …; or after nouns indicating purpose, intention, decision, etc. The conjunction **ukuthi** can replace **ukuba** in these environments.):

<u>babengafuni</u> ukuba <u>ashade</u> noSebata 'they did not want her to marry Sebata (lit. did not want that she should marry)'

<u>ngenhloso</u> yokuba <u>ngiyogeza</u> izithombe 'with the aim that I should go and have developed photos' [Note that *ngiyogeza* is in the subjunctive. It does not end in *-e* because this suffix is not found in andative constructions.]

wama kulendawo <u>ngenhloso</u> **yokuba** <u>ayothenga</u> **uhlobo lwensipho** 'he stopped at this place with the intention of going and buying a kind of soap'

<u>isinqumo</u> ukuba <u>aphumele</u> obala <u>atshele</u> amalunga 'the decision that they should come out into the open and tell their members' [Note that there are two verbs in the subjunctive here]

Ngenxa yokuthi abafundi abanawo umkhandlu obamele bonke <u>bebengathandi</u> ukuba <u>badalulwe</u> amagama abo 'Due to the fact that the pupils do not have a representative body, they did not want their names to be disclosed (lit. did not want that their names should be disclosed)'

ngokuzovimbela o-mosquito ukuba bangangeni 'to prevent the mosquitoes from entering'

ngokucela abafowethu nodade abayizintatheli ukuba bazihlwaye yonke indawo izindaba 'by asking my fellow reporters to disseminate this information widely'

uhlelo lokugwema ukuba izingane zihlale emigwaqweni 'a plan to prevent children from being on the streets'

owesilisa akadalelwanga ukuba kuyiwe naye ocansini 'a male was not created to be the passive partner in sex (purpose)'

Ukungatholakali kwezincwadi sekwenze ukuba abafundi bazidube izifundo 'Not receiving the books made the pupils boycott classes'

UZama uhlaba umkhosi kuzo zonke izingane ukuba ziphume ngobuningi bazo 'Zama sends out word to all children that they should come out in large numbers'

ngesikhathi emenywa ukuba ayodlulisela ulwazi ayeselutholile 'at the time he was invited to go and pass on the knowledge'

(b) + *subjunc:* 'to, for, from'
(in clauses of necessity or obligation; these are frequently introduced by the auxiliaries *-fanel-* and *-mel-* both meaning 'must, should, ought, have to,' *-ding-* 'require, need,' *-dingek-* 'be necessary, be required,' or by verbs such as *-phiq-/-phoq-* 'force, compel,' *-khubaz-* 'disable, hinder,' and *-nqand-* 'prevent, check'):

kufanele ukuba usebenzele phezu kwamaphutha 'you have to work to overcome the mistakes'

kuyaye kudingeke ukuba basebenzise indluzula 'it is sometimes necessary for them to use force (lit. that they should use force)'

Kwadingeka ukuba ngibancenge 'It was necessary for me to beg them'

nokuyisikhundla <u>esasidinga</u> ukuba <u>aphathe</u> abasebenzi abangu-150 'and which is a position which required him to manage 150 workers'

Lesihluku engangisithola ekhaya <u>sangiphiqa</u> ukuba <u>ngiyohlal'</u> **emigwaqweni** 'this cruelty which I experienced at home forced me to go and live on the streets'

lokho akuzange <u>kubakhubaze</u> **abahlengikazi ukuba** <u>benze</u> **umsebenzi wabo** 'this never prevented the nurses from doing their work'

ubiyelwe ngothango olusiza <u>ngokunqanda</u> **izinkomo ukuba** <u>zingangeni</u> **kuwo** 'it has been enclosed by a fence to prevent the cattle from entering it (lit. to check the cattle that they should not enter into it)'

Yinkantolo kuphela enegunya <u>lokukuphoqa</u> **ukuba** <u>ukhokhele</u> **isikweleti sakho.** 'It is only a court which has the power to compel you to repay your debt.'

(c) + *subjunc:* 'for, to'
(in clauses of desirability (often introduced by *kuhle* 'it would be good' or some other construction involving the adjective *-hle* 'good'), preference (often following a construction involving -*ngcono* 'better'), or importance (involving the verb *-balulek-* 'become important'):

Lesi yisikhathi <u>esihle</u> **sokuba** <u>uzihlelisise</u> **izinto zakho** 'This is a good time for you to arrange your affairs'

<u>kuhle</u> <u>zazi</u> **ukuthi ...** 'it would be good for them to know that ...'

Ngibona kungcono ukuba siqikelele ... 'I think it would be better to look out for ...'

nokuthi <u>kubaluleke</u> **kangakanani ukuba** <u>baye</u> **emtholampilo wokuhlelwa kwemindeni** 'and how important it is for them to go to a family planning clinic'

<u>kubalulekile</u> **ukuthi uma umuntu ohlala noma obevaka-shele endaweni eyingozi kakhulu ephethwe wumkhuhlane** <u>abonane</u> **nodokotela ngokushesha futhi** <u>amchazele</u> **ngendawo abekuyo** 'it is important that when a person who lives in or has visited a high

risk area has a cold, (s)he should immediately consult a doctor and explain to him or her where (s)he has been'

(d) + *subjunc:*
(after the phrase *phambi kokuba* 'before') [Note that *phambi kokuthi* occurs as an alternative to *phambi kokuba*]:

ngaphambi kokuba <u>zithathe</u> izinqumo 'before they take decisions'

ngaphambi kokuba <u>adlondlobale</u> 'before (s)he gets very excited'

(e) + *subjunc:*
(in clauses indicating repeated, common, usual, normal, actions; these are often preceded by the auxiliary verb *-vam-* 'do usually, often, ...' It would appear that the use of *ukuthi* is more common in such cases.)

<u>**Kuvame**</u> **ukuba <u>uzithole</u> zifihle ibhodlela le-glue ezingutsheni zabo** 'One usually finds them with a bottle of glue hidden in their clothes'

(f) + *subjunc:*
It is difficult to formulate a specific rule for the occurrence of the subjunctive in the following example:

Kwakungokokuqala ngqa ukuba uVuma <u>aboshwe</u>. 'It was the very first time that Vuma was arrested (lit. that Vuma should be arrested).'

(g) + *participial:*
(after the phrase *emva kokuba* 'after'):

emva kokuba umngani wakhe e<u>zibulale</u> ngokuziphonsa esitimeleni sihamba 'after his friend committed suicide by throwing him- or herself in front of a moving train'

Umngani wakhe wazibulala emva kokuba abazali bakhe <u>bengafunanga</u> ukulalela izinkinga zakhe. 'His friend committed suicide after his/her parents did not want to listen to his/her problems.'

Lesinambuzane singena kumuntu emva kokuba <u>elunywe</u> ngu-mosquito wesifazane onalesinambuzane. 'This parasite enters a human being after (s)he has been bitten by a female mosquito that is a carrier of the parasite.'

Emva kokuba eseyibonile impumelelo yesivuno sakhe sokuqala
'After he had seen the success of his first crop'

(h) + *indicative (principal or participial) or subjunctive:* 'if'
(in the clause expressing the condition in conditional sentences). The articles selected have only one instance of **ukuba** in a conditional sentence, and here the underlined verb or copulative is in the indicative mood.

Sengike ngadlula ebunzimeni obukhulu kanti ukuba angizange ngiye eThuthukani Outreach Centre ngabe sengifile manje. 'I once went through great hardship and if I had not gone to the Thuthukani Outreach Centre I would be dead by now.' [Note that while the auxiliary *angizange* is itself in the indicative mood, it requires a subjunctive complement – *ngiye*.]

Ngabe angikho kulelizinga engikulo manje ukuba akungenxa yabo 'I would not be at the level I am at now if it were not for them'

2.3.2. **nakuba** 'although, even though'

This conjunction is followed by the participial form of either the indicative or the potential moods, according to the meaning.

nakuba iSadtu yasho uqala u-1994 ... 'although Sadtu stated at the beginning of 1994 ...'

Nakuba singayazi ingqikithi yendaba ... 'although we don't know the essence of the matter ...'

Nakuba kungekho ukungabaza ... 'Although it is not to be wondered at (lit. although there is not wonder) ...'

Nakuba lesibalo singabukeka sisincane ... "Although this figure may be considered as low ..."

In the second and third examples above, the prefixes *-nga-* and *-nge-* are participial negative prefixes. In the last example, *-nga-* is a potential prefix, corresponding to the English *may*.

2.3.3. **ngokuba** 'that, so that'
+ *subjunctive:*
(in clauses expressing purpose, intention, desirability, ...)

babezimisele ngokuba **ngibe** ngudokotela 'they were determined that I should become a doctor'

sekuyisikhathi sokuba imithandazo nezifiso zakho ziphumelele ngokuba uthole umuntu ozothandana naye. 'it is now time for your prayers and desires to succeed so that you find a person to love.

2.3.4. ngoba 'because, seeing that, since'
+ principal or participial

In some cases there is a clear distinction in significance depending upon whether a principal or a participial form is used:

Abamqashanga, ngoba uyisoka lami 'They did not employ him, because he is my boyfriend' [principal]

Abamqashanga ngoba eyisoka lami, kodwa ngoba ejwayele lomsebenzi kahle 'They did not employ him because he is my boyfriend, but because he is thoroughly *au fait* with this work' [participial]

[Note that in the first example the boyfriend was *not* employed, whereas in the second, he *was*. The difference here is equivalent to the distinction between the conjoint and disjoint forms of the present and past tenses.]

Akezi emsebenzini, ngoba uyagula 'He doesn't come to work, because he is ill (in general).' [principal]

Akezanga emsebenzini ngoba egula. 'He didn't come to work because he was ill (at that time).' [participial]

[As emerges in the above two examples participial forms occurring in clauses introduced by *ngoba* frequently emphasize that the action or state is concurrent with that in the main clause of the sentence, while principal forms lack this emphasis.]

Further examples:

(a) Examples with a participial complement:

Kukhona abazali abadutshulwe yisoka lengane yabo ngoba nje bekhuza umsindo phakathi kwalezi zinthandani. 'There are parents who have been shot merely because they were trying to calm a quarrel between the lovers.'

(b) Examples with a principal complement:

Ngiyawazonda amaphoyisa ngoba ahlale esishaya 'I hate the police because they keep on hitting us' [Though **ahlale** seems to have the subjunctive structure, this is not the case. The suffix *-e* here is not the subjunctive suffix, but the suffix which is generally used to change an ordinary verb into an auxiliary verb. The fact that the SC is *a-* in place of *e-* indicates that this verb is principal and not participial.]

Asilali ebusuku ngoba bayasinukubeza ngesikhathi silele. 'We don't sleep at night because they sexually interfere with us while we are asleep.'

ngoba akukho okwenziwayo ukuthuthukisa isikole 'because there is nothing being done to uplift the school'

(c) Examples in which the complement could be either principal or participial depending on their semantic and or syntactic interpretation, and with tone possibly differ-entiating the two:

Ngibona kungcono ukuba siqikelele ukuphepha kwa-bantwana bethu ngoba kusazothatha isikhathi ukuba kutholakale indlela yokunqanda lo mkhuba. 'I'm of the opinion that it would be better for us to be careful about our children's safety because it will be some time yet before a way is found to prevent this practice."

Umshado wabo waqala ngokuba nezinkinga ngoba abazali bakhe babengafuni ukuba ashade noSebata. 'Their marriage started off with problems because her parents did not wan her to marry Sebata.'

babengahambisani nalokho ngoba babezimisele ngokuba ngibe ngudokotela 'they did not go along with that because they were determined that I should become a doctor'

2.3.5. **njengoba** 'because, seeing that, since'
+ *principal or participial*

(a) Examples with a participial complement:

uyaziqhenya ngomsebenzi wakhe njengoba eyi-Principal Telecommunications Operator ... 'he is proud of his work, since he is Principal Telecommunications Operator ...'

Njengoba kungenamigwaqo neziphawu zomgwaqo esibhakabhakeni, ... 'Since there are no roads or road signs in the sky, ...'

Njengoba iningi labantu abahlala kulezozindawo eziyingozi lingakunaki ukusebenzisa imithi yokuzivikela kulesifo, ... 'Since the majority of people who live in high risk areas take no notice about using preventatives against this disease, ...'

njengoba esezidayisela izinto azenzele zona ngezandla zakhe 'since she is already selling her own handicaft'

(b) Examples which, without tonal data, could be either principal or participial:

ukukhishwa kwezisu kwanda kakhulu njengoba sibhekene nesimo sokuntenga komnotho 'abortions are on the increase since we are facing volatility in the economy'

Njengoba kukhona obhekene nakho ngalesisikhathi, ... 'Seeing that there is something you are faced with at this time, ...'

2.3.6. **ukuthi** 'that'

2.3.6.1. non-influencing 'that'
(i.e. can be followed by the indicative, subjunctive, or potential depending on context: (after verbs of knowing, believing, thinking, feeling, seeing, hearing, saying, asking, promising, finding ...). The situation in Zulu here is similar to what holds in English):

indicative (in a statement of fact or belief):

Ngicabanga ukuthi uyazama 'I think that (s)he is trying'

subjunctive (in a statement of obligation, necessity, etc.):
Ngicabanga ukuthi azame 'I think that (s)he should try'

potential (in a statement of possibility, etc.):
Ngicabanga ukuthi <u>angazama</u> 'I think that (s)he might try'

[Note that in Zulu the conjunction *ukuthi* may not occur after the verb *-th-i* 'say.' In English 'that' is optional: he says (that) he is ill; in Zulu only *Uthi uyagula* is acceptable, with **Uthi ukuthi uyagula* being incorrect.

USebata uthi ukungaboni kwakhe ... 'Sebata said (that) his blindness ...

uthi angathokoza kakhulu 'he says (that) he would be very happy'

Uthe wethemba ukuthi ... 'He said (that) he hoped that ...

Other verbs of 'saying, stating, etc.' *are* followed by *ukuthi*:
noma ungqongqoshe <u>esho</u> <u>ukuthi</u> akakhishwe 'although the minister stated that (s)he should be removed'

iSadtu <u>yasho</u> uqala u-1994 <u>ukuthi</u> <u>akuphenywe</u> 'Sadtu said at the beginning of 1994 that it should be investigated']

Other examples

(a) + *indicative* (in a statement of fact or belief):

uzothola ukuthi abaholi be-ANC <u>balokhu</u> becela uxolo 'you will find that ANC leaders keep on asking for peace'

lokho akusho ukuthi uMnuz Mandela <u>ukhaliphe</u> kakhulu kunoMnuz Mbeki 'this does not mean to say (that) Mr. Mandela is cleverer than Mr. Mbeki'

Abanye bake bangibuze ukuthi <u>ngishefa</u> kanjani 'Others sometimes ask me how I shave (lit. that I shave how)'

Izingane kufanele zazi ukuthi abazali <u>bayathinteka</u> ezimpilweni zazo 'Children must know that their parents are affected by heir lives'

Apparent counter-examples may not actually conflict with the above statement:

Lapho ngathola ukuthi <u>kufe</u> abadayisa ezitaladini aba-yishumi
'There I found that ten street traders had died'

The verb *kufe* might be thought to be subjunctive, since it has the subjunctive, positive, structure SC-R-e. But in fact this is an instance of the past conjoint, which has the same pattern. On paper they appear identical but tone and stress would differentiate them in speech.

(b) + *potential* (in a statement of doubt, possibility, ...)

Kukhona nokwesabela ukuthi isifo se-AIDS <u>singanda</u> emajele.
'There is also a fear that the AIDS disease could increase in prisons.'

2.3.6.2. *influencing*
(in certain contexts, or with certain significances, *ukuthi* has a particular influence on the mood or aspect of any verb or copulative that follows it. For example, it may require a subjunctive or a participial.)

(a) + *subjunc:* 'so that, in order that, to'
(in clauses of purpose or desire; often, though not necessarily, after verbs of desire, intention, instructing, requesting, ordering, preventing, causing, ...; or after nouns indicating purpose, intention, decision, etc. The conjunction *ukuba* can replace *ukuthi* in these environments, as can *ukuze* in at least some cases.) In the following examples, both the word requiring a subjunctive as well as the subjunctive itself are underlined):

izincwadi zokuthi <u>baboshwe</u> 'warrants of arrest (lit. letters of that they should be arrested)'

izizathu <u>ezibangela</u> ukuthi <u>bangangeni</u> ezindlini zoku-fundela
'the reasons that caused them not to enter (lit that caused that they should not enter) the classrooms'

ngenxa yokuthi abafundi <u>bebefuna</u> i-stationery nokuthi <u>kusikwe</u> utshani 'due to the fact that the students wanted stationery and that the grass should be cut' [Note that after *yokuthi* the verb *bebefuna* is in the indicative, since it is a factual element, whereas after *nokuthi* the verb *kusikwe* is in the subjunctive following the verb of wanting – *fun-a*.]

isiboshwa sathi besitshelwe ngamaphoyisa ukuthi asithini 'the prisoner said that he had been told by the police what to say (lit. that let him say what)'

Ijaji lithe ngesigwebo elisikhiphile liqonde ukuthi lo mbulali ahlale impilo yakhe yonke ejele. 'The judge said that with the sentence she imposed, she intended that this killer should spend the rest of his life in jail.'

(b) + *subjunc:* 'that'
(in a statement of obligation, necessity; after verbs of ordering, instructing, requesting, ...; after forms indicating preference or importance):

babe sebecela ukuthi balungiselwe le nkinga 'they asked that they should have this problem resolved for them'

okubalulekile wukuthi bafunde 'what is important is that they should study'

(c) + *subjunc:*
(in clauses indicating repeated, common, usual, normal, actions; these are often preceded by the auxiliary verb *-vam-* 'do usually, often, ...' The conjunction *ukuba* may also be used in such cases.)

Kuvamile ukuthi izinhlamvu zangasese zingalingani 'It is normal for the testes not to be the same'

Akuvamile ukuthi lesifo usithole kulezozindawo 'It is not usual to find this disease in those places (lit it is not usual that this disease you should find it ...)'

(d) + *subjunc:*
(after the phrase *ngaphandle kokuthi* 'unless, without'):

bese sifika esivumelwaneni naye ngaphandle kokuthi kube khona olimalayo noma oboshwayo 'then we come to an agreement with him/her without there being anyone who gets hurt or arrested'

waphumelela ngaphandle kokuthi azame '(s)he succeeded without trying'

izilwanyazana zingenile ngaphandle kokuthi sizinake 'the insects got in without us noticing them'

xxxiv

(e) + *subjunc:*
(after the phrase ***esikhundleni sokuthi*** 'instead of, in place of, rather than'):

esikhundleni sokuthi <u>kube</u> yimina engihamba phambi kwakhe
'instead of it being me who walked ahead of him'

Sesifundise nalabo abelapha ngamakhambi ukuthi bangawatshala kanjani amakhambi esikhundleni sokuthi <u>basebenzise</u> izihlahla. 'We have also taught herbalists how to cultivate medicinal herbs rather than their using shrubs'

The following sentence has three occurrences of ***ukuthi***. Can you tell the mood of the following verb or copulative, and why that particular mood is found?

Sekuyisikhathi sokuthi umphakathi ubone ukuthi lokhu kuyinkinga ngempela nokuthi lobugebengu buyabu-thikameza ubudoda bomuntu wesilisa. 'It is now time that the community should see that this is indeed a problem and that this crime has a negative impact on male sexuality.'

(f) + *subjunc:*
(in a clause indicating expectation)
Lokhu kusiphatha kabi sinonkosikazi wami ngoba sicabanga ukuthi <u>singazitholi</u> izingane. 'This badly affects my wife and me because we think that we won't have children.'

abafana abancane abahlukunyezwe ngabanye abantu besilisa ngokocansi bangaba sethubeni lokuthi <u>babe</u> yizinkonkoni 'young boys who are sexually abused by older males have the chance that they will become homosexuals'

(g) + *subjunc:*
It is difficult to formulate a specific rule for the occurrence of the subjunctive in the following examples:

Isifo sikamalaleveva sidlange ezindaweni ezikhethekile ezweni ... Kuyenzeka futhi ukuthi <u>sitholakale</u> eNorth West nakwiMolopo ne-Orange River. 'The disease malaria is rife in particular areas of the country ... It also happens that it is found in the North West and around the Molopo and Orange Rivers.'

Njengoba KULULA ukuthi abantu baphathwe ngumalaleveva ... 'Since it is EASY for people to contract malaria ...'

2.3.7. **ngokuthi** 'that, in that'
non-influencing (see 2.3.6.1 above)

(a) + *indicative* (in a statement of fact or belief):

Ngifisa ukwazisa ezinye izingane ngokuthi kufanele zikhulume nabazali bazo 'I wish to let other children know that they should speak to their parents' [Although the English translation contains the auxiliary 'should,' the Zulu auxiliary *kufanele* itself is in the indicative mood, though itself governing a subjunctive complement.]

bafuna ukuchazeleka ngokuthi izimali ziyaphi 'they want to have an explanation about where the monies go (lit. that the monies go where)'

Babuye bagxeka ukukhuphuka kwemali yokufunda ngokuthi isuke ku-R50 ... iye ku-R120 'They again opposed the rise in tuition fees that went from R50 rands to R120'

(b) + *subjunctive* (in a statement of obligation, necessity, etc.):

Ngingakweluleka ngokuthi ubonane nodokotela ukuze akwazi ukuhlola. 'I can advise you that you should consult your doctor so that (s)he can (lit. (s)he should) examine you.'

(c) + *subjunctive* (in clauses indicating repeated, common, usual, normal, actions):
iziboshwa zivamise ukuzifikisa ezinye iziboshwa ngokuthi bazihlukumeze ngokocansi 'prisoners generally mistreat new prisoners in that they sexually assault them'

Kulesosimo kungenzeka noma yini, njengokuthi kube khona ogcina nokuphangalala 'In that situation anything is possible, such as someone ending up dying (lit. like that there should be one who end up dying)'

2.3.8. **ukuze** 'in order that'

2.3.8.1. + *subjunc:* 'so that, in order that, to, so ... should'
(in clauses of purpose or desire; often, though not necessarily after verbs of desire, intention, instructing, requesting, ordering, preventing, causing ...; or after nouns indicating purpose, intention,

decision, etc. The conjunctions **ukuba** and **ukuthi** can replace **ukuze** in these environments.):

Kufanele ugxile ezintweni okufanele uzenze neziyisibopho sakho ukuze <u>wazi</u> ukuthi uzobhekana nazo kanjani. 'You should be steadfast in things which you have to do and which are your obligation so that you (should) know how to face them.'

Ngingakweluleka ngokuthi ubonane nodokotela ukuze <u>akwazi</u> ukuhlola. 'I can advise you that you should consult your doctor so that (s)he can (lit. (s)he should) examine you.'

Inhloso yabo kwakungukuthi ngelinye ilanga ngiwu-thokozele lomkhuba ukuze <u>ngijwayele</u>! 'Their intention was that one day I would enjoy this practice so I should start getting used to it!'

2.3.9. **uma, ma** 'if, when' (the English translation will depend on context)
+ *participial (either indicative, or potential:* (in clauses expressing condition or simultaneity)

Othandweni uma <u>ungumuntu</u> ongayedwana … 'In love, if you are a person who is not alone …'

Uma <u>ufunda</u> amaphepha, <u>ulalela</u> nomsakazo … 'When you read the neswspapers, or listen to the radio …'

uma sivotela I-ANC <u>siyobe</u> sivotela imfundo enhle 'if we vote for the ANC, we shall be voting for good education'

uma <u>singayitholanga</u> imali eyanele 'if we haven't obtained enough money'

uma esekhaya 'when (s)he's at home'

uma lowomuntu <u>enodlame</u> 'if that person is violent'

uma kwenzeka 'if it happens' [indicative, participial]

uma kungenzeka 'if it were to happen' [participial potential]

noma baye kuzo <u>uma</u> izulu lingani kakhulu 'or they should go to them when it is not very rainy'

2.3.10. **noma** 'although, or, whether'
noma … noma 'whether … or'

2.3.10.1. *non-influencing* 'or, whether'
(i.e. can be followed by the indicative, subjunctive, potential, or participial depending on context: (after verbs of knowing, believing, thinking, feeling, seeing, hearing, saying, asking, promising, finding …).

(a) + *indicative principal (i.e. non-participial)* (in a statement of fact or belief):
[Including **noma … noma** 'whether … or']

Ukungazi ukuthi ipuleti lokudla uzolitholaphi noma <u>uzolalaphi</u> **ebusuku …** 'Not knowing where you will get a plate of food or where you will sleep at night …'

angazi noma <u>bayakhohlwa</u> **yini ukuthi angiboni emehlweni** 'I don't know whether or not they forget that I am blind'

kukhona isifo owake waba naso noma <u>yake</u> **yalimala leyonhlamvu** 'there is a disease which you once had or that testicle was once injured'

Uma usubhekene nabo noma <u>uxoxisana</u> **nabo** 'When you are face-to-face with them or are negotiating with them,'

(b) + *potential* (in a statement of doubt, possibility, …)

singaphuma nabo noma <u>singasala</u> **la siphekele abavakashi** 'we could go out with them or we could stay here and cook for the guests'

(c) + *subjunctive* (in a statement of obligation, necessity, …):

sekufanele ehlele phansi noma <u>asuke</u> **kuleso naleso sikhumulo sezindiza** '(s)he must land or take off from some or other airport'

zama ukumboza amafasitela … noma <u>uvale</u> **ebusuku** 'try to screen the windows … or close up at night'

noma <u>baye</u> **kuzo uma izulu lingani kakhulu** 'or they should go to them when it is not very rainy'

(d) + *subjunctive* (in a statement of frequency, the norm, expectation, …):

bavame ukusishaya noma **basethembise** ukusibulala 'they often hit us or they threaten to kill us'

Kungalesosikhathi lapho kuyaye kushise noma kutholakale imvula eningi kakhulu … 'It is at that time when it is normally hot or (when) there is a great deal of rain …'

2.3.10.2. *influencing:* 'although, even though, even if'
Occurs in the conjunctive phrase *yize noma* with the same meanings and behavior.
(With the above significances, *noma* is followed by the participial, either indicative or potential.)

noma uNgqongqoshe kaZwelonke … esho ukuthi … akakhishwe 'although the National Minister stated that he should be removed (from office)'

yize noma ngingenazo izibalo eziqondile 'even thoug I don't have accurate figures'

yize noma ekhona umuntu oshayela imoto yakhe 'even though there is somebody to drive his car'

Singeke sikhathale nakancane noma engafa khona manjalo. 'We would not care in the least, even if (s)he were to die right now.' [potential, participial]

2.3.11. **lapho** 'when'
+ *participial*

lapho sekuyisikhathi sesidlo sasemini … 'when it is lunch time …'

lapho eseneminyaka eyishumi … 'when (s)he was ten years old …'

2.3.12. **futhi** 'and, also, again, moreover, in addition'
non-influencing
(See 2.3.6.1 above):

(a) + *indicative* (in a statement of fact or belief):

kubaluleke kakhulu, futhi <u>kuyasiza</u>, uma ufuna ukuphepha kumalaleveva 'it is very important, and it is useful, if you want to escape malaria

UDkt Labuschagne uyavuma futhi <u>uyexwayisa</u> ngokuthi ... 'Dr. Labuschagne agrees and warns that ...'

Ngeke ngihlukane nokufunda futhi <u>akekho</u> oyonginqanda kulokho. 'I will never give up study and there is noboy who will turn me away from it.'

(b) + *indicative participial* (in a statement of doubt, possibility, ..., when there is another conjunction which requires a participial form, or where a concurrent action or state is indicated):

<u>Uma</u> ingekho nhlobo enye inhlamvu futhi i-scrotum <u>singenalutho</u> ... 'If it is completely absent and the scrotum is empty ...'

(c) + *potential* (in a statement of doubt, possibility, ...):

Kubukeka sengathi abantu besimame ... banawo umdlandla, futhi <u>bangaphumelela</u> ezimakethe zomsebenzi 'it seems as if women have the enthusiasm, and can succeed in the job market'

(d) + *subjunctive* (in a statement of obligation, necessity, importance, ...):

<u>kubalulekil</u>e ukuthi abonane nodokotela futhi <u>amchazele</u> ngendawo abekuyo 'it is important that (s)he see a doctor and explain to him/her where (s)he was been'

Amadoda angaboni emehlweni <u>kufanele</u> azethembe futhi <u>akhumbule</u> ukuthi ayafana namadoda abonayo. 'Blind men should have faith in themselves and remember that they are the same as other men.'

(e) + *subjunctive* (in a statement of frequency, repetition, the norm, expectation, ...):

Amadoda ayahlukunyezwa ngokocansi futhi <u>kulalwe</u> nawo nangaphandle kwasemajele. 'Men are sexually assaulted and people have sex with hem even outside prisons.'

ngoba bazibona sengathi banecala futhi bathole nokuphoxeka 'because they feel as if they are to blame and they experience being made fun of'

balahlekelwa yithemba, baphinde bazibone bengcolile futhi bangabinakho ukukhululeka 'they lose hope, and see themselves as dirty and are unable to relax'

2.3.13. **kodwa, kepha** 'but, however, yet'
non-influencing
(See 2.3.6.1 above):

(a) + *indicative* (in a statement of fact or belief):

Umphakathi uyakwamukela ukuthi abantu besifazane bayehlulwa ngamandla kodwa abantu besilisa bayakwazi ukuzivikela. 'People accept that women are overpowered, but that men are able to defend hemselves.'

Iningi lethu lavota okhethweni lonyaka ka 1994 kodwa uhulumeni akakazifezi izethembiso zakhe. 'The majority of us voted in the 1994 election, but the government has not yet carried out its promises.'

(b) + *indicative participial* (in a statement of fact or belief, where there is another conjunction which requires a participial form, or where a concurrent action or state is indicated):

bebengathandi ukuba badalulwe amagama abo ephepheni kodwa bezimisele ukuthi basho izizathu ... 'they were not happy to have their names divulged in the paper, (but) were prepared to state the reasons ...' [their being prepared to state the reason is concurrent with their unhappiness about having their names divulged]

(c) + *potential* (in a statement of doubt, possibility, ...):

Kubukeka sengathi abantu besimame ... banawo umdlandla, futhi bangaphumelela ezimakethe zomsebenzi 'it seems as if women have the enthusiasm, and can succeed in the job market'

indoda ngeke itholakale inecala lokudlwengula omunye umuntu wesilisa, kodwa ingabekwa icala lokuhluku-mezeka ngokocansi

'a man would never be found guilty of raping another male, but he could be charged with sexual assault'

(d) *subjunctive* (in a statement of obligation, necessity, importance, ...):

kubalulekile ukuthi abonane nodokotela futhi <u>amchazele</u> ngendawo abekuyo 'it is important that (s)he see a doctor and explain to him/her where (s)he was been'

Amadoda angaboni emehlweni <u>kufanele</u> azethembe futhi <u>akhumbule</u> ukuthi ayafana namadoda abonayo. 'Blind men should have faith in themselves and remember that they are the same as other men.'

(e) *subjunctive* (in a statement of frequency, repetition, the norm, expectation, ...):

Amadoda ayahlukunyezwa ngokocansi futhi <u>kulalwe</u> nawo nangaphandle kwasemajele. 'Men are sexually assaulted and people have sex with hem even outside prisons.'

ngoba bazibona sengathi banecala futhi <u>bathole</u> nokuphoxeka 'because they feel as if they are to blame and they experience being made fun of'

balahlekelwa yithemba, baphinde bazibone bengcolile futhi <u>bangabinakho</u> ukukhululeka 'they lose hope, and see themselves as dirty and are unable to relax'

2.3.14. **kanti** 'whereas, while, after all, but, and'
non-influencing (all examples in the selections are followed by the *indicative*)
(See 2.3.6.1 above):

+ *indicative* (in a statement of fact or belief):

UMnuz Mandela ufunde ngezomthetho, kanti uMnuz Mbeki ufunde ngezomnotho. 'Mr. Mandela studies Law, whereas Mr. Mbeki studied Economics.'

Zigqoka izingubo ezinukayo futhi ezingcolile, kanti nemizimba yazo <u>imbozwe</u> yizibazi zokulimala. 'They wear smelly and dirty clothes, while their bodies are covered with the scars of injuries.'

UThulani eneminyaka engu-10 kanti <u>walishiya</u> ikhaya lakhe eminyakeni emine eyedlule. 'Thulani is ten years old and he left his home four years ago.'

Njengamanje usaqhubeka nezifundo zakhe kanti <u>wenza</u> neziqu zikaBA kwezokuhatha. 'At present (s)he is continuing with his/her studies and is doing a BA degree in Management.'

2.3.15. **ngakho(ke)** 'therefore, thus, so'
non-influencing (all examples in the selections are followed by the *indicative*)
(See 2.3.6.1 above):

(a) + *indicative* (in a statement of fact or belief):

Ngakho-ke umnotho <u>yiwo</u> olawula izwe 'Thus it is economics that governs the country'

Akadli kahle; ngakhoke <u>wondile</u>. '(S)he doesn't eat properly; therefore she is thin.'

(b) + *potential* (in a statement of doubt, possibility, …):

Liyakhithika; ngakhoke ikhehla <u>lingefike</u> namhlanje. 'It is snowing; so the old may may not come today.'

Uyathetha; ngakhoke <u>angezwa</u> ukuthi labobantu bathini. '(S)he speaks Xhosa; therefore she might understand what those people are saying.'

(c) *subjunctive* (in a statement of obligation, necessity, importance, …):

Sengathi lingana; ngakhoke abantwana <u>bathathe</u> iza-mbulela. 'It looks as if it may rain; therefore the children should take umbrellas.'

2.3.16. **selokhu** 'ever since'
+ *participial*

Imi kanje imiklomelo selokhu <u>kuhoxe</u> inkampani yakwaWakefield JHI 'The prizes remained thus ever since the company of Wakefield JHI withdrew'

bafuna ukuchazeleka ngokuthi izimali ziyaphi ngoba selokhu <u>baqala</u> ukukhokha abakaze bababone onogada 'they want an explanation of where the monies go because ever since they started paying, they have never seen any guards' [At first glance it may seem that *baqala* is principal, since the SC would appear to be *ba-* instead of *be-*. However, the correct segmentation of this word is:

be- SC + -a- remote past prefix + qala

with the vowel of *be-* being elided before the vowel of the remote past prefix.]

2.3.17. **kade** 'until (in the distant future), and then, already, for a long time'
+ *participial* [the significances and syntax of this item are much more complex than indicated here, but since there is only

Kusazothatha iminyaka eminingi kade iNkatha yazi ukuthi iyini ipolitiki. 'It will still take many years until Inkatha knows what politics is.'

Yekani umuntu omdala aziphumulele kade ayidonsa ku le ndima yokuhola abantu. 'Let the old man just rest "since for a long time he carried the burden" of leading the people.'

3. Tables of Nominal Prefixes and Concords

Table 1. Noun Prefixes

Cl	1	2	3	4
1	um-	um-	umu-	
2	aba-	ab-	abe-	
1a	u-			
2a	o-		bo-	awo-
3	um-	um-	umu-	
3a	u-			
4	imi-	im-		
5	i-		ili-	
6	ama-		ame-	
7	isi-	is-		
8	izi-	iz-		
9	iN-			
9a	i-			
10	iziN-			
10a	izi-			

11	u-	ulw-	ulu-	
14	ubu-	ub-	u-	
15	uku-	ukw-/uk-		
16	pha-		phe-	
17	ku-			

Notes:
1. The prefixes in Column 1 may be taken as the basic, most widely found prefixes in each class, which is not to say that they are the original forms in all classes (e.g. in Cls. 5 and 11, the forms in Column 3 are the historical basis of the other forms).
2. In Cls. 9 and 10 the symbol *N* represents a homorganic nasal (written either *n* or *m*), i.e. a nasal that adapts to the following sound (as in the English *im_possible* and *i_mbalance* versus *in_tolerable* and *in_credible*).
3. The prefixes of certain classes have special forms that occur before vowels. These are found in Column 2. In Cl. 15, there are two variants: **ukw-** which occurs before the vowels *a, e* and *i:* and **uk-** which occurs before *o*.
4. The 3rd column represents a number of different rules:
(a) In Cls. 1 and 3, **umu-** is found before monosyllabic stems.
(b) In Cl. 2b, **bo-** occurs in vocatives (while **awo-** is a dialectal variant to the first form).
(c) In Cl. 2 **abe-** is restricted to a few nouns: *abeLungu* 'White people,' *abeSuthu* 'Sotho people' and *abeTshwana* 'Tswana people.'
(d) Likewise in Cl. 6 **ame-** is restricted to the nouns *amehlo* 'eyes' and *ameva* 'horns.' An alternative analysis is that in these cases the plural prefix **ama-** is superimposed onto the singular nouns *ihlo* and *iva*, respectively.
(e) In C. 16 **phe-** occurs in *phezulu* 'above, on top' and *phezolo* 'during the early evening, yesterday afternoon.' An alternative analysis is for these nouns to be analysed as the prefix **pha-** being superimposed on the nouns *izulu* and *izolo*.
(f) In Cls. 5 and 11 **ili-** (sometimes known as the full form of the prefix) is used by some speakers before monosyllabic stems, particularly in events where the initial vowel is not used.
(g) In Cl. 14 **u-** occurs only in *utshani* 'grass' and *utshwala* 'beer, alcohol.'

Table 2. Adjective Concords

Cl	NP	1	2
1	um(u)-	om-	omu-
2	aba-	aba-	
3	um(u)-	om-	omu-
4	imi-	emi-	
5	i(li)-	eli-	
6	ama-	ama-	
7	isi-	esi-	
8	izi-	eziN-	
9	iN-	eN-	
10	iziN-	eziN-	
11	u(lu)-	olu-	
14	ubu-	obu-	
15	uku-	uku-	
17	ku-	oku-	

Notes:
1. The adjective concords can be derived by prefixing **a-** to the noun prefix, and for this reason we have given the NP in the first column.
2. In Cls. 1 and 3 the variant **omu-** occurs before mono-syllabic stems.
3. In Cls. 5 and 11 the adjective concords derive from the 'full form' of the noun prefix.
4. It is clear that some confusion emerged between the concords of Cls. 8 and 10, and that over time the Cl. 8 form gave way to the Cl. 10 form. Note that in Xhosa there is still a distinction between the two classes, with Cl. 8 being *ezi-* and Cl. 10 *eziN-* as would be expected from the derivational rule.
5. Note that Cls. 1a, 2b, 3a, and 9a do not have their own concords, but use those of the classes without the *a* or *b*.
6. Cl. 16 does not have its own concords, but always useds those of Cl. 17.

Table 3. Relative Concords

Cl	SC	1	2	3
1	u-	o-	ow-	a-
2	ba-	aba-	ab-	
3	u-	o-	ow-	
4	i-	e-	ey-	
5	li-	eli-	el-	
6	a-	a-	Ø-	
7	si-	esi-	es-	
8	zi-	ezi-	ez-	
9	i-	e-	ey-	
10	zi-	ezi-	ez-	
11	lu-	olu-	olw-	ol-
14	bu-	obu-	ob-	
15	ku-	uku-	okw-	ok-
17	ku-	ku-	okw-	ok-

Notes:
1. The relative concords are said to derive by prefixing *a-* to the basic subject concord in each case, and for this reason we give this SC in the first column. This *a* then *coalesces* with the SC when it consists of a vowel, and *assimilates* to the vowel of the SC where the SC is of the structure CV. In this assimilation *a > e* before *i*: *a > a* before *a*: and *a > o* before *u*.
2. The concords used in direct and indirect relative constructions are the same, except in the case of Cl. 1, which has *a-* as indirect relative concord, and *o-* or *ow-* as direct relative concord.
3. Column 1 gives the concords found before consonants.
4. In Cls. 11, 15 and 17, the variants in Column 3 occur before the vowel *o*, while the variants in Column 2 occur before the vowels *a* and *e*.
5. In all other classes the variants in Column 2 occur before any vowel.

Table 4. Enumerative Concords

Cl	NP	Enum	
1	umu-	mu-	
2	aba-	ba-	
3	umu-	mu-	
4	imi-	mi-	
5	ili-	li-	
6	ama-	ma-	
7	isi-	si-	
8	izi-	zi-	
9	iN-	i-	yi-
10	iziN-	zi-	
11	ulu-	lu-	
14	ubu-	bu-	
15	uku-	ku-	
17	ku-	ku-	

Notes:
1. The enumerative concord resembles the full form of the noun prefix without the initial vowel, and in Cls. 9 and 10, without the homorganic nasal *N-*.
2. In Cl. 9 there is a dialectal variant *yi-*

Table 5. Possessive Concords

Cl	SC	1	2
1	u-	w-a-	ka-
2	ba-	b-a-	baka-
3	u-	w-a-	ka-
4	i-	y-a-	ka-
5	li-	l-a-	lika-
6	a-	Ø-a-	ka-
7	si-	s-a-	sika-
8	zi-	z-a-	zika-
9	i-	y-a-	ka-
10	zi-	z-a-	zika-
11	lu-	lw-a-	luka-
14	bu-	b-a-	buka-
15	ku-	kw-a-	kuka-
17	ku-	kw-a-	kuka-

Notes:
1. In most cases the structure of the possessive concord is *SC* + *-a-* or *SC* + *-ka-*. In the so-called nasal classes (Cls. 1, 3, 4, 6 and 9) however, instead of *SC* + *-ka-*, we find just *ka-*.
2. The forms in Column 2 occur only when the possessive stem is a noun of Cl. 1a. In all other cases one finds the form in Column 1.
3. In Cl. 6, there is one additional form, not given in the table, and that is **-wa-** which occurs in the formation of possessive pronouns. Thus: *amadodakazi ami* 'my daughters,' but *awami awabhemi* 'mine (daughters) don't smoke.'

Table 6. Quantitative Concords

	SC	*basic*	*+ -dwa*
Persons			
1st p.s.	**ngi-**	**ngo-**	**nge-**
pl.	**si-**	**so-**	
2nd p.s.	**u-**	**wo-**	**we-**
pl.	**ni-**	**no-**	
Classes			
1	**u-**	**wo-**	**ye-**
2	**ba-**	**bo-**	
3	**u-**	**wo-**	
4	**i-**	**yo-**	
5	**li-**	**lo-**	
6	**a-**	**o-**	
7	**si-**	**so-**	
8	**zi-**	**zo-**	
9	**i-**	**yo-**	
10	**zi-**	**zo-**	
11	**lu-**	**lo-**	
14	**bu-**	**bo-**	
15	**ku-**	**ko-**	
17	**ku-**	**ko-**	

Notes:
In most cases, the structure of the quantitative concord is *SC* + *-o-*. Only for the 1st and 2nd p. s. and Cl. 1 is the structure *SC* + *-e-* before the stem *-dwa* 'only, alone'

FREQUENCY LIST

We present as a learning tool the following word frequency count, imperfect as it may be, and based as it is on a limited corpus. It is obvious that a learner of a language should ideally first acquire the forms they are most likely to come across in speech or the written word.

The following words or stems are listed according to their frequency of occurrence in the reading selections. They may occur on their own as separate words, or may constitute part of a larger inflected form. Thus *umuntu* 'person' might occur on its own, or as part of the word *nakumuntu* 'and to the person.' In the case of verbal radicals, they always occur in combination with various prefixes or suffixes; e.g. *-cel-* 'request' is found in *abasicelanga* 'they did not request us.' They are presented from most frequently to least frequently occurring items. Since this word count is based on a limited corpus, certain words have a higher overall percentage than they would in a larger corpus. There is also the problem of a biased or skewed frequency endemic to any corpus which contains specialized materials; thus the word for 'rape' occurs very frequently, since there is a lengthy article on rape. Similarly the words for 'malaria,' 'disease,' and 'mosquito' occur often, since there is an article on malaria, and since the writer of that article uses the English-derived word for 'mosquito,' the Zulu equivalent never appears in our corpus. On the other hand certain words, such as *wena* 'you,' that would occur fairly frequently in conversation are not found in this list.

Altogether, the 28 selections contain a corpus of some 7,800 words (tokens) representing 4,659 lexical entries, i.e., many forms were used more than once. Those presented below are intentionally unglossed so as to provide a study tool, since their meanings and the articles in which they appeared can be found in the Glossary. In a few instances, however, the part of speech of an item is indicated. Note that most of the items towards the beginning of the list are grammatical forms, as is the case of just about any frequency study of any of the world's languages.

The student should be well aware of the problem of homographs which confront him or her. In working through these high-frequency words, it is important to understand that many of the grammatical forms, e.g., **ukuthi**, **ukuba**, or **lapho** can have different functions and/or different meanings.

We have excluded forms which occur in the names of companies, institutions and so on. Also excluded are purely foreign names, such as *u-Gladys*. Other foreign forms that have not been Zuluized are also excluded, e.g. *for*, *school*. In Zulu most personal given names derive from other forms, rather like the English *Faith*, *Hope* and *Charity*. Nevertheless, since the counting of such forms would overinflate the number of occurrences of the source, we have counted the name only once under that source. Thus the word *-and-* occurs 6 times in the readings. If one included the name *uSandile*, which occurs six times, this would double the count of *-and-* to 12. By counting *uSandile* only once, the total for *-and-* is a more realistic 7. A separate listing of Zulu given names and surnames is included, however, at the end of the general list.

Presentation of Frequency List
Forms given in **bold** capitals represent a base form (this may be an actual word, or a stem) from which all the indented items below them are derived, and the number appearing after them represents the sum of all these items. Likewise, a capitalized, bold item further indented, below an already indented item, derives from the one above it. Thus:

-M-	**50**
-m-	6
-MO	**20**
(i)simo	13
nesimo	3
esimweni	2
izimo	1
umumo	1
-mel-	6
ummeli	2
-mel-e [aux]	5
-melan-	2
-misel-	6
ngangizimisele	3

The verbal radical represented **-M-** occurs 50 times in the readings. Of these 50 times, it occurs as such in verbal forms 6 times. This verbal form functions as a base for a nominal stem -MO (note the use of small, bold capitals) that occurs 20 times in different words. These are the indented forms *(i)simo, nesimo, esimweni, izimo* and *umumo*. Note that *(i)simo* is not capitalized or bold, and thus the items *nesimo* and *esimweni* are not included within the count **13**, although they *are* derived from this noun. The basic verbal form *-m-* is also the base of the more complex verbal forms *-mel-*, *-melan-* and *-misel-*.

Though it would generally be argued that in the majority of cases, plural nouns derive from their singulars by substitution of prefix, we have taken an arbitrary decision to have singulars and plurals at the same level of indentation. Likewise many abstract nouns derive from concrete ones by a similar process (e.g. *ubuntu* 'humanity' < *umuntu* 'human being'), in order to simplify the table below, we present them at the same level of indentation. The parenthesis within *(i)simo* indicates that the prefix *i-* may or may not occur in the item. Similarly in the case of extended verbs, we indicate only their derivation from the basic verb stem, and not possible derivation of one extended verb from another. Thus in the following hypothetical entry, all the items below and to the right of *-bhal-* can be taken as derivations from *-bhal-*. Whether *-bhalisel-* is derived from *-bhalel-* or from *-bhalis-* is a moot point, as is the derivation of *-bhalelw-* (does it derive from *-bhalw-*, or *-bhalel-*, or in fact directly from *-bhal-*?).

-bhal-
-bhalel-
-bhalis-
-bhalisel-
-bhalw-
-bhalelw-

An entry *other* indicates all other words or forms not already identified that derive from the less indented item above it.

As can be seen from the example above, the word frequency count serves not only as a pointer to useful words in the language, but also gives an indication of a web of interrelated items. So, from the verb *-m-* 'stand, stop,' nouns meaning 'state, status, standing, situation' are derived, as is the extended verb *-mel-* 'stand for, represent,' which in turn gives the noun *ummeli* 'advocate, representative, lawyer,' and so on.

-TH-I	**272**		ekubeni	2
-THI	**69**		kwakungukuba	1
uthe	10		kuba	4
wathi	10		uba	1
uthi	7		eba	1
lithe	5		ziba	1
kwathi	5		zaziba	1
ethi	3		yiba	1
ngithi	3		(o)kwaba	4
bathi	4		waba	2
kuthi	3		baba	1
sengathi	8		saba	1
-thiw-	1		yaba	1
kuthiwa	3		bangaba	1
other	7		kube	13
UKUTHI	**203**		babe	6
(u)kuthi	123		abe	3
nokuthi	20		ibe	1
wukuthi	18		ube	3
ngokuthi	14		ngibe	1
sokuthi	10		ukungabi	1
yokuthi	6		angabi	2
lokuthi	6		bangabi	2
kokuthi	3		singabi	1
other	3		kungaba	4
-B-	**203**		okungaba	2

(We have divided forms derived from the verb -*b*- into 3 categories — copulatives, conjunctions, and auxiliaries — though they undoubtedly have the same historical origin. We have also given a full list of these forms since they are often difficult for learners.)

			Conjunctives	
			-B-	**117**
			ukuba	28
			ngokuba	1
			ngoba	43
			njengoba	17
			kangangoba	2
			kokuba	9
			sokuba	4
			yokuba	2
Copulatives			nakuba	4
-B-	**79**		ukube	1
ukuba	11		ngabe	6
sokuba	2			
ngokuba	5			

Auxiliaries

(We have only counted forms which function as independent auxiliaries, and not those that have been reduced to mere prefixes.)

-B-	**7**
kube	2
ube	2
bebe	1
babe	1
wabe	1
-NTU	**155**
(A)BANTU	**121**
(a)bantu	72
labantu	11
labobantu	7
walabobantu	3
nabantu	9
kubantu	5
sabantu	5
kwabantu	4
ngabantu	4
other	1
(U)MUNTU	**34**
(u)muntu	22
ngumuntu	8
kumuntu	4
-ENZ-	**113**
-enz-	54
(u)kwenza	6
awenzayo	4
(i)senzo	3
ngezenzo	3
-enzek-	17
ukwenzeka	1
kwenzeka	3
kungenzeka	6
kuyenzeka	4
-enziw-	9
-enzel-	1
-enzelw-	1

other	1
-SEBENZ-	**107**
-sebenz-	24
ukusebenza	4
(u)msebenzi	24
lomsebenzi	13
(i)misebenzi	6
nemisebenzi	3
abasebenzi	1
-SEBENZIS-	**19**
ukusebenzisa	5
basebenzise	3
-sebenzel-	4
-sebenzisel-	1
-setshenzisw-	7
-setshenziselw-	1
-KHULU	**100**
(cf. *-khul-*)	
kakhulu	61
ikakhulu	4
ikakhulukazi	4
omkhulu	6
umkhulu	2
(e)sikhulu	5
elikhulu	4
enkulu	3
yinkulu	1
uNkulunkulu	2
(a)makhulu	3
okukhulu	2
ezinkulu	1
other	2
-NYE	**98**
abanye	9
other	5
omunye	11
amanye	8
enye	7
other	4
ezinye	6
kwezinye	5
nezinye	3

other	2		-DAWO	65
elinye	4		indawo	6
okunye	3		endaweni	8
ESINYE	4		kulendawo	4
ngesinye	3		kuleyondawo	3
other	1		izindawo	18
kanye	15		ezindaweni	13
other	7		kulezozindawo	12
-THOL-	74		*other*	1
-thol-	45		KHO	65
(u)kuthola	4		kho	19
bathola	3		ngakho(-ke)	6
bathole	3		akukho	5
-tholakal-	10		khona	26
kutholakale	3		kukhona	9
-tholel-	3		LE	63
-tholan-	2		-Z-E [aux]	63
-tholis-	1		kuze	11
UMA	71		ukuze	27
-FUND-	70		-z-ang-e	8
-fund-	8		akuzange	3
ukufunda	6		*other*	14
ufunde	3		-BON-	59
izifundo	16		-bon-	32
ezifundweni	1		ubona	3
imfundo	10		ukubona	3
umfundi	4		ukungaboni	6
abafundi	12		umbono	1
-fundis-	6		-bonakal-	4
other	1		-bonan-	3
-fundel-	3		-bonel-	3
BO	67		isibonelo	1
bona	3		izibonelo	1
nabo	12		-bonis-	1
yabo	13		-bonisan-	1
zabo	7		-KHATHI	59
wabo	5		isikhathi	12
abo	5		ngesikhathi	26
kwabo	5		ngalesosikhathi	6
labo	3		esikhathini	4
abafowabo	3		sekuyisikhathi	4
other	11		kwesikhathi	4

izikhathi	2	ummeli	2
(i)nkathi	1	-mel-e [aux]	5
-AZ-I	**57**	-melan-	2
-az-i	34	-misel-	9
ukwazi	2	ngangizimisele	3
zazi	3	**NOMA**	**53**
ulwazi	2	noma	51
nolwazi	4	kunoma	2
other	2	**-SHO**	**50**
-aziw-	5	-sh-o	11
-azis-	3	kusho	27
-azisw-	1	okusho	2
-azek-	1	ngisho	3
-THO	**56**	ukusho	1
into	7	ngokusho	4
yinto	2	-shiw-o	1
kuyinto	6	*other*	1
other	1	**-NINGI**	**47**
other	1	-ningi	5
(i)zinto	20	(e)ziningi	6
ezintweni	4	(a)baningi	7
other	2	eningi	3
lutho	13	*other*	5
-KHE	**55**	iningi	18
zakhe	12	ubuningi	1
wakhe	10	kaningi	1
yakhe	8	-ningana	1
kwakhe	8	**-KATHI**	**45**
lakhe	7	phakathi	7
bakhe	5	ngaphakathi	7
sakhe	3	(u)mphakathi	16
other	2	emphakathini	3
LO	**53**	nomphakathi	5
-M-	**53**	omphakathi	3
-m-	6	*other*	4
-MO	**20**	**KODWA**	**45**
(i)simo	13	(see also -*dwa*)	
nesimo	3	**NJENGA-**	**44**
esimweni	2	njenga-	27
izimo	1	njengoba	17
umumo	1	**-F-**	**43**
-mel-	6	-f-a	7

ukufa	1	**ISIMAME**	**35**
ekufeni	2	besimame	10
-fel-	1	abesimame	11
-fo	5	labesimame	3
(i)sifo	5	*other*	7
lesifo	11	wesimame	3
lesisifo	6	owesimame	1
yilesifo	2	omame	3
(i)zifo	3	**-QAL-**	**38**
-FANEL-	**40**	-qal-	18
-fanel-	9	ukuqala	7
kufanele	23	okokuqala	3
okufanele	5	wokuqala	6
efanele	3	kuqala	1
-BULAL-	**39**	(i)ziqalo	1
-bulal-	16	-qalw-	2
ukuzibulala	13	**-SIZ-**	**37**
-bulalan-	1	-siz-	17
-bulalw-	1	(u)kusiza	7
-bulaw-	4	(u)sizo	8
umbulali	4	(u)msizi	3
-PHIL-	**39**	-sizakal-	1
-phil-	7	-sizw-	1
-philis-	2	**-SUK-**	**37**
-PHILISW-	**1**	-suk-	13
uPhilisiwe	1	basuke	3
impilo	12	abasuke	10
lempilo	4	kusukela	5
ngempilo	2	osuke	4
empilweni	2	-sus-	2
other	5	**-THATH-**	**37**
izimpilo	3	-thath-	21
ezimpilweni	1	ukuthatha	5
-FUN-	**38**	-thathw-	5
-fun-	19	-thathis-	3
befuna	11	-thathel-	1
bafuna	4	izintatheli	1
ufuna	3	-thathelan-	1
-funel-	1	**-HAMB-**	**35**
KANTI	**38**	-hamb-	12
-MAME	**38**	ukuhamba	3
(see also *-mama*)		ngokuhamba	3

other	3		(i)miphumela	4
uhambo	1		-phumelel-	7
-hambel-	3		(i)mpumelelo	7
-hanjelw-	1	**MI**		**33**
-hambisan-	9		wami	9
-LISA	**35**		zami	5
ISILISA	**35**		lami	4
besilisa	19		yami	3
abesilisa	9		*other*	5
wesilisa	5		mina	7
owesilisa	2	**-ZULU**		**33**
FUTHI	**34**		izulu	2
-NKE	**34**		sezulu	3
bonke	7		**PHEZULU**	**28**
zonke	6		phezulu	8
wonke	8		phezu	10
yonke	5		ngaphezu	10
konke	4	**-HLAL-**		**31**
other	4		-hlal-	11
-NYAKA	**34**		abahlala	7
(u)nyaka	3		ohlala	4
ngonyaka	6		ezihlala	3
(i)minyaka	11		(i)sihlalo	1
neminyaka	9		-hlezi	1
eminyakeni	3		-hlal-e [aux]	4
other	2	**LABO**		**31**
-PHATH-	**34**		labo	18
-phath-	7		kulabo	5
-phethe	2		nalabo	4
abaphathi	4		yilabo	4
-phathw-	3	**-(E)DLUL-**		**30**
(u)kuphathwa	3	(*-dlul-* and *-edlul-* are variants)		
aphathwe	3		-dlul-	9
-phethwe	3		edlule	3
other	3		odlule	3
-phathel-	1		-dlulel-	2
-PHATHELAN-	**4**		-dlulis-	1
eziphathelene	3		-dlulisel-	3
-phathis-	1		-dlulw-	1
-PHUM-	**34**		-edlul-	4
-phum-	13		eyedlule	3
-phumel-	3		-edlulel-	1

-GANE	30
izingane	18
lezingane	3
other	4
ingane	2
other	3
-PHEL-	30
-phel-	10
-phelel-	2
-phelelw-	1
kuphela	11
phela	3
IMPELA	3
okusempeleni	1
ngempela	2
-KINGA	29
(i)zinkinga	14
nezinkinga	2
(i)nkinga	8
(s)enkingeni	2
other	3
LESI	29
LOKHU [dem]	27
-MALI	27
imali	22
izimali	5
-Y-	26
-y-	11
kuya	4
ukuya	6
-yiw-	2
-yis-	1
-yisw-	1
-YELAN-	1
mayelana	1
-ZW-	26
-zw-	7
-zwakal-	9
-zwakalis-	1
-zwan-	4
-zwel-	1
uzwelo	1
imizwa	2
other	1
-HLE	25
-hle	12
kahle	9
kuhle	3
ubuhle	1
-KHO	25
yakho	7
other	1
zakho	7
sakho	4
wakho	3
other	3
LAPHO	25
lapho	21
nokuyilapho	3
other	1
-HLUKUMEZ-	24
-hlukumez-	6
ukuhlukumeza	3
-hlukumezek-	1
ukuhlukumezeka	7
-hlukunyezw-	7
LELI	24
LOKHO	24
lokho	12
kwalokho	4
other	8
-THAND-	24
-thand-	14
(u)thando	4
othandweni	1
-thandan-	2
(i)zithandani	1
-thandek-	1
-thandisis-	1
-CANSI	23
UCANSI	23
ocansini	6
zocansi	2
ezocansi	5

ngokocansi 10
-KHIPH- 23
  -khiph- 4
    (u)kukhipha 7
  -khishw- 4
    (u)kukhishwa 7
  -khishelw- 1
-KOLE 23
  (i)sikole 11
  esikoleni 8
  (i)zikole 1
  ezikoleni 3
LESO 23
-ZAL- 23
  -ZAL- 23
  (a)bazali 9
  (u)mzali 2
  -zalel- 1
    ukuzalela 3
  -zalelw- 2
  -zalw- 5
  -zalan- 1
-DABA 22
  (u)daba 9
  (i)ndaba 7
  other 3
  (i)zindaba 3
-(E)THEMB- 22
(*-themb-* and *-ethemb-* are variants)
  -(e)themb- 4
    uzethembe 1
    uZethembe 1
    ithemba 3
    uThemba 1
    amathemba 2
  -thembel- 3
  -ethembis- 3
    izethembiso 2
  -thenjisw- 1
  -thembakal- 1
-K-E 22

-k-e 12
  ngeke 7
  angeke 1
  abangeke 1
  ake 1
-BAL- 21
  -bal- 2
  isibalo 6
    lesibalo 3
  izibalo 2
  -balw- 3
  -mbalwa 3
  -balelw- 2
-BHEK- 21
  -bhek- 4
  -bhekan- 4
  -bhekene 7
  ababhekene 3
  -bhekel- 2
  -bhekelel- 1
-HLANGAN- 21
  -hlangan- 5
  -hlangene 1
  -HLANGANO 12
    (i)nhlangano 10
    izinhlangano 2
  -hlanganis- 1
  -hlanganisw- 1
  -hlanganyel- 1
-KHOKH- 21
  -khokh- 4
    ukukhokha 6
  -khokhel- 4
    ukuzikhokhela 4
    (i)zinkokheli 1
  -khokhek- 1
  other 1
MANJE 21
  (see also *-nje*)
  manje 14
  njengamanje 7
-NCANE 21

-ncane	11
(a)bancane	4
kancane	1
nakancane	5
-NDLE	**21**
PHANDLE	**20**
ngaphandle	13
angaphandle	3
nangaphandle	3
other	1
AMAPHANDLE	**1**
semaphandleni	1
-NUMZANE	**21**
(u)mnumzane	2
uMnuz [abbrev]	19
-VA	**21**
emuva	1
emva	20
YE	**21**
yena	11
naye	8
other	2
-ZWE	**21**
(see also *-fundazwe*)	
(i)zwe	3
ezweni	2
(i)zwelonke	3
amazwe	5
(s)emazweni	6
isizwe	1
esizweni	1
LEZO	**20**
ZO	**20**
zo	13
kuzo	5
zona	2
-ANSI	**19**
phansi	6
ngaphansi	10
ophansi	3
-CHAZ-	**19**
-chaz-	4
kuchaza	8
-chazel-	5
incazelo	1
-chazelek-	1
-GCIN-	**19**
-GOZI	**19**
(I)NGOZI	**18**
-yingozi	7
eziyingozi	10
other	1
(i)zingozi	1
-KHAYA	**19**
(i)khaya	1
(s)ekhaya	5
(a)makhaya	2
(s)emakhaya	8
ezisemakhaya	3
-QHUB-	**19**
-qhub-	4
(u)kuqhuba	3
-qhubek-	11
-qhutshekelw-	1
-BHANOYI	**18**
(a)mabhanoyi	9
(i)bhanoyi	9
-CEL-	**18**
-cel-	4
(u)kucela	3
ngicela	9
(i)sicelo	1
-celel-	1
-DLWENGUL-	**18**
-dlwengul-	2
ukudlwengula	4
-dlwengulw-	7
ukudlwengulwa	5
-DODA	**18**
indoda	8
(i)ndodana	2
(i)ndodakazi	1
ubudoda	1
amadoda	6

-LIM-	18		*other*	3
-lim-	1		**-TSHAL-**	17
(a)balimi	7		-tshal-	4
(u)mlimi	3		(i)zitshalo	4
ULIMO	7		(u)kutshala	4
ezolimo	4		-tshalw-	1
kwezolimo	3		(u)kutshalwa	3
-MOSQUITO	18		-tshalel-	1
u-mosquito	2		**WO**	17
ngu-mosquito	6		wo	12
o-mosquito	10		nawo	3
-NGEN-	18		wona	2
-ngen-	15		**-HLEL-**	16
-ngenw-	1		-hlel-	2
-ngenelw-	1		(u)mhleli	6
-ngenis-	1		uhlelo	2
-THEL-	18		izinhlelo	2
-thel-	3		-hlelw-	2
-thelel-	1		-hlelelw-	1
intela	8		-hlelisis-	1
bentela	4		**-KHETH-**	16
other	2		-kheth-	8
-VAM-	18		-khethel-	5
-vam-	12		-khethek-	1
bavame	5		*other*	2
-vamis-	1		**-KWELET-**	16
-ZAM-	18		**-KWELET-**	16
-zam-	11		obakweletayo	3
bazame	3		izikweleti	4
imizamo	3		nezikweleti	3
uZama	1		ezikweletini	2
-BUY-	17		(i)sikweleti	4
-buy-	2		**LEZI**	16
-buy-e [aux]	7		lezi	13
wabuye	3		kwalezi	3
-buyel-	3		**-PHOYISA**	16
-buyisel-	1		amaphoyisa	14
-buyiselw-	1		iphoyisa	2
-THETH-	17		**-MALALEVEVA**	16
ukuthethwa	1		(u)malaleveva	16
(u)mthetho	10		**-CALA**	15
ezomthetho	3		(a)macala	6

(i)cala	9		iziboshwa	5
-FIK-	**15**		isiboshwa	1
-fik-	11		umboshwa	1
-fikelw-	2		-boshelw-	1
-fikis-	1		**-DING-**	**14**
-fikisel-	1		-ding-	8
-KHOSI	**15**		(i)zidingo	2
inkosi	1		-dingek-	4
other	2		**-FAN-**	**14**
inkosikazi	1		-fan-	13
unkosikazi	1		**-FANISWAN-**	**1**
(u)Nkk [abbrev]	3		umfaniswano	1
other	2		**-JELE**	**14**
UNKOSAZANA	**5**		ijele	1
(u)Nksz [abbrev]	5		ejele	6
LOLU	**15**		amajele	1
NJE	**15**		emajele	6
(see also *manje*)			**KWAZULU-NATAL**	**14**
nje	11		KwaZulu-Natal	8
kanje	2		saKwaZulu-Natal	5
NJENA	**2**		*other*	1
kanjena	2		**-SHAY-**	**14**
-QEQESH-	**15**		-shay-	10
-QEQESH-	**15**		-shayw-	3
-qeqeshw-	4		*other*	1
abaqeqeshiwe	3		**-TSHEL-**	**14**
abangaqeqeshiwe	2		-tshel-	11
-qeqeshel-	1		-tshelw-	3
-qeqeshelw-	5		**-ZE**	**14**
-SOUTH AFRICA	**15**		**IZE**	**14**
(see also *iNingizimu Afrika*)			yize	7
i-South Africa	1		neze	7
(s)e-South Africa	9		**-BANG-**	**13**
lase-South Africa	5		-bang-	1
YO	**15**		-bangel-	2
yo	10		imbangela	4
ngayo	3		yimbangela	4
yona	2		-bangelw-	1
-BOPH-	**14**		-bangw-	1
-boph-	1		**-BEK-**	**13**
isibopho	1		-bek-	7
-boshw-	4		wabeka	5

-bekw-	1		**UBUHOLI**	**1**
-BHAL-	**13**		ebuholini	1
-bhal-	4		amaholo	2
unobhala	2		umholo	1
-bhalel-	1		komholo	2
ukubhalela	3		-holel-	1
-bhalis-	1		**-KHUL-**	**13**
-bhalisel-	1		(cf. *-khulu*)	
-bhalw-	1		-khul-	9
-BILI	**13**		-khulis-	1
amabili	2		-khulisw-	1
ababili	3		-khulelw-	2
other	2		**LOWO**	**13**
ezimbili	2		**-LUNG-**	**13**
zimbili	1		-lung-	1
kabili	1		ulungile	1
isibili	2		uLungile	1
-BUZ-	**13**		-lungel-	1
-buz-	8		ilungelo	3
umbuzo	1		amalungelo	1
imibuzo	2		-lungisw-	3
-buzw-	2		-lungisel-	1
-DLELA	**13**		-lungiselw-	1
(i)ndlela	5		**-MNYAMA**	**13**
ngendlela	4		**-MNYAMA**	**13**
other	1		abamnyama	7
(i)zindlela	3		*other*	6
-HLUK-	**13**		**-PHEPH-**	**13**
(This has variants *-ahluk-* and			-pheph-	7
-ehluk- that are included here.)			(u)kuphepha	3
-ehluk-	1		-phephis-	2
umehluko	1		-phephel-	1
-hlukan-	5		**-PHIND-**	**13**
-hlukahlukan-	1		-phind-	9
-ehlukahlukan-	1		-phindaphind-	1
-ahlukan-	2		-phindw-	1
-hlukanis-	1		-phindiselw-	1
-ehlukanis-	1		-phindelel-	1
-HOL-	**13**		**-QOND-**	**13**
-hol-	2		-qond-	4
abaholi	3		umqondo	3
umholi	1		ingqondo	1

enggqondweni	1	(i)zifiso	3
ezengqondo	1	**-KHUBA**	**12**
-QONDIS-	**1**	(u)mkhuba	8
umqondisi	1	lomkhuba	4
-qondisis-	1	**-NAMBUZANE**	**12**
-qondan-	1	izinambuzane	8
-SUKU	**13**	isinambuzane	3
UBUSUKU	**8**	lesinambuzane	1
(s)ebusuku	8	**NGENXA**	**12**
(i)zinsuku	2	**-THUMB-**	**12**
other	3	-thumb-	1
-THISHA	**13**	umthumbi	2
(u)thisha	1	abathumbi	1
nothisha	2	-thunjw-	5
uthishanhloko	1	kuthunjwe	3
uthishomkhulu	1	**-VIKEL-**	**12**
othisha	8	-vikel-	3
-XOX-	**13**	ukuzivikela	4
-xox-	3	yokuzivikela	3
-xoxisan-	3	*other*	1
(u)kuxoxisana	4	-vikelan-	1
-xoxel-	2	**-BI**	**11**
other	1	kabi	5
-AKH-	**12**	embi	2
-akh-	3	mibi	2
ukwakha	1	(u)bubi	2
other	2	**-DL-**	**11**
-akhel-	3	-dl-	2
-AKHELW-	**1**	ukudla	5
omakhelwane	1	esokudla	1
-akhiw-	1	isidlo	1
umakhi	1	**-DLEK-**	**2**
-DAYIS-	**12**	izindleko	2
-dayis-	4	**-DOKOTELA**	**11**
(u)kudayisa	4	udokotela	2
-dayisel-	1	nodokotela	3
dayiselw-	2	uDkt [abbrev]	4
-dayisw-	1	odokotela	1
-FIS-	**12**	ngodokotela	1
-fis-	5	**-ELAPH-**	**11**
ngifisa	3	-elaph-	2
(i)sifiso	1	ukwelapha	1

ezokwelapha	4		isiqiniseko	3
-ELASHW-	**3**		-qinisekis-	1
ukwelashwa	3		**-SHAYEL-**	**11**
-elashelw-	1		-shayel-	4
-ETHU	**11**		umshayeli	4
-ethu	7		abashayeli	2
zethu	3		-shayelel-	1
other	1		**-THI**	**11**
-FANA	**11**		**UMUTHI**	**3**
(see also *-fo*)			ngomuthi	2
(a)bafana	7		*other*	1
(a)bafanyana	1		(i)mithi	6
umfana	1		kwemithi	2
(u)mfanyana	2		**-VEL-**	**11**
-LULA	**11**		-vel-	2
-lula	4		-vel-e [aux]	1
kalula	4		imvelo	2
kulula	3		-velel-	1
-NDENI	**11**		-vez-	5
(u)mndeni	6		**-ZATHU**	**11**
(i)mindeni	4		isizathu	4
abomndeni	1		ngesizathu	3
-NQUM-	**11**		zizathu	4
-NQUM-	**11**		**-GEBENGU**	**10**
(i)sinqumo	7		ezigebengu	5
(i)zinqumo	2		*other*	2
-nqunyelw-	2		(u)bugebengu	3
-PHAHLA	**11**		**-GWAQO**	**10**
(u)phahla	2		umgwaqo	2
(i)zimpahla	7		emgwaqweni	2
ezimpahleni	1		(i)migwaqo	1
impahla	1		emigwaqweni	5
-QEMBU	**11**		**-GWEB-**	**10**
amaqembu	8		-gweb-	1
other	1		isigwebo	5
(i)qembu	2		-gwetshw-	4
-QIN-	**11**		**-GWEM-**	**10**
-qin-	2		-gwem-	6
-qinis-	1		(u)kugwema	4
iqiniso	2		**-HLABA**	**10**
amaqiniso	2		umhlaba	6
-QINISEK-	**3**		emhlabeni	4

-HLOS-	10		-SU	10
-hlos-	1		izisu	2
inhloso	1		kwezisu	7
ngenhloso	7		isisu	1
-hlosw-	1		**-VAKASH-**	10
LEYO	10		-vakash-	1
-MBILI	10		ezokuvakasha	4
PHAMBILI	10		izivakashi	2
ngaphambi	7		abavakashi	1
phambi	1		-vakashel-	2
phambilini	2		**YINI**	10
			-BALULEK-	9
-MOTO	10		**-DLAL-**	9
(i)zimoto	5		-dlal-	4
other	1		imidlalo	2
(i)moto	3		(u)mdlali	1
other	1		-dlalel-	1
-NCWADI	10		-dlalw-	1
(i)ncwadi	1		**-EHL-**	9
encwadini	2		-ehl-	3
(i)zincwadi	4		-ehlel-	2
kwezincwadi	3		-ehlelw-	2
-NDLA	10		-ehlis-	1
(a)mandla	10		-ehliselw-	1
NJANI	10		**-ESAB-**	9
-njani	3		-esab-	3
kanjani	6		ukwesaba	3
other	1		-(e)sabis-	2
-QASH-	10		-esabel-	1
-qash-	4		**-FAZI**	9
umqashi	1		(see also *-fo*)	
-qashw-	5		**-ISIFAZANE**	9
-QHAMUK-	10		wesifazane	4
-qhamuk-	4		besifazane	4
-QHAMUKIS-	6		abesifazane	1
-li-qhamukis-	6		**-HLONI**	9
-SHA	10		amahloni	1
(a)basha	2		-hloniph-	3
omusha	1		(i)nhlonipho	2
intsha	2		-hlonishw-	2
entsheni	1		-hloniphek-	1
kabusha	4		**-HULUMENI**	9

uhulumeni	6	**-THI**	9
kuhulumeni	3	thina	4
-GAMA	9	kithina	1
igama	6	kithi	4
amagama	3	**-THOKOZ-**	9
-HLO/IHLO/EHLO/SO	9	-thokoz-	4
amehlo	3	-thokozel-	4
emehlweni	5	-thokozis-	1
(i)so	1	**-THUBA**	9
-JAJI	9	ithuba	4
(i)jaji	7	nethuba	2
other	2	sethubeni	1
-KE [enclitic]	9	amathuba	2
-KHEMISI	9	**-ANC**	8
IKHEMISI	5	(i)-ANC	5
kulelikhemisi	1	*other*	3
other	3	**-BUK-**	8
ekhemisi	1	-buk-	2
USOKHEMISI	2	izibuko	1
other	2	-bukek-	3
AMAKHEMISI	2	-bukel-	2
other	2	**-FAK-**	8
-LAWUL-	9	-fak-	3
-lawul-	5	-fakw-	3
umlawuli	2	-fakel-	1
abalawuli	1	-fakelw-	1
-lawulw-	1	**-FUNDAZWE**	8
-LUNGU	9	(see also *-funda* and *-zwe*)	
(see also *-lunga*)		**ISIFUNDAZWE**	8
amalungu	7	lesisifundazwe	1
ilungu	2	*other*	3
-NDIZ-	9	*other*	4
-ndiz-	2	**-HLANU**	8
(i)zindiza	7	emihlanu	3
-NTWANA	9	isihlanu	2
(cf. *ntu*) abantwana	4	uLwesihlanu	2
nabantwana	3	*other*	1
umntwana	2	**-KHUBAZ-**	8
-PHIKO	9	-khubaz-	3
(u)phiko	3	-khubazek-	2
loluphiko	5	abakhubazekile	3
other	1	**-KHULUM-**	8

-khulum-	5	**-BHIZINISI**	7
izinkulumo	1	amabhizinisi	6
-khulumel-	1	ibhizinisi	1
-khulunyw-	1	**-BIZ-**	7
-KHUNDLA	8	-biz-	5
isikhundla	1	-bizw-	2
esikhundleni	5	**-CABANG-**	7
INKUNDLA	1	**-DALA**	7
enkundleni	1	omdala	4
IZINKUNDLA	1	*other*	3
ezinkundleni	1	**-DE**	7
-NZIMA	8	-de	4
-nzima	7	kade	3
ebunzimeni	1	**-ELULEK-**	7
-PHI?	8	-elulek-	1
SO	8	izeluleko	5
so	6	umeluleki	1
sona	2	**-HLAMVU**	7
-STRAWBERRY	8	inhlamvu	4
i-strawberry	1	izinhlamvu	2
ama-strawberry	3	uhlamvu	1
lama-strawberry	3	**-HLANHLA**	7
other	1	**(I)NHLANHLA**	7
-THILE	8	zenhlanhla	4
-VOT-	8	ngenhlanhla	2
-vot-	1	uNhlanhla	1
-votel-	7	**-HLENG-**	7
-ZINGA	8	**-HLENG-**	7
(i)zinga	6	abahlengi	1
ezingeni	1	(a)bahlengikazi	4
(a)mazinga	1	**-HLENGW-**	2
-AND-	7	(u)Hlengiwe	1
-and-	5	**-HLOBO**	7
(u)Sandile	1	(u)hlobo	3
-andis-	1	izinhlobo	1
-BAMB-	7	(i)nhlobo	1
-bamb-	1	(ii)nhlobonhlobo	2
ibamba	1	**-KAMPANI**	7
-bamban-	1	(i)nkampani	5
-bambel-	1	(i)zinkampani	2
-bambek-	1	**-KHOMB-**	7
-bambisan-	2	-khomb-	2

-khombis-	5
-KHULUL-	7
-khulul-	1
-khululek-	5
inkululeko	1
-LUM-	7
-lum-	1
-lunyw-	3
UKULUNYWA	3
ekulunyweni	2
other	1
-ML	7
(u)-ml	7
-NGUBO	7
(i)zingubo	6
ezingutsheni	1
-NSIZWA	7
(i)nsizwa	6
(i)zinsizwa	1
-NYANGA	7
(i)nyanga	3
other	1
(i)zinyanga	3
-ONGAMEL-	7
-ONGAMEL-	7
(u)mongameli	7
-PULAZI	7
(i)pulazi	5
epulazini	1
AMAPULAZI	1
emapulazini	1
-SHAD-	7
-shad-	4
(u)mshado	3
-SHESH-	7
-shesh-	3
ngokushesha	4
-SHIS-	7
-shis-	3
-shisel-	1
-shisw-	1
shisisw-	2

-THINT-	7
-thint-	3
ezithinta	3
-thintek-	1
-VAL-	7
(cf. **-vul-** in the overall glossary)	
-val-	3
-valw-	1
-valelw-	3
-VIMB-	7
-vimb-	2
-vimbel-	1
ukuvimbela	4
-AFRIKA	6
I-AFRIKA	3
ase-Afrika	3
(a)ma-Afrika	3
-BHEDLELA	6
(i)sibhedlela	5
izibhedlela	1
-DOJ-	6
-doj-	4
(a)badoji	2
-DOLOBHA	6
(I)DOLOBHA	2
edolobheni	2
(A)MADOLOBHA	4
-(s)emadolobheni	4
-DWA	6
-dwa	5
-dwana	1
-FO	6
(See also *-fana* and *-fazi*)	
(u)mfowabo	2
(a)bafowabo	2
(a)bafowethu	1
umfoka-	1
-FUNDA	6
(see also *-fundazwe*)	
isifunda	1
esifundeni	1
izifunda	4

other	1
-KHAL-	6
-khal-	5
-khalel-	
-KHANYAMBA	6
inkanyamba	1
lenkanyamba	4
other	1
-KHATHAL-	6
-khathal-	1
-khathaz-	1
-KHATHAZEK-	4
okhathazekile	4
-KHIQIZ-	6
-khiqiz-	2
(i)mikhiqizo	3
umkhiqizo	1
-KHOL-	6
-kholw-	4
-kholelw-	1
izinkolelo	1
-LAL-	6
-lal-	3
-lele	1
-lalw-	2
LAPHA	6
lapha	5
other	1
LAWO	6
-NJALO	6
njalo	5
manjalo	1
-NYATHEL-	6
-NYATHEL-	6
(i)sinyathelo	2
(i)zinyathelo	3
other	1
-NZI	6
amanzi	5
other	1
-PHEPHA	6
(i)phepha	2

amaphepha	1
-PHEPHANDABA	3
(i)phephandaba	2
emaphephandabeni	1
-PHIK-	6
-phik-	1
-phikis-	2
-phikisan-	2
-phikelel-	1
R [rand(s)]	6
-THOMBE	6
izithombe	1
nezithombe	3
isithombe	2
-VUM-	6
-vum-	1
uVuma	1
-vumel-	1
-vumelan-	1
-VUMELWAN-	2
ISIVUMELWANA	2
esivumelwaneni	2
-ZI	6
umuzi	2
emzini	1
other	2
imizi	1
-BANI	5
UBANI?	4
ngubani?	4
usibanibani	1
-CHWEPHESHE	5
(u)chwepheshe	5
-DAL-	5
-dal-	1
-dalw-	3
-dalelw-	1
-DUBUL-	5
-dubul-	2
-dutshulw-	2
-dubulek-	1
-DUZE	5

(s)eduze	4	-LIMAL-	5
maduze	1	-LOKHU [aux]	5
-FAKAZI	5	-MUNCU	5
ofakazi	1	-NE	5
ubufakazi	4	-NGCONO	5
-FEZ-	5	-NGQONGQOSHE	5
-fez-	5	ungqongqoshe	5
-G [gram(s)]	5	-NOTHO	5
(u)-g	5	umnotho	2
-GCIZELEL-	5	ezomnotho	3
-gcizelel-	2	-NQAND-	5
wagcizelela	3	-nqand-	1
-GCOB-	5	(u)kunqanda	3
-gcob-	3	yokunqanda	1
-gcotshw-	1	-PHETH-	5
-gcotshisw-	1	-pheth-	4
-GQUGQUZEL-	5	amaphethelo	1
-gqugquzel-	2	-QIWI	5
umgqugquzeli	1	(i)ziqiwi	1
-gqugquzelw-	2	leziziqiwi	4
-HLUPH-	5	-SE [aux]	5
-hluph-	3	-SHIY-	5
-hluphek-	1	-SHUMI	5
inhlupheko	1	ISHUMI	5
-KHANKAS-	5	eyishumi	3
-KHANKAS-	4	other	2
(u)mkhankaso	4	-SONTO	5
emkhankasweni	1	(i)sonto	2
-KHATHA	5	amasonto	1
inkatha	4	impelasonto	1
other	1	other	1
-KHUMBUL-	5	-THELO	5
-khumbul-	4	(i)sithelo	2
-khumbulek-	1	izithelo	3
-KOLISHI	5	-THUTHUK-	5
(i)kolishi	2	THUTHUK-	5
lelikolishi	3	intuthuko	2
-LAHL-	5	-THUTHUKIS-	3
-LAHL-	5	ukuthuthukisa	3
-lahlek-	1	-THWAL-	5
-lahlekelw-	4	-thwal-	4
-LALEL-	5	other	1

-XWAYIS-	5	**-GAZI**	4
-(e)xwayis-	4	(i)gazi	3
isexwayiso	1	ugazi	1
-Y-E [aux]	5	**-GCWAL-**	4
-ANDLA	4	-gcwal-	1
(i)sandla	2	-gcwele	3
IZANDLA	2	**-GLUE**	4
ngezandla	2	(i)-glue	4
-BABA	4	**-GODL-**	4
(u)baba	1	-godl-	3
nobaba	2	-godlw-	1
usingababa	1	**-HLUL-**	4
-BALEK-	4	(This has variant -*ehlul*- that is
-balek-	1	included here.)
-balekel-	3	**-(E)HLUL-**	4
-BANDAKANY-	4	-hlulek-	2
-BIK-	4	-ehlulek-	1
-bik-	2	-ehlulw-	1
imibiko	1	**-HLUNGU**	4
-bikel-	1	ubuhlungu	2
-BONG-	4	-buhlungu	2
-bong-	3	**-KANTOLO**	4
isibongo	1	(i)nkantolo	3
-BUS-	4	izinkantolo	1
-BUS-	4	**-KHAKHA**	4
-busis-	1	(u)mkhakha	1
(u)Sibusiso	1	emkhakheni	2
-busisw-	1	**(I)MIKHAKHA**	1
(u)Busisiwe	1	emikhakheni	1
-DLANGE	4	**-KHAMBI**	4
-DONS-	4	(i)khambi	2
-dons-	3	amakhambi	2
-donsel-	1	**-KHANGIS-**	4
-FASITELA	4	**-KHANGIS-**	4
amafasitela	3	(i)sikhangiso	3
(i)fasitela	1	abakhangisi	1
-FEBRUARY	4	**-KHUMBI**	4
U-FEBRUARY	4	umkhumbi	4
ngo-February	4	**-KHUNGO**	4
-FIHL-	4	(i)sikhungo	2
-fihl-	3	(i)zikhungo	2
-fihlw-	1	**-KILASI**	4

(I)KILASI	2	-phumulel-	2
ekilasini	2	**-QED-**	**4**
amakilasi	1	-qed-	3
emakilasini	1	-qedw-	1
-KLOMEL-	**4**	**-QHENY-**	**4**
-KLOMEL-	**4**	-zi-qheny-	4
umklomelo	2	**-QHUDELWANO**	**4**
imiklomelo	2	(u)mqhudelwano	4
LABA	**4**	**SELOKHU**	**4**
-LANDEL-	**4**	**-SINDO**	**4**
-landel-	3	(u)msindo	3
-landelan-	1	imisindo	1
-LETH-	**4**	**-SOL-**	**4**
-LILI	**4**	-zi-sol-	4
(u)bulili	4	**-THUM-**	**4**
-MAMA	**4**	**-THUM-**	**4**
umama	3	-thumel-	1
other	1	-thunyelw-	3
-MOYA	**4**	**-TOLO**	**4**
UMOYA	**4**	(I)SITOLO	3
onomoya	3	esitolo	3
(s)emoyeni	1	**IZITOLO**	**1**
-NAK-	**4**	ezitolo	1
-nak-	2	**-VALO**	**4**
-nakw-	2	(u)valo	4
NGASESE	**4**	**-XAZULUL-**	**4**
NGQA	**4**	-xazulul-	3
-NKONKONI	**4**	-xazululek-	1
(i)zinkonkoni	4	**-XHUM-**	**4**
-PHAWU	**4**	-xhum-	1
-PHAWU	**4**	-xhuman-	2
izimpawu	1	**-XHUMANIS-**	**1**
(one case of *izimpawo* not		umxhumanisi	1
included)		**-XOL-**	**4**
(i)ziphawu	1	**-XOL-**	**4**
-phawul-	2	uxolo	3
-PHENDUL-	**4**	-xolis-	1
-phendul-	2	**-YEK-**	**4**
impendulo	1	-yek-	3
-phendulel-	1	-yekw-	1
-PHUMUL-	**4**	**-ZIMBA**	**4**
-phumul-	2	(u)mzimba	1

emzimbeni	2	-HIV	3
(i)mizimba	1	(i-)HIV	3
-AIDS	3	-HLAHLA	3
(i)-AIDS	1	izihlahla	3
other	2	-HLAKANI	3
-BALA	3	ubuhlakani	1
UBALA	3	other	2
(s)obala	3	-KHONZ-	3
-BANDLA	3	-KHWABANIS-	3
ibandla	1	-KHWABANIS-	3
amabandla	2	abakhwabanisi	3
BESE	3	-LANGA	3
-BHOLA	3	ilanga	3
ibhola	3	-LING-	3
-BINDI	3	-LING-	3
isibindi	2	-lingw-	1
esibindini	1	-lingan-	1
-CABHA	3	-linganiselw-	1
izicabha	3	-LUNGA	3
-DIDA	3	(see also -lungu)	
indida	3	amalunga	2
-DLAME	3	emalungeni	1
udlame	3	-MANGA	3
-DONGA	3	-MANGA	3
udonga	1	izimanga	1
izindonga	2	-mangal-	1
-DUM-	3	-mangaz-	1
EKUSENI	3	-MBONI	3
-GAMEKO	3	imboni	1
isigameko	1	izimboni	1
izigameko	2	ezimbonini	1
-GESI	3	-MELIKA	3
ugesi	1	iMelika	1
ngogesi	2	other	2
-GUQU	3	NAKHU	3
-guqul-	1	-NGABAZ-	3
-guquk-	1	-ngabaz-	2
-guquguquk-	1	-ngabazek-	1
-GXIL-	3	-NGANI	3
-HHOVISI	3	umngani	3
(i)hhovisi	2	-NGCOL-	3
(a)mahhovisi	1	-NINGIZIMU AFRIKA	3

(see also *i-South Africa*)		-sakazw-	1
INiNGIZIMU AFRIKA	3	-sakazek-	1
neNingizimu Afrika	1	-SAND-	3
(s)eNingizimu Afrika	2	-SHINTSH-	3
-NYUK-	3	-shintsh-	1
-nyuk-	2	-shintshan-	1
-enyuk-	1	-shintshel-	1
(the latter is a variant of the		-SHUSHIS-	3
first)		-SHUSHIS-	1
-ONAKAL-	3	umshushisi	1
-ONAKAL-	2	-shushisw-	1
umonakalo	2	-shushiselw-	1
-onakalelw-	1	-TALADI	3
-ONG-	3	IZITALADI	3
-ONG-	3	ezitaladini	3
-ONGIW-	3	-TESHI	3
ukongiwa	3	(i)siteshi	2
-PHAKETHE	3	*other*	1
IPHAKETHE	3	-THANDAZ-	3
ephaketheni	3	-thandaz-	1
-PHAS-	3	(i)mithandazo	2
-phas-	1	-THE	3
-phasisw-	2	amathe	2
-PHUZ-	3	-sematheni	1
-phuz-	2	-THIMBA	3
-phuzel-	1	(i)thimba	1
-QAPH-	3	*other*	2
-QAPH-	3	-THUL-	3
abaqaphi	3	-THUPHA	3
-QHATH-	3	ISITHUPHA	2
-QHATH-	3	-yisithupha	2
-qhathanisw-	2	izithupha	1
-qhathw-	1	-VUN-	3
-QOQ-	3	-vun-	1
-qoq-	1	isivuno	2
-qoqw-	2	-W-	3
-RAMA	3	-w-	2
i-rama	2	-wel-	1
other	1	-YISE	3
-SAKAZ-	3	(u)yise	3
-SAKAZ-	3	-Z-	3
umsakazo	1		

Personal names (in alphabetical order)		*Place names* (in alphabetical order)	
(u)Dlamini	4	iBochum	3
(u)Dudu	4	iShowe	3
(u)Khoza	3	i-South Africa	15
(u)Madlala	4	iThekwini	5
(u)Mandela	8	KwaZulu-Natal	13
(u)Mbeki	5	uMgungundlovu	3
(u)Mfeka	4	uMlazi	3
(u)Mpanza	6	uMtata	5
(u)Ngcobo	3		
(u)Sipho	14		

(u)Vuma   4

Selections

Ama-Orange Citrus Cakes

(Kuphuma angu 12[4])
Izithako
60g [u-60 grams][5] (60ml) [noma u-60 millimeters] iRama
100g [u-100 grams] (100ml) [noma u-100 mills] i-castor sugar
150g [u-150 grams] (270ml) [noma 270 mill] i-self-raising flour
3 amaqanda [amaqanda amathathu] ashayiwe
80ml [u-80 mill] i-orange juice

Izithako ze-Frosting
100g [u-100 grams] (200ml) [or 200 mill] i-icing sugar eshaywe
yahlanganiswa no-15ml [no-15 mill] we-orange juice kanye no-30g
[u-30 grams] (30ml) [or 30 mill] weRama ikhasi lewolintshi
eligreythiwe.

Indlela Yokwenza
Shaya iRama noshukela. Thela ufulawa namaqanda kanye nojusi.
Kuthele kuma-patty pans agcotshisiwe noma emathinini okubhaka
angu 2 x 20cm [angu-two by 20 centimeters]. Kubhake imizuzu engu
25 kuhhavini oshisiswe ngezinga elingu 160°C kuze kukhukhumale
kahle kube nsundu. Kupholise bese ukugcoba nge-orange frosting
ngaphezulu. Kuvuvuzele ngekhasi lewolintshi eligreythiwe.

Numerals, weights, measures …
Zulu writers are very inconsistent in the presentation of numerals. They
ought to be written together with any preceding prefix as a single word, but
separated therefrom by a hyphen, e.g. *u-12*, *ngo-1997*. Some writers omit
the hyphen as in *u12* and *ngo1997*, while others write them as separate
words as in *u 12* and *ngo 1997*. For numbers, especially higher numbers,
Zulu speakers tend to use English forms (with varying types of accent). The
same applies to certain weights and measures. Recipes are generally written
as is customary for English recipes, but would be read differently. Thus, *3
amaqanda*, above, is read as *amaqanda amathathu*. Weights and measures
will also normally be assigned to an appropriate noun class. Thus, what is
written *60g* is read as *u-60grams* (Cl. 1a or 3a).

---

[4] See box below on numbers, weights and measures.
[5] We have given in square brackets what was actually read.

Vocabulary

kuphuma it yields (lit. there comes out) [pres, conjoint]
ku- it, there [indefinite SC, Cl. 17]
-phum-a come/go out, come from, emerge, leave, depart [v.i.]
-a [default (basic) verb suffix]
angu-12 twelve (lit. which are twelve) [relative Cl. 6]
a- which, that, who(m) [relativizer used when the SC in the verb concerned has the vowel **a**]
angu-12 they are twelve (i.e. there are twelve of them) [identificative copulative, pres]
ng- is, are [ident cop pref]
u-12 twelve [n Cl. 1a]
uØ- [NP Cl. 1a]
izithako ingredients [n Cl. 8; sg **isithako**; < **isi-** NP Cl. 7 + **-thak-** mix, concoct + **-o** nominalizing suffix (henceforth: nom suff. With few exceptions the nom suff **-o** derives product or process nouns, always non-personal, while the nom suff **-i** forms agent nouns, which are generally personal.)]
izi- [NP Cl. 8]
u-60 grams [n phr Cl. 3a] {Eng}
noma or [conjunction]
u-60 millimeters [n phr Cl. 3a]
iRama Rama margarine (Rama is a brand name; without the capital letter **irama** is the generic term for margarine) [n Cl. 9a]
iØ- [NP Cl. 9a]
i-castor sugar bakers' sugar [n Cl. 9a]

i-self-raising flour self-rising flour [n Cl. 9a]
amaqanda eggs [n Cl. 6; sg **iqanda** Cl. 5]
ama- [NP Cl. 6]
amathathu three [adj Cl. 6]
ama- [adjective concord, Cl. 6]
-thathu three [adj stem]
ashayiwe (that have been) beaten [relative Cl. 6; < **a-** relativizer + **ashayiwe**]
ashayiwe they have been beaten [stative, disjoint (relative forms of the verb are very similar to those of the participial aspect, but they often differ in tone]
a- they, it [SC Cl. 6]
-shayiwe have been beaten [v-pass-stative]
-i... e [stative suff used in passive]
-shayw-a be hit, be beaten [v-pass]
-shay-a hit, beat, strike [v.t.]
-w- be VERB-ed, be VERB-en [passive extension]
i-orange juice [n Cl. 9a] {Eng}
ze-frosting of frosting [possessive Cl. 8]
ze- of [poss concord Cl. 8 coalesced with following **i**]
za- of [poss concord Cl. 8]
i-frosting [n Cl. 9a] {American English (South African English has "icing")}
i-icing sugar confectioner's sugar [n Cl. 9a] {Eng}
eshaywe that/which has been beaten [relative Cl. 9]
e- which, that, who(m) [relativizer used when the SC in the verb concerned has the vowel **i**]

ishaywe it has been beaten [stative, conjoint form]
i- it, he, she [SC Cl. 9]
-e [suffix of past, conjoint form; the conjoint form indicates that the vb phrase continues, while the disjoint suffix **-ile** would indicate the end of the vb phrase]
yahlanganiswa and (it was) mixed [narrative aspect]
y- it, he, she [SC Cl. 9]
-a- [narrative aspect marker]
-hlanganisw-a be mixed or joined [v-caus-pass]
-hlangan-a meet, join [v.i.]
-is- make VERB, cause to VERB [causative extension]
no-15ml with 15ml [assoc adv]
no- [assoc pref coalesced with **u**]
na- with, and, also, too, even [assoc pref]
u-15ml 15ml [n Cl. 1a/3a]
we-orange juice of orange juice [possessive Cl. 1/3]
we- of [poss concord Cl. 1/3 coalesced with following **i**]
wa- of [poss concord Cl. 1a/3a]
kanye no-30g (30ml) together with 30g (30ml)
kanye na- together with [adv phr]
u-30g [n Cl. 1a/3a]
weRama of (Rama) margarine [possessive Cl. 1/3]
ikhasi peel, shell [n Cl. 5; pl **amakhasi** Cl. 6]
iØ- [NP Cl. 5]
lewolintshi of an orange [poss Cl. 5]
le- of [poss concord Cl. 5 coalesced with following **i**]
la- of [poss concord Cl. 5]

iwolintshi orange [n Cl. 5; pl **amawolintshi** Cl. 6] {Eng}
eligreythiwe (that has been) grated [rel Cl. 5]
eli- which, that, who [rel conc Cl. 5; < **a-** relative marker + **li-** SC]
ligreythiwe it has been grated [stative]
li- it, he, she [SC Cl. 5]
-greythiwe has been grated [v-pass-stative]
-greythw-a be grated [v-pass]
-greyth-a grate [v.t.] {Eng}
indlela path, road, way, method [n Cl. 9; pl **izindlela** Cl. 10]
in- [NP Cl. 9]
yokwenza for making [possessive Cl. 9]
yo- of [poss concord Cl. 9 coalesced with following **u**]
ya- of [poss concord Cl. 9]
ukwenza making, to make [vn Cl. 15]
ukw- to VERB, VERB-ing [prefix of verbal nouns; NP Cl. 15; var of **uku-** found before **a, i, e**]
-enz-a make, do [v.t.]
shaya beat! [imperative]
noshukela and sugar [assoc adv; < **na- + ushukela**]
ushukela sugar [n Cl. 1a/3a] {Eng}
uØ- [NP Cl. 1a/3a]
thela pour! [imperative]
-thel-a pour [v-appl]
-el- [applied extension; here semantically imprecise]
-th-a pour into vessel with narrow aperture [v.t.]
ufulawa flour [n Cl. 3a] {Eng}
namaqanda and eggs [assoc adv; < **na- + amaqanda**]
kanye nojusi together with the juice

ujusi juice [n Cl. 1a/3a] {Eng}
kuthele pour it [imper + obj]
ku- it [indefinite OC Cl. 17]
-e [imperative suffix used when object concord is present]
kuma-patty pans in cupcake tins, in patty pans [locative]
  ku- to, from, in, at, on [loc pref]
  ama-patty pans cupcake tins, patty pans [n Cl. 6; sg **i-patty pan** Cl. 9a] {Eng}
agcotshisiwe that/which have been greased [rel Cl. 6; < **a-** relativizer + **agcotshisiwe**]
  agcotshisiwe they have been greased [stative]
  -gcotshisw-a be greased [v-caus-pass; < **-gcobis-w-a**; **b** ... **-w-** > **tsh** ... **w**]
  -gcobis-a grease [the causative suffix **-is-** is semantically empty here]
  -gcob-a grease, smear, rub with oil, lubricate [v.t.]
emathinini in tins [loc]
  amathini tins, cans [n Cl. 6; sg **ithini** Cl. 5] {Eng}
  e- ... **-ini** to, from, in, at, on [loc marker]
okubhaka for baking [poss Cl. 6]
  o- of [poss concord Cl. 6 coalesced with following **u**]
  a- of [poss conc Cl. 6]
  ukubhaka baking, to bake [vn Cl. 15] {Afrikaans *bak*}
  uku- to VERB, VERB-ing [prefix of verbal nouns; NP Cl. 15]
  -bhak-a bake [v.t.]
angu-2 x 20cm two of 20cm (lit. which are two times 20cm) [rel phr Cl. 6]
kubhake bake it [imper + obj]
imizuzu minutes [n Cl. 4; sg **umzuzu** Cl. 3]
  imi- [NP Cl. 4]

engu-25 twenty-five [rel Cl. 4]
ingu-25 it is 25 [identificative copulative, pres]
u-25 25 [n Cl. 1a]
kuhhavini in the oven [loc]
  uhhavini oven [n Cl. 1a; pl **ohhavini** Cl. 2b] {Eng}
oshisiswe that/which has been heated [rel Cl. 1]
  o- which, that, who(m) [relativizer used when the SC in the verb concerned has the vowel **u**]
  ushisiswe it has been heated [past, conjoint form]
  u- it, he, she [SC Cl. 1]
  -shisis-a heat [v-caus-caus]
  -shis-a be hot, burn (t.) [v-caus]
  -sh-a burn, get burnt [v.i.]
ngezinga elingu 160°C to 160°C
  ngezinga with a level [adv]
  nge- [instr adv pref coalesced with following **i**]
  nga- by means of, with, through, about, on, at, in, during, on account of, in the vicinity of, in the direction of, towards [instr adv pref]
  izinga degree (not academic); elevation between two closely placed grooves, level, standard, rate [n Cl. 5; pl **amazinga** Cl. 6]
  elingu-160 °C (a hyphen is normally used before numerals) [rel Cl. 5]
  lingu-160°C it is 160°C [ident cop, pres]
  u-160°C [n Cl. 1a] {Eng}
kuze kukhukhumale until it rises
  kuze until it, so that finally, until eventually [aux; subjunctive]
  -ze until [aux; followed by the narrative in the past and the subjunctive elsewhere]

kukhukhumale it rises [subjunc]

-khukhumal-a swell, expand; rise (of dough) [v.i.]

-e [subjunctive suff]

kahle well, properly [manner adv]

ka- **-ly** [adverb formative, prefixed to qualificative stems]

-hle good, nice, lovely, pretty, beautiful, handsome [adjective stem]

kube nsundu and becomes brown [descr cop, inch, subjunctive]

kube it should become [copula, subjunc]

-b-a become, be [copula]

-nsundu dark brown [rel stem]

kupholise cool it [imperative]

-pholis-a cool [v-caus]

-phol-a become cool [v.i.]

bese and then [conjunction]

ukugcoba you spread it [pres, conjoint]

u- you [SC 2 p sg]

nge-orange frosting with orange frosting [instrumental adv]

ngaphezulu on top [instrumental adv]

phezulu top, above, high [loc n Cl. 16]

kuvuvuzele sprinkle it [imperative]

-vuvuzel-a sprinkle (with sugar, powder, ...) [v.t.]

ngekhasi with rind or zest [instrumental adv]

Bayabonga kwaMpanza

Umndeni wakwaMpanza eNewlands East, ubonga bonke abawusingathile usefwini elimnyama ushonelwe yindodana yawo endala uMnuz Sipho Steven Mpanza.

Ubezalwa nguMfundisi waseWeseli uJoe noNkk Abegail Mpanza. Ushone ngoFebruary 2, 1999 wafihlwa ngoFebruary 6, 1999.

USipho ufundise eMandlethu High School naseFunimfundo lapho eshone efundisa khona.

Ushiye emhlabeni inkosikazi yakhe uNkk Constance Lovey Matseng MaMote Mpanza nabantwana abane.

UNkulunkulu anibusise nonke nize nenze njalo nakwabanye. Makaphumule ngobuhle, Amen.

Ngu: Nkk Matseng Constance Lovey Mpanza, Newlands East

Vocabulary

bayabonga they give thanks [pres, disjoint]
  ba- they [SC Cl. 2]
  -ya- [marker of the disjoint form of the present indicative, positive; indicates the end of the verb phrase]
  -bong-a give thanks, be(come) grateful; recite the praises of [v.i. & t.]
kwaMpanza at the Mpanzas' place [loc]
  kwa- at the place of [loc prefix]
  uMpanza (surname) [n Cl. 1a]
umndeni wakwaMpanza the Mpanza family
  umndeni family [n Cl. 3; **imindeni** Cl. 4]
  um- [NP Cl. 3]
wakwaMpanza of the place of Mpanza [poss Cl. 3]
  wa- of [poss conc Cl. 3]

eNewlands East in Newlands East [loc]
  e- to, from, in, at, on [loc prefix]
  iNewlands East (place) [n Cl. 5]
ubonga it thanks [pres, conjoint]
  u- it [SC Cl. 3]
bonke everyone, all, every [quantitative Cl. 2]
  bo- [quant concord Cl. 2, referring to **abantu** people]
  -nke all, every [quant stem]
abawusingathile who supported it [rel Cl. 2]
bawusingathile they supported it [past, disjoint form]
  -wu- it [OC Cl. 3]
  -singath-a support, hold in the arms [v.t.]
  -ath- [fossilized contactive extension indicating bodily contact]
  -ile [past tense suffix]

8

usefwini elimnyama while it was
under a black cloud [locational
cop phr]
usefwini it is under a cloud [loc
cop, pres, partic]
sefwini under a cloud [loc; <
efwini < **e-** + **ifu** + **-ini**]
ifu cloud [n Cl. 5; pl **amafu**
Cl. 6]
-se- ... -ini to, from, in, at, on
[loc marker; **-se-** occurs after
vowels]
elimnyama black, dark [rel Cl. 5]
limnyama it is black, it is dark
[descr cop]
-mnyama black, dark [rel stem]
**ushonelwe yindodana yawo
endala** having lost or having
been bereaved of its elder son
ushonelwe it has been bereaved
[past tense, participial aspect,
conjoint]
-shonelw-a y- be bereaved of
-shonelw-a have set, disappear
or die to one's detriment [v-
appl-pass]
-shonel-a set in the direction of;
set, disappear or die to the
detriment of [v-appl]
-shon-a set (of sun), disappear;
die (euph); fail (in an exam); go
bankrupt [v.i.]
i n d o d a n a son [n Cl. 9; pl
amadodana Cl. 6]
yawo its [poss Cl. 9]
wo it [abs pron Cl. 3]
endala eldest (old) [adjective
Cl. 9]
en- [adj conc Cl. 9]
-dala old [adj stem]
uMnuz Mr. (abbreviation for
uMnumzane)
umnumzane family head;
gentleman, mister [n Cl. 1; pl
abanumzane]

um- [NP Cl. 1]
uSipho (male name) [n Cl. 1a; <
isipho gift]
Mpanza (surname) [n Cl. 1a]
ubezalwa (s)he was born to (lit.
(s)he was being given birth to)
[past present tense]
u- he, she [SC Cl. 1]
-b- [aux indicating past relative
tenses; < **-be**]
-e- he, she [SC Cl. 1; used in
participial]
-zalw-a be given birth to, be
born [v-pass]
-zal-a give birth (to) (not
considered polite with reference
to people) [v.t.]
nguMfundisi by the Reverend
[agentive adv]
ng- by [agentive adv pref]
umfundisi minister, pastor,
priest (**uMfundisi** X the
Reverend X) [n Cl. 1; < **um-** NP
+ **-fundis-** teach + **-i** nom suff;
pl **abefundisi** or **abafundisi**
Cl. 2]
waseWeseli of the Wesleyan
Church [poss Cl. 1]
iWeseli the Wesleyan Church [n
Cl. 5] {Eng}
uJoe (name) [n Cl. 1a] {Eng}
noNkk Abegail Mpanza and Mrs.
Abegail Mpanza [assoc adv phr]
noNkk and Mrs. [assoc adv; < **na-**
+ **uNkk**]
uNkk Mrs. (abbreviation for
unkosikazi)
unkosikazi lady, missus, wife [n
Cl. 1a; pl **onkosikazi** Cl. 2b]
u s h o n e (s)he passed away
(euphemism; lit. set (as of the
sun)) [past tense, conjoint form]
ngo-February 2, 1999 on
February 2, 1999 [instr adverb
phr]

ngo- [instr pref nga- coalesced with u]

u-February (February is usually uFebhuwari in Zulu) [n Cl. 1a]

wafihlwa and (s)he was buried [narrative aspect]

w- he, she [SC Cl. 1; occurs before vowels]

-fihl-w-a be hidden, buried [v-pass]

-fihl-a hide, conceal; bury (euphemism) [v.t.]

ufundise (s)he taught [past tense, conjoint]

-fundis-a teach [v-caus]

-fund-a learn, study; read [v.t.]

eMandlethu High School at Mandlethu High School [loc]

naseFunimfundo and at Funimfundo

seFunimfundo at Funimfundo (school) [loc; < eFunimfundo]

-se- to, from, in, at, on [loc prefix; found after vowels]

iFunimfundo [n Cl. 5]

lapho ... khona where ... [2nd position dem Cl. 16 + abs pron Cl. 17]

eshone (s)he died [past tense, participial aspect, conjoint]

efundisa while teaching [pres, participial aspect]

ushiye (s)he left [past tense, conjoint]

-shiy-a leave (behind) [v.t.]

emhlabeni to, from, in, on the world or earth [loc]

umhlaba world, earth; land [n Cl. 3]

e- ... -eni to, from, in, at, on [loc marker]

inkosikazi wife, woman (in this sense, considered more polite than umfazi) [n Cl. 9; pl

amakhosikazi Cl. 6; n + kh > nk]

yakhe his, her, its [poss Cl. 9]

-khe his, her, its [abs pron Cl. 1, used in possessives]

uNkk Constance Lovey Matseng MaMote Mpanza Mrs. Constance ...

nabantwana and children [assoc adv]

abantwana children [n Cl. 2; sg umntwana Cl. 1]

aba- [NP Cl. 2]

abane four [adjective Cl. 2]

aba- [adj conc Cl. 2]

-ne four [adj stem]

uNkulunkulu God [n Cl. 1a]

anibusise may (s)he bless you [subjunctive]

a- he, she, it [SC Cl. 1]

-ni- you (plural) [OC 2 p pl]

-busis-a bless [v-caus]

-bus-a enjoy life [v.i.]

nonke you all [quant 2 p pl]

no- [quant conc 2 p pl]

nize (and) may you [aux, subjunctive]

ni- you [SC 2 p pl]

-ze eventually VERB [auxiliary]

nenze (may you) do [subjunctive]

n- you [SC 2 p pl]

njalo always [adverb]

nakwabanye and to others

kwabanye to, from others [loc; < ku- + abanye]

abanye other(s), some [adjective Cl. 2]

-nye other, some [adj stem]

makaphumule may (s)he rest [subjunctive]

ma- may, let [hortative prefix]

-ka- he, she [SC Cl. 1]

-phumul-a rest [v.i.]

ngobuhle in beauty [instr adv]

ubuhle beauty [n Cl. 14]

ubu- [noun prefix Cl. 14]
-hle beauty [noun stem; < **-hle**
good, beautiful [adj stem]]

Amen [interjective]
NguNkk by Mrs. (written by)
[agent adv]

Luphi Ubisi Noju?

Wayaphi umhlaba wobisi noju? Iningi lethu lavota okhethweni lonyaka ka 1994 kodwa kuze kube yimanje uhulumeni akakazifezi izethembiso zakhe. Esikhundleni salokho kuyadilizwa ezimbonini, amalungelo awatholakali, kwenyuke izinga lobugebengu, amanani ezimpahla anyukile kanti futhi sibona kugcwala abantu abaqhamuka emazweni angaphandle bezothatha imisebenzi. Ngabe asikafiki isikhathi sokuthi uhulumeni afeze izethembiso zakhe?

J. N., Roodepoort

Vocabulary

luphi? where is it, (s)he? [loc cop, pres]
  lu- it, he, she [SC Cl. 11]
  -phi? where? [interrogative adv]
ubisi milk [n Cl. 11]
  uØ- [NP Cl. 11]
noju and honey [assoc adv; < **na- + uju**]
  uju honey [n Cl. 11]
wayaphi? where did it go? [v phr]
  waya it went [remote past tense]
  -a- [remote past pref]
  -y-a go to (direction to a place always implied if not stated) [v.i.]
wobisi of milk [poss Cl. 3]
  wo- of [poss conc Cl. 3 coalesced with following **u**]
iningi majority, a large number [n Cl. 5; < **-ningi** many [adj st]]
lethu of us, our [possessive Cl. 5; < **la- + -ithu**]
  le- of [poss conc Cl. 5 coalesced with following **i**]
  -ithu [abs pron 1 p pl, used in possessives]
lavota voted [remote past tense]
  l- it, he, she [SC Cl. 5 found before vowels]
  -vot-a vote [v.i.] {Eng}

okhethweni in the election [loc; < **o- + ukhetho + -eni**]
  o- ... -eni to, from, in, at, on [loc marker]
  o- [loc pref used with nouns of Cl. 11]
  ukhetho election [n Cl. 11; < **-kheth-** choose, select, vote; pl **izinketho**]
lonyaka the year, this year [dem phr Cl. 3]
  lo this [1st position dem Cl. 3]
  unyaka year, season [n Cl. 3a; pl **iminyaka** Cl. 4]
ka-1994 of 1994 [poss Cl. 3]
  ka- of [poss conc Cl. 3]
  u-1994 [n Cl. 1a]
kodwa but [conjunction]
kuze kube yimanje up to now, until now
kuze kube up to, until [aux phrase]
yimanje it is now [ident cop, present]
  yi- is, are [ident cop prefix; often follows above construction]
  manje now [time adv]
uhulumeni government [n Cl. 1a; pl **ohulumeni** Cl. 2b] {Afr *goewerment*}

akakazifezi it has not yet fulfilled (them) [present, negative, exclusive aspect]
  a- not [neg pref]
  -ka- he, she [SC Cl. 1]
  -ka- yet [aspect marker]
  -zi- them [OC Cl. 8]
  -fez-a finish, complete, fulfill, effect, accomplish [v.t.]
  -i [neg suff]
izethembiso promises [n Cl. 8; sg **isethembiso**; < **is-** NP + **-ethembis-** promise]
  iz- [NP Cl. 8]
esikhundleni sa- in place of, instead of [loc phrase]
  esikhundleni in (the) place, to, from, in the position [loc]
  isikhundla place, situation [n Cl. 7]
  isi- [NP Cl. 7]
salokho of that, thereof [poss Cl. 7]
  sa- of [poss conc Cl. 7]
  lokho that [2nd position dem Cl. 17]
kuyadilizwa they are retrenching (lit. there is being retrenched) [present tense, disjoint form]
  -dilizw-a be pulled down; be retrenched [v-pass]
  -diliz-a pull down, cause to fall down; retrench [v.t.]
ezimbonini in the factories [loc]
  izimboni factories [n Cl. 10; sg **imboni** Cl. 9]
  izim- [NP Cl. 10; occurs before stems starting in **b, bh, p, ph, f**]
amalungelo rights [n Cl. 6; sg **ilungelo** Cl. 5]
awatholakali are not received [present tense, neg]
  -wa- they, it [SC Cl. 6; found after vowels]

-tholakal-a get found, be found, be available, be obtainable [v-neut]
-thol-a obtain, get, find, receive; experience [v.t.]
  -akal- get VERB-ed, be VERB-able/-ible [neuter extension]
kwenyuke there has gone up, there has risen [past tense, conjoint]
  kw- it, there [indefinite SC; Cl. 17]
  -enyuk-a go up, rise, ascend [v.t.; variant **-nyuk-a** (see below: **a-nyuk-ile**)]
lobugebengu of crime [poss Cl. 5; < **la-** + **ubugebengu**]
  lo- of [poss conc Cl. 5 coalesced with following **u**]
  ubugebengu crime, criminality, gangsterism [n Cl. 14]
amanani numbers; prices [n Cl. 6; sg **inani** Cl. 5]
ezimpahla of goods [poss Cl. 6]
  ezim- [< **a-** + **izim-**]
  e- of [poss conc Cl. 6 coalesced with following **i**]
  izimpahla goods, property, belongings, luggage [n Cl. 10; sg **impahla** (same meaning as plural); < **im-** + **-phahla**; **m** + **ph** > **mp**]
anyukile they have increased [past tense, disjoint]
  -nyuk-a go up, rise, ascend [v.t.; variant **-enyuk-a** (see above)]
kanti after all, whereas, while, but [conj]
futhi again, in addition, also [adv]
sibona we see [pres, conjoint]
  si- we [SC 1 p pl]
  -bon-a see, witness, understand [v.t.]
kugcwala the influx (lit. there becoming full) [present tense, participial aspect]

13

-gcwal-a become full, be abundant, abound in [v.i., inch]

abaqhamuka who come from [rel Cl. 2]

baqhamuka they come from [pres, conjoint]

-qhamuk-a proceed from, come from, come suddenly into view, appear unexpectedly [v.i.]

emazweni to, from, in countries [loc]

amazwe lands, countries [n Cl. 6; sg **izwe** Cl. 5]

angaphandle that are outside [rel Cl. 6]

angaphandle they are outside [locational cop]

ngaphandle outside [loc]

phandle outside [loc noun, Cl. 16]

pha- [NP Cl. 16]

bezothatha (they) coming to take [present tense, participial aspect, venitive]

be- they [SC Cl. 2; used in partic]

-zo- come to, come and [venitive marker]

-thath-a take, carry away [v.t.]

imisebenzi jobs [n Cl. 4; sg **umsebenzi** Cl. 3; < **-sebenz-** work **-i +** nom suff]

ngabe asikafiki isikhathi sokuthi ...? isn't it about time that ...?

ngabe ought, is it the case (that), it would be, it could be, could it be that [conj]

asikafiki it hasn't yet arrived [present, negative, exclusive aspect]

-si- it, he, she [SC Cl. 7]

-fik-a arrive (at), reach [v.i.]

isikhathi time [n Cl. 7; pl **izikhathi** Cl. 8]

sokuthi (for) that [poss Cl. 7]

so- of [poss conc **sa-** of Cl. 7 coalesced with following **u**]

ukuthi that [conj]

Roodepoort (town)

Izinkanyezi

Virgo
(August 24 — September 22)
Njengoba kukhona obhekene nakho ngalesisikhathi, kufanele ukuba usebenzele phezu kwamaphutha esikhathi esedlule. Kufanele uziseshe ngokwenzeke esikhathini esedlule ukuze ube nekusasa elikhanyayo, uwagweme lawo maphutha angaphindi enzeke. Ukuba nogazi kwakho kubantu bobunye ubulili yikho okuzokwenza ukuba uthandeke.
Izinsuku zenhlanhla mhlaka 2 no-3.
Izinombolo zenhlanhla 2 no-3.

Libra
(September 23 — October 22)
Lesi yisikhathi esihle sokuba uzihlelisise izinto zakho. Yisikhathi sokucabanga ngempilo yakho nangekusasa lakho. Kufanele ugxile ezintweni okufanele uzenze neziyisibopho sakho ukuze wazi ukuthi uzobhekana nazo kanjani. Othandweni uma ungumuntu ongayedwana, sekuyisikhathi sokuba imithandazo nezifiso zakho ziphumelele ngokuba uthole umuntu ozothandana naye.
Izinsuku zenhlanhla mhlaka 4, 5 no-6.
Izinombolo zenhlanhla 4, 5 no-6.

Vocabulary

izinkanyezi stars [n Cl. 10; sg **inkanyezi** Cl. 9; < **-khany-** shine; **n + kh > nk**]

njengoba since, just as, seeing that [conj]

kukhona there is ..., there are ... [loc cop, pres; may also introduce an exist cop]
  khona it, there, present [abs pron Cl. 17]
  kho it, there, present [abs pron Cl. 17]

-na [stabilizer (a syllable added to a monosyllabic form to make it disyllabic. Monosyllabic forms are rare in Zulu.)]

obhekene nakho that/which you are facing (lit. that you are look-ing at each other with it) [ind rel of assoc adverbial relationship, 2 p sg]

o- you who, which you, that you, who(m) you [rel conc 2 p sg]

ubhekene you are facing [stative; < **-bhekan-** + **-i...e**]

-i...e [stative suffix used with radicals ending in **al, an, am, ath**; coalescence takes place between the **a** and the **i**]

-bhekan-a na- ... bec faced with ..., be opposite ...

-bhekan-a look at each other, face each other, be opposite [v-recip]

-an- each other, one another

[recip ext]

-bhek-a look (at), watch, keep a watch on, watch over, look after [v.t.]

ngalesisikhathi at this time [instr adv phr]

lesisikhathi this time [dem phr Cl. 7]

lesi this [1st position dem Cl. 7]

kufanele ukuba usebenzele phezu kwamaphutha you need to work on the basis of the mistakes

kufanele it is necessary [stative tense]

-fanel-a must, should, ought, have to, be necessary [v.inch]

-e [stative suff found with verbs ending in **el, ol, ul**]

ukuba (so) that [conj; followed by subjunc]

usebenzele you should work from [subjunc]

-sebenzel-a work for, work towards, work from [v-appl]

-el- for, on behalf of, with respect to, to the detriment of, in or from the direction of [appl ext]

-sebenz-a work, operate [v.i.]

phezu kwa- above, over [loc phr; < **phezulu** (the final syllable is elided when followed by **kwa-**) + **kwa-**]

kwa- [poss conc Cl. 17; link between certain loc nouns and a following nominal]

amaphutha failings, shortcomings, errors, mistakes [n Cl. 6; sg **iphutha**]

esikhathi of time [poss Cl. 6]

esedlule that/which has passed [rel Cl. 7]

sedlule it has passed [stative]

s- it, he, she [SC Cl. 7]

-edlul-a pass, surpass [v.t.;

variant of **-dlul-a**]

uziseshe you should ask yourself, you should look into yourself [subjunc]

-zi- self (myself, yourself, himself, herself, itself), selves (ourselves, yourselves, themselves) [reflexive pref]

-sesh-a search, pump for information, crossquestion [v.t.] {Eng}

ngokwenzeke about what has happened [instr adv]

ng- by means of, with, through, on account of, about, on, at, in, during, in the vicinity of [instr adv prefix with elision of **a**]

okwenzeke that which has happened [rel Cl. 17]

kwenzeke it happened [past, conjoint form]

-enzek-a occur, happen, take place, be feasible [v-neut]

-ek- get VERB-ed, be VERB-able/-ible [neuter ext]

esikhathini in (the) time [loc; < **isikhathi**]

ukuze so that, in order to [conj; followed by subjunctive]

ube nekusasa you should have a future (lit. you should be with a tomorrow) [assoc cop, inch, subjunc]

ube you should be [subjunc]

nekusasa with a future [assoc adv; < **na- + ikusasa**]

ne- with, and, also, too, even [assoc pref coalesced with **i**]

ikusasa tomorrow, the future [n Cl. 5]

elikhanyayo that/which is bright, that/which shines [rel Cl. 5]

liyakhanya it is bright, it shines [pres, disjoint]

-khany-a shine, glow, gleam,

be bright [v.i.]
-yo [rel suff]
uwagweme and you should avoid them [subjunc]
-wa- them, it [OC Cl. 6]
-gwem-a avoid, evade [v.t.]
lawo those, that [2nd position dem Cl. 6]
angaphindi enzeke they should not reoccur
angaphindi they should not again [aux, subjunc, neg]
-nga- not [neg pref, used in participials, relatives and the subjunctive]
-phind-a VERB repeatedly, VERB again, VERB also [aux indicating repetition of an action]
enzeke they should happen, occur [subjunc]
Ø- they, it [SC Cl. 6; var of a- found before vowels]
ukuba nogazi kwakho your having charm [assoc cop, vn Cl. 15]
ukuba na- ... having ..., to have ... (lit. to be with) [vn of assoc cop]
ugazi personality, charm [n Cl. 11]
kwakho your [poss Cl. 15]
kwa- of [poss conc Cl. 15]
-kho your [abs pron 2 p sg, used in possessives]
kubantu to people [loc; < ku- + abantu]
abantu people [n Cl. 2; sg umuntu Cl. 1]
bobunye of the other, of another [poss Cl. 2]
b- of [poss conc Cl. 2; < ba- by deletion of a before o]
obunye other, another [adj Cl. 14]
obu- [adj conc Cl. 14]

ubulili gender, sex; sexuality [n Cl. 14]
yikho is that, is what [ident cop, pres]
okuzokwenza that/which will make [rel Cl. 17]
kuzokwenza it will make [future]
ku- it [SC Cl. 15]
-zo- will, shall [fut pref]
-kw- [prefix inserted to separate two vowels in the future tense]
uthandeke you should be lovable or likable or popular [subjunc]
-thandek-a be lovable, be likable, be popular [v-neut]
-thand-a like, love [v.t.]
izinsuku days (of 24 hours) [n Cl. 10; sg usuku]
izin- [NP Cl. 10]
zenhlanhla lucky, of luck, of good fortune [poss Cl. 10]
inhlanhla good luck, good fortune [n Cl. 9]
mhlaka 2 the second (day) [< umuhla ka-2]
mhlaka the day of
umuhla day [n Cl. 3; pl. imihla Cl. 4]
umu- [NP Cl. 3]
u-2 two [n Cl. 1a; the initial vowel is elided after the poss conc]
no-3 and three
u-3 three [n Cl. 1a]
izinombolo numbers [n Cl. 10a; sg inombolo Cl. 9a] {Eng/Afr?}
iziØ- [NP Cl. 10a]
yisikhathi esihle sokuba uzihlelisise is a good time to put them in order [ident cop phr]
yisikhathi it is time [ident cop, pres]
y- is, are [ident cop pref used before the vowel i]
esihle good [adj Cl. 7]

esi- [adj conc Cl. 7]

sokuba for ... to ..., for becoming [poss Cl. 7]

so- of [poss conc Cl. 7 coalesced with following u]

uzihlelisise you should put them in good order [subjunc]

-hlelisis-a put in good order, arrange thoroughly [v-intens]

-isis- thoroughly, very well, forcefully [intensive ext]

-hlel-a put in order, arrange [v.t.]

izinto things [n Cl. 10; sg utho Cl. 11; n + th > nt]

zakho your [poss Cl. 10]

za- of [poss conc Cl. 10]

yisikhathi sokucabanga it is time to think [ident cop phr]

sokucabanga for thinking [poss Cl. 7]

ukucabanga to think, thinking [vn Cl. 15]

-cabang-a think [v.i. & t.]

ngempilo about life [instr adv; < nga- + impilo]

impilo life, health, good health [n Cl. 9; < -phil- live, be well, be in good health; m + ph > mp]

yakho your [poss Cl. 9]

nangekusasa and about the future, and about tomorrow [assoc adv]

ngekusasa about the future, about tomorrow [instr adv]

lakho your [poss Cl. 5]

ugxile you must be firm [subjunc]

-gxil-a stand firm, stand fast, be steadfast [v.i.]

ezintweni okufanele uzenze in the things you have to do

ezintweni in things [loc; < izinto]

okufanele uzenze that/which you have to do [ind rel of plain objectival relationship, Cl. 17]

kufanele uzenze you have to do them [v phr]

uzenze you should do them [subjunc]

-z- them [OC Cl. 10]

neziyisibopho and which are an obligation [assoc adv]

n- with, and, also, too [assoc pref with vowel elision]

eziyisibopho that/which are an obligation [rel Cl. 10]

ziyisibopho they are an obligation [ident cop, pres]

zi- they, it [SC Cl. 10]

isibopho obligation, duty, necessity [n Cl. 7; < -boph- tie (up), bind, make fast; pl izibopho Cl. 8]

sakho your [poss Cl. 7]

ukuze wazi ukuthi so that you should know that

wazi you should know [subjunc]

-az-i know [irregular verb taking the suffix -i in all tenses and moods except for the past tense (Here -i occurs in place of the expected -e.)]

uzobhekana nazo kanjani how you will face them

nazo with them [assoc adv]

zo them, they, their [abs pron Cl. 10]

kanjani? how? [interrogative adverb]

ka- [adv formative that is semantically redundant here]

-njani? what sort or kind of? [rel stem; < interrogative adv]

njani? how? [interrogative adverb; sometimes interchangeable with kanjani?]

othandweni in love [loc < o- + uthando + -eni]

uthando love [n Cl. 11; < -thand- love]

uma if, when [conj; followed by the participial aspect]
ungumuntu you are a person [ident cop, pres]
  umuntu person [n Cl. 1]
  umu- [NP Cl. 1]
ongayedwana who is not alone/on his own [rel Cl. 1]
  akayedwana (s)he is not on his or her own [descr cop, pres, neg]
  yedwana sole, completely alone [quant]
  ye- [quant conc Cl. 1]
  -dwana sole, completely alone [quant stem]; < **-dwa** only, alone + **-ana** [dimin suff] (In this instance the diminutive suffix intensifies rather than lessens the meaning of the base stem.)
sekuyisikhathi it is now time, it is high time [ident cop, present tense, exclusive aspect]
  se- already, now, soon [exclusive aspect marker]
  kuyisikhathi it is time [ident cop, pres]
imithandazo prayers [n Cl. 4; sg **umthandazo** Cl. 3; < **-thandaz-** pray]

nezifiso and desires [assoc adv]
  izifiso desires, wishes [n Cl. 8; sg **isifiso** Cl. 7; < **-fis-** desire, wish for]
zakho your [poss Cl. 8]
ziphumelele they should succeed [subjunc]
  zi- they [SC Cl. 8]
  -phumelel-a succeed [v-perfective]
  -elel- completely, perfectly [perfective ext]
ngokuba through (that) [instr adv; < **nga-** + **ukuba**]
uthole you should find [subjunc]
ozothandana naye with whom you will share love [ind rel of plain adverbial relationship, 2 p sg]
  uzothandana naye you and he or she will love each other (lit. you will love each other with her or him) [fut v phr]
naye with him, with her
  ye him, her, it [abs pron Cl. 1]
(u-)4 four [n Cl. 1a]
(u-)5 five [n Cl. 1a]
no-6 and six [assoc adv]
u-6 six [n Cl. 1a]

Abantu Manje Abavotele Imfundo

Mhleli

Ngicela isikhala kengibonisane nomphakathi wakithi Kwa-Zulu/Natal, njengoba kuza ukhetho ngithi awuvotele imfundo noxolo ngalezi zizathu.

Inhlangano ye-IFP ihlulekile ukukhipha imiphumela emihle kaSTD 10 ngo1999, nalonyaka isazoba mibi kakhulu.

UNgqongqoshe osewaphuma wehluleka ukubeka imfundo ezingeni elifanele kwala noma uNgqongqoshe kazwelonke uProf Sibusiso Bhengu esho ukuthi uDr Vincent Zulu akakhishwe.

INkatha yakushaya indiva lokho. Buka nje ukuqedwa kwezipoki nothisha bomgunyathi kuthathwe iminyaka emihlanu yonke kungenziwa lokhu nakuba iSadtu yasho uqala u-1994 ukuthi akuphenywe. Namanje ezikoleni zethu kugcwele othisha abangaqeqeshiwe.

Isikole ngasinye, othisha abaqeqeshiwe bayingcosana kuna-bangaqeqeshiwe. Baningi othisha abaqeqeshiwe abahlezi emakhaya, kodwa uNgqongqoshe akafuni ukuqasha othisha abawufundele umsebenzi, ufuna kuqhubeke laba abangazi lutho.

Ngaleyo ndlela imiphumela isazoba mibi.

Ngakho ukuvotela iNkatha kusho ukuvotela imfundo efile.

Bakhohlisa abantu bakhala ngoHulumeni kazwelonke, kodwa kwezinye izifunda ukutshalwa kabusha nokuqashwa kothisha kuya kuqhubeka.

Lapha uNgqongqoshe wemfundo ulokhu ethithiza nje.

Kuzo zonke izifunda udlame lwepolitiki selwaphela, kodwa lapha KwaZulu/Natal lusaqhubeka.

Uma ufunda amaphepha, ulalela nomsakazo, uzothola ukuthi abaholi be-ANC balokhu becela uxolo; ezindaweni lapho iNkatha iningi khona, kusahlukunyezwa abantu abayi-ANC, kodwa ezindaweni lapho i-ANC iningi khona ayikwenzi lokho kwabeNkatha.

20

Lokhu kubangwa wukuthi abaholi bayo kabathembele ebuholini obunobuhlakani, kodwa bathembele ekuhlukumezeni.

Kusazothatha iminyaka eminingi kade iNkatha yazi ukuthi iyini ipolitiki.

Ngithi-ke mphakathi wakithi uma sivotela i-ANC siyobe sivotela imfundo enhle yezingane zethu ngoba kuyoqashwa othisha abaqeqeshiwe ibe mihle imiphumela, nodlame luyophela ngoba i-ANC inabaholi abafuna uxolo njalo.

Votela i-ANC imele imfundo nokuthula. Viva ANC, Viva!

Ngicela ugodle igama lami nekheli.

Okhathazekile, Bergville

Vocabulary

abavotele may they vote for, let them vote for [subjunc]
a- let, may, if only [hortative pref]
-votel-a vote for [v-appl]
imfundo education [n Cl. 9; < -fund- study, learn, read]
mhleli [vocative of **umhleli**]
umhleli editor [n Cl. 1; < -hlel- arrange, edit; pl. **abahleli** Cl. 2]
ngicela I would like, I request [pres, conjoint]
ngi- I [SC 1 p sg]
-cel-a ask for, request [v.t.]
isikhala opening, opportunity [n Cl. 7; pl **izikhala** Cl. 8]
kengibonisane in order that I can exchange views [subjunc]
ke in order that, so that [subjunc prefix]
-bonisan-a exchange views (lit. show one another) [v-caus-recip]
-bonis-a show (to) [v-caus]
nomphakathi with, even, and, also the community [assoc adv]

umphakathi community [n Cl. 3; < **um-** + **phakathi** inside; pl **imiphakathi** Cl. 4]
wakithi of our home, of our country [poss Cl. 3]
kithi to, from, in, at our place or country, the place to which I or we belong [loc]
ki- to, from, in, at, on [loc pref; variant found before pronouns **mi(na)**, **thi(na)** and **(ni)na**]
thi we, us [abs pron 1 p pl]
KwaZulu/Natal KwaZulu-Natal (province of South Africa) [loc]
kuza there is going to be (lit. there is coming) [pres, conjoint]
-z-a come [v.i.]
ngithi I say, I think [present, pos]
-th-i say; think (be of the opinion) [irregular verb taking the suffix **-i** in all tenses and moods except for the past tense]
awuvotele let it vote for [subjunc]
noxolo and peace [assoc adv]
uxolo peace [n Cl. 11; < -xol-bec peaceful, tranquil, calm]

ngalezi for these [instr adv]
  lezi these [1st pos dem Cl. 8]
zizathu [< **izizathu**]
  izizathu reasons [n Cl. 8; sg
  isizathu Cl. 7]
inhlangano meeting, assembly;
  association, society,
  organization [n Cl. 9; <
  -hlangan- meet, assemble; pl
  izinhlangano Cl. 10]
ye-IFP of the IFP (Inkatha
  Freedom Party) [poss Cl. 9]
  i-IFP IFP [n Cl. 9a]
ihlulekile it has been unable
  [stative]
  -hlulek-a be beaten, be overcome, be defeated, be conquered; be unable, fail [v-neut]
  -hlul-a defeat, conquer, overcome [v.t.]
ukukhipha to take out, to withdraw, to produce (to view) [vn
  Cl. 15]
  -khiph-a take out, withdraw,
  produce (to view) [v.t.]
imiphumela results [n Cl. 4; sg
  umphumela; < **-phumel-** come
  out for + **-a** nom suff]
emihle good [adj Cl. 4]
  emi- [adj conc Cl. 4]
ka-STD 10 for Std (Standard) 10
  (This was formerly the highest
  level of secondary education)
  [poss Cl. 4]
  u-STD 10 Std 10 [n Cl. 1a]
  {Eng}
ngo-1999 in 1999 [instr adv]
  u-1999 1999 [n Cl. 1a]
nalonyaka and this year, even this
  year [assoc adv]
isazoba mibi they will still be bad
  [descr cop, inch, future]
  i- they [SC Cl. 4]
  -sa- still [persistive aspect
  prefix]

mibi bad [adjective minus
  initial vowel **e-**]
  -mi- [2nd half of adj conc,
  Cl. 4]
  -bi bad [adj stem]
kakhulu very, a lot, a great deal,
  highly [manner adv; < **ka-** +
  -khulu big, great [adj stem]]
ungqongqoshe minister of state,
  cabinet minister [n Cl. 1a; pl
  ongqongqoshe Cl. 2b]
osewaphuma who already left
  some time ago [rel Cl. 1]
  sewaphuma (s)he already left
  long ago [rem past, exclusive; <
  se- + **-w-** SC Cl. 1 + **-a-** rem
  past pref]
wehluleka (s)he was unable
  [remote past; < **w-** SC Cl. 1 +
  -Ø:- rem past pref that merges
  with the following **e** to produce
  a long vowel]
  -Ø:- remote past prefix [the
  colon **:** represents a lengthening
  of the following vowel]
  -ehlulek-a [v-neut; variant of
  -hlulek-a (see ABOVE) and
  -ahlulek-a]
**ukubeka imfundo ezingeni
elifanele** to place education on a
  proper level
ukubeka to put, to place [vn Cl.
  15]
  -bek-a put, place [v.t.]
ezingeni to, from, at, on a level or
  degree [loc; < **izinga**]
elifanele that/which is necessary,
  that/which is proper [rel Cl. 5]
  lifanele it is necessary, it is
  proper [stative]
  -fanel-a bec proper [v.inch]
kwala even though, not
  withstanding the fact that [conj]
noma although, as if [this conjunction is redundant here]

kazwelonke the national (minister) [poss Cl. 1]
uzwelonke the nation [n Cl. 1a; < **izwe** country + **lonke** the whole [quant]]
uProf Prof. [n Cl. 1a; pl **oProf** Cl. 2b] {Eng}
Sibusiso (male name) [n Cl. 1a; < **isibusiso** blessing]
Bhengu (surname) [n Cl. 1a]
esho (s)he being of the opinion, (s)he states [pres, partic]
  -sh-o say, say that, say so, state, mean, be of the opinion that, intend [irregular verb taking the suffix **-o** in all tenses and moods except for the negative of the past tense]
uDr Dr. [n Cl. 1a] {Eng}
Vincent (name) [n Cl. 1a] {Eng}
Zulu (surname) [n Cl. 1a]
akakhishwe (s)he should be removed [subjunc]
  -khishw-a be taken out, be brought out, be removed [v-pass; < **-khiphw-a**; **phw** > **shw**]
iNkatha Inkatha (Zulu cultural and political organization; < **inkatha** headpad (on which to carry loads), tribal emblem believed to ensure the solidarity and loyalty of members of the tribe) [n Cl. 9; < **in-** + **-khatha**; **n + kh > nk**]
yakushaya indiva dismissed it as worthless [v phr, rem past]
  -ku- it [OC Cl. 15; see the note under **lokho** below]
  -shay-a indiva dismiss as worthless
  indiva castoff, castaway, worthless thing [n Cl. 9]
lokho that [2nd pos dem Cl.15; although applied to the Cl. 9 noun **indiva**, the Cl. 15

demonstrative (referring to **ukunto** thing [n Cl. 15]) indicates contempt]
buka nje just look
buka look [imperative]
  -buk-a look (at), watch [v.t.]
nje just, only, merely, then, so [manner adv]
ukuqedwa the removal, to be ended, to be finished [vn Cl. 15]
  -qedw-a be ended [v-pass]
  -qed-a bring to an end, finish [v.t.]
kwezipoki of ghosts (teachers) [poss Cl. 15]
  izipoki ghosts (i.e. ghost teachers—non-existent teachers who are on the salary role) [n Cl. 8; sg **isipoki** Cl. 7] {Afr *spook*}
nothisha and teachers [< **na-** + **othisha**]
  othisha teachers [n Cl. 2b; sg **uthisha** Cl. 1a] {Eng}
  o- [NP Cl. 2b]
bomgunyathi bogus [poss Cl. 2]
  umgunyathi backdoor methods [n Cl.3]
kuthathwe it took (lit. there was taken) [past, conjoint]
  -thathw-a be taken [v-pass]
iminyaka years [n Cl. 4; sg **unyaka** Cl. 3a]
emihlanu five [adj Cl. 4]
  -hlanu five [adj stem]
yonke every, all, the whole [quant Cl. 4]
  yo- [quant conc Cl. 4]
kungenziwa without this being done [present, partic, negative]
  -ng- not [neg prefix; variant of **-nga-** found before vowels]
  -enziw-a be done, be made [v-pass]
  -iw- be VERB-ed, be VERB-en

[pass ext found after verbs having C or VC structure]
-a [present negative suffix found with verbs ending in **w** (mainly passive)]
lokhu this [1st pos dem Cl. 17]
nakuba although, even though [conj, followed by participial]
iSadtu Sadtu (South African Democratic Teachers Union) [n Cl. 9a]
yasho it said so [remote past, partic]
uqala (when) it began [present, partic]
-qal-a begin, start, do for the first time [v.i. & t.]
akuphenywe let it be investigated [subjunc]
-phenyw-a be investigated [v-pass]
-pheny-a turn over (a leaf, page); investigate, search [v.t.]
namanje even now [assoc adv]
ezikoleni to, from, in, at schools [loc]
izikole schools [n Cl 8; **isikole** Cl. 7] {Afr *skool*}
ngasinye each [instr adv]
zethu our [poss Cl. 8]
kugcwele are full of, it is full (of) [stative; < **-gcwal-** + **-i...e**]
-gcwele be full (of), abound (in)
abangaqeqeshiwe who are not trained, who are not qualified [rel Cl. 2]
abaqeqeshiwe they have not been trained [stative; < **-qeqesh-** + **-w-** + **-i...e**]
-qeqesh-a train, coach, instruct [v.t.]
sinye one [enumerative]
si- [enum conc Cl. 7]
-nye one [enum stem]
abaqeqeshiwe who are qualified,

who are trained [rel Cl. 2]
baqeqeshiwe they have been trained [stative]
bayingcosana there are few, they are a small number [ident cop, pres]
ingcosana a small quantity or number, few, a little [n Cl. 9; < **in-** + **-cosana**; **n + c > ngc**]
kunabangaqeqeshiwe compared with those who are unqualified [comparative adv]
kuna- compared to, in comparison with, more than [compar adv pref]
baningi there are many (lit. they are many) [descr cop, pres]
ba- [2nd half of adj conc Cl. 2]
-ningi many, a lot of, much, plentiful, numerous [adj stem]
abahlezi who sit [rel Cl. 2]
bahlezi they are sitting, they are seated [stative]
-hlezi sitting, seated [irregular stative form of **-hlal-a**]
-hlal-a sit (down) [v.inch]
emakhaya at home, (to) home, from home (lit. at, to, from homes) [loc; one of the exceptions that does not take a locative suffix]
amakhaya homes [n Cl. 6; sg **ikhaya** Cl. 5]
akafuni (s)he does not want [pres, neg]
-fun-a want [v.t.]
ukuqasha to employ [vn Cl. 15]
-qash-a employ, hire, rent [v.t.]
abawufundele umsebenzi who have studied for the job [rel phr Cl. 2]
abawufundele who have studied for it [rel Cl. 2]
bawufundele they have studied for it [past, disjoint]

-fundel-a study or read in, or at, or for, or towards [v-appl]

umsebenzi work, job, task; use [n Cl. 3; < **-sebenz-** + **-i** (though the nominal suffix **-i** is generally associated with agent nouns, this is one of the few exceptions)]

ufuna kuqhubeke laba abangazi lutho (s)he wants those who know nothing to continue

ufuna (s)he wants [pres, conjoint]
  u- he, she [SC Cl. 1]

kuqhubeke that there should continue [subjunc]
  -qhubek-a continue, proceed, carry on [v-neut; the neut ext does not have its usual significance here]
  -qhub-a continue, carry on, proceed, make progress [v.i.]

laba these [1st pos dem Cl. 2]

abangazi who do not know [rel Cl. 2]
  abazi they do not know [pres, neg]

lutho something, anything, nothing [< **ulutho** n Cl. 11; initial vowel elided due to preceding neg verb]
  ulu- [NP Cl. 11; var of **uØ-** used by some people before monosyllabic noun stems]

ngaleyo ndlela in that way [instr adv phr]

ngaleyo through that [instr adv]
  leyo that [2nd pos dem Cl. 9]
  ndlela [< **indlela**]

ngakho ukuvotela by voting for [instr adv phr]

ngakho by it, through it [instr adv]
  kho it [abs pron Cl. 15]

ukuvotela voting for, to vote for [vn Cl. 15]

kusho that means [pres, conjoint]

efile that/which is dead, that/which is broken (down) [rel Cl. 9

ifile it or (s)he is dead, it is broken (down) [stative]

-file(yo) dead, broken (down) [rel stem]

-f-a die; be ill, suffer [v.i.]

-ile [stative suff]

bakhohlisa they deceive, mislead, cheat [pres, conjoint]
  -khohlis-a deceive, mislead, cheat [v-caus]
  -khohl-a slip the mind, escape the memory; perplex, puzzle [v.t.]

bakhala they complain [pres, conjoint]
  -khal-a cry, weep, scream; complain, voice a grievance; request [v.i.]

ngohulumeni kazwelonke about the national government [instr adv phr]

ngohulumeni about the government [instr adv]

kwezinye in other(s), amongst other(s) [loc; < **ku-** + **ezinye**]
  ezinye other [adj Cl. 8]
  eziØ- [adj conc Cl. 8]

izifunda districts, regions, provinces [n Cl. 8; sg **isifunda**]

ukutshalwa kabusha renewal, revitalization, rejuvenation

ukutshalwa to be planted or sown [vn Cl. 15]
  -tshalw-a be planted, be sown [v-pass]
  -tshal-a plant, sow [v.t.]

kabusha anew, afresh [manner adv]
  busha anew, afresh [manner adv (the adverb prefix **ka-** is redundant here); < **ubusha** newness, freshness [n Cl. 14; < **-sha** new, fresh, young [adj

25

stem]]

nokuqashwa and the appointment [assoc adv]

ukuqashwa appointment, employment, to be hired or appointed or employed [vn Cl. 15]

-qashw-a be employed, be hired, be appointed [v-pass]

kothisha of teachers [poss Cl. 15; < **kwa-** + **othisha**]

ko- of [< **kwa-** poss conc Cl. 15 + **o**]

kuya kuqhubeka it still continues [v phr]

-y-a still [aux indicating present continuous action]

lapha here [1st pos dem Cl 16]

wemfundo of education [pos Cl. 1]

ulokhu ethithiza (s)he keeps on bumbling [v phr]

-lokhu keep on VERB-ing [aux, followed by the participial; < **lokhu** [1st pos dem Cl 15]

ethithiza bumbling [present, partic]

-thithiz-a hesitate, be confused, bumble [v.i.]

kuzo zonke in all these [loc phr]

kuzo to, from, in them [loc]

zo them, they, their [abs pron Cl. 8]

zonke all, every [quant Cl. 8]

zo- [quant conc Cl. 8]

udlame violence [n Cl. 11]

lwepolitiki of politics [poss Cl. 11]

lwe- [poss conc Cl. 11 coalesced with **i**]

lwa- of [poss conc Cl. 11]

ipolitiki politics [n Cl. 9a] {Afr *politiek*}

selwaphela it ceased a long time ago [remote past, exclusive aspect]

-lw- it, he, she [SC Cl. 11]

-phel-a come to an end, cease, get finished [v.i.]

lusaqhubeka it still continues [pres, persistive aspect]

ufunda you read [present, partic]

amaphepha papers [n Cl. 6; sg **iphepha** Cl. 5] {Eng}

ulalela (and) you listen to [present, partic]

-lalel-a listen (to) [v.i. & t.]

nomsakazo the radio too [assoc adv]

umsakazo radio, broadcast [n Cl. 3; < **-sakaz-** broadcast]

uzothola you will find [fut]

abaholi leaders [n Cl. 2; sg **umholi** Cl. 1; < **-hol-** lead]

be-ANC of the ANC (African National Congress) [poss Cl. 2]

be- of [poss conc Cl. 2 coalesced with **i**]

i-ANC the ANC [n Cl. 9a]

balokhu they keep on [aux]

becela (they) asking for [present, partic]

ezindaweni to, from, in, at, the places [loc]

izindawo places [n Cl. 10; sg **indawo** Cl. 9]

lapho iNkatha iningi khona where Inkatha is found in large numbers [ind rel of plain loc rel]

iningi it is plentiful, there are many [descr cop, pres]

kusahlukunyezwa abayi-ANC those of the ANC are still attacked or assaulted

kusahlukunyezwa there is or are still attacked [pres, persistive]

-hlukunyezw-a be attacked, assaulted, violated, harassed, jolted [v-pass; < **-hlukumez-w-a**; m ... **-w-** > **ny** ... **-w-**]

-hlukumez-a attack, assault, be violent, violate; shock, jolt, offend, annoy, harass [v.t.]
abayi-ANC who are ANC [rel]
bayi-ANC they are (the) ANC [ident cop, pres]
ayikwenzi it does not do it [pres, neg]
-yi- it, (s)he [SC Cl. 9]
-kw- it [indefinite OC Cl. 17]
kwabeNkatha to, from those of Inkatha [loc]
abeNkatha those of Inkatha [poss pron Cl. 2]
a- [pronominalizer (forms pronouns from possessives)]
beNkatha of Inkatha [poss Cl. 2]
lokhu kubangwa wukuthi this is caused by the fact that (lit. this is caused by that)
kubangwa it is caused [pres, conjoint]
-bangw-a be caused [v-pass]
-bang-a cause, produce [v.t.]
wukuthi by (the fact) that, because, due to [agentive adv]
w- by [agentive adv pref]
bayo its [poss Cl. 2]
yo it, he, him, she, her [abs pron Cl. 9]
kabathembele they do not have faith in, they do not believe in [stative, neg; Note: with different tones, this word could also mean "let them have faith in" — subjunc with hortative pref]
ka- not [neg pref; variant of **a-**]
-thembel-a have faith in, have confidence in, trust, rely on [v-appl, inch]
-themb-a hope, trust, expect [v.t.]
ebuholini in leadership [loc]

ubuholi leadership [n Cl. 14]
obunobuhlakani intellectual (lit. that has cleverness) [rel Cl. 2]]
bunobuhlakani it has cleverness [assoc cop, pres]
bu- it, they [SC Cl. 14]
-na- with [assoc pref]
ubuhlakani cunning, craftiness, cleverness [n Cl. 14]
bathembele they believe in [stative]
ekuhlukumezeni in violence [loc]
ukuhlukumeza violence, violation, (to) assault, (to) attack, harassment [vn Cl. 15]
kusazothatha it will still take [fut, persistive aspect]
kade before, and then [conj]
yazi it knows [pres, partic]
iyini? it is what? [ident cop, pres; < **i-** it [SC] + **-y-** is [ident cop pref] + **ini?**]
ini what? [enum Cl. 9]
i- [enum conc Cl. 9]
-ni? what?, what kind?, what sort of?, of what sex? [enum stem]
ngithi-ke I believe then
-ke then, so [enclitic attached to last word of phrase]
sivotela we vote for [pres, partic]
siyobe sivotela we shall be voting for [rem future present]
siyobe we shall be [aux, rem fut]
-yo- will, shall [rem fut marker]
-be [aux marking relative tenses; followed by partic]
enhle good [adj Cl. 9]
yezingane for, of children [poss Cl. 9]
ye- of [poss conc Cl. 9 coalesced with **i**]
izingane children [n Cl. 10; sg **ingane** Cl. 9]

zethu our [poss Cl. 10]
kuyoqashwa they will appoint (lit. there will be appointed) [rem fut]
ibe mihle imiphumela and the results will be good
ibe mihle and they will be good [descr cop, subjunc]
  ibe they should be [copula, subjunc]
  mihle [adjective minus initial vowel **e-**]
luyophela it will come to an end [rem fut]
inabaholi it has leaders [assoc cop, pres]
abafuna who want [rel Cl. 2]
  bafuna they want [pres, conjoint]
imele so that it can stand for or represent [subjunc]
  -mel-a stand (up) for, represent; manage, look after, oversee, superintend [v-appl]
  -m-a stand (up); wait; stop [v.i., inch]
nokuthula and peace [assoc adv]
  ukuthula to be quiet, quiet,

tranquillity, peacefulness [vn Cl. 15]
-thul-a be quiet, be tranquil [v.i. (normally inch)]
viva [interj] {Portuguese}
ugodle that you should withhold [subjunc]
  -godl-a hold back, reserve, withhold, suppress [v.t.]
igama name [n Cl. 5]
lami my [poss Cl. 5]
  mi I, me, my [abs pron 1 p sg]
ikheli address [n Cl. 5] {Eng *care of*}
okhathazekile one who is worried [rel Cl. 1]
  ukhathazekile (s)he is worried [stative]
  -khathazekile [v-caus-neut-stative]
  -khathazek-a be worried, be disturbed [v-caus-neut]
  -khathaz-a tire; worry, disturb, bother, pester [v-caus; < **-khathal- + -Y-**; l + Y > z]
  -Y- cause to [caus ext]
  -khathal-a bec tired [v.inch]
Bergville (place)

Sikhala Ngogesi Nje

Mhleli

Ngingumfundi ongathandi ukudlulwa amaqiniso aleli phephandaba.

Ngicela ukudlulisa nanku umbono ohlupha abaningi endaweni yangakithi, kwesenkosi uCalalakubo Khawula.

Umphakathi wakule ndawo ukhathazekile ngokungayiboni intuthuko, ikakhulu ugesi, nokuyinto ebaluleke kangaka. Futhi kuyatholakala ukuthi kukhona izimali esezike zaqoqwa ebantwini, bathenjiswa ukuthi kuzoyiwa kwa-Eskom, kodwa lutho impendulo. Yashona imali.

Ngisho noKhansela uMntomuhle Khawula ozalwa yiyona inkosi akabenzeli lutho abantu, usebenza ngesandla esifana nesikayise.

Kuleya ndawo akukho ngisho isigxobo sokushaya ucingo lolu. Ugesi ungawuthola kwasibanibani abaseduze nekhwapha lezikhulu.

Kunezigodi okunabantu ababizwa ngamalungu enhlangano ethile, kuze kushiwo ukuthi ngeke bawuthole bona ugesi, kodwa abasho lokhu, bona nemindeni yabo baphelele ngezidingo zempilo.

Ngicela uligodle igama lami.

Okhathazekile, EMZUMBE

Vocabulary

ngogesi about, with, by electricity [instr adv]
  ugesi electricity [n Cl. 1a/3a] {Eng *gas*}
ngingumfundi I am a reader [ident cop, pres]
  umfundi reader, student, pupil [n Cl. 1; < **-fund-**; pl **abafundi**]
ongathandi who doesn't like [rel Cl. 1]
  akathandi (s)he does not like [pres, neg]
ukudlulwa to be passed by, to be

bypassed [vn Cl. 15]
  -dlulw-a be passed (by) [v-pass]
  -dlul-a pass, pass by, surpass [v.t.; variant **-edlul-a**]
amaqiniso by truths [agentive adv]
  Ø- by [agent adv pref; in speech equates with breathy voice and a rising tone]
  amaqiniso truths [n Cl. 6; sg **iqiniso** Cl. 5; < **-qinis-** confirm, speak the truth]
aleli of this [poss Cl. 6]

leli this [1st pos dem Cl. 5]

phephandaba [< **iphephandaba**]

iphephandaba newspaper [n Cl. 5; < **iphepha** + **indaba** news]

ukudlulisa to pass on [vn Cl. 15]

-dlulis-a pass on, forward [v-caus]

nanku ... here is ... [presentative dem Cl. 3, 1st pos; var **nawu**]

umbono view(point) [n Cl. 3; < **-bon-** see; pl **imibono**]

ohlupha that/which is bothering [rel Cl. 3]

   uhlupha it is bothering [pres, conjoint]

   -hluph-a bother, disturb, cause problems or trouble [v.t.]

endaweni yangakithi in our area [loc phr]

endaweni to, from, in, at, a place [loc]

   indawo place, locality [n Cl. 9]

   yangakithi (of) around our area or district [poss Cl. 9]

   ngakithi in the vicinity of our place [instr adv phr]

kwesenkosi uCalalakubo in the jurisdiction of Chief Calalakubo Khawula [loc phr]

   kw- at the place of [loc pref; form of **kwa-** found before vowels]

   esenkosi that of a chief [poss pron Cl. 7; refers to **isifunda**]

   e- [form of the pronominalizer **a-** with assimilation to following **e**]

   senkosi of chief [poss Cl. 7; < **sa-** + **inkosi**]

   inkosi chief [n Cl. 9; pl. **amakhosi**; **n** + **kh** > **nk**]

uCalalakubo Khawula (name) [n phr Cl. 1a]

ukhathazekile it is disturbed, it is distressed [stative]

wakule ndawo from this place [poss Cl. 3]

kule ndawo to, from, at, in this place [loc phr]

le ndawo this place [dem phr Cl. 9]

   le this [1st pos dem Cl. 9]

ngokungayiboni by not seeing it [instr adv]

   ukungayiboni not to see it, not seeing it [vn Cl. 15]

intuthuko increase, progress, development [n Cl. 9; < **-thuthuk-** increase, progress; **n** + **th** > **nt**]

ikakhulu especially, particularly [adv; < **kakhulu**]

nokuyinto and that/which is something [assoc adv phr]

   okuyinto that/which is something [rel Cl. 17]

   kuyinto it is something, it is a thing [ident cop, pres]

   yinto it is something, it is a thing [ident cop, pres]

ebaluleke that/which is important [rel]

   ibaluleke it is important [past, conjoint]

   -balulek-a bec important [v.i.] {Xhosa}

kangaka so (much), to this extent [manner adv]

   -ngaka of this size, as big as this [rel stem]

izimali monies [n Cl. 10a; sg **imali** Cl. 9a]

esezike zaqoqwa that/which were already once collected [rel phr Cl. 10]

   sezike they already once [aux, past, exclusive, conjoint]

   -ke do once, do ever [aux; followed by the narrative in the past, and the subjunctive

elsewhere]
zaqoqwa (and) they were collected [narrative]
z- they [SC Cl. 10]
-qoqw-a be collected, be gathered; be tidied up [v-pass]
-qoq-a gather (together), collect, tidy up, clear up [v.t.]
ebantwini from people [loc; < **abantu**]
bathenjiswa and they were promised [narrative]
-thenjisw-a be promised [v-caus-pass; < **-thembis-w-a**; mb ... -w- > nj ... -w-]
-thembis-a promise, give hope (to) [v-caus]
kuzoyiwa they would go, one would go (lit. there would be gone) [fut]
-yiw-a be gone to [v-pass]
kwa-Eskom to Eskom [loc]
u-Eskom Eskom (national electricity supplier; originally: Electricity Supply Commission) [n Cl. 1a]
impendulo answer, response, reply [n Cl. 9; < **-phendul-** answer, reply; m + ph > mp]
yashona it disappeared [narrative]
ngisho I mean, I am of the opinion that [pres, conjoint, pos]
noKhansela even Councilor
ukhansela councilor [n Cl. 1a] {Eng}
uMntomuhle (given name; lit. Goodperson, Beautifulperson)
Khawula (surname) [n Cl. 1a]
ozalwa who was born [rel]
uzalwa (s)he is born [pres, conjoint]
yiyona inkosi by him the chief [agent adv phr]
yi- by [agent adv pref]
yona it, he, him, she, her [abs

pron Cl. 9]
akabenzeli lutho abantu (s)he does nothing for them the people
akabenzeli (s)he does not do for them
-b- them [OC Cl. 2]
-enzel-a do for, make for [v-appl]
usebenza ngesandla esifana nesikayise (s)he acts like his or her father does (lit. (s)he works with a hand that is like that of his or her father) [v phr]
usebenza (s)he works [pres, conjoint]
ngesandla with a hand [instr adv]
isandla hand [n Cl. 7; pl **izandla** Cl. 8]
is- [NP Cl. 7]
esifana that/which is like, that/which resembles [rel Cl. 7]
sifana it resembles, it is like [pres, conjoint]
-fan-a na- ... be similar to ..., resemble ..., be like ..., be the same as ...
esikayise that of his father [poss pron Cl. 7]
e- [pronominalizer; used with following **i**]
sikayise of his father [poss Cl. 7]
sika- [poss conc Cl. 7; used with Cl. 1a noun bases]
uyise his or her father [n Cl. 1a]
kuleya in that [loc]
leya that (over there) [3rd pos dem Cl. 9]
akukho ngisho isigxobo sokushaya ucingo lolu I mean there isn't a telegraph pole
akukho there isn't, there aren't [loc cop, pres, neg; may also introduce an exist cop]

31

isigxobo sokushaya ucingo telegraph pole [n Cl. 7]
isigxobo stake, sharpened pole [n Cl. 7]
ukushaya ucingo to phone (lit. to hit the wire) [vn phr Cl. 15]
ucingo wire; telephone, telegraph [n Cl. 11; pl **izingcingo** Cl. 10; n + c > **ngc**]
lolu this [1st pos dem Cl. 11]
ungawuthola you may find it [pres, potential]
-nga- can, could, may, might, would, should [marker of the potential mood]
kwasibanibani at the place of certain people [loc]
  osibanibani some people or other, certain people [n Cl. 2b; sg **usibanibani** Cl 1a]
abaseduze nekhwapha lezikhulu those with patronage from, or influence with, important people (lit. those close to the armpit(s) of important people) [rel phr Cl. 2]
abaseduze na- ... who are near to ... [rel phr Cl. 2]
  baseduze they are nearby, close by [loc cop, pres]
    seduze [< **eduze**]
    eduze nearby, close by [loc]
  ikhwapha armpit [n Cl. 5]
  lezikhulu of important people [poss Cl. 5]
    izikhulu people of rank or social standing, important people [n Cl. 8; sg **isikhulu**; < -**khulu** big, important [adj stem]]
kunezigodi there are districts (lit. it with districts) [assoc cop, pres]
  kune- there is, there are [< **kuna-** + **i**]
  kuna- there is, there are [though

made up of the SC **ku-** and the assoc pref **-na-**, this is conveniently treated as an entity]
  izigodi districts [n Cl. 8; sg **isigodi**]
okunabantu where there are people [rel]
  kunabantu there are people (lit. it with people) [assoc cop, pres]
ababizwa nga- who are called (by) [rel phr Cl. 2]
  babizwa they are called, they are named as [pres, conjoint]
    -bizw-a nga- be called (by a name, title, etc.; e.g. **ubizwa ngombulali** (s)he is called a murderer)
    -bizw-a be called [v-pass]
    -biz-a nga- call (by a name, title, etc.; **bambiza ngophulofesa** they call her professor)
    -biz-a call [v.t.]
ngamalungu they are members [ident cop, pres]
  amalungu members [n Cl. 6; sg **ilungu** Cl. 5]
enhlangano of an organization or party [poss Cl. 6]
ethile certain, particular [rel Cl. 9]
  · **-thile** some, (a) certain, particular [rel stem; < **-th-i** say; var **-thize**]
kuze until, so that eventually, until eventually [aux]
kushiwo it is said [subjunc]
  -shiw-o be said [v-pass; < **-sh-o**]
ngeke bawuthole they could never get it [pres, potential, neg]
  ngeke never [aux; followed by the subjunctive]
  bawuthole bona *they* should get it [subjunc]
    bona they, them, their [abs pron

Cl. 2]

bo they, them, their [abs pron Cl. 2]

-na [stabilizer (see R04)]

abasho those who say [rel]

basho they say, they state [pres, conjoint]

nemindeni and families [assoc adv]

yabo their [poss Cl. 4]

ya- [poss conc Cl. 4]

baphelele they are well catered for [stative]

-phelel-a bec fully satisfied, bec well catered for [v.i.]

ngezidingo with regard to the needs, as far as the needs are concerned [instr adv]

izidingo needs, requirements [n Cl. 8; sg **isidingo** need; < **-ding-** need, require]

zempilo of life; of health [poss Cl. 8]

uligodle you should withhold it [subjunc]

eMzumbe at Umzumbe [loc]

uMzumbe (place) [n Cl. 3]

Yekani Umuntu Omdala Aziphumulele Kade Ayidonsa Indima

Mhleli

Abantu baseNingizimu Afrika mabaqine idolo njengoba sekuzongena uMnuz Thabo Mbeki ezicathulweni zikaMnuz Nelson Mandela.

Ngikusho lokhu nje yingoba iningi labantu liyakungabaza ukuphatha kukaMnuz Thabo Mbeki uma kuqhathaniswa nokukaMnuz Mandela.

Lalelani-ke nginichazele le nto ibe sobala.

Nakhu okuhlukanisa lezi zinkokheli, uMnuz Mandela udume umhlaba wonke ukwedlula uMnuz Mbeki, kodwa lokho akusho ukuthi uMnuz Mandela ukhaliphe kakhulu kunoMnuz Mbeki.

UMnuz Mandela ufunde ngezomthetho, kanti uMnuz Mbeki ufunde ngezomnotho. Ngakho-ke umnotho yiwo olawula izwe njengoba ubona iMelika, iJaphani, iJalimani, njll.

Yekani umuntu omdala aziphumulele, kade adonsa kule ndima yokuhola abantu.

Wilson S Mnyandu, KWADABEKA

Vocabulary

yekani let go (of) [imperative]
  -yek-a let go (of), leave (alone, out), stop VERBing [v.t.]
  -ni [pluralizing suffix used in imperatives]
omdala the old one, old, elder [adj Cl. 1]
  om- [adj conc Cl. 1]
aziphumulele so that (s)he can just rest [subjunc]
  -zi-phumulel-a rest for oneself, just rest [v-refl-appl]
  -phumulel-a rest for [v-appl]
kade for a long time [conj followed here by the participial]

ayidonsa (s)he carried [rem past, partic]
  Ø- he, she [SC Cl. 1; the participial SC e- > Ø- before a vowel]
  -a- [rem past pref]
  -dons-a pull, haul, tug, drag, draw, attract [v.t.]
indima cultivated plot, field; task [n Cl. 9; < -lim- cultivate; n + l > nd]
baseNingizimu Afrika of South Africa [poss Cl. 2]

34

seNingizimu Afrika to, from, in South Africa [loc; < **eNingizimu Afrika**]

iNingizimu Afrika South Africa [n Cl. 5]

mabaqine idolo let them be strong (lit. let them be firm in the knee)

mabaqine let them be firm [subjunc]

-qin-a bec firm, bec solid, bec hard, bec tough, bec strong [v.i.]

idolo knee [n Cl. 5]

sekuzongena there will soon enter [future, exclusive]

-ngen-a enter, come in(to), go in(to) [v.i.]

Thabo Mbeki (name of South African President) [n phr Cl. 1a]

uThabo (male name; lit. 'happiness' [n Cl. 1a] {Sotho}

uMbeki (surname) [n Cl. 1a]

ezicathulweni to, from, in(to), on the shoes [loc]

izicathulo shoes [n Cl. 8; sg **isicathulo**]

zikaMnuz Nelson Mandela of Mr. Nelson Mandela [poss phr Cl. 8]

zika- [poss conc Cl. 8; used before nouns of Cl. 1a]

Nelson Mandela (name of former South African President) [n phr Cl. 1a]

ngikusho I say it [pres, conjoint]

yingoba it is because [ident cop, pres]

labantu of people [poss Cl. 5]

liyakungabaza they are uncertain about, they doubt [pres, disjoint]

-ngabaz-a be uncertain, doubt [v.i. & t.]

ukuphatha handling, management, command [vn Cl. 15]

kukaMnuz of Mr. [poss Cl. 15]

kuka- [poss conc Cl. 15]

kuqhathaniswa (it) being compared [pres, partic]

-qhathanisw-a be compared [v-recip-caus-pass]

-qhathanis-a compare; place side by side; set to fight each other [v-recip-caus]

-qhath- set to fight, place in opposition to [v.t.]

nokukaMnuz Mandela with that of Mr. Mandela [assoc adv phr]

okukaMnuz Mandela that of Mr. Mandela [poss pron phr Cl. 15]

o- [form of the pronominalizer **a-** with assimilation to following **u**]

lalelani-ke listen then [imperative]

nginichazele le nto ibe sobala so that I can explain this thing to you openly [v phr]

nginichazele so that I can explain to you [subjunc]

-chazel-a explain to [v-appl]

-chaz-a explain [v.t.]

nto thing [< **into** n Cl. 9; deletion of initial vowel due to preceding dem]

ibe sobala so that it should be out in the open [loc cop, inch, subjunc]

sobala in the open [loc]

so- to, from, in, at, on [loc pref; the presence of **s** in the loc prefix suggests that though the above phrase is written as two words, it constitutes one phonological word]

ubala unoccupied, open country; the open [n Cl. 11]

nakhu ... here is ... [presentative dem Cl. 17, 1st pos; var **naku**]

okuhlukanisa that which

distinguishes [rel Cl. 17]
kuhlukanisa it distinguishes [pres, conjoint]
-hlukanis-a separate, make a distinction between [v-recip-caus; **-ahlukanis-a** is a more common variant]
-hlukan-a part from one another; differ from one another [v-recip]
-hluk-a deviate, separate [v.i.]
lezi these [1st pos dem Cl. 10]
zinkokheli leaders [< **izinkokheli** n Cl. 10; deletion of init vowel due to preceding dem; sg **inkokheli**]
udume (s)he is famous, (s)he is well-known [past, conjoint]
-dum-a bec famous, bec renowned; resound, thunder, rumble [v.i.]
wonke the whole, all, every [quant Cl. 3]
wo- [quant conc Cl. 3]
ukwedlula to surpass, more than [vn used to express degree of comparison]
akusho it doesn't mean (that) [pres, neg]
ukhaliphe kakhulu kuna-... (s)he is cleverer than ...
ukhaliphe (s)he is clever [past, conjoint]
-khaliph-a bec clever, smart, intelligent [v.inch]
ufunde (s)he has studied [past, conjoint]
ezomthetho Law (as an academic subject), legal matters [poss pron Cl. 10]

zomthetho those of law [poss Cl. 10]
zo- of [poss conc Cl. 10 (agrees with **izindaba** affairs, matters) coalesced with following **u**]
umthetho law [n Cl. 3]
ezomnotho financial affairs, finance, economy, Economics (as an academic discipline) [poss pron Cl. 10]
umnotho wealth; economics, finance [n Cl. 3]
ngakho-ke therefore, thus, so (lit. through this then) [conj; < instr adv]
yiwo olawula it is what rules [ident cop phr]
yiwo it is it [ident cop, pres]
olawula that which controls [rel Cl. 3]
ulawula it controls, regulates [pres]
-lawul-a give commands, order; control, regulate, marshal [v.t.]
izwe country [n Cl. 5]
ubona you see [pres, conjoint]
iMelika America [n Cl. 5] {Eng}
iJaphani Japan [n Cl. 5] {Eng}
iJalimani Germany [n Cl. 5] {Eng}
njll. etc., and so on [abbreviation of **njalonjalo**]
yokuhola of leading [poss Cl. 9]
ukuhola to drag, to haul, to pull along; to lead, to guide [vn Cl. 15]
-hol-a drag, haul, pull along; lead, guide [v.t.]
uMnyandu (surname) [n Cl. 1a]
KwaDabeka (place: at Dabeka's)

Ezomame kwelamaQiniso
Eziphuma ebhodweni loMhleli zishisa

Izingane kufanele zazi ukuthi
abazali bayathinteka ezimpilweni zazo

«1»

Impelasonto edlule ibinezigameko eziningana ezithinta impilo yemindeni ngezindlela ezahlukene, kusukela kubantu besifazane abangenelwe bukhoma badutshulwa eKapa, kuya kulabo abalahlekelwe yimiphefumulo ngenxa yezingozi zomgwaqo.

«2»

Kukhona abazali abadutshulwe yisoka lengane yabo ngoba nje bekhuza umsindo phakathi kwalezi zithandani.

Isizathu salokhu, kuzwakala ukuthi isoka beselifuna zonke izingubo elazithengela indodakazi yabo.

«3»

Nakuba singayazi ingqikithi yendaba, kepha sengathi lokhu kungaba yisifundo nakwezethu izingane.

Izingane zamantombazane kuhle zazi ukuthi kunezinqumo ezizenzayo, ezingagcini ngokuthinta impilo yazo kuphela, kodwa ezithinta nomndeni wonke.

«4»

Ngokunjalo nezingane zabafana kuhle zazi ukuthi noma ngubani omdala kumele zimhloniphe, zimthathe njengomzali wazo, futhi kuhle umuntu angavumeli ukulawulwa yimizwa yakhe, angabi namawala.

«5»

Kunezigameko eseziqala ukuba inhlalayenza lapho kulahleka khona izingane zidlala egcekeni, kuthiwe ibonakale ithathwa "yindoda-thizeni" kwaba ngukunyamalala kwayo njalo.

«6»

Ngiyacela komame, lesi sisho esithi ukubona kanye wukubona kabili, asisisebenzise ngempela ukuze singalindi amathonsi abanzi, ubone ngoba sekwenzeka kweyakho ingane, ngaphambi kokuthatha izinyathelo. Ngiyazi kukhona asebe-buza ukuthi yini engenziwa ukuvimbela lo mshophi.

«7»

Ngibona kungcono ukuba siqikelele ukuphepha kwabantwana bethu ngoba kusazothatha isikhathi ukuba kutholakale indlela yokunqanda lo mkhuba.

Kunganjani nje singomakhelwane sihlanganyele ekwakheni uthango,

37

kuqalwe ngomuzi okuvame ukudlalela khona abantwana, kuqhutshekelwe nakweminye imizi?

Dudu Khoza

Vocabulary

ezomame things for the ladies, women's matters [poss pron Cl. 10]
omame mothers, ladies [n Cl. 2b; sg **umame** Cl. 1a]
kwelamaqiniso in true words [loc]
elamaqiniso that of truths [poss pron Cl. 5, agrees with **izwi** word]
eziphuma ebhodweni loMhleli zishisa that which comes hot from the editor's pot (comparison of news items to ingredients being added to a stew) [rel phr Cl. 10]
eziphuma that which comes from [rel Cl. 10; refers to **izindaba** news, matters]
ziphuma they come from, they go out [pres, conjoint]
ebhodweni into, from, in a pot [loc]
ibhodwe pot [n Cl. 5] {Afr}
loMhleli of the editor [poss Cl. 5]
zishisa they being hot [pres, partic]
zazi they should know [subjunc]
abazali parents [n Cl. 2; sg **umzali**; < **-zal-** give birth (to)]
bayathinteka they are touched, they are affected [pres, disjoint]
-thintek-a be touched, be affected [v-neut]
-thint-a touch, handle; affect [v.t.]
ezimpilweni in lives [loc; < **izimpilo**]
zazo their, of them [poss Cl. 10]

«1»
impelasonto weekend [n Cl. 9; < **im- + -phel-a** end + **isonto** week; **m + ph > mp**]
edlule last, that/which has passed [rel Cl. 9]
idlule it has passed [past, disjoint]
ibinezigameko it had repeated events [assoc cop, past pres; **i-** SC + **-b-** aux + **i-** SC + **-na-** assoc pref + **izigameko**]
izigameko repeated incidents [n Cl. 8; sg **isigameko**]
eziningana rather many, quite a number [adj Cl. 8]
-ningana rather many, quite a number [< **-ningi + -ana** dimin suff]
ezithinta that/which touch, handle, or affect [rel Cl. 8]
zithinta they touch, handle, affect [pres, conjoint]
yemindeni of families [poss Cl. 9]
ezahlukene various, different [rel Cl. 10]
zahlukene they are different [stative; < **-ahlukan-** bec different + **-i...e** stative suff]
-ahlukan-a bec different, part from one another, part company [v.inch; var **-ehlukan-**, **-hlukan-**]
kusukela from [conj; < **kusukela** it originates at or in]
-sukel-a originate at [v-appl]
-suk-a go away, leave (from),

set off, originate (at, from) [v.i.]
besifazane female [poss Cl. 2]
   isifazane female gender [n Cl. 7]
abangenelwe who were attacked [rel Cl. 2]
   bangenelwe they were attacked unawares [past, conjoint]
   -ngenelw-a be attacked unawares [v-appl-pass]
   -ngenel-a attack unawares [v-appl]
bukhoma at close range [loc]
badutshulwa and they were shot [narrative]
   -dutshulw-a be shot [v-pass; < **-dubul-w-a**; b ... -w- > tsh ... -w-]
   -dubul-a shoot [v.t.]
eKapa in Cape Town [loc]
   iKapa Cape Town [n Cl. 5] {Afr *Kaap*}
kuya to, up to, as far as [conj; < **kuya** it goes to]
kulabo to those, from those, among those [loc]
   labo those [2nd position dem Cl. 2]
abalahlekelwe yimiphefumulo who lost their lives (lit. who were lost for by lives) [rel phr Cl. 2]
   abalahlekelwe who lost [rel Cl. 2]
   balahlekelwe they lost [past, conjoint]
   -lahlekelw-a + AGENTIVE PREFIX lose [v-neut-appl-pass]
   -lahlek-a get lost, go missing [v-neut]
   -lahl-a throw away [v.t.]
   yimiphefumulo by lives [agent adv]
   imiphefumulo lives; breaths [n Cl. 4; sg **umphefumulo**; <

-phefumul- breathe]
ngenxa ya- because of, on account of, due to, owing to [instr adv phr]
   inxa origin, cause [n Cl. 9a]
yezingozi of accidents [poss Cl. 9]
   izingozi accidents [n Cl. 10; sg **ingozi**]
zomgwaqo of the road [poss Cl. 10]
   umgwaqo road [n Cl. 3]

«2»

abadutshulwe who were shot [rel Cl. 2]
   badutshulwe they were shot [past, conjoint]
yisoka by the boyfriend [agent adv]
   isoka bachelor; boyfriend [n Cl. 5]
lengane of the child [poss Cl. 5]
bekhuza they were calming [pres, partic]
   -khuz-a calm, soothe, quieten [v.t.]
umsindo noise; quarrel [n Cl. 3]
phakathi kwa- in, inside, between, amongst [loc phr]
zithandani [< **izithandani**]
   izithandani lovers [n Cl. 8; no singular; < **-thandan-** love each other]
isizathu reason [n Cl. 7]
salokhu for this, of this, hereof [poss Cl. 7]
kuzwakala it is understood, there is heard, it is audible [pres, conjoint]
   -zwakal-a be audible, be comprehensible, be understandable, be reasonable [v-neut]
beselifuna (s)he then wanted [past pres, exclusive]
izingubo clothing, clothes [n Cl.

10; sg **ingubo** garment, blanket]
elazithengela that/which (s)he bought for [ind rel of plain obj rel, Cl. 5]
  el- which, that, who [rel conc Cl. 5; < **a-** relative marker + **li-** SC]
  lazithengela (s)he bought them for [rem past]
  -zi- them [OC Cl. 10]
  -thengel-a buy for [v-appl]
  -theng-a buy [v.t.]
indodakazi daughter [n Cl. 9; pl **amadodakazi** Cl. 6]

«3»
singayazi we don't know (it) [pres, partic, neg]
  -y- it [OC Cl. 9; found before vowels]
ingqikithi essence [n Cl. 9]
yendaba of the matter [poss Cl. 9]
  indaba matter, affair, item of news [n Cl. 9]
kepha but [conj]
sengathi if only, would that [conj, followed by potential mood]
kungaba yisifundo it could be a lesson [ident cop, inch, pres, potential]
  kungaba it could be(come), it would be(come) [copula, pres, potential]
  yisifundo it is a lesson [ident cop, pres]
  isifundo lesson, subject (in education), course [n Cl. 7; < **-fund-**]
nakwezethu also to ours (children)
  kwezethu to, from, at, in, on ours [loc]
  ezethu ours [poss pron Cl. 10]
  ze- of [poss conc Cl. 10 coalesced with following **i**]
izingane zamantombazane girls

(lit. children of girls) [n phr Cl. 10]
  zamantombazane of girls [poss Cl. 10]
  amantombazane young girls (up to puberty; but often used for young women as well) [n Cl. 6; sg **intombazane** Cl. 9]
kuhle it is good [descr cop, pres]
  ku- [2nd half adj conc **oku-**, Cl. 17]
kunezinqumo there are decisions [assoc cop, pres]
  izinqumo decisions, verdicts, judgments [n Cl. 8; sg **isinqumo**; < **-nqum-** decide]
ezizenzayo that/which they make [ind rel of plain objectival relationship, Cl. 8]
  ziyazenza they make them [pres, disjoint]
  -z- them [OC Cl. 8; found before vowels]
ezingagcini that/which do not end [rel Cl. 8]
  azigcini they do not end (up) [pres, neg]
  -gcin-a end, end up VERBing, eventually VERB; last VERB, VERB for the last time [v.i. & t.]
ngokuthinta by affecting, by touching [instr adv]
  ukuthinta to touch, to handle; to affect [vn Cl. 15]
yazo their [poss Cl. 9]
kuphela only, alone [adv]
nomndeni also the family [assoc adv]

«4»
ngokunjalo in this way [instr adv phr]
  okunjalo something like this, or like that [rel Cl. 17]
  kunjalo it is so, it is like that

[descr cop, pres]

njalo thus, so, like that [adv]

nezingane zabafana also boys, boys too, even boys [assoc adv phr]
   izingane zabafana boys (lit. children of boys) [n phr Cl. 10]
   zabafana of boys [poss Cl. 10]
   abafana boys [n Cl. 2; sg **umfana**]

noma ngubani omdala any older person, no matter who the older person is
   ngubani? who is it? [ident cop, pres, partic]
   ubani? who? (sg) [n Cl. 1a; pl **obani?**]

kumele it is obligatory, it is requisite, must, should, ought [stative]
   -mel-a bec obligatory [aux, inch; followed by subjunc when it has a Cl. 17 SC]

zimhloniphe they should respect him or her [subjunc]
   -m- him, her [OC Cl. 1]
   -hloniph-a respect, honor [v.t.]

zimthathe that they should take him/her [subjunc]

njengomzali as a parent, like a parent [compar adv]
   njengo- [compar adv pref coalesced with following **u**]
   njenga- like, as, such as [compar adv pref]

wazo their [poss Cl. 1]

angavumeli (s)he should not agree to, should not accept [subjunc, neg]
   -vumel-a agree to, accept, permit, allow [v-appl]
   -vum-a agree, assent, consent, be willing [v.i. & t.]

ukulawulwa to be governed [vn Cl. 15]

yimizwa by feelings, by emotions [agent adv]
   imizwa feelings, emotions [n Cl. 4; sg **umuzwa**; < **-zw-** feel]

angabi namawala s(h)e should not take (lit. be with) hasty action [assoc cop, inch, subjunc, neg]
   amawala hasty action [n Cl. 6; neutral]

«5»

kunezigameko there are repeated events [assoc cop, pres]

eseziqala that/which are already beginning [rel Cl. 8]
   seziqala they are already beginning [pres, exclusive]
   ziqala they are beginning [pres, conjoint]

ukuba to become, to be [vn Cl. 15]

inhlalayenza a common occurrence, daily event, tendency [n Cl. 9; no pl]

lapho kulahleka khona izingane where children go missing [ind rel of plain loc relationship]
   kulahleka there go missing, there get lost [pres, partic]

zidlala they play(ing) [pres, partic]

egcekeni in the open ground [loc]
   igceke open ground [n Cl. 5]

kuthiwe (then) it's said, (then) "they" say [subjunc]
   -thiw-a be said [v-pass]

ibonakale it was visible [past, conjoint]
   -bonakal-a be visible, appear, be apparent, seem [v-neut]

ithathwa it (the child) being taken [present, part]

yindoda-thizeni by a certain man [agent adv]
   indoda-thizeni a certain man [n

Cl. 9; < **indoda** + **-thizeni** [noun suffix indicating 'a certain']

kwaba ngukunyamalala and then it became the disappearance [ident cop, inch, narrative]

kwaba and it became [copula, narrative]

ngukunyamalala it is disappearance [ident cop, pres]

ukunyamalala disappearance [vn Cl. 15]

-nyamalal-a disappear [v.i.]

kwayo its, his, her [poss Cl. 15]

«6»

ngiyacela I am requesting [pres, disjoint]

komame from, to the ladies [loc]

sisho [<**isisho**]

isisho saying [n Cl. 7; < **-sh-o** say (so), mean]

esithi that/which goes, that/which says [rel Cl. 7]

sithi (s)he, it goes; (s)he, it says [pres, conjoint, pos]

ukubona kanye wukubona kabili to see once is to see twice (proverb; once bitten twice shy; experience is the best taskmaster)

ukubona to see, sight [vn Cl. 15]

kanye once (adv; < **ka-** + **-nye** one]

wukubona (it) is to see [ident cop, pres]

w- (it) is [ident cop pref]

kabili twice [adv; < **ka-** + **-bili** two]

asisisebenzise let us use it [subjunc; **a-** hortative + **-si-** us [SC] + **-si-** it [OC 7] + **-sebenzis-**]

-sebenzis-a use, employ, make work, put into operation; help work [v-caus]

ngempela indeed, really [instr adv]

impela truth [n Cl. 9]

singalindi we should not wait [subjunc, neg]

-lind-a wait (for), expect [v.i. & t.]

amathonsi abanzi severe problems (idiom; lit. wide drops (i.e. tears)) [n phr Cl. 6]

amathonsi drops [n Cl. 6; sg **ithonsi** Cl. 5]

abanzi wide, broad [rel Cl. 6]

-banzi wide, broad [rel stem]

ubone and you understand (lit. see) [subjunc]

sekwenzeka it is now happening [pres, exclusive]

kweyakho to yours [loc]

eyakho yours [poss pron Cl. 9]

ngaphambi kokuthatha before taking [instr adv phr]

phambi kwa- before, ahead of, in front of [loc phr; < **phambili** in front, ahead; before, beforehand [the final syllable is elided when followed by **kwa-**, the Cl 17 poss conc that follows certain loc nouns]

ukuthatha taking, to take [n Cl. 15]

izinyathelo steps [n Cl. 8; sg **isinyathelo**; < **-nyathel-** tread, step]

ngiyazi I know [pres, disjoint]

asebebuza those who are already asking [rel Cl. 2]

sebebuza they are already asking [pres, exclusive]

-buz-a ask, question [v.t.]

yini? it is what? [ident cop, pres]

engenziwa that can be done [rel Cl. 9]

ingenziwa it can be done, performed, carried out [pres, potential]

-ng- can, could, may, might, would, should [potential mood pref; variant of **-nga-** found before vowels]
ukuvimbela to prevent [vn Cl. 15]
   -vimbel-a prevent, repel [v-appl]
   -vimb-a block, bar, prevent, hinder, stop [v.t.]
mshophi epidemic [< **umshophi**]
   umshophi epidemic [n Cl. 3]

«7»
ngibona I am of the opinion [pres, conjoint]
kungcono it is better, it is preferable [descr cop, pres]
   -ngcono better [rel stem]
siqikelele we should be on the lookout for, guard against [subjunc]
   -qikelel-a be on the lookout for, guard against [v.t.]
ukuphepha safety, security [vn Cl. 15]
kwabantwana of children [loc]
bethu our [poss Cl. 2: < **ba-** + **-ithu**]
kutholakale there should be found [subjunc]
yokunqanda of preventing, of checking [poss Cl. 9]
   ukunqanda preventing, checking [vn Cl. 15]
   -nqand-a prevent, check [v.t.]
mkhuba [< **umkhuba**]
   umkhuba custom, practice; (bad) habit [n Cl. 3]
kunganjani nje ... how would it be if ...?, why not...? [followed by subjunc]
singomakhelwane us being neighbors [ident cop, pres, partic]
   omakhelwane neighbors [n Cl.

2b; sg **umakhelwane** Cl. 1a]
sihlanganyele we should unite in, collaborate in [subjunc]
   -hlanganyel-a unite against, act together [v.i. & t.]
ekwakheni in the building [loc]
   ukwakha to build [vn Cl. 15]
   -akh-a build, construct [v.t.]
uthango fence [n Cl. 11; pl **izintango; n + th > nt**]
kuqalwe there should be begun, one should begin [subjunc]
   -qalw-a be started, be initiated [v-pass]
ngomuzi with the household [instr adv]
   umuzi household, homestead, village; family [n Cl. 3]
okuvame ukudlalela khona abantwana where children customarily play [ind rel of plain locative relationship, Cl. 17]
okuvame where one normally VERBs, where they usually VERB
   kuvame one normally (does), they normally (do), it normally [aux, past, conjoint]
   -vam-a normally VERB, bec accustomed to VERB [aux; inch; followed by vn]
ukudlalela to play at or in [vn Cl. 15]
   -dlalel-a play at, in, for [v-appl]
   -dlal-a play [v.i. & t.]
kuqhutshekelwe and one should proceed to, and there should be proceeded to [subjunc]
   -qhutshekelw-a be proceeded towards [v-neut-appl-pass; < **-qhubekel-w-a; b ... -w- > tsh ... -w-**]
   -qhubekel-a proceed to [v-neut-appl]
nakweminye also to other [assoc adv]

kweminye to, from, at, in, on other [loc]

eminye other [adj Cl. 4]

Dudu (female name) [n. Cl. 1a]

Khoza (surname) [n Cl. 1a]

Izingane Ezihlala Ezitaladini

«1»
Ukungazi ukuthi ipuleti lokudla uzolitholaphi noma uzo-lalaphi ebusuku... izinto ezenza impilo yezingane ezihlala emigwaqweni ibenzima.

Namuhla sekuyinto eyejwayelekile emadolobheni amakhulu aseNingizimu Afrika ukubona izingane ezingenamakhaya zizulazula emigwaqweni.

«2»
Iningi lazo licela imali kubashayeli bezimoto noma kwaba-hamba ngezinyawo. Umphakathi—ikakhulukazi ohamba nge-zimoto—uvame ukuzithathisa okwezigebengu lezingane.

Ziba ngumndeni owodwa uma zihamba ziyiqembu, kanti futhi ziyavikelana. Ziyabelana lokho kudla okuncane ezikutholayo.

«3»
Zigqoka izingubo ezinukayo futhi ezingcolile, kanti nemi-zimba yazo imbozwe yizibazi zokulimala. Kuvame ukuba uzi-thole zifihle ibhodlela le-glue ezingutsheni zazo, kanti futhi zihlale zidakwe yile-glue eziphinde ziyisebenzisele nokuthiba indlala.

Ukuzwana kwazo lezingane kuzinikeza ubunye nokuthandana ezingazange zikuthole emakhaya nasezihlotsheni. Kodwa ukuhlangana kwazo sekwakhe ibutho eliyingozi, nokuletha uvalo emalungeni omphakathi, ikakhulukazi emadolobheni.

«4»
Labafanyana amaphoyisa bawathathisa okwezitha. USandile Memela oneminyaka engu-9 uyilungu leqembu elaziwa ngele-Mdlwembe Gang ePoint Road eThekwini, wathi amaphoyisa avame ukubathatha abayise esiteshini samaphoyisa lapho bephoqelelwa khona ukuwasha izimoto zamaphoyisa nama-trucks. "Ngiyawazonda amaphoyisa ngoba ahlale esishaya," kusho uSandile.

«5»
"Amalungu omphakathi nawo ayasishaya aphinde asihluku-meze ngokocansi," kugcizelela uThulani Khanyile, oliqha-mukisa eMpangeni, KwaZulu-Natal.

"Kodwa ifaqafaqa (glue) sizichithela ngayo isikhathi," kusho umholi weSantoshi Young Killers, u-Innocent Shezi wase-Mgungundlovu.

«6»
"Sibhema i-glue ukuze singalambi, ikakhulukazi uma singayitholanga imali eyanele yokuthenga ukudla.

"Ayisisuthisi, kodwa siyayithokozela," kusho uClive Wilkes,
waseWentworth.

UThulani Makhathini, ophinda aziwe ngelikaSnoopy enemi-nyaka
engu 10 kanti walishiya ikhaya lakhe eliseBhambayi eminyakeni
emine eyedlule.

«7»
"Usingababa (stepfather) wami wayevame ukungishaya nsuku-zonke
umama angasho lutho — esikhundleni salokho wayemlekelela,"
kusho lomfanyana. "Lesihluku engangisithola ekhaya sangiphiqa
ukuba ngiyohlal' emigwaqweni yaseThe-kwini. Kodwa impilo
inzima lapha. Sengike ngadlula ebunzi-meni obukhulu kanti ukuba
angizange ngiye eThuthukani Outreach Centre ngabe sengifile
manje.

«8»
"Amalungu omphakathi namaphoyisa asithathisa okwezi-gebengu
kanti futhi bavame ukusishaya noma basethembise ukusibulala.
Ngifisa ukwazisa ezinye izingane ngokuthi kufa-nele zikhulume
nabazali bazo noma osoNhlalakahle ngapha- mbi kokuba zithathe
izinqumo zokuyohlal' emigwaqweni. Impilo lapha inzima futhi
iyingozi."

Abanye abafana abancane basetshenziswa njengezinto zocansi
ngabafan' abadala. "Asilali ebusuku ngoba bayasinukubeza
ngesikhathi silele," kusho uXolani Khambule oneminyaka
eyisishiyagalombili.

«9»
Kwezinye izindawo kuleli kunamaqembu ezigebengu ayingozi
kakhulu. Zihlukumeza ziphinde zibulale abantu. Ukulwa
kwamaqembu ezigebengu eCape Flats kuhlale kusemithonjeni
yabezindaba. Amaqembu ezigebengu kulendawo afana ne-
Americans, Young Boys kanye neNotorious Mongrel Gang
abulalana ngezibhamu ezinkulu ekuxazululeni izinkinga zokubanga
ukukhonya nezidakamizwa.

«10»
UJoan van Niekerk onguMqondisi kwiChildline esifundeni
saKwaZulu-Natal wathi uhulumeni, umphakathi kanye nezinhlangano zezenhlalakahle kufanele baqhamuke nohlelo loku-

gwema ukuba izingane zihlale emigwaqweni nolokuqeda[6] amaqembu ezigebengu.

"Kufanele sizisize lezingane ukuze ziphinde ziphile ngendlela efanele," kusho uJoan. "Izingane ezihlala emgwaqweni namaqembu ezigebengu yizinto ezisihluphayo ezweni lethu kanti futhi kunzima ukubuyisela isimo endaweni efanele."

Ngu: Linda Manyoni

Vocabulary

ezihlala who live [rel Cl. 10]
  zihlala they live [pres, conjoint]
  -hlal-a reside, live, stay [v.i.]
ezitaladini on streets [loc]
  izitaladi streets [n Cl. 8] {Afr *straat*}

«1»
ukungazi not knowing [vn Cl. 15, neg]
ipuleti plate [n Cl. 5] {Eng}
lokudla of food [poss Cl. 5]
  ukudla food; to eat, eating [vn Cl. 15]
uzolitholaphi (s)he will get it where [v phr]
  uzolithola (s)he will get it [fut]
  -li- it, him, her [OC Cl. 5]
uzolalaphi (s)he will sleep where [v phr]
  uzolala (s)he will (go to) sleep, (s)he will go to bed, (s)he will lie down [fut]
  -lal-a (go to) sleep, go to bed [v.inch]
ebusuku at night [loc]
  ubusuku night(s) [n Cl. 14; neutral]

ezenza that/which make [rel Cl. 10]
  zenza they make, do, act, perform, cause [pres, conjoint]
emigwaqweni on the streets [loc]
  imigwaqo streets, roads [n Cl. 4; sg **umgwaqo**]
ibenzima (that) it should be difficult or hard [descr cop, inch, subjunc]
  -nzima heavy; hard, difficult [rel stem]
namuhla today [time adv]
sekuyinto it is something [ident cop, pres, exclusive aspect]
eyejwayelekile usual, normal, regular, customary [rel Cl. 9]
  yejwayelekile it is usual [stative]
  -ejwayelek-a bec customary, bec usual, bec normal [v-neut; var **-jwayelek-a**]
  -ejwayel-a grow accustomed to, get used to, adjust to [v.t.; var **-jwayel-a**]
emadolobheni in towns, in cities [loc]

---

[6] The original text had this as ***nelokuqeda**, mistakenly using a Cl. 5 form.

amadolobha towns, cities [n Cl. 6; sg idolobha Cl. 5] {Afr *dorp*}

amakhulu large, big [adj Cl. 6]

-khulu big, large, great, important, adult, grown-up, senior, chief [adj st]

aseNingizimu Afrika of South Africa [poss Cl. 6]

ezingenamakhaya homeless (lit. who are not with homes) [rel Cl. 10]

zingenamakhaya they don't have homes [assoc cop, pres, rel, neg]

-nge- not [neg pref found in copulatives]

azinamakhaya [assoc cop, pres, neg]

zizulazula roaming about homelessly [pres, partic]

-zulazul-a roam about homelessly [reduplicated form of -zul-a]

-zul-a wander, roam homelessly [v.i.]

«2»

lazo of them [poss Cl. 5]

licela it (the majority) asking for [pres, partic]

imali money [n Cl. 9a; pl izimali Cl. 10a]

kubashayeli from drivers [loc] abashayeli drivers [n Cl. 2; sg umshayeli; < -shayel- drive]

bezimoto of cars [poss Cl. 2] izimoto cars [n Cl. 10a; sg imoto] {Eng *motor(car)*}

kwabahamba ngezinyawo from pedestrians [loc phr] abahamba ngezinyawo pedestrians (lit. those who go on feet) [rel phr Cl. 2]

abahamba those who go or travel [rel Cl. 2 (referring to abantu)]

bahamba they go, they travel [pres, conjoint]

-hamb-a go, travel [v.i.]

ngezinyawo on foot (lit. by feet) [instr adv]

izinyawo feet [n Cl. 10a; sg unyawo Cl. 11]

umphakathi occupant [n Cl. 1; < um- NP + phakathi inside]

ikakhulukazi especially, particularly [adv; alternative to ikakhulu]

ohamba who travels [rel Cl. 1] uhamba (s)he travels [pres, conjoint]

ngezimoto by car(s) [instr adv]

uvame (s)he normally (does) [stative, conjoint]

ukuzithathisa okwezigebengu to take them as criminals [vn phr Cl. 15]

-is- + POSS PRON like [The caus ext -is- followed by a possessive pronoun translates "like X," with X being the base of the pronoun]

okwezigebengu that of criminals [poss pron Cl. 17] izigebengu criminals, robbers, gangsters [n Cl. 8]

lezingane these children [dem phr Cl. 10] le this, these [1st position dem, Cl. 10; in some dialects the abbreviated form le is used for all demonstratives that have i as 2nd vowel]

ziba ngumndeni [ident cop, inch, pres] ziba they become [copula, pres, conjoint]

ngumndeni it is, they are a family [ident cop, pres]
owodwa (the) only [rel Cl. 3]
   wodwa alone, only [quant Cl. 3]
   wo- [qua.it conc Cl. 3]
   -dwa alone, only [quant stem]
zihamba they travel, they move about [pres, conjoint]
ziyiqembu they being a small group [ident cop, pres, partic]
   iqembu small group, band, team [n Cl. 5]
ziyavikelana they stand up for one another, they protect one another [pres, disjoint]
   -vikelan-a stand up for one another, protect one another [v-appl-recip]
   -vikel-a stand up for, protect, defend [v-appl]
   -vik-a ward off, parry [v.t.]
ziyabelana they share amongst themselves [pres, disjoint]
   -y- [disjoint form marker; variant found before vowels]
   -abelan-a share among one another [v-appl-recip]
   -abel-a distribute among, apportion to [v-appl]
   -ab-a distribute, apportion, allot [v.t.]
kudla food [< **ukudla**]
okuncane little [adj Cl. 15]
   oku- [adj conc Cl. 15]
   -ncane small, (a) little, juvenile [adj stem]
ezikutholayo that/which they get [ind rel of plain obj rel, Cl. 10]
   ziyakuthola they get it, they obtain it [pres, disjoint]

«3»
zigqoka (they) wearing [pres, partic]

-gqok-a put on (clothes), wear [v.t.]
ezinukayo smelly (lit. that smell) [rel Cl. 10]
   ziyanuka they smell [pres, conjoint]
   -nuk-a smell [v.i. & t.]
ezingcolile that/which are dirty [rel Cl. 10]
   zingcolile they are dirty [stative]
   -ngcol-a bec dirty [v.inch]
nemizimba and bodies [assoc adv]
   imizimba bodies [n Cl. 4; sg **umzimba**]
imbozwe they are covered [past, disjoint]
   -mbozw-a be covered [v-pass]
   -mboz-a cover (over), screen [v.t.]
yizibazi by scars [agent adv]
   izibazi scars [n Cl. 8; sg **isibazi**]
zokulimala from getting injured [poss Cl. 8]
   ukulimala to bec injured, hurt, wounded [vn Cl. 15]
   -limal-a bec injured, get hurt, get wounded, get damaged [v.inch]
uzithole you find them [subjunc]
zifihle they having hidden [past, partic, conjoint]
ibhodlela bottle [n Cl. 5] {Eng/Afr?}
le-glue of glue [poss Cl. 5]
   i-glue glue [n Cl. 9a] {Eng}
ezingutsheni in clothes [loc; < **ezingubweni** < e- + izingubo + -eni; bw > tsh]
zihlale they continually VERB, they keep on VERBing [aux]
   -hlal-e continually VERB, keep on VERBing [aux, followed by partic]

49

zidakwe they are intoxicated [past, partic, conjoint]
  -dakw-a bec intoxicated, get drunk [v-pass, inch]
  -dak-a intoxicate, make drunk [v.t.]
yile-glue by this glue [agent adv]
  le-glue this glue [dem phr Cl. 9]
eziphinde ziyisebenzisele nokuthiba indlala that/which they repeatedly use also to prevent hunger [ind rel of plain loc rel, Cl. 10]
  ziphinde they repeatedly VERB, they again VERB [aux]
  -phind-e VERB repeatedly, VERB again, VERB also [aux; followed by the subjunc]
  ziyisebenzisele they use it for [subjunc]
  -yi- it [OC Cl. 9]
  -sebenzisel-a use for, use in order to [v-caus-appl]
nokuthiba also to ward off [assoc adv]
  ukuthiba to ward off [vn Cl. 15]
  -thib-a ward off [v.t.]
indlala hunger [n Cl. 9; neutral]
ukuzwana mutual understanding, getting on together [n Cl. 15]
  -zwan-a hear one another, understand one another, get on together, communicate with one another; be addicted to, be very much inclined to [v-recip]
  -zw-a feel, hear, understand [v.t.]
kwazo their [poss Cl. 15]
kuzinikeza it hands them [pres, conjoint]
  -nikez-a hand to [v-appl-caus; < -nikel- + -Y-; l + -Y- > z]
  -nikel-a give for, hand over to, donate [v-appl]

-nik-a give (not as a gift), hand to [v.tt.]
ubunye unity, togetherness [n Cl. 14; < -nye one]
nokuthandana and mutual love [assoc adv]
  ukuthandana mutual love, to love or like each other [vn Cl. 15]
  -thandan-a love one another, like one another [v-recip]
ezingazange zikuthole mutual love that they have never found [ind rel of plain obj rel, Cl. 10]
  ezingazange that/which they have never [rel Cl. 10]
  zingazange they have never [aux, past, rel, neg; < azizange]
  azizange they have never [aux, past, neg]
  -z-ang-e never [aux, followed by the subjunc]
  -ang-e [past neg suff; var of
  -anga used with certain auxiliaries ending in **-e**]
  -z-e do eventually, do ever [aux; followed by subjunc]
  zikuthole they find it [subjunc]
nasezihlotsheni or in families [assoc adv]
  sezihlotsheni in families [loc; < sezihlobweni < e- + izihlobo + -eni; bw > tsh]
  izihlobo relatives [n Cl. 8; sg isihlobo]
ukuhlangana to meet, meeting, coming together [vn Cl. 15]
sekwakhe it has already built [past, exclusive, conjoint]
  kw- it [SC Cl. 15]
ibutho band, troop, regiment [n Cl. 5; < -buth- gather together, recruit]
eliyingozi that/which is dangerous [rel Cl. 5]

liyingozi it is danger [ident cop, pres]
yingozi it is danger [ident cop, pres]
ingozi danger [n Cl. 9]
nokuletha and to bring [assoc adv]
  ukuletha to bring [vn Cl. 15]
  -leth-a bring [v.t.]
uvalo fear, anxiety (lit. diaphragm; Zulus see the diaphragm as the seat of fear) [n Cl. 11; pl **izimvalo**]
emalungeni among the members [loc]
  amalunga members [n Cl. 6; sg **ilunga** Cl. 5; var of **ilungu**]
omphakathi of the community [poss Cl. 6; < **a-** + **umpha-kathi**]

«4»
labafanyana these good-for-nothing youths [< **la** + **abafanyana**]
  la these [1st position dem; in some dialects the abbreviated form **la** is used for the Cl. 2 demonstrative **laba**]
  abafanyana good-for-nothing boys or youths [< **abafana** + **-Yana**]
  -Yana little, small; dear, sweet; wretched, awful, good-for-nothing [dimin suffix; significance depends on context]
amaphoyisa the police, policemen, policewomen [n Cl. 6; sg **iphoyisa** Cl. 5] {Eng}
bawathathisa okwezitha they take them as enemies
  izitha enemies [n Cl. 8; sg **isitha**]
uSandile (male name) [n Cl. 1a;

< **sandile** we (the family) have increased in number (the tones on the stem are all LOW; more rarely one finds the name with the tones HIGH LOW LOW which would mean "it (the nation, i.e. isizwe) has increased," a name more likely to be given to a prince)]
Memela (surname) [n Cl. 1a]
oneminyaka who has years [rel Cl. 1]
  uneminyaka (s)he has years [assoc cop, pres]
engu-9 that/which are 9 [rel Cl. 4]
  ingu-9 there are 9 of them [ident cop, pres]
  u-9 nine [n Cl. 1a]
uyilungu (s)he is a member [ident cop, pres]
leqembu of the group [poss Cl. 5]
elaziwa that/which is known [rel Cl. 5]
  laziwa it is known [pres, conjoint]
  -aziw-a be known [v-pass]
ngeleMdlwembe Gang by that (name) of the Mdlwembe Gang [instr adv phr]
  eleMdlwembe Gang that of the Mdlwembe Gang [poss pron Cl. 5]
  leMdlwembe Gang of the Mdlwembe Gang [poss Cl. 5]
  iMdlwembe Gang the Mdlwembe Gang [n Cl. 9a; < **umdlwembe** undisciplined person; wild, uncontrolled animal [n Cl. 1 or 3; pl **imidlwembe**]
ePoint Road in Point Road [loc]
  iPoint Road (place; notorious for prostitution and other crime) [n Cl. 5]

eThekwini in Durban (place; large harbor city) [loc; < ethekwini place of the harbor; < itheku harbor]
wathi (s)he said [rem past]
avame they normally [past, conjoint]
ukubathatha to take them [vn Cl. 15]
-ba- them [OC Cl. 2]
abayise and they take them to [subjunc]
-yis-a take to [v-caus]
esiteshini samaphoyisa to, from, in, at the police station [loc]
isiteshi samaphoyisa police station [n phr Cl. 7]
esiteshini to, from, at the station [loc] {Eng station}
isiteshi station [n Cl. 7] { back formation from the locative esiteshini derived from the English}
samaphoyisa of the police [poss Cl. 7]
lapho bephoqelelwa khona where they are forced [ind rel of plain loc rel]
bephoqelelwa they are forced [pres, partic]
-phoqelelw-a be continually forced, be compelled, be pressurized [v-perfective-pass]
-phoqelel-a urge continually, pressurize [v-perfective]
-phoq-a force, compel [v.t.]
ukuwasha to wash [vn Cl. 15]
-wash-a wash [v.t.] {Eng}
zamaphoyisa of the police [poss Cl. 10]
nama-trucks and trucks or vans [assoc adv]
ama-trucks trucks, vans [n Cl. 6; sg i-truck Cl. 5] {Eng}

ngiyawazonda I hate them [pres, disjoint]
-zond-a hate [v.t]
ahlale they keep on, they continually [aux]
esishaya they hitting us [pres, partic]
e- they, it [SC Cl. 6; used in participial]
kusho ... said ... [past, conjoint]
-o [past conjoint suffix; differs in tone and length or stress from the default suffix]

«5»
nawo they too [assoc adv]
wo they, them, their [abs pron Cl. 6]
ayasishaya they hit us [pres, disjoint]
aphinde and they repeatedly [aux, subjunc]
asihlukumeze ngokocansi they indecently assault us
asihlukumeze they assault us [subjunc]
ngokocansi indecently, sexually [instr adv phr]
okocansi sexual matters (i.e. (things) of the sleeping-mat; euph) [poss pron Cl. 17]
kocansi of the sleeping-mat [poss Cl. 17; < kwa- + ucansi]
ucansi sleeping-mat [n Cl. 11; pl amacansi Cl. 6]
kugcizelela emphasizes [pres, conjoint]
-gcizelel-a emphasize, stress [v.i. & t.]
uThulani (male name) [n Cl. 1a; < imper thulani! settle down! (this name might be given when there is strife within a family)]
Khanyile (surname) [n Cl. 1a]

oliqhamukisa who comes from [rel Cl. 1]
uliqhamukisa (s)he comes from there [pres, conjoint]
-li-qhamukis-a come from a place [idiom; The Cl. 5 OC refers to any place mentioned. The caus ext is used idiomatically here.]
eMpangeni from Empangeni [loc]
iMpangeni Empangeni (place) [n Cl. 5]
ifaqafaqa glue [n Cl. 9a]
sizichithela we just spend [pres, conjoint]
-zi- VERB **-el-** just VERB, merely VERB, VERB for no particular reason [reflexive prefix + appl ext]
-chith-a spill, waste, spend [v.t]
ngayo through it [instr adv]
weSantoshi Young Killers of the Santoshi Young Killers [poss Cl. 1]
iSantoshi Young Killers (gang name) [n Cl. 9a]
u-Innocent (male name) [n Cl. 1a]
Shezi (surname) [n Cl. 1a]
waseMgungundlovu of Pietermaritzburg [poss Cl. 1]
uMgungundlovu Pietermaritzburg (capital of KwaZulu-Natal Province) [n Cl. 3]

«6»
sibhema we sniff, we smoke [pres, conjoint]
-bhem-a smoke, sniff (a substance) [v.i. & t.]
singalambi we should not get hungry [subjunc, neg]
-lamb-a get hungry [v.inch]
singayitholanga we have not got [past, partic, neg]

-anga not + past [past neg suffix]
eyanele that/which is sufficient, that/which is enough [rel Cl. 9]
yanele it is sufficient, it is enough [stative]
-anel-a bec sufficient (for), bec enough (for) [v.i. & t., inch]
yokuthenga for buying [poss Cl. 9]
ukuthenga to buy, buying [vn Cl. 15]
ayisisuthisi it does not satisfy us, make us full [pres, neg]
-si- us [OC 1st p pl]
-suthis-a satisfy (of food), make full [v-caus]
-suth-a have enough to eat, bec satiated [v.inch]
siyayithokozela we are glad for it [pres, disjoint]
-thokozel-a be happy about or for, be glad about or for, enjoy [v-appl]
-thokoz-a be happy, be glad [v.i.]
uClive Wilkes (name) [n phr Cl. 1a]
waseWentworth of Wentworth [poss Cl. 1]
iWentworth (place) [n Cl. 5]
Makhathini (surname) [n Cl. 1a]
ophinda who also [rel Cl. 1]
uphinda (s)he also VERBs, (s)he again VERBs [aux; followed by subjunc]
aziwe (s)he is known [subjunc]
Ø- he, she, it [SC Cl. 1]
ngelikaSnoopy by that (name) of Snoopy [instr adv phr]
elikaSnoopy that of Snoopy [poss pron Cl. 5]
lika- of [poss conc Cl. 5; occurs before nouns of Cl. 1a]
uSnoopy (name) [n Cl. 1a]

53

eneminyaka having years [assoc cop, pres, partic]

engu-10 that/which are 10 [rel Cl. 4]

ingu-10 there are ten of them [ident cop, pres]

u-10 ten [n Cl. 1a]

walishiya (s)he left it [rem past]

lakhe his, her [poss Cl. 5]

eliseBhambayi that/which is in Bhambayi [rel Cl. 5]

liseBhambayi it, (s)he is in Bhambayi [loc cop, pres]

iBhambayi (place) [n Cl. 5]

eminyakeni in years, during years [loc]

emine four [adj Cl. 4]

eyedlule that/which have passed [rel Cl. 4]

yedlule they have passed [stative]

y- they [SC Cl. 4]

«7»

usingababa (stepfather) father-figure (*not* stepfather) [n Cl. 1a]

-singa- something like [prefix deriving nouns; means 'some-thing like']

wami my [poss Cl. 1]

wayevame (s)he used [aux, rem past past, conjoint]

-ye- he, she, it [SC Cl. 1]

ukungishaya to beat me [vn Cl. 15]

-ngi- me [OC 1 p sg]

nsukuzonke daily, every day [adv; < (izi)nsuku days + zonke all]

umama (my) mother [n Cl. 1a; var umame]

angasho not saying [narr, partic, neg; < Ø- SC + -a- narr pref + -nga- neg pref + -sh-o]

wayemlekelela (s)he used to assist him or her [rem past pres]

-lekelel-a assist, help, aid [v.t.]

lomfanyana this little boy [dem phr Cl. 1; < lo + umfanyana]

lo this [1st position dem Cl. 1]

umfanyana little boy [n Cl. 1; < umfana + -Yana]

lesihluku this cruelty [1st pos dem Cl. 7; < le + isihluku]

isihluku cruelty, ill-will [n Cl. 7]

engangisithola that/which I experienced (it) [ind rel of plain obj rel, 1 p sg]

ngangisithola I experienced (found) it [rem past pres]

ng- I [SC 1 p sg; found before vowels]

-si- it, him, her [OC Cl. 7]

ekhaya at home [loc]

ikhaya home [n Cl. 5]

sangiphiqa it forced me [rem past]

-phiq-a force, compel [v.t.]

ngiyohlal' (final -a is elided) I should go and live [subjunc]

-yo- go and, go to [andative marker]

-a [subjunctive pos suffix found in andatives and venitives]

yaseThekwini of (in) Durban [poss Cl. 4]

inzima it is hard, it is difficult [descr cop, pres]

sengike I have already [aux, past, exclusive, conjoint]

ngadlula I passed [narrative]

ebunzimeni through or in hardship [loc]

ubunzima hardship, difficulty [n Cl. 14; < -nzima hard, difficult [rel stem]]

obukhulu great [adj Cl. 14]

ukuba because, since [conj]

angizange ngiye I have never gone (to) [v phr]

angizange I have not ever [aux, past, neg; < **-z-e** + **-ange**]
-z-e do ever [aux, followed by subjunc]
ngiye I went [subjunc]
eThuthukani Outreach Centre to the Thuthukani Outreach Center [loc]
   iThuthukani Outreach Centre Thuthukani Outreach Center [n Cl. 9a; < **t h u t h u k a n i !** progress!, go forward!]
sengifile I am already dead [stative, exclusive]

«8»

namaphoyisa and the police [assoc adv]
asithathisa okwezigebengu they take us as criminals [v phr]
kanti futhi and also [conj phr]
bavame they generally VERB [past, conjoint]
ukusishaya to beat us [vn Cl. 15]
basethembise they promise (i.e. threaten) us [subjunc]
   -s- us [OC 1 p pl]
   -ethembis-a promise [v-caus]
   -ethemb-a hope, trust [v.t.; var of **-themb-a**]
ukusibulala to kill us [vn Cl. 15]
   -bulal-a kill [v.t.]
ukwazisa to inform [vn Cl. 15]
   -azis-a notify, inform, let know [v-caus]
ngokuthi that (lit. about that), so that, about what [instr adv]
zikhulume they should talk [subjunc]
   -khulum-a talk, speak [v.t.]
nabazali with parents [assoc adv]
bazo their, of them [poss Cl. 2]
osohlalakahle social workers [n Cl. 2b; sg **usohlalakahle**]

ngaphambi kokuba before (V E R B ing) [conj phrase; followed by the subjunc]
zithathe they take [subjunc]
zokuyohlal' (final **-a** is elided) to go and live (lit. of going to live) [poss Cl. 8]
   ukuyohlala to go and live [vn Cl. 15, andative]
abancane little, small [adj Cl. 2]
basetshenziswa they are used [pres, conjoint]
   -setshenzisw-a be used, be utilized, be employed [v-caus-appl; < **-sebenzisw-a**; b ... **-w**- > tsh ... **-w**-]
njengezinto zocansi as sexual objects [compar adv phr]
   njenge- [compar adv pref coalesced with following **i**]
   izinto zocansi sexual objects (lit. things of the sleeping-mat)
   zocansi sexual [poss Cl. 10]
ngabafan' (final **-a** is elided) by boys [agentive adverb]
abadala old, older [adj Cl. 2]
asilali we don't sleep [pres, neg]
bayasinukubeza they sexually abuse us [pres, disjoint]
   -nukubez-a abuse sexually [v.t.]
ngesikhathi at the time (when), during the time (that), while [instr adv; followed by partic]
silele we are sleeping [stative, partic]
   -lele [< **-lal-** + **-i...e**]
uXolani (male name) [n Cl. 1a; < imper **xolani!** forgive! (this name might be given when the mother has done something wrong, e.g. had an illegitimate child)]
   Khambule (surname) [n Cl. 1a]

eyisishiyagalombili eight (adj) [rel Cl. 4]
yisishiyagalombili it is eight [ident cop]
isishiyagalombili eight (n) [n Cl. 7]

«9»
kuleli to, from, in this (country) [loc; short for **kuleli zwe** in this country]
kunamaqembu there are groups or gangs [assoc cop, pres]
ezigebengu of criminals [poss Cl. 6]
ayingozi that/which are dangerous [rel Cl. 6]
ziphinde and they repeatedly [aux, subjunc]
zibulale they kill [subjunc]
ukulwa fighting, to fight [n Cl. 15]
-lw-a fight [v.i.]
kwamaqembu of the gangs [poss Cl. 15]
eCape Flats on the Cape Flats (area of Greater Cape Town to which the former apartheid government relocated Coloreds (people of mixed race), who had been removed by law from their homes that were considered to be in White areas. This area is now infamous for crime, and gang warfare.) [loc]
iCape Flats (place) [n Cl. 5]
kuhlale it continues to be, it remains [aux]
kusemithonjeni it is in the sources [loc cop, pres]
semithonjeni in the sources [loc; < **emithombweni** < **se-** + **imithombo** + **-eni**; **mbw** > **nj**]
imithombo springs; sources [n Cl. 4; sg **umthombo**]

yabezindaba of journalists, or reporters [poss Cl. 4; < **ya-** + **abezindaba**]
abezindaba journalists, reporters (lit. those of the news) [poss pron Cl. 2]
bezindaba of the news [poss Cl. 2]
izindaba affairs, matters, news [n Cl. 10]
kulendawo to, from, in, at, this place [loc]
afana like (that resemble) [rel Cl. 6]
afana they resemble, they are like [pres, conjoint]
i-Americans the Americans (a gang) [n Cl. 9a]
Young Boys (gang name)
iNotorious Mongrel Gang (gang name) [n Cl. 9a]
abulalana they kill one another [pres, conjoint]
-bulalan-a kill one another [v-recip]
ngezibhamu with guns [instr adv]
izibhamu guns [n Cl. 8; sg **isibhamu**]
ezinkulu large [adj Cl. 8; < **ezin-** + **-khulu**; **n** + **kh** > **nk**]
ezin- [adj conc Cl. 8]
ekuxazululeni in the settlement (of quarrels, etc.) [loc]
ukuxazulula settlement, to settle, resolution, to resolve [vn Cl. 15]
-xazulul-a settle or resolve (a quarrel, dispute) [v.t.]
izinkinga problems [n Cl. 10; sg **inkinga**]
zokubanga of creating [poss Cl. 10]
ukubanga creating, to create [n Cl. 15]

ukukhonya power, superiority; influence; turf (lit. bellowing (as a bull), to roar (as a lion)) [vn Cl. 15]
-khony-a bellow (as a bull), roar (like a lion) [v.i.]
nezidakamizwa and drugs [assoc adv]
izidakamizwa drugs [n Cl. 8; sg **isidakamizwa**; < **-dak-a** intoxicate, stupefy + **imizwa** feelings]

«10»
UJoan van Niekerk (name) [n phr Cl. 1a]
ongumqondisi who is a director [rel Cl. 1]
    ungumqondisi (s)he is a director [ident cop, pres]
    umqondisi director [n Cl. 1; < **-qondis-** direct (steer in a direction) [v-caus]
kwiChildline at Childline [loc]
    iChildline Childline (call center for crisis counseling for or about children) [n Cl. 9a]
esifundeni in the province [loc]
    isifunda province, district [n Cl. 7]
saKwaZulu-Natal of KwaZulu-Natal [poss Cl. 7]
nezinhlangano and organizations, societies, associations [assoc adv]
    izinhlangano organizations, societies, associations [n Cl. 10; sg **inhlangano**]
zezenhlalakahle for social welfare [poss Cl. 10; < **za-** + **ezenhlalakahle**]
    z- of [pos conc Cl. 10]
    ezenhlalakahle social welfare [poss pron Cl. 10; < **izindaba zenhlalakahle**]

inhlalakahle social welfare [n Cl. 9; < **-hlal-a** live + **kahle** well]
baqhamuke they should come up (lit. they should appear) [subjunc]
nohlelo with a system [assoc adv]
    uhlelo arrangement, system, program [n Cl. 11; < **-hlel-** put in order, arrange; pl **izinhlelo**]
lokugwema for avoiding [poss Cl. 11]
zihlale they should stay [subjunc]
nolokuqeda and one (plan) for bringing to an end [assoc adv phr]
    olokuqeda one for bringing to an end [poss pron Cl. 11]
    lokuqeda for bringing to and end [poss Cl. 11]
    lo- of [poss conc Cl. 11, **lwa-**, coalesced with following **u**]
    ukuqeda to bring to an end, to finish [vn Cl. 15]
sizisize we should help them [subjunc]
    -siz-a help, assist, aid [v.t.]
ziphinde ziphile they should again live [v phr]
    ziphile they (should) live [subjunc]
ngendlela in a way [instr adv]
efanele proper [rel Cl. 9]
    ifanele it is proper, it is fitting [stative]
emgwaqweni on the street [loc; var **emgwaqeni**; < **umgwaqo**]
yizinto are things [ident cop, pres]
ezisihluphayo that/which bother us [rel Cl. 10]
    ziyasihlupha they bother us [pres, disjoint]
ezweni in a or the country [loc; < **izwe**]
kunzima it is difficult [descr cop, pres]

ukubuyisela to restore to, to return to [vn Cl. 15]
-buyisel-a restore to, return to [v-caus-appl]
-buyis-a return (v.t.), send back [v-caus]
-buy-a return (v.i.), return from, go back, come back from [v.i.]
isimo standing, status, condition, situation; nature, form, character [n Cl. 7; < **-m-** stand]
uLinda (name) [n Cl. 1a]
Manyoni (surname) [n Cl. 1a]

Isandla esiqinile kubakhokhi-ntela

Ngu: Sandile Mdadane

«1»
Bazalelwe yinja endlini ababalekela ukukhokha intela njengoba umnyango obhekele ukuqoqwa kwentela i-South African Revenue Services (Sars) [iSars] ibambisene nophiko lwamacala emali i-Saps Commercial Crime Unit noMnyango wezobuLungiswa beqale umkhankaso wokubopha bonke abantu nabamabhizinisi abaqinisa ikhanda ekukhokheni intela.

«2»
Kusukela ngenyanga edlule eThekwini sebengu-896 abantu asebefakwe ohlwini lwabazoshushiselwa amacala okubalekela ukukhokha intela, kuthi nabangu-300 asebekhishelwe izincwadi zokuthi baboshwe.

«3»
Umbhidlango walolu phiko usanda kubonakala ekuboshweni nasekushushisweni kukayise nendodana balapha eThekwini ababhekene necala lika-R15mln lokudoja ukukhokha intela yezimpahla ezithengwa ngaphandle kwemingcele yeNingizimu Afrika.

«4»
Laba ababili babe yizisulu zokuqala zomthetho omusha i-Proceeds of Crime Act lapho uHulumeni ethathe impahla yabo wavala izimali zabo emabhange ezingaphezu kuka-R1mln, umuzi nezimoto ezinhlanu kuze kube kuphuma isinqumo secala.

«5»
Amagama abo bonke labo abadoja ukukhokha intela asezosakazwa emaphephandabeni kungekudala.

Abakhwabanisi

Iningi labantu lidoja ukukhokha intela i-Value Added Tax ([i]VAT), intela yabaqashwa, nama-Annual Tax Returns.

«6»
Ongumshushisi omkhulu ezinkantolo eziyisipesheli uMnuz Barend Groen uthe okumele kwaziwe ngabantu ngukuthi kunomehluko phakathi kwabadoji bentela nabakhwabanisi bentela.

"Lezi zinhlobo ezimbili zezaphuli-mthetho zehluke kakhulu.

«7»
"Uma kukhulunywa ngabakhwabanisi bentela, sikhuluma ngabantu abadla imali eyizinkulungwane ngezinkulungwane," kuchaza uMnuz Groen.

Uqhube wathi abadoji bentela yize bephula umthetho abajwayele ukuthi benze imali eningi.

Uphethe ngokuthi akakholwa neze ukuthi kukhona abantu abadoja intela bengazi ukuthi baphula umthetho.

Vocabulary

esiqinile firm, sturdy [rel Cl. 7]
  siqinile it is firm [stative]
kubakhokhi-ntela towards taxpayers [loc]
  abakhokhi-ntela taxpayers [n Cl. 2; sg. **umkhokhi-ntela**; < **umkhokhi** payer + **intela** tax]
Mdadane (surname) [n Cl. 1a]

«1»
bazalelwe yinja endlini they have a huge problem (idiom; lit. they have had a dog born in the house)
bazalelwe they have had born to them [stative, conjoint]
yinja by a dog [agent adv]
  inja dog [n Cl. 9]
endlini in the house [loc]
  indlu house [n Cl. 9]
ababalekela those who run away from [rel Cl. 2]
  babalekela they run away from, they evade [pres, conjoint]
  -balekel-a run away from, evade, run away to, flee to [v-appl]
  -balek-a run away (from), flee [v.i. & t.]
ukukhokha paying, to pay [vn Cl. 15]
  -khokh-a pay; repay; draw out, withdraw [v.t.]
intela tax [n Cl. 9; < **-thel-** pay tax; **n + th > nt**]
umnyango state department

[n Cl. 3]
obhekele that/which is looking towards [rel Cl. 3]
  ubhekele it is looking towards or at [past, conjoint]
ukuqoqwa collection, to be collected [n Cl. 15]
kwentela of tax [poss Cl. 15]
i-South African Revenue Services (Sars) [i-Sars] [n Cl. 9a]
ibambisene it is cooperating [stative]
  -bambisan-a cooperate with each other, assist each other in [v-caus-recip]
  -bambis-a assist in doing [v-caus]
nophiko with the department [assoc adv]
  uphiko wing, department, section [n Cl. 11; pl. **izimpiko**; **m + ph > mp**]
lwamacala of prosecutions [poss Cl. 11]
  amacala prosecutions, court cases [n Cl. 6; sg **icala** Cl. 5]
emali financial, commercial [poss Cl. 6]
  -imali financial, commercial [poss base; < **imali** money]
i-Saps (South African Police Services) **Commercial Crime Unit** [n Cl. 9a]
noMnyango and the Department [assoc adv]

wezobuLungiswa of Correctional Services (i.e. Prisons) [poss Cl. 3]
w- of [poss conc Cl. 3; found before **a**, **e** and **o**]
ezobuLungiswa Correctional Services [poss pron Cl. 10]
beqale they having started [past, partic, conjoint]
umkhankaso tactic, scheme (originally a horseshoe movement in order to outmaneuver an enemy) [n Cl. 3; < **-khankas-** move in a horseshoe formation in order to outmaneuver]
wokubopha of arresting [poss Cl. 3]
ukubopha to arrest [vn Cl. 15]
-boph-a arrest, tie (up), bind, make fast [v.t.]
nabamabhizinisi and business-owners [assoc adv]
abamabhizinisi business-owners [poss pron Cl. 2; sg **owamabhizinisi**]
bamabhizinisi (people) of businesses [poss Cl. 2]
amabhizinisi businesses, firms [n Cl. 6; sg **ibhizinisi** Cl. 5] {Eng}
abaqinisa ikhanda who are obstinate [rel phr Cl. 2]
baqinisa ikhanda they are obstinate (lit. they make (their) head strong) [v phr]
-qinis-a ikhanda be obstinate, be stubborn, be headstrong (lit. make the head strong or hard)
-qinis-a strengthen, tighten, make firm [v-caus]
ikhanda head [n Cl. 5]
ekukhokheni in paying [loc]

«2»
ngenyanga monthly, during the month, within a month [instr adv]
inyanga month [n Cl. 9a]
sebengu-896 there are now 896 [ident cop, pres, exclusive]
ngu-896 it is 896 [ident cop, pres]
u-896 896 [n Cl. 1a]
asebefakwe who have been placed [rel Cl. 2]
sebefakwe [past, exclusive, conjoint]
-fakw-a be placed, be put in, be installed [v-pass]
-fak-a place, put in, instal [v.t.]
ohlwini on the list [loc; < **o-** + **uhlu** + **-ini**]
o- ... -ini to, from, in, at, on [loc marker]
uhlu list, roll [n Cl. 11; pl **izinhlu**]
lwabazoshushiselwa of those who will have cases prosecuted against them [poss, Cl. 11; < **lwa-** poss conc + **abazoshushiselwa**]
abazoshushiselwa who will have cases prosecuted against them [rel Cl. 2]
bazoshusiselwa they will have cases brought against them [fut]
-shushiselw-a be sued for, have cases brought against one [v-caus-appl-pass]
-shushisel-a sue for, prosecute for [v-caus-appl]
-shushis-a prosecute, sue [v-caus]
-shush-a harass, press [v.t.]
okubalekela ukukhokha intela for tax evasion [poss phr Cl. 6]
okubalekela of evading, of running away from [poss Cl. 6]

kuthi it being so that [conj]

nabangu-300 and 300 [assoc adv]

    abangu-300 300 of them [rel Cl. 2]

    bangu-300 there are 300 of them [ident cop, pres]

    u-300 300 [n Cl. 1a]

asebekhishelwe who have already had taken out against them [rel Cl. 2]

    sebekhishelwe they have already had taken out against them [past, exclusive, conjoint]

izincwadi zokuthi baboshwe warrants of arrest (lit. letters that they should be arrested) [n phr Cl. 10a]

    izincwadi letters; books [n Cl. 10a; sg **incwadi** Cl. 9a]

    zokuthi of to say, of that [poss Cl. 10]

    baboshwe they should be arrested [subjunc]

    -boshw-a be arrested [v-pass; < -boph-w-a; phw > shw]

«3»

umbhidlango campaign [n Cl. 3]

walolu of this [poss Cl. 3]

phiko [< **uphiko**]

usanda it has just [aux, pres, conjoint]

    -sand-a do just [aux, followed by vn]

kubonakala (with elision of initial **u**) to become apparent [vn Cl. 15]

ekuboshweni in the arrest [loc]

    ukuboshwa arrest, to be arrested [vn Cl. 15]

nasekushushisweni and in the prosecution [assoc adv]

    -sekushushisweni in the prosecution [loc; < **ekushushisweni**]

ukushushiswa prosecution, to be prosecuted [vn Cl. 15]

kukayise of the father (lit. of his or her father) [poss Cl. 15; < **kuka- + uyise**]

balapha of here, local [poss Cl. 2]

ababhekene necala who are faced with a charge [rel phr Cl. 2]

lika-R15mln of 15 million rands [poss Cl. 5]

    u-R15mln 15 million rands [n Cl. 1a]

lokudoja of evading [poss Cl. 5]

    ukudoja evasion, to evade, to dodge [vn Cl. 15]

    -doj-a evade, avoid, dodge [v.t.] {Eng}

yezimpahla for goods [poss Cl. 9]

ezithengwa that/which are bought [rel Cl. 10]

    zithengwa they are bought [pres, conjoint]

    -thengw-a be bought [v-pass]

kwemingcele of the borders [poss Cl. 17]

    imingcele borders [n Cl. 4; sg **umngcele**]

«4»

ababili two [adj Cl. 2]

    -bili two [adj stem]

babe yizisulu they became victims [ident cop, inch, past, conjoint]

    yizisulu it is victims [ident cop, pres]

    izisulu victims [n Cl. 8; sg **isisulu**]

zokuqala first [poss Cl. 8]

    zo- of [poss conc Cl. 8 coalesced with following **u**]

    ukuqala to begin, to start; first, initial [vn Cl. 15]

omusha new [adj Cl. 3]

omu- [adj conc Cl. 3; used before monosyllabic stems] **-sha** new, young, fresh [adj stem]

i-Proceeds of Crime Act [n Cl. 9a] {Eng}

lapho when [conj; followed by participial]

ethathe it, (s)he took [past, partic, conjoint]

wavala and it, (s)he froze (lit. closed) [narr] **-val-a** close, shut [v.t.]

izimali accounts (lit. monies) [n Cl. 10a]

zabo their [poss Cl. 10]

emabhange in banks [loc] **amabhange** banks [sg **ibhange** Cl. 5] {Afr *bank*}

ezingaphezu kuka-R1mln that/which are above R1m [rel phr Cl. 10] (R = rand, the unit of South African currency) **zingaphezu kuka-R1mln** they are above R1m [loc cop, pres] **ngaphezu kuka-** above, over, more than [instr adv phr] **kuka-R1mln** of R1m [poss Cl. 17] **kuka-** of; link between locative noun and following noun of Cl. 1a [poss conc Cl. 17]

nezimoto and cars [assoc adv]

ezinhlanu five [adj Cl. 10]

«5»

amagama names [n Cl. 6; sg **igama** Cl. 5]

abo their [poss Cl. 6]

abadoja who evade [rel Cl. 2] **badoja** they evade, they dodge [pres, conjoint]

asezosakazwa they will soon be published [fut, exclusive; < **a-** they + **-s-** soon + **-e-** they + **-zo-** will + **-sakazw-a**] **-sakazw-a** be broadcast, be published [v-pass] **-sakaz-a** broadcast, publish, disseminate [v.t.]

emaphephandabeni in newspapers [loc]

kungekudala before long [loc cop, pres, partic; < **ku-** SC Cl. 17 + **-nge-** neg pref + **kudala**] **kudala** long ago, a long time [loc n Cl. 17] **ku-** [NP Cl. 17]

abakhwabanisi embezzlers, frauds [n Cl. 2; sg **umkhwabanisi**; < **-khwabanis-** embezzle]

lidoja it evades [pres, conjoint]

i-Value Added Tax (VAT) [n Cl. 9a] {Eng}

yabaqashwa employees' [poss Cl. 9] **abaqashwa** employees, staff [n Cl. 2; sg **umqashwa**; < **-qashw-** be employed, hired + **-a** nominalizing suffix found with passive verbs]

nama-Annual Tax Returns and annual ... [assoc adv] **ama-Annual Tax Returns** [n Cl. 6; sg **i-Annual Tax Return** [n Cl. 9a]

«6»

ongumshushisi (s)he who is prosecutor [rel Cl. 1] **ungumshushisi** (s)he is the prosecutor [ident cop, pres] **umshushisi** prosecutor [n Cl. 1; < **-shushis-** persecute, prosecute]

omkhulu senior [adj Cl. 1]

ezinkantolo in the courts [loc; one of the exceptions that does not take a locative suffix]
izinkantolo courts [n Cl. 10; sg **inkantolo** Cl. 9] {Afr *kantoor* office}
eziyisipesheli (that are) special [rel Cl. 10]
ziyisipesheli they are special [ident cop, pres]
isipesheli special thing [n Cl. 7] {Eng}
Barend (male name) [n Cl. 1a] {Afr}
Groen (surname) [n Cl. 1a] {Afr}
uthe (s)he said [past, conjoint]
okumele what must [rel Cl. 17]
kwaziwe it should be known [subjunc]
ngabantu by people [agent adv]
ngukuthi (it) is that [ident cop, pres]
kunomehluko there is a difference [assoc cop, pres]
kuno- there is, there are [< **kuna-** + **u**]
umehluko difference, distinction [n Cl. 4; < **-ehluk-** differ; pl **imehluko**; **im-** NP Cl. 4; occurs before vowels]
phakathi kwabadoji between evaders [loc phr]
abadoji evaders, avoiders [n Cl. 2; sg. **umdoji**; < **-doj-** dodge, evade]
bentela of tax [poss Cl. 2]
nabakhwabanisi and frauds [assoc adv]
zinhlobo < **izinhlobo** types, sorts, kinds [n Cl. 10; sg **uhlobo** Cl. 11]
ezimbili two [adj Cl. 10]
ezim- [adj conc Cl. 10]
zezaphuli-mthetho of law-breakers [poss Cl. 10]

izaphuli-mthetho law-breakers [n Cl. 8; sg **isaphuli-mthetho** Cl. 7; < **-aphul-** break + **umthetho**]
zehluke they are different [past, conjoint]
-ehluk-a bec different, differ [v.i., inch; var of **-ahluk-a** and **-hluk-a**]

«7»

kukhulunywa one speaks (lit. there is spoken) [pres, partic]
-khulunyw-a be spoken, be talked [v-pass; < **-khulumw-**; **m** + **w** > **nyw**]
ngabakhwabanisi about frauds [instr adv]
sikhuluma we speak [pres, conjoint]
abadla who embezzle [rel Cl. 2]
badla they embezzle; they eat [pres, conjoint]
-dl-a embezzle (lit. eat) [v.t.]
eyizinkulungwane ngezinkulungwane thousands upon thousands [rel phr Cl. 9]
iyizinkulungwane there are thousands [ident cop, pres]
izinkulungwane thousands [n Cl. 10; sg **inkulungwane** Cl. 9]
ngezinkulungwane upon thousands [instr adv]
kuchaza ... explains ... [pres, conjoint]
uqhube (s)he continued [past, conjoint]
yize it is to no avail, it is for nothing, it is useless [ident cop, pres]
ize nothing, a thing of no value [n Cl. 5]
bephula (that) they break [pres, partic]
-phul-a break [v.t.; var of

-aphul-a and **-ephul-a**]
abajwayele they are not used (to),
they are not wont (to) [stative,
neg]
-jwayel-a get used to, grow
accustomed to, adjust to [v.t.;
var **-ejwayel-a**]
benze they should make or do
[subjunc]
b- they [SC Cl. 2]
eningi a lot, much [adj Cl. 9]
eØ- [adj conc Cl. 9]
uphethe (s)he concluded [past,
conjoint]

-pheth-a complete, conclude,
finish, have the last say [v.i. &
t.]
ngokuthi by saying [instr adv]
ukuthi saying, to say [vn Cl. 15]
akakholwa (s)he does not believe
[pres, neg]
-kholw-a believe [v.i. & t.]
neze at all, in the slightest [assoc
adv; < **na-** + **ize**]
bengazi without knowing, they not
knowing [pres, partic, neg]
baphula they are breaking [pres,
conjoint]

Ingaphinda izenzele kalula
ikwaShaka kwiSoccer Festival?

Ngu: Zwelakhe Ngcobo

«1»

Ukuvikela kwekaShaka [sic] High School isicoco seGirls Soccer okwesithathu iminyaka ilandelana kuzophelekezelwa isiqubulo sokongiwa kwamanzi kwi-Umlazi Soccer Festival engoLwesine eKing Zwelithini Stadium eqala ngo-9 ekuseni.

«2»

Lo mqhudelwano ozobe ugubha iminyaka emihlanu wasungulwa kuzokwenzeka okungajwayelekile njengoba uzobe uhanjelwe ngu-Ngqongqoshe weZamanzi neZamahlathi kuzwelonke, uProf Kader Asmal, nozobe ephelekezelwa yiMeya yaseDurban South Central uTheresa Mthembu noDudu Khoza woKhozi FM abazonikezela ngemiklomelo emaqenjini adle ubhedu.

«3»

Ngokusho kukaMorgan Zama ongumgqugquzeli walo mqhudelwano amaqembu aqhathwe kanje; Kwi-Boys U/11 – i-Entuthukweni yaseLamontville izotholana phezulu neVumokuhle; Kwi-Girls U/14 iManyuswa izwane amandla neBhekithemba; Kwi-Boys U/14 iManyuswa igadulisane neBhekithemba; Kwi-Girls Open – iKwaShaka High School idudulane ne-Umlazi Comtech kuvale oweLamontville High School ezobambana ngezihluthu nezi-kaSiyavuma Mfeka ikwaMgaga High School engompetha banyakenye.

«4»

Imi kanje imiklomelo yalo mqhudelwano ozodlalwa okokuqala ngqa selokhu kuhoxe inkampani yakwaWakefield JHI ebingenye yabeseki balo mqhudelwano phambilini.

Umklomelo wokuqala kuzohlomulwa ngenkomishi, indondo zegolide, ijezi lebhola, isikhwama esikhulu nezikibha.

«5»

Umklomelo wesibili: Izindondo zesiliva, ijezi lebhola, isikhwama esisodwa esikhulu nezikibha.

Owomdlali ovelele kuzoba yi-track suit namakhokho amabili anikelwe ngabakwa-Adidas.

UZama uhlaba umkhosi kuzo zonke izingane ezakhele uMlazi namaphethelo ukuba ziphume ngobuningi bazo zizozitika ngonqambothi lwemidlalo.

Vocabulary

ingaphinda it can again [pres, potential]

izenzele it just do [subjunc]

-z- ... -el- just, merely [reflexive prefix (before vowels) + appl ext]

kalula easily [manner adv]

-lula easy, light [rel stem]

iKwaShaka the KwaShaka (football team) [n Cl. 9a; < **KwaShaka** the kingdom of Shaka]

uShaka (Zulu king who molded disparate Nguni tribes into the Zulu nation) [n Cl. 1a]

kwi-Soccer Festival at the Soccer Festival [loc]

i-Soccer Festival [n Cl. 9a] {Eng}

«1»

ukuvikela defence, to defend, protection, to protect [n Cl. 15]

(**kwekaShaka**) this should read: **kwekwaShaka High School** of the Shaka High School [poss Cl. 15]

iKwaShaka High School [n Cl. 9a] {Eng}

isicoco se-Girls Soccer girls' soccer title [n Cl. 7]

isicoco title [n Cl. 7]

se-Girls Soccer for girls' soccer [poss Cl. 7]

i-Girls Soccer [n Cl. 9a] {Eng}

okwesithathu third [poss pron Cl. 15; refers to **ukuvikela**]

ilandelana successive (lit. they following one other) [pres, partic]

-landelan-a follow one

another [v-recip]

-landel-a follow [v.t.]

kuzophelekezelwa it (the defence) will be accompanied [fut]

-phelekezelw-a be accompanied [v-pass]

-phelekez-a accompany [v.t.; var **-phekelez-a**]

isiqubulo by a slogan [agent adv; < Ø- by + **isiqubulo**]

isiqubulo slogan [n Cl. 7]

sokongiwa of the conservation [poss Cl. 7]

ukongiwa conservation [n Cl. 15]

uk- [vn pref; NP Cl. 15; found before **o**]

-ongiw-a be saved, preserved, conserved [v-pass]

-ong-a save; economize [v.i. & t.]

kwamanzi of water [poss Cl. 15]

amanzi water [n Cl. 6]

kwi-Umlazi Soccer Festival at the Umlazi Soccer Festival [loc]

i-Umlazi Soccer Festival [n Cl. 9a] {Eng}

uMlazi (town) [n Cl. 3]

engoLwesine that/which is on Thursday [rel Cl. 9]

ingoLwesine it is on Thursday [loc cop, pres]

ngoLwesine on Thursday [instr adv; can be analysed as **nga- + oLwesine** or **nga- + uLwesine**]

oLwesine Thursday [poss pron; **o-** pronominalizer + **lwa-** poss conc Cl. 11 (agreeing with understood **usuku** day) + **isine** fourth]

uLwesine [n Cl. 1a; < poss
Cl. 11]
e-King Zwelithini Stadium at
the King Zwelithini Stadium
[loc]
i-King Zwelithini Stadium [n
Cl. 9a] {Eng}
uZwelithini (male name;
name of the present Zulu
King) [n Cl. 1a]
eqala that/which begins [rel
Cl. 9]
iqala it begins [pres, conjoint]
ngo-9 at 9 [instr adv]
ekuseni in the morning [loc;
< **ukusa** to dawn]

«2»
mqhudelwano < **umqhudelwano** competition, challenge
[n Cl. 3]
ozobe ugubha that/which will be
celebrating [rel Cl. 3]
uzobe ugubha it will be
celebrating [fut pres]
-gubh-a celebrate, observe (a
festival, occasion) [v.t.]
wasungulwa since it was
inaugurated [rem past, partic]
-sungulw-a be inaugurated,
be established [v-pass]
-sungul-a inaugurate, initiate,
establish, found, set up [v.t.]
kuzokwenzeka there will
happen, it will happen [fut]
okungajwayelekile something
unusual [rel Cl. 17]
kungajwayelekile it not being
usual [stative, rel, neg; <
akujwayelekile]
uzobe uhanjelwe it will be
attended [fut stative]
-hanjelw-a be attended
[v-appl-pass]
-hambel-a attend, visit, travel

towards, travel for [v-appl,
inch]
**nguNgqongqoshe wezamanzi
nezamahlathi kuzwelonke**
by the National Minister of
Water Affairs and Forestry
[agent adv]
wezamanzi of water affairs [poss
Cl. 1]
ezamanzi water affairs [poss
pron Cl. 10]
nezamahlathi and forestry
[assoc adv]
ezamahlathi forestry [poss
pron Cl. 10]
zmahlathi of forests [poss
Cl. 10]
amahlathi forests [n Cl. 6; sg
ihlathi]
kuzwelonke to, from, in the
nation [loc]
Kader (male name) [n Cl. 1a]
{Arabic}
Asmal (surname) [n Cl. 1a]
{Arabic}
nozobe ephelekezelwa and who
will be accompanied [assoc
adv phr]
ozobe ephelekezelwa who
will be accompanied [rel phr
Cl. 1]
uzobe ephelekezelwa (s)he
will be accompanied [fut pres]
yiMeya by the Mayor [agent
adv]
imeya mayor [n Cl. 9a; pl
izimeya Cl. 10a] {Eng}
yase-Durban South Central of
Durban South Central [poss
Cl. 9]
se-Durban South Central to,
from, in, at ... [loc; < e-Durban South Central]
i-Durban South Central
[n Cl. 9a] {Eng}

uTheresa (female name) [n Cl. 1a] {Eng}
Mthembu (surname) [n Cl. 1a]
noDudu and Dudu [assoc adv]
woKhozi FM of Khozi FM [poss Cl. 1]
wo- of [poss conc Cl. 1 coalesced with following **u**]
uKhozi FM (name of radio station) [n Cl. 11]
abazonikezela who will present [rel Cl. 2]
bazonikezela they will present [fut]
-nikezel-a present (to) [v-appl-caus-appl]
ngemiklomelo with prizes [instr adv]
imiklomelo prizes, awards, rewards [n Cl. 4; sg **umklomelo**; < **-klomel-** reward, give a prize or bonus]
emaqenjini to the teams [loc; < **emaqembwini**; < **e-** + **amaqembu** + **-ini**; **mbw** > **nj**]
adle ubhedu that/which have won a challenge, that/which have attained their goal (lit. that/which have eaten the fat around the heart – considered the reward for a herdboy who has won a challenge) [rel phr Cl. 6]
adle who have eaten [rel Cl. 6; < **a-** rel marker + **adle**]
adle they have eaten [past, conjoint]
-dl-a eat, consume [v.t.]
ubhedu heart fat; prize [n Cl. 11]

«3»
ngokusho kuka- according to [instr adv phr; used before a noun of Cl. 1a]
ngokusho according to (lit. by the saying so) [instr adv]
ukusho saying (so), statement [n Cl. 15]
kukaMorgan Zama of Morgan Zama [poss Cl. 15]
Morgan (male name) [n Cl. 1a] {Eng}
Zama (surname) [n Cl. 1a]
ongumgqugquzeli who is the coordinator [rel Cl. 1]
ungumgqugquzeli (s)he is the coordinator [ident cop, pres]
umgqugquzeli coordinator [n Cl. 1]
walo of this [poss Cl. 1]
aqhathwe they have been teamed up against one another [past, conjoint]
-qhathw-a be teamed up against, be set up against [v-pass]
kanje thus, like this, in this way [adv]
-nje like this [rel stem]
kwi-Boys U/11 in the Boys U(nder)/11 [loc]
i-Boys U/11 Boys U(nder)/11 [n Cl. 9a] {Eng}
i-Entuthukweni (team name) [n Cl. 9a]
yaseLamontville of Lamontville [poss Cl. 9]
seLamontville to, from, in Lamontville [loc; < **eLamontville**]
iLamontville (place) [n Cl. 5]
izotholana it will be in contention with [fut]
-tholan-a fight, be in contention [v-recip]
neVumokuhle with Vumokuhle [assoc adv]
iVumokuhle (team name) [n Cl. 9a]
kwi-Girls U/14 in the Girls

U(nder)/14 [loc]
i-Girls U/14 Girls U(nder)/14
[n Cl. 9a] {Eng}
iManyuswa Manyuswa (team
name) [n Cl. 9a]
izwane amandla it will test (its)
strength (lit. it will feel each
other strength)
izwane "it will feel each
other" [subjunc]
amandla strength, power, force
[n Cl. 6]
neBhekithemba against
Bhekithemba [assoc adv]
iBhekithemba (team name)
[n Cl. 9a]
igadulisane will tackle [subjunc]
-gadulisan-a tackle [v-caus-
recip]
kwi-Girls Open in the Girls
Open [loc]
i-Girls Open [n Cl. 9a] {Eng}
idudulane will come against (lit.
it will mutually fend off an
attack) [subjunc]
-dudulan-a fend off one
another's attack [v-recip]
-dudul-a repel an attack [v.t.]
ne-Umlazi Comtech (with)
Umlazi Comtech [assoc adv]
i-Umlazi Comtech (name of a
technical school offering
commerce) [n Cl. 9a]
kuvale and the close will be (lit.
it will close) [subjunc]
oweLamontville High School
that (game) of Lamontville
High School [poss pron Cl. 3
(agrees with **umdlalo**)]
ezobambana ngezihluthu
that/which will go head to
head (idiom) [rel phr Cl. 9]
ezobambana that/which will
take each other on, that/which
will go into battle with each

other [rel Cl. 9]
izobambana it will go into
battle (with each other) [fut]
-bamban-a wrestle, go into
battle with, take each other on
[v-recip]
-bamb-a undertake, engage in
battle [v.t.]
izihluthu long mass of hair
[n Cl. 8]
nezikaSiyavuma Mfeka with
those of Siyavuma Mfeka
[assoc adv phr]
ezikaSiyavuma Mfeka those
of Siyavuma Mfeka [poss
pron Cl. 8]
Mfeka (surname) [n Cl. 1a]
iKwaMgaga High School [n
Cl. 9a]
engompetha who were the
finalists [rel Cl. 9]
ingompetha they are the
finalists [ident cop, pres]
ompetha finalists [n Cl. 2b]
banyakenye last year [poss
Cl. 2]
nyakenye last year [adv]

«4»
imi they stand [stative]
-i [irregular stative suff]
yalo of this [poss Cl. 4]
ozodlalwa that/which will be
played [rel Cl. 3]
uzodlalwa it will be played
[fut]
-dlalw-a be played [v-pass]
okokuqala first [adv; < poss
pron "that of to start"]
ngqa be first [ideophone]
selokhu ever since [conj;
followed by partic]
kuhoxe there withdrew [past,
partic, conjoint]
-hox-a hide, withdraw [v.i.]

inkampani company, firm [n Cl. 9] {Eng}
yakwaWakefield JHI of Wakefield JHI [poss Cl. 9]
ebingenye that/which was one [rel Cl. 9]
  ibingenye it was one [ident cop, past pres]
yabeseki of the sponsors [poss Cl. 9]
  abeseki sponsors, supporters [n Cl. 2; sg. **umeseki**; < **-esek-** sponsor, support (var **umseki** < **-sek-**)]
  ab- [NP Cl. 2; occurs before vowels]
balo of this [poss Cl. 2]
phambilini previously, in the past [adv]
wokuqala first [poss Cl. 3]
kuzohlomulwa one will be rewarded [fut]
  -hlomulw-a be rewarded [v-pass]
  -hlomul-a reward [v.t.]
ngenkomishi with a cup [instr adv]
  inkomishi cup [n Cl. 9] {Afr *kommetjie* small basin}
indondo medals (pronounced: **iindondo**; sg **indondo**)
  iin- [NP Cl. 10 (common in speech, but less so in writing); var of **izin-**]
zegolide of gold, golden [poss Cl. 10]
  igolide gold [n Cl. 5] {Eng}
ijezi jersey [n Cl. 5] {Eng}
lebhola of football, of soccer [n Cl. 5]
  ibhola ball; football, soccer [n Cl. 5] {Eng}
isikhwama bag [n Cl. 7]
esikhulu large, big [adj Cl. 7]
nezikibha and T-shirts [assoc adv]
  izikibha T-shirts [n Cl. 8; sg **isikibha**] {< Eng. *skipper*}

«5»
wesibili second [poss Cl. 3]
  isibili second (ordinal number) [n Cl. 7; < **-bili** two [adj stem]]
izindondo medals [n Cl. 10]
zesiliva of silver [poss Cl. 10]
  isiliva silver [n Cl. 7] {Eng}
esisodwa one [rel Cl. 7]
  sodwa only, alone [quant Cl. 7]
  so- [quant conc Cl. 7]
owomdlali that (prize) of the player [poss pron Cl. 3]
  womdlali of the player [poss Cl. 3]
  umdlali player [n Cl. 1; < **-dlal-** play]
ovelele the top (lit. who came to the fore) [rel Cl. 1]
  uvelele (s)he is outstanding, (s)he is prominent [past, disjoint]
  -velel-a be prominent, stand out [v-appl]
  -vel-a come from, be prominent, stand out [v.i.]
kuzoba yi-track suit will be a track suit [ident cop, inch, fut]
  kuzoba it will be [copula, fut]
  yi-track suit it is a track suit [ident cop, pres]
  i-track suit [n Cl. 9a] {Eng}
namakhokho and soccer boots [assoc adv]
  amakhokho soccer boots [n Cl. 6; sg **ikhokho** Cl. 5]
amabili a pair, two [adj Cl. 6]
anikelwe that/which have been donated [rel Cl. 6]

anikelwe they have been donated [past, conjoint]

-nikelw-a be donated, be handed over [v-appl-pass]

ngabakwa-Adidas by people from Adidas [agent adv]

abakwa-Adidas those (people) from Adidas [poss pron Cl. 2]

u-Adidas [n Cl. 1a] {Eng}

uhlaba umkhosi (s)he sends out word (lit. sounds the alarm)

umkhosi call of alarm, warning cry [n Cl. 3]

ezakhele who live at or in [rel Cl. 10]

zakhele they live at or in [stative, disjoint]

-akhel-a live at, live in [v-appl, inch]

-akh-a establish residence, bec a citizen of [v.inch]

namaphethelo and suburbs [assoc adv]

amaphethelo suburbs, outskirts, environs [n Cl. 6; sg **iphethelo**; < **-phethel-** border on]

ziphume they should come out [subjunc]

ngobuningi in large numbers [instr adv]

ubuningi large numbers, abundance, plenty [n Cl. 14; < **-ningi** many [adj stem]]

zizozitika they should come and participate to the fullest [subjunc, venitive]

-zi-tik-a overindulge, do in excess [v-refl]

-tik-a get the better of, overcome [v.t.]

-a [subjunc pos suffix found in venitives and andatives]

ngonqambothi with the entertainment (lit. with the nice flavor, nice smell) [instr adv]

unqambothi nice flavor, nice smell [n Cl. 11]

lwemidlalo of the games [poss Cl. 11]

uZwelakhe (male name) [n Cl. 1a]

Ngcobo (surname) [n Cl. 1a]

Inhlangano yomame esemkhankasweni wokusungula izimboni ezincane zomphakathi

Ngu: Nash Ngcobo

«1»

ISiyaphezulu Womens Club yaseNazareth ePhayindane iphezu komkhankaso wokuqala amabhizinisi amancane azogcina ngokusabalalisa ukusizakala kwamalungu ayo angasebenzi ngokuthola imisebenzi enhlobonhlobo.

«2»

Lokhu kuzokwenzeka ngokuqalwa kwezifundo zokuphathwa kwamabhizinisi anhlobonhlobo okubalwa kuwo ukuthunga, ukusungulwa kwezinhlelo zokudayiswa kwemikhiqizo eqhamuka emazweni angaphandle nemisebenzi ezotholakala kuMasipala wase-Inner West Council.

«3»

Lezi zifiso ezizwakala zinomqondo ophusile zivuke emva kokugqugquzelwa kwale nhlangano nguNksz Dudu Ngcongo ozimele osezuze lukhulu eMnyangweni wezoMnotho nezoku-Vakasha kuHulumeni wakwaZulu/Natal.

«4»

ISiyaphezulu itshelwe ngamathuba amakhulu enawo okuqala inkampani yabangcwabi, ukusungulwa kwebhange elizosiza kakhulu umphakathi osendaweni yawo ngezindlela ezahlukene.

Ukuphathwa kwamakhaza okugcina asebeshonile, ukuthunyelwa kwezingubo zomfaniswano ezikoleni, emafemini, izinkampani zokupheka yizinto iSiyaphezulu ezimisele ngokuzithatha njengoba inamalungu awenzayo lo msebenzi.

«5»

Kuthiwa iningi lale misebenzi izonikwa wonke amalungu ale nhlangano okumanje aqashiwe ukuze kunciphe izindleko zokuqasha abantu abathile ngaphandle kwalabo abaqeqeshelwe imisebenzi ethile.

UNksz Dudu uthi konke lokhu okungenhla kungaba lula uma iSiyaphezulu isibhalisile ngokusemthethweni njengenkampani kuHulumeni ukuze ithembakale kulabo abafisa ukusebenzisana nayo.

Vocabulary

inhlangano yomame women's organization [n phr Cl. 9]
  yomame of women (lit. of mothers) [poss Cl. 9]
  y- of [poss conc Cl. 9; found before **a, e** and **o**]
esemkhankasweni that/which is involved in a scheme or program (lit. that/which is in a scheme) [loc cop, pres, partic]
  isemkhankasweni it is in a scheme [loc cop, pres]
  semkhankasweni in a scheme [loc; < **semkhankasweni** < **umkhankaso**]
  wokusungula of setting up [poss Cl. 3]
ezincane small, little [adj Cl. 10]
  eziØ- [adj conc Cl. 10]
isiyaphezulu Womens Club yaseNazareth the Siyaphezulu Womens' Club of Nazareth [n Cl. 9a; < **siya phezulu** we are going upward]
ePhayindane in Pinetown [loc]
  iPhayindane Pinetown (town) [n Cl. 5]
iphezu kwa- it is in control of, it is heading (lit. is on top of) [loc cop, pres]
komkhankaso of the scheme or program [poss Cl. 17; < **kwa-** + **umkhankaso**]
amancane small [adj Cl. 6]
azogcina that/which will eventually [rel Cl. 6]
  azogcina they will eventually [fut]
ngokusabalalisa by furthering [instr adv]
  ukusabalalisa to further [vn Cl. 15]
  -sabalalis-a spread, further [v-caus]
  -sabalal-a spread out [v.i.]
ukusizakala to get helped, assistance, relief, development [vn Cl. 15]
  -sizakal-a get help, be assisted, get relief [v-neut]
kwamalungu of members [poss Cl. 15]
ayo its [poss Cl. 6]
angasebenzi who don't work [rel Cl. 6]
  angasebenzi they don't work [pres, rel, neg; < **akasebenzi/ awasebenzi**]
ngokuthola in the finding, by obtaining, by acquiring [instr adv]
enhlobonhlobo various, diverse [rel Cl. 4]
  -nhlobonhlobo various, diverse [rel stem; < **i(z)inhlobonhlobo**]

«2»

ngokuqalwa through the initiation [instr adv]
  ukuqalwa initiation, to be begun [vn Cl. 15]
kwezifundo of studies, of lessons [poss Cl. 15]
  kwe- of [poss conc Cl. 15 coalesced with **i**]
zokuphathwa in or for the running, in the management [poss Cl. 8]
  ukuphathwa management, to be managed, to be handled, to be treated, to be held [vn Cl. 15]
  -phathw-a be handled, be treated, be managed; suffer from [v-pass]
  -phath-a take hold of, handle; affect; treat, manage [v.t.]
kwamabhizinisi of businesses

[poss Cl. 15]
anhlobonhlobo of various types
[rel Cl. 6]
okubalwa to be counted [poss Cl.
6]
   ukubalwa to be counted [vn Cl.
   15]
   -balw-a be counted, be included
   [v-pass]
   -bal-a count, calculate [v.t.]
kuwo among them, to them, from
them [loc]
ukuthunga is sewing [ident cop,
pres: < Ø- + ukuthunga]
   Ø- it is, they are [ident cop pref;
   in speech equates with breathy
   voice and a rising tone]
   ukuthunga sewing, to sew [vn
   Cl. 15]
   -thung-a sew [v.t.]
kwezinhlelo of programs [poss Cl.
15]
zokudayiswa for marketing [poss
Cl. 10]
   ukudayiswa to be marketed,
   offered for sale, sold, traded [vn
   Cl. 15]
   -dayisw-a be marketed, be
   offered for sale, be sold, be
   traded [v-pass]
   -dayis-a market, auction, trade,
   offer for sale [v.t.]
kwemikhiqizo of surpluses [poss
Cl. 15]
   imikhiqizo surpluses, production (normally refers to mass
   production) [n Cl. 4; sg **umkhiqizo** surplus, produce; <
   -khiqiz- produce in abundance,
   turn out in large quantities,
   produce a surplus]
eqhamuka that/which come from
[rel Cl. 4]
   iqhamuka they come from
   [pres, conjoint]

emazweni angaphandle to, from,
in foreign countries [loc]
   amazwe angaphandle foreign
   countries (countries of outside)
   [n phr Cl. 6]
nemisebenzi and jobs, also jobs,
even jobs [assoc adv]
ezotholakala that/which will be
obtainable [rel Cl. 4]
   izotholakala they will be
   obtainable [fut]
kuMasipala from the municipality
[loc]
   umasipala municipality [n Cl.
   1a]
wase-Inner West Council of (in)
Inner West Council [poss Cl. 1]

«3»
zifiso [< izifiso]
ezizwakala that/which are
understandable [rel Cl. 10]
   zizwakala they are understandable [pres, conjoint]
zinomqondo as having sense
[assoc cop, pres, partic]
   u m q o n d o understanding,
   comprehension, intelligence,
   sense, mind [n Cl. 3; < **-qond-**
   understand, comprehend]
ophusile solid [rel Cl. 3]
   uphusile it is solid [stative]
   -phus-a bec solid [v.inch]
zivuke they arose [past, conjoint]
emva kwa- behind, at the back of,
after [loc phr]
emva (contracted form of **emuva**
used when followed by a
complement)
   emuva behind, at the back, after
   [loc]
   umuva hind part, rear [n Cl. 3]
kokugqugquzelwa [poss Cl. 17; <
   kwa- + ukugqugquzelwa]
   ko- of [< **kwa-** poss conc Cl. 17

+ **o**; the poss conc links the loc with the following noun]
ukugqugquzelwa prodding, persuasion [vn Cl. 15]
-gqugquzelw-a be prodded, be persuaded [v-appl-pass]
-gqugquzel-a prod, nag, persuade, try to win over [v-appl]
-gqugquz-a prod, pierce, poke [v.t.]
kwale of this [poss Cl. 15]
nhlangano [< **inhlangano**]
nguNksz by Miss [agent adv]
    uNksz Miss [abbrev of **uNkosazana** Miss [n Cl. 1a; < **inkosazana** young lady, princess]
Ngcongo (surname) [n Cl. 1a]
ozimele who is independent [rel Cl. 1]
    uzimele (s)he is independent [stative]
    -zi-mel-a stand up for one's self, bec independent [v-refl-appl]
osezuze who has already earned or achieved [rel Cl. 1]
    usezuze (s)he has already earned or achieved [past, conjoint; < **u-** (s)he + **-s-** already + **-e-** (s)he + **-zuz-** achieve + **-e** past]
    -s- already, now, soon [exclusive aspect marker]
    -zuz-a earn, achieve, acquire, obtain [v.t.]
lukhulu much, a lot [n Cl. 11, with elision of initial **u-**]
eMnyangweni in the Department [loc; < **umnyango**]
wezoMnotho of Finance [poss Cl. 3]
nezokuVakasha and of Tourism [assoc adv]
    ezokuvakasha tourism affairs, tourism [poss pron Cl. 10]
    zokuvakasha of visiting [poss Cl. 10]
ukuvakasha to visit [vn Cl. 15]
    -vakash-a visit [v.i.]
kuHulumeni to, from, in, with the government [loc]
wakwaZulu/Natal of KwaZulu-Natal [poss Cl. 1]

«4»
itshelwe it has been told [past, conjoint]
    -tshelw-a be told [v-pass]
    -tshel-a tell [v.t.]
ngamathuba about opportunities [instr adv]
    amathuba opportunities, chances [n Cl. 6; sg **ithuba** Cl. 5]
enawo that/which it has [rel Cl. 9]
    inawo it has it [assoc cop, pres]
okuqala of starting (up) [poss Cl. 6]
inkampani yabangcwabi burial company, company of undertakers
    yabangcwabi of buriers, of undertakers [poss Cl. 9]
    abangcwabi buriers, undertakers, morticians [n Cl. 2; sg **umngcwabi**; < **-ngcwab-** bury]
ukusungulwa foundation, establishment [n Cl. 15]
kwebhange of a bank [poss Cl. 15]
elizosiza that/which will help [rel Cl. 5]
    lizosiza it, (s)he will help [fut]
osendaweni that/which is in a place or locality [rel Cl. 3]
    usendaweni it, (s)he is in a place or locality [loc cop, pres]
    sendaweni in a place or locality [loc; < **endaweni** < **indawo**]
yawo its [poss Cl. 9]
ngezindlela with ways, in ways [instr adv]

ukuphathwa kwamakhaza okugcina asebeshonile the cold storage of the deceased [vn phr Cl. 15]
kwamakhaza of cold [poss Cl. 15]
  amakhaza cold (temperature) [n Cl. 6]
okugcina of keeping, of preserving [poss Cl. 6]
  ukugcina to keep, to preserve, preservation [vn Cl. 15]
  -gcin-a keep, preserve, store [v.t.]
asebeshonile those who have already passed away [rel Cl. 2]
  sebeshonile they have already passed away [stative, exclusive]
ukuthunyelwa dispatch, to be dispatched, to be sent [vn Cl. 15]
  -thunyelw-a be sent (to) [v-appl-pass; < **-thumel-w-a**; m ... -w- > ny ... -w-]
  -thumel-a send to, send (an object), send for, order [v-appl]
  -thum-a send (a person) [v.tt.]
kwezingubo zomfaniswano of uniforms [poss phr Cl. 15]
kwezingubo of clothes [poss Cl. 15]
izingubo zomfaniswano uniforms (lit. clothing of uniformity) [n phr Cl. 10]
zomfaniswano of uniformity [poss Cl.10]
umfaniswano uniformity [n Cl. 3; < **-faniswan-** be made mutually alike]
ezikoleni to schools [loc; < **izikole**]
emafemini to firms [loc]
  amafemu firms [n Cl. 6; sg **ifemu** Cl. 5] {Eng}
izinkampani zokupheka catering companies (lit. companies of cooking) [n phr Cl. 10]
  ukupheka cooking [vn Cl. 15]

-phek-a cook [v.t.]
ezimisele ngokuzithatha which they were prepared to take on [ind rel of plain adv rel]
ezimisele that/which it is ready, that/which it is prepared for [rel Cl. 9]
  izimisele it, (s)he is prepared or ready [stative]
  -zi-misel-a get ready for, prepare for, be determined [v-refl-caus-appl; < **-zi-** self + **-m-** stand + **-is-** caus + **-el-** for]
ngokuzithatha in taking them (on) [instr adv]
  ukuzithatha to take them (on) [vn Cl. 15]
inamalungu it has members [assoc cop, pres]
awenzayo who do it [rel Cl. 6]
  -w- it [OC Cl. 3; occurs before vowels]
  ayawenza they do it [pres, disjoint]
msebenzi [< **umsebenzi** work, job, task; use]

«5»
kuthiwa it is said, they say [pres, conjoint]
lale of these [poss Cl. 5]
  le these[1st pos dem Cl. 4]
misebenzi [< **imisebenzi**]
izonikwa they will be given (to) [fut]
  -nikw-a be given (to) [v-pass]
wonke every, all, the whole [quant Cl. 6]
  wo- [quant conc Cl. 6; var **o-**]
ale of this [poss Cl. 6]
okumanje for now [adv; < rel]
aqashiwe who are employed [rel Cl. 6]
  aqashiwe they are employed [stative]

kunciphe there should become less, there should be a decrease (in) [subjunc]
   -nciph- grow less, diminish [v.i.]
izindleko costs, expenses [n Cl. 10; sg **indleko**]
zokuqasha of hiring, of employing [poss Cl. 10]
abathile certain, particular [rel Cl. 2]
kwalabo of those [poss Cl. 17]
abaqeqeshelwe who have been trained for [rel Cl. 2]
   baqeqeshelwe they have been trained for [stative]
   -qeqeshelw-a be trained for [v-appl-pass]
   -qeqeshel-a train for [v-appl]
   -qeqesh-a train, coach, instruct [v.t.]
ethile certain, particular [rel Cl. 4]
uthi (s)he says [pres, conjoint]
konke lokhu all this [quant phr]
konke everything, all [quant]
   ko- [quant conc Cl. 17]
okungenhla the above, which is above [rel Cl. 17]
   kungenhla it is above [loc cop, pres]
   ngenhla above [instr adv]
   enhla higher up, upstairs, upcountry [loc]
isibhalisile it had already had registered [past, disjoint,

exclusive; < **i-** SC Cl. 9 + **-s-** already + **-i-** SC Cl. 9 + **-bhalisile**]
   -bhalis-a cause to register, make write, help write [v-caus]
   -bhal-a write, register [v.t.]
ngokusemthethweni legally (lit. by that which is in the law) [instr adv phr]
   okusemthethweni that which is legal [rel Cl. 17]
   kusemthethweni it is legal, it is in the law [loc cop, pres]
   semthethweni in the law [loc; < **emthethweni** < **umthetho**]
njengenkampani as a company [comp adv]
ithembakale it should be trustworthy [subjunc]
   -thembakal-a be trustworthy, be trustable [v-neut]
abafisa who desire, who wish [rel Cl. 2]
   bafisa they desire, they wish [pres, conjoint]
   -fis-a desire, wish for [v.t.]
ukusebenzisana to work together, to cooperate [vn Cl. 15]
   -sebenzisan-a work together, cooperate [v-caus-recip]
   -sebenzis-a help work [v-caus]
   -is- help VERB [caus ext]
nayo with it [assoc adv]
uNash (male name) [n Cl. 1a]{Eng}

Abafundi batelekele ukungafiki kwezincwadi zokubhalela ePM Burg

«1»
Ukungatholakali kwezincwadi zokufunda nezokubhalela sekwenze ukuba abafundi eGeorge Town High School ese-Edendale emgungundlovu, bazidube izifundo kuze kulungiswe le nkinga.

«2»
Lokhu kuqale ukugqama ngomsombuluko odlule ngenkathi abafundi beveza ukungagculiseki kwabo ngokungatholi izincwadi zokubhalela, babe sebecela ukuthi balungiselwe le nkinga.

«3»
Ngenxa yokuthi abafundi abanawo umkhandlu obamele bonke bebengathandi ukuba badalulwe amagama abo ephepheni kodwa bezimisele ukuthi basho izizathu ezibangela ukuthi bangangeni ezindlini zokufundela.

«4»
Ngokwabafundi ukungabi khona kwezidingo kube sekwenza ukuthi bathole nethuba lokuveza ezinye izinkinga ababhekene nazo.

«5»
"Okusempeleni akukhona ukuthi sinenkinga yama-exercise kuphela lapha esikoleni kodwa ziningi izinkinga esibona ukuthi kumele zilungiswe kuyima siya ekilasini," kuchaza omunye umfundi.

«6»
Izinkinga
Baqhubeka bathi ngoMsombuluko baxoxisana nothisha omkhulu uMnuz Ngubane ngezinkinga zabo wabe esethembisa ukuthi uzobalungisela kodwa kuze kwashaya uLwesihlanu abafundi bewadubile amakilasi.

«7»
Ezinye izinkinga abanazo ngaphandle kwezincwadi, bafuna kuqashwe abazosika utshani esikoleni sonke, kufakwe amafasitela nezicabha, bafuna ukwazi uhlahlomali lwesikole, bafuna ukwazi ukuthi izimali zenzani ngoba akukho okwenziwayo ukuthuthukisa isikole nokuthi kuyekwe ukushaywa kwabafundi.

«8»
Omunye umfundi uqhubeke wathi bafuna ukuchazeleka ngokuthi izimali abazikhokhela abaqaphi besikole ziyaphi ngoba selokhu baqala ukukhokha abakaze bababone onogada esikoleni.

«9»
"Abazali bakhokhiswa izimali kodwa umsebenzi wazo ugcine ungabonakalanga.

«10»
"Siyazi ukuthi ukukhokhwa kwale mali kwaba ukuvumelana phakathi kwabazali nothisha omkhulu kodwa abazali abezi esikoleni futhi abazazi izinto ezenzekayo ngaphakathi," kuchaza lo mfundi.

«11»
Zithunyeliwe
Babuye bagxeka kakhulu ukukhuphuka kwemali yokufunda ngokuthi isuke ku-R50 wangonyaka odlule iye ku-R120 kulo nyaka. Into exakayo bathi kule mali kubalwa neyabonogada laba abangekho esikoleni.

«12»
Bathi uma kuwukuthi lezi zinkinga azilungi angeke babuyele emakilasini.

«13»
Akazange atholakale uthishomkhulu walesi sikole uMnuz Ngubane ukuba aphefumule ngale nkinga esesikoleni sakhe kodwa okhulumela uMnyango weZemfundo eMgungundlovu, uMnuz Muzi Kubheka, uthe bese bezitholile lezi zinkinga zabafundi. Ube eseqhubeka ethi uMnyango wakhe ube sewuthumela izincwadi zokubhala ngoLwesihlanu.

«14»
"Sesitholile ukuthi kuke kwabanokuphazamiseka kokufunda kulesi sikole ngenxa yokuthi abafundi bebefuna i-stationery nokuthi kusikwe utshani ezinkundleni zesikole," kusho uMnuz Kubheka.

«15»
Uthe wethemba ukuthi emva kokuthola i-stationery, yonke into izobuyela esimweni esijwayelekile.

Vocabulary

batelekele they are striking for, they are on strike over [stative, conjoint]
-telekel-a strike for, strike over [v-appl]
-telek-a go on strike [v.i.]
ukungafiki the non-arrival, not to arrive [vn Cl. 15, neg]
kwezincwadi of books [poss Cl. 15]
zokubhalela for writing in [poss Cl. 10]
ukubhalela to write in, to write to, to write for [vn Cl. 15]
-bhalel-a write in, write for, write to [v-appl]
e-PM Burg in Pietermaritzburg (city) [loc]

«1»
ukungatholakali non-receipt, non-obtainability [vn Cl. 15, neg]
zokufunda of reading, of study [poss Cl. 10]
ukufunda study, to study, to learn, learning, to read, reading [vn Cl. 15]
nezokubhalela and for writing in [assoc adv]
ezokubhalela for writing in

[poss pron Cl. 10]
sekwenze it has already made or caused [past, exclusive, conjoint]
eGeorge Town High School at George ... [loc]
ese-Edendale that/which is in Edendale [rel Cl. 9]
   ise-Edendale it is in Edendale [loc cop, pres]
   i-Edendale (town) [n Cl. 5]
eMgungundlovu in Pieter-maritzburg [loc]
bazidube that they (should) throw or give up [subjunc]
   -dub-a give up, throw up; ignore; boycott, go on strike [v.i. & t.]
kulungiswe they sort out (lit. there should be fixed) [subjunc]
nkinga [< **inkinga** problem, puzzle, fix]

«2»
kuqale it began [past, conjoint]
ukugqama to be clear, to stand out [vn Cl. 15]
   -gqam-a be clear, be evident, stand out, be obvious [v.i.]
ngoMsombuluko on Monday [instr adv]
   uMsombuluko Monday [n Cl. 3; no plural]
odlule last, (that/which has) passed [rel Cl. 3]
   udlule it has passed [past, disjoint]
ngenkathi at the time [instr adv; followed by the participial]
   inkathi time, period, age, epoch [n Cl. 9; < **in-** + **-khathi** (cf. **isikhathi**); n + kh > nk]
beveza they were (lit. are) expressing [pres, partic]

-vez-a bring out, exhibit, show; disclose, reveal [v-caus; < **-vel-** + **-Y-**]
ukungagculiseki dissatisfaction, not being satisfied [vn Cl. 15, neg]
   -gculisek-a bec satisfied [v-neut]
   -gculis-a satisfy [v.t.]
kwabo their [poss Cl. 15]
ngokungatholi about not receiving [instr adv]
   ukungatholi not to receive, non-receipt, not to acquire, not to find [vn Cl. 15, neg]
babe sebecela they then requested [rem past pres, exclusive]
   babe they then (in rem past) [aux, rem past]
   -be [aux indicating past or future relative tenses]
   sebecela they now request [pres, exclusive, partic]
balungiselwe they should have sorted out for them [subjunc]
   -lungiselw-a have sorted out for (one) [v-caus-appl-pass]
   -lungisel-a sort out for, fix for [v-caus-appl]
   -lungis-a fix, repair, make right, make good, rectify, correct, sort out, arrange, put in order [v-caus]
   -lung-a bec in order, bec correct, bec OK [v.i., inch]

«3»
ngenxa yokuthi due to the fact that [instr adv phr]
yokuthi (of)that [poss Cl. 9]
abanawo umkhandlu they don't have an organization [assoc cop]
   umkhandlu organization [n Cl. 3]
   obamele that/which represents

them [rel Cl. 3]

ubamele it represents them [stative]

bebengathandi they were not keen or happy [past pres, neg]

badalulwe they should be divulged [subjunc]

-**dalulw-a** be exposed, be divulged [v-pass]

-**dalul-a** expose, divulge [v.t.]

ephepheni in the paper [loc]

iphepha paper [n Cl. 5] {Eng}

bezimisele they being prepared [stative, partic]

ezibangela that/which cause to/that [rel Cl. 8]

zibangela they cause to/that [pres, conjoint]

-**bangel-a** cause for, cause to, cause that [v-appl]

bangangeni they should not enter [subjunc, neg]

ezindlini zokufundela into educational institutions [loc]

izindlu zokufundela educational institutions (lit. houses for studying in)

izindlu houses [n Cl. 10]

zokufundela for studying in [poss Cl. 10]

ukufundela to study in or for [vn Cl. 15]

«4»

ngokwabafundi according to the students [instr adv; **nga-** + POSS PRON CL. 17 = according to]

ngokwa- according to

okwabafundi that of the students [poss pron Cl. 17]

ukungabi khona absence (lit. not being there) [infin of loc cop]

ukungabi not being [copula, vn Cl. 15, neg]

kube sekwenza it then caused

[past pres]

kube "it past" [aux]

sekwenza it now causes [pres, partic, exclusive]

bathole they should get [subjunc]

nethuba also an opportunity [assoc adv]

ithuba opportunity, chance [n Cl. 5]

lokuveza of raising, of bringing out [poss Cl. 5]

ukuveza to bring out, to produce to view [vn Cl. 15]

«5»

okusempeleni in truth, indeed (lit. that which is in truth) [rel Cl. 17]

kusempeleni it is in truth [loc cop; < **ku-** SC 17 + -**se-** loc pref + **impela** truth + -**eni** loc suff]

akukhona ukuthi sinenkinga yama-exercise kuphela it isn't just that we have a problem with exercise books [exist cop phr, pres, neg]

akukhona it or there isn't, there aren't [loc cop, pres, neg; often introduces an exist cop]

sinenkinga we have a problem [assoc cop, pres]

yama-exercise of exercise books [poss Cl. 9]

ama-exercise exercise books [n Cl. 6; sg **i-exercise** Cl. 9a]

esikoleni to, from, in, at school [loc]

ziningi there are many [descr cop, pres]

esibona that/which we see, that/which we are of the opinion [ind rel of plain obj rel, 1 p pl]

zilungiswe they must be rectified [subjunc]

kuyima before [conj; followed by

partic]
siya we go (to) [pres, partic]
ekilasini to, from, in class [loc]
  ikilasi class, classroom [n Cl. 5]
  {Eng or Afr}
omunye a certain, some, one (not in enumeration), another [adj Cl. 1]
  omu- [adj conc Cl. 1 (occurs with monosyllabic stems]

«6»
baqhubeka they carried on, they continued [narr]
bathi (and) they said [narr]
baxoxisana na- ... they had a conversation with ..., they negotiated with ... [rem past]
  -xoxisan-a chat, converse, negotiate [v-caus-recip]
  -is-an- the combination of caus and recip extensions means 'together'
  -xox-a chat, converse, narrate, tell [v.i.]
nothisha omkhulu with the head teacher or principal [assoc adv phr]
Ngubane (surname) [n Cl. 1a]
ngezinkinga about problems [instr adv]
wabe esethembisa (s)he then promised [rem past pres, exclusive]
  esethembisa (s)he now promises [pres, exclusive, partic]
uzobalungisela he will make things right for them [fut]
kuze kwashaya uLwesihlanu Friday came (lit. it eventually hit Friday) [v phr]
kwashaya there hit [narr]
uLwesihlanu Friday [n Cl. 1a]
bewadubile they having boycot-

ted them [past, partic, disjoint]

«7»
abanazo that/which they have [ind rel of plain cop rel, Cl. 2]
  banazo they have them [assoc cop, pres]
ngaphandle kwa- apart from, except for, without [instr adv phr]
  kwezincwadi of books [poss Cl. 17]
kuqashwe they should employ, there should be employed [subjunc]
abazosika who will cut or mow [rel Cl. 2]
  bazosika they will cut or mow [fut]
  -sik-a cut, mow [v.t.]
utshani grass, lawn [n Cl. 14]
  uØ- [NP Cl. 14]
sonke the whole, all, every [quant Cl. 7]
kufakwe they should put in, there should be put in [subjunc]
amafasitela windows [n Cl. 6; sg **ifasitela** Cl. 5] {Afr *venster*}
nezicabha and doors [assoc adv]
  izicabha doors [n Cl. 8; sg **isicabha**]
ukwazi to know, knowledge [vn Cl. 15]
uhlahlomali budget [n Cl. 11; no plural; < **uhlahlo** division, distribution [< **-hlahl-** divide, distribute] + **imali** money]
  lwesikole of the school [poss Cl. 11]
zenzani? what are they doing?
akukho okwenziwayo there is nothing being done [exist cop, pres, neg]
  okwenziwayo that which is being done [rel Cl. 17]

kwenziwa it is made, it is done, it is caused [pres, conjoint]
ukuthuthukisa to develop, to uplift [vn Cl. 15]
-thuthukis-a develop, uplift, enlarge [v-caus]
nokuthi and that, also that, even that, with that [assoc adv]
kuyekwe they should stop, there should be stopped [subjunc]
-yekw-a be stopped, be left (alone, out, off) [v-pass]
ukushaywa beating, to be beaten, corporal punishment [vn Cl. 15]
kwabafundi of students [poss Cl. 15]

«8»
uqhubeke he carried on [past, conjoint]
ukuchazeleka to get an explanation [vn Cl. 15]
-chazelek-a get an explanation (lit. get explained to) [v-appl-neut]
abazikhokhela that/which they pay to or for [ind rel of plain obj rel, Cl. 2]
bazikhokhela they pay them to or for [pres, conjoint]
-khokhel-a pay to, pay for, pay on behalf of, pay off, repay [v-appl]
abaqaphi security personnel, guards, warders [n Cl. 2; sg **umqaphi**; < **-qaph-** watch intently, be on the look-out]
besikole of the school [poss Cl. 2]
ziyaphi? where do they go?
ziya they go (to) [pres, conjoint]
baqala they started [rem past, partic]
abakaze they have not yet ever [aux, pres, exclusive, neg; < **a-** neg pref + **-ba-** SC + **-ka-**

yet + **-ze** ever [aux]]
bababone they see them [subjunc]
onogada guards, watchmen [n Cl. 2b; sg **unogada**]

«9»
bakhokhiswa they are made to pay, they are charged [pres, conjoint]
-khokhisw-a be made to pay, be charged [v-caus-pass]
-khokhis-a make pay, charge, fine [v-caus]
ugcine it ended up [past, conjoint]
ungabonakalanga it not being visible [past, partic, neg]
-bonakal-a be visible, be apparent, appear, seem [v-neut]

«10»
siyazi we know [pres, disjoint]
ukukhokhwa payment, to be paid [vn Cl. 15]
-khokhw-a be paid [v-pass]
mali money [< **imali**]
kwaba ukuvumelana it became an agreement, it was an agreement [ident cop, inch, rem past]
kwaba it became [copula, rem past]
ukuvumelana it is an agreement [ident cop, pres; < Ø- cop pref + **ukuvumelana**]
ukuvumelana mutual agreement, to agree with each other [vn Cl. 15]
-vumelan-a be in agreement, agree with each other, concur [v-appl-recip]
abezi they do not come [pres, neg; < **a-** + **-ba-** + **-iz-** + **-i**]
-iz-a come [variant of **-z-a** found after **a**; then **a + i > e**]
abazazi they do not know them [pres, neg]

84

ezenzekayo that/which occur [rel Cl. 10]
  ziyenzeka they occur, happen, take place [pres, disjoint]
mfundi [< **umfundi** student, pupil, reader]

«11»
zithunyeliwe they have been sent for, they have been ordered [past, disjoint]
babuye they again [aux]
  -buy-e again VERB [aux]
bagxeka they opposed [narr]
ukukhuphuka the rise [n Cl. 15]
  -khuphuk-a rise, go up, ascend [v.i.]
kwemali of money [poss Cl. 15]
yokufunda for study [poss Cl. 9]
ngokuthi because [conj]
isuke it went from [past, conjoint]
ku-R50 from R50 [loc; < **ku-** + **u-R50**]
  u-R50 R50 [n Cl. 1a]
wangonyaka of the year (lit. of in the year) [poss Cl. 1a]
  ngonyaka in the year, in a year, per year, annually [instr adv]
iye (and) it went [past, conjoint]
ku-R120 to R120 [loc]
  u-R120 R120 [n Cl. 1a]
kulo nyaka (also **kulonyaka**) this year [loc]
kulo to, from, in this [loc]
nyaka year [< **unyaka**]
into thing, object [n Cl. 9; < **-tho** (cf. **utho**); **n + th > nt**]
exakayo that causes difficulties [rel Cl. 9]
  iyaxaka it causes difficulties [pres, disjoint]
  -xak-a put into difficulties [v.t.]
kule to, from, in, at, on this [loc]
kubalwa there is included, there is counted [pres, conjoint]

neyabonogada also that for guards [assoc adv]
  eyabonogada that of or for guards [poss pron Cl. 9]
  yabonogada of guards [poss Cl. 9]
  abonogada guards [n Cl. 2b; sg **unogada**]
  abo- [extremely rare var of: NP Cl. 2b]
abangekho esikoleni who are not at school [rel Cl. 2]
  bangekho esikoleni they are not at school [loc cop, pres, rel, neg]

«12»
kuwukuthi it is (the case) that [ident cop, pres; < **ku-** SC 17 + **w-** cop pref + **ukuthi** conj]
azilungi they are not coming right [pres, neg]
angeke never [aux; followed by the subjunctive]
babuyele they will return to [subjunc]
  -buyel-a return to, go back to [v-appl]
emakilasini to, from, at, in classes or classrooms [loc]

«13»
akazange (s)he has never [aux, past, neg; < **-z-e**]
atholakale (s)he should be found [subjunc]
uthishomkhulu head teacher, principal [n Cl. 1a; < **uthisha + omkhulu**]
walesi of this [poss Cl. 1]
sikole [< **isikole**]
aphefumule (s)he would give an opinion [subjunc]
  -phefumul-a give an opinion [v.i.]

ngale about this [instr adv]
esesikoleni that/which is at or in school [rel Cl. 9]
   isesikoleni it is at or in school [loc cop, pres]
sakhe his, of his, her, of hers [poss Cl. 7]
okhulumela spokesperson for (lit. (s)he who speaks for) [rel Cl. 1; pl **abakhulumela**]
   ukhulumela (s)he speaks for [pres, conjoint]
   -khulumel-a speak for [v-appl]
wezemfundo of education [poss Cl. 3]
   ezemfundo educational affairs [poss pron Cl. 10]
   zemfundo of education [poss Cl. 10]
Muzi (male name) [n Cl. 1a]
Kubheka (surname) [n Cl. 1a]
bese bezitholile they had already had or received them [past past, exclusive, disjoint]
   bese already (in the past) [aux]
   bezitholile they have received them [past, partic, disjoint]
zabafundi of the students [poss Cl. 10]
ube eseqhubeka he then continued [past present, exclusive]
   ube (s)he was [aux, indicating relative tense]
   eseqhubeka (s)he is now continuing [pres, exclusive, partic]
ethi (s)he saying, (s)he says [pres, partic]
wakhe his, her [poss Cl. 3]
ube sewuthumela it was already sending [past pres, exclusive]
   ube it was [aux, indicating relative tense]
   sewuthumela it is already sending [pres, partic, exclusive]

zokubhala for writing [poss Cl. 10]
ngoLwesihlanu on Friday [instr adv]

«14»
sesitholile we have already found [past, disjoint, exclusive]
kuke kwaba nokuphazamiseka there was sometimes an interruption [assoc cop, inch, rem past, occasional]
   kuke it sometimes PAST VERB [aux, past, conjoint]
   kwaba nokuphazamiseka there was interruption (lit. it became with interruption) [assoc cop, inch, narr]
   nokuphazamiseka with interruption [assoc adv]
   ukuphazamiseka interruption, to get interrupted, to get disturbed [vn Cl. 15]
   -phazamisek-a get interrupted, get disturbed [v-caus-neut]
   -phazamis-a interrupt, disturb [v-caus]
   -phazam-a be disturbed, be interrupted [v.i.]
kokufunda of study [poss Cl. 15]
kulesi to, from, in, at this [loc]
bebefuna they were wanting [past pres]
i-stationery [n Cl. 9a] {Eng}
kusikwe they should cut, there should be cut [subjunc]
ezinkundleni in the playgrounds, yards [loc]
   izinkundla playgrounds [n Cl. 10; sg **inkundla**]
zesikole of the school [poss Cl. 10]

«15»
wethemba (s)he hopes [pres, disjoint]

kokuthola (of) obtaining, of (receipt) [poss Cl. 17; following **emva**]

ukuthola to obtain, to acquire, to get, to find [vn Cl. 15]

yonke into everything [quant phr Cl. 9]

yonke every, all, the whole [quant Cl. 9]

izobuyela it will return to [fut]

esimweni to, from, at the status [loc; < **isimo** status]

esijwayelekile customary, usual, normal [rel Cl. 7]

sijwayelekile it is customary, usual, normal [stative]

USebata – Indoda Engazenyezi Ngokungaboni Kwayo!

«1»
USebata uthatha ukungaboni kwakhe emehlweni njengento eyisipho. "Ukungaboni kwami kungenze ngazibona ngamanye amehlo izinto futhi kungenze ngazethemba. Sengifunde ukuzimela ezintweni eziningi kanti nabantu ngifuna bangangidabukeli," kusho uSebata.

«2»
Ngesikhathi ngihlangana noSebata esangweni lesibhedlela asebenza kuso, kwaba nguyena owangihola sesiya ehhovisini lakhe esikhundleni sokuthi kube yimina engihamba phambi kwakhe. Kuthe lapho sekuyisikhathi sesidlo sasemini, wangithatha saya enkantini wangidonsela nesihlalo.

«3»
USebata uthi ukungaboni kwakhe kwadalwa wukuthi umndeni wakubo wawungenayo incazelo egcwele ngezempilo ngesikhathi esakhula. Ngesikhathi ezalwa wayebona kahle emehlweni kodwa kwathi lapho eseneminyaka eyishumi waphathwa yisimungumungwane. Lesisifo sagcina sesikhubaze namehlo akhe.

«4»
USebata akazenyezi neze ngokungaboni kwakhe futhi uyaziqhenya ngomsebenzi wakhe njengoba eyiPrincipal Tele-communications Operator eBlouberg Hospital. Umsebenzi wakhe ubandakanya ukubheka ukusebenza kwezingcingo ezingenayo neziphumayo kulesisibhedlela.

«5»
Njengamanje usaqhubeka nezifundo zakhe e-University of South Africa (UNISA) kanti wenza neziqu zikaBA kwezokuphatha. "Ngeke ngihlukane nokufunda futhi akekho oyonginqanda kulokho," kusho yena. Ngo-1971 usebata wayefunda eSiloam School okuyisikole sabantu abangaboni emehlweni kanti abamsiza ngokumfunela lesosikole kwaba ngu-anti wakhe nenhlangano yeSouth African National Council for the Blind.

«6»
Kulesosikole waphothula uGrade 12. Ngo-1984 wathola isitifiketi sokuba yi-switchboard operator ePhoneficiency College eGoli. Umsebenzi wakhe wokuqala njenge-switch-board operator wawenza eGeorge Maseba Hospital ePotgietersrus. Wasebenza kulesosibhedlela iminyaka eyisithupha ngaphambi kokuba bamdlulisele eBlouberg Hospital ngo-1990.

«7»
Lensizwa yazalelwa eBochum kwelaseNorthern Province ngo-1961. Yakhuliswa ngumama wayo uMoiporoti. "Umama wangikhulisa

88

yedwa wangithanda kusukela ngalesosikhathi kuze kube yimanje,"
kusho uSebata.

«8»
USebata ushade noGladys Molokomme kanti babusiswe
ngabantwana abane, uSolly (11), Mahlatse (6), Moosa (4) noTshepo
(1). U-Gladys uneziqu zikaBA kwezeMfundo kanti umshado wakhe
uwuthatha njengesipho esivela kuNkulunkulu.

«9»
Umshado wabo waqala ngokuba nezinkinga ngoba abazali bakhe
babengafuni ukuba ashade noSebata. "Kwadingeka ukuba ngibancenge ngaze ngabatshela nokuthi kufanele bakhumbule ukuthi
ngizikhethele mina ukushada naye," kusho u-Gladys.

«10»
U-Gladys unesifiso sokusungula inhlangano yabesimame abashade
nabantu abakhubazekile ukuze abasize ngokubafundisa ukuthi
kufanele bawaphathe kanjani amadoda abo. "Ngifisa sengathi abantu
bangabona izinto ngendlela engizibona ngayo. Amadoda angaboni
emehlweni kufanele azethembe futhi akhumbule ukuthi ayafana
namadoda abonayo," kusho u-Gladys.

«11»
USebata uyindoda ehloniphekile emphakathini wase-Bochum.
UnguMongameli weBochum After-Care Centre kanti futhi
ukwezokuXhumana noMphakathi enhlanganweni yabakhubazekile
eBochum.

«12»
Lenhlangano isiza ngokuthuthukisa izimpilo zabantu abakhubazekile
ibuye ibatholele nemisebenzi.

Ukhonze ukudlala amabhayisikili kanti uma esewadlala ungafunga
ukuthi akanankinga! Yize noma ekhona umuntu oshayela imoto
yakhe, uSebata uyakwazi ukuzishayelela.

«13»
Uma esekhaya uthanda ukulalela umculo kaLionel Richie, Brenda
Fassie kanti kweze-jazz ukhonze uDoctor Philip Tabane
ongumshayi-siginci.

"Abantu bavame ukungibuza imibuzo eyindida njengokuthi nje
ngambona kanjani unkosikazi wami, angazi noma bayakhohlwa yini
ukuthi angiboni emehlweni. Abanye bake bangibuze ukuthi ngishefa
kanjani — phela mina nginonkosikazi ongumsizi wami.

«14»
"Ngicela ukudlulisela lesisicelo emphakathini: ningabafihli ezindlini
abantu abakhubazekile. Bavezeni ukuze umphakathi ube nolwazi
ngabo. Abazali abafihla izingane ezikhubazekile kufanele bavalelwe
emajele ngoba bazincisha ilungelo lempilo engcono.

«15»
"Abantu abakhubazekile ngeke bakwazi ukuziphilisa ngemali yempesheni — okubalulekile wukuthi bafunde. Uma umnike imfundo usuke usukuqede nya ukukhubazeka kwakhe!" kuphetha uSebata.

Ngu: Noko Mashilo

Vocabulary

uSebata (male name) [n Cl. 1a] {Sotho}

indoda man [n Cl. 9; pl amadoda Cl. 6]

engazenyezi who does not make him- or herself miserable or allow him- or herself to get despondent [rel Cl. 9]

ingazenyezi (s)he does not make him- or herself miserable or allow him- or herself to get despondent [pres, rel, neg; < ayizenyezi]

-z- self (myself, yourself, himself, herself, itself), selves (ourselves, yourselves, themselves) [reflexive pref; found before vowels]

-enyez-a dissatisfy, displease, hurt the feelings of [v-caus; < -enyel- + -Y-]

-enyel-a bec dissatisfied, bec displeased, have one's feelings hurt [v.i.]

ngokungaboni about not seeing, about blindness [instr adv]

ukungaboni not seeing, blindness [vn Cl. 15, neg]

uthatha he takes [pres, conjoint]

kwakhe his, her [poss Cl. 15]

emehlweni into, from, in eyes [loc; < amehlo]

amehlo eyes [n Cl. 6; sg iso or ihlo Cl. 5]

ame- [NP Cl. 6; this could also

be taken as ama- superimposed on ihlo with coalescence of a + i]

njengento as something, like a thing [comp adv]

eyisipho that/which is a gift [rel Cl. 9]

iyisipho it is a gift [ident cop, pres]

isipho gift, present [n Cl. 7; < -ph- give]

kwami my [poss Cl. 15]

kungenze it has made me [past, conjoint]

-ng- me [OC 1 p sg]

ngazibona I saw them [narr]

ngamanye with other, through other [instr adv]

amanye other, some, certain [adj Cl. 6]

ngazethemba I had faith in myself [narr]

sengifunde I have already learnt [past, exclusive, conjoint]

ukuzimela to stand up for myself, to bec independent [vn Cl. 15]

eziningi many, numerous [adj Cl. 10]

nabantu also people, people too, and people, even people, with people[assoc adv]

ngifuna I want [pres, conjoint]

bangangidabukeli they should not pity me [subjunc, neg]

-dabukel-a pity, feel sorry for

90

[v-appl]
-dabuk-a bec sad, bec sorry, bec contrite, repent [v.inch]

«2»
ngihlangana I met (lit. I (was) meeting) [pres, partic]
noSebata with Sebata [assoc adv]
esangweni to, from, at the gate [loc; < isango]
isango gate, gateway; main entrance to cattle-kraal [n Cl. 5]
isibhedlela hospital [n Cl. 7] {Eng spittal?}
asebenza kuso that/which (s)he works at [ind rel of plain loc rel, Cl. 1]
a- that/which (s)he ... [ind rel conc Cl. 1]
kuso at, to, from, in it [loc]
so it, its, him, his, her, hers [abs pron Cl. 7]
kwaba nguyena it was him or her [ident cop, inch, rem past]
nguyena it is him or her [ident cop, pres]
ngu- it is [ident cop pref; occurs before abs prons we(na) and ye(na)]
yena he, him, she, her [abs pron Cl. 1]
owangihola who led me [rel]
wangihola (s)he led me [rem past]
sesiya we were (lit. are) then going [pres, partic, exclusive]
ehhovisini to, from, in, at office [loc; var ehhovisi]
ihhovisi office, bureau [n Cl. 5] {Eng}
kube yimina it should be me [ident cop, inch, subjunc]
yimina it is me, it is I [ident cop, pres]
engihamba I who am walking [rel

1 p sg]
ngihamba I walk, I go, I travel [pres, conjoint]
phambi kwakhe ahead of him or her [loc phr]
kwakhe of him, of her [poss Cl. 17]
kuthe lapho just as (in the past) [conj phr]
sesidlo sasemini for lunch [poss phr Cl. 7]
isidlo sasemini lunch [n phr Cl. 7]
isidlo meal [n Cl. 7; < -dl- eat]
sasemini of noon [poss Cl. 7]
semini at midday, at noon; during the day [loc; < emini; one of the exceptions that does not take a locative suffix]
imini day, daytime [n Cl. 9; no pl]
wangithatha (s)he took me [rem past]
saya (and) we went [narr]
-s- we [SC 1 p pl]
enkantini to, from, in, at the cafeteria [loc; one of the exceptions that does not take a locative suffix]
inkantini cafeteria, canteen [n Cl. 7] {Eng}
wangidonsela (and) (s)he pulled out for me [narr]
-donsel-a pull (up) for, draw (up) for [v-appl]
nesihlalo even, also, and a chair [assoc adv]
isihlalo chair, seat, stool [n Cl. 7; < -hlal- sit]

«3»
uthi (s)he believes, (s)he thinks, (s)he is of the opinion [pres, conjoint]
kwadalwa it was caused [rem

past]
-dalw-a be created, be caused, be formed, be brought into being [v-pass]
-dal-a create, form, bring into being, cause [v.t.]
wakubo of his, her, their home or family [poss Cl. 3]
kubo to, from, at, in, his, her, their home, place or country [loc]
wawungenayo incazelo it did not have information (long ago) [assoc cop, rem past pres]
incazelo explanation, information, solution [n Cl. 9; < **-chazel-** explain to; **n + ch > nc**]
egcwele (that is) full or complete [rel]
igcwele it is full (of), it is complete [stative]
ngezempilo about health matters [instr adv]
ezempilo health matters [poss pron Cl. 10]
zempilo of health, of life [poss Cl. 10]
esakhula (s)he was (lit. is) still growing up [pres, partic, persistive; < **e-** SC 1 + **-sa-** still + **khula**]
-khul-a grow, grow up; age [v.i.]
ezalwa (s)he was (lit. is) born [pres, partic]
wayebona (s)he saw [rem past pres]
kwathi it happened that; then (in the past) [conj]
eseneminyaka eyishumi (s)he was ten years old (lit. (s)he already has ten years)
eseneminyaka ... she is now ... years old (lit. she now has

years) [assoc cop, pres, partic, exclusive]
eyishumi ten [rel Cl. 4]
iyishumi they are ten [ident cop, pres]
ishumi ten (n) [n Cl. 5]
waphathwa y- (s)he suffered from (lit. was taken hold of by) [v phr]
yisimungumungwane from measles [agent adv]
isimungumungwane measles [n Cl. 7]
lesisifo this disease [dem phr Cl. 7]
isifo disease, illness [n Cl. 7]
sagcina it ended in [rem past]
sesikhubaze it has already damaged [past, exclusive, conjoint]
-khubaz-a disable, make ineffective; damage, injure, hurt; intimidate [v-caus; < **-khubal-** + **-Y-**; l + **-Y-** > z]
-khubal-a get hurt, damaged, injured, disabled; be disappointed; be ineffective, fail [v.i.]
namehlo even eyes [assoc adv]
akhe his, her [poss Cl. 6]

«4»
uyaziqhenya (s)he is proud [pres, disjoint]
-zi-qheny-a be proud [v-refl]
-qheny-a show off [v.i.]
ngomsebenzi about work, about a job [instr adv]
eyi-Principal Telecommunications Operator (s)he being principal telecommunications operator [ident cop, pres, partic]
i-Principal Telecommunications Operator [n Cl. 9a] {Eng}
eBlouberg Hospital at Blouberg

Hospital [loc]
iBlouberg Hospital [n Cl. 9a]
ubandakanya it involves [pres, conjoint]
-bandakany-a involve, include [v.t.]
ukubheka checking, to check, supervising, to supervise, to look (at); to head for [n Cl. 15]
ukusebenza working, to work, to operate, to function [n Cl. 15]
kwezingcingo of calls, of phones [poss Cl. 15]
ezingenayo incoming [rel Cl. 10]
ziyangena they come or go in, they enter [pres, disjoint]
neziphumayo and outgoing [assoc adv]
eziphumayo outgoing [rel Cl. 10]
ziyaphuma they come or go out, they exit [pres, disjoint]
kulesisibhedlela to, from, at, in this hospital [loc]
lesisibhedlela this hospital [dem phr Cl. 7]

«5»
njengamanje right now, at the moment, at present [adv]
usaqhubeka (s)he is still continuing [pres, persistive]
nezifundo with studies [assoc adv]
zakhe his, her [poss Cl. 8]
e-University of South Africa (UNISA) at the University ... [loc]
i-University of South Africa [n Cl. 9a] {Eng}
wenza (s)he is doing, making [pres, conjoint]
neziqu also a degree [assoc adv]
iziqu degree(s) (the plural is frequently used with singular meaning) [n Cl. 8; sg **isiqu**]

zika-BA of BA [poss Cl. 8]
u-B.A. B.A. [n Cl. 1a]
kwezokuphatha in Management or Administration [loc]
ezokuphatha management or administrative affairs [poss pron Cl. 10]
zokuphatha of management or administration [poss Cl. 10]
ngihlukane na- ... I would separate from ..., I would give up ... [subjunc]
-hlukan-a na- part company with; differ from; get away from; give up [v phr]
nokufunda with studying [assoc adv]
akekho oyonginqanda there is nobody who will turn me away [exist cop, pres, neg]
akekho (s)he is not there, is not present; there is no ... [loc cop, pres, neg; may also introduce an exist cop]
-ke- he, she [SC Cl. 1, found only in this construction]
oyonginqanda one who will turn me away, who will prevent me [rel Cl. 1]
uyonginqanda (s)he will turn me away, will prevent me [rem fut]
kulokho from this (lit. from that) [loc]
ngo-1971 in 1971 [instr adv]
u-1971 1971 [n Cl. 1a]
wayefunda (s)he was studying (long ago) [rem past pres]
eSiloam School at Siloam School [loc]
iSiloam School [n Cl. 9a]
okuyisikole that/which is a school [rel Cl. 17]
kuyisikole it is a school [ident cop, pres]

sabantu for people, of people [poss Cl. 7]

abangaboni emehlweni who do see (in the eyes) [rel phr Cl. 2]

bangaboni they do not see [pres, rel, neg; < ababoni]

abamsiza those who helped him or her [rel Cl. 2]

bamsiza they helped him or her [rem past]

ngokumfunela by seeking out for him or her [instr adv]

ukumfunela to seek out for him or her [vn Cl. 15]

-funel-a look for for, seek out for [v-appl]

lesosikole that school [dem phr Cl. 7]

leso that [2nd pos dem Cl. 7]

ngu-anti were (lit. are) aunt [ident cop, pres]

u-anti aunt [n Cl. 1a] {Eng auntie}

wakhe his, her [poss Cl. 1]

nenhlangano and the association or society [assoc adv]

ye-South African National Council for the Blind of the South African ... [poss Cl. 9]

i-South African National Council for the Blind [n Cl. 9a]

«6»

kulesosikole at that school [loc]

waphothula (s)he completed [rem past]

-phothul-a complete [v.t.]

u-Grade 12 (final year of school) [n Cl. 1a]

ngo-1984 in 1984 [instr adv]

u-1984 1984 [n Cl. 1a]

wathola (s)he obtained [rem past]

isitifiketi certificate [n Cl. 7] {Eng}

yi-switchboard operator (s)he is a switchboard operator [ident cop, pres]

i-switchboard operator a switchboard operator [n Cl. 9a] {Eng}

ePhoneficiency College at the Phoneficiency College [loc]

i-Phoneficiency College [n Cl. 9a]

eGoli to, from, in Johannesburg [loc]

iGoli Johannesburg (largest city in South Africa) [n Cl. 5]

njenge-switchboard operator as a switchboard operator [compar adv]

wawenza (s)he did it [rem past]

eGeorge Maseba Hospital at George Maseba Hospital [loc]

i-George Maseba Hospital [n Cl. 9a]

e-Potgietersrus to, from, in Potgietersrus [loc]

i-Potgietersrus (town) [n Cl. 5]

wasebenza (s)he worked [rem past]

kulesosibhedlela to, from, at, in that hospital [loc]

lesosibhedlela that hospital [dem phr Cl. 7]

eyisithupha six [rel Cl. 4]

iyisithupha there are six of them [ident cop, pres]

isithupha thumb; six (in counting on the fingers, one moves from five on one hand to the thumb of the other for 'six') [n Cl. 7]

bamdlulisele they transferred or seconded him or her to [subjunc]

-dlulisel-a transfer, second, pass on to [v-caus-appl]

ngo-1990 in 1990 [instr adv]

u-1990 1990 [n Cl. 1a]

«7»
lensizwa this young man [dem phr Cl. 9
insizwa young man, youth [n Cl. 9]
yazalelwa (s)he was born in [rem past]
-zalelw-a be born in (lit. be given birth to in) [v-appl-pass]
eBochum to, from, in Bochum [loc]
iBochum (place) [n Cl. 5]
kwelase-Northern Province to, from, in the Northern Province (lit. in that of in the Northern Province) [loc]
elase-Northern Province that of the Northern Province [poss pron Cl. 5; agrees with understood **izwe** country, land]
lase-Northern Province of the Northern Province [poss Cl. 5]
se-Northern Province to, from, in Northern Province [loc]
i-Northern Province [n Cl. 5]
ngo-1961 in 1961 [instr adv]
u-1961 1961 [n Cl. 1a]
yakhuliswa (s)he was brought up [narr]
-khulisw-a be brought up, be raised [v-caus-pass]
-khulis-a bring up, raise; grow, enlarge [v-caus]
ngumama by mother [agent adv]
wayo his, her, its [poss Cl. 1]
uMoiporoti (name) [n Cl. 1a] {Sotho}
wangikhulisa (s)he brought me up [rem past]
yedwa alone, on his or her own [quant Cl. 1]
wangithanda (and) she loved me [narr]

ngalesosikhathi at that time [instr adv phr]
lesosikhathi that time [dem phr Cl. 7]

«8»
ushade (s)he got married, (s)he married [past, disjoint]
-shad-a marry, get married, wed [v.i. & t.]
noGladys to Gladys, with Gladys [assoc adv]
uGladys [n Cl. 1a] {Eng}
Molokomme (surname) [n Cl. 1a] {Sotho}
babusiswe they have been blessed [past, conjoint]
-busisw-a be blessed [v-caus-pass]
ngabantwana with (or by) children [agent adv]
uSolly (name) [n Cl. 1a]
Mahlatse (female name) [n Cl. 1a] {Sotho}
Moosa (name; this could be an Indian name, or it could be a misspelling of the Sotho male name Mosa) [n Cl. 1a]
noTshepo and Tshepo [assoc adv]
uTshepo (male name meaning 'hope') [n Cl. 1a] {Sotho}
uneziqu she has a degree [assoc cop, pres]
kwezeMfundo in Education [loc]
umshado marriage, wedding [n Cl. 3; < -shad- marry]
uwuthatha (s)he takes it [pres, conjoint]
esivela that/which comes from [rel Cl. 7]
sivela it, he, she comes from [pres, conjoint]
-vel-a come from, originate in; appear, come into view [v.i.]
kuNkulunkulu to, from God [loc]

«9»

wabo their, of them [poss Cl. 3]

waqala it began [rem past]

ngokuba nezinkinga by having problems [instr adv phr]

bakhe his, her [poss Cl. 2]

babengafuni they did not want (lit. they were not wanting) [rem past pres, neg]

ashade (s)he should get married [subjunc]

kwadingeka it was necessary [rem past]

-dingek-a be necessary, be required, be needed [v-neut]

-ding-a need, require [v.t.]

ngibancenge that I should plead with them [subjunc]

-nceng-a beg, plead with [v.i. & t.]

ngaze (and) I eventually [aux, rem past]

ngabatshela I told them [narr]

ngizikhethele I have chosen for myself [past, conjoint]

-khethel-a choose for, decide on for, select for, elect for [v-appl]

-kheth-a choose, decide on, opt, select, elect [v.t.]

ukushada to marry, to get married [vn Cl. 15]

«10»

unesifiso (s)he has a wish [assoc cop, pres]

sokusungula of establishing [poss Cl. 7]

ukusungula to establish, establishment, to found, foundation [vn Cl. 15]

yabesimame of women [poss Cl. 9]

abesimame women [poss pron

Cl. 2; < a- pronominalizer + ba- poss conc Cl. 2 (agrees with abantu) + isimame female gender]

besimame female [poss Cl. 2]

isimame womenfolk [n Cl. 7]

abashade who have got married [rel Cl. 2]

bashade they married [past, conjoint]

abakhubazekile who are disabled or handicapped, the handi- capped, the disabled [rel Cl. 2]

bakhubazekile they are disabled or handicapped [stative]

-khubazek-a bec disabled or handicapped, get injured [v-neut]

abasize (s)he should assist them [subjunc]

ngokubafundisa by teaching them [instr adv]

ukubafundisa to teach them [vn Cl. 15]

bawaphathe they should treat them [subjunc]

amadoda men, husbands [n Cl. 6; sg indoda Cl. 9]

ngifisa I wish [pres, conjoint]

bangabona they could see [pres, potential]

engizibona that I see (them) [ind rel of plain obj rel, 1 p sg]

ngizibona I see them [pres, conjoint]

angaboni emehlweni who are blind (lit. who do not see in the eyes) [rel phr Cl. 6]

angaboni who do not see [rel Cl. 6]

angaboni they do not see [pres, rel, neg; < akaboni/ awaboni]

azethembe they should believe in themselves, they should have faith in themselves [subjunc]

akhumbule they should remember [subjunc]

ayafana they are like, they are similar, they resemble [pres, disjoint]

namadoda with men, and men, men too, men also, even men [assoc adv]

abonayo who can see, sighted [rel Cl. 6]

   ayabona they see [pres, disjoint]

«11»

uyindoda he is a man [ident cop, pres]

ehloniphekile who is respected, respectable [rel Cl. 9]

   ihloniphekile (s)he is respected, (s)he is respectable [stative]

   -hloniphek-a bec respected [v-neut; inch]

emphakathini to, from, in the community [loc]

waseBochum of (in) Bochum [poss Cl. 3]

ungumongameli (s)he is president [ident cop, pres]

   umongameli president [n Cl. 1; < **-ongamel-** lean over; preside over; pl **abongameli**]

weBochum After-Care Centre of the Bochum ... [poss Cl. 1]

   iBochum After-Care Centre [n Cl. 9a]

ukwezokuXhumana noMpha-kathi (s)he is in Community Relations [loc cop, pres]

   kwezokuXhumana noMpha-kathi in Community Relations [loc]

   ezokuXhumana noMphakathi Community Relations affairs [poss pron phr Cl. 10]

ukuxhumana linkage, to link up, relations, to join [vn Cl. 15]

   -xhuman-a link up, join [v-recip]

   -xhum-a join, splice, link [v.t.]

enhlanganweni to, from, in the society or organization [loc; < **inhlangano**]

yabakhubazekile of the disabled [poss Cl. 9]

«12»

lenhlangano this society, this organization [dem phr Cl. 9]

ngokuthuthukisa by uplifting, by developing [instr adv]

izimpilo lives [n Cl. 10]

zabantu of people [poss Cl. 10]

ibuye it, (s)he again [aux]

ibatholele it, (s)he finds for them [subjunc]

   -tholel-a find for, get for, obtain for [v-appl]

ukhonze (s)he is a fan of, is passionate about [past, conjoint]

   -khonz-a bec passionate about, bec keen on; worship; pay respect(s) to [v.inch; v.t.]

ukudlala amabhayisikili to cycle, cycling [vn phr Cl. 15]

ukudlala to play [vn Cl. 15]

amabhayisikili bicycles [n Cl. 6; sg **ibhayisikili**; var **ibhayisekili**]

esewadlala (s)he is playing them [pres, partic, exclusive]

ungafunga you would or could swear [pres, potential]

   -fung-a swear, swear by, take an oath [v.i. & t.]

akanankinga (s)he has no problem [assoc cop, pres, neg]

yize it is a little, it is a bit, it is almost [ident cop, pres]

   ize a little, a bit [n Cl. 5]

ekhona there is ... [exist cop, pres, partic]
oshayela one who drives [rel Cl. 1]
   ushayela (s)he drives [pres, conjoint]
   -shayel-a drive [v.t.]
uyakwazi (s)he is able, (s)he knows how, (s)he can [pres, disjoint; < **u-** (s)he + **-ya-** disjoint pref + **-kw-** OC Cl. 15 (agreeing with **ukuzishayelela**) + **-azi** know]
   -yakwazi be able to, can, know how to [< **-ya-** pres disjoint marker + **-kw-** OC Cl. 15 + **-az-i** know]
ukuzishayelela to drive for oneself [vn Cl. 15]
   -zi- VERB **-el-** VERB for oneself
   -shayelel-a drive for, drive to [v-appl]

«13»
esekhaya (s)he is at home [loc cop, pres, partic]
   sekhaya to, from, at home [loc; < **ekhaya**]
uthanda (s)he likes, (s)he loves [pres, conjoint]
ukulalela to listen (to), listening (to) [vn Cl. 15]
umculo music [n Cl. 3; < **-cul-** sing]
kaLionel Richie of Lionel Richie [poss Cl. 3]
   uLionel Richie (name of an American singer and composer) [n Cl. 1a]
Brenda Fassie (name of a South African singer) [n Cl. 1a]
kweze-jazz in jazz [loc]
   eze-jazz jazz matters [poss pron Cl. 10]

i-jazz [n Cl. 9a] {Eng}
uDoctor Philip Tabane (South African musician) [n phr Cl. 1a]
ongumshayi-siginci who is a guitarist [rel Cl. 1]
   umshayi-siginci guitarist [n Cl. 1a; < **-shay-** hit, play + **isiginci** guitar]
ukungibuza to ask me [vn Cl. 15]
imibuzo questions [n Cl. 4; sg **umbuzo**; < **-buz-** ask]
eyindida puzzling, that/which are a puzzle, strange [rel Cl. 4]
   iyindida they are a puzzle or riddle [ident cop, pres]
   indida puzzle, riddle, confusing thing [n Cl. 9]
njengokuthi nje such as [conj phr]
ngambona I saw her or him (in this context: I was attracted to her) [rem past]
angazi I do not know [pres, neg]
bayakholwa they believe [pres, disjoint]
yini or not [tag]
angiboni emehlweni I am blind
   angiboni I do not see [pres, neg]
bake they sometimes VERB [aux]
   -ke do sometimes, do occasionally [aux; followed by subjunc]
bangibuze they (should) ask me [subjunc]
ngishefa I shave [pres, conjoint]
   -shef-a shave [v.i. & t.] {Eng}
phela indeed, truly [adv]
nginonkosikazi I have a wife [assoc cop, pres]
ongumsizi who is a helper
   umsizi helper, assistant [n Cl. 1; < **-siz-** help, assist]

«14»
ukudlulisela to pass on [vn Cl. 15]
lesisicelo this request [dem phr

Cl. 7]

isicelo request [n Cl. 7; < **-cel-** ask for, request]

ningabafihli you (pl) should not hide them [subjunc, neg]

bavezeni bring them out [imper pl]

ube nolwazi it should have (the) knowledge [assoc cop, inch, subjunc]

ulwazi knowledge [n Cl. 11; < **-az-i** know]

ulw- [NP Cl. 11; occurs before **a** and **e**]

ngabo about them [instr adv]

abafihla who hide [rel Cl. 14]

bafihla they hide [pres, conjoint]

ezikhubazekile disabled, handicapped [rel Cl. 10]

zikhubazekile they are disabled, handicapped [stative]

bavalelwe they should be shut up in or at [subjunc]

-valelw-a be shut up in or at [v-appl-pass]

-valel-a shut up in or at [v-appl]

emajele in jails [loc]

amajele jails, prisons [n Cl. 6; sg **ijele** Cl. 5] {Eng}

bazincisha they deprive them [pres, conjoint]

-ncish-a deprive (of), stint [v.t.]

ilungelo right [n Cl. 5; < **-lungel-** be right for]

lempilo to (of) a life [poss Cl. 5]

engcono better [rel Cl. 9]

ingcono it is better [descr cop, pres]

«15»

bakwazi they should know, they should be able [subjunc]

ukuziphilisa to earn their living, to keep themselves alive (lit. to make themselves live) [vn Cl. 15]

ngemali with money [instr adv]

yempesheni of a welfare grant [poss Cl. 9]

impesheni welfare grant, pension [n Cl. 9] {Eng}

okubalulekile what is important [rel Cl. 17]

kubalulekile it is important [stative, disjoint]

wukuthi it is that [ident cop, pres]

bafunde they should study [subjunc]

umnike you have given him or her [past, conjoint]

usuke you have just [aux]

-suk-e just VERB, merely VERB, happen to VERB [aux]

usukuqede you have already brought to an end [past, exclusive, conjoint; < **u-** you + **-s-** already + **-u-** you + **-ku-** it + **-qed-** end + **-e** past]

nya be nothing, be silent (can translate as: completely, utterly, perfectly, absolutely) [ideo]

ukukhubazeka disability, handicap [n Cl. 15]

kuphetha X X finish(es) up, X has/have the last word, X clinch(es) the argument

Noko (personal name) [n Cl. 1a]

Mashilo (surname) [n Cl. 1a] {Sotho}

99

Izinhlamvu zesitho
sangasese ezincane

Uhlamvu lwami lwesitho sangasese langakwesobunxele luncane kunolwesokudla. Lokhu kusiphatha kabi sinonkosikazi wami ngoba sicabanga ukuthi kungenzeka singazitholi izingane.

A.S.D., Bloemfontein

Kuvamile ukuthi izinhlamvu zangasese zingalingani kodwa uma enye incane kunenye kunokwenzeka ukuthi kukhona isifo owake waba naso noma yake yalimala leyonhlamvu. Uma ingekho nhlobo enye inhlamvu futhi i-scrotum singenalutho enye inhlamvu isuke ingehlanga. Ngenhlanhla enkulu, enye inhlamvu ephile kahle ingakwazi ukutholisa abantwana. Ngingakweluleka ngokuthi ubonane nodokotela ukuze akwazi ukuhlola.

Vocabulary

izinhlamvu zesitho sangasese ezincane small testicles (lit. small berries of the private parts) [n phr Cl. 10]

izinhlamvu zesitho testicles [n phr Cl. 10; sg **uhlamvu lwesitho**]

izinhlamvu grains, berries, pips, stones (of fruit); testicles (euph) [n Cl. 10; sg **uhlamvu** Cl. 11]

zesitho of the body (lit. of limbs or body parts) [poss Cl. 10]

isitho limb, part of the body [n Cl. 7]

sangasese private [poss Cl. 7]

ngasese privately, secretly [manner adv]

lwami my [poss Cl. 11]

lwangakwesobunxele (of the) left-hand [poss Cl. 11]

ngakwesobunxele on the left [instr adv phr]

kwesobunxele to, from, on the left [loc]

esobunxele left-hand one [poss pron Cl. 7; refers to **isandla** hand]

sobunxele of the left [poss Cl. 7]

ubunxele the left [n Cl. 14]

luncane kunolwesokudla it is smaller than the right-hand one

luncane it is small [descr cop, pres]

lu- [2nd half adj conc Cl. 11]

kunolwesokudla more than or compared with that of the right [compar adv]

kun- [compar adv pref **kuna-** with elision of a before o]

olwesokudla the right-hand one [poss pron Cl. 11]

lwesokudla of the right [poss Cl. 11]

esokudla right-hand one [poss pron Cl. 7; refers to **isandla** hand]

sokudla of the right; for eating (in Zulu custom, it is the right hand that is used for eating) [poss Cl. 7]

kusiphatha it affects us (the 1 p pl OC is used, since the wife is also affected by the problem)

kabi badly, awfully, terribly, very [adv; < **-bi** bad [adj stem]]

sinonkosikazi wami when I am (lit. we are) with my wife (the 1 p pl SC is often used in Zulu in place of the singular **ngi-** when someone associated with the subject is included in the sentence as part of the predicate)

sinonkosikazi I am with my wife (lit. we are with a wife) [assoc cop, pres, partic]

sicabanga we think [pres, conjoint]

kungenzeka it could happen, it is possible [pres, potential]

singazitholi that we do not have (lit. get) them [subjunc, neg]

A.S.D. (initials)

Bloemfontein (city; capital of Free State Province)

kuvamile it is normal [aux, stative]

izinhlamvu zangasese testicles [n phr Cl. 10; sg **uhlamvu lwangasese**]

zingalingani they should not be the same [subjunc, neg]

-lingan-a be equal, be the same; bec sufficient [v.i.]

enye another, the other, some, one, a certain [adj Cl. 9]

incane is small(er) [descr cop, pres; < **i-** SC Cl. 9 + **-ncane**]

kunenye (more) than the other [compar adv]

kunokwenzeka it is possible, it could happen (lit. it is with to happen) [assoc cop, pres]

owake waba naso that/which you have had [ind rel of assoc adv rel, 2 p sg]

owake that/which you have once (in the distant past) [rel 2 p sg]

wake waba naso you have once had [assoc cop, rem past, experiential]

wake you once [aux, rem past]

-w- you [SC 2 p sg; occurs before vowels]

waba naso you had it [assoc cop, inch, narr]

yake it once [aux, rem past]

yalimala it got injured [narr]

leyonhlamvu that testicle [dem phr Cl. 9]

ingekho there is no, it is not present [loc cop, pres, partic, neg; may also introduce an exist cop]

nhlobo in any way, at all [adv; < **inhlobo** sort, kind, type]

i-scrotum [n Cl. 7; **is** is interpreted as being the Cl. 7 NP]

singenalutho it is empty (lit. it does not have anything) [assoc cop, pres, partic, neg]

enye inhlamvu the other testicle [adj phr Cl. 9]

isuke ingehlanga it is merely undescended [v phr]

isuke it merely [aux]

ingehlanga it has not descended [past, partic, neg]

-ehl-a descend, come down, go down [v.i.]

ngenhlanhla fortunately, luckily [instr adv]

enkulu the large one, large, big [adj Cl. 9]

ephile kahle that/which is healthy **ephile** that/which is in good health [rel Cl. 9]

iphile it is in good health [past, conjoint]

ingakwazi it would be able [pres, potential]

ukutholisa to provide, to secure [vn Cl. 15]

-tholis-a provide, secure [v-caus]

ngingakweluleka I would advise you [pres, potential]

-elulek-a advise, counsel [v.t.]

ubonane you should consult [subjunc]

-bonan-a see each other, consult [v-recip]

nodokotela with a doctor [assoc adv]

udokotela doctor [n Cl. 1a] {Eng}

akwazi (s)he can, (s)he should be able [subjunc]

ukuhlola to carry out an examination; to examine [vn Cl. 15]

-hlol-a examine, test, inspect [v.t.]

Uzethembe Uphephisa
Abantu Ekufeni

UZethembe Dlamini ungomunye walabobantu abaqeqeshelwe ukusiza abantu abasuke befuna ukuzibulala nabathunjiwe.

«1»

UZethembe Dlamini wathatha isinqumo sokwenza umsebenzi wokuphephisa labobantu abasuke befuna ukuzibulala emva kokuba umngani wakhe ezibulale ngokuziphonsa esitimeleni sihamba. Kungumsebenzi osemahlombe akhe ukusindisa abantu abasuke bethunjiwe nalabo abasuke befuna ukuzibulala e-South Africa nasemazweni aphesheya.

«2»

Lensizwa eyiphoyisa neneminyaka engu 24 iliqhamukisa eNtuzuma eThekwini kanti yasitshela ukuthi siyanda isibalo sabantu abazibulalayo nabathunjwayo e-South Africa. Ngenxa yalesosizathu yagcina isikhethe ukwenza izifundo eziphathelene nokusindisa abantu ekufeni. UZethembe ungunobhala ngaphansi kophiko lwe-South African Police Service's Finance [Department] eMzimkhulu kanti waphothula izifundo ezihambisana nalomsebenzi emva kokuqeqeshwa amasonto amabili ePietermaritzburg.

«3»

"Njengomsizi walabobantu abasuke befuna ukuzibulala nabathunjiwe, umsebenzi wami owokuxoxisana nalowo osuke ethumbe ibhanoyi, ibhasi, imoto, umkhumbi, noma lowo osuke efuna ukuzibulala. Uma kwenzekile kwathunjwa ibhanoyi, sixoxa nomthumbi bese sifika esivumelwaneni naye ngaphandle kokuthi kube khona olimalayo noma oboshwayo. Siqhuba ngendlela efanayo futhi uma kuthunjwe umkhumbi noma uthishanhloko esikoleni," kuchaza uZethembe.

«4»

Wagcizelela nephuzu lokuthi uma lowo osuke efuna ukuzibulala noma umthumbi engafuni ukubalalela, kuyaye kudingeke ukuba basebenzise indluzula.

"Labo abaxoxisana nabathumbi noma abasuke befuna ukuzibulala bahambisana nethimba leSpecial Task Force eliqeqeshiwe ukuze kuthi uma lowomuntu enodlame, lelithimba liyixazulule kalula leyonkinga. Kulesosimo kungenzeka noma yini, njengokuthi kube khona ogcina ngokuphangalala – nokuyinto esizama ukuyigwema kakhulu leyo."

«5»

UZethembe wabuye wasichazela nokuthi labobantu abasuke befuna ukuzibulala bavame ukuma phezu kwamabhilidi amade noma emabhulohweni. Kwesinye isikhathi bazikhomba ngezibhamu befuna ukuzidubula.

"Esikhathini esiningi lababantu basuke befuna ukunakwa. Uma usubhekene nabo noma uxoxisana nabo, kuyenzeka bawuguqule umqondo wabo," kusho uZethembe.

«6»

UZethembe wasixoxela ngokwenzekayo uma kuthunjwe ibhanoyi noma umkhumbi wakuleli emazweni angaphandle: "Uma kuthunjwe ibhanoyi lase-South Africa noma umkhumbi kwelaseMelika noma e-Europe, siyahamba siye kulezozindawo ngokushesha ukuze siyosiza. Imbangela yalokho wukuthi thina sisiqonda kangcono isimo sempilo yezwe lase-South Africa ngaphezu kwabanye abantu."

«7»

Ngokusho kukaZethembe, isibalo sabantu abazibulalayo sikhula ngesivinini esikhulu minyaka yonke. Wasitshela ukuthi kungenzeka ukuthi imbangela yalokhu kube yizinkinga eziphathelene nomsebenzi noma zasekhaya. Lomkhuba kuthiwa usudlange kakhulu kubantu abamnyama ngoba iningi labo selihlala ezindaweni ezisemadolobheni nokuyilapho kuyilowo nayilowo enake izinkinga zakhe engenandaba nezomunye umuntu.

«8»

"Thina ma-Afrika sesijwayele ukuxoxela abanye abantu izinkinga zethu kodwa manje abantu sebekhetha ukuzithulela uma behlangabezana nezinkinga ngoba iningi labo selihlala ezindaweni okwakungezabaMhlophe kuphela kuqala."

Abanye bazama ukuzibulala emva kokuzwa ukuthi bane-HIV.

«9»

UZethembe wathi iningi labantu likhetha ukuzibulala ngoku-zidubula, lizibulale ngokuphuza amaphilisi ngokweqile, liziphonse emfuleni noma esitimeleni.

Wabuye wagcizelela nokuthi abantu abasuke befuna ukuzibulala kufanele banakwe. Umngani wakhe wazibulala emva kokuba abazali bakhe bengafunanga ukulalela izinkinga zakhe.

UZethembe wathi uma ufuna ukuqeqeshelwa lomsebenzi kufanele uqale ngokuba yilungu lombutho wamaphoyisa. Kufanele ube ngumuntu ozithobileyo, osondelene nomphakathi nokwaziyo ukuxazulula izinkinga zabantu ngaphandle kokuchema.

«10»

Lensizwa isihambele amazwe afana ne-Germany, Belgium nemelika ngenhloso yokwengeza ulwazi oluzoyisiza ekuqhubeni lomsebenzi.

"Abantu abacabanga ukuzibulala kufanele bazame ukuxhumana nekamu lamaphoyisa eliseduze nabo ukuze bathole usizo. Usizo lutholakala mahhala," kuchaza uZethembe.

Indaba nezithombe ngu: **Themba Ntshingila**

Vocabulary

uZethembe (male name) [n Cl. 1a]

uphephisa ekufeni (s)he treats trauma related to death (lit. he helps to escape death) [v phr]

uphephisa (s)he causes to recover, (s)he cures [pres, conjoint]
-**phephis-a** help escape; help recover, cure [v-caus]
-**pheph-a** escape; recover, get well; bec safe, bec secure [v.i.]

ekufeni to, from, in death [loc]
ukufa death, to die [vn Cl. 15]

Dlamini (surname) [n Cl. 1a]

ungomunye (s)he is one [ident cop, pres]

walabobantu of those people [poss Cl. 1]
labobantu those people [dem phr Cl. 2]

ukusiza to help, to assist, to aid [vn Cl. 15]

abasuke who have just [rel Cl. 2]
basuke they have just [aux]

befuna they are on the point of, they are about to; they want [pres, partic]
-**fun-a** be about to, be on the point of [aux, followed by vn]

ukuzibulala to commit suicide [vn Cl. 15]
-**zi-bulal-a** commit suicide, kill oneself [v-refl]

nabathunjiwe and who have been taken hostage or hijacked [assoc adv]
abathunjiwe who have been taken hostage, who have been hijacked [rel Cl. 2]
bathunjiwe they have been taken hostage, they have been hijacked [stative; < ba- + -thumb- + -w- + -i...e; mb ... -w- > nj ... -w-]
-**thunjw-a** be taken hostage, be hijacked, be taken prisoner [v-pass]
-**thumb-a** capture, take hostage, hijack, take slyly [v.t.]

«1»

wathatha (s)he took [rem past]
sokwenza of doing [poss Cl. 7]
wokuphephisa of helping to recover [poss Cl. 3]
emva kokuba after [conj phr]
umngani friend [n Cl. 1; var **umngane**]
ezibulale (s)he has committed suicide [past, partic, conjoint]
ngokuziphonsa by throwing themselves (himself, herself,

oneself, etc) [instr adv]
-phons-a throw [v.t.]
esitimeleni to, from, in, on, in front of a train [loc]
isitimela train [n Cl. 7] {Eng *steamer*}
sihamba (it) moving, while it is in motion [pres, partic]
kungumsebenzi it is a task [ident cop, pres]
osemahlombe that/which is on shoulders [rel Cl. 3]
semahlombe [< emahlombe to, from, in, on the shoulders; loc; one of the exceptions that does not take a locative suffix]
amahlombe shoulders [n Cl. 6; sg ihlombe Cl. 5]
ukusindisa to save, to rescue [vn Cl. 15]
-sindis-a save, rescue [v-caus]
-sind-a escape, bec saved [v.i.]
bethunjiwe they have been taken hostage, they have been hijacked [stative, partic]
nalabo and those, with those, also those, even those [assoc adv]
e-South Africa to, from, in South Africa [loc]
i-South Africa [n Cl. 5] {Eng}
nasemazweni and to, from, in countries [assoc adv]
semazweni to, from, in countries [loc; < emazweni]
aphesheya overseas, abroad [rel poss Cl. 6]
phesheya on the other side, abroad, overseas [loc noun Cl. 16]

«2»
eyiphoyisa who is a policeman [rel Cl. 9]
iyiphoyisa (s)he is a policeman [ident cop, pres]

iphoyisa policeman, police-woman [n Cl. 5]
neneminyaka engu 24 and who is 24 [assoc adv phr]
neneminyaka and who is one who has years [assoc adv]
eneminyaka one who has years [rel Cl. 9]
engu-24 (that/which are) 24 [rel Cl. 4]
u-24 24 [n Cl. 1a]
iliqhamukisa (s)he comes from it [pres, conjoint]
eNtuzuma to, from, in Ntuzuma [loc]
iNtuzuma (place) [n Cl. 5]
yasitshela (s)he told us [rem past]
siyanda it is increasing [pres, disjoint]
-and-a increase, multiply [v.i.]
isibalo number, figure, sum [n Cl. 7; < -bal- count]
abazibulalayo who commit suicide [rel Cl. 2]
bayazibulala they commit suicide [pres, disjoint]
nabathunjwayo and who are hijacked or taken hostage [assoc adv]
abathunjwayo those hijacked, hostages [rel Cl. 2]
bayathunjwa they are hijacked or taken hostage [pres, disjoint]
yalesosizathu of, for that reason [poss Cl. 9]
lesosizathu that reason [dem phr Cl. 7]
yagcina (s)he ended up, (s)he eventually [rem past]
isikhethe (s)he already having chosen [past, exclusive, conjoint; < i- SC + -s- already + -i- SC + -kheth- + e]
eziphathelene that/which concern, that/which relate to, that/which

go together with [rel Cl. 8]

ziphathelene they go together, they concern, they relate to [stative, disjoint]

-phathelan-a na- ... bec related to ..., bec concerned with ...[v-appl-recip]

-phathel-a hold for; treat for, manage for [v-appl]

nokusindisa with saving [assoc adv]

ungunobhala (s)he is a secretary [ident cop, pres]

unobhala secretary [n Cl. 1a; < **u-** NP + **-no-** noun formative, often (but not necessarily) used to form feminine nouns) + **-bhal-a** write]

ngaphansi kophiko in the department or section (lit. under the wing) [instr adv phr]

ngaphansi under(neath), below, down [instr adv]

phansi kwa- under [loc phr]

phansi underneath, below, down [loc noun Cl. 16]

lwe-South African Police Service's Finance «Department» [poss Cl. 11]

eMzimkhulu to, from, in Umzimkhulu [loc]

uMzimkhulu (place) [n Cl. 3]

ezihambisana that/which go together [rel Cl. 8]

zihambisana they go together [pres, conjoint]

-hambisan-a na- ... go together with ..., accompany ..., go along with ... (i.e. agree with), accord with ...

-hambisan-a accompany each other, go with each other [v-caus-recip]

-hambis-a cause to go, go with [v-caus]

nalomsebenzi with this job [assoc adv]

lomsebenzi this job, this task, this work [dem phr Cl. 3]

kokuqeqeshwa (of) being trained [poss Cl. 17]

ukuqeqeshwa to be trained, training [vn Cl. 15]

-qeqeshw-a be trained, be coached, be instructed [v-pass]

amasonto weeks [n Cl. 6; sg **isonto**]

ePietermaritzburg to, from, in Pietermaritzburg [loc]

iPietermaritzburg (city; capital of the province KwaZulu-Natal; the Zulu name for the city is **uMgungundlovu**) [n Cl. 5]

«3»

njengomsizi as assistant [compar adv]

wami my [poss Cl. 3]

owokuxoxisana is to negotiate [ident cop, pres; < **Ø-** ident cop pref (realized as breathy voice on the 1st vowel together with a tonal change) + **owoku-xoxisana**]

owokuxoxisana that of negotiating [poss pron Cl. 3]

wokuxoxisana of negotiating [poss Cl. 3]

ukuxoxisana to negotiate [vn Cl. 15]

nalowo with that one [assoc adv]

lowo that (one) [2nd pos dem Cl. 1]

osuke who has just, who has merely [rel Cl. 1]

usuke (s)he has just, (s)he has merely [aux]

ethumbe (s)he has hijacked [past, partic, conjoint]

ibhanoyi aeroplane [n Cl. 5]

ibhasi bus [n Cl. 5] {Eng}

umkhumbi ship [n Cl. 3]

efuna (s)he is on the point of, (s)he is about to; (s)he wants [pres, partic]

kwenzekile it has happened, it has occurred [past, disjoint]

kwathunjwa there was a hijacking or a hostage-taking [narr]

sixoxa we mention, we narrate, we discuss, we chat [pres, conjoint]

nomthumbi with a hijacker or hostage-taker [assoc adv]

sifika we reach, we arrive [pres, conjoint]

esivumelwaneni at an agreement [loc]

    isivumelwana agreement, contract [n Cl. 7; var **isivumelwano**; < **-vumelwan-** be mutually agreed to]

kokuthi of that [poss, following the loc noun **phandle**]

olimalayo one who gets hurt or injured [rel Cl. 1]

    uyalimala (s)he gets hurt, injured [pres, disjoint]

oboshwayo one who is arrested [rel Cl. 1]

    uyaboshwa (s)he is arrested [pres, disjoint]

siqhuba we make progress, we proceed [pres, conjoint]

efanayo similar [rel Cl. 9]

    iyafana it or (s)he resembles, it or (s)he is like [pres, disjoint]

kuthunjwe they have hijacked, there has been a hijacking, they have held hostage [past, conjoint]

uthishanhloko head teacher, principal [n Cl. 1a; < **uthisha** teacher + **(i)nhloko** head]

«4»

wagcizelela (s)he emphasized, stressed [narr]

nephuzu also the point [assoc adv]

    iphuzu point (of discussion) [n Cl. 5]

engafuni (s)he does not want [pres, partic]

ukubalalela to listen to them [vn Cl. 15]

kuyaye it sometimes [pres, disjoint]

    -ye VERB sometimes [aux, followed by subjunc]

kudingeke it is necessary [subjunc]

basebenzise they use [subjunc]

indluzula force, violence [n Cl. 9]

abaxoxisana who negotiate [rel Cl. 2]

    bayaxoxisana they negotiate [pres, disjoint]

nabathumbi with hijackers or hostage-takers [assoc adv]

bahambisana they accompany [pres, conjoint]

nethimba (with) a group [assoc adv]

    ithimba group [n Cl. 9]

le-special task force of a special task force [poss Cl. 5]

eliqeqeshiwe that/which has been trained [rel Cl. 5]

    liqeqeshiwe it, (s)he has been trained [stative]

kuthi it should happen [subjunc]

lowomuntu that person [dem phr Cl. 1]

enodlame (s)he is violent (lit. (s)he has violence [assoc cop, pres, partic]

lelithimba this team [dem phr Cl. 5]

liyixazulule it would resolve or settle it [subjunc]

leyonkinga that problem, that difficulty [dem phr Cl. 9]

kulesosimo in that manner [loc]

noma yini nonetheless, nevertheless, no matter what, anything at all (even if it is what)

njengokuthi such as that [conj]

ogcina one who ends up [rel Cl. 1]
  ugcina (s)he ends up, (s)he finally [pres, conjoint]

ngokuphangalala by dying [instr adv]
  ukuphangalala to die, to collapse, to faint [vn Cl. 15]
  -phangalal-a die, faint, collapse [v.i.]

esizama ukuyigwema that/which we try to avoid [ind rel of plain obj rel, 1 p pl]

esizama that/which we try [rel 1 p pl]
  sizama we try [pres, conjoint]
  -zam-a try [v.i. & t.]
  ukuyigwema to avoid it [vn Cl. 15]

«5»

wabuye (s)he again [rem past or narr]

wasichazela (s)he explained to us [narr]

ukuma to stand [vn Cl. 15]

phezu kwa- on, on top of, above, in control of; in addition to; in spite of [loc phr]

kwamabhilidi of buildings [poss Cl. 17]
  amabhilidi buildings [n Cl. 6; sg **ibhilidi** Cl. 5] {Eng}

amade tall, long [adj Cl. 6]
  -de tall, long, lengthy [adj stem]

emabhulohweni to, from, on bridges [loc; < **amabhuloho**]
  amabhuloho bridges [n Cl. 6;

sg **ibhuloho** Cl. 5] {Afr *brug*}

kwesinye isikhathi sometimes, at other times [loc phr]

esinye some, other, certain, one [adj Cl. 7]

bazikhomba they point at themselves [pres, conjoint]
  -khomb-a point (at), point out [v.i. & t.]

esiningi a lot [adj Cl. 7]

lababantu these people [dem phr Cl. 2]

ukunakwa to be noticed, to be taken notice of [vn Cl. 15]
  -nakw-a be noticed, be taken notice of [v-pass]
  -nak-a notice, take notice of, be concerned about, be troubled by [v.t.]

usubhekene you are already confronted [past, exclusive, conjoint; < **u-** SC + **-s-** already + **-u-** SC + **-bhekan-** + **-i...e**]

nabo with them, them too, also them, even them [assoc adv]

uxoxisana you are negotiating [pres, conjoint]

bawuguqule they change it [subjunc]

«6»

wasixoxela (s)he related to us [rem past]

ngokwenzekayo about what happens [instr adv]
  okwenzekayo what happens, what occurs, what takes place [rel Cl. 17]
  kuyenzeka it happens, it takes place, it occurs [pres, disjoint]

wakuleli of this (the noun **izwe** 'country' is understood) [poss Cl. 3]

lase-South Africa of South Africa [poss Cl. 5]

se-South Africa [< **e-South Africa** to, from, in South Africa]

kwelaseMelika in that (country) of America [loc]

elaseMelika that of America [poss pron Cl. 5; agrees with **izwe**]

laseMelika of America [poss Cl. 5]

semelika to, from, in America [loc; < **eMelika**]

e-Europe to, from, in Europe [loc]

i-Europe Europe[n Cl. 5] {Eng}

siyahamba we travel [pres, disjoint]

siye (and) we go [subjunc]

kulezozindawo to, from, in, at those places [loc]

lezozindawo those places [dem phr Cl. 10]

ngokushesha hurriedly, quickly [instr adv]

ukushesha to hurry, to rush, to be quick [vn Cl. 15]

-shesh-a hurry, rush, be quick, speed [v.i.]

siyosiza so that we go and help [subjunc, andative]

imbangela cause [n Cl. 9; < **-bangel-** cause for]

yalokho of that [poss Cl. 9]

thina we, us [abs pron 1 p pl]

sisiqonda we understand it [pres, conjoint]

kangcono better [manner adv]

sempilo of life [poss Cl. 7]

yezwe of the country [poss Cl. 9]

ngaphezu kwa- above, more than [instr adv phr]

«7»

sikhula it grows [pres, conjoint]

ngesivinini at a speed [instr adv]

isivinini speed [n Cl. 7]

esikhulu great, large [adj Cl. 7]

minyaka yonke annually, yearly, every year [n phr Cl. 4]

minyaka years [< **iminyaka**]

wasitshela (s)he told us [rem past]

yalokhu of this [poss Cl. 9]

kube yizinkinga it should be problems [ident cop, inch, subjunc]

yizinkinga it is problems [ident cop]

eziphathelene that/which relate to, that/which go together with [rel Cl. 8]

zasekhaya domestic, of home [poss Cl. 10]

lomkhuba this custom, this practice [dem phr Cl. 3]

umkhuba custom, (bad) practice, (bad) habit [n Cl. 3]

usudlange has gained force, has taken hold [past, exclusive, conjoint; < **u-** SC + **-s-** already + **-u-** SC + **-dlang-** + **-e**]

-dlang-a rage, overwhelm, be overpowering, take the upper hand [v.i.]

abamnyama black [rel Cl. 2]

ngoba because [conj]

labo of them, their [poss Cl. 5]

selihlala he, she, it already lives [pres, exclusive]

ezisemadolobheni that/which are in town, urban [rel Cl 10]

zisemadolobheni they are in towns or cities [loc cop, pres]

semadolobheni to, from, in towns [loc; < **emadolobheni**]

nokuyilapho and that is where [assoc adv phr]

okuyilapho that is where [rel Cl. 17]

kuyilapho it is where [ident cop, pres]

lapho there, where [2nd pos dem Cl. 16]
kuyilowo nayilowo each and every, individually (lit. it being that one and that one) [ident cop phr]
    kuyilowo it is that one [ident cop, pres]
    nayilowo and it is that one [assoc adv phr]
enake (s)he is concerned about, being troubled by [past, partic, conjoint]
zakhe his, her [poss Cl. 10]
engenandaba (s)he not caring, (s)he not bothered (lit. not having a matter) [assoc cop, pres, partic, neg]
nezomunye with or about those (troubles) of another [assoc adv]
    ezomunye those of another [poss pron Cl. 10]
    zomunye [poss Cl. 10]

«8»

ma-Afrika Africans [< **ama-Afrika** (loss of initial vowel is due to the preceding abs pron)]
sesijwayele we are already accustomed [stative, exclusive]
ukuxoxela to communicate to [vn Cl. 15]
    -xoxel-a communicate to, converse for [v-appl]
zethu our [poss Cl. 10]
sebekhetha they now choose, they already choose [pres, exclusive]
ukuzithulela just to keep quiet [vn Cl. 15]
behlangabezana they come up against [pres, partic]
    -hlangabezan-a come up against, compete, vie with one another, go out to meet one another [v-recip]

-hlangabez-a go out to meet or welcome an arrival [v.t.]
okwakungezabaMhlophe that/ which were those of Whites [rel Cl. 17]
    kwakungezabaMhlophe they were those of Whites [ident cop, rem past pres; < **kw-** SC Cl. 17 + **-a-** rem past pref + **-ku-** SC + **-ng-** cop pref + **ezabaMhlophe**]
    ezabaMhlophe those of the Whites [poss pron Cl. 10]
    zabaMhlophe of White people [poss Cl. 10]
    abaMhlophe White people [rel Cl. 2]
    -mhlophe white [rel stem]
kuqala at first, in the beginning [time adv]
bazama they try [pres, conjoint]
emva kokuzwa after hearing [loc phr]
    ukuzwa to hear, hearing, to feel, to understand [vn Cl. 15]
bane-HIV they have HIV [assoc cop, pres]
i-HIV [n Cl. 9a] {Eng}

«9»

likhetha he, she, it chooses [pres, conjoint]
ngokuzidubula by shooting themselves [instr adv]
    ukuzidubula to shoot oneself [vn Cl. 15]
lizibulale (or) they commit suicide [subjunc]
ngokuphuza by drinking [instr adv]
    ukuphuza to drink [vn Cl. 15]
    -phuz-a drink [v.t.]
amaphilisi pills, tablets, capsules [n Cl. 6; sg **iphilisi** Cl. 5] {Eng}
ngokweqile in excess, in overdose [instr adv; < **nga-** + **uku-** +

VERB + -ile, a formula for deriving adverbs from verbs]
-eq-a exceed, jump (across), skip (over); transgress (a law); cross (a boundary) [v.t.]
liziphonse (or) they throw themselves [subjunc]
emfuleni to, from, in(to) a river [loc]
umfula river [n Cl. 3]
banakwe they should be taken notice of [subjunc]
wazibulala (s)he killed him- or herself [rem past]
bengafunanga they did not want [past, partic]
wathi (and) he said [narr]
ufuna you want [pres, partic]
ukuqeqeshelwa to be trained for [vn Cl. 15]
uqale you should begin [subjunc]
ngokuba yilungu by becoming a member [instr adv phr]
ukuba yilungu to become a member [vn form of ident cop, inch]
lombutho wamaphoyisa of the police force [poss Cl. 5]
umbutho wamaphoyisa police force [n phr Cl. 3]
umbutho gathering [n Cl. 3]
wamaphoyisa of the police [poss Cl. 3]
ube ngumuntu you should become a person [ident cop, inch, subjunc]
ngumuntu it is a person [ident cop, pres]
ozithobileyo who is humble [rel Cl. 1]
uzithobile (s)he is humble [stative]
-zi-thob-a bec humble [v-refl]
-thob-a bend, lower, bow; humble, humiliate [v.t.]

osondelene who is close [rel Cl. 1]
usondelene (s)he is close [stative; < -sondelan- + -i...e]
-sondelan-a bec close to one another, approach one another [v-recip]
-sondel-a approach, come or go near [v.i. & t.]
nokwaziyo and who knows [assoc adv phr]
okwaziyo who knows how [rel Cl. 1; < uyakwazi]
ukuchema bias, to be prejudiced, to be biased [vn Cl. 15]

«10»
isihambele (s)he has already visited [past, exclusive, conjoint]
i-Germany [n Cl. 5] {Eng}
(i-)Belgium [n Cl. 5]
neMelika and America [assoc adv]
ngenhloso with the intention or aim [instr adv]
inhloso intention, aim [n Cl. 9; < -hlos- intend, aim]
yokwengeza to increase [poss Cl. 9]
ukwengeza to increase [vn Cl. 15]
-engez-a add to, increase, supplement [v.t.]
oluzoyisiza that/which would help him or her [rel Cl. 11]
luzoyisiza it will help him or her [fut]
ekuqhubeni in the development [loc]
ukuqhuba to develop, to progress [vn Cl. 15]
abacabanga who think [rel Cl. 2]
bacabanga they think [pres, conjoint]
bazame they should try [subjunc]
nekamu lamaphoyisa with a

police station [assoc adv phr]
ikamu lamaphoyisa police station [n phr Cl. 5]
ikamu (military) camp [n Cl. 5]
lamaphoyisa of the police [poss Cl. 5]
eliseduze that/which is near [rel Cl. 5]
liseduze it, (s)he is near [loc cop, pres]
seduze near, close by [loc; < **eduze**]
eduze na- ... close to ..., near to ... [loc phr]

usizo help, aid, assistance [n Cl. 11; pl **izinsizo**; < -**siz**- help]
lutholakala it is available [pres, conjoint]
mahhala for free, free of charge, for nothing, in vain [adv]
nezithombe and pictures, and photos [assoc adv]
i z i t h o m b e pictures, photographs [n Cl. 8; sg **isithombe**]
Themba (male name) [n Cl. 1a]
Ntshingila (surname) [n Cl. 1a]

Ifu elimnyama eMtata!

«1»
Isigigaba sokuhlasela kwenkanyamba edolobheni laseMtata ngo-
December 15 nyakenye siyohlale sikhumbuleka empilweni ngoba
kulapho kwacishe kwasala enkundleni uMongameli odume umhlaba
wonke uDkt Nelson Mandela. Ukubakhona kukaMongameli
kulendawo ngesikhathi kuhlasela inkanyamba, kwanika abantu
bakulendawo ithemba elikhulu.

«2»
Ilanga lalilihle konke kuhamba kahle edolobheni laseMtata
ngesikhathi ngingena kwelinye lamakhemisi ngenhloso yokuba
ngiyogeza izithombe zomshado engangiwuhambele ngempelasonto
eyayandulele ukuqala kwalelosonto. Ngangisematasatasa ngixoxa
nosokhemisi ngesikhathi sizwa imisindo yama-sirens izwakala
ezimotweni.

«3»
Kwathi lapho siqalaza ngefasitela sabona izimoto zishaye uhhide
ziza ngakulelikhemisi nokuyilapho zafika zema. Kwavuleka izicabha
kwaphuma izidlakela zezinsizwa ezazidlubhe izingubo ezimnyama.
Emotweni eyayiphahlwe ngezinye kwehla uMongameli Mandela
wangena ekhemisi. Ngalesosikhathi izulu lase lijikile laguqubala
kwamnyama – labaniza.

«4»
UMongameli wama kulendawo ngenhloso yokuba ayothenga uhlobo
lwensipho aqala ukuyisebenzisa ngesikhathi esaseRobben Island.
Ngesikhathi ngisondela ngathola ithuba lokuxoxisana nomunye
wabaqaphi bakhe. Umbuzo engnginawo washabalala ngesikhathi
sizwa ukuduma okwangqangqazelisa kwabulala amafasitela
akulelikhemisi ngomkhulu umsindo owadala ukwesaba kunoma
ngubani. Ngalesosikhathi uMongameli Mandela wayesehlengiwe
wayiswa kwelinye lamahhovisi akulelikhemisi nokuyilapho
ayephahlwe ngabaqaphi bakhe. UMongameli wama esikhulu isibindi
kodwa ubona ukuthi naye wethukile.

«5»
Ngenhlanhla bonke abantu ababengaphakathi kulelikhemisi
babephephile. Kwathi lapho ngiqalaza emgwaqeni...ngabona
okushaqisayo. Kwakudilika izindonga zezindlu kusuka kuphephukisa okwamaphepha, kwawa namatshe esichotho ayemakhulu
njengenqindi yomuntu. Khona manjalo kwakuzwakala nomsindo
wokukhala kwabantu becindezelwa yizindlu ezaziwela kubona.
Ngokushesha, konke kwanyamalala kwaphela sengathi akuzange
kwenzeke lutho.

«6»

Ngaphuma ngiyobheka umonakalo emnyango. Ngangihlangana nabantu begijima bekhala "Umntwana wami uphi?". Abantu abaphela ngesikhathi kudlula lenkanyamba yilabo abadayisa ezitaladini bonakalelwa nayizimpahla abazidayisayo. Ngahamba ngehla ngoYork Road. Ngahlangana nowesimame owayekhala ethi, "Bafile, bafile bonke." Ngasuka ngaqonda lapho lona wesimame ayeme khona erenki yamatekisi. Lapho ngathola ukuthi kufe abadayisa ezitaladini abayishumi nanye kanye nengane nokungabantu ababulalwa wudonga olwawela phezu kwabo.

«7»

Abatakuli nabahlengi bezimpilo base beqalile bekhipha abantu ababecindezelekile. Yayingekho indlela umshayeli ayengabalekela ngayo ukufa. Isibhedlela saseMtata yiso esadicileka phansi kakhulu. Indawo yeziguli yayintanta emanzini kanti amanye amagumbi akulesisibhedlela alimala aphela kodwa lokho akuzange kubakhubaze abahlengikazi ukuba benze umsebenzi wabo wokusiza abantu.

«8»

IBandla labasePresbyterian[7] Church of Southern Africa laligubha ukuhlanganisa iminyaka elikhulu ngesikhathi inkanyamba isusa uphahla. Abazibonela ngamehlo bathi lenkanyamba yayiphakeme cishe ngamamitha angu-450 kanti phezulu kwakundiza okwakubukeka sengathi amaphepha nokwathi emva kwesikhathi sabona ukuthi uphahla lwezindlu. Ihhovisi elibhekele isimo sezulu kulendawo yaseMtata labika ukuthi lenkanyamba yayihamba ngesivinini esingu-60 kuya ku-65km/h.

«9»

Ehhotela engangikulo, abaningi lenkanyamba babeyibiza bethi yi-'Hurricane Nelson' kanti yashiya abantu abangu-18 befile kwathi abangu-168 balimala. Umonakalo usuwonke kulesisifunda ubalelwa ku-R90 million.

Ngu: Ponko Masiba

---

[7] The original text had **labePresbyterian** a form rejected by the reader, but which is perfectly acceptable in our view. Below we give a grammatical analysis of both forms.

Vocabulary

eMtata in Umtata [loc]
uMtata (town) [n Cl. 3; according to the current Xhosa orthography, this ought to be **uMthatha**]

«1»
isigigaba major event, serious affair [n Cl. 7]
sokuhlasela of striking, attacking, invading [poss Cl. 7]
ukuhlasela to attack, to invade [vn Cl. 15]
-hlasel-a attack, invade [v.t.]
kwenkanyamba of a tornado [poss Cl. 15]
inkanyamba tornado [n Cl. 9]
edolobheni in town [loc]
idolobha town [n Cl. 5] {Afr *dorp*}
laseMtata of Umtata [poss Cl. 5]
seMtata to, from, in Umtata [loc; < **eMtata**]
ngo-December 15 on December 15 [instr adv]
u-December (December is usually **uDisemba** in Zulu) [n Cl. 1a] {Eng}
siyohlale it will continue, it will always [aux, rem fut]
sikhumbuleka it is memorable or remembered [pres, partic]
-khumbulek-a be memorable, be remembered [v-neut]
-khumbul-a remember, miss [v.t.]
empilweni in life, in health [loc; < **impilo**]
kulapho it was when [loc cop, pres]
kwacishe there almost [rem past, partic]
-cish-e almost VERB, VERB

nearly [aux]
kwasala enkundleni there died (lit. there stayed behind in the incident)
kwasala there stayed behind [narr]
-sal-a remain, stay behind [v.i.]
enkundleni in the incident, in the situation [loc]
inkundla incident, situation [n Cl. 9]
odume famous, renowned [rel Cl. 1]
uDkt Dr [n Cl. 1a; abbrev: **uDokotela**]
ukubakhona the presence [loc cop, vn phr]
kukamongameli of the president [poss Cl. 15]
kuhlasela there struck (lit. there strikes) [pres, partic]
kwanika it gave [rem past]
bakulendawo of that place [poss Cl. 2]
ithemba hope, faith [n Cl. 5; < **-themb-** hope]
elikhulu great, large, big [adj Cl. 5]
eli- [adj conc Cl. 5]

«2»
ilanga sun, day [n Cl. 5]
lalilihle it, he, she was beautiful [descr cop, rem past pres; < l- SC Cl. 5 + **-a-** rem past pref + **-li-** SC + **-li-** 2nd half adj conc + **-hle** adj stem]
kuhamba it going [pres, partic]
ngingena I went in (lit. I go into) [pres, partic]
kwelinye to one, to a certain [loc]
elinye one, some, another, a certain [adj Cl. 5]

116

lamakhemisi of the pharmacies [poss Cl. 5]

amakhemisi pharmacies [n Cl. 6; sg **ikhemisi** Cl. 5] {Eng *chemist*}

yokuba (of) that [poss Cl. 9]

ngiyogeza I should go and have developed [subjunc, andative]
-**gez-a** wash; develop (photos) [v.i. & t.]

zomshado of a wedding [poss Cl. 8]

engangiwuhambele that/which I had attended [ind rel of plain obj rel, 1 p sg]
ngangiwuhambele I had attended it [rem past past, conjoint]
-**hambel-a** attend, visit, travel towards, travel for [v-appl]

ngempelasonto during, at the weekend [instr adv]

eyayandulele that/which preceded [rel Cl. 9]
yayandulele it had preceded [rem past past, conjoint; < **y**- SC + -**a**- rem past + -**y**- SC + -**andulel**- + -**e**]
-**andulel-a** anticipate, come before, precede [v.t.]

kwalelosonto of that week [poss Cl. 15]
lelosonto that week [dem phr Cl. 5]
lelo that [2nd pos dem Cl. 5]
sonto [< **isonto**]

ngangisematasatasa I was still busy [descr cop, rem past pres, persistive]
-**se**- still [persistive pref; var of -**sa**- used in copulatives]
-**matasatasa** busy, occupied [rel stem; < **amatasatasa** busyness [n Cl. 6]]

ngixoxa (I) chatting [pres, partic]

nosokhemisi with the pharmacist, with the chemist [assoc adv]

usokhemisi pharmacist, chemist [n Cl. 1a]

sizwa we heard (lit. we hear) [pres, partic]

yama-sirens of sirens [poss Cl. 4]
ama-sirens sirens [n Cl. 6; sg **i-siren** Cl. 9a] {Eng}

izwakala (they) being heard, being audible [pres, partic]

ezimotweni to, from, in cars [loc; < **izimoto**]

«3»

siqalaza we look(ed) about [pres, partic]
-**qalaz-a** look about, peer around [v.i.]

ngefasitela through the window [instr adv]
ifasitela window [n Cl. 5] {Afr *venster*}

sabona we saw [rem past]

zishaye uhhide they have formed a convoy (lit. having hit a long line)
zishaye they have hit [past, partic, con-joint]
uhhide long line of things, convoy [n Cl. 11; pl **izihhide** Cl. 10a]

ziza (they) coming [pres, partic]

ngakulelikhemisi towards this pharmacy [instr adv phr]
kulelikhemisi to this pharmacy [loc]
lelikhemisi this pharmacy [dem phr Cl. 5]

zafika they arrived [rem past, partic]

zema and they stopped [narr; < **za**- + -**im-a**]
-**im-a** stand (up); wait; stop [v.i.; var of -**m-a** used when preceded

by a]
kwavuleka there opened [narr]
   -vulek-a open (v.i.) [v-neut]
   -vul-a open (v.t.) [v.t.]
kwaphuma (and) there came out [narr]
izidlakela well-built people [n Cl. 8]
zezinsizwa of youths, of young men [poss Cl. 8]
ezazidlubhe who were smartly dressed, or wearing their best [rel Cl. 8]
   zazidlubhe they were smartly dressed, they were wearing their best [rem past past, conjoint]
   z- they [SC Cl. 8; found before vowels]
   -dlubh-a put on one's best clothes, dress up in (finery) [v.t.]
ezimnyama black [rel Cl. 10]
emotweni to, from, in a car [loc; < **imoto**]
eyayiphahlwe that/which was surrounded [rel Cl. 9]
   yayiphahlwe it was surrounded [rem past past, conjoint]
   -phahlw-a be surrounded [v-pass]
   -phahl-a surround [v.t.]
ngezinye by others [agent adv]
   ezinye other(s) [adj. Cl. 10]
kwehla there descended [rem past; < **kw-** SC + **-Ø:-** rem past prefix the colon : represents a lengthening of the following vowel) + **-ehl-a**]
wangena (and) (s)he went into [narr]
izulu sky, heaven; weather [n Cl. 5]
lase it already [aux, narr]
   -se VERB already, VERB then, VERB now, VERB soon [aux; translation depends on context]

lijikile it has turned [past, disjoint]
   -jik-a turn [v.i.]
laguqubala (and) it became cloudy, overcast [narr]
   -guqubal-a bec cloudy or overcast [v.i.]
kwamnyama and became black [abbreviation of **kwaba mnyama**]
labaniza and it flashed with lightning [narr]
   -baniz-a flash (referring to lightning) [v.i.]

«4»
wama (s)he stopped [rem past]
ayothenga that (s)he should go and buy [subjunc, andative]
uhlobo type, sort, kind [n Cl. 11]
lwensipho of soap [poss Cl. 11]
   insipho soap [n Cl. 9] {Afr *seep*}
aqala ukuyisebenzisa that/which (s)he started (long ago) to use (it) [ind rel of plain obj rel, Cl. 1]
   aqala that/which (s)he started [rem past, rel; < **Ø-** that/which (s)he ... [ind rel conc Cl. 1; var of **a-** found before vowels] + **-a-** rem past pref + **qal-** + **-a**]
esaseRobben Island that (s)he was on Robben Island (island off Cape Town that has been used as a penitentiary or place for lepers over the centuries. Infamous as a prison for political prisoners during the apartheid era.) [loc cop, pres, partic, persistive]
ngisondela I approached [pres, partic]
ngathola I found [rem past]
lokuxoxisana of chatting [poss Cl. 5]

nomunye with one, with a certain [assoc adv]

wabaqaphi of guards [poss Cl. 1]

umbuzo question [n Cl. 1; < **-buz-ask**]

enganginawo that/which I had [ind rel of associative rel, 1 p sg]

nganginawo I had it [assoc cop, rem past pres]

washabalala it disappeared, it came to nought [narr]

-shabalal-a disappear, come to nought, evaporate [v.i.]

ukuduma thunder, rumbling [n Cl. 15]

okwangqangqazelisa that/which rattled [rel Cl. 15]

kwangqangqazelisa it caused to rattle or tremble [rem past]

-ngqangqazelis-a cause to shiver, tremble, have the shakes; make rattle [v-caus]

-ngqangqazel-a shiver, tremble, have the shakes [v.i.]

-ngqangq-a tremble with anger [v.i.]

kwabulala and smashed (lit. and killed) [narr]

akulelikhemisi of this pharmacy [poss Cl. 6]

ngomkhulu with a huge [instr adv]

omkhulu large, big [adj Cl. 3]

om- [adj conc Cl. 3]

owadala that/which created [rel Cl. 3]

wadala it created [rem past]

ukwesaba fear [n Cl. 15]

-esab-a fear, be afraid (of) [v.i. & t.]

kunoma ngubani to no matter whom, to whomever [loc]

kunoma to no matter, to even [loc]

wayesehlengiwe (s)he had already been escorted [rem past past,

disjoint; < **w-** SC + **-a-** rem past + **-ye-** SC + **-s-** already + **-e-** SC + **-hleng-** + **-w-** + **-i...e**]

-hlengw-a be escorted [v-pass]

-hleng-a escort [v.t.]

wayiswa (and) (s)he was taken [narr]

-yisw-a be taken (to) [v-caus-pass]

lamahhovisi of the offices [poss Cl. 5]

amahhovisi offices [n Cl. 6; sg **ihhovisi** Cl. 5]

lapho ayephahlwe where (s)he had been surrounded [ind rel of plain loc rel]

ayephahlwe (s)he had been surrounded [rem past past, partic, conjoint]

isibindi courage, bravery; liver (according to Zulu culture, the liver is said to be the seat of bravery) [n Cl. 7]

naye (s)he too, (s)he also, even (s)he [assoc adv]

wethukile (s)he got a fright [past, disjoint]

-ethuk-a get a fright [v.i.]

«5»

ababengaphakathi who were inside [rel Cl. 2]

babengaphakathi they were inside (long ago) [loc cop, rem past pres]

ngaphakathi inside [instr adv]

phakathi inside [loc noun Cl. 16]

babephephile they had escaped [rem past past, disjoint]

ngiqalaza I look(ed) about [pres, partic]

emgwaqeni to, from, in, on the street [loc; var **emgwaqweni**; < **umgwaqo**]

ngabona I saw [rem past]
okushaqisayo something amazing [rel Cl. 17]
  kuyashaqisa it is amazing [pres, disjoint]
  -shaqis-a amaze, astonish, shock [v-caus]
  -shaq-a bec amazed, astonished, shocked [v.i.]
kwakudilika there were collapsing [rem past pres]
  -dilik-a fall down, collapse [v.i.]
izindonga walls [n Cl. 10; sg **udonga** Cl. 11]
zezindlu of houses [poss Cl. 10]
kusuka it just, it merely [aux, pres, conjoint]
kuphephukisa it blew about [pres, conjoint]
  -phephukis-a blow about [v-caus]
  -phephuk-a get blown away or about [v.i.]
okwamaphepha something like papers [poss pron Cl. 17]
  okwa- ... something like ... [poss pron pref Cl. 17]
kwawa (and) there fell [narr]
  -w-a fall, collapse [v.i.]
namatshe also stones [assoc adv]
esichotho of hail [poss Cl. 6]
  isichotho hail [n Cl. 7]
ayemakhulu that/which were large [descr cop, rem past pres]
njengenqindi like a fist [compar adv]
  inqindi fist [n Cl. 9a]
yomuntu of a person [poss Cl. 9]
khona manjalo at that time [conj phr]
kwakuzwakala there was audible [rem past pres]
nomsindo also the sound [assoc adv]
wokukhala of the crying,

screaming [poss Cl. 3]
kwabantu of people [poss Cl. 15]
becindezelwa they being crushed [pres, partic]
  -cindezelw-a be crushed, be pressed down, be squeezed [v-pass]
  -cindezel-a press down, squeeze, crush; oppress [v.t.]
yizindlu by houses [agent adv]
ezaziwela that/which were falling onto, into [rem past pres]
  -wel-a fall onto, into [v-appl]
kubona to, from, in, at, on them [loc]
kwanyamalala it disappeared [rem past or narr]
kwaphela (and) it ended [narr]
sengathi as if [conj]
akuzange there had never, it never [aux, past, neg; < -z-e]

«6»

ngaphuma I went out [rem past]
ngiyobheka (I) going to look at [pres, partic, andative]
umonakalo damage, mess [n Cl. 3; < -onakal- get spoilt]
emnyango from or in the doorway [loc; one of the exceptions that does not take a locative suffix]
  umnyango doorway [n Cl. 3]
ngangihlangana I was meeting, I was coming across [rem past pres]
begijima (they) running [pres, partic]
  -gijim-a run [v.i.]
bekhala (they) crying [pres, partic]
umntwana child [n Cl. 1]
uphi? where is (s)he? [loc cop, pres]
abaphela who met their end (lit. who came to an end) [rel Cl. 2]

baphela they met their end, they came to an end [rem past]

kudlula there passed [pres, partic]

lenkanyamba this tornado [dem phr Cl. 17]

yilabo are those [ident cop, pres]

abadayisa who traded, who offered for sale [rel Cl. 2]

badayisa they trade, they offer for sale [pres, conjoint]

bonakalelwa nayizimpahla and they also had their goods destroyed (lit. and they were destroyed for even by the goods) [v phr]

bonakalelwa and who had had destroyed [narr]

b- they [SC Cl. 2]

-Ø- [pref of narrative aspect; var of **-a-** found before vowels]

-onakalelw- have sg spoilt or damaged [v-neut-appl-pass]

-onakalel-a spoil for, damage for [v-neut-appl]

-onakal-a get spoilt, damaged, injured; bec corrupt, sinful [v-neut]

-on-a spoil, damage, injure; sin, do wrong; corrupt [v.i. & t.]

nayizimpahla also the goods, even the goods [assoc adv phr]

yizimpahla by the goods [agent adv]

abazidayisayo that/which they were trading in [ind rel of plain obj rel, Cl. 2]

bayazidayisa they trade them, they offer them for sale [pres, disjoint]

ngahamba I walked [rem past]

ngehla and went down [narr]

ngoYork Road via York Road [instr adv]

uYork Road [n Cl. 3a]

ngahlangana I met [narr]

nowesimame with a lady [assoc adv phr]

owesimame lady, woman [poss pron Cl. 1; pl **abesimame**]

owayekhala who was crying [rel Cl. 1]

wayekhala (s)he was crying or complaining [rem past pres]

bafile they are dead, they have died [stative]

ngasuka I soon [aux, rem past]

-suk-a soon VERB [aux; followed by narr in the past]

ngaqonda I understood [narr]

-qond-a understand, comprehend, realize [v.t.]

lona this [1st pos dem Cl. 1]

lapho ayeme khona where (s)he was standing [ind rel of plain loc rel]

ayeme (s)he was standing [rem past past, partic, conjoint]

erenki to, from, at the rank [loc; one of the exceptions that does not take a locative suffix]

irenki rank [n Cl. 9a]

yamatekisi of taxis [poss Cl. 9]

amatekisi taxis, cabs [n Cl. 6; sg **itekisi** Cl. 5] {Eng}

kufe there had died [past, conjoint]

abayishumi nanye eleven (adj) [rel Cl. 2]

abayishumi ten (adj) [rel Cl. 2]

bayishumi there are ten (lit. they are ten) [ident cop, pres]

nanye and one [assoc adv]

kanye nengane together with a child [adv phr]

ingane child [n Cl. 9]

nokungabantu and people-like things [assoc adv]

okungabantu things like people, hominoids [rel Cl. 17]

-nga- like [prefix added to nouns forming a relative stem indicating 'like, as if']

ababulalwa who were killed [rel Cl. 2]

babulalwa they were killed [rem past]

-bulalw-a be killed [v-pass; var **-bulaw-a**]

wudonga by a wall [agent adv]

udonga wall [n Cl. 11]

olwawela that/which fell onto [rel Cl. 11]

lwawela it fell onto [rem past]

«7»

abatakuli life-savers, rescue teams [n Cl. 2]

nabahlengi bezimpilo and, with, also, even life-savers or paramedics [assoc adv]

abahlengi nurses [n Cl. 2]

bezimpilo of lives [poss Cl. 2]

base they already [aux]

beqalile they (had) begun [past, partic, disjoint]

bekhipha (they) taking out [pres, partic]

ababecindezelekile who had been crushed [rel Cl. 2]

babecindezelekile they had been crushed [rem past past, disjoint]

-cindezelek-a get crushed; get injured; get pressurized; get oppressed [v-neut]

yayingekho indlela there was no way [exist cop, rem past pres, neg]

yayingekho it, (s)he was not there [loc cop, rem past pres, neg; may also introduce an exist cop]

indlela umshayeli ayengabale-kela ngayo ukufa a way or road by which a driver could run away from death

umshayeli driver [n Cl. 1; < **-shayel-** drive]

ayengabalekela ngayo ukufa by which (s)he could run away from death [ind rel of plain adv rel, Cl. 1]

ayengabalekela (s)he could run away from [rem past pres, potential, rel; < **wayenga-balekela** by replacement of the SC **w-** with the ind rel conc **a-**, that becomes **Ø-** before the vowel **a** of the remote past pref]

wayengabalekela (s)he could run away from [rem past pres, potential]

saseMtata of Umtata [poss Cl. 7]

yiso is the one, is it, is him, is her [ident cop, pres]

esadicileka that/which collapsed, got thrown down [rel Cl. 7]

sadicileka it got thrown down [rem past]

-dicilek-a get thrown down, fall flat [v.i.]

indawo yeziguli ward (lit. place of patients) [n phr Cl. 9]

yeziguli of patients [poss Cl. 9]

iziguli patients, sick people [n Cl. 8; sg **isiguli**; < **-gul-** be sick]

yayintanta was floating [rem past pres]

-ntant-a float [v.i.]

emanzini in, to, from, on water [loc]

amagumbi rooms [n Cl. 6; sg **igumbi** Cl. 5]

akulesisibhedlela of (at) this hospital [poss phr Cl. 6]

alimala they got damaged [rem past]

aphela and 'came to an end' (i.e. were severely damaged) [narr]

akuzange kubakhubaze it never disable them

kubakhubaze it should disabled them [subjunc]
-khubaz-a disable, make ineffective; damage, injure [v.t.]
abahlengikazi nurses (female) [n Cl. 2; sg **umhlengikazi**]
-kazi -ess, -lady, -woman, female … [feminine suff]
wokusiza of helping [poss Cl. 3]

«8»
iBandla labe-Presbyterian Church of Southern Africa the Presbyterian Church of Southern Africa [n phr Cl. 5]
ibandla assembly of men (for discussion, trial, etc.; these days may include women); congregation, church, denomination [n Cl. 5]
labase-Presybeterian Church of Southern Africa of those in the Presbyterian … [poss Cl. 5]
l- of [poss conc Cl. 5; found before vowels **a, e** and **o**]
abase-Presbyterian … those who are in the Presbyterian …[rel Cl. 2]
base-Presbyterian they are in the Presbyterian … [loc cop, pres]
se-Presbyterian in the Presbyterian … [loc; < **e-Presbyterian**]
i-Presbyterian Church of Southern Africa [n Cl. 9a] {Eng}
OR **labe-Presbyterian** … of those of the Presbyterian … [poss Cl. 5]
abe-Presbyterian … those of the Presbyterian … [poss pron Cl. 2]
be-Presbyterian … of the Presbyterian … [poss Cl. 2]

laligubha it was observing [rem past pres]
ukuhlanganisa iminyaka elikhulu the centenary (lit. the bringing together or completion of 100 years)
ukuhlanganisa bringing together; completion [n Cl. 15]
-hlanganis-a bring together, assemble; join, add up [v-caus]
elikhulu a hundred [rel Cl. 4]
ilikhulu there are a hundred [ident cop, pres]
l- it is [ident cop prefix; used by some speakers before nouns of Cl. 5 and 11]
ikhulu hundred (n) [n Cl. 5]
isusa it removes [pres, conjoint]
-sus-a remove, take away [v-caus; < **-suk-** + **-Y-**; k + **-Y-** > s]
uphahla roof [n Cl. 11; pl. **izimpahla**; m + ph > mp]
abazibonela those who saw for themselves [rel Cl. 2]
bazibonela they saw for themselves [rem past]
-zi-bonel-a see for oneself [v-refl-appl]
-bonel-a see for [v-appl]
ngamehlo through eyes [instr adv]
yayiphakeme it had risen, it had gone up [rem past stative]
-phakam-a rise up, mount, bec elevated [v.inch]
ngamamitha it is meters [ident cop, pres]
amamitha meters [n Cl. 6; sg **imitha** Cl. 5] {Eng}
angu-450 450 (lit. that/which are 450) [rel Cl. 6]
u-450 450 [n Cl. 1a]
kwakundiza there flew [rem past pres]
okwakubukeka something remarkable [rel Cl. 17]

kwakubukeka it was remarkable, it was attractive [rem past pres]
-bukek-a be attractive, remarkable [v-neut]
amaphepha they are/it is papers [ident cop, pres; < Ø - + **amaphepha**]
nokwathi and which then [assoc adv]
okwathi which then [rel Cl. 17]
emva kwesikhathi after a time, after a while [loc phr]
uphahla is the roof [ident cop; < Ø- + **uphahla**]
lwezindlu of houses [poss Cl. 11]
elibhekele that/which watches [rel Cl. 5]
libhekele it watches [stative]
-bhekel-a watch for, watch at [v-appl]
isimo sezulu the weather (lit. the state of the weather)
sezulu of the weather [poss Cl. 7]
yaseMtata of (in) Umtata [poss Cl. 9]
labika it reported [rem past]
-bik-a report, announce [v.t.]
yayihamba it was travelling [rem past pres]
esingu-60 kuya ku-65km/h of 60 to 65 km/h (lit. that is 60 ...) [rel phr Cl. 7]
kuya up to, as far as (lit. going to)

«9»

ehhotela in, at, to, from the hotel [loc; one of the exceptions that does not take a locative suffix]
ihhotela hotel [n Cl. 5] {Eng or

Afr *hotel*}
engangikulo in which I was [ind rel of plain loc rel, 1 p sg; < **e-**rel pref + **ng-** I + **-a-** rem past + **-ngi-** I + **-ku-** loc pref + **-lo** abs pron Cl. 7]
ngangikulo I was in it [loc cop, rem past pres]
abaningi many [adj Cl. 2]
babeyibiza they were calling it [rem past pres]
bethi (they) saying [pres, partic]
yi-Hurricane Nelson it is Hurricane Nelson [ident cop, pres]
i-Hurricane Nelson [n Cl. 9a] {Eng}
yashiya it left (behind) [rem past]
abangu-18 eighteen [rel Cl. 2]
u-18 18 [n Cl. 1a]
befile (they) dead [stative, partic]
kwathi and they say [narr]
abangu-168 168 [rel Cl. 2]
u-168 168 [n Cl. 1a]
balimala they were injured [rem past]
usuwonke it is already in total [descr cop, pres, exclusive]
kulesi sifunda in this province [loc phr]
ubalelwa it is calculated at, is reckoned at [pres, conjoint]
-balelw-a be calculated at, be reckoned at [v-appl-pass]
-balel-a calculate at, reckon at [v-appl]
ku-R90million at R90 million [loc]
u-R90million R90 million [n Cl. 1a] {Eng}
uPonko (name) [n Cl. 1a]
Masiba (surname) [n Cl. 1a]

Olawula ukuhamba kwamabhanoyi

«1»

USandile Maphanga oneminyaka engu-24 uthi umsebenzi awenzayo wokulawula ukuhamba kwamabhanoyi esikhumulweni sezindiza eThekwini umenza azizwe ekhululekile.

Umfanyana owayevame ukubukela izindiza zidlula eMseleni okuyindawo eseNyakatho nesifundazwe saKwaZulu-Natal waqopha umlando ngesikhathi eba ngumlawuli wokuhamba kwezindiza (air-traffic controller) omnyama wokuqala ngqa ukuqeqeshelwa lomsebenzi eSouth Africa.

«2»

"Ngangingazi ukuthi nami ngiyosebenza ngaphansi kwemboni yezindiza ngelinye ilanga, angisayiphathi-ke eyokugibela ibhanoyi," kusho uSandile Maphanga. "Into engangizimisele ngokuyenza kwakungukuba ngummeli ngangingayingeni eyamabhanoyi yize noma ngangivame ukuwabukela eMseleni."

Lensizwa yaphasa ibanga leshumi ngo-1992 kanti ngonyaka owalandela lowo yayizibambela amatoho ngoba yayingenayo imali yokuqhuba izifundo zayo.

«3»

"Ngo-1994, ngabona isikhangiso ephepheni. Kulesosikhangiso kwakubhalwe ukuthi abe-South African Airways (SAA) babedinga abantu ababezobaqeqeshela ukushayela amabhanoyi. Ngesikhathi ngifunda lesosikhangiso, engqondweni yami kwabuya lesosithombe samabhanoyi engangivame ukuwabuka ngesikhathi ngisakhula. Ngavele ngazibonela ukuthi akukho okunye engangingaphephela kukho ngaphandle kokuqeqeshelwa lowomsebenzi!"

«4»

USandile waba ngomunye walabobantu abamnyama ababezo-qeqeshwa yinkampani yakwaSAA ukushayela amabhanoyi.

Ngesikhathi beqeqeshwa, kwadingeka ukuba baye eGoli kanti wayeziphuzela kalula nje ezifundweni zakhe. Ngokuhamba kwesi-khathi, uSandile wabona ukuthi wayengakuthandisisi kahle ukuba ngumshayeli wamabhanoyi.

«5»

"Ngo-1996 ngabhalisela ukufundela ukuba ngumlawuli wokuhamba kwezindiza nokuyizifundo ezazingaphansi kwe-Airports Company of South Africa (ACSA). Lesosinyathelo engangizikhethele sona sasingelula neze kodwa manje ngithokoza kakhulu ngoba angikaze ngizisole ngaso."

«6»
Njengamanje uSandile uyaziqhenya ngoba umsebenzi awenzayo awujwayelekile entsheni engama-Afrika. "Esikhathini esedlule, intsha yakithi ibivame ukukhetha ukuba ngodokotela, othisha, abahlengikazi noma amaphoyisa – abacabangi ukuthi ziningi izinto abangazenza ngaphandle kwalezi esengizibalile."

Ngokusho kukaSandile, bambalwa kabi abantu abamnyama abawuqondisisa kahle lomsebenzi awenzayo. "Bayamangala nje uma sengibachazela ngawo."

«7»
Ngesikhathi sisaxoxa nosandile, kwezwakala umshayeli webhanoyi esememezela ukuthi ibhanoyi selizosuka. USandile waphendula echaza ukuthi konke kwakumi ngomumo kulowomzila owawuzo-hamba ibhanoyi.

«8»
Ngalesosenzo sabo basuke befuna ukwenza isiqiniseko sokuthi ibhanoyi lizohamba ngokuphepha nangaphandle kokuphazamiseka lize lifike kuleyondawo eliphikelele kuyo. "Abalawuli bamabhanoyi basebenzisa i-radar okuyiyona ekhombisa umshayeli ukuthi sekufanele ehlele phansi noma asuke kuleso naleso sikhumulo sezindiza. Njengoba kungenamigwaqo neziphawu zomgwaqo esibhakabhakeni, abashayeli bamabhanoyi babeka amathemba abo kithina."

«9»
"Ukuze lomsebenzi uwenze ngaphandle kwezingqinamba, kufanele ufunde ukusebenza ngaphansi kwesimo esibucayi, uzethembe futhi ujwayele ukusebenza ngokubambisana nabanye abantu," kusho uSandile.

Lensizwa isazimisele ngokuqhubeka nezifundo zayo ukuze igcine isikwazi ukulawula nezindiza ezihambela emazweni aphesheya kwezilwandle.

Ngu: Pearl Mzoneli

Vocabulary

olawula ukuhamba kwama-bhanoyi air-traffic controller (lit. one who controls the traveling of airplanes) [rel phr Cl. 1]
olawula one who controls, regulates, marshals, orders [rel Cl. 1]

ulawula (s)he controls, regulates, marshals, orders [pres, conjoint]
ukuhamba (to) travel, movement, to go, to walk; traffic [n Cl. 15]
kwamabhanoyi of airplanes [poss Cl. 15]

Maphanga (surname) [n Cl. 1a]
awenzayo that/which (s)he does [ind rel of plain obj rel, Cl. 1]
uyawenza (s)he does it [pres, disjoint]
wokulawula of controlling, of regulating [poss Cl. 3]
ukulawula to give commands, to order; to control, to regulate, to marshal [vn Cl. 15]
esikhumulweni sezindiza at the airport [loc phr]
esikhumulweni port, harbor, depot [loc]
isikhumulo place of outspan-ning or unharnessing [n Cl. 7; < -khumul- outspan, unharness]
sezindiza of airplanes [poss Cl. 7]
izindiza airplanes [n Cl. 8; < -ndiz- fly]
umenza it makes him or her [pres, conjoint]
azizwe that (s)he should feel him- or herself [subjunc]
ekhululekile (s)he is free [stative, partic]
-khululek-a bec free or eman-cipated, be released [v-neut]
-khulul-a free, release, emanci-pate [v.t.]
owayevame who used (to) [rem past past, conjoint]
ukubukela to watch [vn Cl. 15]
-bukel-a watch [v-appl]
zidlula (while) they are passing [pres, partic]
eMseleni (place) [loc]
okuyindawo that/which is a place [rel Cl. 17]
kuyindawo it is a place [ident cop, pres]
esenyakatho that/which is to the north [rel Cl. 9]

isenyakatho it is in the north [loc cop, pres]
senyakatho to, from, in the north [loc; < enyakatho]
enyakatho na- ... (to or in the) north of ... [loc phr]
inyakatho north [n Cl. 9a]
nesifundazwe of the province, and the province [assoc adv]
isifundazwe province [n Cl. 7]
waqopha umlando (s)he carved out history [v phr]
waqopha (s)he carved out, notched [rem past]
-qoph-a cut out, notch; peck holes (e.g. a woodpecker) [v.t.]
umlando history [n Cl. 3; < -land-relate]
eba ngumlawuli wokuhamba kwezindiza (s)he became an air-traffic controller (lit. becomes) [ident cop, pres, partic]
eba (s)he, becoming, (s)he becomes [pres, partic]
ngumlawuli wokuhamba kwezindiza (s)he, it is a controller [ident cop, pres]
umlawuli wokuhamba kwezi-ndiza air-traffic controller [n phr Cl. 1; pl **abalawuli bokuhamba kwezindiza**]
umlawuli marshal, controller [n Cl. 1; < -lawul- control, mar-shal]
wokuhamba of travel, of movement [poss Cl. 1]
kwezindiza of airplanes [poss Cl. 15]
omnyama black [rel Cl. 1]
umnyama (s)he is black [descr cop, pres]
wokuqala first [poss Cl. 1]

«2»

ngangingazi I didn't know [rem past pres, neg; < **ng-** SC **-a-** rem past **-ngi-** SC **-ng-** not **-az-i** know]

nami I too, even I [assoc adv]

ngiyosebenza I shall work [rem fut]

ngaphansi kwemboni yezindiza within the airline industry

kwemboni of the industry, business, factory [poss Cl. 15 or 17]

yezindiza of aircraft, of planes [poss Cl. 9]

ngelinye ilanga some day, one day [instr adv phr]

ngelinye on, by, about a certain [instr adv]

angisayiphathi-ke I need not mention (idiom; lit. I no longer take it then) [pres, persistive, neg]

eyokugibela ibhanoyi that (industry) of air travel [poss pron Cl. 9]

yokugibela of riding, of boarding, of traveling by [poss Cl. 9]

ukugibela to ride, to mount (as a horse), to board, to travel by [vn Cl. 15]

-gibel-a ride, mount (as a horse), board, travel by [v.t.]

into engangizimisele ngokuyenza the thing that I had prepared myself to do (it) [ind rel of plain adv rel, 1 p sg]

engangizimisele that I had prepared myself for [rel 1 p sg]

ngangizimisele I had prepared myself [rem past stative]

ngokuyenza for, about doing it [instr adv]

ukuyenza to do it [vn Cl. 15]

kwakungukuba ngummeli it was to become a lawyer [ident cop, rem past pres; < **kw-** SC + **-a-**

rem past + **-ku-** SC + **-ng-** is + **ukuba** to become + **ngummeli** it is a lawyer]

ngummeli (s)he, it is a lawyer [ident cop, pres]

ummeli lawyer, representative, spokesperson [n Cl. 1; < **-mel-** stand for, represent]

ngangingayingeni I had no desire (lit. I was not entering it (referring to **into**)) [rem past pres, neg]

eyamabhanoyi that (subject) of airplanes [poss pron Cl. 9]

yamabhanoyi of airplanes [poss Cl. 9]

yize noma even though [conj phr]

yize even though [conj]

ngangivame I was accustomed [rem past past, conjoint]

ukuwabukela to watch them [vn Cl. 15]

yaphasa (s)he passed [rem past]

-phas-a pass (a test or exam) [v.t.] {Eng}

ibanga standard, grade [n Cl. 5]

leshumi (of) ten [poss Cl. 5]

ngo-1992 in 1992 [instr adv]

u-1992 [n Cl. 1a]

owalandela that followed [rel Cl. 3]

walandela it followed [rem past]

lowo that [2nd pos dem Cl. 3]

yayizibambela amatoho (s)he took on day jobs

yayizibambela (s)he used to take on, (s)he held or caught for him- or herself [rem past pres]

-bambel-a take hold of for, catch for; deputize for, take the place of [v-appl]

amatoho day jobs [n Cl. 6; sg **itoho**] {Afr *tog* journey, expedition}

yayingenayo imali (s)he did not have the money [assoc cop, rem past pres, neg; < **y-** SC **-a-** rem past **-yi-** SC **-nge-** not **-na-** with **-yo** it]
yokuqhuba for, of continuing [poss Cl. 9]
izifundo lessons, studies [n Cl. 8]
zayo his, her, its [poss Cl. 9]

«3»
ngo-1994 in 1994 [instr adv]
isikhangiso advertisement [n Cl. 7; < **-khangis-** advertise; < **-khang-a** be attractive, attract admiration or desire]
kulesosikhangiso in, from that advertisement [loc]
lesosikhangiso that advertisement [dem phr Cl. 7]
kwakubhalwe there was written [rem past past, conjoint]
-bhalw-a be written [v-pass]
abe-South African Airways (SAA) those (people) from SAA [poss pron Cl. 2]
i-South African Airways [n Cl. 9a] {Eng}
babedinga they were needing [rem past pres]
ababezobaqeqeshela whom they would train to or for [ind rel of plain obj rel, Cl. 2]
babezobaqeqeshela they were going to train them for [rem past fut]
ukushayela to drive, to pilot [vn Cl. 15]
ngifunda I read [pres, partic]
engqondweni in mind [loc; < **ingqondo**]
ingqondo mind, intelligence, understanding, common sense; meaning, sense [n Cl. 9; < **-qond-** understand]

yami my [poss Cl. 9]
kwabuya there came back [rem past]
lesosithombe that picture, that image [dem phr Cl. 7]
isithombe picture, image, photograph [n Cl. 7]
samabhanoyi of airplanes [poss Cl. 7]
ukuwabuka to look at them [vn Cl. 15]
ngisakhula I was, I am still growing up [pres, partic, persistive]
ngavele I in advance [aux, rem past]
-vel-e VERB in advance, VERB with premeditation, VERB with foresight [aux; followed by subjunc, and in the past by the narrative]
ngazibonela I simply saw [narr]
akukho okunye there is nothing else [ident cop, pres, neg]
okunye something else, another thing [adj Cl. 17]
oku- [adj conc Cl. 17]
engangingaphephela kukho in which I could take refuge [ind rel of plain loc rel, 1 p sg]
engangingaphephela that/which I could take refuge [rel 1 p sg]
ngangingaphephela I could take refuge [rem past pres, potential]
-phephel-a take refuge [v-appl]
kukho to, from, in, at, on it [loc]
kokuqeqeshelwa (of) being trained for [poss Cl. 17]
lowomsebenzi that job, work, or task [dem phr Cl. 3]

«4»
waba ngomunye (s)he became one [ident cop, inch, rem past]
waba (s)he became [rem past]

ngomunye (s)he, it is one [ident cop]

ababezoqeqeshwa who were going to be trained [rel Cl. 2]

babezoqeqeshwa they were going to be trained [rem past fut]

yinkampani by the company [agent adv]

yakwaSAA of (at) SAA [poss Cl. 9]

kwaSAA at SAA [loc]

uSAA South African Airways [n Cl. 1a]

beqeqeshwa they were hired [pres, partic]

baye they should go [subjunc]

wayeziphuzela (s)he passed with ease [rem past pres]

-zi-phuzel-a pass with ease [idiom; v-refl-appl]

ezifundweni in studies, in lessons [loc; < izifundo]

ngokuhamba kwesikhathi in the passage of time [instr adv phr]

ngokuhamba through, by, in going; in, through the passage [instr adv]

kwesikhathi of time [poss Cl. 15]

wayengakuthandisisi (s)he did not like it very much [rem past pres, neg]

-thandisis- like greatly, like very much, love passionately [v-intens]

ukuba ngumshayeli wamabhanoyi to become a pilot [vn form of ident cop, inch]

ngumshayeli (s)he, it is a driver, pilot [ident cop, pres]

wamabhanoyi of airplanes [poss Cl. 1]

«5»

ngo-1996 in 1996 [instr adv]

u-1996 [n Cl. 1a]

ngabhalisela I registered for [rem past]

-bhalisel-a register for [v-caus-appl]

ukufundela ukuba to study to become [vn phr Cl. 15]

nokuyizifundo and which were studies [assoc adv phr]

okuyizifundo which were studies [rel Cl. 17]

kuyizifundo it is, they are studies [ident cop, pres]

ezazingaphansi that/which were under [loc cop, rem past pres]

kwe-Airports Company of South Africa (ACSA) of the Airports Company of South Africa [poss Cl. 17]

lesosinyathelo that step [dem phr Cl. 7]

isinyathelo step [n Cl. 7; < -nyathel- tread, step]

engangizikhethele sona that I had chosen for myself [ind rel of plain obj rel, 1 p sg]

ngangizikhethele I had chosen for myself [rem past past, conjoint]

sona it, its, he, him, his, she, her [abs pron Cl. 7]

sasingelula it was not easy [descr cop, rem past pres, neg]

ngithokoza I am happy [pres, conjoint]

angikaze I have not yet ever [aux, pres, exclusive, neg]

ngizisole I blamed myself, I regretted [subjunc]

-zi-sol-a blame oneself, regret, be contrite, show remorse [v-refl]

-sol-a find fault (with), grumble, blame, criticize, reprove; express doubt or dissatisfaction, be suspicious or doubtful [v.i. & t.]

ngaso about it, him, her; through it, him her [instr adv]

«6»

awujwayelekile it is not usual, it is not customary [stative, neg]

-jwayelek-a bec customary, bec usual, bec normal [v-neut]

entsheni to, from, among the youth or young people [loc]

intsha youth, young people [n Cl. 9; < **-sha** new, young [adj stem]; **n + sh > ntsh**]

engama-Afrika African (lit. who are Africans, i.e. Black Africans) [rel Cl. 9]

ngama-Afrika it is, they are Africans [ident cop, pres]

ama-Afrika Africans [n Cl. 6; sg **um-Afrik**a Cl. 1]

yakithi of my or our home [poss Cl. 9]

ibivame (s)he, they used to, were accustomed to [past past, conjoint]

ukukhetha to choose, to select, to elect, to vote [vn Cl. 15]

ngodokotela it is, they are doctors [ident cop, pres]

abacabangi they do not think [pres, neg]

abangazenza that/which they can do or make [ind rel of plain obj rel, Cl. 2]

bangazenza they can do or make them [pres, potential]

kwalezi from these, of these [poss Cl. 17]

esengizibalile that/which I have already enumerated [ind rel of plain obj rel, 1 p sg]

sengizibalile I have already enumerated them [past, exclusive, disjoint]

bambalwa there are few [descr cop, pres]

-mbalwa few [rel stem]

abawuqondisisa who understand it thoroughly [rel Cl. 2]

bawuqondisisa they understand it thoroughly [pres, conjoint]

-qondisis-a understand thoroughly [v-intens]

bayamangala they are surprised [pres, disjoint]

-mangal-a bec surprised, wonder [v.i.]

sengibachazela I then explain to them [pres, partic, exclusive]

ngawo about, with, through it [instr adv]

«7»

sisaxoxa I was still chatting (lit. we are still chatting; note the use of **si-** 'we,' which is used instead of **ngi-** 'I' because the other participant in the conversation (Sandile) is included as part of the subject. cf. **sisebenza naye** 'I work with him or her,' or, 'We work with him or her.') [pres, partic, persistive]

kwezwakala there was audible [rem past]

esememezela (s)he is now announcing [pres, partic, exclusive; < **e-** SC + **-s-** already, now + **-e-** SC + **-memezela**]

-memezel-a shout for, proclaim loudly , announce [v-appl]

-memez-a shout, call out (to) [v.i. & t.]

selizosuka it, (s)he will soon depart [fut, exclusive]

waphendula (s)he answered [rem past]

echaza (s)he explains [pres, partic]

kwakumi ngomumo it was in order [idiom; lit. it stood in character)

  kwakumi it was standing [rem past stative]

  ngomumo normally (lit. by state, by characteristic) [instr adv]

    umumo state, characteristic [n Cl. 3; < **-m-** stand]

kulowomzila to, from, in that broad track [loc]

  lowomzila that broad track [dem phr Cl. 3]

    mzila [< **umzila** broad track [n Cl. 3]]

owawuzohamba on which would travel [rel Cl. 3]

  wawuzohamba it would travel, it would give access to travel [rem past fut]

«8»

ngalesosenzo by that action [instr adv phr]

  lesosenzo that action [dem phr Cl. 7]

    isenzo act, action, deed [n Cl. 7; pl **izenzo**; < **-enz-** do, act]

sabo their, of theirs [poss Cl. 7]

ukwenza isiqiniseko to make sure [vn phr, Cl. 15]

  -enz-a isiqiniseko make sure [v phr]

    isiqiniseko surety, guarantee, certainty, conviction [n Cl. 7; < **-qinisek-** be proved true, be fulfilled]

lizohamba it will travel [fut]

ngokuphepha safely, in safety, securely [instr adv]

nangaphandle and without, and outside [assoc adv]

kokuphazamiseka of being disturbed [poss Cl. 17]

lize until it [aux, subjunc]

lifike it, (s)he should arrive [subjunc]

kuleyondawo to, from, at, in that place [loc]

  leyondawo that place [dem phr Cl. 9]

eliphikelele kuyo where it was headed [ind rel of plain loc rel, Cl. 5]

eliphikelele that/which was headed [rel Cl. 5]

  liphikelele it is headed [past, conjoint]

    -phikelel-a persist, persevere [v-perfective]

      -phik-a be obstinate; argue, compete; deny, contradict, repudiate [v.i. & t.]

  kuyo to it, him, her [loc]

abalawuli bamabhanoyi air-traffic controllers [n phr Cl. 2]

  bamabhanoyi of airplanes [poss Cl. 2]

basebenzisa they use [pres, conjoint]

i-radar [n Cl. 9a] {Eng}

okuyiyona which is what, which is the thing [rel Cl. 17]

  yiyona it is it, him, her [ident cop, pres]

ekhombisa that/which shows [rel Cl. 9]

  ikhombisa it, (s)he shows [pres, conjoint]

    -khombis-a point out, show [v-caus; the caus ext is here used idiomatically]

sekufanele it is now necessary [aux, stative, exclusive]

ehlele (s)he should descend
[subjunc; < Ø- SC + -ehlel-e]
-ehlel-a descend to(wards),
come or go down to(wards),
come down upon, happen to [v-
appl]
asuke (s)he should leave [subjunc]
kuleso naleso from, to this or that
[loc phr]
    leso naleso this or that (lit. that
    or that) [dem phr Cl. 7]
    naleso and that [assoc adv]
s i k h u m u l o sezindiza   [<
    isikhumulo sezindiza airport [n
    phr Cl. 7; pl izikhumulo
    zezindiza]]
kungenamigwaqo there are no
roads [assoc cop, pres, partic,
neg]
neziphawu and signs [assoc adv]
    iziphawu signs [n Cl. 8; sg
    isiphawu]
esibhakabhakeni in the sky [loc]
    isibhakabhaka sky [n Cl. 7]
babeka they place, they put [pres,
conjoint]
kithina to, from, at, on us [loc]

«9»

uwenze you should do it [subjunc]
kwezingqinamba of weakness of
the knees, of nervousness [poss
Cl. 17]
    izingqinamba weakness of the
    knees, nervousness [n Cl. 10; the
    sg ingqinamba and pl have the
    same meaning]
ufunde you should learn [subjunc]
ngaphansi kwesimo under con-
dition(s) [instr adv phr]

kwesimo of condition, status
[poss Cl. 17]
esibucayi unpleasant, uncomfortable [rel Cl. 7]
    -bucayi unpleasant, uncom-
    fortable [rel stem; < ubucayi
    uncomfortable position, fix,
    dilemma]
uzethembe you should believe in
yourself [subjunc]
ujwayele you should get used to
[subjunc]
ngokubambisana by cooperating,
through cooperation [instr adv]
isazimisele (s)he is still determined [stative, persistive]
ngokuqhubeka by continuing
[instr adv]
    ukuqhubeka to continue, to
    proceed, to carry on [vn Cl. 15]
igcine (s)he should end up
[subjunc]
isikwazi (s)he already knows
[pres, partic, exclusive]
nezindiza even airplanes, also
airplanes [assoc adv]
ezihambela that/which are
traveling to [rel Cl. 10]
    zihambela they are traveling to
    [pres, conjoint]
phesheya kwezilwandle overseas
(lit. on the other side of seas)
[loc phr]
    phesheya kwa- on the other side
    of, across [loc phr]
    izilwandle seas, oceans [n Cl.
    10a; the prefix izi- is super-
    imposed on the pref (u)lw- of
    Cl. 11; sg ulwandle Cl. 11]
Mzoneli (surname) [n Cl. 1a]

Abesimame abenza imisebenzi okwakungeyabesilisa

«1»
Ngesikhathi iningi labesimame abasebasha likhetha imisebenzi yezokwelapha nezomthetho, abesimame abase-Pretoria West College of Technology bathola ukuthi nemisebenzi yezobunjiniyela iyabudinga ubuhlakani.

«2»
Abantu besimame abasebancane benza izifundo zobunjiniyela e-Pretoria West College of Technology. Lelikolishi lisanda kukhipha intokazi yokuqala yomdabu ephumelele emsebenzini wokuba ngumakhenikha (fitter and turner). Abanye abafundi besimame benza izifundo emikhakheni efana ne-electronics, civil engineering kanye ne-mechanical engineering.

Kunabafundi besimame ababalelwa ku-200 kulelikolishi, nokwenza babe ngu-11% ekolishi lonke.

«3»
"Nakuba lesibalo singabukeka sisincane, linyukile inani labantu besimame kuleminyaka emihlanu eyedlule," kusho uJudy Ferreira, ongumxhumanisi aphinde abe nguthisha kulelikolishi. "Izinto eziletha abantu besilisa emkhakheni wezobunjiniyela ziyabathinta nabo abantu besimame.

"Uma sethula sazisa ikolishi ngokuvakashela ezikoleni, asehlukanisi phakathi kwabantu besilisa nabesimame. Ukungena emkhakheni wezobunjiniyela akuyi ngobulili, kodwa kuya ngekhono lomuntu.

«4»
"Ngikholwa wukuthi akukho okuvimbe abantu besimame ekutheni baphumelele kulokho abakufisayo. Abantu besimame bano-kuzimisela okukhulu."

U-Minah Sono (21) [oneminyaka engu-21] ongowokuqala kubafundi besimame abamnyama ukuphumelela ekubeni ngu-fitter and turner, wathi: "Iyangithokozisa impumelelo yami, kodwa ngifisa nabanye abantu besimame balandele ezinyathelweni zami. Lomkhakha akusiwo owabantu besilisa kuphela.

«5»
"Yimi kuphela ekhaya umntwana owakhula nobaba owenza umsebenzi wokushisela izinsimbi. Ngangikuthokozela ukumsiza uma esebenza. Esikoleni ngangenza i-technical drawing kanye nesifundo se-welding, nokwangenza ngathanda ukwenza izifundo zobunjiniyela."

Babili kuphela abantu besimame ekilasini akulo, kodwa uMinah akumkhubazi nakancane ukufunda nabantu besilisa. "Umama wami wayengahambisani nokuthi ngenze lomsebenzi. Wayefuna ngenze izifundo zezokwelapha ngesizathu sokuthi wayekholwa wukuthi zifanele umuntu wesimame. Nganqaba, ngafuna ukufeza iphupho lami."

«6»

URebecca Maitsapo (22) [oneminyaka engamashumi amabili nambili] ugxile kakhulu kweze-turner. "Ngesikhathi ngikhula ngangidlala imidlalo yabafana, njengebhola lezinyawo. Angizange ngizithathe izifundo zezokwelapha ngoba angithandi ukusebenza nabantu. Ngingumuntu othandayo ukusebenzisa ingqondo ezintweni ezifana nemishini futhi ngizenze zisebenze."

U-Moira Kgopane, owenza izifundo ze-instrumentation (ebandakanya ukusebenzisa izinto ezisetshenziselwa ukulawula i-pressure, izinto ezihambayo kanye nezithinta izinga lemikhiqizo emafemini), wathi: "Yinye kuphela into ebalulekile ngezobunjiniyela – ngeke uhlale ungasebenzi. Ungakwazi nokuzisebenza. Ngingu-bufakazi bokuthi indawo yomuntu wesimame ayikho ekhishini."

«7»

U-Charmaine Phega (22) wenza izifundo ze-electrical engineering. "Eminyakeni eyishumi eyedlule, ngangizibuza ukuthi kwenziwa yini abantu abahlala emakhaya bangabi nawo ugesi, kodwa bebe benawo abasemadolobheni," kusho lentokazi. "Ngangizimisele ngokwenza okuthile uma sengikhulile, kodwa ugogo nomkhulu babenga-hambisani nalokho ngoba babezimisele ngokuba ngibe ngudokotela.

"Kodwa ke ngangizimisele ngokwenza okuthile okungaba yinselelo kimina. Ngangazi ukuthi ezobunjiniyela kwakungumsebenzi wabantu besilisa odinga amandla. Nginawo amandla adingekayo." Kubukeka sengathi abantu abesimame abathanda umsebenzi ofana nezobunjiniyela banawo umdlandla, futhi bangaphumelela ezimakethe zomsebenzi.

Indaba nezithombe ngu: Bongani Hlatshwayo

Vocabulary

abenza who do [rel Cl. 2]
  benza they are doing, making [pres, conjoint]
okwakungeyabesilisa that/which were ones for males [rel Cl 17]

kwakungeyabesilisa they were those for males [ident cop, rem past pres]
ngeyabesilisa they are those for males [ident cop, pres]
  eyabesilisa [poss pron Cl. 4]

yabesilisa of males [poss Cl. 4]
abesilisa males [poss pron Cl. 2; sg owesilisa]
besilisa of the masculine gender or sex [poss Cl. 2]
isilisa menfolk, male-kind [n Cl. 7]

«1»
labesimame of women [poss Cl. 5]
abasebasha who are still young [rel Cl. 2]
basebasha they are still young [descr cop, pres, persistive]
basha they are young [descr cop, pres]
yezokwelapha of healing (i.e. nursing, or medicine) [poss Cl. 4]
ezokwelapha health sciences, those (studies) of healing [poss pron Cl. 8]
zokwelapha of healing, health [poss Cl. 8]
ukwelapha healing, to heal, to cure, to treat [vn Cl. 15]
-elaph-a heal, cure, treat [v.t.]
nezomthetho and of law [assoc adv]
abase-Pretoria West College of Technology who are at the Pretoria West College of Technology [rel Cl. 2]
base-Pretoria West College of Technology they are at the Pretoria ... [loc cop, pres]
bathola they find [pres, conjoint]
yezobunjiniyela in (of) engineering [poss Cl. 4]
ezobunjiniyela (those (studies) of) engineering [poss pron Cl. 8]
zobunjiniyela of engineering [poss Cl. 8]

ubunjiniyela engineering [n Cl. 14] {Eng}
iyabudinga they require it [pres, disjoint]
-bu- it [OC Cl. 14]

«2»
abasebancane who are still few in number; who are still little or small [rel Cl. 2]
basebancane there are still few of them, they are still small [descr cop, pres, persistive]
bancane there are few of them, they are small [descr cop, pres]
lelikolishi this college [dem phr Cl. 5]
ikolishi college [n Cl. 5; var ikholishi, ikholiji]
lisanda kukhipha it, (s)he has just produced [aux v phr]
lisanda it, (s)he has just VERBed [aux, pres, conjoint]
intokazi young woman [n Cl. 9]
yokuqala first [poss Cl. 9]
yomdabu native, indigenous, aboriginal [poss Cl. 9]
umdabu origin [n Cl. 3]
ephumelele who succeeded [rel Cl. 9]
iphumelele (s)he succeeded [stative]
emsebenzini in the job [loc]
wokuba of being [poss Cl. 3]
ukuba ngumakhenikha to be(come) a mechanic [ident cop, inch, vn phr Cl. 15]
ngumakhenikha it, (s)he is a mechanic [ident cop, pres]
umakhenikha mechanic [n Cl. 1a] {Eng}
emikhakheni in directions or fields (as of study, knowledge) [loc]

imikhakha directions, fields [n Cl. 4; sg **umkhakha**]

efana such as, like, that/which resemble [rel Cl. 4]

ifana they resemble, they are like, they are similar [pres, conjoint]

ne-electronics with, and, also electronics [assoc adv]

i-electronics [n Cl. 9a] {Eng}

kunabafundi there are students [assoc cop, pres]

ababalelwa who number, who are counted [rel Cl. 2]

babalelwa they are numbered, they are counted [pres, conjoint]

ku-200 at 200 [loc]

kulelikolishi at this college [loc]

nokwenza and to constitute, and to make [assoc adv]

babe ngu-11% they should be 11% [ident cop, inch, subjunc]

babe they should become [subjunc]

ngu-11% it is, they are 11% [ident cop, pres]

ekolishi to, from, at, in college [loc]

lonke all, the whole [quant Cl. 5]

lo- [quant conc Cl. 5]

«3»

lesibalo this figure, this number [dem phr Cl. 7; < le + isibalo]

sibalo [< isibalo]

singabukeka it, (s)he can be considered, can be regarded as, may seem [pres, potential]

-bukek-a seem, be considered, be regarded (as) [v-neut]

sisincane it is small [descr cop, pres, partic]

linyukile it, (s)he has risen, has gone up [past, disjoint]

inani number [n Cl. 5]

kuleminyaka during, in these years [loc]

leminyaka these years [dem phr Cl. 4]

uJudy Ferreira (name) [n phr Cl. 1a]

ongumxhumanisi who is the public relations officer [rel Cl. 1]

ungumxhumanisi (s)he is a public relations officer [ident cop, pres]

umxhumanisi public relations officer [n Cl. 1; < -xhumanis- cause to link up]

aphinde abe nguthisha and who also became a teacher [aux v phr]

aphinde and (s)he also [aux, subjunc]

abe nguthisha and (s)he became a teacher, (s)he should bec a teacher [ident cop, inch, subjunc]

abe (s)he should become [copula, subjunc]

nguthisha (s)he, it is a teacher [ident cop, pres]

uthisha teacher [n Cl. 1a] {Eng}

eziletha that/which bring [rel Cl. 10]

ziletha they bring [pres, conjoint]

emkhakheni in the field [loc; < umkhakha]

wezobunjiniyela of engineering [poss Cl. 3]

ziyabathinta they influence (lit. touch) them [pres, disjoint]

sethula we present (for information) [pres, partic]

-ethul-a present (for information) [v.t.]

sazisa we make known, we advertise [pres, conjoint]

137

ngokuvakashela by visiting [instr adv]

ukuvakashela to visit (v.t.) [vn Cl. 15]

-vakashel-a visit (v.t.) [v-appl]

asehlukanisi we do not differentiate [pres, neg]

-ehlukanis-a differentiate, distinguish [v-recip-caus; var **-hlukanis-, -ahlukanis-**]

-ehlukan-a bec different [v.inch; var **-ahlukan-, -hlukan-**]

nabesimame and females [assoc adv]

ukungena to enter [vn Cl. 15]

akuyi it does not go [pres, neg]

ngobulili according to sex or gender [instr adv]

kuya it goes [pres, conjoint]

ngekhono according to ability [instr adv]

ikhono skill, dexterity, ability [n Cl. 5]

lomuntu of a person [poss Cl. 5]

«4»

ngikholwa I believe [pres, conjoint]

akukho okuvimbe there is nothing that prevents [exist cop, pres, neg]

okuvimbe that that prevents [rel Cl. 17]

kuvimbe it prevents [past, conjoint]

ekutheni that [conj]

baphumelele they should succeed [subjunc]

abakufisayo that/which they desire [rel Cl. 2]

bayakufisa they wish it, they desire it [pres, disjoint]

banokuzimisela they have determination [assoc cop, pres]

ukuzimisela determination [n Cl. 15]

okukhulu great [adj Cl. 15]

uMinah (name) [n Cl. 1a]

Sono (surname) [n Cl. 1a]

(21) oneminyaka engu-21 who is 21 years old [rel Cl. 1]

ongowokuqala who was (lit. is) the first one [rel Cl. 1]

ungowokuqala (s)he is the first one [ident cop, pres]

owokuqala the first one [poss pron Cl. 1]

kubafundi to, from, among students [loc]

bafundi students [< **abafundi**]

ukuphumelela to succeed [vn Cl. 15]

ekubeni in becoming [loc]

ngu-fitter and turner (s)he is a fitter and turner [ident cop]

u-fitter and turner [n Cl. 1a]

iyangithokozisa it makes me happy [pres, disjoint]

-thokozis-a make happy, gladden [v-caus]

impumelelo success [n Cl. 9; < **-phumelel-** succeed]

nabanye also other(s) [assoc adv]

balandele they should follow [subjunc]

ezinyathelweni in the steps [loc; < **izinyathelo**]

zami my [poss Cl. 8]

lomkhakha this field, this direction [dem phr Cl. 3]

umkhakha field, direction [n Cl. 3]

akusiwo owabantu it is not one of people [ident cop, pres, neg]

-si- [neg cop pref]

owabantu one of people [poss pron Cl. 3]

wabantu of people [poss Cl. 3]

«5»

owakhula who grew up [rel Cl. 1]
  wakhula (s)he grew up [rem past]
nobaba with, also, even a father; and mister [assoc adv]
  ubaba (my) father; mister [n Cl. 1a]
owenza who does, who makes [rel Cl. 1]
wokushisela of forging [poss Cl. 3]
  ukushisela to forge, to burn for [vn Cl. 15]
  -shisel-a forge; burn for [v-caus-appl]
izinsimbi metals [n Cl. 10; sg **insimbi** iron, metal; bell]
ngangikuthokozela I was happy about it [rem past pres]
ukumsiza helping him or her, to help him or her [vn Cl. 15]
esebenza (s)he works [pres, partic]
ngangenza I did, I was doing [rem past pres]
i-technical drawing [n Cl. 9a] {Eng}
nesifundo and, with the subject [assoc adv]
se-welding of welding [poss Cl. 7]
  i-welding [n Cl. 9a]
nokwangenza and which made me [assoc adv phr]
  okwangenza that which made me [rel Cl. 17]
  kwangenza it made me [rem past]
ngathanda to like (lit. and I liked) [narr]
babili there are two [descr cop; < **ababili** minus initial vowel]
akulo in which (s)he is [ind rel of plain loc rel, Cl. 1; < **a-** which (s)he [ind rel conc Cl. 1] + **ku-**

in [loc pref] + **lo** it [abs pron Cl. 5]]
akumkhubazi it doesn't intimidate or disable her/him, or make her/ him ineffective [pres, neg]
  -khubal-a get hurt, damaged, injured, disabled; be disappointed; be ineffective, fail [v.i.]
nakancane in the slightest, in the least, even a little (found after negative verbs) [assoc adv]
  kancane a little, somewhat, a bit; slowly [adv]
wayengahambisani (s)he did not go along with [rem past pres, neg]
ngenze I should do or make [subjunc]
wayefuna (s)he wanted [rem past pres]
zezokwelapha of health, of healing [poss Cl. 8]
ngesizathu for the reason [instr adv]
wayekholwa (s)he believed [rem past pres]
zifanele they suit, they fit, they are appropriate to [stative]
  -fanel-a bec suitable (for), bec fitting, bec appropriate (for, to) [v.inch; v.i. & t.]
nganqaba I rejected (that) [rem past]
  -nqab-a refuse, reject [v.i. & t.]
ngafuna and I wanted [narr]
iphupho dream [n Cl. 5; < **-phuph-** dream]

«6»

uRebecca (name) [n Cl. 1a]
Maitsapo (surname) [n Cl. 1a] {Sotho/Tswana}
(22) oneminyaka engamashumi amabili nambili who is 22 years old [rel Cl. 1]

engamashumi amabili nambili twenty-two [rel phr Cl. 4]

ingamashumi amabili nambili there are twenty-two [ident cop, pres]

amashumi amabili nambili twenty-two (lit. two tens and two) [n phr Cl. 6]

amashumi amabili twenty (lit. two tens)

nambili and two [assoc adv]

-mbili two [adj Cl. 9 minus initial vowel]

ugxile (s)he was determined, (s)he stood firm [past, conjoint]

kweze-turner in those (studies) of a turner [loc]

eze-turner those (studies) of a turner [poss pron Cl. 8]

i-turner trade of a turner [n Cl. 9a]

ngikhula I am growing up [pres, partic]

ngangidlala I used to play [rem past pres]

imidlalo games, sports [n Cl. 4; sg **umdlalo**; < **-dlal-** play]

yabafana of boys [poss Cl. 4]

njengebhola lezinyawo such as football, soccer [compar adv phr]

ibhola lezinyawo football, soccer (lit. ball of feet) [n phr Cl. 5]

lezinyawo of feet [poss Cl. 5]

ngizithathe I took them, I should take them [subjunc]

angithandi I do not like [pres, neg]

ngingumuntu I am a person [ident cop, pres]

othandayo who likes, who loves [rel Cl. 1]

uyathanda (s)he likes, loves [pres, disjoint]

ukusebenzisa to use, using, to employ (i.e. use), employment [vn Cl. 15]

ezifana such as, like, that/which resemble [rel Cl. 10]

zifana they resemble, they are like [pres, conjoint]

nemishini with, and, even, also machines [assoc adv]

imishini machines [n Cl. 4; sg **umshini**] {Eng}

ngizenze I should make them [subjunc]

zisebenze they should work [subjunc]

uMoira (name) [n Cl. 1a]

Kgopane (surname) [n Cl. 1a] {Sotho/Tswana}

ze-instrumentation of instrumentation [poss Cl. 8]

i-instrumentation [n Cl. 9a]

ebandakanya that/which involves [rel Cl. 9]

ibandakanya it involves [pres, conjoint]

ezisetshenziselwa that/which are used or employed for [rel Cl. 10]

zisetshenziselwa they are used or employed for [pres, conjoint]

-setshenziselw-a be used for, be employed for [v-caus-appl-pass; < **-sebenzisel-w-a**; b ... -w- > tsh ... -w-]

i-pressure [n Cl. 9] {Eng}

izinto ezihambayo moving things (i.e. moving parts of machinery)

ezihambayo that/which move [rel Cl. 10]

ziyahamba they travel, they go [pres, conjoint]

izinga lemikhiqizo level of production [n phr Cl. 5]

lemikhiqizo of production [poss Cl. 5]

yinye there is one [descr cop, pres]

yinye one [enum Cl. 9]
yi- [enum conc Cl. 9]
ebalulekile that/which is important [rel Cl. 9]
ibalulekile it is important [stative]
ngezobunjiniyela about engineering [instr adv phr]
uhlale you should continue [aux, subjunc]
ungasebenzi you (are) not working [pres, partic]
ungakwazi you would be able [pres, potential]
nokuzisebenza also to work for yourself [assoc adv]
ukuzisebenza to work for yourself [vn Cl. 15; var **ukuzisebenzela**]
ngingubufakazi I am witness, I am evidence [ident cop, pres]
ubufakazi evidence, witness, testimony [n Cl. 14]
bokuthi of that [poss Cl. 14]
ayikho ekhishini it is not in the kitchen [loc cop, pres, neg]
ayikho it is not there [loc cop; may also introduce an exist cop]
ekhishini in the kitchen [loc] {Eng}
ikhishi kitchen [n Cl. 5; back-formation from the locative]

«7»
uCharmaine (name) [n Cl. 1a]
Phega (surname) [n Cl. 1a]
ze-electrical engineering of electrical engineering [poss Cl. 8]
i-electrical engineering [n Cl. 9a]
ngangizibuza I used to wonder, I asked myself [rem past pres]
-zi-buz-a wonder, ask oneself [v-refl]

kwenziwa yini what causes (lit. it is caused by what)
yini by what [agent adv]
abahlala who stay, who live [rel Cl. 2]
bahlala they stay, they live [pres, conjoint]
bangabi nawo ugesi they should not have electricity [assoc cop, inch, subjunc, neg]
bangabi they should not be(come) [copula, subjunc, neg]
nawo with it [assoc adv]
bebe benawo they had it [assoc cop, past pres, partic]
bebe they PAST [aux, partic; < **be-** SC + **-be** aux stem]
benawo they have it [assoc cop, pres, partic]
abasemadolobheni urban-dwellers, those who are in towns [poss pron Cl. 2]
basemadolobheni they are of towns [poss Cl. 2]
lentokazi this young lady [dem phr Cl. 9]
ngokwenza about doing [instr adv]
okuthile something [rel Cl. 17]
sengikhulile I am already grown up [stative, exclusive]
ugogo (my) grandmother [n Cl. 1a]
nomkhulu and my grandfather [assoc adv]
umkhulu (my) grandfather [n Cl. 1a]
babengahambisani they did not go along [rem past pres, neg]
nalokho with that [assoc adv]
babezimisele they were determined [rem past stative]
ngokuba that [conj]
ngibe ngudokotela I should become a doctor [ident cop, inch, subjunc]

ngibe I should become [copula, subjunc]

ngudokotela it, (s)he is a doctor [ident cop, pres]

okungaba yinselelo that/which would be a challenge [rel Cl. 17]

kungaba yinselelo it would or could be a challenge [ident cop, inch, pres, potential]

yinselelo it is a challenge [ident cop, pres]

inselelo challenge [n Cl. 9; no pl.; var **inselele**]

kimina to, from, at, on me [loc]

ngangazi I knew [rem past pres]

kwakungumsebenzi it was a job, it was work [ident cop, rem past pres]

odinga that/which requires, that/which needs [rel Cl. 3]

udinga it requires, it needs [pres, conjoint]

nginawo I have it [assoc cop, pres]

adingekayo that/which is needed or required [rel Cl. 6]

ayadingeka it is (or, they are) needed, it is (or, they are) required [pres, disjoint]

kubukeka it seems [pres, conjoint]

abathanda who like, who love [rel Cl. 2]

bathanda they like, love [pres, conjoint]

ofana such as, like, that/which resembles [rel Cl. 3]

nezobunjiniyela and, with, also, even engineering [assoc adv]

banawo they have it [assoc cop, pres]

umdlandla enthusiasm, keenness [n Cl. 3]

bangaphumelela they can, could, would succeed [pres, potential]

ezimakethe in the markets [loc]

izimakethe markets [n Cl. 10a; sg **imakethe** Cl 9a] {Eng}

zomsebenzi of jobs [poss Cl. 10]

Bongani (name) [n Cl. 1a]

Hlatshwayo (surname) [n Cl. 1a]

Zivikele Kumalaleveva

«1»
Isifo sikamalaleveva siyingxenye yalezozifo esezibhubhise iningi labantu. Ngonyaka, bangaphezu kuka-500 million abantu abaphathwa yilesisifo – u-90% wabo uliqhamukisa emazweni ase-Afrika. Abangu-750 000 balahlekelwa yizimpilo zabo ngonyaka ngenxa yaso – kulesosibalo u-85% uliqhamukisa emazweni ase-Afrika.

«2»
Kwelase-South Africa, sesiyanda kakhulu isibalo sabantu ababulawa yilesifo. Ngokwezibalo ezikhishwe yi-Communicable Disease Control of the Department of Health, balinganiselwa ku-23 282 abantu ababenomalaleveva ngonyaka odlule, kulesosibalo abangu-158 badlula emhlabeni.

«3»
Isizathu esiyimbangela yokuthi lesibalo sikhuphuke kangaka, yisimo sezulu esihlala siguquguquka zikhathi zonke kulezozindawo okudlange kuzo lesifo kanti nokuntuleka kwemithi yokuzivikela kwenza isimo sibe muncu kakhulu. Okunye okwenza lesibalo sikhule kakhulu, wukuthutheleka kwabantu abaliqhamukisa kwamanye amazwe nabavela kulawomazwe ase-Afrika anesibalo esikhulu sabantu asebephethwe ngumalaleveva. Labobantu bathwala lesifo basilethe e-South Africa. Enye inkinga wukuthi labantu abaliqhamukisa kulawomazwe anabantu abanalesifo kakhulu, bathwala o-mosquito abasuke becashe ezimpahleni zabo noma ezintweni zokuhamba nokuyaye kuthi uma sebefikile e-South Africa, lezilwanyazana zithole ithuba lokuphumela ngaphandle zithelele abantu ngalesifo.

«4»
NGABE UYINI UMALALEVEVA?

Umalaleveva ungesinye salezozifo ezithathelana kakhulu emhlabeni kanti lesifo simandla kulezozindawo ezinamazinga okushisa aphezulu kakhulu. Lesisifo abantu basithola uma belunywe ngu-mosquito wesifazane. O-mosquito besilisa abawuthwali umalaleveva.

«5»
NGABE UMALALEVEVA UDALWA YINI?

Uhlobo lukamalaleveva oluyingozi kakhulu ludalwa yisinambuzane esibizwa ngokuthi yi-Plasmodia falciparum. Lesinambuzane sidinga izinto ezimbili ezehlukene ukuze sizalele kahle – lezozinto kuba ngumuntu no-mosquito. Lesinambuzane singena kumuntu emva

143

kokuba elunywe ngu-mosquito wesifazane onalesinambuzane. U-mosquito umunca igazi lalowomuntu onomalaleveva, uthathe nezinambuzane ezifike ziqhubeke nokuzalela ku-mosquito. Uma lowo-mosquito usuluma omunye umuntu, izinambuzane zingena emzimbeni wakhe ngokusebenzisa amathe alowo-mosquito. Uma lezinambuzane sezingene emzimbeni womuntu olunywe ngu-mosquito, zidlulela esibindini. Emva kokukhula kwazo, zingena egazini zifike zizalane zande.

«6»

IZINDAWO EZIYINGOZI KAKHULU

Isifo sikamalaleveva sidlange ezindaweni ezikhethekile ezweni – njengase-Northern Province, Mpumalanga nasezingxenye ezithile zesifundazwe saKwaZulu-Natal. Kuyenzeka futhi ukuthi sitholakale eNorth West nakwiMolopo ne-Orange River. Akuvamile ukuthi lesifo usithole kulezozindawo ezingaphandle kwalezi esezibaliwe kanti abantu abagcina besitholile basithola emva kokulunywa ngu-mosquito osuke unaso.

«7»

IZIKHATHI EZIYINGOZI KAKHULU

Kwelase-South Africa, izinyanga eziphakathi kuka-October no-May zithathwa njengezinyanga eziyingozi kakhulu. Kungalesosikhathi lapho kuyaye kushise noma kutholakale imvula eningi kakhulu (o-mosquito besifazane bayazwana kakhulu nokuzalela ngalesosikhathi) kulezozindawo eziyingozi.

ABANTU OKUFANELE BAKUGWEME KAKHULU UKUNGENWA YILESIFO

Kunabantu okufanele bazame ukugwema ukuya kulezozindawo ezithathwa njengeziyingozi kakhulu. Kulabobantu singabala izingane ezisanda kuzalwa noma ezineminyaka engaphansi kweyisi-hlanu, abesimame abakhulelwe, yilabobantu abane-AIDS, yilabo abelashelwa umdlavuza nalabo asebekhishwe ubende (i-spleen). Labobantu abasengozini yokuphathwa yilesifo kakhulu kufanele bazame ukubonana nodokotela ukuze abanike izeluleko ngokusetshenziswa kwemithi yokunqanda umalaleveva.

«8»

IZIMPAWO ZASO

Umuntu onalesifo uba nemfiva, angqangqazele, aphathwe yikhanda, ajuluke, akhathale, aphathwe yiqolo, kuqaqambe amalungu omzimba, kubebuhlungu kwesingezansi, akhishwe isisu, angakuthandi ukudla, aphathwe yinzululwane uma emile, abe nenhliziyo encane, abe ne-jaundice kancane, akhwehlele, kuvuvukale isibindi nobende. Izimpawu zingadonsa kuze kuphele izinyanga eziyisithupha emva kokuba beshiye kuleyondawo okudlange kuyo lesisifo.

«9»

UKUZIVIKELA

UKUZIVIKELA EKULUNYWENI NGU-MOSQUITO kubaluleke kakhulu, futhi kuyasiza, uma ufuna ukuphepha kumalaleveva. Ukuzivikela ekulunyweni ngu-mosquito kufanele kusetshenziswe kakhulu kulezozindawo eziyingozi kakhulu. O-mosquito abanomalaleveva baziphilisa ngokudla kusukela ekuseni kuze kube sebusuku. Nakhu okufanele ukwenze ukuze uphephe kulesisifo:

«10»

• Uma kungenzeka, zama ukuba sendlini ekuseni nantambama.
• Uma kwenzeka uphumela ngaphandle ebusuku, gqoka izingubo ezinemikhono emide, amabhulukwe amade namasokisi.
• Gcoba isikhumba nezingubo ngomuthi wokuzivimbela izinambuzane. Kuphindaphinde lokho kodwa ungeqi kulesosikalo onqunyelwe sona.
• Uma kungenzeka, zama ukumboza amafasitela nezicabha ngokuzovimbela o-mosquito ukuba bangangeni ngaphakathi endlini noma uvale ebusuku.
• Abantu abayizivakashi nabahlala ezindaweni eziyingozi kakhulu kufanele balale phansi kwe-mosquito net egcotshwe imithi yokuvimbela izinambuzane. Leyomithi itholakala ezitolo nasemakhemisi.
• Ungasisebenzisa i-spray sezinambuzane ezindizayo ikakhulu kulezozindawo okulalwa kuzo.
• Ungasebenzisa i-mosquito mat noma i-mosquito coil ebusuku.

«11»

Abavakashi bangasigwema lesifo ngokungayi kulezozindawo eziyingozi kakhulu noma baye kuzo uma izulu lingani kakhulu, noma uma kunesomiso futhi basebenzise imithi yokuzivikela kulesifo. Ungabuza kudokotela noma kusokhemisi ngaleyomithi esetshenziswayo ngaphambi kokuya kuleyondawo eyingozi kakhulu.

Njengoba iningi labantu abahlala kulezozindawo eziyingozi lingakunaki ukusebenzisa imithi yokuzivikela kulesifo, nakhu okungabasiza uma befuna ukwehlisa izinga lo-mosquito:

«12»

• Bangakha izindlu zabo ezindaweni eziqhelile emaxhophozini nezingenamswakama ngoba o-mosquito bayakuthanda ukuzalela kulezozindawo.

145

• Yiba nesiqiniseko sokuthi kunamapayipi athwala amanzi eduze kwendlu yakho.
• Thela imithi yokunqanda izinambuzane kulawomanzi okungelula ukuwasusa.
• Gcoba izindonga ngaphakathi ngomuthi wokubulala izinambuzane.

«13»

UKWELASHWA KWALESISIFO

Njengoba KULULA ukuthi abantu baphathwe ngumalaleveva phezu kokusebenzisa izindlela zokuzivikela, kubalulekile ukuthi uma umuntu ohlala noma obevakashele endaweni eyingozi kakhulu ephethwe wumkhuhlane abonane nodokotela ngokushesha futhi amchazele ngendawo abekuyo. Kufanele uqale ukwelashwa NGOKUSHESHA ngoba umalaleveva uyabulala uma ungasheshanga ukwelashwa!

Vocabulary

zivikele protect yourself [imper]
kumalaleveva from, against malaria [loc]
  umalaleveva malaria [n Cl. 1a] {Eng *malaria fever*}

«1»
sikamalaleveva of malaria [poss Cl. 7]
siyingxenye it is one (part) [ident cop, pres]
  ingxenye one part, one half [n Cl. 9]
yalezozifo of those diseases [poss Cl. 9]
  lezozifo those diseases [dem phr Cl. 8]
esezibhubhise that/which have already wiped out [rel Cl. 8]
  sezibhubhise they have already wiped out [past, exclusive, conjoint]
  -bhubhis-a wipe out, annihilate, kill, destroy [v-caus]
  -bhubh-a die, suffer annihilation [v.i.]

bangaphezu kuka-500 million there are more than 500 million [loc cop, pres]
  kuka-500 million of 500 million [poss Cl. 17]
  500 million [< u-500 million]
abaphathwa who suffer [rel Cl. 2]
  baphathwa they suffer [pres, conjoint]
yilesisifo from this disease [agent adv]
u-90% 90% [n Cl. 1a]
ase-Afrika of Africa [poss Cl. 6]
  se-Afrika to, from, in Africa [loc; < e-Afrika]
abangu-750 000 750,000 (of them) [rel Cl. 2]
  bangu-750 000 there are 750,000 of them [ident cop, pres]
  u-750 000 [n Cl. 1a]
balahlekelwa they lose [pres, conjoint]
yizimpilo (by) lives [agent adv]
yaso of it [poss Cl. 9]
kulesosibalo to, from that figure or

146

number [loc]

lesosibalo that figure, that number [dem phr Cl. 8]

u-85% 85% [n Cl. 1a]

«2»

kwelase-South Africa to, from, in that (country) of South Africa [loc]

    elase-South Africa that of South Africa [poss pron Cl. 5; agrees with **izwe**]

    se-South Africa to, from, in South Africa [loc]

eziyingozi dangerous [rel Cl. 8]

    ziyingozi they are dangerous [ident cop, pres]

sesiyanda is now increasing [pres, exclusive, disjoint]

ababulawa who are killed [rel Cl. 2]

    babulawa they are killed [pres, conjoint]

    -bulaw-a be killed [v-pass; var **-bulalw-a**; < **-bulal-**]

yilesifo by this disease [agent adv]

    lesifo this disease [dem phr Cl. 7; < **le** + **isifo**]

    sifo [< **isifo**]

ngokwezibalo according to the figures [instr adv; < **okwezibalo** poss pron Cl. 17; **nga-** + POSS PRON = 'according to …']

    ngokwe- according to [< **ngokwa-** + the vowel **i**; **nga-** + POSS PRON = 'according to …']

ezikhishwe that/which were brought out [rel Cl. 8]

    zikhishwe they have been brought out [past, conjoint]

yi-Communicable Disease Control of the Department of Health [agent adv]

balinganiselwa they are measured or calculated at [pres, conjoint]

-linganiselw-a be measured or calculated at [v-recip-caus-appl-pass]

-linganisel-a gauge at, weigh at, calculate at [v-recip-caus-appl]

-linganis-a measure, weigh, survey, calculate [v-recip-caus]

ku-23 282 at 23,282 [loc]

    u-23 282 [n Cl. 1a]

ababenomalaleveva who had malaria [rel Cl. 2]

    babenomalaleveva they had malaria [assoc cop, rem past pres]

abangu-158 158 (of them) [rel Cl. 2]

    bangu-158 there are 158 of them [ident cop, pres]

    u-158 [n Cl. 1a]

badlula emhlabeni they passed away (lit. they passed from earth)

    badlula they passed [rem past]

    -dlul-a emhlabeni pass away (idiom; lit. pass from earth)

«3»

esiyimbangela that/which is the cause [rel Cl. 7]

    siyimbangela it is the cause [ident cop, pres]

    yimbangela it is the cause [ident cop, pres]

sikhuphuke it should go up [sub-junc]

yisimo sezulu it is the weather [ident cop phr]

    yisimo it is the state

esihlala that/which keeps on, that/which continually [rel Cl. 7]

    sihlala it, (s)he keeps on VERBing; it, (s)he continually VERBs [aux, pres conjoint]

-hlal-a continually VERB, keep on VERBing [aux, followed by partic]

siguquguquka it is changeable, it keeps changing [pres, partic]
-guquguquk-a be changeable, keep altering, keep turning over [v-redup]
-guquk-a change, alter; turn, turn over [v.i.]

zikhathi times [< izikhathi]

okudlange kuzo where it is rife [ind rel of plain loc rel, Cl. 17]

okudlange where there is rife [rel Cl. 17]
kudlange it is rife [past, conjoint]

nokuntuleka and the lack [assoc adv]
ukuntuleka lack, to be missing, to be required [vn Cl. 15]
-ntulek-a be missing, be lacking, be required [v.i.]

kwemithi of medicines [poss Cl. 15]
imithi medicines [n Cl. 4; sg umuthi]

yokuzivikela for protecting oneself [poss Cl. 4]
ukuzivikela to protect or defend oneself [vn Cl. 15]

kwenza it makes, it does, it causes [pres, conjoint]

sibe it should be(come) [copula, subjunc]

muncu nasty, unpleasant, unhappy; sour, bitter [rel stem]

okwenza that/which makes [rel Cl. 17]

sikhule it should grow [subjunc]

wukuthutheleka it is the increase, it is the growth [ident cop, pres]
ukuthuthuleka to increase, to grow [v-neut]
-thuthulek-a increase, grow [v.i.]

abaliqhamukisa who come from [rel Cl. 2]
baliqhamukisa they come from [pres, conjoint]

kwamanye to, from, at, in, on (the) other [loc]

nabavela and who come from [assoc adv]
abavela who come from [rel Cl. 2]
bavela they come from [pres, conjoint]

kulawomazwe from those countries [loc]
lawomazwe those countries [dem phr Cl. 6]

anesibalo that/which have a number [rel Cl. 6]
anesibalo they have a number [assoc cop, pres]

asebephethwe who are already infected [rel Cl. 2]
sebephethwe they are already infected [stative, exclusive]

ngumalaleveva by malaria [agent adv]

bathwala they carry [pres, conjoint]
-thwal-a carry or wear (on the head, in the hands, on the feet) [v.t.; inch]

basilethe and they bring it [subjunc]

labantu these people [dem phr Cl. 2; < la + abantu]

anabantu who have people [rel Cl. 6]
anabantu they have people [assoc cop, pres]

abanalesifo who have this disease [rel Cl. 2]
banalesifo they have this disease [assoc cop, pres]

o-mosquito mosquitoes [n Cl. 2b; sg u-mosquito; the Zulu word is umiyane Cl. 1a] {Eng}

becashe they have hidden [past, partic, conjoint]
ezimpahleni in luggage [loc]
zokuhamba for travel [poss Cl. 10]
nokuyaye kuthi and what sometimes happens [assoc adv phr]
  nokuyaye and what sometimes [assoc adv phr]
  okuyaye that which sometimes [rel Cl. 17]
kuthi it happens that [pres, conjoint]
sebefikile they have already arrived [past, exclusive, disjoint]
lezilwanyazana these insects [dem phr Cl. 8]
  zilwanyazana [< izilwanyazana insects [n Cl. 8]]
zithole they find [subjunc]
ithuba opportunity, chance [n Cl. 5]
lokuphumela for coming out into [poss Cl. 5]
  ukuphumela to come out for, into [vn Cl. 15]
  -phumel-a come out for, into; go out to [v-appl]
ngaphandle outside [instr adv]
zithelele they spread among, the pour for, they scatter for [subjunc]
  -thelel-a pour for, pour onto, pour into, scatter for, spread among [v-appl-appl]
ngalesifo with this disease [instr adv phr]

«4»
ngabe uyini? what could it be?
ungesinye it is one [ident cop, pres]
  ngesinye it is one [ident cop, pres]
salezozifo of those diseases [poss phr Cl. 7]
ezithathelana contagious [rel

Cl. 8]
zithathelana they are contagious [pres, conjoint]
  -thathelan-a contract from one another, be contagious [v-appl-recip]
simandla it is strong [descr cop, pres]
  -mandla strong, powerful, mighty [rel stem; < **amandla** strength, power, might]
ezinamazinga okushisa that/which have temperatures [rel Cl. 10]
  zinamazinga okushisa they have temperatures [assoc cop, pres]
  amazinga okushisa temperatures (lit. degrees of heat) [n phr Cl. 6; sg **izinga lokushisa**]
  okushisa of heat [poss Cl. 6]
  ukushisa to be hot, to burn, heat [vn Cl. 15]
aphezulu high, that/which are high [rel Cl. 6]
  aphezulu they are on top, they are above [loc cop, pres]
basithola they get it [pres, conjoint]
belunywe they have been bitten [past, partic, conjoint]
  -lunyw-a be bitten, be stung [v-pass; < **-lum-w-a**; mw > nyw]
  -lum-a bite, sting [v.t.]
ngu-mosquito by a mosquito [agent adv]
wesifazane female [poss Cl. 1]
abawuthwali they do not carry it [pres, neg]

«5»
udalwa it is caused [pres, conjoint]
lukamalaleveva of malaria [poss Cl. 11]
  luka- of [poss conc Cl. 11]
oluyingozi that/which is dangerous

[rel Cl. 11]

ludalwa it is caused, it is created [pres, conjoint]

yisinambuzane by a parasite [agent adv]

isinambuzane insect, parasite (lit. small slow-moving person or animal) [n Cl. 7; < **-nambuz-** move lazily; act lethargically]

esibizwa ngokuthi yi- that/which is called ... [rel phr Cl. 7]

+ **-bizw-a ngokuthi** IDENT COP PREF ... be called ...

esibizwa that/which is called [rel Cl. 7]

sibizwa it, (s)he is called [pres, conjoint]

yi-Plasmodia falciparum it is *Plasmodia falciparum* [ident cop, pres]

lesinambuzane this parasite, this insect [dem phr Cl. 7; < **le** + **isinambuzane**]

sidinga it needs, it requires [pres, conjoint]

ezehlukene different, various [rel Cl. 10]

zehlukene they are different [stative; < **-ehlukan-** b e c different + **-i...e** [stative suff]

sizalele it should lay eggs [subjunc]

-zalel-a lay eggs; give birth for, at [v-appl]

lezozinto those things [dem phr Cl. 10]

kuba ngumuntu are a person [ident cop, inch, pres, conjoint]

kuba it becomes [copula, pres, conjoint]

no-mosquito and a mosquito [assoc adv]

singena it enters [pres, conjoint]

kumuntu to, from, on, at, into a person [loc]

elunywe (s)he has been bitten

[past, partic, conjoint]

onalesinambuzane that/which has this parasite [rel Cl. 1]

unalesinambuzane (s)he, it has this parasite [assoc cop, pres]

umunca it sucks [pres, conjoint]

-munc-a suck [v.t.; var **-muny-a**]

igazi blood [n Cl. 5]

lalowomuntu of that person [poss Cl. 5]

onomalaleveva who has malaria [rel Cl. 1]

unomalaleveva (s)he has malaria [assoc cop, pres]

uthathe (and) it takes [subjunc]

nezinambuzane also parasites, also insects [assoc adv]

ezifike that/which immediately [rel Cl. 8]

zifike they immediately [aux, pres, conjoint]

-fik-e V E R B first, V E R B immediately [aux; followed by subjunctive]

ziqhubeke they proceed, they carry on [subjunc]

nokuzalela also to lay eggs [assoc adv]

ukuzalela to lay eggs; to give birth to ... at [vn Cl. 15]

ku-mosquito in, to, from, on the mosquito [loc]

lowo-mosquito that mosquito [dem phr Cl. 1]

usuluma it then bites [pres, exclusive; note that though **u-mosquito** is a Cl. 1a noun, in this case it uses the SCs of Cl. 3. If it had been those of Cl. 1, the form would have been **useluma**]

zingena they come or go in, they enter [pres, conjoint]

emzimbeni to, from, in, on a body [loc]

ngokusebenzisa by using [instr adv]

amathe saliva, spit [n Cl. 6]

alowo-mosquito of that mosquito [poss Cl. 6]

lezinambuzane these parasites [dem phr Cl. 8]

sezingene they have already entered [past, exclusive, conjoint]

womuntu of a person [poss Cl. 3]

olunywe who has been bitten [rel Cl. 1]

ulunywe (s)he has been bitten [past, disjoint]

zidlulela they pass on to [pres, conjoint]

-dlulel-a pass on to [v-appl]

esibindini to, from, in liver [loc]

ukukhula growing, to grow (up) [vn Cl. 15]

egazini in(to), from blood [loc]

zizalane they breed prolifically [subjunc]

-zalan-a breed prolifically [v-recip]

zande and they multiply [subjunc]

«6»

eziyingozi dangerous [rel Cl. 10]

sidlange it is rife [past, conjoint]

ezikhethekile particular [rel Cl. 10]

zikhethekile they are differentiated, picked out, selected [stative]

-khethek-a be picked out, selected, differentiated, be particular [v-neut]

njengase-Northern Province such as in Northern province [compar adv phr]

iMpumalanga east; also an eastern province of South Africa [n Cl. 9; < **im-** + **-phum-a** come out + **ilanga** sun; **m + ph > mp**]

nasezingxenye and in parts [assoc adv]

sezingxenye in parts [< **ezingxenye** [loc]

ezithile certain [rel Cl. 10]

zesifundazwe of the province [poss Cl. 10]

sitholakale it is found [subjunc]

e-North West in the North West (Province) [loc]

nakwiMolopo and around the Molopo [assoc adv]

kwiMolopo at, around the Molopo (River) [loc]

iMolopo Molopo River [n Cl. 9a]

ne-Orange River and the Orange River [assoc adv]

i-Orange River (The Zulu name is **isAngqu** Cl. 7) [n Cl. 9a]

akuvamile it is not usual [stative]

usithole you should find it [subjunc]

ezingaphandle that/which are outside [rel Cl. 10]

zingaphandle they are outside [loc cop, pres]

esezibaliwe that/which have already been enumerated [rel Cl. 10]

sezibaliwe they have already been enumerated [past, exclusive, disjoint]

abagcina who end up [rel Cl. 2]

bagcina they end up [pres, conjoint]

besitholile (they) having contracted it [past, partic, disjoint]

emva kokulunywa after being bitten

ukulunywa to be bitten, stung [vn Cl. 15]

unaso it has it (the mosquito has the disease) [assoc cop, pres]

«7»
izinyanga months [n Cl. 10a]
eziphakathi kuka- (that/which are) between [rel Cl. 10]
 ziphakathi kuka- they are between [loc cop, pres]
 kuka-October of October [poss Cl. 17]
  u-October [n Cl. 1a]
no-May and May [assoc adv]
 u-May [n Cl. 1a] {Eng}
zithathwa they are taken [pres, conjoint]
njengezinyanga as months [compar adv]
kungalesosikhathi it is at that time [loc cop, pres]
kushise it is hot [subjunc]
imvula rain [n Cl. 9]
bayazwana they are much inclined to [pres, disjoint]
okufanele bakugweme what they must avoid [ind rel of plain obj rel, Cl. 17]
okufanele that which is necessary [rel Cl. 17]
 bakugweme they should avoid it [subjunc]
ukungenwa to be entered, to be invaded [vn Cl. 15]
abantu okufanele bazame people who have to try [n phr Cl. 2]
ukugwema to avoid [vn Cl. 15]
ukuya going to, to go to [vn Cl. 15]
ezithathwa that/which are taken [rel Cl. 10]
njengeziyingozi as dangerous ones [compar adv phr]
kulabobantu to, from, amongst those people [loc]
singabala we can count [pres, potential]
ezisanda who (or that/which) have just [rel Cl. 10]
 zisanda they have just [aux,

pres, conjoint]
kuzalwa to be born [< **ukuzalwa**]
e z i n e m i n y a k a engaphansi kweyisihlanu those younger than five (lit. those who have years which are under five)
 ezineminyaka who are aged (lit. who have years) [rel Cl. 10]
  zineminyaka they are aged (lit. they have years) [assoc cop, pres]
 engaphansi which are under [rel Cl. 4]
  ingaphansi they are under [loc cop, pres]
 kweyisihlanu to, from five [loc]
  eyisihlanu five (adj) [rel Cl. 4]
   iyisihlanu there are five (of them) [ident cop, pres]
    isihlanu five, a fifth [n Cl. 7]
abakhulelwe who are pregnant [rel Cl. 2]
 bakhulelwe they are pregnant (euph; lit. they have been grown for) [stative]
  -khulelw-a bec pregnant (euph) [v-appl-pass]
   -khulel-a grow for, grow towards, grow up in [v-appl]
yilabobantu they are those people [ident cop, pres]
abane-AIDS who have AIDS [rel Cl. 2]
 bane-AIDS they have AIDS [assoc cop, pres]
  i-AIDS [n Cl. 9a]
abelashelwa who are being treated for [rel Cl. 2]
 belashelwa they are being treated for [pres, conjoint]
  -elashelw-a be treated for [v-appl-pass; < **-elaphel-** + **-w-**; ph ... -w- > sh ... -w-]
   -elaphel-a treat for [v-appl]
umdlavuza cancer [n Cl. 3]

asebekhishwe who have already
had removed [rel Cl. 2]
  sebekhishwe they have already
had removed, they have already
been removed [past, exclusive,
conjoint]
ubende spleen [n Cl. 11; pl
izimbende]
i-spleen [n Cl. 9a] {Eng}
abasengozini who are in danger
[rel Cl. 2]
  basengozini they are in danger
[loc cop, pres]
  sengozini in danger [loc; <
engozini]
yokuphathwa of being infected
[poss Cl. 9]
  ukuphathwa to be infected, to
be held, to be handled [vn Cl.
15]
ukubonana na- to consult (lit. to
see one another with) [vn Cl. 15]
abanike (s)he should give them
[subjunc]
izeluleko advice [n Cl. 8; <
-elulek- advise]
ngokusetshenziswa about the use
[instr adv]
  ukusetshenziswa use, to be used
[vn Cl. 15]

«8»
izimpawo symptoms, marks,
brand-marks, birthmarks [n Cl.
10; sg **uphawo** Cl. 11; var
uphawu]
zaso its, his, her [poss Cl. 10]
onalesifo who has this disease [rel
Cl. 1]
  unalesifo (s)he has this disease
[assoc cop, pres]
uba nemfiva (s)he develops a fever
(lit. becomes with a fever) [assoc
cop, inch, pres]
  uba (s)he becomes [copula, pres

conjoint]
  nemfiva with, and, also fever
[assoc adv]
  imfiva fever [n Cl. 9] {Eng}
angqangqazele and (s)he shivers,
trembles, has the shakes [sub-
junc]
aphathwe yikhanda and (s)he gets
a headache (lit. (s)he is held by
the head)
  aphathwe and (s)he suffers
[subjunc]
  yikhanda from a headache
[agent adv]
ajuluke and (s)he sweats [subjunc]
  -juluk-a sweat, perspire [v.i.]
akhathale and (s)he gets tired
[subjunc]
yiqolo from the small of the back
[agent adv]
  iqolo small of the back [n Cl. 5]
kuqaqambe and there aches or
throbs [subjunc]
  -qaqamb-a ache, throb [v.i.]
amalungu joints [n Cl. 6; sg
ilungu Cl. 5]
omzimba of the body [poss Cl. 6]
  umzimba body [n Cl. 3]
kubebuhlungu (or **kube
buhlungu**) and there becomes
painful, and one has pain [descr
cop, inch, subjunc]
  buhlungu painful, sore [rel
stem; < **ubuhlungu** pain]
kwesingezansi in the pelvic region
[loc]
  esingezansi pelvic region (euph)
[rel Cl. 7, refers to **isiqu** root,
basis, bottom end]
  singezansi it is lower down [loc
cop, pres]
  ezansi low, on the coast, down-
country, downstairs [loc]
  izansi coastal belt, low country
[n Cl. 5]

akhishwe isisu and (s)he has diarrhea (lit. and (s)he is taken out the stomach) [subjunc]
akhishwe (s)he should be taken out, (s)he should have ... taken out [subjunc]
-khishw-a isisu have diarrhea (lit. be taken out the stomach) [vn phr Cl. 15]
isisu stomach [n Cl. 7]
angakuthandi and (s)he is not fond of it [subjunc, neg]
yinzululwane by giddiness [agent adv]
inzululwane giddiness [n Cl. 9]
emile (s)he is standing up [stative, partic, conjoint]
abe nenhliziyo encane and (s)he becomes nauseous (lit. and (s)he becomes with a small heart) [assoc cop, inch, subjunc]
inhliziyo encane nausea (lit. a small heart; the heart is considered to be the seat of nausea (and irritability)) [n phr Cl. 9]
inhliziyo heart [n Cl. 9]
encane small, little [adj Cl. 9]
abe ne-jaundice and (s)he becomes jaundiced (lit. and (s)he becomes with jaundice) [assoc cop, inch, subjunc]
akhwehlele and (s)he coughs [subjunc]
-khwehlel-a cough [v.i.]
kuvuvukale and there swells [subjunc]
-vuvukal-a swell (up) [v.i.]
nobende and spleen [assoc adv]
zingadonsa they can drag on [pres, potential]
eziyisithupha six [rel Cl. 10]
  ziyisithupha there are six of them [ident cop, pres]
beshiye they have left [past, partic, conjoint]

okudlange kuyo the place where it is rife [ind rel of plain loc rel, Cl. 17]

«9»
ekulunyweni from, in being bitten [loc; < ukulunywa]
kubaluleke it is important [past, conjoint]
kuyasiza it helps [pres, disjoint]
ukuphepha to recover, to get well [vn Cl. 15]
kusetshenziswe one should use, there should be used [subjunc]
abanomalaleveva that/which/who have or carry malaria [rel. Cl. 2]
  banomalaleveva they have or they carry malaria [assoc cop, pres]
baziphilisa they keep themselves alive [pres, conjoint]
  -zi-philis-a keep oneself alive [v-refl-caus]
  -philis-a keep alive, keep healthy, make well [v-caus]
  -phil-a live, be alive; be well, be healthy [v.i.]
ngokudla by eating [instr adv]
sebusuku at night [loc; < ebusuku]
ukwenze you must do it [subjunc]
uphephe you should escape [subjunc]

«10»
uma kungenzeka if possible
zama try [imper]
ukuba sendlini to be in the house [descr cop, vn]
  sendlini in the house [< endlini]
nantambama and in the afternoon [assoc adv]
  ntambama in the afternoon [time adv; < intambama afternoon [n Cl. 9; < -thambam-slant, decline (of sun in afternoon); n + th > nt]]

kwenzeka it happens [pres, partic]
uphumela you go out to [pres, conjoint]
gqoka wear [imper]
ezinemikhono with sleeves [rel Cl. 10]
   zinemikhono they have sleeves [assoc cop, pres]
   imikhono sleeves [n Cl. 4; sg **umkhono**]
emide long [adj Cl. 4]
amabhulukwe trousers [n Cl. 6; sg **ibhulukwe** Cl. 5]
namasokisi and socks [assoc adv]
   amasokisi socks [n Cl. 6; sg **isokisi**] {Eng}
gcoba rub, smear [imper]
isikhumba skin, hide; leather [n Cl. 7]
nezingubo and clothes [assoc adv]
ngomuthi with medicine, with ointment, with oil [instr adv]
   umuthi woku(zi)vimbela repellent [n Cl. 3]
kuphindaphinde keep repeating it [imper, with OC, Cl. 17]
   -phindaphind-a keep repeating [v-redup]
   -phind-a repeat, do again; reduplicate; return, go back [v.i. & t.]
ungeqi you should not exceed [subjunc, neg]
kulesosikalo to, from that dose [loc]
   lesosikalo that dose [dem phr Cl. 7]
   isikalo dose [n Cl. 7] {Afr *skaal* scale}
onqunyelwe sona that/which you have been set, prescribed [ind rel of plain obj rel, 2 p sg]
   unqunyelwe you have been set, you have been prescribed, you have had mapped out [past, disjoint]
   -nqunyelw-a be set, be prescribed, be allocated, be mapped out (of work), be assigned, be allocated [v-appl-pass; < **-nqumel-w-a; m ... -w- > ny ... -w-**]
   -nqumel-a set work for, map out work for, prescribe, assign to, allocate [v-appl]
   -nqum-a decide, give a decision, fix positively [v.t.]
ukumboza to screen [vn Cl. 15]
ngokuzovimbela in order to prevent [instr adv]
   ukuzovimbela to come and prevent [vn Cl. 15, venitive]
uvale you should close up [subjunc]
abayizivakashi who are visitors [rel Cl. 2]
   bayizivakashi they are visitors [ident cop, pres]
   izivakashi visitors [n Cl. 8; sg **isivakashi**; < **-vakash-** visit]
nabahlala and who stay [assoc adv]
balale they should sleep [subjunc]
i-mosquito net mosquito net [n Cl. 9a]
egcotshwe that/which has been spread [rel Cl. 9]
   igcotshwe it has been spread, greased, smeared [past, conjoint]
   -gcotshw-a be smeared, be greased, be rubbed with oil [v-pass; < **-gcobw-a; bw > tshw**]
leyomithi those medicines, those oils [dem phr Cl. 4]
   leyo those (near the addressee) [2nd pos dem Cl. 4]
   mithi [< **imithi**]
itholakala they are obtainable [pres, conjoint]
ezitolo in shops, in stores [loc; one

of the exceptions that does not take a locative suffix]
izitolo shops, stores [n Cl. 8; sg **isitolo**] {Eng}
nasemakhemisi and in pharmacies [assoc adv]
  semakhemisi in pharmacies [loc; < **emakhemisi**]
ungasisebenzisa you can use it [pres, potential]
i-spray [n Cl. 7; the **s** of 'spray' is taken as part of the noun pref **is-**]
sezinambuzane of insects, of parasites [poss Cl. 7]
ezindizayo flying [rel Cl. 8]
  ziyandiza they fly [pres, disjoint]
okulalwa kuzo in which people sleep (lit. that which there is slept in it) [ind rel of plain loc rel, Cl. 17]
  okulalwa that/which is slept [rel Cl. 17]
  kulalwa one sleeps, they sleep, there is slept [pres, conjoint]
  -lalw-a be slept [v-pass]
ungasebenzisa you can use [pres, potential]
i-mosquito mat [n Cl. 9a]
i-mosquito coil [n Cl. 9a]

«11»
abavakashi visitors [n Cl. 2; sg **umvakashi**; < **-vakash-** visit]
bangasigwema they can avoid it [pres, potential]
ngokungayi by not going [instr adv]
  ukungayi not to go, not going [vn Cl. 15, neg]
izulu lingani it is not raining (lit. the sky is not raining)
  lingani it is not raining [pres, partic]

-n-a rain [v.i.]
kunesomiso there is a drought [assoc cop, pres]
isomiso drought, dry spell [n Cl. 7; < **-omis-** bec dry (of the weather) < **-om-** dry up, bec dry]
ungabuza you can ask [pres, potential]
kudokotela from a doctor [loc]
kusokhemisi to, from a pharmacist [loc]
ngaleyomithi about those medicines [instr adv phr]
esetshenziswayo that are used [rel Cl. 4]
  iyasetshenziswa they are used [pres, disjoint]
lingakunaki it, (s)he does not notice it [pres, partic]
okungabasiza something that can help them [rel Cl. 17]
  kungabasiza it can help them [pres, potential]
ukwehlisa to lower [vn Cl. 15]
  -ehlis-a lower; go down along; reduce [v-caus]
lo-mosquito of mosquitoes [poss Cl. 5]

«12»
bangakha they can build [pres, potential]
eziqhelile that/which are remote [rel Cl. 10]
  ziqhelile they are remote [stative]
  -qhel-a bec remote [v.i.]
emaxhophozini to, from, in, at swamps [loc]
  amaxhophozi swamps [n Cl. 6; sg **ixhophozi** Cl. 5]
nezingenamswakama and that are not damp [assoc adv]
  ezingenamswakama that/which are not damp (lit. that do not

have dampness or moisture) [rel Cl. 10]

zingenamswakama they are not damp [assoc cop, pres, rel]

mswakama [< **umswakama** dampness or moisture rising from the ground [n Cl. 3; < **-swakam-** bec damp or moist]

bayakuthanda they like it [pres, disjoint]

yiba nesiqiniseko make sure, ensure, make certain (lit. become with certainty) [assoc cop, inch, imper]

yiba become [copula, imper]

yi- [stabilizer (a syllable added to a monosyllabic form to make it disyllabic. Monosyllabic forms are unusual in Zulu.)]

kunamapayipi there are pipes [assoc cop, pres]

amapayipi pipes [n Cl. 6; sg **ipayipi** Cl. 5] {Eng}

athwala that/which carry [rel Cl. 6]

athwala they carry [pres, conjoint]

eduze kwa- close to, near to [loc n + link]

kulawomanzi to, from, in, on that water [loc]

lawomanzi that water [dem phr Cl. 6]

okungelula that/which is not easy [rel Cl. 17]

ukuwasusa to remove (it) (i.e. standing water not easily drained) [vn Cl. 15]

wokubulala for killing [poss Cl. 3]

«13»

ukwelashwa treatment, to be treated, cure, to be cured [vn Cl. 15]

-elashw-a be treated, be cured [v-pass; < **-elaph-w-a**; **phw** > **shw**]

kwalesisifo of this disease [poss Cl. 15]

kulula it is easy [descr cop, pres, partic]

baphathwe they should suffer from, they should be treated, they should be handled [subjunc]

phezu kokusebenzisa in spite of the use [loc phr]

zokuzivikela of protecting oneself [poss Cl. 10]

ohlala who resides [rel Cl. 1]

uhlala (s)he resides, (s)he lives [pres, conjoint]

obevakashele who had visited [rel Cl. 1]

ubevakashele (s)he had visited [past past, conjoint]

eyingozi dangerous (lit. that is a danger) [rel Cl. 9]

ephethwe (s)he suffers from [stative, partic]

wumkhuhlane it is a cold (and fever) [agent adv]

umkhuhlane cold or cough, normally accompanied by a fever [n Cl. 3]

abonane (s)he should consult [subjunc]

amchazele and (s)he should explain to him or her [subjunc]

ngendawo about the place [instr adv]

abekuyo in or at which (s)he was [ind rel of plain loc rel, Cl. 1]

ubekuyo (s)he was at or in it [descr cop, past]

ungasheshanga if you have not quickly [past, partic]

Ayazenzela amaphoyisa endaweni yaseNkume

Mhleli

«1»

Kwelakho engilithembile ngithi ake ngizwakalise ukulila kwemizwa yami ngokwenzeka ngoFebruary ka-1996 endaweni yakithi eNkume ngaphansi kweNkosi uMpungose.

Ngalo nyaka kwenzeka into eyashaqisa umphakathi wonke waKwaMpungose kangangoba wasuka wamasha wayokhalaza kumphathi-siteshi eShowe ngesenzo samaphoyisa.

«2»

Kodwa kuze kube manje akuzwakali lutho, futhi lolu daba aluphumanga phezu kokuthi sesifuna izwe lazi ngalo.

Amaphoyisa afika ngesikhathi sasebusuku emzini waKwaNgcobo ahlukumeza umndeni wakhona kwaze kwadubuleka umnumzane wakhona, washona, kwafa nenkomo yakhe emithi.

«3»

Emva kwalokho kwasuka esinamandla kwaze kwasiza amasosha ukudambisa isimo.

Umasiteshi wethembisa uphenyo olusheshayo ngalolu daba.

Okwaba muncu kakhulu wukuthi umndeni ubese umpofu, waziphathela izindleko zokungcwaba ulekelelwa ngumphakathi.

«4»

Okucanula kakhulu wukuthi leli phoyisa elenza izimanga alazi nakwazi, liyazisebenzela njengokwejwayelekile.

Esifisa ukukwazi wukuthi lolu daba lwafika yini kumhlonishwa wezokuPhepha ubaba uNyanga Ngubane, nobaba u(Sydney) Mufamadi ngoba lapha eShowe akukho okubambekayo ngabantu ababulawa emini kwabha, kugcina kungezwakali lutho ngabo.

«5»

Sifuna lolu daba lufakelwe izibuko, abahlonishwa abaphethe kulo Mnyango balusukumele. Lo mnumzane owabulawa bekungumuntu ozihloniphayo, esebenzela umphakathi, ewakhela izindlu.

«6»

Manje izingane zakhe zincela izithupha. Ngiphethe ngokucela abafowethu nodade abayizintatheli, ikakhulu KwaZulu/Natal ukuba bazihlwaye yonke indawo izindaba, ikakhulu ezabelweni ukuze ukuhlukumezeka komphakathi kwazeke kuHulumeni.

«7»
Ngomusa wakho ngibonga ukushicilelwa kwalolu daba kuze kuqwashiseke iziphathimandla ngokuhlukunyezwa okusasetshenziswa ngamaphoyisa emakhaya.

Ngicela igama nesibongo kuhoxiswe.

Okhathazekile
ESHOWE

Vocabulary

ayazenzela they just do what they like, they act for no reason [pres, disjoint]
-z-enzel-a make for oneself, do for oneself; do for no apparent reason, just do [v-refl-appl]
yaseNkume of Nkume [poss Cl. 9]
seNkume to, from, in, Nkume [< **eNkume**]
iNkume (place) [n Cl. 9]

«1»
kwelakho in yours (newspaper is understood) [loc]
elakho yours [poss pron Cl. 5]
engilithembile in which I have faith, that/which I trust [ind rel of plain obj rel, 1 p sg]
ngilithembile I trust or have faith in it, him, her [past, disjoint]
ake please, would (you/(s)he/they) be so good as to, may (I, we, they ...) [conj; followed by subjunc]
ngizwakalise let me voice, let me express [subjunc]
-zwakalis-a make audible, make heard, voice, express [v-neut-caus]
ukulila weeping, lament [vn Cl. 15]
-lil-a weep, cry, wail, lament [v.i.]

kwemizwa of feelings [poss Cl. 15]
ngokwenzeka about what happened [instr adv]
ka-1996 of 1996 [poss Cl. 1]
uMpungose (name) [n Cl. 1a]
ngalo about it, in this [instr adv]
kwenzeka there happened [rem past]
eyashaqisa that/which shocked [rel Cl. 9]
yashaqisa it, (s)he shocked [rem past]
waKwaMpungose of KwaMpungose (Mpungose's place) [poss Cl. 3]
KwaMpungose at the place of Mpungose [loc]
kangangoba since, inasmuch as, so much so that [conj]
wasuka it was given cause [rem past]
-suk-a start or arise from some cause [v.i.]
wamasha it marched [narr]
-mash-a march [v.i.] {Eng}
wayokhalaza and it went and protested [narr, andative]
-khalaz-a complain, protest [v.i.]
kumphathi-siteshi to, from the station commander [loc]
umphathi-siteshi station

159

commander [n Cl. 1]
eShowe to, from, in Eshowe [loc]
iShowe (place) [n Cl. 5]
ngesenzo about the incident, about the act [instr adv]

«2»
akuzwakali lutho nothing is heard, nothing is said [v phr]
akuzwakali there is not heard [pres, neg]
daba serious matter [< **udaba** [n Cl. 11]]
aluphumanga it did not emerge [past, neg]
phezu kokuthi in spite of the fact that [conj phr]
sesifuna we now want [pres, exclusive]
lazi it, (s)he should know [subjunc]
afika they arrived [rem past]
sasebusuku of (at) night [poss Cl. 7]
emzini at, in, to, from the village [loc]
waKwaNgcobo of KwaNgcobo (Ngcobo's place) [poss Cl. 3]
ahlukumeza and they assaulted [narr]
wakhona local, of, from there [poss Cl. 3]
kwaze until [aux, narr]
kwadubuleka there was shot [narr]
    -dubulek-a get shot [v-neut]
wakhona local, of or from there [poss Cl. 1]
washona and (s)he died [narr]
kwafa and there died [narr]
nenkomo a cow too, also a cow [assoc adv]
    inkomo head of cattle, "cow," "beast" [n Cl. 9; < **in-** + **-khomo**; n + kh > nk]

emithi that/which is (i.e. was) in calf [rel Cl. 9]
imithi it is in calf, it is pregnant [stative; **-i** irregular stative suffix]
    -mith-a bec pregnant (used only of animals) [v.i.; var **-emith-a**]

«3»
e m v a kwalokho after that, thereafter, then [loc phr]
kwasuka there arose [rem past]
esinamandla a fierce one (it is not clear what is referred to here; possibilities are **isiphepho** or **isivunguvungu** both meaning 'gale' [rel Cl. 7]
sinamandla it is strong (lit. it has strength) [assoc cop, pres]
kwasiza there helped [narr]
amasosha soldiers [n Cl. 6; sg **isosha** Cl. 5] {Eng}
ukudambisa to cause to subside; to assuage, to calm down [vn Cl. 15]
    -dambis-a cause to subside; assuage, calm down [v-caus]
    -damb-a go down (of a swelling), subside; calm down, be allayed [v.i.]
umasiteshi station commander, chief of station [n Cl. 1a]
wethembisa (s)he promised [rem past]
uphenyo investigation, examination [n Cl. 11; pl **izimpenyo; m + ph > mp**; < **-pheny-** investigate]
olusheshayo quick, speedy [rel Cl. 11]
    luyashesha it is quick, it hurries [pres, disjoint]
ngalolu into, about, concerning this [instr adv]
okwaba muncu what was sad (lit.

160

that which became bitter) [rel
Cl. 17]
kwaba muncu it became bitter
or unpleasant [descr cop, inch,
rem past]
ubese umpofu it was already poor
[descr cop, past, exclusive]
umpofu it is poor [descr cop,
pres]
-mpofu poor [rel stem]
waziphathela they carried by
themselves, they bore for
themselves [rem past]
zokungcwaba of burying [poss Cl.
10]
ukungcwaba burying, to bury
[vn Cl. 15]
-ngcwab-a bury [v.t.]
ulekelelwa it being assisted [pres,
partic]
-lekelelw-a be assisted, be aided
[v-pass]
ngumphakathi by the community
[agent adv]

«4»
okucanula what is disgusting [rel
Cl. 17]
kucanula it disgusts, it
nauseates [pres, conjoint]
-canul-a disgust, nauseate [v.t.]
phoyisa policeman [< **iphoyisa**]
elenza who caused [rel Cl. 5]
lenza (s)he, it caused [rem past]
izimanga unbelievable events [n
Cl. 8; sg **isimanga**]
alazi nakwazi (s)he does not even
know [a neg verb followed by
na- + the infinitive form of that
verb means 'does not even';
akaphuzi nokuphuza (s)he
does not even drink;
asimthandi nokumthanda we
don't even like him or her)]
liyazisebenzela (s)he just works

[pres, disjoint]
njengokwejwayelekile as usual
[compar adv phr]
okwejwayelekile that which is
usual, normal, customary [rel
Cl. 17]
kwejwayelekile it is usual,
normal, customary [stative]
esifisa that which we wish [ind rel
of plain obj rel, 1 p pl]
sifisa we wish [pres, conjoint]
ukukwazi to know it [vn Cl. 15]
lwafika it arrived [rem past]
kumhlonishwa to the honorable
[loc]
umhlonishwa respected person,
the honorable [n Cl. 1; <
-hlonishw- be respected, be
honored, be honorable; <
-hloniph- respect, honor]
wezokuPhepha of Security
(Minister is understood here)
[poss Cl. 1]
ezokuphepha security matters
[poss pron Cl. 10]
uNyanga (male name) [n Cl. 1a]
uSydney Mufamadi (name;
former Minister of Police) [n
phr Cl. 1a]
Mufamadi (surname) [n Cl. 1a]
{Sotho}
akukho okubambekayo there is
nothing tangible [exist cop,
pres, neg]
okubambekayo that which is
tangible [rel Cl. 17]
kuyabambeka it is tangible
[pres, disjoint]
-bambek-a be held, be tangible
[v-neut]
ngabantu about people [instr adv]
babulawa they were killed [rem
past]
ababulawa who were killed [rel
Cl. 2]

kwabha in the open country, in a bare place; openly, in full view [loc; cf. **bhaa** be open, be clear, be bare [ideo]]

kugcina there ending up [aux, pres, partic]

kungezwakali there not being heard [pres, partic]

«5»

sifuna we want [pres, conjoint]

lufakelwe izibuko it should be placed under scrutiny [v phr]
  lufakelwe that it should have placed on it [subjunc]
  -fakelw-a be placed in or on, be put in or on, be installed in [v-appl-pass]
  -fakel-a place in or on, put in or on, install in [v-appl]
  izibuko spectacles, glasses, mirrors [n Cl. 8; sg **isibuko**]

abaphethe who are in charge, who manage, who run [rel Cl. 2]
  baphethe they manage, they run, they are in charge of [stative]

mnyango doorway; department [< **umnyango**]

balusukumele they must take action about it (lit. they should stand up for it) [subjunc]
  -sukumel-a stand up for, rise for [v-appl]
  -sukum-a stand up, get up [v.i.]
  -lu- it, him, her [OC Cl. 11]

mnumzane [< **umnumzane**]

owabulawa who was killed [rel Cl. 1]
  wabulawa (s)he was killed [rem past]

bekungumuntu it was a person [ident cop, past pres]

ozihloniphayo self-respecting [rel Cl. 1]

uyazihlonipha (s)he is self-respecting [pres, disjoint]

esebenzela (s)he is working for [pres, partic]

ewakhela (s)he is building for it [pres, partic]
  -akhel-a build for [v-appl]

«6»

zincela izithupha they are helpless (idiom; lit. they suck (their) thumbs)
  zincela they suck [pres, conjoint]
  -ncel-a suck [v.t.]
  izithupha thumbs [n Cl. 8; sg **isithupha**]

ngiphethe I must conclude [subjunc]

ngokucela by requesting [instr adv]
  ukucela to request, to ask for [vn Cl. 15]

abafowethu my or our brothers [n Cl. 2; sg **umfowethu**]

nodade and my sisters [assoc adv]
  odade my sisters [n Cl. 2b; sg **udade**]

abayizintatheli who are reporters, journalists [rel Cl. 2]
  bayizintatheli they are reporters, journalists [ident cop, pres]
  izintatheli reporters, journalists [n Cl. 10; sg **intatheli**; < **-thathel-** forage, gather what has been stored]

bazihlwaye they should spread them [subjunc]
  -hlway-a spread, scatter [v.t.]

yonke indawo everywhere [quant phr Cl. 9]

ezabelweni in the media [loc]
  izabelo the media [n Cl. 8; < **-abel-** distribute among]

ukuhlukumezeka the assault, the

attack, violation; to be shocked, jolted, annoyed, offended, harassed [vn Cl. 15]
-hlukumezek-a get attacked, assaulted, violated, harassed, shocked, jolted, annoyed, offended [v-neut]
komphakathi of the community [poss Cl. 15]

«7»
kwazeke it should bec known [subjunc]
-azek-a be known, be knowable [v-neut]
ngomusa with or through kindness [instr adv]
umusa kindness [n Cl. 3]
wakho your [poss Cl. 3]
ngibonga I am grateful for, I give thanks for [pres, conjoint]
ukushicilelwa the publication, to be printed [vn Cl. 15]
-shicilelw-a be printed, be published [v-pass]
-shicilel-a print, publish [v.t.]
kwalolu of this [poss Cl. 15]
kuqwashiseke they should be put on the look out, they should be alerted [subjunc]
-qwashisek-a be on the look out, be alerted [v-caus-neut]

-qwashis-a put on the look out, alert to [v-caus]
-qwash-a be on the watch [v.i.]
iziphathimandla the authorities, those in control [n Cl. 8; sg **isiphathimandla**]
ngokuhlukunyezwa about the violence, assaults, attacks [instr adv]
ukuhlukunyezwa be assaulted, be attacked, violence [vn Cl. 15]
okusasetshenziswa that/which is still used [rel Cl. 15]
kusasetshenziswa it is still used, employed [pres, persistive]
ngamaphoyisa by the police [agent adv]
emakhaya in rural areas (lit. where the homes are – in former times, the large majority of Black people lived in rural areas) [loc]
nesibongo and surname [assoc adv]
isibongo surname [n Cl. 7]
kuhoxiswe it should be withheld, it should be hidden [subjunc]
-hoxisw-a be withheld, be hidden [v-caus-pass]
-hox-a hide (v.i.), withdraw [v.i.]

Ngifuna Usisi Oyisingili[8]
Nonomoya Ophansi

Ngingumakhi wezindlu osafufuzayo ono-40; ngicela usisi oyisingili onomoya ophansi nonenhlonipho ofuna ukwakha umuzi nobhuti ongahluphi nongaphuzi.

Onengane engenayise, owadivosa, owashonelwa noyintandane ulungile uma nje enenhlonipho, ukuzithoba, angalifaki ibhulukwe, abenothando lokuba nekwakhe elihle, athande isonto, angabi owakwaNdlovu, kwaShezi, koMkhize, koMthembu, koDlamini, koShozi, Sibisi Msomi.

Nginamathalente nothando lweGospel Music, iRadio, iTV, ukubhala, ukufunda, izingane nokupheka, abanothando nozwelo.

Ngicela isithombe, sizobuya, uzichaze encwadini; ikheli: New Love Order, PO Box 706, Pinetown, 3600.

Ngicela, Mhleli, uligodle igama lami ngolisho kulabo abazongiphendula.

Okhathazekile, PINETOWN

Vocabulary

usisi young lady, lass; (my) younger sister [n Cl. 1a] {Afr *sussie* little sister}
oyisingili who is single [rel Cl. 1]
  uyisingili (s)he is single [ident cop, pres]
  isingili person who is single [n Cl. 5] {Eng}
nonomoya ophansi and who is reserved or gentle [assoc adv]
  onomoya ophansi one who is reserved or gentle (lit. has a spirit that is down)

unomoya ophansi (s)he is reserved or gentle [assoc cop]
umoya wind, air, breath, spirit, soul, personality, nature [n Cl. 3a; pl imimoya]
ngingumakhi I am a builder [ident cop, pres]
  umakhi builder [n Cl. 1; < -akh- build]
wezindlu of houses [poss Cl. 1]
osafufuzayo who is still passionate [rel Cl. 1]
  usafufuza (s)he is still passionate [pres, persistive]

---

[8] Pronounced here as **oyisingil**.

-fufuz-a act passionately, act impetuously [v-caus; < **-fuful-** + **-Y-**; l + **-Y-** > z]

-fuful-a sweep away, carry off in a rush [v.t.]

ono-40 who is forty (lit. who has 40) [rel Cl. 1]

uno-40 (s)he is forty (lit. (s)he has forty) [assoc cop, pres]

u-40 [n Cl. 1a]

nonenhlonipho and who has respect [aaoc adv]

onenhlonipho and who has respect [rel Cl. 1]

unenhlonipho (s)he has respect [assoc cop, pres]

inhlonipho respect, honor [n Cl. 9; < **-hloniph-** respect, honor]

ofuna who wants [rel Cl. 1]

nobhuti with a guy, with a chap (lit. older brother) [assoc adv]

ubhuti (my) brother [n Cl. 1a] {Afr *boetie* little brother}

ongahluphi who causes no trouble [rel Cl. 1]

ungahluphi (s)he does not cause trouble, or disturb [pres, rel, neg; < akahluphi]

nongaphuzi and who does not drink [assoc adv phr]

ongaphuzi who does not drink [rel Cl. 1]

ungaphuzi (s)he does not drink [pres, rel, neg; < akaphuzi]

onengane engenayise a single mother (lit. one with a child who has no father) [rel phr Cl. 1]

onengane who has a child [rel Cl. 1]

unengane (s)he has a child [assoc cop, pres]

owadivosa a divorcee (lit. one who got divorced) [rel Cl. 1]

wadivosa (s)he (got) divorced [rem past]

-divos-a divorce, get divorced [v.i. & t.] {Eng}

owashonelwa a widow(er) (lit. one who has been died for) [rel Cl. 1]

washonelwa (s)he was bereaved [rem past]

noyintandane and or even one who is an orphan [assoc adv phr]

oyintandane one who is an orphan [rel Cl. 1]

uyintandane (s)he is an orphan [ident cop, pres]

intandane orphan [n Cl. 9]

ulungile (s)he is OK, fine, in order [stative]

uma nje just as long as [conj phr]

enenhlonipho (s)he has respect [assoc cop, pres, partic]

ukuzithoba humility, to be humble [vn Cl. 15]

angalifaki ibhulukwe (s)he should not wear the pants

angalifaki (s)he should not put it or them on [subjunc]

ibhulukwe pair of trousers, pants [n Cl. 5] {Afr *broek*}

abenothando lokuba nekwakhe elihle (s)he should be house-proud (lit. should have a liking to have a beautiful home) [assoc cop, inch, subjunc]

abenothando (s)he should have a liking or love [assoc cop, inch, subjunc]

lokuba nekwakhe to have a home [poss Cl. 11]

ukuba nekwakhe to have a home [assoc cop, inch, vn Cl. 15]

ikwakhe a home, a place of his or her own [n Cl. 5; < **kwakhe** at his or her place]

elihle beautiful, nice [adj Cl. 5]

athande (s)he should like [subjunc]

isonto church, week; with capital 's': **iSonto** Sunday [n Cl. 5] {Afr *Sondag*}

angabi (s)he should not be(come) [copula, subjunc]

owakwaNdlovu one of the Ndlovu clan [poss pron Cl. 1]

wakwaNdlovu of Ndlovu's place [poss Cl. 1]

kwaNdlovu at Ndlovu's place [loc]

uNdlovu (surname, clan name) [n Cl. 1a]

kwaShezi the Shezi clan, Shezi's place [loc]

koMkhize the Mkhize clan, the Mkhizes' place [loc]

oMkhize the Mkhizes [n Cl. 2b; sg **uMkhize** (surname, clan name)]

koMthembu the Mthembu clan, the Mthembus' place [loc]

oMthembu the Mthembus [n Cl. 2b; sg **uMthembu** surname, clan name]

koDlamini the Dlamini clan, the Dlaminis' place [loc]

koShozi the Shozi clan, the Shozis' place [loc]

oShozi the Shozis [n Cl. 2b; sg **uShozi** surname, clan name]

Sibisi Msomi (name) refers here to the Sibisi Msomi clan [n Cl. 1a]

uSibisi (name) [n Cl. 1a]

uMsomi (surname, clan name) [n Cl. 1a]

nginamathalente I am talented (lit. I have talents) [assoc cop, pres]

amathalente talents [n Cl. 6; sg. **ithalente** Cl. 5] {Eng}

nothando and love [assoc adv]

lweGospel Music of gospel music [poss Cl. 11]

i-gospel music [n Cl. 9a]

iradio radio [n Cl. 9a]

iTV TV [n Cl. 9a]

ukubhala writing, to write [vn Cl. 15]

nokupheka and cooking [assoc adv]

abanothando those who are loving (lit. who have love) [rel Cl. 2]

banothando they are loving, they have love or a liking [assoc cop, pres]

nozwelo and sensitivity [assoc adv]

uzwelo sensitivity [n Cl. 11; < **-zwel-** be sensitive]

sizobuya it will return (i.e. it will be returned) [fut]

uzichaze you should describe yourself [subjunc]

encwadini in, from, on a book or letter [loc]

incwadi book, letter [n Cl. 9a]

ngolisho at the request of [instr adv]

abazongiphendula who will reply to me [rel Cl. 2]

bazongiphendula they will reply to me [fut]

Amadoda Adlwengula Amanye

«1»

Kwakungokokuqala ngqa ukuba uVuma (igama lakhe langempela ligodliwe) aboshwe. Wayesaba enovalo eqhaqhazela ... ngoba phela kukaningi ezwa ngempilo engeyinhle yeziboshwa ejele. Wayelokhu ethandaza buthule efisa ukuthi sengathi yena angaphepha kulempilo yobugebengu yasejele.

«2»

Phezu kwemithandazo yakhe, lafika ilanga eliyisilima lapho wayezovalelwa esitokisini okokuqala ngqa. Ezinye iziboshwa ezase zinesikhathi zivalelwe[9] zajabula zimbona zasho ngezinhliziyo ukuthi 'nansi inyama.'

Kwakuyimigulukudu ezibiza ngokuthi ngama'28' ekubeni yena wayengumfana wesikole.

«3»

UVuma wazama ukubamba izinyembezi kodwa phezu kwalokho wawuzizwela nje nangezwi lakhe ukuthi lendaba ayilandayo yokudlwengulwa kwakhe ngezinye iziboshwa zishintshana ngaye imfikisela ubuhlungu.

«4»

Ngokukachwepheshe owelapha okumayelana nezocansi ... isimo sokudlwengulwa sidlulele kowesilisa. "Ngaphandle kokuhlu-kumezeka ngokomqondo, ubuhlungu obuzwakalayo bedlulele lokhu; phela owesilisa akadalelwanga ukuba kuyiwe naye ocansini," kuchaza uchwepheshe wezocansi.

«5»

"Ngazizwa ngifikelwe wukudinwa, ukwesaba kanye nokula-hlekelwa yisithunzi, ikakhulukazi njengoba yayingekho into engangingayenza ukuze ngibavimbe kulobubi ababekwenza," kusho uVuma. "Ngingumuntu onomoya ophansi, futhi ngangihlangene nezinkakha zezigelekeqe. Kwangicacela ukuthi alikho ithuba engingalithola njengoba ngangingesiye nomuntu okwazi ukulwa kakhulu. Ngangiqhaqhazeliswa wukwesaba.

«6»

"Ubuhlungu babungaphezu kwamandla ami. Ngacabanga ukuthi lezizigilamkhuba zizongiyeka uma sengopha, kodwa akuzange kubenjalo! Baqhubeka, behleka ukuthi bonke abantu abaqalayo ukuya ocansini bayafana. Inhloso yabo kwakungukuthi ngelinye ilanga ngiwuthokozele lomkhuba ukuze ngijwayele!"

---

[9] In a slip of the tongue, this was read as **zivalwelwe**.

«7»
UVuma uthi lokhu kwakwenzeka ebusuku. Babemesabisa uma ebazisa ukuthi uzobikela abaphathi. Inhlupheko yakhe yaba nemiphumela eyindida. Ukuhlolwa kwegazi okwenziwa ngabaphathi basejele kwaveza ukuthi unegciwane elandulela isifo se-AIDS, i-HIV.

«8»
Nakuba kungekho ukungabaza ukuthi baningi abesimame abadlwengulwayo, kodwa nabesilisa bayadlwengulwa. Ngokwabe-Life Line: "Ukudlwengulwa kwabantu besilisa yinto ejwayelekile emajele. Lokhu kuyenzeka futhi nakulezozindawo lapho kuhlala abantu besilisa bodwa bengekho abesimame.

«9»
"Lokhu kubandakanya izikole ezingama-boarding school zabesilisa kuphela, ezinkanjini zamasosha, nasezinkanjini lapho kuhlala khona abesilisa kuphela. Kutholakale ukuthi bakhona abantu abasha basemaphandleni abagila lomkhuba.

«10»
"Ukudlwengulwa kwezingane kuvame ukwenzeka emakhaya mhlawumbe kwenziwa ngumzali, umkhulu, ubhuti omdala, umzala, umalume noma ngumuntu ongumngani wabomndeni. Abafana abancane ababaleka emakhaya nabo basengcupheni yokwehlelwa yilomshophi.

«11»
"Kukhona nezinye izindawo noma izimo eziyingozi ngokufanayo kwabesilisa nabesimame," kuxwayisa abe-Life Line. "Lezizindawo ngezifana nama-night clubs, ukucela ama-lift endleleni, ukuhamba wedwa ezindaweni eziyizinkangala lapho kungekho abantu, kanye nasezindlini zangasese ezisetshenziswa ngumphakathi nakwezinye nje izindawo."

«12»
Ngokwabe-Life Line, "Iningi labantu besilisa elisuke lehlelwe yilenkinga liye lingathathi zinyathelo, ngoba libona ukuthi abantu nabaphathi yinto abangeke bayishaye mkhuba. Iningi labantu, ngisho nochwepheshe bezokwelapha, abanalwazi lokuthi nabesilisa baya-hlukunyezwa ngokocansi.

«13»
"Ngenxa yesimo sezocansi, abesilisa abakhululeki nakancane ukukhuluma ngokudlwengulwa. Iningi labantu lokhu likuthatha njengehlazo uma kwenzeka kumuntu wesilisa. Nabo bavame ukufela ngaphakathi ngoba besaba ukuthi abanye abantu bazobabiza ngezinkonkoni – lesi ngesinye sezizathu esenza besabe ukubika lelihlazo."

«14»

Okwandisa lenkinga wuhlangothi lwezomthetho ngoba lubhekelela ukuthi abantu besifazane kuphela abadlwengulwayo. Ukudlwengula kuyicala elenziwa ngumuntu weSILISA kumuntu weSIFAZANE. Ngakhoke indoda ngeke itholakale inecala lokudlwengula omunye umuntu wesilisa, kodwa ingabekwa icala lokuhlukumeza ngokocansi.

«15»

Ukwenza isibonelo ... abe-Child Protection Unit babhekana namacala okudlwengulwa kwamantombazane angu 8 992 aneminyaka engaphansi kuka 18 ngonyaka ka 1995. Kodwa amacala angu 600 athinta abafana abangaphansi kweminyaka engu 18 athathwa njenge-sodomy – okusho ukuya kwabesilisa bobabili ocansini. Yini ebangela ukuthi indoda ize idlwengule enye indoda? Nokuthi yindoda enjani engangena enkingeni yokudlwengulwa?

«16»

UDkt Irma Labuschagne oyi-Forensic Criminologist wabeka wathi: "Umenzi usuke ekhungatheke ngaphezu kwenkanuko yezocansi. Amadoda ahlukumeza amanye amadoda ngokocansi (ngaphakathi nangaphandle kwamajele) ngenhloso yokukhipha ukudinwa, ukuhlukumeza noma ukukhombisa amandla noma ukukhombisa ukucasuka.

«17»

"Ngaphakathi emajele ukuhlukumeza ngokocansi kubangelwa yizizathu ezihlukene, kwezinye zazo kunezibonelo eziningi lapho sithola abantu besilisa beboshelwe ukuxhaphaza izingane noma benukubeze izingane ngokocansi, bahlukunyezwe ngokocansi yilabo abahlala nabo "ngenhloso yokubabeka endaweni yabo" kanti futhi lokhu kungcola kuphindwe kwenziwe nangamaqembu athile "ngesizathu sokuthi bezwe ukuthi kunjani." Ngake ngezwa ukuthi iziboshwa zivamise ukuzifikisa ezinye iziboshwa ngokuthi bazihlukumeze ngokocansi.

«18»

"Emajele abanye abantu besilisa bake baziphathise okwezinkonkoni ngenhloso yokwanelisa izinkanuko zabo zocansi. Uma sebekhululekile babuyela esimweni esejwayelekile. Kukhona nokwesabela ukuthi isifo se-AIDS singanda emajele.

«19»

"Amadoda ayahlukunyezwa ngokocansi futhi kulalwe nawo nangaphandle kwasemajele. Sengike ngabhekana nomsebenzi wokusiza abantu besilisa asebeke bathola lokhu kuhlukunyezwa. Noma yimuphi umuntu wesilisa uyakuthola ukuhlukumezeka – kodwa abantu besilisa abayizinkonkoni yibo abahlukumezeka kakhulu."

169

«20»
Kunzima kakhulu kubantu besilisa abadlwenguliwe ngoba bazibona sengathi banecala futhi bathole nokuphoxeka. Umphakathi uyakwamukela ukuthi abantu besifazane bayehlulwa ngamandla kodwa abantu besilisa bayakwazi ukuzivikela. Ngakhoke indoda edlwenguliwe izibona ingendoda yalutho.

«21»
UDkt Labuschagne uyavuma futhi uyexwayisa ngokuthi nabo abantu besilisa abathole lokhu kuhlukumezeka bayaludinga usizo ukuze bakwazi ukumelana nalesisimo. "Kunokuhlukumezeka okuthatha isikhathi eside nokuthatha isikhathi esincane. Lokhu kungaba ngaphezu kwalokho okwenzeka kumuntu wesifazane. Abantu besilisa bazithola besenkingeni enkulu emva kwalesisehlo – balahlekelwa yithemba, baphinde bazibone bengcolile futhi bangabinakho ukukhululeka uma becabanga ngalesigameko.

«22»
"Lokhu bangakunqoba ngosizo lochwepheshe – lokhu kuyaku-khulula nasemoyeni. Abantu besilisa kufanele basizwe ukuze babone ukuthi akusikho ukuphoxeka ukucela usizo. Sekuyisikhathi sokuthi umphakathi ubone ukuthi lokhu kuyinkinga ngempela nokuthi lobugebengu buyabuthikameza ubudoda bomuntu wesilisa. I-Rape Crisis Services enganyelwe ngabakwa-Life Line yenzelwe ukusiza abesilisa abathole ukuhlukumezeka.

«23»
Ekuphikiseni okuningi abantu abakholelwa kukho, kunezindaba ezinhle eziqhamuka noDkt Labuschagne ezithi, "Kunobufakazi obuncane obukhomba ukuthi abafana abancane abahlukunyezwe ngabanye abantu besilisa ngokocansi bangaba sethubeni lokuthi babe yizinkonkoni – okuphikisa lokhu okungaba yiqiniso.

«24»
"Engikutholile wukuthi labo abake bathola ukuhlukumezeka baba nezinkinga ngokwejwayela ubulili babo – bahlale benezinkinga uma sebeya ocansini nabesifazane ngokuhamba kwesikhathi – kodwa lokho akuchazi nakancane ukuthi sekumele babe nothando lokuya ocansini nabantu abanobulili obufana nalobo babo."

Vocabulary

adlwengula who rape [rel Cl. 6]
  adlwengula they rape [pres, conjoint]
  -dlwengul-a rape [v.t.]

«1»
kwakungokokuqala it was the first (time) [ident cop, rem past pres; **kw-** SC Cl. 17 + **-a-** rem past + **-ku-** SC + **-ng-** + **okokuqala**]

ngokokuqala it is the first (time) [ident cop, pres]
okokuqala the first (time) [poss pron Cl. 17]
kokuqala of beginning [poss Cl. 17]
uVuma (male name) [n Cl. 1a]
langempela real, true [poss Cl. 5]
ligodliwe it has been withheld [past, disjoint]
aboshwe (s)he was arrested (lit. (s)he should be arrested [subjunc]
wayesaba (s)he was afraid [rem past pres]
-y- (s)he [partic SC Cl. 1; var of -ye- found before vowels]
enovalo (s)he having fear [assoc cop, pres, partic]
eqhaqhazela (s)he is shivering, trembling [pres, partic]
-qhaqhazel-a shiver, tremble [v.i.]
kukaningi it is often [loc cop, pres]
kaningi often [adv; < -**ningi** many, much]
ezwa (s)he hears [pres, partic]
engeyinhle that/which is not good [rel Cl. 9]
ingeyinhle [descr cop, pres, rel, neg; < **i-** SC Cl. 9 + -**nge**- neg pref + -**yi-** Cl. 9 pref + -**n**- 2nd half adj conc + -**hle** good]
yinhle it, (s)he is good, nice, pretty [descr cop, pres]
yi- (s)he, it is [descr cop pref used with monosyllabic stems in Cl. 9]
yeziboshwa of prisoners [poss Cl. 9]
iziboshwa prisoners [n Cl. 8; sg **isiboshwa**; < -**boshw**- b e arrested]

ejele to, from, in jail or prison [loc; one of the exceptions that does not take a locative suffix]
ijele jail, prison [n Cl. 5] {Eng}
wayelokhu (s)he kept on, (s)he always [aux, rem past pres]
ethandaza (s)he is praying [pres, partic]
-thandaz-a pray [v.i.]
buthule silently [adv; < **bu**- + **thul-e** < -**thul-a** be silent; this is a very rare form of adverbial derivation]
efisa (s)he wishes [pres, partic]
angaphepha (s)he could escape [pres, potential]
kulempilo to, from, in this life [loc]
lempilo this life [dem phr Cl. 9]
yobugebengu of gangsterism, of crime [poss Cl. 9]
yasejele of in prison [poss Cl. 9]
sejele [< **ejele**, see ABOVE]

«2»
phezu kwemithandazo in spite of prayers (lit. at the top of ...)
yakhe his, her, its [poss Cl. 4]
lafika it, (s)he arrived [rem past]
eliyisilima that/which is difficult, hard [rel Cl. 5]
liyisilima it is a difficult thing, it is a deformity [ident cop, pres]
isilima deformed person or thing [n Cl. 7]
wayezovalelwa (s)he would be locked up [rem past fut]
esitokisini in a prison cell [loc]
isitokisi prison cell [n Cl. 7] {Eng *stocks*}
ezase zinesikhathi zivalelwe who had already been locked up for some time [rel Cl. 8]

171

ezase zinesikhathi who already had time [rel Cl. 8]

zase zinesikhathi they already had long ago [assoc cop, rem past pres, exclusive]

zinesikhathi they have time [assoc cop, pres, partic]

zivalelwe they are imprisoned [stative, partic]

zajabula they were happy [rem past]

-jabul-a be or become happy [v.i.]

zimbona (when) they saw (lit. see) him or her [pres, partic]

zasho and said [narr]

ngezinhliziyo with desire (lit. with hearts – the seat of emotions, including desire) [instr adv]

izinhliziyo hearts [n Cl. 9]

nansi here is [presentative dem Cl. 9, 1st pos; var **nayi**]

inyama meat, flesh [n Cl. 9a]

kwakuyimigulukudu it was hardened or habitual criminals [ident cop, rem past pres]

imigulukudu hardened criminals, habitual criminals [n Cl. 4; sg **umgulukudu** Cl. 1 or 3]

ezibiza ngokuthi ng- who call themselves

ezibiza who call themselves [rel Cl. 4]

izibiza they call themselves [pres, conjoint]

-biz-a ngokuthi + IDENT COP PREF ... call someone or something ...

ngama-28 it is, they are the 28s [ident cop, pres]

ama-28 the 28s (an infamous prison gang, known particularly for homosexuality and male rape) [n Cl. 6]

ekubeni whereas [conj]

wayengumfana wesikole he was a schoolboy [ident cop phr]

wayengumfana he was a boy [ident cop, rem past pres]

umfana boy, young man [n Cl. 1]

wesikole of school [poss Cl. 1]

«3»

wazama (s)he tried [rem past]

ukubamba to hold back, to keep back [vn Cl. 15]

-bamb-a hold (back), take hold of, catch [v.t.]

izinyembezi tears [n Cl. 10a; sg **inyembezi**]

wawuzizwela you just heard, you heard for yourself [rem past pres]

-zi-zwel-a just hear, just feel, hear for yourself [v-refl-appl]

-zwel-a hear for, feel for, feel sorry for, sympathize with [v-appl]

nangezwi even by voice [assoc adv]

ngezwi by, through voice [instr adv]

izwi voice, word [n Cl. 5]

lendaba this matter, this affair [dem phr Cl. 9]

ayilandayo that/which (s)he relates [ind rel of plain obj rel, Cl. 1]

uyayilanda (s)he relates it [pres, disjoint]

-land-a relate [v.t.]

yokudlwengulwa of being raped [poss Cl. 9]

ukudlwengulwa to be raped [vn Cl. 15]

-dlwengulw-a be raped [v-pass]

zishintshana they taking turns [pres, partic]

-shintshan-a take turns [v-recip]

-shintsh-a change [v.t.]

ngaye with, by, through him or her [instr adv]

imfikisela it (the matter) brings him [pres, conjoint]

-fikisel-a bring to (lit. cause to arrive to) [v-caus-appl]

-fikis-a cause to arrive, bring [v-caus]

ubuhlungu pain [n Cl. 14]

«4»

ngokukachwepheshe according to an expert [instr adv phr; **nga-** + POSS PRON CL. 17 = according to]

ngokuka- according to [instr adv phr; used before nouns of Cl. 1a]

okukachwepheshe that of an expert [poss pron Cl. 17]

kukachwepheshe of an expert [poss Cl. 17]

chwepheshe expert, specialist [< **uchwepheshe** n Cl. 1a]

owelapha who treats [rel Cl. 1]

welapha (s)he treats [pres, conjoint]

okumayelana that which concerns [rel Cl. 17]

mayelana na- ... with regard to ..., with respect to ..., concerning ... [conj phr]

ezocansi sexual matters [poss pron Cl. 10 (refers to **izindaba**)]

sokudlwengulwa of being raped [poss Cl. 7]

sidlulele it is extreme for [past, conjoint]

kowesilisa to, from, at males [loc; < **ku-** + **owesilisa**]

owesilisa a male [poss pron Cl. 1; pl **abesilisa**]

wesilisa of the male sex or gender [poss Cl. 1]

ngaphandle kokuhlukumezeka ngokomqondo apart from the emotional (mental) shock [instr adv phr]

obuzwakalayo that/which is felt or experienced [rel Cl. 14]

buyezwakala it is felt or experienced [pres, disjoint; < **bu-** + **-ya-** + **-izwakal-a**]

-zwakal-a be felt, be experienced [v-neut; var **-izwakal-** occurs after the vowel a]

bedlulele it (sur)passed, it went beyond [past, conjoint]

b- it [SC Cl. 14]

-edlulel-a pass on to, go past to or for [v-appl]

akadalelwanga (s)he was not created for [past, neg]

-dalelw-a be created for [v-appl-pass]

-dalel-a create for [v-appl]

ukuba kuyiwe naye ocansini that he should be the passive partner sexually (lit. that there should be gone with him to bed)

kuyiwe there should be gone [subjunc]

ocansini to bed, to, from, on a sleeping-mat [loc; < **ucansi**]

wezocansi in sexual matters [poss Cl. 1]

w- of [poss conc Cl. 1; found before **a, e** and **o**]

«5»

ngazizwa I felt (lit. I felt myself) [rem past]

ngifikelwe I have experienced [past, partic, conjoint]

-fikelw-a experience (lit. have arrive to one) [v-appl-pass]

-**fikel-a** befall, happen to [v-appl]

wukudinwa (by) being sickened [agent adv]

ukudinwa to be sickened, to be wearied [vn Cl. 15]

-**dinw-a** bec sickened, bec wearied, bec troubled, bec bored [v-pass]

-**din-a** weary, tire, sicken [v.t.]

ukulahlekelwa yisithunzi loss of self-worth [vn phr Cl. 15]

ukulahlekelwa to lose (lit. to have something get lost to one's detriment) [vn Cl. 15]

isithunzi shadow; moral weight, influence, prestige; personality, soul [n Cl. 7]

yayingekho into there was nothing [exist cop, rem past pres, neg]

engangingayenza that/which I could do (it) [ind rel of plain obj rel, 1 p sg]

ngangingayenza I could do it [rem past pres, potential]

ngibavimbe I should stop them [subjunc]

kulobubi in this evil [loc]

lobubi this evil [dem phr Cl. 14; < lo + ububi]

lo this, these [1st position dem, Cl. 14; in some dialects the abbreviated form **lo** is used for all demonstratives that have **u** as 2nd vowel]

ububi evil, wickedness, ugliness [n Cl. 14]

ababekwenza that/which they were doing (it) [ind rel of plain obj rel, Cl. 2]

babekwenza they were doing it [rem past pres]

onomoya ophansi who is reserved or gentle [rel Cl. 1]

unomoya ophansi (s)he is reserved or gentle (lit. (s)he has a spirit that is down) [assoc cop phr]

ngangihlangene I had met [rem past past]

nezinkakha with skilled people [assoc adv]

izinkakha zezigelekeqe master criminals [n phr Cl. 10]

izinkakha skilled people [n Cl. 10; sg **inkakha**]

zezigelekeqe of criminals [poss Cl. 10]

izigelekeqe criminals [n Cl. 8; sg **isigelekeqe**]

kwangicacela it became clear to me [rem past]

-**cacel-a** bec clear to [v-appl]

-**cac-a** bec clear [v.i.]

alikho ithuba there is no chance [exist cop, pres, neg]

alikho it, (s)he is not there [loc cop; may also introduce an exist cop]

engingalithola that/which I could find [ind rel of plain obj rel, 1 p sg]

ngingalithola I can find or obtain it [pres, potential]

ngangingesiye nomuntu I was not even a person [ident cop, rem past pres, neg]

ngangingesiye I was not him or her [ident cop, rem past pres, neg; **ng-** SC + -**a**- rem past + -**ng**- SC + -**nge**- neg partic pref found in copulatives + -**si**- neg pref found in ident copulatives + **ye** abs pron]

nomuntu even, with, also, a person [assoc adv]

ngangiqhaqhazeliswa I was made to tremble [rem past pres]

wukwesaba by fear [agent adv]

«6»

babungaphezu kwamandla it was beyond (lit. above) strength [loc cop, rem past pres]

ami my [poss Cl. 6]

ngacabanga I thought [rem past]

lezizigilamkhuba these evil-doers [dem phr Cl. 8]

izigilamkhuba evil-doers [n Cl. 8; sg **isigilamkhuba**]

zizongiyeka they will leave me alone [fut]

sengopha I am already bleeding [pres, partic, exclusive]

-oph-a bleed [v.i.]

akuzange kubenjalo it never happened (lit. it never became so) [descr cop phr, inch, past, neg]

kubenjalo (or **kube njalo**) it should be so [descr cop, inch, subjunc]

baqhubeka they carried on, they continued [rem past]

behleka they (are) laughing [pres, partic]

-hlek-a laugh (at) [v.i. & t.]

abaqalayo who are for the first time, who are beginning [rel Cl. 2]

baqala they start, they do for the first time [(aux) pres, conjoint]

ukuya ocansini to have sex (lit. to go to the sleeping-mat) [vn phr]

bayafana they are the same, they are similar [pres, disjoint]

yabo their [poss Cl. 9]

kwakungukuthi it was that [ident cop, rem past pres]

ngiwuthokozele I would enjoy it, I would be glad for it [subjunc]

ngijwayele I should get used to (it) [subjunc]

«7»

kwakwenzeka it used to happen [rem past pres]

babemesabisa they used to scare him [rem past pres]

-esabis-a scare, make afraid [v-caus; var **-sabis-a**]

ebazisa (s)he informs them [pres, partic]

uzobikela (s)he will report to [fut]

-bikel-a report to [v-appl]

abaphathi warders, wardens, authorities, those in charge, guardians, superintendents, managers, officials [n Cl. 2; sg **umphathi**; < **-phath-** handle]

inhlupheko suffering [n Cl. 9; < **-hluphek-** suffer, be worried, be troubled]

yaba nemiphumela it, (s)he had results [assoc cop, inch, rem past]

yaba it, (s)he became [copula, rem past]

nemiphumela with results [assoc adv]

ukuhlolwa the examination [vn Cl. 15]

-hlolw-a be examined, inspected [v-pass]

kwegazi of blood [poss Cl. 15]

okwenziwa that/which was done, made [rel Cl. 15]

kwenziwa it was done, made [rem past]

ngabaphathi by the wardens, by the managers [agent adv]

basejele of the prison [poss Cl. 2]

kwaveza it brought to light, it revealed [rem past]

unegciwane (s)he has a germ, a virus [assoc cop, pres]

igciwane particle, bit of dust floating in air; germ, virus, microbe [n Cl. 5]

elandulela that/which precedes, that/which is the precursor of

el- which, that, who [rel conc Cl. 5]

landulela it precedes [pres, conjoint]

-andulel-a precede [v.t.]

se-AIDS of AIDS [poss Cl. 7]

«8»

kungekho ukungabaza there is no doubt [exist cop, pres, partic]

kungekho ... there is no..., there being no ..., there are no ... [introduces: exist cop, pres, partic, neg]

ukungabaza doubt, to doubt, to conjecture, to imagine [vn Cl. 15]

abadlwengulwayo who are raped [rel Cl. 2]

bayadlwengulwa they are raped [pres, disjoint]

nabesilisa males too, even males [assoc adv]

ngokwabe-Life Line according to people from Life Line [instr adv]

abe-Life Line those from Life Line [poss pron Cl. 2]

i-Life Line (call center for crisis counseling) [n Cl. 9a]

ejwayelekile that/which is normal, usual, common [rel Cl. 9]

ijwayelekile it is normal, usual, common [stative]

nakulezozindawo and to, from, in, at those places [assoc adv]

kuhlala there live [pres, conjoint]

bodwa only, alone [quant Cl. 2]

bengekho abesimame in the absence of women [exist cop, pres, partic, neg]

bengekho they not being there, they being absent; there being no ... [loc cop, pres, partic, neg; introduces exist cop, pres, partic, neg]

«9»

kubandakanya it involves [pres, conjoint]

ezingama-boarding school that/which are boarding schools [rel Cl. 8]

zingama-boarding school they are (or it is) boarding schools [ident cop, pres]

ama-boarding school [n Cl. 6; sg Cl. 9] {Eng}

zabesilisa boys' (lit. of males) [poss Cl. 8]

ezinkanjini to, from, in, at, camps [loc; < ezinkambwini < e- + izinkambu + -ini; mbw > nj] {Afr kamp}

zamasosha of soldiers [poss Cl. 10]

nasezinkanjini and in camps [assoc adv]

kutholakale it has been found [past, conjoint]

bakhona abantu there are people [exist cop, pres]

bakhona they are there [loc cop, pres; may introduce an exist cop]

abasha young [adj Cl. 2]

basemaphandleni from rural areas [poss Cl. 2]

semaphandleni to, from, in rural areas [loc; < emaphandleni]

amaphandle rural areas, outskirts of a village [n Cl. 6; neutral; < **phandle**]
abagila lomkhuba who practise this evil [rel phr Cl. 2]
  bagila they practise [pres, conjoint]
  -gil-a umkhuba practise an evil
  -gil-a perform [v.t.]

«10»
kwezingane of children [poss Cl. 15]
ukwenzeka to happen, to occur, to take place, to be feasible [vn Cl. 15]
mhlawumbe perhaps [conj]
ngumzali by a parent [agent adv]
umzala cousin [n Cl. 1]
umalume maternal uncle [n Cl. 1a]
ngumuntu by a person [agent adv]
ongumngani who is a friend [rel Cl. 1]
  ungumngani (s)he is a friend [ident cop, pres]
wabomndeni of the family [poss Cl. 1]
  abomndeni family members [poss pron Cl. 2]
  bomndeni of the family [poss Cl. 2]
ababaleka who run away (from) [rel Cl. 2]
  babaleka they run away (from) [pres, conjoint]
basengcupheni they are in danger [loc cop, pres]
  sengcupheni in danger [loc; < **engcupheni**]
  ingcuphe danger, dangerous position [n Cl. 9; < **in-** + **-cuphe**; n + c > **ngc**]
yokwehlelwa of being overcome [poss Cl. 9]

ukwehlelwa to be overcome, to have happen to one [vn Cl. 15]
  -ehlelw-a be overcome, have happen to one [v-appl-pass]
yilomshophi by this plague [agent adv]
  lomshophi this plague or epidemic [dem phr Cl. 3]

«11»
nezinye also other(s), other(s) too, and other(s) [assoc adv]
ngokufanayo equally, similarly [instr adv]
  okufanayo that which is similar or the same [rel Cl. 17]
  kuyafana it is similar, it is the same [pres, disjoint]
kwabesilisa for, to, from males [loc]
kuxwayisa there warns [pres, conjoint]
  -xwayis-a warn, caution, alert, put on guard [v-caus; var **-exwayis-a**]
  -xway-a be on the alert, be cautious, be wary [v.i.; var **-exway-**]
lezizindawo these places [dem phr Cl. 10]
ngezifana na- ... are one's such as ... [ident cop phr, pres]
nama-night clubs with, and night clubs [assoc adv]
  ama-night clubs [n Cl. 6; sg **i-night club** Cl. 9a]
ukucela i-lift hitch (a lift, a ride) [vn phr Cl. 15]
  ama-lift lifts, rides [n Cl. 6; sg **i-lift** Cl. 9a] {Eng}
endleleni on the way; to, from, on, in, the road [loc]
wedwa on your own, (you) alone [quant 2 p sg]
  we- [quant conc 2 p sg]

eziyizinkangala that/which are deserted [rel Cl. 10]
ziyizinkangala they are deserted places [ident cop, pres]
izinkangala open, treeless country [n Cl. 10; sg **inkangala**]
nasezindlini zangasese and to, from, in toilets [assoc adv]
sezindlini zangasese to, from, in toilets [loc phr; < **ezindlini zangasese**]
izindlu zangasese toilets [n phr Cl. 10; sg **indlu yangasese**]
ezisetshenziswa that/which are used [rel Cl. 10]
zisetshenziswa they are used [pres, conjoint]
nakwezinye and in other [assoc adv]

«12»
elisuke who have just [rel Cl. 5]
lisuke it, (s)he, have just [aux]
lehlelwe it is overcome [subjunc]
yilenkinga by this problem [agent adv]
lenkinga this problem [dem phr Cl. 9]
liye it sometimes [aux]
lingathathi it, (s)he does not take [subjunc, neg]
zinyathelo steps [< **izinyathelo**]
libona it, (s)he thinks [pres, conjoint]
nabaphathi and the warders, and the authorities, and the managers [assoc adv]
abangeke bayishaye mkhuba that/which they would never take seriously [ind rel of plain obj rel, Cl. 2]
bangeke bayishaye mkhuba they would never take it seriously [v phr]

bangeke they would never [aux, pres, potential, neg]
bayishaye they should hit it [subjunc]
-shay-a mkhuba take seriously [idiom]
nochwepheshe even experts [assoc adv; < **na-** + **ochwepheshe**]
bezokwelapha (they) coming to treat [pres, partic, venitive]
abanalwazi they do not have (the) knowledge [assoc cop, pres, neg]
lwazi knowledge [< **ulwazi**]
lokuthi that [poss Cl. 11]
bayahlukunyezwa they are assaulted [pres, disjoint]

«13»
abakhululeki they are not free [pres, neg]
ukukhuluma to speak, to talk [vn Cl. 15]
ngokudlwengulwa about being raped [instr adv]
likuthatha they take it [pres, conjoint]
njengehlazo as a disgrace [compar adv]
ihlazo disgrace, dishonor, shame [n Cl. 5; **-hlaz-** dis-grace, dishonor, shame]
ukufela (nga)phakathi suffer in silence, control one's feelings, hide one's rage
ukufela to die in [vn Cl. 15]
-fel-a die in, die for, die because of [v-appl]
besaba they are afraid [pres, conjoint]
bazobabiza ngezinkonkoni they will call them homosexuals [fut]
bazobabiza they will call them [fut]

ngezinkonkoni (as) homosexuals [instr adv]

izinkonkoni homosexuals; wildebeest [n Cl. 10]

sezizathu of the reasons [poss Cl. 7]

esenza that/which makes or causes [rel Cl. 7]

senza it, (s)he makes, causes, does [pres, conjoint]

besabe that they should be afraid [subjunc]

ukubika to report [vn Cl. 15]

lelihlazo this shame, this dishonor [dem phr Cl. 5]

«14»

okwandisa that which increases [rel Cl. 17]

kwandisa it increases [pres, conjoint]

-andis-a increase, make greater, multiply [v-caus]

wuhlangothi it is the section [ident cop, pres]

uhlangothi side, section [n Cl. 11]

lwezomthetho of the law [poss Cl. 11]

lubhekelela it definitely considers [pres, conjoint]

-bhekelel-a consider definitely [v-perfective]

abantu it is people [ident cop, pres]

ukudlwengula rape, to rape [vn Cl. 15]

kuyicala it is an offence [ident cop, pres]

icala crime, offence, felony; guilt; wrong, defect; court case; charge [n Cl. 5]

elenziwa that/which is done or performed [rel Cl. 5]

lenziwa it is done, made, performed [pres, conjoint]

itholakale (s)he should be found [subjunc]

inecala (s)he is guilty (lit. has guilt) [assoc cop, pres, partic]

lokudlwengula of raping [poss Cl. 5]

ingabekwa icala (s)he can be charged with the offence

ingabekwa (s)he, it can be placed, or have placed on her/him/it [pres, potential]

-bekw-a icala be found guilty

-bekw-a be placed, have placed on one [v-pass]

lokuhlukumeza of assault [poss Cl. 5]

«15»

ukwenza isibonelo to give an example (lit. to make an example) [vn phr Cl. 15]

isibonelo example [n Cl. 7]

abe-Child Protection Unit the people from the Child Protection Unit [poss pron Cl. 2]

babhekana they are looking at, are faced [pres, conjoint]

namacala with cases [assoc adv]

okudlwengulwa of rape (i.e. of being raped) [poss Cl. 6]

kwamantombazane of girls [poss Cl. 15]

angu-8 992 8,992 [rel Cl. 6]

aneminyaka engaphansi kuka-18 who are aged under 18

aneminyaka who are aged (lit. who have years) [rel Cl. 6]

aneminyaka they are aged [assoc cop, pres]

engaphansi kuka- that/which are under [rel phr Cl. 4]

ka-1995 of 1995 [poss Cl. 3]

u-1995 [n Cl. 1a]

179

angu-600 600 [rel Cl. 6]
u-600 [n Cl. 1a]
athinta that/which concern or deal with [rel Cl. 6]
athinta they concern, they deal with [pres, conjoint]
abangaphansi who are under [rel Cl. 2]
bangaphansi they are under [loc cop, pres]
athathwa they are taken [pres, conjoint]
njenge-sodomy as sodomy [compar adv]
i-sodomy [n Cl. 9a]
okusho which is to say, which means [rel Cl. 17]
kwabesilisa of males [poss Cl. 15]
bobabili both [quant Cl. 2; < bo-quant conc + **babili** two [adj minus initial vowel]]
ebangela that causes [rel Cl. 9]
ibangela it causes (for) [pres, conjoint]
ize (s)he, it should ever [aux, subjunc]
idlwengule (s)he should rape [subjunc]
yindoda it, he is a man [ident cop, pres]
enjani? what kind of? [rel Cl. 9]
engangena who can get into [rel Cl. 9]
ingangena (s)he, it can enter, can get into [pres, potential]
enkingeni into, from, in a problem [loc]

«16»
Irma Labuschagne (name) [n Cl. 1a] {Afr}
oyi-forensic criminologist who is a forensic criminologist [rel Cl. 1]

uyi-forensic criminologist (s)he is a forensic criminologist [ident cop, pres]
i-forensic criminologist [n Cl. 9a]
wabeka wathi (s) he put in (to a conversation)
wabeka (s)he put in, added [rem past]
-bek-a state, add (to what is said), put in, contribute [v.t.]
umenzi doer, maker, perpetrator [n Cl. 1; pl **abenzi**; < **-enz-** do, make]
ekhungatheke ngaphezu kwenkanuko yezocansi (s)he is more than overwhelmed by sexual desire or lust
ekhungatheke (s)he is overwhelmed, frustrated [past, partic, conjoint]
-khungathek-a be overwhelmed, bec frustrated, be placed in a dilemma [v-neut]
-khungath-a frustrate, place in a dilemma, perplex; embarrass, shame [v.t.]
inkanuko urge, lust, strong desire; jealousy, envy [n Cl. 9; < -khanuk- lust, desire strongly; be jealous, be envious]
yezocansi sexual [poss Cl. 9]
ahlukumeza they assault, violate [pres, conjoint]
kwamajele of jails [poss Cl. 17]
yokukhipha of taking out [poss Cl. 9]
ukukhipha ukudinwa to alleviate boredom [vn phr Cl. 15]
ukudinwa to bec bored [vn Cl. 15]
-dinw-a bec bored [v.inch]
ukukhombisa to show [vn Cl. 15]
ukucasuka contempt (lit. nausea) [vn Cl. 15]

«17»
kubangelwa it is caused [pres, conjoint]
-bangelw-a be caused for, to or because of [v-appl-pass]
yizizathu by reasons [agent adv]
kunezibonelo there are examples [assoc cop, pres]
  izibonelo examples [n Cl. 8]
eziningi many, numerous [adj Cl. 8]
sithola we find [pres, conjoint]
beboshelwe they are imprisoned for [past, partic, conjoint]
-boshelw-a be imprisoned for, be arrested for [v-appl-pass; < -bophel-w-a; ph ... -w- > sh ... -w-]
ukuxhaphaza to exploit, exploitation [vn Cl. 15]
-xhaphaz-a exploit [v.t.]
benukubeze they having sexually abused [past, partic, conjoint]
bahlukunyezwe they are assaulted [subjunc; different tones to item ABOVE]
yilabo by those [agent adv]
abahlala nabo whom they live with [ind rel of plain adverbial rel, Cl. 2]
yokubabeka of putting them [poss Cl. 9]
  ukubabeka to put them, putting them [vn Cl. 15]
lokhu kungcola this immorality
  kungcola [< **ukungcola** be corrupt, be immoral, be dirty]
kuphindwe it is repeatedly [aux, subjunc]
-phindw-e be done repeatedly [aux, pass; followed by the subjunc]
kwenziwe it is done [subjunc]
ngamaqembu in groups [instr adv]

athile certain [rel Cl. 6]
bezwe they should feel [subjunc; < ba- SC Cl. 2 + -izw- feel + -e]
kunjani what is it like, how is it [descr cop, pres]
ngake I once [aux, rem past]
ngezwa I heard [narr; < nga- + -izw-a]
zivamise they generally [aux]
-vamis-a VERB generally, usually [aux v-caus]
ukuzifikisa to mistreat a newcomer (as bullying a new child at school or when a new member of staff who doesn't know the ropes is given extra work by old staff) [vn Cl. 15]
bazihlukumeze they should assault them [subjunc]

«18»
baziphathise okwezinkonkoni they behave like homosexuals [subjunc v phr]
-zi-phath-a behave (lit. carry oneself, hold oneself) [v-refl]
yokwanelisa of satisfying [poss Cl. 9]
-anelis-a satisfy, fill a deficiency, convince [v-caus]
izinkanuko urges, strong desires, lust; jealousies [n Cl. 10; sg **inkanuko**; < -khanuk- lust, desire strongly; be jealous, be envious [v.i.]
sebekhululekile once they have been released [past, exclusive, disjoint]
babuyela they return to [pres, conjoint]
esejwayelekile usual, customary, normal [rel Cl. 7]
  sejwayelekile it is usual, customary, normal [stative]

nokwesabela also fear of [assoc adv]
ukwesabela fear of, fear that [vn Cl. 15]
-esabel-a ukuthi be afraid that, fear that
se-AIDS of AIDS [poss Cl. 7]
singanda it could increase [pres, potential]

«19»
ayahlukunyezwa they are assaulted [pres, disjoint]
kulalwe there is slept, they have intercourse [subjunc]
semajele in jails [loc; < emajele]
ngabhekana I faced, I handled [narr]
asebeke who have already once [rel Cl. 2]
   sebeke they have already once [aux, past, exclusive, conjoint]
bathola they found, they experienced [narr]
kuhlukunyezwa [< ukuhluku-nyezwa]
noma yimuphi umuntu no matter what person, anybody at all (lit. although it is which person)
   yimuphi? it is which one? [ident cop, pres]
   muphi? which? [enum Cl. 1]
uyakuthola (s)he experiences or finds it [pres, disjoint]
abayizinkonkoni who are homo-sexuals [rel Cl. 2]
   bayizinkonkoni they are homo-sexuals [ident cop, pres]
   yizinkonkoni they are or it is homosexuals or wildebeest [ident cop, pres]
yibo it is they or them [ident cop, pres]
abahlukumezeka who are assaulted [rel Cl. 2]

bahlukumezeka they are assaulted, attacked [pres, conjoint]

«20»
abadlwenguliwe who have been raped [rel Cl. 2]
badlwenguliwe they have been raped [past, disjoint]
bazibona they see themselves [pres, conjoint]
banecala they are guilty, they are at fault (lit. they have guilt) [assoc cop, pres]
bathole they experience [subjunc]
nokuphoxeka also being mocked, being the butt of jokes too [assoc adv]
ukuphoxeka to be mocked, to be the butt of jokes, to be made fun of, embarrassment, shame [vn Cl. 15]
-phoxek-a be mocked, be the butt of jokes, be made fun of [v-neut]
-phox-a make feel stupid, mock, embarrass [v.t.]
uyakwamukela it accepts it [pres, disjoint]
-amukel-a accept; welcome [v.t.]
bayehlulwa they are overcome [pres, disjoint]
-ehlulw-a be overcome, be defeated, be conquered [v-pass]
-ehlul-a defeat, conquer, overcome [v.i.; var -hlul-a]
ngamandla by force, strongly, powerfully [instr adv]
bayakwazi they can, they are able, they know how to [pres, disjoint]
edlwenguliwe who has been raped [rel Cl. 9]
idlwenguliwe (s)he has been

raped [past, disjoint]
izibona (s)he sees her- or himself
ingendoda not being a man at all [ident cop, pres, partic]
yalutho of any use, in any way (lit. of anything) [poss Cl. 9]

«21»
uyavuma (s)he agrees [pres, disjoint]
uyexwayisa (s)he focuses attention, alerts, warns [pres, disjoint]
   -exwayis-a warn, caution, alert, put on guard [v-caus; var **-xwayis-a**]
   -exway-a be on the alert, be cautious, be wary [v.i.; var **-xway-a**]
abathole who have experienced [rel Cl. 2]
   bathole they experienced [past, conjoint]
bayaludinga they need it [pres, disjoint]
ukumelana na- ... to cope with ... [vn phr Cl. 15]
   -melan-a stand up for or against one another, support one another, defend one another, wait for one another [v-appl-recip]
lesisimo this situation [dem phr Cl. 7]
kunokuhlukumezeka there is subjection to violence or assault [assoc cop, pres]
okuthatha that/which takes [rel Cl. 15]
   kuthatha it takes [pres, conjoint]
eside long [adj Cl. 7]
nokuthatha and that which takes [assoc adv]
esincane little, small [adj Cl. 7]

ngaphezu kwalokho in addition to that [conj phr]
bazithola they find themselves [pres, conjoint]
besenkingeni they are in difficulty, they have a problem [loc cop, pres, partic]
lesisehlo this shock [dem phr Cl. 7]
   isehlo shock, surprising event [n Cl. 7; pl **izehlo**; < **-ehl-** take by surprise, befall, happen to]
yithemba (by) hope [agent adv]
baphinde and they repeatedly [aux, subjunc]
bazibone they see themselves [subjunc]
bengcolile they are dirty [stative, partic]
bangabinakho ukukhululeka and they have no peace of mind [assoc cop, inch, subjunc, neg; < **ba-** they **-nga-** neg **-b-** become **-i** neg **-na-** with **-kho** it]
   ukukhululeka to be freed, to be released, to bec emancipated; relief [vn Cl. 15]
becabanga they think [pres, partic]
ngalesigameko about this re-peated incident [instr adv phr]
   lesigameko this repeated inci-dent [dem phr Cl. 7; < **le** + **isigameko**]

«22»
bangakunqoba they can over-come or conquer it [pres, potential]
   -nqob-a overcome, conquer, defeat [v.t.]
ngosizo with help, with assistance [instr adv]
lochwepheshe of an expert [poss Cl. 11]

kuyakukhulula it frees you, sets you free, releases you, emancipates you [pres, disjoint]

nasemoyeni also spiritually, also psychologically [assoc adv]

semoyeni in spirit, in soul, psychologically; to, from, in the air, wind, breath [loc; < **emoyeni**]

basizwe they should be helped [subjunc]

-sizw-a be helped, assisted, aided [v-pass]

babone they should see [subjunc]

akusikho ukuphoxeka it is not something shameful [ident cop phr, pres, neg]

ubone it should see [subjunc]

kuyinkinga it is a problem, it is a puzzle, it is a difficulty [ident cop, pres]

lobugebengu this crime [dem phr Cl. 14; lo- + ubugebengu]

buyabuthikameza it disturbs it, it has a negative impact on it, it interferes with it [pres, disjoint]

-thikamez-a disturb, distract, interrupt, have a negative impact on [v.t.]

ubudoda manhood, manliness, virility; semen [n Cl. 14]

bomuntu of a person [poss Cl. 14]

i-Rape Crisis Services [n Cl. 9a]

enganyelwe that/which is run or administered by [rel Cl. 9]

yenganyelwe it is run or administered, it is presided over [past, conjunc]

-enganyelw-a be presided over, be run, be administered; be overhung [v-positional-appl-pass; < **-engamel-w-a**; m ... -w- > ny ... -w-]

-engamel-a lean over (for), over-hang; preside over,

administer [v-positional-appl; var **-ongamel-a**; **-angamel-**]

-engam-a lean over, overhang; preside over, administer [v-positional; var **-ongam-a**; **-angam-a**]

ngabakwa-Life Line (by) the people from Life Line [agent adv]

yenzelwe it was founded in order to [past, conjoint]

-enzelw-a be made for, be done for [v-pass]

«23»

ekuphikiseni in contradiction to; to, from, in the debate or dispute [loc]

ukuphikisa (to) dispute, (to) debate, to contradict [vn Cl. 15]

-phikis-a dispute, debate, contradict [v-caus]

okuningi much, a lot [adj Cl. 15]

abakholelwa kukho in which they believe [ind rel of plain loc rel, Cl. 2]

bakholelwa they believe in [pres, conjoint]

-kholelw-a believe in [v-appl-pass]

kunezindaba there is news, there are matters [assoc cop, pres]

ezinhle good, beautiful, pretty, handsome [adj Cl. 10]

eziqhamuka that/which come(s) from [rel Cl. 10]

ziqhamuka they come from [pres, conjoint]

noDkt with Dr. [assoc adv]

ezithi that/which say, namely [rel Cl. 10]

zithi they say [pres, conjoint]

kunobufakazi there is evidence [assoc cop, pres]

obuncane (a) little, small [adj

Cl. 14]

obukhomba that/which points [rel Cl. 14]

 bukhomba it points [pres, conjoint]

abahlukunyezwe who have been assaulted [rel Cl. 2]

 bahlukunyezwe they have been assaulted [past, conjoint]

ngabanye by other [instr adv]

bangaba sethubeni they stand the chance (lit. they could bec in the chance) [loc cop, inch, pres, potential]

lokuthi that [poss Cl. 5]

b a b e yizinkonkoni they should become homosexuals [ident cop, inch, subjunctive]

okuphikisa lokhu okungaba yiqiniso the opposite could be true

okuphikisa that which contradicts [rel Cl. 17]

 kuphikisa it contradicts [pres, conjoint]

okungaba yiqiniso it is what could be the truth [ident cop, pres; < Ø- + okungaba]

 okungaba yiqiniso that which could be the truth [rel phr Cl. 17]

 kungaba yiqiniso it could be the truth [ident cop, inch, pres, potential]

 kungaba it could become [copula, pres, potential]

 yiqiniso it is the truth [ident cop, pres]

 iqiniso truth [n Cl. 5]

«24»

engikutholile what/that/which I have found [ind rel of plain obj rel, 1 p sg]

 ngikutholile I have found it

[past, disjoint]

abake who have once [rel Cl. 2]

 bake they once [aux, rem past]

b a b a nezinkinga they have problems or difficulties [assoc cop, inch, pres]

 baba they become [copula, pres, conjoint]

ngokwejwayela in adjusting to, in getting used to [instr adv]

 ukwejwayela to adjust to, to get used to, to bec accustomed to [vn Cl. 15]

babo their [poss Cl. 14]

bahlale they continually [aux]

benezinkinga they have problems [assoc cop, pres, partic]

sebeya they then go [pres, partic, exclusive]

nabesifazane with women [assoc cop]

 abesifazane females, (polite term for) women [poss pron Cl. 2; < a- pronominalizer + -ba- poss conc Cl. 2 (agrees with **abantu**) + isifazane female gender; sg **owesifazane**]

akuchazi it does not explain [pres, neg]

sekumele it is now necessary [aux, stative, exclusive]

babe nothando they should want (lit. they should bec with the liking) [assoc cop, inch, subjunc]

lokuya of going [poss Cl. 11]

abanobulili who have a gender or sex [rel Cl. 2]

 banobulili they have a gender or sex [assoc cop, pres]

obufana that/which is the same [rel Cl. 14]

 bufana it is the same, it resembles, it is like [pres,

conjoint]
nalobo with that [assoc adv]
   lobo that [2nd position dem
   Cl. 14]

Ukuhlomula Komphakathi Wasemakhaya

«1»

Kuyinto engangabazeki ukuthi umphakathi ohlala ezindaweni ezisemakhaya awuyinambithisisi neze kahle indaba yeziqiwi ezigcwele eSouth Africa. Imbangela yalokhu wukuthi abantu basuke bezitshela ukuthi ngaleziziqiwi kuhloswe ukuthi baphucwe umhlaba wabo.

«2»

Phambilini iziphathimandla zaleziziqiwi zazenza isimo sibe muncu kakhulu ngoba zaziba nesiqiniseko sokuthi labo ababetholakala bezingela kuleziziqiwi bayaboshwa.

«3»

Uphiko olubhekene nokongiwa kwemvelo esifundazweni saKwaZulu-Natal seluthathe isinyathelo sokwakha ubudlelwane obuhle nomphakathi ohlala eduze kwaleziziqiwi.

«4»

Loluphiko selwakhe izikhungo okuzodayiselwa kuzo izinto ezenziwe ngezandla lwabuye lwatholela nomphakathi indawo yoku-tshala izitshalo eziluhlaza. Lezizinto zidayiselwa izivakashi ezisuke zivakashe kulesisifundazwe. UMaureen Mndaweni osebenza ngaphansi kweKZN Nature Conservation Service wathi loluphiko luphezu komkhankaso wokufundisa umphakathi ngokongiwa kwemvelo ubuye uzitholele nendlela yokungenisa imali.

«5»

"Sesifundise nalabo abelapha ngamakhambi ukuthi bangawatshala kanjani amakhambi esikhundleni sokuthi basebenzise izihlahla. Labo abahlala ezindaweni ezisemakhaya sebengakwazi ukusebenzisa izihlahla abazitshalele zona ekwenzeni imithi yokwelapha."

«6»

Ngesikhathi kunomkhankaso wokutshalwa kwezihlahla, loluphiko lwahlela uhambo lwezinsuku ezinthathu ngenhloso yokuthuthukisa impilo yomphakathi ohlala ezindaweni ezisemakhaya kules-isifundazwe.

«7»

ULungile Biyela waseDukuduku ungomunye wabesimame abangu-50 abahlala emakhaya nosethole ukusizakala njengoba esezidayisela izinto azenzele zona ngezandla zakhe eSiyabonga Crafts Centre. Lesisikhungo singesinye salezo esezakhiwe eNyakatho yesi-fundazwe saKwaZulu-Natal.

«8»

"Yimina engondlayo ekhaya kanti nginabantwana abayisihlanu. Ngalemali engiyithola kulesisikhungo sengiyakwazi ukondla izingane zami kanye nomyeni wami owalahlekelwa wumsebenzi eminyakeni emine edlule."

«9»

Njengamanje abamele ezokuvakasha KwaZulu-Natal sebesungule uhlelo oluzokwenza ukuthi intuthuko yalesisifundazwe yaziwe nakwamanye amazwe nokuthi kugqugquzelwe abantu abahlala emakhaya ukuthi bazibandakanye kwezamabhizinisi noma kwezo-kuvakasha.

«10»

"Sizimisele ngokusiza umphakathi ngokuwufundisa ngokubaluleka kwezikhungo zezamabhizinisi ezingagcina ziwusizile uma udinga ukudayisa imikhiqizo yawo," kusho uRonnie Naidoo oyimenenja emnyangweni wezokuvakasha.

Indaba nezithombe nguLinda Manyoni

Vocabulary

ukuhlomula to give a share (especially the meat of a game animal), rewarding [vn Cl. 15]
wasemakhaya of rural areas [poss Cl. 3]

«1»

engangabazeki that/which is undoubted [rel Cl. 9]
ingangabazeki it is undoubted [pres, rel, neg; < **ayingabazeki**]
-ngabazek-a be doubted [v-neut]
ohlala that/which resides [rel Cl. 3]
uhlala it resides [pres, conjoint]
ezisemakhaya that/which are in rural areas [rel Cl. 10]
zisemakhaya they are in rural areas [loc cop, pres]
awuyinambithisisi it does not understand it fully [pres, neg]
-nambithisis-a understand fully [v-intens]
-nambith-a understand [v.t.]
yeziqiwi of game reserves [poss Cl. 9]

iziqiwi game reserves [n Cl. 8; sg **isiqiwi**]
ezigcwele that/which abound [rel Cl. 8]
zigcwele they abound, they are full [stative]
basuke they just [aux, pres]
bezitshela they tell themselves [pres, partic]
ngaleziziqiwi by, about, concerning these reserves [instr adv phr]
leziziqiwi these reserves [dem phr Cl. 8]
kuhloswe it is intended [past, conjoint]
-hlosw-a be intended, be aimed for [v-pass]
-hlos-a intend, aim at [v.t.]
baphucwe they should be deprived (of), they should have taken away [subjunc]
-phucw-a be deprived of, have taken away; be shaved [v-pass]
-phuc-a shave; deprive (of), take away [v.i. & t.]

«2»

zaleziziqiwi of these reserves [poss Cl. 8]

zazenza they used to make [rem past pres]

zaziba nesiqiniseko they were intent (lit. they bec with determination) [assoc cop, inch, rem past pres]

zaziba they were becoming [copula, rem past pres]

ababetholakala those who were found [rel Cl. 2]

babetholakala they were found [rem past pres]

bezingela they are hunting [pres, partic]

-zingel-a hunt [v.i. & t.]

bayaboshwa they are arrested [pres, disjoint]

«3»

olubhekene na- ... that/which deals with ... [rel Cl. 11]

lubhekene na- ... it deals with ... [past, conjoint]

-bhekene deal with, be facing [< -bhekan- + -i...e]

nokongiwa with conservation [assoc adv]

kwemvelo of nature [poss Cl. 15]

imvelo nature [n Cl. 9]

esifundazweni in the province [loc; < isifundazwe]

seluthathe it has now taken [past, exclusive, conjoint]

sokwakha of building [poss Cl. 7]

ubudlelwane friendship, good relationship [n Cl. 14]

obuhle good [adj Cl. 14]

«4»

loluphiko this branch [dem phr Cl. 11]

selwakhe it has already built [past, exclusive, conjoint]

izikhungo covered stalls [n Cl. 8; sg **isikhungo**]

okuzodayiselwa kuzo where there will be sold [ind rel of plain loc rel, Cl. 17]

kuzodayiselwa they will market in or at (lit. there will be marketed in or at) [fut]

-dayiselw-a be offered for sale to, be marketed to [v-appl-pass]

-dayisel- market to, for, in or at [v-appl]

ezenziwe that/which have been made [rel Cl. 10]

zenziwe they have been made [past, conjoint]

ngezandla by hand (lit. by hands), about hands, with hands [instr adv]

lwabuye and it again [aux, narr]

lwatholela it found for [narr]

yokutshala for or of planting [poss Cl. 9]

ukutshala to plant, to sow [vn Cl. 15]

izitshalo crops [n Cl. 8; sg **isitshalo**]

eziluhlaza green [rel Cl. 8]

-luhlaza green [rel stem]

lezizinto these things [dem phr Cl. 10]

zidayiselwa they are sold to [pres, conjoint]

ezisuke who happen to, who just [rel Cl. 8]

zisuke they happen to, they just [aux]

zivakashe they visit [past, partic, conjoint]

kulesisifundazwe to, from, in this province [loc]

lesisifundazwe this province [dem phr Cl. 7]

u-Maureen [n Cl. 1a]

Mndaweni (surname) [n Cl. 1a]

osebenza who works [rel Cl. 1]

i-KZN Nature Conservation Service (KZN = KwaZulu-Natal) [n Cl. 9a]

luphezu komkhankaso it is in control of the scheme [loc cop, pres]

wokufundisa of teaching [poss Cl. 3]

    ukufundisa to teach, teaching [vn Cl. 15]

ngokongiwa about conservation, about preservation [instr adv]

ubuye and it also [subjunc]

uzitholele it should find for itself [subjunc]

nendlela also a way [assoc adv]

yokungenisa of bringing in [poss Cl. 9]

    ukungenisa to bring or put in, to insert [vn Cl. 15]

    -ngenis-a bring or put in, insert [v-caus]

«5»

sesifundise we have already taught [past, exclusive, conjoint]

abelapha ngamakhambi herbalists (lit. those who treat with medicinal herbs) [rel phr Cl. 2; sg **owelapha ngamakhambi**]

    abelapha those who treat or cure [rel Cl. 2]

    ngamakhambi with medicinal herbs [instr adv]

amakhambi medicinal herbs; herbal decoctions for medicine [n Cl. 6; sg **ikhambi** Cl. 5]

bangawatshala they can plant them [pres, potential]

izihlahla bushes, shrubs [n Cl. 8; sg **isihlahla**]

sebengakwazi they are now able [pres, potential, exclusive]

abazitshalele zona that/which they have planted for themselves [ind rel of plain obj rel, Cl. 2]

    bazitshalele they have planted for themselves [past, conjoint]

    -tshalel-a plant for [v-appl]

ekwenzeni to, from, in the making [loc]

yokwelapha for medical treatment [poss Cl. 4]

«6»

kunomkhankaso there is a scheme [assoc cop, pres]

wokutshalwa for the planting [poss Cl. 3]

kwezihlahla of trees, bushes, shrubs [poss Cl. 15]

lwahlela it arranged [rem past]

uhambo trip, journey, tour [n Cl. 11; < **-hamb-** go, travel; pl **izihambo** Cl. 10a or **izinkambo** Cl. 10; n + h > nk]

lwezinsuku of days [poss Cl. 11]

ezinthathu three [adj Cl. 10; < **ezin-** + **-thathu**; n + th > nt]

yokuthuthukisa of uplifting [poss Cl. 9]

yomphakathi of the community [poss Cl. 9]

«7»

uLungile (female name) [n Cl. 1a]

Biyela (surname) [n Cl. 1a]

waseDukuduku of Dukuduku [poss Cl. 1]

    seDukuduku to, from, in, at Dukuduku (a forest reserve) [loc; < **eDukuduku**]

wabesimame of the women [poss Cl. 1]

abangu-50 50 [rel Cl. 2]

bangu-50 there are fifty of them [ident cop, pres]
u-50 fifty [n Cl. 1a]
nosethole and who has already received [assoc adv]
  osethole who has already received [rel Cl. 1]
  usethole (s)he has already received [past, exclusive, conjoint]
esezidayisela (s)he is already selling for herself [pres, partic, exclusive]
azenzele that/which she or he has made for her- or himself [ind rel of plain obj rel, Cl. 1]
  uzenzele (s)he has made for her- or himself [past, conjoint]
  -z-enzel-a make for oneself, do for oneself [v-refl-appl]
eSiyabonga Crafts Centre at the Siyabonga ... [loc]
iSiyabonga Crafts Centre [n Cl. 9a]
lesisikhungo this stall [dem phr Cl. 7]
singesinye it is one [ident cop, pres]
salezo of those [poss Cl. 7]
  lezo those [2nd position dem Cl. 8]
esezakhiwe that/which have already been built [rel Cl. 8]
  sezakhiwe they have already been built [stative, exclusive]
yesifundazwe of the province [poss Cl. 9]

«8»

engondlayo who am the bread-winner (lit. who raises, who nourishes) [rel 1 p sg]
  ngiyondla I bring up, I rear [pres, disjoint]

-ondl-a nourish, rear, bring up [v.t.]
nginabantwana I have children [assoc cop, pres]
abayisihlanu five [rel Cl. 2]
ngalemali with this money [instr adv]
  lemali this money [dem phr Cl. 9]
engiyithola that/which I get [ind rel of plain obj rel, 1 p sg]
  ngiyithola I get it [pres, conjoint]
kulesisikhungo from this stall [loc]
sengiyakwazi I am now able, I can now [pres, disjoint, exclusive]
ukondla to bring up, to raise, to rear [vn Cl. 15]
zami my [poss Cl. 10]
kanye nomyeni together with my husband [adv phr]
  umyeni husband, bridegroom [n Cl. 1]
owalahlekelwa who lost (long ago) [rel Cl. 1]
  walahlekelwa (s)he lost [rem past]
wumsebenzi by work, by a job [agent adv]

«9»

abamele ezokuvakasha tourism authorities [rel phr Cl. 2]
sebesungule they have already initiated [past, exclusive, conjoint]
oluzokwenza that/which will produce [rel Cl. 11]
  luzokwenza it will produce [fut]
yalesisifundazwe of this province [poss Cl. 9]
yaziwe it is known [past, disjoint]
nakwamanye also in other [assoc adv]

kugqugquzelwe they should be prodded [subjunc]

bazibandakanye they should involve themselves [subjunc]

kwezamabhizinisi in business affairs [loc]

ezamabhizinisi business affairs [poss pron Cl. 10]

zamabhizinisi of businesses [poss Cl. 10]

kwezokuvakasha in tourism affairs [loc]

«10»

sizimisele we are determined or prepared [stative]

ngokusiza in aiding [instr adv]

ngokuwufundisa by teaching it [instr adv]

ukuwufundisa to teach it [vn Cl. 15]

ngokubaluleka about the importance [instr adv]

ukubaluleka importance, to bec important [vn Cl. 15]

kwezikhungo of shelters [poss Cl. 15]

zezamabhizinisi for trade [poss Cl. 8]

ezingagcina that/which could eventually [rel Cl. 8]

zingagcina they could eventually, they could end up [pres, potential]

ziwusizile they have assisted it [past, partic, disjoint]

uRonnie (name) [n Cl. 1a]

Naidoo (surname) [n Cl. 1a] {Indian}

oyimenenja who is a manager [rel Cl. 1]

uyimenenja he is a manager [ident cop, pres]

imenenja manager [n Cl. 9a; pl Cl. 10a] {Eng}

wezokuvakasha of tourism [poss Cl. 3]

Ukukhishwa kwezisu
kuqubule izinkulumo eziningi

«1»
Ukukhishwa kwezisu kusewudaba olusematheni noluyindida kakhulu emphakathini kusukela ekuphasisweni komthetho owawukugunyaza lokho ephalamende lase-South Africa ngoFebruary 1997.

«2»
Yize noma kwakunezinye izinhlangano zezepolitiki kanye namaKhrestu ayengahambisani nalomthetho, iningi labesimame lasishayela elikhulu ihlombe lesosinqumo sikahulumeni.

«3»
Imizamo yokuphikisana nalesisinqumo ayizange iphumelele yize noma labo ababephikisana naso babezama ngawowonke amandla ukubhikisha kuleyomitholampilo eqhuba lomsebenzi.

Ababhikishi babephatha izingqwembe ezazikubeka ngokusobala ukuthi ingane engakazalwa inelungelo lokuphila.

«4»
Lawomaqembu ayehambisana nalesosinqumo asithakasela kakhulu isenzo seNkantolo yoMthethosisekelo kanti ayesho nokusho ukuthi abesimame abahluphekayo bazosizakala ngalomthetho.

«5»
Abahlengikazi bakwezinye izibhedlela nabo babengazibekile neze phansi bezama ngawowonke amandla ukubonisa abesimame ukuthi ukukhipha isisu kuyinto embi kangakanani. Labobahlengikazi bagcina sebenqunyelwe ugwayi katiki batshelwa ukuthi kungenzeka babhekane nengalo yomthetho uma beqhubeka nemizamo yabo yokuvimbela abesimame ababezikhethele bona ngokwabo ukukhipha izisu.

«6»
UWeziwe Thusi oyiBamba leSekela likaNobhala kwi-ANC Women's League KwaZulu-Natal, ungomunye walabo abasethimbeni elibhekene neziphathelene nodaba lokukhishwa kwesisu kulenhlangano kanti waphawula kanjena ngalo: "Ukuphasiswa kwalomthetho kulethe inkululeko enkulu kwabesimame. Baningi asebedlulile emhlabeni ngenxa yokukhipha izisu ezindaweni ezingafanele manje sebengakwenza lokho ngendlela ephephile."

«7»
UWeziwe uphethe naseMnyangweni wezoKwasiza kuloluPhiko lwabesiMame kanti wabeka nokuthi yena nalabo asebenza nabo bavame ukuhlangana neningi labesimame uma kunezinhlelo ezithile eziqondene nalomnyango. "Sesithole ukuthi iningi labesimame liyahambisana nalomthetho. Thina umsebenzi wethu kulenhlangano

owokubanika izeluleko labo abazikhethela ukukhipha izisu sibatshele nokuthi kubaluleke kangakanani ukuba baye emtholampilo
wokuhlelwa kwemindeni."

«8»
Wabeka nokuthi bayawagqugquzela nalawomabandla angahambisani nalesisinqumo ukuba aphumele obala atshele amalunga
awo ngezocansi. "Amanye amabandla akathandi neze ukukhuluma
ngaloludaba. Kuwoṅa luseyinto embi nenyanyekayo kanti-ke thina
sibona kungcono ukuthi abesimame baziswe ngokubaluleka kokuya
ocansini uphephile nokugwema ukukhulelwa okungahlelelwanga
kanye nezifo ezinjenge-HIV."

«9»
Ngokusho kukaSister Nonsikelelo Khuzwayo osemnyangweni
wezokuhlelwa kwemindeni, ukukhishwa kwezisu kuyinto
engakajwayeleki kahle esizweni sama-Afrika. "Intsha isikhombise
ukukuthakasela kakhulu ukukhishwa kwezisu yize noma ngingenazo
izibalo eziqondile.

"Mina ngokwami ngingathi ukukhishwa kwezisu kwanda kakhulu
njengoba sibhekene nesimo sokuntenga komnotho kulelizwe
lakithi."

«10»
NgokukaNonsikelelo, ukukhishwa kwezisu kuzobasiza kakhulu
abesimame abasuke bedlwenguliwe noma abaphethwe yizo ezibeka
impilo yabo engcupheni.

UGertrude Mzizi osophikweni lwabesimame kwi-IFP wabeka ukuthi
inhlangano yabo iyazihlonipha kabi izinkolelo namasiko abantu
abahlukahlukene. "Amalunga ethu anelungelo lokuzikhethela –
ngeke siwatshele ukuthi yikuphi okufanele akwenze."

J. N., Roodepoort

Vocabulary

ukukhishwa kwezisu abortions
(lit. taking out of the stomachs)
[vn phr Cl. 15; sg **ukukhishwa
kwesisu**]
kwezisu of stomachs [poss Cl.
15]
kuqubule it has caused to erupt
[past, conjoint]
-qubul-a cause to erupt; scatter
at full speed, drive off (as birds);

sing loudly in chorus [v.t.]
izinkulumo conversations,
discussions [n Cl. 10; sg
inkulumo; < **-khulum-** speak]

«1»
kusewudaba it is now a serious
matter [ident cop, pres
exclusive]

olusematheni that/which is on everyone's lips (lit. that is in the saliva) [rel Cl. 11]
lusematheni it is in the saliva, it is on the lips [loc cop, pres]
sematheni on the lips (lit. in the saliva) [loc; < **ematheni**]
noluyindida and which is a confusing thing [assoc adv phr]
ekuphasisweni to, from, at, in the passing [loc]
ukuphasiswa to be passed (of a law or student) [vn Cl. 15]
-phasisw-a be passed (of a law or student) [v-caus-pass]
-phasis-a pass (v.t.; a law or student) [v-caus]
-phas-a pass (a test or exam) [v.i. & t.]
komthetho of the law [poss Cl. 15]
owawukugunyaza that/which endorsed it [rel Cl. 3]
wawukugunyaza it endorsed it [rem past pres]
-gunyaz-a force down; endorse, sanction [v.t.]
ePhalamende to, from, in, at Parliament [loc]
iPhalamende Parliament [n Cl. 5] {Eng}

«2»
kwakunezinye there were certain [assoc cop, rem past pres]
zezepolitiki political [poss Cl. 10]
ezepolitiki politics, political matters [poss pron Cl. 10]
amaKhrestu Christians [n Cl. 6; sg **iKhrestu** Cl. 5/**umKhrestu** Cl. 1]
ayengahambisani who did not go along with [rel Cl. 6]
ayengahambisani they did not go along with [rem past pres, neg]

nalomthetho with this law [assoc adv]
lomthetho this law [dem phr Cl. 3]
lasishayela elikhulu ihlombe they greatly applauded it (lit. it beat for it a big shoulder)
lasishayela it, (s)he beat for it/him/her [rem past]
-shayel-a elikhulu ihlombe applaud greatly
-shay-a ihlombe clap rhythmically, applaud [idiom; lit. hit the shoulder]
lesosinqumo that decision [dem phr Cl. 7]
sikahulumeni of the government [poss Cl. 7]

«3»
imizamo attempts, efforts, trials [n Cl. 4; sg **umzamo**; < **-zam-** try, attempt]
yokuphikisana to contest [poss Cl. 4]
ukuphikisana na- ... to contest ..., to argue against ..., to defy ... [vn phr Cl. 15]
lesisinqumo this decision [dem phr Cl. 7]
ayizange it never [aux, past, neg; < **-z-e**]
iphumelele it succeeds [subjunc]
ababephikisana who were contesting or arguing against [rel Cl. 2]
babephikisana they were contesting or arguing against [rem past pres]
naso with it [assoc adv]
babezama they tried, they were trying [rem past pres]
ngawowonke with all [instr adv phr; < **nga-** instr pref + **wo** abs pron Cl. 6 + **wonke** all]

ukubhikisha to protest, to fight against [vn Cl. 15]

kuleyomitholampilo to, from, at, in those clinics [loc]
leyomitholampilo those clinics [dem phr Cl. 4]
imitholampilo clinics [n Cl. 4; sg. **umtholampilo**]

eqhuba that/which continue with, that/which carry on [rel Cl. 4]
iqhuba it continues with, it carries on [pres, conjoint]

ababhikishi demonstrators [n Cl. 2; sg **umbhikishi**; < -bhikish- protest, fight against]

babephatha they held [rem past pres]

izingqwembe demonstrations, protests [n Cl. 10]

ezazikubeka that/which put it [rel Cl. 10]
zazikubeka they put it [rem past pres]

ngokusobala in public, publicly, in the open [instr adv phr]
okusobala that which is public, that which is out in the open [rel Cl. 17]
kusobala it is public, it is in the open [loc cop, pres]

engakazalwa unborn, who has not yet been born [rel Cl. 9]
ingakazalwa it, (s)he has not yet been born [pres, rel, exclusive, neg; < ayikazalwa]

inelungelo it, (s)he has the right [assoc cop, pres]

lokuphila to life, of living [poss Cl. 5]
ukuphila to live, to be alive, to be well, to be healthy [vn Cl. 15]

«4»
lawomaqembu those groups [dem phr Cl. 6]

ayehambisana that/which went along with [rel Cl. 6]
ayehambisana they went along with [rem past pres]
nalesosinqumo with that decision [assoc adv]

asithakasela they welcomed it [rem past]
-thakasel-a be kind to, be genial towards; welcome, laud, praise flatteringly; congratulate [v-appl]
-thakas-a show kindness, be genial; praise [v.i. & t.]

seNkantolo yoMthethosisekelo of the Constitutional Court [poss Cl. 7]
iNkantolo yoMthethosisekelo the Constitutional Court (South African equivalent to the Supreme Court)
yomthethosisekelo of the constitution [poss Cl. 9]
umthethosisekelo constitution (legal foundation) [n Cl. 3; < **umthetho** law + **isisekelo**]
isisekelo foundation stone [n Cl. 7; < -sekel- prop up, support]

ayesho nokusho they even thought [v phr]
ayesho they thought, they said [rem past pres]

abahluphekayo underprivileged, suffering, troubled [rel Cl. 2]
bayahlupheka they suffer, they are troubled, they are afflicted [pres, disjoint]
-hluphek-a suffer, be troubled, be afflicted, be in difficulties [v-neut]

bazosizakala they will be assisted [fut]

ngalomthetho by, through this law [instr adv phr]

«5»

bakwezinye from some [poss Cl. 2]

babengazibekile phansi they had not stopped [lit. they had not put themselves down]
  babengazibekile they had not put themselves [rem past stative, neg]
  ukuzibeka phansi to stop what one is doing (lit. to put oneself down)

bezama they try [pres, partic]
  ukubonisa to show [vn Cl. 15]
  ukukhipha isisu to abort [vn phr Cl. 15]

embi bad, naughty, wicked, ugly [adj Cl. 9]
  em- [adj conc Cl. 9]

kangakanani to what extent?, how much?, to what degree? [adv]
  -ngakanani? how much? [rel stem]

labobahlengikazi those nurses [dem phr Cl. 2]

bagcina they ended up, they eventually [aux, rem past]

sebenqunyelwe ugwayi katiki they were cautioned, given a warning
  -nqunyelw-a ugwayi katiki be cautioned, given a warning (idiom; lit. to be allocated three-pence worth of tobacco or snuff)
  sebenqunyelwe they have already been allocated, assigned [past, exclusive, conjoint]
  ugwayi tobacco, snuff [n Cl. 1a or 3a]
  katiki for three pence, for a tickey (South African word for three pence) [poss Cl. 1 or 3]
  utiki three-penny piece [n Cl. 1a] {S.A. English *tickey*}

batshelwa and they were told [narr]

babhekane they will have to face [subjunc]

nengalo with the arm [assoc adv]
  ingalo arm [n Cl. 9]

yomthetho of the law [poss Cl. 9]

beqhubeka they continue [pres, partic]

nemizamo with attempts [assoc adv]

yokuvimbela (of) to prevent [poss Cl. 4]

ababezikhethele who had made a personal choice [rel Cl. 2]
  babezikhethele they had chosen for themselves, they had made a personal choice [rem past past, disjoint]

ngokwabo on their own, independently, according to them [instr adv]

«6»

uWeziwe (female name) [n Cl. 1a]

Thusi (surname) [n Cl. 1a]

oyibamba who is deputy [rel Cl. 1]
  uyibamba (s)he is a deputy [ident cop, pres]
  ibamba deputy [n Cl. 5; < **-bamb-** undertake]

lesekela of the assistant [poss Cl. 5]
  isekela assistant [n Cl. 5; < **-sekel-** assist, stand in for]

likanobhala of the secretary [poss Cl. 5]

kwi-ANC Women's League in the ANC (African National Congress) Women's League [loc]

walabo of those [poss Cl. 1]

abasethimbeni who are in a group of unmarried girls or women [rel Cl. 2]

197

basethimbeni they are in a group of unmarried girls or women [loc cop, pres]

elibhekene na- ... that/which deals with ... [rel Cl. 5]

libhekene na- ... it, (s)he deals with or faces ... [past, conjoint]

neziphathelene with those (matters) that concern [assoc adv]

nodaba with the serious matter [assoc adv]

lokukhishwa kwezisu of abortions [poss Cl. 11]

kulenhlangano to, from, in this organization [loc]

waphawula (s)he pointed out, indicated [rem past]

kanjena thus, in this way, in this fashion [adv]

kwalomthetho of this law [poss Cl. 15]

kulethe it has brought [past, conjoint]

inkululeko freedom, emancipation [n Cl. 9]

kwabesimame to, from women [loc]

asebedlulile who have already passed [rel Cl. 2]

sebedlulile they have already passed [past, exclusive, disjoint]

ezingafanele that/which are not suitable [rel Cl. 10]

zingafanele they are not suitable [stative, rel, neg; < azifanele]

sebengakwenza they are now able to do it [pres, potential, exclusive]

ephephile that/which is safe [rel Cl. 9]

iphephile (s)he, it is safe or secure; (s)he it has escaped [stative]

«7»

uphethe (s)he handles, is in charge of, runs, manages [stative]

naseMnyangweni also in the Department [assoc adv]

wezoKwazisa of Information [poss Cl. 3]

ezokwazisa information affairs [poss pron Cl. 10]

kuloluphiko to, from, in this section or branch [loc]

lwabesimame of women, women's [poss Cl. 11]

asebenza nabo with whom (s)he works [ind rel of plain adverbial rel, Cl. 1]

neningi with a great number, with a majority [assoc adv]

kunezinhlelo there are arrangements [assoc cop, pres]

eziqondene na- ... that/which concern ... [rel Cl. 10]

ziqondene na- ... they concern ... [stative]

-qondan-a na- ... concern ...

-qondan-a be opposite each other, be in line with each other; understand one another [v-recip]

nalomnyango with this department [assoc adv]

lomnyango this department [dem phr Cl. 3]

sesithole we have now or already found [past, exclusive, conjoint]

liyahambisana it agrees with [pres, disjoint]

wethu our [poss Cl. 3]

owokubanika is one of giving them [ident cop, pres; Ø- cop pref + owokubanika]

owokubanika that of giving them [poss pron Cl. 3]

wokubanika of giving them [poss Cl. 3]

ukubanika to give to them [vn Cl. 15]

abazikhethela who choose for themselves [rel Cl. 2]

bazikhethela they choose for themselves, they just choose [pres, conjoint]

sibatshele we inform them [subjunc]

e m t h o l a m p i l o wokuhlelwa kwemindeni to, from, in, at a family planning clinic [loc phr]

emtholampilo to, from, in, at a clinic [loc]

u m t h o l a m p i l o wokuhlelwa kwemindeni family planning clinic [n phr Cl. 3]

umtholampilo clinic [n Cl. 3; < -thol-a find, get + impilo health]

wokuhlelwa for planning, of being arranged [poss Cl. 3]

ukuhlelwa to be arranged, to be put in order [vn Cl. 15]

-hlelw-a be arranged, be put in order [v-pass]

«8»

bayawagqugquzela they nag them, they try to win them over, they persuade them [pres, disjoint]

nalawomabandla with those groups [assoc adv]

lawomabandla those groups [dem phr Cl. 6]

angahambisani who do not go along (with) [rel Cl. 6]

angahambisani they do not go along with [pres, rel, neg: < akahambisani/awahambisani]

aphumele they should come out (in)to [subjunc]

atshele they should tell [subjunc]

awo their [poss Cl. 6]

akathandi they do not like [pres, neg]

-ka- they [neg SC Cl. 6]

ngaloludaba about this grave matter [instr adv phr]

loludaba this grave matter [dem phr Cl. 11]

kuwona to them [loc]

wona them, it [abs pron Cl. 6]

luseyinto it is still something [ident cop, pres, persistive]

n e n y a n y e k a y o and which is objectionable or deplorable [assoc adv]

enyanyekayo objectionable, deplorable [rel Cl. 9]

iyanyanyeka it is objectionable, deplorable [pres, disjoint]

-nyanyek-a be objectionable, deplorable [v-neut]

-nyany-a have an aversion for, dislike strongly [v.t.]

baziswe they should be informed [subjunc]

-azisw-a be informed, be notified [v-caus-pass]

kokuya ocansini of having sex [poss Cl. 15]

uphephile you being safe [stative, partic]

nokugwema and to avoid [assoc adv]

ukukhulelwa pregnancy, to bec pregnant [vn Cl. 15]

okungahlelelwanga unplanned for [rel Cl. 15]

kungahlelelwanga it was not planned for [past, rel, neg; < akuhlelelwanga]

-hlelelw-a be planned for, be arranged for [v-appl-pass]

-hlelel-a arrange for, plan for, put in order for [v-appl]

ezinjenge-HIV such as HIV (lit. that are like HIV) [rel Cl. 8]

zinjenge-HIV they are like HIV [descr cop, pres]
njenge-HIV such as, like HIV [compar adv]

«9»
Sister (nursing rank) [n Cl. 1a; < **uSister**] {Eng}
Nonsikelelo (female name) [n Cl. 1a]
Khuzwayo (surname) [n Cl. 1a]
osemnyangweni who is in the department [rel Cl. 1]
usemnyangweni (s)he is in the department [loc cop, pres]
wezokuhlelwa kwemindeni of family planning [poss Cl. 3]
e z o k u h l e l w a kwemindeni family planning (matters) [poss pron phr Cl. 10]
ezokuhlelwa of planning matters [poss pron Cl. 10]
zokuhlelwa of planning [poss Cl. 10]
kwemindeni of families [poss Cl. 15]
engakajwayeleki that/which is not yet customary, normal [rel Cl. 9]
ingakajwayeleki it is not yet customary, normal [pres, rel, exclusive, neg; < **ayikajwa-yeleki**]
esizweni in the nation, among the people [loc]
isizwe nation, a people [n Cl. 7]
sama-Afrika of Africans [poss Cl. 7]
isikhombise it has already shown [past, exclusive, conjoint]
ukukuthakasela to welcome it [vn Cl. 15]
ngingenazo izibalo I do not have the figures [assoc cop, pres, partic, neg]
eziqondile accurate [rel Cl. 8]

ziqondile they are straight, direct, accurate [stative]
-qond-a make straight for, go directly towards, head straight for [v.i.]
ngokwami personally, according to me, in my view [instr adv]
ngingathi I believe (that), I am of the opinion (that) [pres, potential, pos]
sibhekene we are facing [stative]
sokuntenga cyclic, volatile [poss Cl. 7]
ukuntenga to sway back and forth, to oscillate, oscillation, volatility [vn Cl. 15]
-nteng-a sway back and forth, oscillate [v.i.]
komnotho of the economy [poss Cl. 15]
kulelizwe in this country [loc]
lelizwe this country [dem phr Cl. 5]
zwe country [< **izwe**]
lakithi of ours [poss Cl. 5]

«10»
ngokukaNonsikelelo according to Nonsikelelo [instr adv phr]
kuzobasiza it will help them [fut]
bedlwenguliwe they have been been raped [past, partic, disjoint]
abaphethwe who suffer [rel Cl. 2]
baphethwe they suffer [stative]
yizo ezibeka impilo yabo engcu-pheni life-threatening situations (lit. from those (things) that put their life in danger) [agent adv phr]
yizo by them [agent adv]
ezibeka that/which place [rel Cl. 10]
zibeka they place [pres, conjoint]
uGertrude (name) [n Cl. 1a]

Mzizi (surname) [n Cl. 1a]
osophikweni who is in the league
or wing or section [rel Cl.
1] **usophikweni** (s)he is in the
league or wing or section [loc
cop, pres] **sophikweni** to, from, on the
wing; to, from, in the section,
league, division [loc;
< **ophikweni**; < **uphiko**]
kwi-IFP to, from, in the IFP [loc]
iyazihlonipha it respects them
[pres, disjoint]
izinkolelo beliefs [n Cl. 10; sg
inkolelo; < **-kholelw-** believe in]
namasiko and customs, and
culture [assoc adv] **amasiko** customs, manners,
practices, culture [n Cl. 6; sg
isiko]
abantu of people [poss Cl. 6]
abahlukahlukene different,
various [rel Cl. 2]

bahlukahlukene they differ,
they vary [stative]
-ahlukahlukan-a differ in
various ways, vary [reduplicated
form of **-ahlukan-**]
ethu our [poss Cl. 6]
anelungelo they have the right
[assoc cop, pres]
lokuzikhethela to choose for
themselves [poss Cl. 7]
siwatshele we should tell them
[subjunc]
yikuphi okufanele akwenze what
to do [ident cop phr]
yikuphi it is which [ident cop,
pres]
kuphi? which? [enum Cl. 17]
ku- [enum conc Cl. 17]
okufanele akwenze that (s)he
should do (it) [ind rel of plain
obj rel, Cl. 17]
akwenze (s)he should do it
[subjunc]

Kugwetshwa umabulalephindelela

«1»

Umabulalephindelela onguSipho Thwala (31) [oneminyaka enga-mashumi amathathu nanye] ugwetshwe ngeledlule iminyaka engu-506 ngawokudlwengula nawokuzama ukubulala, uthi imbangela yokungazikhaleli kwakhe ejajini esegwetshwa kube ngenxa yokunengwa yileli jaji.

«2»

USipho ongowaKwaBester eNanda, ukusho lokhu engxoxweni nolobela UMAFRIKA esegwetshiwe emuva kwezinsuku ezine abelokhu enikwe ithuba lokuveza ilaka lakhe, kodwa elokhu ethi akakakulungeli ukuziphendulela.

«3»

USipho uthe okumnenge ngaleli jaji wukuthi belimbuza sengathi belikhona lapho kuthiwa ubenza khona amacala.

Ukuphela kwaleli cala kusho ukukhululeka kuNksz[10] Busisiwe Mfeka ongudadewabo kaHlengiwe Theresa Mfeka ongomunye odlwe-ngulwe wabulawa nguSipho.

«4»

Ekhuluma nolobela leli phephandaba uNksz Mfeka, uthe selokhu liqalile leli cala ubenovalo lokuthi uzophunyula uSipho, abuye azombulala naye njengoba ubengomunye wofakazi.

Uthi lukhule kakhulu lolu valo emva kwemibiko eke yasakazeka yokuthi uSipho uphumile ejele nokuholele ekushisweni komuzi wakubo kwenswelaboya enguSipho.

«5»

IJaji uNksz Vivianne Niles-Duner ugwebe uSipho ngamacala angu-16 okubulala, angu-10 okudlwengula nawokuzama ukubulala.

Ekhipha isigwebo uJustice Niles-Duner uthe selokhu liqalile ukuthethwa leli cala, akuzange kubonakale nakancane ukuthi uyazisola ngezenzo zakhe uSipho, 'ungumbulali ongenanembeza.'

«6»

Leli jaji lithe ukube isigwebo sentambo sisekhona nakanjani besimfanele lo mbulali.

UDr Micky Pretorius onguchwepheshe wezengqondo nowethule ubufakazi ngocwaningo alwenzile ngoThwala ukuqinisekisile ukuthi awekho amathemba okuguquka kwesimilo kulo mbulali.

---

[10] Incorrectly read as **kaNkosazana.**

«7»
Lo chwepheshe wexwayise ngokuthi uma engaphuma uyophuma eseyingozi ngaphezu kwalokhu.

Uthe ijele ngukuphela kwendawo engazama ukumqoqa ukuthi angenzi ububi obungaphezu kwasebenzile.

Ummeli kaSipho, uMnuz Kenneth Samuel, uthe uSipho uyazisola ngezenzo zakhe ngoba encwadini okuthiwa uyibhalele umphakathi esejele, kukhona lapho esho khona ukuthi uyaxolisa nokuthi uyazisola ngezenzo zakhe.

«8»
Ijaji lithe isiboshwa esinguSipho siyiphikile leyo ncwadi, sathi besitshelwe ngamaphoyisa ukuthi asithini, ngakho-ke lokho ukuthatha ngokuthi bekungaphumi kuye.

Ijaji lithe ngesigwebo elisikhiphile liqonde ukuthi lo mbulali ahlale impilo yakhe yonke ejele.

Ebuzwa ngUMAFRIKA umboshwa ukuthi uthini ngesigwebo asitholile uthe asimfanele ngoba akenzanga lutho.

«9»
Ebuzwa ukuthi kungani engazicelelanga ukwehliselwa isigwebo ejajini, uthe akezwani nejaji ngoba ngesikhathi limbuza imibuzo limtshela nangobufakazi obukhona walibuza ukuthi lambona yini ekwenza lokhu akutshele inkantolo ukuthi wakwenza.

Ngu: Philisiwe Mjoli

Vocabulary

kugwetshwa judgement is given, sentence is passed [pres, conjoint]
-gwetshw-a be decided (of a court case), be passed of judgment, be sentenced [v-pass]
-gweb-a pass judgment, decide a court case, sentence [v.t.]
umabulalephindelela serial killer [n Cl. 1a]

«1»
onguSipho namely, Sipho (lit. who is Sipho) [rel Cl. 1]

unguSipho he is Sipho [ident cop, pres]
Thwala (surname) [n Cl. 1a]
ugwetshwe (s)he was sentenced [past, conjoint]
ngeledlule yesterday [instr adv]
eledlule that (day) that/which has passed [rel Cl. 5]
ledlule it has passed [past, disjoint]
engu-506 506 [rel Cl. 4]
u-506 [n Cl. 1a]
ngawokudlwengula for those (crimes) of rape [instr adv]

awokudlwengula those of rape [poss pron Cl. 6; agrees with **amacala** crimes, offences] **aw-** [pronominalizer (forms pronouns from possessives); found before vowels] **okudlwengula** of rape [poss Cl. 6]

nawokuzama ukubulala and of attempted murder [assoc adv phr] **awokuzama ukubulala** those of attempted murder [poss pron phr] **okuzama ukubulala** of attempted murder [poss phr Cl. 6] **ukuzama** to attempt, to try [vn Cl. 15] **ukubulala** to kill, to murder [vn Cl. 15]

yokungazikhaleli of not entering a plea on his own behalf [poss Cl. 9] **ukungazikhaleli** not pleading for oneself [vn Cl. 15, neg] **-khalel-a** plead for [v-appl]

ejajini to, from, at the judge [loc] **ijaji** judge [n Cl. 5] {Eng}

esegwetshwa as (s)he is ('was' in this context) being sentenced [pres, partic, exclusive]

kube it was [copula, recent past, conjoint]

ukunengwa to be offended, annoyed, disgusted [vn Cl. 15] **-nengw-a** be disgusted, offended [v-pass] **-neng-a** disgust, nauseate, offend [v.t.]

yileli by this [agent adv]

jaji [< **ijaji**]

«2»

ongowaKwaBester who is from

Bester [rel Cl. 1] **ungowaKwaBester** he is one from Bester's place [ident cop, pres] **owaKwaBester** one from Bester's place [poss pron Cl. 1]

eNanda in Inanda [loc] **iNanda** (place) [n Cl. 5]

ukusho he said this [past, conjoint]

engxoxweni in an interview, in a conversation [loc; < **ingxoxo**] **ingxoxo** conversation, chat, interview; essay [n Cl. 9; < -**xox**-; **n**- + **x** > **ngx**] -**xox-a** converse, chat; narrate [v.i. & t.]

nolobela with the correspondent for (lit.. with the one who writes for) [assoc adv phr] **olobela** ... the correspondent for ... [rel Cl. 1] **ulobela** (s)he writes for [pres, conjoint] -**lobel-a** write for, to [v-appl] -**lob-a** write [v.t.]

UMAFRIKA African (here the name of a newspaper) [n Cl. 1]

esegwetshiwe after (s)he had been sentenced [stative, partic, exclusive]

ezine four [adj Cl. 10]

abelokhu that (s)he was constantly [ind rel of plain loc rel] **ubelokhu** (s)he was constantly, always, continually [aux, past pres]

enikwe (s)he has been given [past, partic, conjoint]

lokuveza of bringing out [poss Cl. 5]

ilaka rage [n Cl. 5; **ulaka** Cl. 11 is more usual]

elokhu (s)he kept on [aux, pres, partic]

akakakulungeli (s)he is not yet

ready for it [pres, exclusive, neg]
-lungel-a be ready for, be right for [v-appl]
ukuziphendulela to defend oneself [vn Cl. 15]
-phendulel-a defend (as in a court of law) [v-appl]

«3»
okumnenge what disgusted him [rel Cl. 17]
kumnenge it disgusted him [past, conjoint]
ngaleli about this [instr adv]
belimbuza (s)he questioned him [past pres]
belikhona (s)he was there, he was present [loc cop, past pres; may also introduce an exist cop]
lapho kuthiwa ubenza khona amacala where it was said he had committed the crimes [ind rel of plain loc rel]
ubenza he was committing, doing, making [past pres]
ukuphela the end, the conclusion, to come to an end [vn Cl. 15]
kwaleli of this [poss Cl. 15]
kuNksz to Miss or Ms [loc]
Busisiwe (female name) [n Cl. 1a]
ongudadewabo who is his or her or their sister [rel Cl. 1]
ungudadewabo she is his, her, their sister [ident cop, pres]
udadewabo his, her, their sister [n Cl. 1a; < **udade** sister + **wabo** their]
kaHlengiwe of Hlengiwe [poss Cl. 1]
Hlengiwe (female name) [n Cl. 1a]
odlwengulwe who was raped [rel Cl. 1]
udlwengulwe (s)he was raped [past, conjoint]

wabulawa and (s)he was killed [narr]
nguSipho by Sipho [agent adv]

«4»
ekhuluma ((s)he) speaking [pres, partic]
liqalile it began [past, disjoint]
cala [< **icala** court case]
ubenovalo (s)he was afraid (lit. (s)he had fear) [assoc cop, past pres]
uzophunyula (s)he will get loose, escape; (s)he will be acquitted [fut]
-phunyul-a get loose, escape; let loose, allow to escape [v.i. & t.]
abuye and (s)he would come back [subjunc]
azombulala and come and kill her or him [subjunc, venitive]
ubengomunye (s)he was one [ident cop, past pres]
wofakazi of the witnesses [poss Cl. 1]
ofakazi witnesses [n Cl. 2b; sg **ufakazi**]
lukhule it grew [past, conjoint]
valo fear [< **uvalo**]
imibiko reports, announcements [n Cl. 4; sg **umbiko**; < **-bik-a** report]
eke that/which once [rel Cl. 4]
ike they once were [aux, past, conjoint]
yasakazeka they got broadcast [narr]
-sakazek-a get broadcast [v-neut]
uphumile (s)he has got out [past, disjoint]
nokuholele and who was implicated in or responsible for [assoc adv]

ukuholele (s)he was implicated in or responsible for [past, conjoint]
-holel-a drag towards; lead to; be responsible for, cause [v-appl]
ekushisweni in the burning [loc]
ukushiswa to be burnt down, to get burnt [vn Cl. 15]
-shisw-a be burnt down, get burnt [v-caus-pass]
komuzi of the village, household, or homestead [poss Cl. 15]
kwenswelaboya by (lit. of) the murderer or evil person [poss Cl. 15, agreeing with **ukushiswa**]
enguSipho who is Sipho [ident cop, pres, partic]

«5»
Vivianne Niles-Duner (name) [n Cl. 1a]
ugwebe (s)he sentenced, passed judgment [past, conjoint]
ngamacala for offences [instr adv]
angu-16 16 (lit. that/which are sixteen) [rel Cl. 6]
u-16 sixteen [n Cl. 1a]
okubulala of murder [poss Cl. 6]
angu-10 10 (that/which are ten) [rel Cl. 6]
ekhipha while (s)he was passing (lit. bringing out) [pres, partic]
isigwebo sentence, judgment [n Cl. 7]
uJustice Justice (judicial title) [n Cl. 1a] {Eng}
Niles-Duner (surname) [n Cl. 1a]
ukuthethwa to be heard (of a court case) [vn Cl. 15]
-thethw-a be tried (in court), be presided over (in court); be found not guilty, have found in one's favor [v-pass]

-theth-a try a court case, preside over a court; find not guilty, give judgment in favor of; scold, nag [v.t.]
kubonakale it is apparent, it should be visible [subjunc]
uyazisola (s)he regrets, (s)he is contrite [pres, disjoint]
ngezenzo about actions, deeds [instr adv]
ungumbulali you are a killer [ident cop, pres]
umbulali killer, murderer [n Cl. 1a]
ongenanembeza who has no conscience [rel Cl. 1]
ungenanembeza (s)he has no conscience [assoc cop, rel, neg; < akananembeza]
unembeza conscience [n Cl. 1a]

«6»
lithe (s)he said [past, conjoint]
ukube if [conj; more usual var **ukuba**]
isigwebo sentambo death sentence (lit. sentence of the rope) [n phr Cl. 7]
sentambo of a rope, of hanging [poss Cl. 7]
intambo rope, string, cord [n Cl. 9; < in- + -thambo; n + th > nt]
sisekhona it is still there, it still exists [loc cop, pres, partic, persistive; may also introduce an exist cop]
nakanjani most decidedly, no matter what [adv]
besimfanele it would have fitted him or her, would have been appropriate for him or her [past past, disjoint]
mbulali [< umbulali]
Micky [n Cl. 1a]

Pretorius (surname) [n Cl. 1a]
{Afr}
onguchwepheshe wezengqondo
who is a psychiatrist [rel phr
Cl. 1]
onguchwepheshe who is an
expert, who is a specialist [rel
Cl. 1]
**unguchwepheshe weze-
ngqondo** (s)he is a psychiatrist
[ident cop phr, pres]
unguchwepheshe (s)he is an
expert [ident cop, pres]
uchwepheshe wezengqondo
psychiatrist or psychologist [n
phr Cl. 1]
wezengqondo of psychological
matters [poss Cl. 1]
ezengqondo matters of the
mind, psychology, psychiatry
[poss pron Cl. 10]
zengqondo of the mind [poss
Cl. 10]
nowethule and who placed before
or laid down [assoc adv phr]
owethule who placed before or
laid down [rel Cl. 1]
wethule (s)he placed before or
laid down [past, conjoint]
ngocwaningo about investigation
[instr adv]
ucwaningo investigation,
research [n Cl. 11; < **-cwaning-**
conduct research (on), investigate [v.i. & t.]
alwenzile that/which (s)he has
carried out [ind rel of plain obj
rel, Cl. 1]
ulwenzile (s)he has done it
[past, disjoint]
-lw- it [OC Cl. 11]
ngoThwala in connection with
Thwala [instr adv]
ukuqinisekisile (s)he showed it
convincingly, (s)he proved it

[past, disjoint]
-qinisekis-a prove true, show
convincingly [v-caus-neut-caus]
awekho amathemba there is no
hope (lit. there are no hopes)
[exist cop, pres, neg]
awekho they are not there, they
are absent [loc cop; may also
introduce a neg exist cop]
-we- they [SC Cl. 6 found in
negative copulatives before
kho]
okuguquka of changing [poss
Cl. 6]
ukuguquka to change (v.i.) [vn
Cl. 15]
kwesimilo of nature, of character
[poss Cl. 15]
isimilo nature, character,
characteristic [n Cl. 7]

«7»
wexwayise (s)he warned [past,
conjoint
engaphuma (s)he were to come
out [pres, potential, partic]
uyophuma (s)he would come out
[rem fut]
eseyingozi (s)he still being a
danger [ident cop, pres, partic,
persistive]
ngaphezu kwalokhu more than
before (i.e. more than that)
[instr adv phr]
ngukuphela kwendawo is the
only place (it is the coming to
an end of a place) [ident cop
phr, pres]
engazama that/which could try
[rel Cl. 9]
ingazama it, (s)he could try
[pres, potential]
ukumqoqa to reform him [vn Cl.
15]
-qoq-a tidy up, clear up, build

up; reform [v.t.]

angenzi (s)he should not perpetrate or do [subjunc, neg]

obungaphezu in addition to, more than [rel Cl. 14]

bungaphezu it is in addition (lit. it is above) [loc cop, pres]

kwasebenzile to what (s)he has committed (lit. worked) [loc]

asebenzile that which (s)he has committed [ind rel of plain obj rel, Cl. 1]

usebenzile (s)he has worked [past, disjoint]

kaSipho Sipho's [poss Cl. 1]

Kenneth Samuel (name) [n phr Cl. 1a]

okuthiwa uyibhalele that/which it is said (s)he wrote to [ind rel of plain obj rel, Cl. 17]

okuthiwa that/which it is said [rel Cl. 17]

uyibhalele (s)he wrote it to [past, conjoint]

esejele while (s)he is in jail [loc cop, pres, partic]

kukhona lapho esho khona there is a place where he states [exist cop, pres]

lapho esho khona where he states [ind rel of plain loc rel]

«8»

esinguSipho who is Sipho [rel Cl. 7]

siyiphikile (s)he has repudiated or denied it [past, disjoint]

ncwadi letter, book [< **incwadi**]

sathi and said [narr]

besitshelwe (s)he had been told [past past, conjoint]

asithini what (s)he should say (lit. let him/her say what) [subjunc; a- let + -si- him/her [SC] + -th-i- say + -ni what]

ukuthatha he takes it [pres, conjoint]

bekungaphumi it was not coming from [past pres, neg]

kuye to, from, at, on him or her [loc]

ngesigwebo about the sentence [instr adv]

elisikhiphile that/which (s)he had delivered (lit. brought out) [ind rel of plain obj rel, Cl. 5]

lisikhiphile (s)he had brought it out, withdrawn it [past, disjoint]

liqonde (s)he determined [past, conjoint]

-qond-a make up one's mind, determine that, decide upon [v.t.]

ahlale (s)he should stay [subjunc]

ebuzwa ((s)he) being asked [pres, partic]

ngUMAFRIKA by *UMAFRIKA* (the newspaper) [agent adv]

umboshwa prisoner [n Cl. 1; **isiboshwa** is more usual]

uthini what (s)he thinks

asitholile that/which (s)he got [ind rel of plain obj rel, Cl. 1]

usitholile (s)he got it, (s)he acquired it, (s)he obtained it [past, disjoint]

asimfanele it is unfair to him/her, it is not right for him/her [stative]

akenzanga (s)he has not done [past, neg]

-k- (s)he [SC Cl. 1]

«9»

kungani? why? [conj; followed by the participial]

engazicelelanga ukwehliselwa isigwebo (s)he did not plead for a reduced sentence

engazicelelanga (s)he did not plead for her- or himself [past,

partic, neg]
-celel-a plead for, request for [v-appl]
ukwehliselwa reduction [vn Cl. 15]
-ehliselw-a have reduced for one, have lowered for one [v-caus-appl-pass]
-ehlisel-a reduce or lower for [v-caus-appl]
akezwani (s)he does not agree, is not "on the same wavelength"
nejaji with the judge [assoc adv]
limbuza (s)he asks him [pres, partic]
limtshela (s)he telling him [pres, partic]
nangobufakazi also about the evidence [assoc adv]

ngobufakazi about the evidence [instr adv]
obukhona that/which there was [rel Cl. 14]
bukhona there is [exist cop, pres]
walibuza he (the prisoner) asked her (the judge) [rem past]
lambona (s)he saw him or her [rem past]
ekwenza (s)he doing it [pres, partic]
akutshele that which (s)he told [ind rel of plain obj rel, Cl. 1]
ukutshele (s)he told it [past, conjoint]
wakwenza (s)he did it [rem past]
Philisiwe (female name) [n Cl. 1a]
Mjoli (surname) [n Cl. 1a]

Umvuzo wokusebenza ngokuzikhandla

«1»
U-Anton Madlala wayeyimfolomane kanti kwathi uma lowomsebenzi umphelela wakhetha ukugxila kwezolimo. Manje usengumlimi omnyama wokuqala KwaZulu-Natal onepulazi lama-strawberry.

«2»
Umhlaba ka-Anton Madlala ungama-hectare angu-0,75 kanti ubiyelwe ngothango olusiza ngokunqanda izinkomo ukuba zingangeni kuwo. Uma ebheka ubuhle besivande sakhe ufikelwa wokukhulu ukuziqhenya. Kulesisivande kutshalwe ama-strawberry aconsisa amathe uma uwabheka.

«3»
"Maningi ama-supermarket nezindawo ezithengisa ngezitshalo eziluhlaza nezithelo ezifuna lama-strawberry," kusho yena ngokuziqhenya.

Ngo-1985 u-Anton waphelelwa wumsebenzi emva kokungaboni ngaso linye nabaphathi baleyonkampani ayeyisebenzela. Lendoda enabantwana abane yagcina isisebenza njengomeluleki epulazini lama-strawberry okwakungelikaGareth Olivier.

«4»
Ngokuhamba kwesikhathi, wakhushulelwa esikhundleni sokuba yimenenja nokuyisikhundla esasidinga ukuba aphathe abasebenzi abangu-150. "Ngangingazi lutho ngezolimo ngesikhathi ngisaqala lomsebenzi. Kuningi engagcina ngikufundile kangangoba manje sengikuthokozela kakhulu ukuwenza," kusho u-Anton.

Kuthe lapho sekuphele iminyaka eyishumi ekulomsebenzi, wawushiya phansi emva kwengxabano eyayiphakathi kwakhe nomqashi neyayiphathelene nezamaholo.

«5»
Ngo-1996, u-Anton waqoka ukuzisungulela ibhizinisi lakhe lezolimo ngoba wayesenolwazi olunzulu ngalo. Wasebenzisa umhlaba okwakungokamfowabo nowawungasetshenziswa ngalesosikhathi. Imali ayeyisebenzisa wayeyiboleke kubafowabo (uLeonard noHenry) kanti ngaleyomali wathenga izithombo ze-strawberry ezimbalwa.

Ngaphandle kosizo lwabafowabo, u-Anton wabuye wathola nemali yomshwalense wakhe kanye no-R20 000 ayewuboleke KwaZulu Finance and Investment Corporation (KFC).

«6»

Lensizwa ibuye ithole nosizo kwabakwa-Agrilek okuyibona abasiza ngokunika abalimi izeluleko. "Abakwa-Agrilek bangifakela i-petrol pump esebenza ngogesi nesingiphungulele umthwalo omkhulu njengoba ngenza lomsebenzi," kusho uMnuz Madlala.

«7»

"Sizimisele ngokuthi abantu abamnyama babonele ku-Anton bahlukane nokukhothama ko-'basi' emapulazini. Kufanele babe nolwazi lokuthi bangazimela ngokwabo kwezolimo," kusho uNhlanhla Dlamini wakwa-Agrilek. UJulius Zondi onguzakwabo naye waphawula kanjena ngaloludaba: "Ezolimo zibalulekile ngoba isizwe sonke sithembele enhlabathini ukuze siphile ngakhoke sithanda ukugqugquzela abamnyama ukuba babe ngabalimi."

«8»

"Noma ngubani ozimisele ngokuvuna izithelo zempumelelo kufanele ahlwayele imbewu efanele ngokusebenza ngokuzikhandla," kusho u-Anton.

"Isivuno sami sokuqala saba sihle kakhulu kodwa ngahlangabezana nezingqinamba ngesikhathi sengifuna ukudayisa umkhiqizo wami ngoba babebaningi abantu esasincintisana nabo. Into eyangenza ngaphumelela wukuthi izithelo zami zaziyikhwalithi," kuqhuba u-Anton.

«9»

Emva kokuba eseyibonile impumelelo yesivuno sakhe sokuqala, u-Anton wathutha endaweni kamfowabo waya kulelipulazi alisebenzisa njengamanje alibiza ngokuthi yi-ALHEBROS neliqanjwe ngeziqalo zamagama abafowabo nelakhe. "Ngabe angikho kulelizinga engikulo manje ukuba akungenxa yabo," kugcizelela yena.

«10»

Wasikhombisa nobuhlakani bakhe ngesikhathi esesichazela ngesizathu esaba yimbangela yokuthi akhethe ukutshala ama-strawberry. "Kulula kabi ukuba ngumlimi otshale ummbila namazambane futhi kuba lukhuni ukudayisa lezozinto ngoba baningi abalimi abazikhiqizayo," kuchaza yena.

Wabeka nokuthi inzuzo ayithola ngokukhiqiza lesisithelo yinkulu kakhulu ngoba bambalwa abalimi abasitshalile. "Njengamanje ngiphezu kwemizamo yokutshala nama-raspberry," kusho u-Anton.

«11»

Izithelo zempumelelo zagqama kakhulu ngesikhathi emenywa ukuba ayodlulisela ulwazi ayeselutholile kubalimi abamnyama aba-beneminyaka engu-13 belime ama-strawberry kodwa bengayiboni impumelelo. U-Anton usenamasheya angu-50% awafake kulabobalimi abasiza kanti nabo sebethole ukwaziwa ezindaweni eziningi ezakhele lesisifundazwe ngenxa yosizo lwakhe.

«12»
Impumelelo ka-Anton iyamangaza kakhulu ngoba nesimo sezulu eMakatini, okuyindawo enepulazi lakhe, asihambisani neze nalesisithelo asitshalile. "Njengamanje sengixhume ama-tunnel okuyiwona azongisiza ngokuvikela izitshalo zami uma kune-sithwathwa," kuchaza yena.

«13»
Lomlimi ongavilaphanga unesexwayiso athanda ukusidlulisela kubantu abakhonze ezolimo. "Uma ungahlomile ngolwazi olufanele kufana nokuthi uyazigangela nje uma uqhuba lomsebenzi," kwexwayisa yena. Wagcizelela nokuthi abantu abafisa ukuba ngabalimi kufanele baqale ngokuthola izeluleko nolwazi olunzulu ngaphambi kokuthi bangene kwezolimo.

«14»
Uzimisele ngokuba wusizo kunoma ngubani odinga izeluleko ngoba naye uyalwazi usizi aqala kulona ngaphambi kokuba adlondlobale ngaloluhlobo.

Uma echaza ngezifiso zakhe, uthi angathokoza kakhulu uma ethola ipulazi elithe xaxa kunaleli alisebenzisa njengamanje. Yize noma impumelelo yakhe imenze waqasha abantu abangu-25, umfokaMadlala ukholwa wukuthi ipulazi elikhulu lingamenza akwazi ukuvula amanye amathuba omsebenzi.

"Lokho kunganginika nethuba lokutshala ezinye izitshalo uma sesidlulile isikhathi sokutshalwa kwama-strawberry," kuphetha yena.

Vocabulary

umvuzo reward [n Cl. 3; < **-vuz-** reward]

wokusebenza of work ing [poss Cl. 3]

ngokuzikhandla without respite, without let-up (lit. by exhausting oneself) [instr adv] **-khandl-a** exhaust, tire out, fatigue, weary [v.t.]

«1»
u-Anton (name) [n Cl. 1a]
Madlala (surname) [n Cl. 1a]
wayeyimfolomane he was a foreman [ident cop, rem past pres]

imfolomane foreman [n Cl. 9] {Eng *foreman* or Afr *voorman*}

umphelela it came to an end for him or her (i.e. (s)he lost his or her job) [pres, partic] **-phelel-a** come to and end for [v-appl]

wakhetha (s)he chose [rem past]

ukugxila to stand firm, to be steadfast [vn Cl. 15]

kwezolimo in agriculture, in farming [loc]

ezolimo agriculture, farming [poss pron Cl. 10]

ulimo farming, cultivation [n Cl. 11; < -lim- cultivate, plough]

usengumlimi (s)he is now a farmer [ident cop, pres, exclusive]

umlimi farmer, cultivator, gardener [n Cl. 1]

onepulazi who has a farm [rel Cl. 1]

unepulazi (s)he has a farm [assoc cop, pres]

ipulazi farm [n Cl. 5] {Afr *plaas*}

lama-strawberry of strawberries [poss Cl. 5]

ama-strawberry strawberries [n Cl. 6; sg **i-strawberry** Cl. 7; **is-** is taken as the Cl. 7 NP]

«2»

ka-Anton Anton's [poss Cl. 3]

ungama-hectare it is hectares [ident cop, pres]

ama-hectare hectares [n Cl. 6; sg **i-hectare** Cl. 9a]

angu-0,75 that/which are 0.75 [rel Cl. 6]

angu-0,75 they are 0.75 [ident cop]

u-0,75 [n Cl. 1a]

ubiyelwe it is fenced [past, conjoint]

-biyelw-a be fenced, be protected by enclosure [v-appl-pass]

-biyel-a fence round, enclose in a fence; construct a fence against [v-appl]

-biy-a make a fence, put up a palisade; ward off a blow [v.i.]

ngothango by a fence [instr adv]

olusiza that/which helps [rel Cl. 11]

lusiza it helps [pres, conjoint]

ngokunqanda by preventing [instr adv]

zingangeni they should not enter [subjunc, neg]

kuwo to, from, at, in(to), on, through it [loc]

ebheka (s)he looks [pres, partic]

besivande of a garden plot [poss Cl. 14]

isivande garden plot [n Cl. 7]

ufikelwa (s)he experiences (lit. (s)he is arrived for) [pres, conjoint]

wokukhulu by a big one [ident cop, pres]

ukuziqhenya pride, to be proud [vn Cl. 15]

kulesisivande in this garden plot [loc]

lesisivande this garden plot [dem phr Cl. 7]

kutshalwe there has or have been planted [past, conjoint]

aconsisa amathe mouth-watering (lit. that causes saliva to drip) [rel Cl. 6]

-consis-a cause to drip, let fall a drop of liquid [v-caus]

-cons-a fall (of a drop of liquid), drip, leak [v.i.]

uwabheka you look at them [pres, partic]

«3»

maningi there are many [descr cop; < **amaningi** adj]

ama-supermarket supermarkets [n Cl. 6; sg **i-supermarket** Cl. 9a]

nezindawo and places [assoc adv]

ezithengisa that/which sell, that/which trade in [rel Cl. 10]

zithengisa they sell, they trade

in [pres, conjoint]

ngezitshalo with, by vegetables [instr adv]

   izitshalo vegetables [n Cl. 8; neutral; < **-tshal-** plant, sow]

nezithelo and fruit [assoc adv]

   izithelo fruit(s) [n Cl. 8]

ezifuna that/which want or require [rel Cl. 10]

   zifuna they want, they require [pres, conjoint]

lama-strawberry these strawberries [dem phr Cl. 6]

   la these [1st position dem Cl. 6]

   ma-strawberry [< **ama-strawberry**]

ngokuziqhenya with pride [instr adv]

ngo-1985 in 1985 [instr adv]

waphelelwa wumsebenzi his or her job came to an end (lit. (s)he was finished for by job)

   waphelelwa (s)he lost [rem past]

   -phelelw-a have come to an end, lose [v-appl-pass]

emva kokungaboni ngaso linye na- ... after not having seen eye to eye with ... (lit. after not seeing with one eye with)

ngaso linye with one eye [instr adv phr]

   so linye one eye [n phr Cl. 5]

   so eye [< **iso**; pl. **amehlo** (var **amaso**); the initial vowel is elided because of the following enumerative]

   linye one [enum Cl. 5]

   li- [enum conc Cl. 5]

baleyonkampani of that company [poss Cl. 2]

   leyonkampani that company [dem phr Cl. 9]

ayeyisebenzela that/which (s)he was working for [ind rel of

plain plain obj rel, Cl. 1; < **a-** rel marker + **-Ø:-** rem past marker + **-ye-** SC + **-yi-** OC + **-sebenzela**]

   wayeyisebenzela (s)he was working for it [rem past pres]

lendoda this man [dem phr Cl. 9]

enabantwana who has children [rel Cl. 9]

   inabantwana (s)he has children, it has young [assoc cop, pres]

isisebenza (s)he now, then or already works [pres exclusive; < **i-** SC + **-s-** exclusive marker + **-i-** SC + **-sebenza**]

njengomeluleki as advisor, as consultant [compar adv]

   umeluleki advisor, counsellor, consultant [n Cl. 1; < **-elulek-** advise, counsel]

epulazini to, from, at, on a farm [loc]

okwakungelikaGareth Olivier that/which belonged to Gareth Olivier (lit. which was that of Gareth Olivier) [rel Cl. 17]

   kwakungelikaGareth Olivier it was that, or it used to be that of Gareth Olivier [ident cop, rem past pres]

   elikaGareth Olivier that of Gareth Olivier [poss pron Cl. 5]

   uGareth Olivier (name) [n phr Cl. 1a]

«4»

wakhushulelwa (s)he was promoted to [rem past]

   -khushulelw-a be promoted to; be raised to [v-appl-pass; **-khuphulel-** + **-w-**; ph ... -w- > sh ... -w-]

   -khuphulel-a promote to, raise to, expose to [v-appl]

-**khuphul-a** promote; raise, hoist; expose [v.t.]

nokuyisikhundla and that is (was) a position [assoc adv phr]

okuyisikhundla that is a position [rel Cl. 17]

kuyisikhundla it is a position [ident cop, pres]

esasidinga that/which required [rel Cl. 7]

sasidinga it, (s)he required or needed [rem past pres]

aphathe (s)he should manage [subjunc]

abasebenzi workers, laborers [n Cl. 2; sg **umsebenzi**; < **-sebenz-** work]

abangu-150 150 [rel Cl. 2]

u-150 [n Cl. 1a]

ngezolimo about agriculture [instr adv phr]

ngisaqala I am still beginning [pres, partic, persistive]

kuningi there is a lot, there is much, there is a great deal [descr cop, pres]

engagcina ngikufundile that/which I had learnt in the end [ind rel of plain obj rel, 1 p sg]

engagcina that/which I in the end (or eventually) [rel 1 p sg]

ngagcina I eventually, I finally, I ended up [aux, rem past]

ngikufundile I having learnt it [past, partic, disjoint]

sengikuthokozela I am now happy about it [pres, exclusive]

ukuwenza to do it, doing it [vn Cl. 15]

sekuphele there ended [past, partic, exclusive, conjoint]

ekulomsebenzi (s)he being in that job [loc cop, pres, partic]

wawushiya phansi (s)he threw it in (lit. (s)he left it down)

wawushiya (s)he left it (behind) [rem past]

kwengxabano of the quarrel [poss Cl. 17]

ingxabano quarrel, dispute [n Cl. 9; < **-xaban-** quarrel; **n + x > ngx**]

eyayiphakathi kwakhe that/which was between him or her [rel Cl. 9]

yayiphakathi it was between, inside, in the middle [loc cop, rem past pres]

nomqashi and the employer [assoc adv]

umqashi employer [n Cl. 1]

neyayiphathelene and which concerned [assoc adv]

eyayiphathelene that/which concerned [rel Cl. 9]

yayiphathelene it (the argument) concerned [rem past stative]

nezamaholo with salary matters [assoc adv]

ezamaholo salary or wage matters [poss pron Cl. 10]

zamaholo of salaries, wages [poss Cl. 10]

«5»

waqoka (s)he decided [rem past]

-**qok-a** decide, choose [v.t.]

ukuzisungulela to set up for himself [vn Cl. 15]

-**sungulel-a** set up for, establish for, found for, initiate for [v-appl]

lezolimo agricultural [poss Cl. 5]

wayesenolwazi (s)he already (or then) had the knowledge [assoc cop, rem past, exclusive]

olunzulu deep, profound [rel Cl. 11]

-**nzulu** deep, profound [rel

stem]

wasebenzisa (s)he used [rem past or narr]

okwakungokamfowabo that/which belonged to his or her brother [rel Cl. 17]

  kwakungokamfowabo it was that of his or her brother [ident cop, rem past pres]

  okamfowabo that of his or her brother [poss pron Cl. 3]

  kamfowabo of his or her brother [poss Cl. 3]

  mfowabo his, her, their brother [< umfowabo]

nowawungasetshenziswa and which was not being utilized [assoc adv phr]

  owawungasetshenziswa one that was not being utilized [rel Cl. 3]

  wawungasetshenziswa it was not being utilized [rem past pres]

ayeyisebenzisa that/which (s)he used [ind rel of plain obj rel, Cl. 1]

  wayeyisebenzisa (s)he was using it [rem past pres]

wayeyiboleke (s)he had borrowed it (Cl. 9) [rem past past, conjoint]

  -bolek- borrow, lend, loan [v.t.; **-bolek-a** + personal noun = lend to; **-bolek-a** + loc pref + personal noun = borrow from]

kubafowabo from his or her brothers [loc]

uLeonard (name) [n Cl. 1a]

noHenry and Henry [assoc adv]

  uHenry (name) [n Cl. 1a]

ngaleyomali with that money [instr adv phr]

  leyomali that money [dem phr Cl. 9]

wathenga (s)he bought [rem past]

izithombo seedlings [n Cl. 8]

ze-strawberry of strawberry [poss Cl. 8]

ezimbalwa a few [rel Cl. 8]

ngaphandle kosizo without the assistance [instr adv phr]

lwabafowabo of his or her brothers [poss Cl. 11]

  abafowabo his or her brothers [n Cl. 2; sg **umfowabo**]

wathola (s)he obtained [narr]

nemali also the money, and money [assoc adv]

yomshwalense from insurance or assurance [poss Cl. 9]

  umshwalense insurance, assurance [n Cl. 3]

u-R20 000 20,000 rands [n Cl. 1a]

ayewuboleke that/which (s)he had borrowed [ind rel of plain obj rel, Cl. 1]

  wayewuboleke (s)he had borrowed it (Cl. 3) [rem past past, conjoint]

KwaZulu Finance and Investment Corporation (KFC) from the KwaZulu Finance … [loc]

«6»

ithole (s)he received or obtained, (s)he should obtain [subjunc]

nosizo further assistance, also assistance [assoc adv]

kwabakwa-Agrilek from the people at Agrilek [loc]

  abakwa-Agrilek those of Agrilek [poss pron phr Cl. 2]

okuyibona who are those [rel Cl. 17]

  kuyibona it is them [ident cop, pres]

abasiza who assist [rel Cl. 2]

  basiza they assist [pres, con-

joint]
ngokunika by providing, by giving [instr adv]
   ukunika to give, to hand (to), to provide, provision [vn Cl. 15]
abalimi farmers [n Cl. 2; sg **umlimi**]
bangifakela they installed for me [rem past]
i-petrol pump [n Cl. 9a]
esebenza that/which works [rel Cl. 9]
   isebenza it, (s)he works [pres, conjoint]
nesingiphungulele and which has already reduced for me [assoc adv]
   esingiphungulele that/which has already reduced for me [rel Cl. 9]
   isingiphungulele it has already reduced for me [past, exclusive, conjoint]
   -phungulel-a lessen for, decrease for, reduce for [v-appl]
   -phungul-a lessen, decrease, reduce, diminish [v.t.]
umthwalo load, burden [n Cl. 3; < **-thwal-** carry]
ngenza I do, I make [pres, conjoint]

«7»
babonele ku-Anton they should copy Anton
   babonele they should copy or imitate [subjunc]
   -bonel-a ku- copy, imitate [v-appl + loc]
bahlukane na- ... they should give up ..., they should part from ..., they should separate from ... [subjunc]
ukukhothama to bend down, to bow; to be humble [vn Cl. 15]

-khotham-a bend over, bow; be humble [v.i.]
-am- [fossilized positional extension indicating bodily position]
kobasi before the White bosses [loc]
   obasi White bosses [n Cl. 2b; sg **ubasi** 1a] {Afr *basie* young boss. In the apartheid era Black people were expected to call White men *baas* 'master, boss' and young White men or even boys *basie* 'young master'}
emapulazini to, from, on farms [loc]
bangazimela ngokwabo they can stand on their own feet, they can be independent
   bangazimela they can stand for themselves [pres, potential]
uNhlanhla (name) [n Cl. 1a; < **inhlanhla** good fortune]
wakwa-Agrilek from Agrilek [poss Cl. 1]
UJulius (name) [n Cl. 1a]
Zondi (surname) [n Cl. 1a]
onguzakwabo who is married into the same family [rel Cl. 1]
   unguzakwabo he is someone married into the same family [ident cop, pres]
   uzakwabo someone married into the same family as him or her [n Cl. 1a]
zibalulekile they are important [stative]
sithembele it relies [stative]
enhlabathini on the soil [loc]
   inhlabathi soil, earth [n Cl. 9]
siphile that it should live [subjunc]
sithanda we like [pres, conjoint]
ukugqugquzela to persuade, to try to win over, to nag, to prod [vn Cl. 15]

abamnyama Black people [rel Cl. 2; sg **omnyama**]

babe ngabalimi they should become farmers [ident cop, inch, subjunc]

ngabalimi they are, it is farmers [ident cop, pres]

«8»

noma ngubani no matter who, anyone (lit. although it is who)

ozimisele who is prepared, who is ready [rel Cl. 1]

   uzimisele (s)he is prepared, (s)he is ready [stative]

ngokuvuna by or about reaping, harvesting [instr adv]

ukuvuna to reap, to harvest [vn Cl. 15]

   -vun-a reap, harvest [v.t.]

zempumelelo of success [poss Cl. 8]

ahlwayele (s)he should sow by scattering [subjunc]

   -hlwayel-a sow by scattering [v-appl; var **-hlwanyel-a**]

imbewu seed(s) [n Cl. 9; neutral]

ngokusebenza by working [instr adv]

   isivuno harvest, crop [n Cl. 7; < **-vun-** reap, harvest]

sami my [poss Cl. 7]

sokuqala first [poss Cl. 7]

saba sihle was good [descr cop, inch, rem past]

ngahlangabezana I came up against [rem past]

nezingqinamba with bouts of nerves [assoc adv]

sengifuna I now want [pres exclusive]

ukudayisa to market, offer for sale, auction, trade [vn Cl. 15]

babebaningi there were many [descr cop, rem past pres]

esasincintisana nabo with whom we were in competition [ind rel of plain adv rel, 1 p pl]

sasincintisana we competed, we were competing [rem past pres]

   -ncintisan-a compete [v-caus-recip]

   -ncint-a excel, be outstanding [v.i.]

eyangenza that/which made me [rel Cl. 9]

   yangenza it made me [rem past]

ngaphumelela that I succeeded [narr]

zaziyikhwalithi they were (of) quality [ident cop, rem past pres]

   ikhwalithi (good) quality [n Cl. 9a]

kuqhuba it continues [pres, conjoint]

«9»

eseyibonile (s)he had already seen it [past, partic, exclusive, disjoint]

yesivuno of the harvest [poss Cl. 9]

wathutha (s)he moved house, (s)he transferred [rem past]

   -thuth-a move house; transfer; convey, transport [v.i. & t.]

kamfowabo of his or her brother [poss Cl. 9]

waya and (s)he went [narr]

kulelipulazi to this farm [loc]

   lelipulazi this farm [dem phr Cl. 5]

alisebenzisa that/which (s)he uses [ind rel of plain obj rel, Cl. 1]

   ulisebenzisa (s)he uses it [pres, conjoint]

alibiza that/which (s)he calls [ind rel of plain obj rel, Cl. 1]

yi-ALHEBROS it is ALHEBROS [ident cop, pres]

neliqanjwe and that was composed [assoc adv]

eliqanjwe that/which was composed [rel Cl. 5]

liqanjwe it has been named, it has been invented, it has been composed [past, conjoint]

-qanjw-a be composed, be invented, be named [v-pass; < -qamb- + -w-; mbw > njw]

-qamb-a compose, invent; give a name [v.t.]

ngeziqalo with the initials [instr adv]

iziqalo origins, beginnings; initials; prefixes [n Cl. 8; sg **isiqalo**; < -qal- begin]

zamagama of the names [poss Cl. 8]

abafowabo of his or her brothers [poss Cl. 6]

nelakhe and his or her (own) [assoc adv]

elakhe his, hers [poss pron Cl. 5]

ngabe angikho kulelizinga engikulo I would not be at the stage or level at which I am

angikho I am not there [loc cop, pres, neg]

kulelizinga at this level, at this stage [loc]

lelizinga this level, this stage, this standard, this degree [dem phr Cl. 5]

ukuba akungenxa yabo if it were not for them

ukuba if [conj]

akungenxa it is not because of, it is not through the reason [ident cop, pres, neg]

«10»

wasikhombisa (s)he showed us [rem past]

nobuhlakani also cleverness [assoc adv]

bakhe his, her [poss Cl. 14]

esesichazela he now explains to us [pres, partic, exclusive]

esaba (s)he is afraid [pres, partic; two analyses are possible: < Ø-SC Cl. 1 + -esab-a verb OR < e-SC Cl. 1 + -sab-a verb (-sab-a and -esab-a are variants)]

yimbangela it is the reason [ident cop]

akhethe (s)he should choose [subjunc]

ukuba ngumlimi to become a farmer [ident cop, inch, vn phr Cl. 15]

otshale who has planted [rel Cl. 1]

utshale (s)he has planted [past, conjoint]

ummbila maize, mealies, corn [n Cl. 3]

namazambane and potatoes [assoc adv]

amazambane potatoes [n Cl. 6; sg **izambane** Cl. 5]

kuba it becomes [copula, pres, conjoint]

lukhuni difficult, hard [rel stem]

abazikhiqizayo who produce them in abundance [rel Cl. 2]

bayazikhiqiza they produce them [pres, disjoint]

-khiqiz-a produce in abundance, turn out in large quantities, produce a surplus [v.t.]

inzuzo profit, gain [n Cl. 9; < -zuz- earn, acquire, obtain]

ayithola that/which (s)he gets [ind rel of plain obj rel, Cl. 1]

ayithola (s)he gets it [rem past]

ngokukhiqiza by producing a surplus or an abundance [instr adv]
ukukhiqiza to produce in abundance, to turn out in large quantities, surplus production [vn Cl. 15]
lesisithelo this fruit [dem phr Cl. 7]
yinkulu it is large, it is big [descr cop, pres]
nkulu big, large [adj Cl. 9 minus initial vowel]
abasitshalile who have planted it [rel Cl. 2]
basitshalile they have planted it [past, disjoint]
ngiphezu kwemizamo I am very busy with trials (lit. I am on top of trials) [loc cop, pres]
nama-raspberry raspberries as well, also raspberries, and raspberries [assoc adv]
ama-raspberry raspberries [n Cl. 6; sg **i-raspberry** Cl. 9a]

«11»
zagqama they became clear or obvious [rem past]
emenywa (s)he is invited [pres, partic]
-menyw-a be invited [v-pass; < **-mem-w-**; **mw > nyw**]
ayodlulisela (s)he should go and pass on [subjunc, andative]
ayeselutholile that/which (s)he had by then acquired [ind rel of plain obj rel, Cl. 1]
wayeselutholile (s)he had already acquired it [rem past past, exclusive, disjoint]
kubalimi to, from, at farmers [loc]
ababeneminyaka engu-13 belime who had been farming for 13 years [rel phr Cl. 2]

ababeneminyaka who had years [rel Cl. 2]
babeneminyaka they had years [assoc cop, rem past pres]
engu-13 thirteen [rel Cl. 4]
ingu-13 there are thirteen [ident cop, pres]
u-13 thirteen [n Cl. 1a]
bengayiboni they not seeing it [pres, partic]
usenamasheya (s)he now has shares [assoc cop, pres, exclusive]
angu-50% that/which are 50% [rel Cl. 6]
angu-50% they are 50% [ident cop, pres]
u-50% 50% [n Cl. 1a]
awafake that/which (s)he has placed [ind rel of plain obj rel, Cl. 1]
uwafake (s)he has placed them [past, conjoint]
kulabobalimi with those farmers [loc]
labobalimi those farmers [dem phr Cl. 2]
abasiza whom he assists [ind rel of plain obj rel, Cl. 1]
sebethole they have now acquired [past, exclusive, conjoint]
ukwaziwa renown, fame, reputation [vn Cl. 15]
ezakhele which are situated in [rel Cl. 10]
yosizo of the assistance [poss Cl. 9]
lwakhe his, her [poss Cl. 11]

«12»
iyamangaza it, (s)he is amazing, is surprising [pres, disjoint]
-mangaz-a amaze, surprise [v-caus; < **-mangal-** + **-Y-**; **l + -Y- > z**]

nesimo and, with, also, even a situation [assoc adv]

eMakatini (pronounced **eMa-kathini**) at Makatini [loc] **iMakatini** (place) [n Cl. 5]

enepulazi where the farm is (lit. that has the farm) [rel Cl. 9] **inepulazi** it, (s)he has a farm [assoc cop, pres]

asihambisani it does not go together, it does not accord [pres, neg]

nalesisithelo with this fruit [assoc adv]

asitshalile that/which he has planted [ind rel of plain obj rel, Cl. 1] **usitshalile** (s)he has planted it [past, disjoint]

sengixhume I have already linked [past, exclusive, conjoint]

ama-tunnel tunnels [n Cl. 6; sg **i-tunnel** n Cl. 9a]

okuyiwona that/which is what [rel Cl. 17] **yiwona** it is them [ident cop, pres]

azongisiza that/which will aid me [rel Cl. 6] **azongisiza** they will aid me [fut]

ngokuvikela by protecting [instr adv]

kunesithwathwa there is frost [assoc cop, pres, partic] **isithwathwa** frost [n Cl. 7]

«13»

lomlimi this farmer [dem phr Cl. 1]

ongavilaphanga who is not lazy [rel Cl. 1] **ungavilaphanga** (s)he is not lazy [past, rel, neg; < **akavila-phanga**]

-vilaph- bec lazy [v.inch; < **ivila** lazy person + **-ph-** suffix that changes nouns and adjectives into verbs]

unesexwayiso (s)he has a warning [assoc cop, pres] **isexwayiso** warning, caution [n Cl. 7; pl **izexwayiso**; < **-exwa-yis-** warn; var **isixwayiso**]

athanda ukusidlulisela that/which (s)he likes to pass on [ind rel of plain obj rel, Cl. 1] **athanda** that/which (s)he likes [rel Cl. 1] **ukusidlulisela** to pass it on [vn Cl. 15]

abakhonze who are keen on [rel Cl. 2] **bakhonze** they are keen on, they are passionate about [past, conjoint]

ungahlomile you are not armed [stative, partic] **-hlom-a** take up arms, arm oneself [v.inch]

ngolwazi with knowledge [instr adv]

olufanele appropriate, necessary [rel Cl. 11] **lufanele** it is appropriate, it must [stative]

kufana it is like, it resembles [pres, conjoint]

uyazigangela you are just playing about, you are just being foolish [pres, disjoint] **-zi-gangel-a** just play about, just be foolish [v-refl-appl] **-gang-a** bec naughty, bec mischievous [v.inch]

uqhuba you continue, you proceed (with) [pres, partic]

kwexwayisa (there) warns [pres, conjoint]

221

wagcizelela (s)he emphasized, stressed [rem past]
nolwazi and, with, also, even knowledge [assoc adv]
ngaphambi kokuthi before [conj phr; followed by subjunctive]
bangene they should go into [subjunc]

«14»
ngokuba by becoming [instr adv]
  ukuba wusizo to be of help, to be of assistance [ident cop, inch, vn phr Cl. 15]
  wusizo it is help, aid, assistance [ident cop, pres]
odinga who requires, who needs [rel Cl. 1]
  udinga (s)he requires, needs [pres, conjoint]
uyalwazi (s)he knows it, is familiar with it [pres, disjoint]
usizi distress, misery, mental pain, sorrow, grief, worry [n Cl. 11]
kulona to, from, at, in, on it [loc]
  lona it, he, him, she, her [abs pron Cl. 11]
adlondlobale (s)he should get greatly excited [subjunc]
  -dlondlobal-a get greatly excited, get highly emotional [v.inch]
ngaloluhlobo in this way [instr adv phr]
  loluhlobo this way, this type, this sort [dem phr Cl. 11]
  hlobo [< **uhlobo**]
ngezifiso about desires, wishes [instr adv]
angathokoza (s)he would be happy [pres, potential]

ethola (s)he gets, acquires [pres, partic]
elithe xaxa that/which is better or larger [rel phr Cl. 5]
  elithe who said, that/which went [rel Cl. 5]
  lithe (s)he said, it went [past, conjoint]
  -th-i go (e.g. it *goes* whiz) [dummy verb which introduces an ideophone]
  xaxa bec improved, bec greater [ideophone]
kunaleli more than this one [compar adv]
imenze it has made him or her [past, partic, conjoint]
waqasha that (s)he hired [narr]
abangu-25 25 [rel Cl. 2]
  bangu-25 there are 25 of them [ident cop, pres]
umfokaMadlala Madlala's brother [n Cl. 1a]
ukholwa (s)he believes [pres, conjoint]
lingamenza it, (s)he could make him or her [pres, potential]
ukuvula to open (up) [vn Cl. 15]
omsebenzi for or of work, for or of employment [poss Cl. 6]
kunganginika it could give me [pres, potential]
lokutshala of planting [poss Cl. 5]
sesidlulile it has already passed [past, exclusive, disjoint]
sokutshalwa for or of being planted [poss Cl. 7]
kwama-strawberry of strawberries [poss Cl. 15]

Ngabe uxakwe yizikweleti?
Likhona ikhambi.

«1»
Sesisenyangeni yesibili onyakeni ka-1999! Ngineqiniso lokuthi iningi lenu likwazile ukufeza lezozinjongo elalihlose ukuzifeza ngaphambi kokuphela konyaka odlule. Siyabahalalisela kakhulu labo abakwazile ukwenza lokho! Mina-ke, enye yezinjongo zami zangalonyaka, wukuhlukana nezikweleti nokugwema ukulingwa yi-credit card.

«2»
Namhlanje iningi labantu libhekene nezikweleti elingakwazi ukuzikhokhela. Isizathu esiyimbangela yalokho wukuthi izinga lempilo yalabobantu lingaphezu komholo abawutholayo. Kulula kabi ukuzithola usucwile ezikweletini. Abantu bathenga izimpahla ezinhle emva kokuba abakhangisi bebayengile babatshela ukuthi kungaba lula ukuzikhokhela.

Okubuhlungu kakhulu ngalokho wukuthi esitolo abakutsheli nakancane ukuthi ngeke ukwazi ukuzikhokhela lezozimpahla ngoba umholo wakho uphansi kakhulu.

«3»
Okunye futhi okugcina ngokuba yimbangela yokuthi abantu babe nezikweleti ezingakhokheki, yiziteleka ezenza bangawatholi amaholo abo nokuwa kwezinkampani ezivalwa ngenxa yesimo sezomnotho. Maduze nje, maningi amabhizinisi amancane agcine esesuliwe kwi-stock exchange emva kokuthi irandi liqhathaniswa ne-dollar. Uma abantu bezithola bebhekene nesimo esimuncu ngenxa yemali, bacabanga ukwenza izinto eziningi ezahlukahlukene. Abanye bayakwazi ukumelana nezinkinga zabo babuye baqale impilo yabo kabusha kanti abanye bayahluleka baze bagcine sebekhethe ukuzibulala ukuze baphumule osizini ababhekene nalo.

«4»
Uma ubona ukuthi izikweleti zikumele ngenhla, khumbula ukuthi lisekhona ithemba nekhambi elingakukhipha kulobobunzima. Izikweleti ungaziqeda kalula ngisho noma ungasenalo nesenti ephaketheni. Bakhona abantu abagcina sebehlele impilo yabo kabusha emva kokucwila kwabo ezikweletini nasebephila impilo engcono kakhulu kunaleyo ababeyiphila esikhathini esidlule. Izinkinga ziqala uma izindleko zakho sezingaphezu komholo wakho wenyanga. Uzothola nokuthi sekunezinye izikweleti ongasakwazi ukuzikhokhela ngenyanga.

«5»
Ungakulindi ukuthola amathonsi abanzi uma usubonile ukuthi izinkinga ziyakulandela. Thatha isinqumo esisheshayo ukuze isimo singabi muncu kakhulu. Zibhale phansi zonke izikweleti zakho ubhale nokuthi unamalini ephaketheni. Khumbula ukuthi abantu obakweletayo abathokozi uma ungasasikhokheli isikweleti sakho ngoba uma bekuthathela izinyathelo zomthetho kuba khona imali abayikhokhayo, okusho ukuthi bangathokoza kakhulu uma nifinyelela esivumelwaneni sokuthi isikweleti sakho ungasikhokhela kanjani.

«6»
Ngokuxoxisana nabo ungagwema nokuthi izimpahla zakho zigcine seziphindiselwe esitolo. Akufanele zikukhathaze kakhulu lezozincwadi ezithunyelwa kuwe nezisuke zikufaka amanzi emadolweni zibasela isikweleti ngoba kuyenzeka ukuthi obakweletayo baqashe umuntu ozokusabisa uma ebasela imali yabo. Zimbili izinto ezingenzeka kuwena uma ungasakhokhi kahle, kunokwenzeka ukuthi izimpahla zakho zibuyiselwe esitolo owazithenga kuso noma igama lakho lifakwe ohlwini lwabantu abangakhokhi kahle.

«7»
Yinkantolo kuphela enegunya lokukuphoqa ukuba ukhokhele isikweleti sakho. Ukuze ugweme leyonkinga, hlela impilo yakho kabusha. Ungabi namahloni okudayisa indlu yakho owayithenga ngemali eshisiwe ushintshele kwengabizi kakhulu. Ungayidayisa nemoto yakho uzijwayeze ukuphila ngaphandle kobukhazikhazi. Uma izinkinga zakho zingaxazululeki noma usuzame ukuxoxisana nobakweletayo, noma usushintshe izinga lempilo yakho, kusho ukuthi sekuyisikhathi sokuthatha isinqumo esinzima kakhulu empilweni yakho—uthathwe njengomuntu ongasenalo ngisho nesenti ephakatheni.
ngu: Premilla Deonath

Vocabulary

uxakwe you are embarrassed, are in a fix, are troubled [past, conjoint]
yizikweleti by debts [agent adv]
  izikweleti debts [n Cl. 8; sg **isikweleti**] {Afr *skuld*}
likhona it, (s)he is there [loc cop, pres; may also introduce an exist cop]
likhona ikhambi there is a remedy [exist cop, pres]

ikhambi remedy; medicinal herb or concoction used as a remedy [n Cl. 5]

«1»
sesisenyangeni we are already in the month [loc cop, pres, exclusive]
  senyangeni in, from the month [loc; < **enyangeni**]
yesibili second [poss Cl. 9]

onyakeni in the year [loc; < **unyaka**]

ka-1999 of 1999 [poss Cl. 9]

ngineqiniso I am sure (lit. I am with truth) [assoc cop, pres]

lenu of you (pl) [poss Cl. 5]

-inu your [abs pron 2 p pl, used in possessives]

likwazile it (the majority) was able [past, disjoint]

lezozinjongo those resolutions, aims [dem phr Cl. 10]

> **zinjongo** [< **izinjongo** aims, purposes, resolutions; sg **injongo**; < **-jong-** have the mind set on]

elalihlose that/which it had intended, aimed at [rem past past, conjoint]

ukuzifeza to accomplish them [vn Cl. 15]

ngaphambi kokuphela before the end [instr adv phr]

konyaka of the year [poss Cl. 15]

siyabahalalisela we congratulate or applaud them [pres, disjoint]

> **-halalisel-a** congratulate, applaud [v-appl; the extension **-el-** is semantically empty here]
>
> **-halalis-a** congratulate, applaud [v.t.]

abakwazile who were able [rel Cl. 2]

> **bakwazile** they were able [past, disjoint]

mina-ke as for me, then

yezinjongo of resolutions [poss Cl. 9]

zangalonyaka of this year [poss phr Cl. 10]

> **ngalonyaka** during, in this year [instr adv phr]

wukuhlukana it is to get away (lit. to part company with) [ident cop, pres]

> **ukuhlukana na-** to part com-

pany with, to get away from [vn phr]

nezikweleti from debts [assoc adv]

ukulingwa to be tempted [vn Cl. 15]

> **-lingw-a** be tempted, be tested, be tried, be attempted [v-pass]
>
> **-ling-a** tempt, test, try, attempt [v.t.]

yi-credit card by the credit card [agent adv]

> **i-credit card** [n Cl. 9]

«2»

libhekene is faced [stative]

elingakwazi ukuzikhokhela that/which it is unable to repay [ind rel of plain obj rel, Cl. 5]

> **elingakwazi** that/which it is unable [rel Cl. 5]
>
> **lingakwazi** it is unable, it cannot [pres, rel, neg; < **alikwazi**]
>
> **ukuzikhokhela** to pay them off, to repay them [vn Cl. 15]

izinga lempilo standard of living [n phr Cl. 5]

yalabobantu of those people [poss Cl. 9]

lingaphezu is greater or higher [loc cop, pres]

komholo than the salary [loc]

> **umholo** salary, wage [n Cl. 3; < **-hol-** draw pay, earn]

abawutholayo that/which they get [ind rel of plain obj rel, Cl. 2]

> **bayawuthola** they get it [pres, disjoint]

ukuzithola to find oneself [vn Cl. 15]

usucwile (you) have already sunk [past, partic, exclusive, conjoint]

> **-cwil-a** sink, dive [v.i.]

ezikweletini into debt(s) [loc]

bathenga they buy [pres, conjoint]

abakhangisi advertisers [n Cl. 2; sg umkhangisi; < -khangis- cause to be desirable, advertise]

bebayengile they have enticed or seduced them [past, partic, disjoint]
-yeng-a entice, seduce [v.t.]

babatshela and they told them [narr]

okubuhlungu what is sad or painful [rel Cl. 17]
kubuhlungu it is painful, it is sad [descr cop, pres]

ngalokho about that [instr adv]

esitolo in the shop [loc]

abakutsheli they do not tell you [pres, neg]

ukwazi you should be able [subjunc]

lezozimpahla those goods [dem phr Cl. 10]

uphansi it is low [loc cop, pres]

«3»

okugcina that ends up [rel Cl. 17]
kugcina it ends up [pres, con- joint]

ngokuba yimbangela by becoming a cause [instr adv]

babe na- ... they should acquire ... [introduces an assoc cop, inch, subjunc]

ezingakhokheki that/which are unpayable [rel Cl. 8]
zingakhokheki they are unpayable [pres, rel, neg; < azikhokheki]
-khokhek-a be payable [v-neut]

yiziteleka it is strikes [ident cop, pres]
iziteleka strikes [n Cl. 8; sg. isiteleka] {Eng}

bangawatholi that they do not get [subjunc, neg]

amaholo wages, salaries [n Cl. 6; sg iholo Cl. 5]

nokuwa and the collapse or bankruptcy [assoc adv]
ukuwa to fall, to collapse, bankruptcy [vn Cl. 15]

kwezinkampani of companies [poss Cl. 15]

ezivalwa that/which are closed (down) [rel Cl. 10]
zivalwa they are closed (down) [pres, conjoint]
-valw-a be shut, be closed (down) [v-pass]

yesimo of the state [poss Cl. 9]

sezomnotho of the economy [poss Cl. 7]

maduze nje not so long ago, just recently [adv phr]

agcine that/which ended up [rel Cl. 6]
agcine they ended up [past, conjoint]

esesuliwe they then being wiped off, they then being removed [past, partic, exclusive, disjoint]
-sulw-a be wiped (off); be removed [v-pass]
-sul-a wipe (off) [v.t.]

kwi-stock exchange to, from, at, in, the stock exchange [loc]
i-stock exchange [n Cl. 9a]

emva kokuthi after [conj phr; followed by partic]

irandi rand (South African currency unit) [n Cl. 5]

liqhathaniswa it, (s)he is compared [pres, partic]

ne-dollar with the dollar [assoc adv]
i-dollar [n Cl. 9a] {Eng}

bezithola they find themselves [pres, partic]

bebhekene (they) facing [past stative, partic]

esimuncu unpleasant, nasty, unhappy [rel Cl. 7]

yemali of money [poss Cl. 9]

ezahlukahlukene different, various [rel Cl. 10]
zahlukahlukene they differ in various ways, they vary [stative]
ukumelana to confront, to stand against [vn Cl. 15]
-melan-a na- ... confront ...
baqale they (should) begin [subjunc]
bayahluleka they are unable, they are defeated [pres, disjoint]
baze until they [aux]
bagcine they eventually [aux, subjunc]
sebekhethe they have already chosen [past, exclusive, conjoint]
baphumule they should rest
osizini to, from, in sorrow [loc; < **usizi**]
nalo with it [assoc adv]

«4»
zikumele they await you, they are standing over you [stative]
khumbula remember [imper]
lisekhona ithemba there is still a remedy [exist cop, pres, persistive]
nekhambi and the remedy [assoc adv]
elingakukhipha that/which can take you out [rel Cl. 5]
lingakukhipha it can take you out [pres, potential]
kulobobunzima from that difficulty [loc]
lobobunzima that difficulty [dem phr Cl. 14]
ungaziqeda you can put an end to them [pres, potential]
ungasenalo you no longer have it [assoc cop, partic, persistive, neg]
nesenti even a cent [assoc adv]
isenti cent [n Cl. 5] {Eng/Afr}

ephaketheni in the pocket [loc]
iphakethe pocket [n Cl. 5] {Eng}
sebehlele they have then arranged [past, exclusive, conjoint]
emva kokucwila after sinking [loc phr]
ukucwila sinking [vn Cl. 15]
nasebephila and who now live [assoc adv]
asebephila who now live [rel Cl. 2]
sebephila they now live, they already live [pres, exclusive]
kunaleyo (more) than that [compar adv]
ababeyiphila that/which they lived (it) [ind rel of plain obj rel, Cl. 2]
babeyiphila they used to live it, they lived it [rem past pres]
sezingaphezu once they are higher [loc cop, pres, exclusive]
wenyanga monthly, of the month [poss Cl. 3]
sekunezinye there are now other [assoc cop, pres, exclusive]
ongasakwazi that/which you are no longer able [rel 2nd p s]
ungasakwazi you are no longer able, you can no longer [pres, persistive, rel, neg; < **awusakwazi**]

«5»
ungakulindi you should not wait for it [subjunc, neg]
amathonsi abanzi severe problems (idiom; lit. wide drops (i.e. tears))
abanzi wide, broad [rel Cl. 6]
-banzi wide, broad [rel stem]
usubonile you have already seen [past, exclusive, disjoint]
ziyakulandela they follow you [pres, disjoint]

esisheshayo quick, speedy [rel Cl. 7]
  siyashesha it is quick [pres, disjoint]
singabi muncu it should not become unpleasant [descr cop, inch, subjunc]
zibhale write them [imper]
ubhale and (you should) write [subjunc]
unamalini you have how much money [assoc cop, pres]
  malini? how much money? [< **imali** money + **ini?** what?]
obakweletayo whom you owe, to whom you are in debt [ind rel of plain obj rel, 2 p sg]
  uyabakweleta you owe them [pres, disjoint]
abathokozi they are not happy [pres, neg]
ungasasikhokheli you no longer pay it off [pres, partic, persistive, neg]
bekuthathela they take against you [pres, partic]
  -thathel-a take for, take against, take from [v-appl]
zomthetho legal, of the law [poss Cl. 8]
kuba khona imali there is money [exist cop, inch, pres]
abayikhokhayo that/which they pay out [ind rel of plain obj rel, Cl. 2]
  bayayikhokha they pay it out [pres, disjoint]
okusho ukuthi that/which means to say [rel phr Cl. 17]
  kusho ukuthi that means to say [v phr]
bangathokoza they would be happy [pres, potential]
nifinyelela you (pl) reach [pres, partic]
  -finyelel-a reach (a destination),

arrive at [v.i.]
esivumelwaneni to, from, at an agreement [loc]
  isivumelwana mutual or legal agreement, contract [n Cl. 7; < **-vumelwan-** be mutually agreed]
ungasikhokhela you can pay it off [pres, potential]

«6»

ngokuxoxisana through negotiation [instr adv]
ungagwema you can avoid [pres, potential]
zigcine they should end up [subjunc]
seziphindiselwe they now having been returned to [past, partic, exclusive, conjoint]
  -phindiselw-a be sent back to, be returned to [v-caus-appl-pass]
  -phindisel-a send back to, return to [v-caus-appl]
  -phindis-a send back, return; retaliate, take vengeance [v-caus]
akufanele it is not necessary (that) [aux, stative, neg]
zikukhathaze they should worry, bother or disturb you [subjunc]
lezozincwadi those letters, those books [dem phr Cl. 10]
ezithunyelwa that/which are sent [rel Cl. 10]
  zithunyelwa they are sent [pres, conjoint]
kuwe to, from, at, on you [loc]
nezisuke and which just [assoc adv]
zikufaka amanzi emadolweni they threaten you (lit. they put you water on the knees) [v phr]
  -fak-a umuntu amanzi emadolweni threaten someone

zikufaka they put or place you [pres, partic]
emadolweni on, from, in the knees [loc; < **amadolo**]
zibasela they make persistent demands for repayment [pres, conjoint]
-basel-a make persistent demands for repayment; make a fire for, kindle for; stir up strife for [v-appl]
-bas-a make, kindle or light a fire; stir up strife [v.t.]
baqashe they employ [subjunc]
ozokusabisa who will scare you [rel Cl. 1]
uzokusabisa (s)he will scare you [fut]
-sabis-a scare, make afraid [v-caus; var **-esabis-a**]
-sab-a be afraid of, fear [v.t.; var **-esab-**]
ebasela (s)he demands repayment [pres, partic]
zimbili there are two [descr cop]
ezingenzeka that/which can happen [rel Cl. 10]
zingenzeka they can happen, occur, take place [pres, potential]
kuwena to, from, at, on you [loc]
ungasakhokhi you no longer pay [pres, partic, persistive, neg]
zibuyiselwe they have to be returned to [subjunc]
-buyiselw-a be returned to [v-caus-appl-pass]
owazithenga kuso from which you bought them [ind rel of plain loc rel, 2 p sg]
wazithenga you bought them [rem past]
lifakwe it should be put [subjunc]
lwabantu of people [poss Cl. 11]
abangakhokhi who do not pay [rel Cl. 2]

bangakhokhi they do not pay [pres, rel, neg; < **abakhokhi**]

«7»

yinkantolo it is a court [ident cop, pres]
enegunya that/which has the authority [rel Cl. 9]
inegunya it has the authority [assoc cop, pres]
igunya authority [n Cl. 5]
lokukuphoqa to force or compel you [poss Cl. 5]
ukukuphoqa to force or compel you [vn Cl. 15]
ukhokhele you should pay off [subjunc]
ugweme you should avoid [subjunc]
ungabi namahloni you should not be ashamed or embarrassed [assoc cop, inch, subjunc, neg]
ungabi you should not become or be [subjunc, neg]
namahloni with embarrassment [assoc adv]
amahloni shame, embarrassment [n Cl. 6]
okudayisa to sell (lit. of selling) [poss Cl. 6]
owayithenga that/which you bought (it) [ind rel of plain obj rel, 2 p sg]
wayithenga you bought it [rem past]
ngemali eshisiwe at great expense, expensively (idiom; lit. with money that has been burnt) [instr adv phr]
eshisiwe that/which has been burnt [rel Cl. 9]
ishisiwe it, (s)he has been burnt [stative, disjoint]
ushintshele and you should change to [subjunc]
-shintshel-a change to, for [v-

appl]

kwengabizi to one that does not cost [loc; < **ku-** + **engabizi**]
engabizi that/which does not cost, that/which does not call [rel Cl. 9]
ingabizi it does not cost or call, (s)he does not call [pres, rel, neg; < **ayibizi**]
-biz-a cost [v.t.]
ungayidayisa you can sell it [pres, potential]
nemoto and a car [assoc adv]
uzijwayeze you should get used to, you should accustom yourself [subjunc]
-zi-jwayez-a get used to, accustom oneself to [v-refl]
-jwayez-a accustom, make get used to [v-caus; < **-jwayel-** + **-Y-**]
ukuphila to live, to be well [vn Cl. 15]
ubukhazikhazi splendor, luxury [n Cl. 14]

zingaxazululeki they do not get resolved [pres, partic]
-xazululek-a get resolved, get settled [v-neut]
usuzame you have already tried [past, partic, exclusive, conjoint]
nobakweletayo with your creditors [assoc adv phr]
usushintshe you have already changed [past, partic, exclusive, conjoint]
sokuthatha for taking [poss Cl. 7]
esinzima difficult, hard, heavy [rel Cl. 7]
uthathwe you have to be taken [subjunc]
njengomuntu as a person, like a person [compar adv]
ongasenalo who no longer has it [rel Cl. 1]
ungasenalo (s)he no longer has it [assoc cop, pres, rel, persistive, neg; < **akasenalo**]

Translations

Selection 1
Orange Citrus Cupcakes

Ingredients:
60 g (60 ml) Rama [brand of margarine]
100 g (100 ml) baker's sugar
150 g (270 ml) self-rising flour
3 eggs, beaten
80 ml orange juice

Frosting ingredients:
100 g (200 ml) confectioner's sugar, creamed with 15 ml orange juice
30 g (30 ml) Rama
the zest of a grated orange

Method:
Cream the Rama and the sugar. Add flour and then the eggs and juice. Pour into either well-greased cupcake tins or 2 x 20 cm baking tins. Bake at 160°C for about 25 minutes, until well risen and light brown. Allow to cool, then spread the top with orange frosting. Sprinkle with orange zest.

Selection 2
The Mpanzas Are Grateful

The Mpanza family of Newlands East thanks everyone who supported them in the dark days after the loss of their eldest son, Mr. Sipho Steven Mpanza.

He was born to a minister of the Methodist Church, the Reverend Joe and Mrs. Abegail Mpanza. He passed away on February 2, 1999, and was laid to rest on February 6, 1999.

Sipho taught at Mandlethu High School and at Funimfundo where he passed away while a teacher there. He leaves behind his wife, Mrs. Constance Lovey Matseng MaMote Mpanza, and four children.

May God bless you all and may you continue to help others. May he rest in peace, Amen.

By Mrs. Matseng Constance Lovey Mpanza, NEWLANDS EAST

Selection 3
Where Are the Milk and Honey?

Where did the land of milk and honey go? The majority of us voted in the elections of the year 1994, but, up to today, the government has not fulfilled its promises. In place of that, we have had retrenchments, rights ignored, rising crime rates, price hikes, and an influx of foreigners taking our jobs. Hasn't the time arrived for the government to keep its promises?

Selection 4
The Stars [Horoscope]

Virgo
(August 24–September 22)
Since you are facing some issue at this time, you need to work to overcome the mistakes of the recent past. You must ask yourself about what happened in the past in order to have a bright future and to avoid those errors so that they never happen again. Having respect for people of the opposite sex is what will make you appealing.
Lucky days: 2nd and 3rd.
Lucky numbers: 2 and 3.

Libra
(September 23–October 22)
This is a good time for you to put your affairs in order. It's a time to think about your life and your future. You should be steadfast in your commitments and know how you will face up to them. In love, if you are not on your own, now is the time for your prayers and desires to be fulfilled because you have found someone to share your love.
Lucky days: 4th, 5th, and 6th.
Lucky numbers: 4, 5, and 6.

Selection 5
People Should Vote for Education Now

Editor,

I would like the opportunity to exchange views with the local community in KwaZulu-Natal. Since elections are coming I feel they should vote for education and peace, for the following reasons.

234

The IFP [Inkatha Freedom Party] organization has failed to produce good results for Std 10 in 1999, and next year will be just as bad. The previous minister, Dr. Vincent Zulu, was unable to get education at an acceptable level, in spite of the Minister of National Education, Prof. Sibusiso Bhengu, having indicated that he [Zulu] should be removed from office.

The Inkatha organization rejected this. Just consider how the removal of "ghost teachers"[11] and bogus teachers took five years, even though Sadtu [South African Democratic Teachers' Union] said at the beginning of 1994 that this matter should be investigated. Even now our schools are full of unqualified teachers.

Each and every school has fewer qualified than unqualified teachers. Many qualified teachers are sitting at home, but the Minister does not want to hire teachers who were trained for the job; he wants those who know nothing to continue.

Accordingly, the results will continue to be bad.

Therefore, voting for Inkatha means voting for an educational system that has broken down.

They deceive people by blaming the national government, but in other regions, renewal and the hiring of teachers still continues.

Here the Minister of Education continues to bumble.

In all regions, political violence has ceased, but here in KwaZulu-Natal it still continues.

If you read the newspapers or listen to the radio, you will find that ANC leaders are always seeking peace. In Inkatha strongholds ANC supporters are assaulted, whereas where the ANC is in the majority, this does not happen to Inkatha people.

This is caused by the fact that its leaders do not believe in intellectual leadership, but rather in violence.

It is going to take years before Inkatha understands what politics is.

---

[11] Ghost teachers are non-existent teachers fraudulently listed on a payroll with their salaries going into the pocket of the school head or some other individual.

So I say, my local community, if we vote for the ANC, we will be voting for a better education for our children, because trained teachers will be employed and school results will improve, and violence will stop, because the ANC has leaders who want lasting peace.

Vote ANC; it stands for education and peace. Viva ANC, Viva!

Please withhold my name and address.
Worried, Bergville

Selection 6
We Need Electricity

Editor,

I am a reader who does not like to miss out on the facts published by this newspaper.

I would like to put forward the following thought that is bothering a lot of people in my neighborhood, which is in the area of chief Calalakubo Khawula.

The local community is bothered by not being able to see any progress, especially with something as important as electricity. In addition, it has been found that funds were collected from the people, and they were promised that these would go to Eskom [national supplier of electricity], but without result. The money disappeared.

I believe that even Councilor Mntomuhle Khawula, who is the chief's son, does not do anything for the people, and that it's a question of like father, like son. At that place there is not even a telephone pole. You will only find electricity in the homes of those who have connections with powerful people.

There are districts where people are said to be members of certain organizations. It's said that *they* will never get electricity, but those who say so, and their families, have all that they need in life.

Please withhold my name.
Troubled, EMZUMBE

Selection 7
Let the Old Man Enjoy His Retirement
After His Long Period of Labor

Editor,

The people of South Africa must show strength now that Mr. Thabo Mbeki is about to take over Mr. Nelson Mandela's shoes.

I say this, because many people question Mr. Thabo Mbeki's leadership compared to that of Mr. Mandela.

So listen, and let me clarify the issue.

Here is what differentiates these leaders: Mr. Mandela is much better known throughout the whole world than Mr. Mbeki, but that does not mean that Mr. Mandela is more intelligent than Mr. Mbeki.

Mr. Mandela studied Law, whereas Mr. Mbeki studied Economics. Thus it is economics that governs the country, just as one sees in America, Japan, Germany, etc.

Let the old man retire in peace, for he has served his term as leader of our people.

Wilson S. Mnyandu, KWADABEKA

Selection 8
True Stories for Women
From the Editor's Hot Pot[12]

Children should be aware that they affect their parents' lives.

«1»

Last weekend saw quite a number of incidents which touched the lives of families in different ways, from the women who were attacked and shot in Cape Town, to those who lost their lives because of road accidents.

«2»

Two parents were shot by their daughter's boyfriend simply because they were calming down a lovers' quarrel.

---

[12] This is a comparison of news items to ingredients being added to a stew that is on the go.

237

The reason for it, apparently, was that the boyfriend wanted all the things that he had bought for their daughter returned to him.

«3»

Even though we may not know the whole story, this incident might yet serve as a lesson to our own children.

Young women should be aware that the decisions they make can end up affecting not only their own lives, but also the lives of their entire family.

«4»

The same is true for young men: they should treat their elders with the same respect that they would their own parents; in addition, it would be in their best interest to be neither controlled by their emotions nor overly impetuous.

«5»

It is becoming common to have children go missing while playing outside: people say that these children are last seen being taken by some anonymous man before they disappear.

«6»

I implore mothers to remember the saying "once bitten, twice shy" and not wait until it's too late—and you see this happen to you own child—before taking precautions. I know that there are some who are already asking what could be done to stop this scourge.

«7»

I believe that it would behoove us to be on the lookout with respect to our children's safety, because it's still going to take a long time to find a way to put a stop to this awful behavior.

Since we are neighbors, how about joining together to erect a fence, starting with the house where the children usually play, and then continuing to the other houses?

Dudu Khoza

Selection 9
Children Who Live on the Streets

«1»

Not knowing where you'll get your next plate of food, or where you'll sleep at night: these are the things that make life difficult for street kids.

These days it is normal to see homeless children roaming the streets in the large cities of South Africa.

«2»

Many of them beg from drivers or pedestrians. People—especially those in cars—generally consider these children to be criminals.

As they go about in groups, these children begin to act like a mutually protective family; they share what little food they get.

«3»

They wear smelly and dirty clothing, and even their bodies are covered with the scars of past injuries. One usually finds them with a bottle of glue hidden in their clothes, and what's more they stay high on this glue which they use repeatedly to ward off hunger.

The understanding between these children provides them with a sense of togetherness and mutual love that they have never experienced at home or among their relatives. But their unity has now resulted in dangerous gangs, and brought fear to members of the community, especially in cities.

«4»

These boys consider the police to be their enemies. Sandile Memela, a nine-year-old member of a gang in Point Road, Durban, known as the Mdlwembe Gang, said that the police often take them to the police station where they are forced to wash the police cars and vans. "I hate the police, because they continually beat us," said Sandile.

«5»

"Members of the community also hit us, and repeatedly abuse us sexually," emphasized Thulani Khanyile, who comes from Empangeni, in KwaZulu-Natal.

"But we pass the time by sniffing glue," said the leader of the Santoshi Young Killers [Gang], Innocent Shezi from Pietermaritzburg.

«6»

"We sniff glue to take away the hunger, especially when we haven't got enough money to buy food. It doesn't fill us, but we are glad for it," said Clive Wilkes of Wentworth.

Thulani Makhathini, who is also known by the name of Snoopy, is 10 years old, yet he left his home in Bhambayi four years ago.

«7»

My stepfather used to hit me every day without my mother saying anything—on the contrary, she used to take part," said this boy. This cruelty that I experienced at home forced me to go and live on the streets of Durban. But life is difficult here. I have already been through much hardship, and if I had not gone to the Thuthukani Outreach Center, I would be dead by now."

«8»

"Members of the community and the police take us as thugs, and also hit us or threaten to kill us. I want to let other kids know that they should speak to their parents or with social workers before making the decision to take to the streets. Life here is difficult and dangerous."

Some of the smaller boys are used as sexual objects by the older boys. "We don't sleep at night because they abuse us sexually while we are asleep," said Xolani Khambule, who is eight years old.

«9»

In some places in this country, there are very dangerous gangs of criminals. They rape and murder people. Gang warfare on the Cape Flats continues to be a topic for journalists. Here, criminal gangs such as the Americans, the Young Boys and the Notorious Mongrel Gang kill one another with big guns to settle problems relating to turf and drugs.

«10»

Joan van Niekerk, who is the director of Childline in the Province of KwaZulu-Natal, said that the state and the community, together with social welfare organizations, must come up with a scheme to prevent children from living on the streets and to bring an end to criminal gangs.

"We must help these children so that they can return to a proper life," said Joan. "Street children and gangs of criminals are a worry to us in our country, but at the same time it is difficult to get the situation back to what it should be."

By Linda Manyoni

Selection 10
A Firm Hand with Taxpayers

By Sandile Mdadane

«1»

Things are going to change for those who evade paying taxes because the department concerned with tax collection, the South African Revenue Services (SARS), has joined forces with the financial crimes division of the SAPS [South African Police Services] Commercial Crime Unit and the Department of Correctional Services [i.e., prisons] and together they have begun the tactic of jailing everyone, including business owners, who evade paying taxes.

«2»

Since last month in Durban, 896 people have already been put on the roll of those who will be prosecuted for tax evasion, and they say that another 300 have had arrest warrants issued against them.

«3»

The campaign of this division has recently been apparent in the arrest and prosecution of a father and son from here in Durban who are faced with a charge of tax evasion to the tune of R15 million on goods they bought outside the borders of South Africa.

«4»

These two became the first victims of the new law, the Proceeds of Crime Act, whereby the state confiscated their goods, froze their bank accounts, which had over R1 million, and took their house and five cars until a verdict is reached.

«5»

The names of all those who evade paying taxes will be published in the newspapers before long.

The Embezzlers

Many people evade paying Value Added Tax (VAT), Employee Tax, and Annual Tax Returns.

«6»

The senior prosecutor in special courts, Mr. Barend Groen, said that people should know that there is a difference between tax evasion and tax fraud.

"These two categories of crime differ greatly.

«7»

"When we speak about tax frauds, we're talking about people who embezzle thousands upon thousands," explained Mr. Groen.

He continued by saying that it is of no avail for tax-evaders to break the law, since they do not normally gain a lot by it.

He ended by saying that he does not believe for a minute that there are people who evade taxes without knowing that they are breaking the law.

Selection 11
Can the KwaShaka Soccer Team Do It Again at the Soccer Festival?

By Zwelakhe Ngcobo

«1»

The KwaShaka High School is defending their Girls' Soccer title for the third time in consecutive years and this will be accompanied by a water conservation program at the Umlazi Soccer Festival which will be held on Thursday at the King Zwelithini Stadium at 9.00 am.

«2»

This competition, which will be celebrating five years since its establishment, will be special because it will be attended by the national Minister of Water and Forestry, Prof. Kader Asmal, who will be accompanied by Mayor Theresa Mthembu of Durban South Central and Dudu Khoza of Khozi FM[13] who will be giving out the awards to the successful teams.

«3»

According to Morgan Zama who is the coordinator of this competition, the team line-up is as follows: Boys under 11 — Entuthukweni from Lamontville will play against Vumokuhle; Girls under 14 — Manyuswa will test its skills against Bhekithemba; Boys under 14 — Manyuswa will tackle Bhekithemba; Girls Open — KwaShaka High School will come up against Umlazi Comtech; and the closing game will be that in which Siyavuma Mfeka comes head to head with Lamontville High School, who were the finalists last year.

«4»

The following are the prizes for this competition, which is being held for the first time since the withdrawal of the Wakefield JHI

---

[13] A radio station.

Company, which was formerly one of the sponsors of the competition.

As first prizes there are a trophy, gold medals, a soccer jersey, a large bag and T-shirts.

«5»

Second prizes: silver medals, a soccer jersey, a big bag and T-shirts.

The sportsperson of the day's award will be a track suit and a pair of soccer boots donated by Adidas.

Zama issues an invitation to all children who live in Umlazi and surrounding areas to come and join in the fun of the games.

Selection 12
Womens' Organization Involved in Setting Up Small Community Industries

By Nash Ngcobo

«1»

The Siyaphezulu Womens' Club of Nazareth, in Pinetown, is heading a scheme to establish small businesses which will, ultimately, extend the assistance given to its unemployed members by providing jobs of various kinds.

«2»

This will happen through the launching of lessons for managing various categories of small business, including needlework; the establishment of programs for selling surplus produce from abroad; and jobs that will come from the Municipality of Inner West Council.

«3»

These aspirations, which make sound sense, came to the fore after some persuasion of this organization by Mrs. Dudu Ngcongo, who has risen quite high in the Department of Trade and Tourism in the Government of KwaZulu-Natal.

«4»

Siyaphezulu was told about the great opportunities it has of starting a company of morticians, the establishment of a bank that will help the community in its area in different ways.

The keeping in cold storage of the deceased, the dispatch of uniforms to schools, factories, and catering companies are things Siyaphezulu is ready to undertake because it has members who do this work.

«5»
They say that in order to decrease the costs of hiring people, most of these jobs will currently be given to members of this organization with the exception of those who are trained for those specific jobs.

Mrs. Dudu said that all the above would be easy once Siyaphezulu is legally registered as a company with the government so that it will give confidence to those who wish to do business with it.

Selection 13
Student Boycott in Maritzburg[14]
over Failed Delivery of Stationery

«1»
The failure to deliver reading books and stationery has led students at George Town High School, which is in Edendale, Pietermaritzburg, to boycott classes until this problem is resolved.

«2»
This problem first arose last Monday when students expressed their dissatisfaction at not receiving books for writing in, and asked that this problem be resolved to their satisfaction.

«3»
Since the students do not have a general representative organization, they did not want their names to be divulged in the paper, but they were prepared to explain why they did not attend their classes.

«4»
According to the students, this lack of basic necessities gave them the opportunity to address the other problems that they face.

«5»
"The thing is not just that we have a problem with workbooks here at school, but there are many problems, which, in our view, must be fixed before we return to class," explained one of the students.

«6»
The Problems

They proceeded to say that on Monday they had had a discussion about their problems with the head teacher[15], Mr. Ngubane, who then promised that he would organize things for them, but Friday came and they were still boycotting classes.

---

[14] Maritzburg is the common abbreviation among English-speakers of Pietermaritzburg, the capital of the KwaZulu-Natal province.
[15] The terms "head teacher" and "principal" are synonymous in South African schools.

«7»

Some of the issues they had, apart from the books, were that they wanted people to be hired to cut the grass around the entire school; they wanted windows and doors to be installed; they wanted information about the school budget; they wanted to know what happened with the monies, since nothing was done to uplift the school; and they thought that corporal punishment should end.

«8»

One of the students added that they wanted an explanation about where the money went that they had to pay for security personnel, because from the time they began paying they had not yet seen any watchmen at the school.

«9»

"Parents have to pay the money, but the fruits thereof are never ultimately seen.

«10»

"We know that the payment of this money was by agreement between the parents and the head teacher, but since the parents do not come to the school they do not know about the things that take place inside it," explained the student.

«11»

They Have Been Ordered

Furthermore, they opposed the raising of school fees because they already went up from R50 last year to R120 this year. A problem with this money, they say, is that it includes money for security personnel who are not actually at the school.

«12»

They say that if these problems are not solved, they will definitely not return to class.

«13»

The principal of the school, Mr. Ngubane, has never been known to offer his opinion about the trouble at his school, but a spokesperson for the Department of Education in Pietermaritzburg, Mr. Muzi Kubheka, said that they had already received these student complaints. He then proceeded to say that his department was already sending out the writing books that Friday.

«14»

"We have already found that there were occasional interruptions of studies at this school due to the students' lack of stationery and the need for the grass to be cut," said Mr. Kubheka.

«15»

He said he hoped that after the arrival of the stationery, everything would return to normal.

"We have already found that there were occasional interruptions of studies at this school due to the students' lack of stationery, and the need for the grass to be cut," said Mr. Kubheka.

He said he hoped that after the arrival of the stationery, everything would return to normal.

Selection 14

Sebata: A Man Who Does Not Let His Blindness Get Him Down!

When I met Sebata at the gates of the hospital where he works, it was he who led me to his office, rather than me walking ahead of him. Then, when it was lunchtime, he took me to the cafeteria and pulled out a chair for me.

Sebata says that his lack of sight was caused by the fact that his family did not have much information about health matters while he was growing up. At the time of his birth he could see well, but apparently when he was ten years old he contracted measles. This disease ended up damaging his eyes.

Sebata doesn't let himself feel even the slightest bit sad about his blindness, and what's more, he is proud of his job as Principal Telecommunications Operator at Blouberg Hospital. His job includes monitoring the incoming and outgoing phone calls at this hospital.

At the moment he is still pursuing his studies at the University of South Africa (UNISA) by doing a B.A. degree in Management. "I will never give up studying, and there is nothing that will turn me away from that," he said. In 1971, Sebata studied at Siloam School, which is a school for the blind. The people who helped him find this school were his aunt and the organization, the South African National Council for the Blind.

At this school he completed twelfth grade. In 1984 he obtained a switchboard operator's certificate at Phoneficiency [sic] College in Johannesburg. His first job as a switchboard operator was at George Maseba Hospital in Potgietersrus. He worked at this hospital for six years before he was transferred to Blouberg Hospital in 1990.

This young man was born in Bochum in the Northern Province in 1961. He was raised by his mother, Moiporoti. "My mother raised me on her own, and has loved me from that time until now," said Sebata.

Sebata married Gladys Molokomme and they have been blessed with four children: Solly (11), Mahlatse (6), Moosa (4), and Tshepo (1). Gladys has a B.A. (Education). She considers her marriage to be a gift from God.

Getting married was problematic at first, because her parents did not want her to marry Sebata. "I had to beg them and tell them that they should remember that I chose to marry him of my own accord," said Gladys.

Gladys wants to establish an organization for women married to disabled people so that she can help them by teaching them how to deal with their husbands. "I wish people could see things the way I see them. Men who can't see should have faith in themselves and should remember that they are the same as sighted men," said Gladys.

Sebata is a respected man in the community of Bochum. He is president of the Bochum After-Care Center and is Community Liaison Officer for the Association for the Disabled in Bochum.

This organization helps to improve the lives of disabled people and also finds them jobs.

He [Sebata] is passionate about cycling, and when he is doing so, you would swear that he has no problem! Even though he has someone to drive him in his car, Sebata is able to drive himself.

When he's at home, he likes listening to the music of Lionel Richie and Brenda Fassie, while in the field of jazz, he is a fan of the guitarist Doctor Philip Tabane.

"People often ask me strange questions such as how I was attracted to my wife. I don't know if they are fooled by the fact that I cannot see with my eyes. On occasion, some ask me how I shave—I have a wife who is such a help to me.

"I would like to pass on this request to the community: you should not hide disabled people in your homes. Bring them out so that the community can learn about them. Parents who hide their disabled children should be locked up in jail, because they deprive them of the right to a better life.

"Disabled people will never be able to support themselves on welfare grants—what is important is that they study. If you have given them education, you have immediately and completely ended their disability!" concluded Sebata.

By Noko Mashilo

Selection 15
Small Testicles

My left testicle is smaller than the one on the right. This greatly bothers my wife and me, because we think that we may not be able to have children.

A.S.D., Bloemfontein

It is common for testes to vary in size, but if one is smaller than the other, this could be due to previous disease or injury to that testicle. If it is not completely absent and yet the scrotum is empty, this is known as an undescended testicle. Fortunately, the healthy one will be adequate to produce children. I would suggest that you consult a doctor so that he can examine you.

Selection 16
Zethembe Is a Lifesaver

Zethembe Dlamini is a suicide-prevention counselor and hostage negotiator.

«1»

After a friend of his killed himself by jumping out of a moving train, Zethembe Dlamini decided to make a career out of helping people who are on the verge of committing suicide. His job is to rescue people who are being held hostage or who want to kill themselves, both in South Africa and abroad.

«2»

This young man, who is a 28-year-old policeman, comes from Ntuzuma in the Durban district. He told us that the number of suicide attempts and hostage situations is on the rise in South Africa. For this reason, he decided to take courses on how to save lives. Zethembe is a secretary with the South African Police Service's financial department in Umzimkhulu and he completed the relevant coursework after two weeks of training in Pietermaritzburg.

«3»

"As an assistant during hostage situations and suicide attempts, my job is to negotiate with the person who has hijacked a plane, bus, car, or ship, or with the person who is thinking about committing suicide. If a plane has been hijacked, we negotiate with the hijacker and then come to an agreement with him or her without anyone getting hurt or arrested. We proceed in a similar manner when a ship has been hijacked or a principal is held hostage at a school," explained Zethembe.

«4»

He emphasized the point that if someone attempting to commit suicide or a hijacker does not want to listen to them, it is sometimes necessary to use force.

"Those who negotiate with a hijacker or a would-be suicide accompany a group of the Special Task Force, which is trained to resolve any problems that might arise with violent individuals. In such a situation, however, someone might end up dying—which is something we try to avoid at all costs."

«5»

Zethembe also explained to us that people threatening suicide often stand on top of high buildings or bridges. Sometimes they threaten to shoot themselves.

"Often, these people just want to be noticed. If you negotiate with them face to face they may change their minds," said Zethembe.

«6»

Zethembe related to us what happens when a plane or ship from this country is hijacked abroad. "When a South African plane or ship is hijacked in America or Europe, we get there as fast as we can to help out. The reason for this is that *we* understand South African culture better than anyone else."

«7»

According to Zethembe, the number of suicides is growing rapidly every year. He told us that this could possibly be due to problems at work or at home. This unfortunate action is said to have increased dramatically among Black people because a very large proportion of them now live in urban areas where people only worry about their own problems and don't care about anyone else.

«8»

We Africans are accustomed to discussing our problems with others, but now people choose to remain silent when dealing with problems because the majority of them now live in areas that were formerly restricted to Whites.

Some attempt suicide after hearing that they are HIV-positive.

«9»

Zethembe said that the majority of suicides choose to kill themselves by shooting themselves, by overdosing on pills, or by throwing themselves into a river or in front of a train.

He also stressed that people who threaten to commit suicide should be taken seriously. His friend killed himself after his parents had not wanted to listen to his troubles.

Zethembe said that if you want to undergo training for this job, you first have to be a member of the police force. You should be a humble person who is close to the community and who is able to resolve peoples' problems objectively.

«10»

This young man has already visited countries such as Germany, Belgium, and America to extend his expertise, which will help him further his career.

"People who are contemplating suicide should try to contact the local police station in order to get help. This service is provided free of charge," explained Zethembe.

Story and photos by Themba Ntshingila.

Selection 17
Dark Clouds over Umtata!

«1»

The tornado that struck the town of Umtata on December 15 of last year will always be remembered because it was when the world-famous president, Dr. Nelson Mandela, nearly lost his life. The president's presence at the time of the tornado greatly reassured the local people.

«2»

It was a nice day and all was well in the town of Umtata when I entered the pharmacy to have photos developed of a wedding I had attended the previous weekend. I was in the midst of chatting to the pharmacist when we heard the sound of car sirens.

«3»

When we peered through the window, we saw a convoy of cars pull up in front of the pharmacy. The doors opened and out came strong young men smartly dressed in black. President Mandela emerged from the central car of the convoy and entered the pharmacy. Then the sky filled with dark clouds and lightning.

«4»

The president stopped here with the intention of buying a kind of soap that he began using at the time he was still on Robben Island[16]. As I approached him I had the opportunity of talking to one of his bodyguards. The question I asked him remained unanswered, however, as we heard a frightening clap of thunder smash the pharmacy windows with an alarming sound. President Mandela was then escorted into one of the pharmacy offices and surrounded by his bodyguards. The president showed great bravery but was also noticeably shaken.

«5»

Fortunately, everyone in the pharmacy was safe. When I looked out into the street, though, I saw an astonishing sight: the walls of houses were collapsing; what appeared to be paper was blowing all around; and hail as big as a man's fist was falling. At that moment, we heard the sound of people screaming as they were crushed by the collapsing houses. And then it ended as abruptly as it began, leaving the surroundings as silent as if nothing had ever happened.

«6»

I went out to survey the destruction from the doorway. I met people running and screaming, "Where is my child?" The people who died when the tornado struck were street merchants whose merchandise was also destroyed. I went up York Road and met a woman crying, "They are dead, everyone is dead!" I immediately headed for the taxi stand where the woman had stood. There I discovered eleven street merchants who had died, together with a child and what appeared to be the bodies of people who were killed by a collapsing wall.

«7»

Rescue services and paramedics were already removing the people who had been crushed. There was no way that people driving on the roads could have survived. The Umtata Hospital was damaged particularly badly. A ward was flooded with water while other rooms at the hospital were damaged or destroyed, but this did not prevent the nurses from carrying out their work of tending to patients.

---

[16] Author's note: Robben Island is an island prison where Dr. Mandela was incarcerated for over two decades.

«8»

The Presbyterian Church of Southern Africa was celebrating its centenary when the tornado removed the roof of their building. Eyewitnesses, who said that the tornado was almost 450 meters high, initially thought that they saw paper flying through the air but later realized that it was roofing material. The weather bureau at Umtata reported that the tornado was traveling at a speed of between 60 and 65 km/h.

«9»

At the hotel where I was staying, many people were calling this tornado "Hurricane Nelson." It left 18 people dead and 168 injured. The total damage in this province is estimated at R90 million.

By Ponko Masiba

Selection 18
The Air-Traffic Controller

«1»

Sandile Maphanga, who is 24 years old, says that the work he does as an air-traffic controller at Durban Airport has made him feel free.

The young boy who used to watch airplanes passing over Mseleni, a place in northern KwaZulu-Natal, made history by becoming the very first Black air-traffic controller trained in South Africa.

«2»

"I didn't know that I too would one day work in the airline industry, let alone travel by plane," said Sandile Maphanga. "I had intended to become a lawyer; I had no inclination for anything to do with aircraft even though I used to watch them at Mseleni."

This youngster passed Standard 10[17] in 1992, and the year thereafter he took on day jobs because he didn't have the money to continue his studies.

«3»

"In 1994, I saw an ad in the paper. The ad said that South African Airways (SAA) needed people to be trained as pilots. As I read the ad, my mind returned to the image of the planes I used to watch when I was growing up. I knew that there was no other option than to be trained for that job!"

---

[17] Author's note: "Standard 10" was the final year of school in South Africa.

«4»

Sandile became one of the Black people chosen to be trained as a pilot by SAA.

Training took them to Johannesburg, where he completed his studies with ease. As time passed, however, Sandile realized that he was not that eager to become a pilot.

«5»

"In 1996 I registered for courses offered by the Airports Company of South Africa (ACSA) to become an air-traffic controller. This was not an easy decision to make, but I have never regretted it and am now very content."

«6»

Right now Sandile is proud that the work he does is unusual among African youth. "In the past, our youth generally decided to become doctors, teachers, nurses, or police officers—they don't think that there are many occupations for them other than these."

According to Sandile, there are very few Black people who truly understand the work he does. "They are just amazed when I explain it to them."

«7»

While I was chatting with Sandile, we heard a pilot announcing that a plane was about to depart. Sandile responded, indicating that the flight path was without problems.

«8»

This pilot just wanted to ensure that the plane would have a safe and undisturbed flight to its destination. "The controllers use radar, which indicates whether the pilot should make his descent or whether he can depart from a particular airport. Since there are no roads or road signs in the skies, pilots place their trust in us."

«9»

"In order to perform this job without getting anxious, you have to learn to work under stressful conditions, to believe in yourself, and to get used to cooperating with others," said Sandile.

This young man is determined to carry on with his studies to prepare himself to direct overseas flights as well.

By Pearl Mzoneli

Selection 19
Women Who Do Jobs
That Were for Men

«1»

At a time when the majority of young women are choosing careers in health or law, women at the Pretoria West College of Technology are finding that engineering careers can also be intellectually demanding.

«2»

Only a few women study engineering at the Pretoria West College of Technology. This college has just produced the first Black female fitter and turner. Other women students are taking courses in fields such as electronics, civil engineering, and mechanical engineering.

There are 200 female students at this college; they make up 11% of the overall student body.

«3»

"Although this might be seen as an insignificant figure, the number of women has risen over the past five years," said Judy Ferreira, a public relations officer who also became a lecturer at the college. "The things that attract men to the engineering field also attract women.

"When we give out information about the college at school visits, we don't discriminate between men and women. Entering the field of engineering has nothing to do with gender, but only with a person's capability.

«4»

"I believe that there is nothing to stop women from succeeding at anything they desire. Women have great determination."

Minah Sono (21), who was the first Black female student to become a fitter and turner, said: "My success pleases me, but I wish other women would follow in my footsteps. This field is not restricted to men.

«5»

"I am the only child who grew up in a home with a father who was a blacksmith. I enjoyed helping him while he was working. At school I took courses in technical drawing and welding, which made me eager to study engineering."

There are only two women in her class, but studying with men doesn't intimidate Minah in the least. "My mother did not support my decision to take this job. She wanted me to do medical studies because she believed that careers in that field were suitable for a woman. I dug in my heels because I wanted to fulfill my dream."

«6»

Rebecca Maitsapo (22) was determined to become a turner. "As I was growing up, I used to play boys' games, like football. I never studied medicine because I don't like working with people. I'm someone who likes to use my brain on mechanical things to get them to work."

Moira Kgopane, who is doing courses in instrumentation (including the use of pressure-regulating equipment, machines with moving parts, and things that affect the production output of businesses), said: "There is one important thing to remember about a career in engineering—you will never be without work. You can also be self-employed. I am witness to the fact that a woman's place is not in the kitchen."

«7»

Charmaine Phega (22) is studying electrical engineering. "Over the past decade, I have wondered why it is that people in rural areas do not have electricity, but those in urban areas do," said this young woman. "I had my mind set on doing something different when I grew up, but my grandmother and grandfather were discouraging because they wanted me to become a doctor.

"However, I was determined to do something different and challenging. I knew that engineering was a male occupation requiring strength, and I have the necessary strength." It appears that women who want to do work such as engineering are enthusiastic and successful.

Story and pictures by Bongani Hlatshwayo

Selection 20
Protect Yourself against Malaria

«1»

Malaria is a devastating disease that has taken many lives. Every year more than 500 million people contract this disease (90% of whom are from Africa), and 750,000 people die from it (85% of whom are from Africa).

«2»

In South Africa the number of people killed by this disease is growing. According to statistics put out by the Communicable

Disease Control Section of the Department of Health, there were 23,282 people with malaria last year, of whom 158 died.

«3»

This figure has risen so high because of the constantly changing weather patterns in the areas where the disease is endemic, and also because a lack of preventive medicines has exacerbated the situation. Another reason for this increase is the growing number of people coming from other African countries with a high incidence of malaria. Carriers of the disease bring it into South Africa. Another problem is that people from countries where the disease is rife carry mosquitoes in their luggage or vehicles, so that often, once they have arrived in South Africa, these insects are able to spread and infect other people.

«4»

What exactly is malaria?

Malaria is a highly communicable worldwide disease that is particularly virulent in countries with very high temperatures. People contract the disease when they are bitten by a female mosquito. Male mosquitoes do not carry malaria.

«5»

What causes malaria?

The strain of malaria that is particularly dangerous is caused by a parasite called *Plasmodia falciparum*. This parasite needs two hosts in order to breed successfully: a human being and a mosquito. The parasite enters the human being via the bite of a female mosquito. When the mosquito sucks the blood of a person with malaria, it ingests parasites that proceed to lay eggs in that mosquito. When these parasites have entered the body of a person who has been bitten by a mosquito, they invade the liver. Once they have matured, they enter the bloodstream where they breed and multiply.

«6»

High-risk areas

Malaria is endemic to certain parts of the country, such as the Northern Province, Mpumalanga, and certain areas in the province of KwaZulu-Natal. It is also found in the North West [Province] and around the Molopo and Orange Rivers. Encountering the disease outside of these areas is uncommon since infected people contract it after having been bitten by a mosquito that carries the disease.

«7»

High-risk periods

In South Africa the months between October and May are considered the most dangerous.

In the high-risk areas of South Africa, female mosquitoes are particularly fond of laying eggs during this dangerous period of normally high temperatures and heavy rainfall.

People who should take extra precautions against this disease
Certain groups of people should try to avoid going to areas that are considered high-risk. These include newborn babies or children under six years of age, pregnant women, people with AIDS, people undergoing cancer treatment, and people who have had their spleens removed. People at risk of being infected by this disease should consult a doctor for advice about taking preventative measures against malaria.

«8»

Symptoms
People suffering from this disease have fevers, shivers, headaches, profuse sweating, fatigue, lower-back pain, aching joints, pain in the pelvic region, diarrhea, lack of appetite, dizziness when standing, nausea, mild jaundice, coughing, and swelling of the liver and spleen. These symptoms can drag on for six months after one has left the malarial area.

«9»

Prevention
PROTECTING ONESELF FROM MOSQUITO BITES is an important and effective step towards avoiding malaria. Protection against mosquito bites is essential in high-risk areas. Malarial mosquitoes feed at any time from morning to night. Steps to take to avoid the disease:

«10»

If possible, try to be indoors in the morning and afternoon.
If you go outdoors at night, wear long-sleeved shirts, long trousers, and socks.
Apply insect repellent to both skin and clothes. Keep reapplying, but do not go beyond the prescribed amount.
If possible, place screens over windows and doors to prevent mosquitoes from getting inside; otherwise, you should close everything at night.
Visitors to, or residents of, high-risk areas should sleep under mosquito nets impregnated with insect repellent. These can be obtained from stores and pharmacies.
You can use a spray against flying insects, especially in bedrooms.
You can use a mosquito mat or mosquito coil at night.

«11»

Tourists can avoid the disease by not going to high-risk areas, or by going at times other than the rainy season or during a drought; they should also use anti-malaria drugs. You can ask your doctor or pharmacist about these drugs, which are taken before visiting a dangerous area.

Since the majority of people living in high-risk areas ignore the use of preventative measures against the disease, here are steps that could help them to reduce the number of mosquitoes.

«12»

They can build their houses far from swamps and damp areas because mosquitoes like to breed in such areas.

Ensure that there is piped water close to your house.

Spray insect repellant on standing water.

Apply insecticide to interior walls.

«13»

Treating the disease

Since it is EASY to contract malaria if you don't take preventative measures, it is vital for anyone who lives in or has visited a malaria area and who develops cold symptoms accompanied by a fever to consult a doctor without delay and to explain to him or her where they have been. You must get treatment IMMEDIATELY because malaria is a fatal disease if it is not promptly treated!

Selection 21
The Police Go Berserk in Nkume

Editor

«1»

Allow me to express, in your reliable newspaper, my outrage at what happened in February 1996 in our area, Nkume, which is under Chief Mpungose.

This year something happened that so shocked the whole community of KwaMpungose[18] that it marched in protest to the commander of the police station at Eshowe about the action of the police.

«2»

As yet, however, nothing has been reported and this serious event has failed to become public knowledge despite our desire to let the nation know about it.

---

[18] Author's note: The prefix *Kwa-* is used in place names to indicate the area of jurisdiction of a tribal chief, or that a place is named after a particular individual.

The police arrived at night in the village of KwaNgcobo and assaulted a local family. A gentleman was shot and killed; his pregnant cow also died.

«3»

Thereafter a riot broke loose that lasted until some soldiers helped to stabilize the situation.

What made it so deplorable is that the family was already so poor that they could only bear the funeral costs with the assistance of the community.

«4»

What is really disgusting is that the policeman who caused these unbelievable events does not even know it; he carries on working as usual.

We want to know whether this matter has come to the attention of the Hon. Minister of Security, Nyanga, Ngubane and Mr. Sydney Mufamadi because here in Eshowe there are no solid facts about the people who were openly killed on that day, and no information has come to light about them even now.

«5»

We want this serious incident to be placed under scrutiny and the honorable people in charge of this department to take action. The gentleman who was killed was a respected person who built houses for the community.

«6»

Now his children are helpless. I conclude by asking my brothers and sisters who are journalists, especially in KwaZulu-Natal, to make this whole affair known in the media so that the violence experienced by this community comes to the attention of the government.

«7»

Thank you for your kind publication of this matter so that the authorities can be alerted to the brutality that is still perpetrated by the police in rural areas.

I request that my name and surname be withheld.

Disturbed. Eshowe

Selection 22
Looking for a Single, Soft-Spoken Young Lady

I am a forty-year-old house builder who has not lost the passion of youth; I would like to meet a single young lady of reserved character and good manners who wants to settle down with a guy who doesn't cause trouble or drink.

A single mother, a divorcee, a widow, or an orphan would all be fine as long as she is respectful, humble, does not try to wear the pants in the family, would like a nice home, is a churchgoer, and is not of the Ndlovu, Shezi, Mkhize, Mthembu, Dlamini, Shozi, or Sibisi Msomi clans.

I am talented and like gospel music, the radio, TV, writing, reading, children, and cooking, as well as loving and sensitive people.

Please send a photograph, which I will return, and give details about yourself in a letter. My address is: New Love Order, P.O. Box 706, Pinetown, 3600.

Please withhold my name, which will only be provided to those who reply.

Lonely, Pinetown

Selection 23
Men Who Rape Men

«1»

Vuma (not his real name) was in jail for the first time. He trembled with fear, having often heard of the terrible life of prisoners behind bars. He prayed silently, hoping that somehow he could escape the gang culture of prison.

«2»

In spite of his prayers, the awful day had arrived when he would be locked into a prison cell for the very first time. The other prisoners, who had already served time, were glad to see him and said lustfully: "Here's some fresh meat."

They were hardened criminals who called themselves the 28s[19], whereas *he* was just a schoolboy.

«3»

Vuma tried to hold back the tears when he related this story, but it was obvious even from the sound of his voice that relating the experience of being gang-raped caused him a great deal of anguish.

«4»

According to one sex therapist, rape is exceedingly painful for males. "Besides the psychological trauma, there is the even worse physical pain; undeniably, males were not created to be the passive partners in sex," this expert explained.

«5»

"I felt sickened, afraid, and worthless, especially since there was nothing I could do to stop this iniquity," said Vuma. "I am a gentle person, and I had now come up against hardened criminals. It was clear to me that I had no chance because I was not someone who could put up a fight. I was shaking with fear.

«6»

"The pain was unbearable. I thought that these monsters would leave me alone because I was bleeding. Not so! They carried on, laughing at the fact that all virgins are the same the first time they have sex. They thought that one day I would enjoy doing this, so I should start getting used to it!"

«7»

Vuma said that this used to happen at night. They threatened him when he told them that he would inform the wardens. His suffering had an unexpected consequence. A blood test by prison authorities revealed that he had the HIV virus, which is the precursor to AIDS.

«8»

Although there is no doubt that a large number of women are raped, men are also raped. According to sources from Life Line, "Male rape is common in prisons. It also occurs in places where men live alone without women.

«9»

"This includes boys' boarding schools, military barracks, and other all-male quarters. One finds young people in rural areas who practice this evil.

«10»

"Child-rape generally takes place in the victim's home and is usually perpetrated by a parent, grandfather, older brother, cousin, maternal

---

[19] Author's note: The 28s are a prison gang found throughout the country, which goes back to the beginning of the last century. It is known as a highly militaristic gang, with homosexuality as one of its key elements.

uncle[20], or friend of the family. Young boys who run away from home are also in danger of becoming victims of this scourge.

«11»

"There are certain places or situations that are equally dangerous for both males and females," Life Line warned. "These include nightclubs, hitchhiking, walking alone in deserted areas, public restrooms, and so on."

«12»

According to Life Line, "The majority of males who have been in this predicament do not take action after the event because they believe that people—and even the authorities—would not take the matter seriously. The majority of people, including medical professionals, do not know that males are also victims of sexual assault.

«13»

"Due to sensitivity about sexual matters, men are unwilling to talk about having been raped. Most people consider it to be something shameful when it happens to a man. The victims suffer in silence because they are afraid that people will call them homosexuals, which is one of the reasons why they are afraid to report this humiliation."

«14»

The law also complicates the issue because, according to its definition, only females can be raped[21]. Rape is a crime committed by a *male* against a *female*. Thus, a man could never be found guilty of raping another male, but he could be charged with sexual assault.

«15»

For example, in 1995 the Child Protection Unit handled 8,992 cases involving the rape of girls under the age of 18. However, the 600 cases involving boys under the age of 18 were treated as sodomy, i.e., sexual intercourse between two males.

What causes a man to rape another man? Also, what kind of man is exposed to the danger of being raped?

«16»

Dr. Irma Labuschagne, who is a forensic criminologist, put it this way: "The perpetrator is simply overwhelmed by lust. Men sexually assault other men—in or out of prison—to give vent to their frustration, to inflict injury, to show power, or to express contempt.

---

[20] Author's note: Maternal uncles are specified here, since according to Xhosa kinship nomenclature, paternal uncles are called "father" or "grandfather".

[21] Author's note: This issue is presently under parliamentary review.

«17»

"In prison, sexual assault has a variety of causes; among them we find many instances of men who have been arrested for the sexual exploitation or sexual abuse of children who are in turn sexually assaulted by their cellmates 'in order to put them in their place,' an act that is repeated, often by gang-rape, 'so that they can feel what it is like.' I have heard that prisoners often maltreat newcomers by sexually assaulting them as a form of initiation. Some men in prison behave as homosexuals in order to satisfy their sexual urges. Once released from prison they return to a normal lifestyle. It is feared that AIDS may increase in prison.

«19»

"Men are sexually assaulted and sodomized outside of prison as well. I once counseled men who had experienced this type of assault. Any man can be violated, but male homosexuals are most likely to be the victims of such assault."

«20»

It is very tough for male rape victims because they blame themselves and because they become the butt of jokes. People believe that men are able to stand up for themselves, but that women lack the necessary strength. Therefore, a man who has been raped considers himself unmanly.

«21»

Dr. Labuschagne agrees, and warns that males who have been raped require help coming to terms with what they've been through. "Sexual assault can take more or less time to recover from, but is likely to take longer for men than for women. Men are severely traumatized after the initial shock: they lose faith, they see themselves as dirty, and they have no peace of mind when thinking of the incident.

«22»

"They can overcome this through professional help, which also brings psychological healing. Men should be helped to realize that seeking help is not shameful. It is time for people to realize that this is a serious problem and that this crime has a negative impact on a man's perception of his manhood. Rape Crisis Services, which is administered by Life Line, was created in order to aid male rape victims.

«23»

Contrary to popular belief, the good news from Dr. Labuschagne is that "There is little evidence to show that young boys who have been sexually abused by other males are likely to become homosexuals; in fact, the opposite could also be true.

«24»

"My findings are that victims of sexual assault have problems of adjustment with respect to their sexuality—over time, they continually experience sexual difficulties with women—but that is not the slightest indication that they necessarily want to have sex with other men."

Selection 24
Coexistence with a Rural Community

«1»

It should come as no surprise that rural communities do not fully understand the issues concerning the game reserves, which are so numerous in South Africa. The reason is that people have convinced themselves that these game reserves are intended to deprive them of their land.

«2»

In the past, game reserve officials created a very negative situation in their determination to arrest anyone found hunting in the reserves.

«3»

The provincial Nature Conservation Service in KwaZulu-Natal has now taken steps towards building a good relationship with communities living alongside the game reserves.

«4»

This organization has already built covered stalls for the sale of handicrafts, and has also found land for the community to grow fresh produce. Both products will be sold to visitors to the province. Maureen Mndaweni, who works for the KZN [KwaZulu-Natal] Nature Conservation Service, said that the organization is in charge of a program designed to teach the community about nature conservation while at the same time providing them with a way to acquire an income.

«5»

"We have also taught herbalists how to grow medicinal plants to replace their use of wild ones. In the production of herbal remedies, those living in rural areas are now able to use bushes they have cultivated for themselves."

«6»

At the time of the planting campaign, the organization arranged a three-day trip with the purpose of improving the lives of rural communities in this province.

«7»

Lungile Biyela of Dukuduku is one of the 50 rural women to receive assistance, and she now sells her own handiwork at the Siyabonga

Crafts Center. Her stall is one of those built in the north of KwaZulu-Natal.

«8»

"I am the breadwinner at home and I have five children. With the money from the stall I am now in a position to support both my children and my husband, who lost his job four years ago."

«9»

At present, tourism officials in KwaZulu-Natal have initiated a program to spread awareness to other provinces about the improvement that has taken place in this province in order to encourage people in rural areas to become involved in tourist commerce.

«10»

"We are prepared to assist the community by communicating the importance of trading stalls that could help them sell their produce," said Ronnie Naidoo, a manager in the Department of Tourism.

Story and pictures by Linda Manyoni.

Selection 25
Abortion: A Major Point of Debate

«1»

Abortion is a matter of serious public debate that has been controversial ever since the South African Parliament passed a bill legalizing it in February 1997.

«2»

Even though some political parties and Christian groups did not support this law, a large number of women applauded the government's policy.

«3»

Attempts to fight this policy were unsuccessful even though opponents did everything they could to protest abortion clinics. The protestors held public pro-life demonstrations.

«4»

Organizations that agreed with the policy praised the verdict of the Constitutional Court and said that poor women would benefit from this law.

«5»

Nurses at some hospitals continued their intense efforts to convince women that abortion is a great evil. These nurses were cautioned and told that they could face legal action if they continued with their attempts to prevent women from having abortions if they had freely chosen to do so.

«6»

Weziwe Thusi, who is the deputy assistant to the secretary of the ANC [African National Congress] Women's League in KwaZulu-Natal and a member of a group of single women that deals with abortion-related issues, made the following point: "The passing of this law has emancipated women. Many have already died from back-alley abortions; now they are able to have abortions safely."

«7»

Weziwe, the head of the information division of this women's league, added that she and those she works with come into contact with many women when there are events concerning her department. "We have found that a large percentage of women support this law. Our job in this organization is to give advice about abortion to those who have chosen this option, and to tell them how important it is that they go to a family planning clinic."

«8»

She added that they attempt to persuade those organizations that disagree with this policy to be open in informing their members about sexual behavior. "Some organizations don't like any discussion of this issue. For them discussion of sexual matters is still something offensive, but our perspective is that women should be informed of the importance of safe sex for avoiding unplanned pregnancies as well as diseases such as HIV."

«9»

According to Sister Nonsikelelo Khuzwayo, who is in the Department of Family Planning, abortions have not traditionally been performed in Africa. "The youth have welcomed abortion, although I don't have the exact figures.

"In my view, abortion is on the rise because we are confronting a volatile economy in this country."

«10»

Nonsikelelo's opinion is that abortion will benefit those who have been raped or have some life-threatening condition.

Gertrude Mzizi of the Women's League of the IFP [Inkatha Freedom Party] stated that their organization would respect the beliefs and cultures of various peoples. "Our members have freedom of choice—we would never tell them what to do."

J.N., Roodepoort

Selection 26
Serial Killer Sentenced

«1»
The serial killer Sipho Thwala (31), who was sentenced yesterday to 506 years for rape and attempted murder,[22] said that the reason that he did not make a plea in mitigation before the judge when he was sentenced was his disgust at the judge.

«2»
Sipho, who is from Bester in the Inanda area, said this in an interview with a correspondent from *UMAFRIKA* four days after having been sentenced, during which time he could have expressed his dissatisfaction at the sentence, but he kept on saying that he was not yet ready to defend himself.

«3»
Sipho said that what appalled him about this judge is that she questioned him as if she had been present when he was alleged to have committed the crimes.

The conclusion of this case means freedom to Miss Busisiwe Mfeka, the sister of Hlengiwe Theresa Mfeka, who was one of those raped and killed by Sipho.

«4»
Speaking to the journalist for this newspaper, Miss Mfeka said that since the beginning of the case, she has been afraid that Sipho would be acquitted and come back and kill her since she was one of the witnesses.

She says that this anxiety grew after reports were broadcast to the effect that Sipho had escaped from prison and that this villain had been implicated in arson against her family home.

«5»
The judge, Ms Vivianne Niles-Duner, found Sipho guilty on 16 charges of murder and ten of rape and attempted murder.

In passing sentence, Justice Niles-Duner, said that from the beginning of the case, there had not been the slightest sign of remorse for his actions on the part of Sipho: "He is a killer with no conscience."

---

[22] This should presumably have read "of murder and attempted murder" since lower in the article it is stated that he was indeed found guilty of sixteen charges of murder.

«6»

The judge said that had the death sentence still been available it would have been fitting for this killer.

Dr. Micky Pretorius, a psychiatrist who testified to his findings on Thwala, is confident that there is no chance of the killer undergoing a change of character.

«7»

The psychiatrist warned that if he were to be released he would be even more dangerous than before.

He said that prison was the only place where they could attempt to reform him so that he would not perpetrate even more evil than he already had.

Sipho's lawyer, Mr. Kenneth Samuel, said that Sipho regretted his actions as is evident from a letter which he supposedly wrote from jail to the community in which he says that he asks forgiveness and regrets his actions.

«8»

The judge said that the defendant, Sipho, had repudiated that letter and said that he had been told by the police what to write; therefore, she could not accept this letter as having come from him.

The judge said that the sentence she was imposing was aimed at ensuring that the killer would spend the rest of his life behind bars.

«9»

Asked by *UMAFRIKA* about his sentence, the prisoner said it was unjust since he was innocent.

Asked why he had not entered an appeal for a lesser sentence, he said that he and the judge would never agree because, at the time she was questioning him about the evidence, he had asked her whether she had been witness to what she told the court he had done.

By Philisiwe Mjoli

Selection 27
The Rewards of Hard Work

«1»

Anton Madlala was a foreman. When his job came to an end, he decided to remain in agriculture. Now he is the first Black farmer to have a strawberry farm in KwaZulu-Natal.

«2»

The size of Anton's land is 0.75 hectares, and it is fenced off in order to prevent cattle from entering. When he looks at the beauty of his plot he is filled with great pride. On his land grow mouth-watering strawberries.

«3»

"There are many supermarkets and other places selling fresh produce which want these strawberries," he said proudly.

In 1985 Anton lost his job after not seeing eye-to-eye with the management of the company for which he worked. This man, who has four children, was last employed as an overseer on the strawberry farm of Gareth Olivier.

«4»

In time, he was promoted to the position of manager, a position that required him to be in charge of 150 laborers. "I knew virtually nothing about agriculture at the time I began this job. I ended up having learned a great deal, so much so that now I enjoy it all," said Anton.

At the end of ten years in this job, he quit after a disagreement between him and the employer dealing with wages.

«5»

In 1996, Anton decided to set up his own agricultural business since he had acquired extensive knowledge in this field. He utilized land which belonged to his brother and which was not being worked at that time. His working capital was borrowed from his brothers, Leonard and Henry, and with it he bought a number of strawberry plants.

Apart from the assistance of his brothers, Anton also received his insurance money and R20,000 that he borrowed from the KwaZulu Finance and Investment Corporation (KFC).

«6»

This young man also obtained assistance from Agrilek, an organization giving advice to farmers. "Agrilek installed an electrically powered gas pump for me that has already reduced my workload," said Mr. Madlala.

«7»

"We anticipate that Black farmers will follow Anton's lead and stop bowing and scraping before White bosses on the farms. They must acquire the know-how to be able to farm on their own," said Nhlanhla Dlamini of Agrilek. Julius Zondi, who is married into the same family that he is, expanded on this matter in this way: "Agriculture is crucial because the whole country depends on the soil; therefore we would like to encourage Black people to become farmers."

«8»

"Anyone who wants to harvest the fruits of success must first plant the essential seed of hard work," says Anton.

"My first crop was very good, but I experienced bouts of nerves when I was about to sell my first produce, because there were many competitors. The thing responsible for my success was that my fruit was of good quality," Anton continued.

«9»

After seeing the success of his first crop, Anton moved from his brother's place and came to this farm that he has been cultivating up to the present. He calls it ALHEBROS, an acronym composed of the initials of his own and his brothers' names. "I would not be where I am today if it were not for them," he emphasized.

«10»

He revealed his shrewdness when explaining to us the reason for his choice of cultivating strawberries. "It is awfully easy to be a farmer who grows maize and potatoes and for it to become difficult to sell them since there are a lot of farmers producing them in abundance," he explained.

He added that he makes a good profit from producing this fruit because there are not many farmers who have planted it. "Right now, I am very busy with test planting of raspberries," says Anton.

«11»

The rewards of his success were obvious when he was invited to pass on his experience to Black farmers who had been unsuccessfully farming strawberries for 13 years. Anton has already passed on 50% of his shares to the farmers whom he helps and they too have become well-known in many places in this province through his assistance.

«12»

Anton's success is quite amazing because in Makatini, where he has his farm, the weather is actually not suited to this fruit. "I have now set up and linked several tunnels that will assist in protecting my plants when there is frost," he explained.

«13»

This by-no-means-lazy farmer has a piece of advice that he likes to pass on to people who are passionate about farming. "If you are not armed with the requisite knowledge, you would be foolish to continue in this line of work," he warns. He also stressed that people wishing to become farmers must first get advice and a depth of knowledge before entering the agricultural field.

«14»

He is ready to be of assistance to anyone who needs advice because he himself knows the stress he first experienced before he became so enthusiastic.

When he outlines his dreams, he says that he would be overjoyed to acquire a larger farm than the one he is farming at present. Even though his success has enabled him to employ 25 people, Mr. Madlala believes that a large farm would enable him to open other avenues of employment.

"That would also give me the opportunity to plant other crops when the strawberry-planting season has passed," he concluded.

Selection 28
Are You Troubled by Debt?
There Is a Solution

«1»

We are already in the second month of the year 1999! I am sure that many of you have been able to fulfill your New Year's resolutions from last year. Congratulations to those of you who were able to do so! For my own part, one of my resolutions for this year was to get out of debt and to avoid the temptations of the credit card.

«2»

Today many people are burdened with debts that they cannot repay. The reason for this is that these people have a standard of living that is higher than their incomes. It is very easy to find yourself submerged in debt. People buy luxuries after having been tempted by advertisers who tell them that they can repay on easy terms.

The tragedy in all of this is that the stores do not tell you that you will never be able to pay off the goods because your income is too low.

«3»

Other things that lead people into insurmountable debt are labor strikes, which mean that they do not receive their wages, and the insolvency of companies that have been shut down because of the economic climate. Just recently, many small businesses have been removed from the stock exchange due to the exchange rate against the dollar. When people are faced with financial difficulties, they think of a variety of ways out. Some are able to confront their problems and start their lives over again, while others are unable to do so and end up choosing suicide as a way out of their woes.

«4»

If you find yourself in debt, remember that there is hope and a course of action which can take you out of your difficulty. You can easily eliminate debt even if you don't have a cent in your pocket. There are people who have reorganized their lives after sinking into debt and who now lead better lives than previously. Problems begin when your expenses exceed your monthly income. You will also find that there are unbudgeted-for expenses that you are unable to repay on a monthly basis.

«5»

Do not procrastinate until you are in dire straits once you have found yourself besieged by debt. Make an immediate decision so that the situation does not become desperate. List all your debts and make a note of any monies in hand. Remember that your creditors will be dissatisfied if you don't pay off your debt since, if they take legal action against you, they incur costs, which means that they would rather come to some agreement about how you can pay off your debt.

«6»

Through negotiation you can avoid having your goods repossessed. Do not be overly concerned if you receive threatening letters making persistent demands for repayment because such letters often come from someone hired by your creditors to pester you about repayment. Two things could happen to you if you default on your repayments: your goods could be repossessed by the store from which you made the purchase; or, your name could be put on a list of debt defaulters.

«7»

Only a court has the power to compel you to repay your debt. In order to avoid this, get your life in order. Do not be embarrassed at having to sell your expensive house and to move into a less expensive one. You could sell your car and get used to living without the luxuries. If your problems are not resolved and you have already tried to negotiate with your creditors and altered your standard of living, now is the time to make a very difficult decision about your life — you have to file for bankruptcy.

Glossary

Ø

Ø- he, she, it [SC Cl. 1; the partici-pial SC e- > Ø- before a vowel] S07

Ø- he, she, it [SC Cl. 1; the sub-junctive SC a- > Ø- before a vowel] S09

Ø- they, it [SC Cl. 6; var of a- found before vowels] S04

Ø- that/which (s)he ... [ind rel conc Cl. 1; var of a- found before vowels] S17

Ø- it is, they are [ident cop pref; in speech equates with breathy voice and a rising tone] S12

Ø- by [agent adv pref; in speech equates with breathy voice and a rising tone] S06

-Ø- [pref of narrative aspect; var of -a- found before vowels] S17

-Ø:- [remote past pref (the colon : represents a lengthening of the following vowel)] S17

A

a- he, she, it [SC Cl. 1] S02

a- they, it [SC Cl. 6] S01

a- not [neg pref; var ka-] S03

a- of [poss conc Cl. 6] S01

a- let, may, if only [hortative pref] S05

a- that, which, who(m) [rel marker used when the SC in the verb concerned has the vowel a] S01

a- that/which (s)he ... [ind rel conc Cl. 1] S14

a- [pronominalizer (forms pro-nouns from possessives)] S05

-a- [remote past pref] S03

-a- and then (in the past) [narrative aspect marker] S01

-a [default (basic) verb suffix] S01

-a [present negative suffix found with verbs ending in w (mainly passive)] S05

-a [subjunctive pos suffix found in venitives and andatives] S11, S09

-a nominalizing suffix (often corresponds to English -er as in 'farmer, writer, killer') [This suffix derives nouns (which may be personal or impersonal) from passive verbs, and from a few miscellaneous other verbs.] S10

ab- [NP Cl. 2; occurs before vowels] S11

aba- [NP Cl. 2] S02

aba- [adj conc Cl. 2; < a- rel marker + aba- NP] S02

aba- who, that [rel conc Cl. 2; < a-rel marker + ba- SC]

-ab-a distribute, apportion, allot [v.t.] S09

ababaleka who run away (from) [rel Cl. 2] S23

ababalekela those who run away from [rel Cl. 2] S10

ababalelwa who number, who are counted [rel Cl. 2] S19

ababecindezelekile who had been crushed [rel Cl. 2] S17

ababekwenza that/which they were doing (it) [ind rel of plain obj rel, Cl. 2] S23

ababeneminyaka who had years [rel Cl. 2] S27

ababeneminyaka engu-13 belime who had been farming for 13 years [rel phr Cl. 2] S27

ababengaphakathi who were inside [rel Cl. 2] S17

ababenomalaleveva who had malaria [rel Cl. 2] S20

ababephikisana who were contesting or arguing against [rel Cl. 2] S25

ababetholakala (those) who were found [rel Cl. 2] S24

ababeyiphila that/which they lived (it) [ind rel of plain obj rel, Cl. 2] S28

ababezikhethele who had made a personal choice [rel Cl. 2] S25

ababezobaqeqeshela whom they would train to or for [ind rel of plain obj rel, Cl. 2] S18

ababezoqeqeshwa who were going to be trained [rel Cl. 2] S18

ababhekene who are faced with [rel Cl. 2] S10

ababhekene necala who are faced with a charge [rel phr Cl. 2] S10

ababhikishi demonstrators [n Cl. 2; sg **umbhikishi**; < -bhikish- protest, fight against] S25

ababili two [adj Cl. 2] S10

ababizwa who are called [rel Cl. 2] S06

ababoni they do not see [pres, neg] S14

ababulalwa who were killed [rel Cl. 2] S17

ababulawa who are killed [rel Cl. 2] S20

ababulawa who were killed [rel Cl. 2] S21

abacabanga who think [rel Cl. 2] S16

abacabangi they do not think [pres, neg] S18

abadala old, older [adj Cl. 2] S09

abadayisa who traded, who offered for sale [rel Cl. 2] S17

abadla who embezzle [rel Cl. 2] S10

abadlwenguliwe who have been raped [rel Cl. 2] S23

abadlwengulwayo who are raped [rel Cl. 2] S23

abadoja who evade [rel Cl. 2] S10

abadoji evaders, avoiders [n Cl. 2; sg **umdoji**; < -doj- dodge, evade] S10

abadutshulwe who were shot [rel Cl. 2] S08

abafana boys [n Cl. 2; sg **umfana**] S08

abafanele who have to [rel Cl. 2] S20

abafanyana good-for-nothing boys or youths [n Cl. 2; sg **umfanyana**; < umfana + -Yana] S09

abafihla who hide [rel Cl. 2] S14

abafisa who desire, who wish [rel Cl. 2] S12

abafowabo his or her brothers [n Cl. 2; sg **umfowabo**] S27

abafowabo of his or her brothers [poss Cl. 6] S27

abafowethu my or our brothers [n Cl. 2; sg **umfowethu**] S21

abafuna who want [rel Cl. 2] S05

abagcina who end up [rel Cl. 2] S20

abagila lomkhuba who practice this evil [rel phr Cl. 2] S23

abahamba those who go or travel [rel Cl. 2 (referring to **abantu**)] S09

abahamba ngezinyawo pedestrians (lit. those who go on feet) [rel phr Cl. 2] S09

abahlala who stay, who live [rel Cl. 2] S19

abahlala nabo whom they live with [ind rel of plain adv rel, Cl. 2] S23

abahlengi nurses [n Cl. 2; sg **umhlengi**] S17

abahlengikazi nurses (female) [n Cl. 2; sg **umhlengikazi**] S17

abahlezi who sit [rel Cl. 2] S05

abahlukahlukene different, various [rel Cl. 2] S25

abahlukumezeka who are assaulted [rel Cl. 2] S23

abahlukunyezwe who have been assaulted [rel Cl. 2] S23

abahluphekayo underprivileged, suffering, troubled [rel Cl. 2] S25

abaholi leaders [n Cl. 2; sg **umholi** Cl. 1; < -hol- lead] S05

abajwayele they are not used (to), they are not wont (to) [stative, neg] S10

abakaze they have not yet ever [aux, pres, exclusive, neg; < a-neg pref + -ba- SC + -ka- yet + -ze ever [aux]] S13

abake who have once [rel Cl. 2] S23

abakhangisi advertisers [n Cl. 2; sg **umkhangisi**; < -khangis-cause to be desirable; advertise] S28

abakhokhi they do not pay [pres, neg] S28

abakhokhi-ntela taxpayers [n Cl. 2; sg **umkhokhi-ntela**; < **umkhokhi** payer + **intela** tax] S10

abakholelwa kukho in which they believe [ind rel of plain loc rel, Cl. 2] S23

abakhonze who are keen on, who are enthusiastic about [rel Cl. 2]

S27

abakhubazekile who are disabled or handicapped, the handicapped, the disabled [rel Cl. 2] S14

abakhulelwe who are pregnant [rel Cl. 2] S20

abakhululeki they are not free [pres, neg] S23

abakhwabanisi embezzlers, frauds [n Cl. 2; sg **umkhwabanisi**; < -**khwabanis**-embezzle] S10

abakufisayo that/which they desire [ind rel of plain obj rel, Cl. 2] S19

abakutsheli they do not tell you [pres, neg] S28

abakwa-Adidas those (people) from Adidas [poss pron Cl. 2] S11

abakwa-Agrilek those of Agrilek [poss pron Cl. 2] S27

abakwazile who were able [rel Cl. 2] S28

abalahlekelwe who lost [rel Cl. 2] S08

abalahlekelwe yimiphefumulo who lost their lives (lit. who were lost for by lives) [rel phr Cl. 2] S08

abalawuli bamabhanoyi air-traffic controllers [n phr Cl. 2; sg **umlawuli wamabhanoyi**] S18

abalimi farmers [n Cl. 2; sg **umlimi**] S27

abaliqhamukisa who come from

[rel Cl. 2] S20

abamabhizinisi business-owners [poss pron Cl. 2; sg **owamabhizinisi**] S10

abamele ezokuvakasha tourism authorities [rel phr Cl. 2] S24

abaMhlophe White people [rel Cl. 2] S16

abamnyama black [rel Cl. 2] S16

abaMnyama Black people [rel Cl. 2; sg **oMnyama**] S27

abamsiza those who helped him or her [rel Cl. 2] S14

abanalesifo who have this disease [rel Cl. 2] S20

abanalwazi they do not have (the) knowledge [assoc cop, pres, neg] S23

abanawo umkhandlu they don't have an organization [assoc cop, pres, neg] S13

abanazo that/which they have [ind rel of plain cop rel, Cl. 2] S13

abancane little, small [adj Cl. 2] S09

abane four (adj) [adj Cl. 2] S02

abane-AIDS who have AIDS [rel Cl. 2] S20

abangaboni who do not see [rel Cl. 2] S14

abangaboni emehlweni who are blind (lit. who do not see in the eyes) [rel phr Cl. 2] S14

abangakhokhi who do not pay [rel Cl. 2] S28

abangaphansi who are under [rel Cl. 2] S23

abangaqeqeshiwe who are not trained, who are not qualified [rel Cl. 2] S05

abangazenza that/which they can do or make [ind rel of plain obj rel, Cl. 2] S18

abangazi who do not know [rel Cl. 2] S05

abangcwabi buriers, undertakers, morticians [n Cl. 2; sg **umngcwabi**] S12

abangeke bayishaye-mkhuba that/which they would never take seriously [ind rel of plain obj rel, Cl. 2] S23

abangekho esikoleni who are not at school [rel phr Cl. 2] S13

abangenelwe who were attacked [rel Cl. 2] S08

abangu- that/which are; when followed by a number, this indicates 'such-and-such a number of them' [introduces a rel based on ident cop]

abangu-150 150 [rel Cl. 2] S27

abangu-158 158 [rel Cl. 2] S20

abangu-168 168 [rel Cl. 2] S17

abangu-18 18 [rel Cl. 2] S17

abangu-25 25 [rel Cl. 2] S27

abangu-300 300 [rel Cl. 2] S10

abangu-50 50 [rel Cl. 2] S24

abangu-750 000 750,000 [rel Cl. 2] S20

abanike (s)he should give them

[subjunc] S20

abaningi many [adj Cl. 2] S17

abanobulili who have a gender or sex [rel Cl. 2] S23

abanomalaleveva that/which/who have or carry malaria [rel Cl. 2] S20

abanothando those who are loving (lit. who have love) [rel Cl. 2] S22

abantu people [n Cl. 2; sg **umuntu** Cl. 1] S04

abantu of people [poss Cl. 6] S25

abantu it is people [ident cop, pres; differs in tone from the foirms above, and has breathy voice on the first syllable] S23

abantu okufanele bazame people who have to try [n phr Cl. 2] S20

abantwana children [n Cl. 2; sg **umntwana** Cl. 1] S02

abanye other(s), some [adj Cl. 2] S02

abanzi wide, broad [rel Cl. 6] S08

abaphathi warders, wardens, authorities, those in charge, guardians, superintendents, managers, officials [n Cl. 2; sg **umphathi**; < **-phath-** handle] S23

abaphathwa who suffer [rel Cl. 2] S20

abaphela who met their end (lit. who came to an end) [rel Cl. 2] S17

abaphethe who are in charge, who

279

manage, who run [rel Cl. 2] S21

abaphethwe who suffer [rel Cl. 2] S25

abaqalayo who are for the first time, who are beginning [rel Cl. 2] S23

abaqaphi security personnel, guards, warders [n Cl. 2; sg **umqaphi**; < -qaph- watch intently, be on the look-out] S13

abaqashwa employees, staff [n Cl. 2; sg **umqashwa**; < -qashw- be employed, hired + - a nominalizing suffix found with passive verbs] S10

abaqeqeshelwe who have been trained for [rel Cl. 2] S12

abaqeqeshiwe they have not been trained [stative; < -qeqesh- + -w- + -i...e] S05

abaqeqeshiwe who are qualified, who are trained [rel Cl. 2] S05

abaqhamuka who come from [rel Cl. 2] S03

abaqinisa ikhanda who are obstinate [rel phr Cl. 2] S10

abasebancane who are still few in number; who are still little or small [rel Cl. 2] S19

abasebasha who are still young [rel Cl. 2] S19

abasebenzi workers, laborers [n Cl. 2; sg **umsebenzi**; < -sebenz- work] S27

abaseduze na- ... who are near to ... [rel Cl. 2] S06

abaseduze nekhwapha lezikhulu those close to the armpit(s) of important people (i.e. those with patronage from or influence with important people) [rel phr Cl. 2] S06

abasemadolobheni urbandwellers, those who are in towns [poss pron Cl. 2] S19

abasengozini who are in danger [rel Cl. 2] S20

abasePretoria West College of Technology who are at the Pretoria West College of Technology [rel phr Cl. 2] S19

abasethimbeni who are in a group of unmarried girls or women [rel Cl. 2] S25

abasha young [adj Cl. 2] S23

abashade who have got married [rel Cl. 2] S14

abashayeli drivers [n Cl. 2; sg **umshayeli**; < -shayel- drive] S09

abasho those who say [rel Cl. 2] S06

abasitshalile who have planted it [rel Cl. 2] S27

abasiza who assist [rel Cl. 2] S27

abasiza whom (s)he assists [ind rel of plain obj rel, Cl. 1] S27

abasize (s)he should assist them [subjunc] S14

abasuke who have just [rel Cl. 2] S16

abatakuli life-savers, rescue teams [n Cl. 2; sg **umtakuli**] S17

abathanda who like, who love [rel Cl. 2] S19

abathile certain, particular [rel Cl. 2] S12

abathokozi they are not happy [pres, neg] S28

abathole who have experienced [rel Cl. 2] S23

abathunjiwe who have been taken hostage, who have been hijacked [rel Cl. 2] S16

abathunjwayo those hijacked, hostages [rel Cl. 2] S16

abavakashi visitors [n Cl. 2; sg **umvakashi**; < -vakash- visit] S20

abavela who come from [rel Cl. 2] S20

abavotele may they vote for, let them vote for [subjunc] S05

abawufundele who have studied for it [rel Cl. 2] S05

abawufundele umsebenzi who have studied for the job [rel phr Cl. 2] S05

abawuqondisisa who understand it thoroughly [rel Cl. 2] S18

abawusingathile who supported it [rel Cl. 2] S02

abawutholayo that/which they get [ind rel of plain obj rel, Cl. 2] S28

abawuthwali they do not carry it [pres, neg] S20

abaxoxisana who negotiate [rel Cl. 2] S16

abayi-ANC who are ANC (African National Congress) [rel Cl. 2] S05

abayikhokhayo that/which they pay out [ind rel of plain obj rel, Cl. 2] S28

abayise and they take them to [subjunc] S09

abayishumi ten (adj) [rel Cl. 2] S17

abayishumi nanye eleven (adj) [rel phr Cl. 2] S17

abayisihlanu five [rel Cl. 2] S24

abayizinkonkoni who are homosexuals [rel Cl. 2] S23

abayizintatheli who are reporters, journalists [rel Cl. 2] S21

abayizivakashi who are visitors [rel Cl. 2] S20

abazali parents [n Cl. 2; sg **umzali**] S08

abazazi they do not know them [pres, neg] S13

abazi they do not know [pres, neg] S05

abazibonela those who saw for themselves [rel Cl. 2] S17

abazibulalayo who commit suicide [rel Cl. 2] S16

abazidayisayo that/which they were trading in [ind rel of plain obj rel, Cl. 2] S17

abazikhethela who choose for themselves [rel Cl. 2] S25

abazikhiqizayo who produce them in abundance [rel Cl. 2] S27

abazikhokhela that/which they pay to [ind rel of plain obj rel, Cl. 2] S13

abazitshalele zona that/which they have planted for themselves [ind rel of plain obj rel, Cl. 2] S24

abazongiphendula who will reply to me [rel Cl. 2] S22

abazonikezela who will be presenting [rel Cl. 2] S11

abazoshushiselwa who will have cases prosecuted against them [rel Cl. 2] S10

abazosika who will cut or mow [rel Cl. 2] S13

abe (s)he should become [copula, subjunc] S19

a b e ne-jaundice and (s)he becomes jaundiced (lit. and (s)he becomes with jaundice) [assoc cop, inch, subjunc] S20

abe nenhliziyo encane and (s)he gets nauseous (lit. and (s)he becomes with a small heart) [assoc cop, inch, subjunc] S20

abe nguthisha (and) (s)he should bec a teacher [ident cop, inch, pres subjunc] S19

abe-child protection unit the people from the child protection unit [poss pron phr Cl. 2] S23

abekuyo in or at which (s)he was [ind rel of plain loc rel, Cl. 1] S20

-abel-a distribute among, apportion to [v-appl] S09

-abelan-a share among one another [v-appl-recip] S09

abelapha those who treat or cure [rel Cl. 2] S24

abelapha ngamakhambi herbalists (lit. those who treat with medicinal herbs) [rel phr Cl. 2; sg **owelapaha ngamakhambi**] S24

abelashelwa who are being treated for [rel Cl. 2] S20

abe-Life Line those from Life Line [poss pron Cl. 2] S23

abelokhu that (s)he was constantly [ind rel of plain loc rel, Cl. 1] S26

abeNkatha those of Inkatha (a Zulu cultural and political organization, with rather traditionalist and nationalistic views) [poss pron Cl. 2] S05

abenothando [also written: **abe nothando**] (s)he should have a liking or love [assoc cop, inch, subjunc] S22

abenothando lokuba nekwakhe elihle (s)he should be house-proud (lit. should have a liking to have a beautiful home) [assoc cop phr, inch, subjunc] S22

abenza who do [rel Cl. 2] S19

abePresbyterian Church of Southern Africa those of the Presbyterian ... [poss pron Cl. 2] S17

abeseki sponsors, supporters [n Cl. 2; sg **umeseki**; < **-esek-** sponsor, support (var **umseki**; < **-sek-a**)] S11

abesifazane females, (polite term for) women [poss pron Cl. 2; < **a-** pronominalizer + **-ba-** poss conc Cl. 2 (agrees with **abantu**) + **isifazane** female gender; sg **owesifazane**] S23

abesilisa males [poss pron Cl. 2; < **a-** pronominalizer + **-ba-** poss conc Cl. 2 (agrees with **abantu**) + **isilisa** male gender; sg **owesilisa**] S19

abesimame women [poss pron Cl. 2; < **a-** pronominalizer + **ba-** poss conc Cl. 2 (agrees with **abantu**) + **isimame** female gender] S14

abe-South African Airways (SAA) those (people) from South African Airways [poss pron Cl. 2] S18

abezi they do not come [pres, neg; < **a-** + **-ba-** + **-iz-** + **-i**] S13

abezindaba journalists, reporters (lit. those of the news) [poss pron Cl. 2; < **a-** pronominalizer + **-ba-** poss conc Cl. 2 (agrees with **abantu**) + **izindaba** news; sg **owezindaba**] S09

abo their [poss Cl. 6] S10

abo- [extremely rare var of **o-**; NP Cl. 2b] *S*13

abomndeni family members [poss pron Cl. 2] S23

abona they see [pres, rel] S14

abonane (s)he should consult [subjunc] S20

abonayo who can see, sighted [rel Cl. 6] S14

abonogada guards, watchmen [n Cl. 2b; sg **unogada**] S13

aboshwe (s)he was arrested (lit. (s)he should be arrested [subjunc] S23

abulalana they kill one another [pres, conjoint] S09

abuye and (s)he would come back [subjunc] S26

aconsisa amathe mouth-watering (lit. that causes saliva to drip) [rel phr Cl. 6] S27

adingeka it is (or, they are) needed, it is (or, they are) required [pres, conjoint] S19

adingekayo that/which is needed, that/which is required [rel Cl. 6] S19

adle they have eaten [past, conjoint] S11

adle who have eaten [rel Cl. 6; < **a-** rel marker + **adle**] S11

adle ubhedu that/which have won a challenge, that/which have attained their goal (lit. that have eaten the fat around the heart —considered the reward for a herdboy who has won a challenge) [rel phr Cl. 6] S11

adlondlobale (s)he should get greatly excited [subjunc] S27

adlwengula they rape [pres, conjoint] S23

adlwengula(yo) who rape [rel Cl. 6] S23

afana they resemble, they are like [pres, conjoint] S09

afana like (that resemble), such as, that/which are like [rel Cl. 6] S09

afika they arrived [rem past] S21

agcine they ended up [past, conjoint] S28

agcine that/which ended up [rel Cl. 6] S28

agcotshisiwe they have been greased [stative] S01

agcotshisiwe(yo) that/which have been greased [rel Cl. 6; < a- rel marker + **agcotshisiwe**] S01

ahlale (s)he should stay [subjunc] S26

ahlale they keep on, they continually [aux] S09

-ahlukahlukan-a differ in various ways, vary [v-redup; < **-ahlukan-**] S25

-ahlukan-a bec different, part from one another, part company [v.inch; var **-ehlukan-, -hlukan-**] S08

ahlukumeza they assault [pres, conjoint] S23

ahlukumeza and they assaulted [narr] S21

-ahlulek-a be beaten, be overcome, be defeated, be conquered; be unable, fail [v-neut; var **-ehlulek-a, -hlulek-a**] S05

ahlwayele (s)he should sow by scattering [subjunc] S27

ajuluke and (s)he sweats [subjunc] S20

akabenzeli (s)he does not do for them [pres, neg] S06

akabenzeli lutho abantu (s)he does nothing for them the people [v phr] S06

akaboni they do not see [pres, neg; var **awaboni**] S14

akadalelwanga (s)he was not created for [past, neg] S23

akafuni (s)he does not want [pres, neg] S05

akahambisani they do not go along with [pres, neg; var **awahambisani**] S25

akahluphi (s)he does not cause trouble, or disturb [pres, neg] S22

akakakulungeli (s)he is not yet ready for it [pres, exclusive, neg] S26

akakazifezi it has not yet fulfilled (them) [pres, exclusive, neg] S03

akakhishwe (s)he should be removed [subjunctive] S05

akakholwa (s)he does not believe [pres, neg] S10

-akal- get VERB-ed, be VERB-able/ -ible [neut ext] S03

akananembeza (s)he has no conscience [assoc cop, pres, neg] S26

akanankinga (s)he has no problem [assoc cop, pres, neg] S14

akaphuzi (s)he does not drink [pres, neg] S22

akasebenzi they don't work [pres,

neg; var **awasebenzi**] S12

akasenalo (s)he no longer has it [assoc cop, pres, persistive, neg] S28

akathandi (s)he does not like [pres, neg] S06

akathandi they do not like [pres, neg] S25

akavilaphanga (s)he is not lazy [past, neg] S27

akayedwana (s)he is not on his or her own [descr cop, pres, neg] S04

akazange (s)he has never [aux, past, neg; < -z-e] S13

ake please, would (you/(s)he/they) be so good as to, may (I, we, they …) [conj; followed by subjunc] S21

akekho (s)he is not there, is not present; there is no … [loc cop, pres, neg; may also introduce an exist cop] S14

akekho oyonginqanda there is nobody who will turn me away [exist cop, pres, neg] S14

akenzanga (s)he has not done [past, neg] S26

akezwani (s)he does not agree, is not "on the same wavelength" [pres, neg] S26

-akh-a build, construct [v.t.] S08

-akh-a establish residence, bec a citizen of [v.inch] S11

akhathale and (s)he gets tired [subjunc] S20

akhe his, her [poss Cl. 6] S14

-akhel-a live at, live in [v.inch; v-appl] S11

-akhel-a build for [v-appl] S21

-akhelwan- be built for one another, be lived in close proximity [v-appl-pass-recip] S08

akhethe (s)he should choose [subjunc] S27

akhishwe (s)he should be taken out, (s)he should have … taken out [subjunc] S20

akhishwe isisu and (s)he has diarrhea (lit. and (s)he is taken out the stomach) [v phr] S20

akhumbule they, (s)he should remember [subjunc] S14

akhwehlele and (s)he coughs [subjunc] S20

akuchazi it does not explain [pres, neg] S23

akufanele it is not necessary (that) [aux, stative, neg] S28

akuhlelelwanga it was not planned for [past, neg] S25

akujwayelekile it is not usual [stative, neg] S11

akukho there isn't, there aren't [loc cop, pres, neg (often used to introduce a negative existential cop)] S06

akukho ngisho isigxobo soku-shaya ucingo lolu I mean there isn't a telegraph pole S06

akukho okubambekayo there is nothing tangible [exist cop, pres] S21

akukho okunye there is nothing else [exist cop, pres, neg] S18

akukho okuvimbe there is nothing that prevents [exist cop, pres] S19

akukho okwenziwayo there is nothing being done [exist cop, pres] S13

akukhona it or there isn't, there aren't [loc cop, pres, neg; often introduces a negative existential cop] S13

akukhona ukuthi sinenkinga yama-exercise kuphela it isn't just that we have a problem with exercise books [exist cop phr, pres, neg] S13

akulelikhemisi of this pharmacy [poss Cl. 6] S17

akulesisibhedlela of (at) this hospital [poss Cl. 6] S17

akulo in which (s)he is [ind rel of plain loc rel, Cl. 1; < a - which/that (s)he [ind rel conc Cl. 1] + ku- in [loc pref] + lo it [abs pron Cl. 5]] S19

akumkhubazi it doesn't intimidate or disable her/him, or make her/him ineffective [pres, neg] S19

akungenxa it is not because of, it is not through the reason [ident cop, pres, neg] S27

akuphenywe let it be investigated [subjunctive] S05

akusho it doesn't mean (that) [pres, neg] S07

akusikho ukuphoxeka it is not something shameful, it is not a

shame [ident cop phr, pres, neg] S23

akusiwo owabantu it is not one of people [ident cop phr, pres, neg] S19

akutshele that which (s)he told [ind rel of plain obj rel, Cl. 1] S26

akuvamile it is not usual [stative] S20

akuyi it does not go [pres, neg] S19

akuzange there had never, it never [aux, past, neg; < -z-e] S17

akuzange kubakhubaze it never disabled them [v phr, past neg] S17

akuzange kubenjalo it never happened (lit. it never became so) [descr cop phr, inch, past, neg] S23

akuzwakali there is not heard [pres, neg] S21

akuzwakali lutho nothing is heard, nothing is said [v phr] S21

akwazi (s)he can, (s)he should be able [subjunc] S15

akwenze (s)he should do it [subjunc] S25

alazi nakwazi (s)he does not even know [v phr; a neg verb followed by na- + the infinitive form of that verb means 'does not even'; **akaphuzi nokuphuza** (s)he does not even drink; **asimthandi nokumthanda** we don't even like him or her)] S21

ale of this [poss Cl. 6] S12

aleli of this [poss Cl. 6] S06

alibiza that/which (s)he calls [ind rel of plain obj rel, Cl. 1] S27

alikho it, (s)he is not there [loc cop; may also introduce a negative exist cop] S23

alikho ithuba there is no chance [exist cop, pres, neg] S23

alikwazi it, (s)he is unable; it, (s)he cannot [pres, neg] S28

alimala they got damaged [rem past] S17

alisebenzisa that/which (s)he uses [ind rel of plain obj rel, Cl. 1] S27

alowo-mosquito of that mosquito [poss Cl. 6] S20

aluphumanga it did not emerge [past, neg] S21

alwenzile that/which (s)he has carried out [ind rel of plain obj rel, Cl. 1] S26

-am- [fossilized positional extension indicating bodily position; cf. **-khotham-a, -phakam-a, -thambam-a**] S17, S20, S27

ama- [NP Cl. 6] S01

ama- [adj conc Cl. 6; < **a-** rel marker + **ama-** NP] S01

ama-28 the 28s (an infamous prison gang, known particularly for homosexuality and male rape) [n Cl. 6] S23

ama-Afrika Africans [n Cl. 6; sg **um-Afrika** Cl. 1] S18

ama-Annual Tax Returns [n Cl. 6; sg **i-Annual Tax Return** Cl. 9a] {Eng} S10

amabhange banks [n Cl. 6; sg **ibhange** Cl. 5] {Afr} S10

amabhayisikili bicycles [n Cl. 6; sg **ibhayisikili**; var **ibhayisekili**] {Eng} S14

amabhilidi buildings [n Cl. 6; sg **ibhilidi** Cl. 5] {Eng} S16

amabhizinisi businesses, firms [n Cl. 6; sg **ibhizinisi** Cl. 5] {Eng} S10

amabhuloho bridges [n Cl. 6; sg **ibhuloho** Cl. 5] {Afr *brug*} S16

amabhulukwe trousers [n Cl. 6; sg **ibhulukwe** Cl. 5] {Afr *broek*} S20

amabili a pair, two [adj Cl. 2] S11

ama-boarding school [n Cl. 6; sg **i-boarding school** Cl. 9] {Eng} S23

amacala offences, crimes; prosecutions, court cases, charges [n Cl. 6; sg **icala** Cl. 5] S10

amacansi sleeping-mats [n Cl. 6; sg **ucansi** Cl. 11] S09

amade tall, long, lengthy [adj Cl. 6] S16

amadoda men, husbands [n Cl. 6; sg **indoda** Cl. 9] S14

amadodakazi daughters [n Cl. 6; sg **indodakazi** Cl. 9] S08

amadodana sons [n Cl. 6; sg **indodana** Cl. 9] S02

ama-dollar [n Cl. 6; sg **i-dollar**

Cl. 9a] {Eng} S28

amadolobha towns, cities [n Cl. 6; sg **idolobha** Cl. 5] {Afr *dorp*} S09

ama-exercise exercise books [n Cl. 6; sg **i-exercise** Cl. 9a] S13

amafasitela windows [n Cl. 6; sg **ifasitela** Cl. 5] {Afr *venster*} S13

amafemu firms [n Cl. 6; sg **ifemu** Cl. 5] {Eng} S12

amagama names [n Cl. 6; sg **igama** Cl. 5] S10

amagumbi rooms [n Cl. 6; sg **igumbi** Cl. 5] S17

ama-hectare hectares [n Cl. 6; sg **i-hectare** Cl. 9a] S27

amahhovisi offices [n Cl. 6; sg **ihhovisi** Cl. 5] S17

amahlathi forests [n Cl. 6; sg **ihlathi**] S11

amahlombe shoulders [n Cl. 6; sg **ihlombe** Cl. 5] S16

amahloni shame, embarrassment [n Cl. 6; neutral] S28

amaholo wages, salaries [n Cl. 6; sg **iholo** Cl. 5] S28

amajele jails, prisons [n Cl. 6; sg **ijele** Cl. 5] {Eng} S14

amakhambi medicinal herbs; herbal decoctions for medicine; remedies [n Cl. 6; sg **ikhambi** Cl. 5] S24

amakhaya homes [n Cl. 6; sg **ikhaya** Cl. 5] S05

amakhaza cold (temperature) [n Cl. 6; neutral] S12

amakhemisi pharmacies [n Cl. 6; sg **ikhemisi** Cl. 5] {Eng *chemist*} S17

amakhokho soccer boots [n Cl. 6; sg **ikhokho** Cl. 5] S11

amakhosi chiefs [n Cl. 6; sg **inkosi** Cl. 9; n + kh > nk] S06

amaKhrestu Christians [n Cl. 6; sg **iKhrestu** Cl. 5/**umKhrestu** Cl. 1] S25

amakhulu large, big [adj Cl. 6] S09

ama-lift lifts, rides [n Cl. 6; sg **i-lift** Cl. 9a] {Eng} S23

amalunga members [n Cl. 6; sg **ilunga** Cl. 5; var **ilungu**] S09

amalungelo rights [n Cl. 6; sg **ilungelo** Cl. 5] S03

amalungu joints (of the body) [n Cl. 6; sg **ilungu** Cl. 5] S20

amalungu members [n Cl. 6; sg **ilungu** Cl. 5; var **ilunga**] S06

amamitha meters [n Cl. 6; sg **imitha** Cl. 5] {Eng} S17

amanani numbers; prices [n Cl. 6; sg **inani** Cl. 5] S03

amancane small [adj Cl. 6] S12

amandla strength, power, might, force [n Cl. 6; neutral] S11

ama-night clubs [n Cl. 6; sg **i-night club** Cl. 9a] S23

amaningi many, a lot, much [adj Cl. 6] S27

amantombazane young girls (up to puberty) [n Cl. 6; sg **intombazane** Cl. 9] S08

amanye other(s), some, certain [adj Cl. 6] S14

amanzi water [n Cl. 6; neutral] S11

ama-patty pans cupcake tins, patty pans [n Cl. 6; sg **i-patty pan** Cl. 9a] {Eng} S01

amapayipi pipes [n Cl. 6; sg **ipayipi** Cl. 5] {Eng} S20

amaphandle rural areas, outskirts of a village [n Cl. 6; neutral; < **phandle**] S23

amaphepha papers [n Cl. 6; sg **iphepha** Cl. 5] {Eng} S05

amaphepha they are/it is papers [ident cop, pres; < Ø- + **amaphepha**; differs tonally from above item] S17

amaphethelo suburbs, outskirts [n Cl. 6; sg **iphethelo**; < -phethel- border on] S11

amaphilisi pills, tablets, capsules [n Cl. 6; sg **iphilisi** Cl. 5] {Eng} S16

amaphoyisa the police, policemen, policewomen [n Cl. 6; sg **iphoyisa** Cl. 5] {Eng} S09

amaphutha failings, shortcomings, errors, mistakes [n Cl. 6; sg **iphutha**] S04

amaqanda eggs [n Cl. 6; sg **iqanda** Cl. 5] S01

amaqiniso truths [n Cl. 6; sg **iqiniso** Cl. 5; < -qinis- confirm, speak the truth] S06

amaqiniso by truths [agentive adv] S06

ama-raspberry raspberries [n Cl.

6; sg **i-raspberry** Cl. 9a] S27

amarenki rank [n Cl. 6; sg **irenki** Cl. 9a] S17

amashumi amabili twenty (lit. two tens) [n phr Cl. 6] S19

amasiko customs, manners, practices, culture [n Cl. 6; sg **isiko**] S25

ama-sirens sirens [n Cl. 6; sg **i-siren** Cl. 9a] {Eng} S17

amaso eyes [n Cl. 6; sg **iso**] S14

amasokisi socks [n Cl. 6; sg **isokisi**] {Eng} S20

amasonto weeks [n Cl. 6; sg **isonto**] S16

amasosha soldiers [n Cl. 6; sg **isosha** Cl. 5] {Eng} S21

ama-strawberry strawberries [n Cl. 6; sg **i-strawberry**; **i-s-** is taken as the Cl. 7 NP] S27

ama-supermarket supermarkets [n Cl. 6; sg **i-supermarket** Cl. 9a] S27

amatekisi taxis, cabs [n Cl. 6; sg **itekisi**] {Eng} S17

amathalente talents [n Cl. 6; sg **ithalente** Cl. 5] {Eng} S22

amathathu three [adj Cl. 6] S26

amathe saliva, spit [n Cl. 6] S20

amathini tins, cans [n Cl. 6; sg **ithini** Cl. 5] {Eng} S01

amathonsi drops [n Cl. 6; sg **ithonsi** Cl. 5] S08

amathonsi abanzi severe problems (idiom; lit. wide drops (i.e. tears)) [n phr Cl. 6] S08

amathuba opportunities, chances [n Cl. 6; sg **ithuba** Cl. 5] S12

ama-trucks trucks, vans [n Cl. 6; sg **i-truck** Cl. 5] {Eng} S09

ama-tunnel tunnels [n Cl. 6; sg **i-tunnel** n Cl. 9a] S27

amawala hasty action [n Cl. 6; neutral] S08

amaxhophozi swamps [n Cl. 6; sg **ixhophozi** Cl. 5] S20

amazambane potatoes [n Cl. 6; sg **izambane** Cl. 5] S27

amazinga okushisa temperatures (lit. degrees of heat) [n phr Cl. 6; sg **izinga lokushisa**] S20

amazwe lands, countries [n Cl. 6; sg **izwe** Cl. 5] S03

amazwe angaphandle foreign countries (countries of outside) [n phr Cl. 6; sg **izwe langaphandle**] S12

amchazele and (s)he should explain to him or her [subjunc] S20

ame- [NP Cl. 6; occurs in **amehlo** 'eyes' and **ameva** 'thorns'] S14

amehlo eyes [n Cl. 6; sg **iso** or **ihlo** Cl. 5] S14

Amen [interjective] S02

ami my [poss Cl. 6] S23

-amukel-a accept; welcome [v.t.] S23

-an- each other, one another [recip ext] S04

-ana little, small; dear, sweet; wretched, awful, good-for-nothing [dimin suffix; signi-

ficance depends on context] S04, S08

anabantu they have people [assoc cop, pres] S20

anabantu who have people [rel Cl. 6] S20

-and-a increase, multiply [v.i.] S16, S23

-andis-a increase, make greater, multiply [v-caus] S23

-andulel-a anticipate, come before, precede [v.t.] S17

-anel-a bec sufficient (for), bec enough (for) [v.i. & t., inch] S09

-anelis-a satisfy, fill a deficiency, convince [v-caus] S23

anelungelo they have the right [assoc cop, pres] S25

aneminyaka they are aged [assoc cop, pres] S23

aneminyaka who are aged (lit. who have years) [rel Cl. 6] S23

aneminyaka engaphansi kuka-18 who are aged under 18) [rel phr Cl. 6] S23

anesibalo they have a number [assoc cop, pres] S20

anesibalo that/which have a number [rel Cl. 6] S20

-anga not + PAST [past neg suffix] S09

angabi (s)he should not be(come) [copula, subjunc] S22

angabi namawala (s)he should not take (lit. be with) hasty action [assoc cop, inch, subjunc, neg] S08

angaboni they do not see [pres, rel, neg] S14

angaboni who do not see [rel Cl. 6] S14

angaboni emehlweni who are blind (lit. who do not see in the eyes) [rel phr Cl. 6] S14

angahambisani they do not go along with [pres, rel, neg; < akahambisani/awahambisani] S25

angahambisani who do not go along (with) [rel Cl. 6] S25

angakuthandi and (s)he is not fond of it [subjunc, neg] S20

angalifaki (s)he should not put it or them on [subjunc] S22

angalifaki ibhulukwe (s)he should not wear the pants [v phr] S22

-angam-a lean over, overhang; preside over, administer [v-positional; var **-ongam-a, -engam-a**] S23

-angamel-a lean over (for), over-hang; preside over, administer [v-positional-appl; var **-ongamel-a, -engamel-a**] S23

angaphandle they are outside [locational cop, pres] S03

angaphandle that are outside [rel Cl. 6] S03

angaphepha (s)he could escape [pres, potential] S23

angaphindi they should not again [aux, subjunc, neg] S04

angaphindi enzeke they should not reoccur [v phr] S04

angasebenzi they don't work [pres, rel, neg] S12

angasebenzi who don't work [rel Cl. 6] S12

angasho and (s)he did not say [narr, partic, neg; < Ø- SC + -a-narr pref + -nga- neg pref + -sh-o] S09

angathokoza (s)he would be happy [pres, potential] S27

angavumeli (s)he should not agree to, (s)he should not accept [subjunc, neg] S08

angazi I do not know [pres, neg] S14

-ang-e [past neg suff; var of **-anga** used with certain auxiliaries ending in **-e**] S09

angeke never [aux; followed by the subjunctive] S13

angenzi (s)he should not perpe-trate or do [subjunc, neg] S26

angiboni I do not see [pres, neg] S14

angiboni emehlweni I am blind (lit. I do not see in my eyes) [v phr] S14

angikaze I have not yet ever, I (have) never [aux, pres, exclusive, neg] S18

angikho I am not there [loc cop, pres, neg] S27

angisayiphathi-ke (idiom; lit. I no longer take it then) [pres, per-sistive, neg] S18

angithandi I do not like [pres, neg] S19

angizange I have not ever [aux, past, neg; < -z-e + -ange] S09

angizange ngiye I have never gone (to) [v phr] S09

angqangqazele and (s)he shivers, trembles, has the shakes [subjunc] S20

angu- they are, it is

angu-0,75 they are 0,75 [ident cop, pres] S27

angu-12 they are twelve (i.e. there are twelve of them) [ident cop, pres] S01

angu-50% they are 50% [ident cop, pres] S27

angu- that/which are [introduces rel based on ident cop]

angu-0,75 that/which are 0,75 [rel Cl. 6] S27

angu-10 10 (lit. that are ten) [rel Cl. 6] S26

angu-12 12 (lit. that are twelve) [rel Cl. 6] S01

angu-16 16 (lit. that are sixteen) [rel Cl. 6] S26

angu-2 x 20cm two of 20cm (lit. that are two times 20cm) [rel Cl. 6] S01

angu-450 450 [rel Cl. 6] S17

angu-50% 50% [rel Cl. 6] S27

angu-600 600 [rel Cl. 6] S23

angu-8 992 8,992 [rel Cl. 6] S23

anhlobonhlobo of various types [poss Cl. 6; < **iinhlobonhlobo** with deletion of **ii-**] S12

anibusise may (s)he bless you [subjunctive] S02

anikelwe they have been donated [past, conjoint] S11

anikelwe that/which have been donated [rel Cl. 6] S11

anyukile they have increased [past, disjoint] S03

aphathe (s)he should manage, run, take hold of [subjunc] S27

aphathwe and (s)he suffers [subjunc] S20

aphathwe yikhanda and (s)he gets a headache (lit. (s)he is held by the head) [v phr] S20

aphefumule (s)he would give an opinion [subjunc] S13

aphela and they came to an end (here: and were severely damaged) [narr] S17

aphesheya overseas, abroad [poss Cl. 6] S16

aphezulu they are on top, they are above [loc cop, pres] S20

aphezulu high, that/which are high [rel Cl. 6] S20

aphinde and they repeatedly [aux, subjunc] S09

aphinde and (s)he also [aux, subjunc] S19

aphinde abe nguthisha and who also became a teacher [aux v phr] S19

-aphul-a break [v.t.; var **-ephul-**, **-phul-**] S10

aphumele they should come out (in)to [subjunc] S25

aqala (s)he started [rem past; < Ø- (s)he [partic SC Cl. 1; var of **e-** found before vowels]] S17

aqala ukuyisebenzisa that/which (s)he started (long ago) to use (it) [ind rel of plain obj rel, Cl. 1] S17

aqashiwe they are employed [stative] S12

aqashiwe who are employed [rel Cl. 6] S12

aqhathwe they have been teamed up against one another [past, conjoint] S11

ase-Afrika of Africa [poss Cl. 6] S20

asebebuza (those) who are already asking [rel Cl. 2] S08

asebedlulile who already have passed [rel Cl. 2] S25

asebefakwe who have already been placed [rel Cl. 2] S10

asebeke who have already once [rel Cl. 2] S23

asebekhishelwe who have already had taken out against them [rel Cl. 2] S10

asebekhishwe who have already had removed [rel Cl. 2] S20

asebenza kuso that/which (s)he works at [ind rel of plain loc rel, Cl. 1] S14

asebenza nabo with whom (s)he works [ind rel of plain adv rel, Cl. 1] S25

asebenzile that which (s)he has committed [ind rel of plain obj rel, Cl. 1] S26

asebephethwe who are already infected [rel Cl. 2] S20

asebephila who now live [rel Cl. 2] S28

asebeshonile those who have already passed away [rel Cl. 2] S12

asehlukanisi we do not differentiate [pres, neg] S19

aseNingizimu Afrika of South Africa [poss Cl. 6] S09

asezosakazwa they will soon be published [fut, exclusive; < **a-** they + **-s-** soon + **-e-** they + **-zo-** will + **-sakazw-a**] S10

ashade (s)he should get married [subjunc] S14

ashayiwe they have been beaten [stative] S01

ashayiwe (that/which have been) beaten [rel Cl. 6; < **a-** rel marker + **ashayiwe**] S01

asihambisani it does not go together, it does not accord [pres, neg] S27

asihlukumeze they assault us [subjunc] S09

asihlukumeze ngokocansi they indecently assault us [v phr] S09

asikafiki it hasn't yet arrived [pres, exclusive, neg] S03

asilali we don't sleep [pres, neg] S09

asimfanele it is unfair to him, it is not right for him [stative, neg] S26

asisisebenzise let us use it [subjunc; **a-** hortative + **-si-** us [SC] + **-si-** it [OC 7] + **-sebenzis-**] S08

asithakasela they welcomed it [rem past] S25

asithathisa okwezigebengu they take us as criminals [v phr] S09

asithini what (s)he should say (lit. let him say what) [subjunc; **a-** let + **-si-** him/her [SC] + **-th-i-** say + **-ni** what] S26

asitholile that/which (s)he got [ind rel of plain obj rel, Cl. 1] S26

asitshalile that/which (s)he has planted [ind rel of plain obj rel, Cl. 1] S27

Asmal (surname) [n Cl. 1a] {Arabic} S11

asuke (s)he should leave [subjunc] S18

-ath- [fossilized contactive extension indicating physical contact; cf. **-khungath-a, -phath-a, -singath-a**] S02

athanda that/which (s)he likes [rel Cl. 1] S27

athanda ukusidlulisela that/which (s)he likes to pass on [ind rel of plain obj rel, Cl. 1] S27

athande (s)he should like [subjunc] S22

athathwa they are taken [pres, conjoint] S23

athile certain [rel Cl. 6] S23

athinta they concern, they deal with [pres, conjoint] S23

athinta that/which concern, that/which deal with [rel Cl. 6] S23

atholakale (s)he should be found [subjunc] S13

athwala they carry [pres, conjoint] S20

athwala that/which carry [rel Cl. 6] S20

atshele they should tell [subjunc] S25

avame they normally [past, conjoint] S09

aw- [pronominalizer (forms pronouns from possessives); found before vowels] S26

awaboni they do not see [pres, neg; var **akaboni**] S14

awafake that/which (s)he has placed [ind rel of plain obj rel, Cl. 1] S27

awahambisani they do not go along with [pres, neg; var **akahambisani**] S25

awasebenzi they don't work [pres, neg; var **akasebenzi**] S12

awatholakali are not received [pres, neg] S03

awekho they are not there, they are absent [loc cop, pres, neg; may also introduce a neg exist cop] S26

awekho amathemba there is no

hope (lit. there are no hopes) [exist cop, pres, neg] S26

awenza they do it [pres, conjoint] S12

awenzayo who do it [rel Cl. 6] S12

awenzayo that/which (s)he does (it) [ind rel of plain obj rel, Cl. 1] S18

awo their [poss Cl. 6] S25

awokudlwengula those of rape [poss pron Cl. 6; agrees with **amacala** crimes, offences] S26

awokuzama ukubulala those of attempted murder [poss pron phr Cl. 6] S26

awujwayelekile it is not usual, it is not customary [stative, neg] S18

awusakwazi you are no longer able, you can no longer [pres, persistive, neg] S28

awuvotele let it vote for [subjunc] S05

awuyinambithisisi it does not understand it fully [pres, neg] S24

ayabona they see [pres, disjoint] S14

ayafana they are like, they are similar, they resemble [pres, disjoint] S14

ayahlukunyezwa they are assaulted [pres, disjoint] S23

ayasishaya they hit us [pres, disjoint] S09

ayazenzela they just do what they

like, they act for no reason [pres, disjoint] S21

ayehambisana they went along with [rem past pres] S25

ayehambisana that/which went along with [rel Cl. 6] S25

ayemakhulu that/which were large [descr cop, rem past pres] S17

ayeme (s)he was standing [rem past past, partic, conjoint] S17

ayengabalekela that/which (s)he could run away from [rel Cl. 1; < **wayengabalekela** by replacement of the SC **w-** with the ind rel conc **a-**, which becomes **Ø-** before the vowel **a** of the remote past pref] S17

ayengabalekela ngayo that/which (s)he could flee or escape by [ind rel of plain adv rel, Cl. 1] S17

ayengabalekela ngayo ukufa by which (s)he could run away from death [ind rel of plain adv rel, Cl. 1] S17

ayengahambisani they did not go along with [rem past pres, neg] S25

ayengahambisani who did not go along with [rel Cl. 6] S25

ayephahlwe (s)he had been surrounded [rem past past, partic, conjoint] S17

ayeselutholile that/which (s)he had acquired [ind rel of plain obj rel, Cl. 1] S27

ayesho they thought, they said [rem past pres] S25

295

ayesho nokusho they even thought [v phr] S25

ayewuboleke that/which (s)he had borrowed [ind rel of plain obj rel, Cl. 1] S27

ayeyisebenzela that/which (s)he was working for [ind rel of plain obj rel, Cl. 1; < **a-** rel marker + **-a-** rem past marker + **-ye-** SC + **-yi-** OC] S27

ayeyisebenzisa that/which (s)he used [ind rel of plain obj rel, Cl. 1] S27

ayibizi it does not cost or call, (s)he does not call [pres, neg] S28

ayidonsa (s)he carried [rem past, partic] S07

ayikajwayeleki it is not yet customary, normal [pres, exclusive, neg] S25

ayikazalwa it, (s)he has not yet been born [pres, exclusive, neg] S25

ayikho it is not there [loc cop, pres, neg; may also introduce a neg exist cop] S19

ayikho ekhishini it is not in the kitchen [loc cop, pres, neg] S19

ayikwenzi it does not do it [pres, neg] S05

ayilandayo that/which (s)he relates [ind rel of plain obj rel, Cl. 1] S23

ayingabazeki it is undoubted [pres, neg] S24

ayingozi that/which are dangerous [rel Cl. 6] S09

ayisisuthisi it does not satisfy us, make us full [pres, neg] S09

ayithola (s)he gets it [rem past] S27

ayithola that/which (s)he gets [ind rel of plain obj rel, Cl. 1] S27

ayizange it never [aux, past, neg; < **-z-e**] S25

ayizenyezi (s)he does not make him- or herself miserable, allow him- or herself to get des-pondent [pres, neg] S14

ayo its [poss Cl. 6] S12

ayodlulisela (s)he should go and pass on [subjunc, andative] S27

ayothenga that (s)he should go and buy [subjunc, andative] S17

-azek-a be known, be knowable [v-neut] S21

azenzele that/which she or he has made for her- or himself [ind rel of plain obj rel, Cl. 1] S24

azethembe they should believe in themselves, they should have faith in themselves [subjunc] S14

-az-i know [irregular verb taking the suffix **-i** in all tenses and moods except for the past tense (Here **-i** occurs in place of the expected **-e.**)] S04

azifanele they are not suitable [stative, neg] S25

azilungi they are not coming right [pres, neg] S13

azigcini they do not end (up) [pres, neg] S08

azikhokheki they are unpayable [pres, neg] S28

aziphumulele so that (s)he can just rest [subjunc] S07

-azis-a notify, inform, let know [v-caus] S09

-azisw-a be informed, be notified [v-caus-pass] S25

-aziw-a be known [v-pass] S09

aziwe (s)he is known [subjunc] S09

azizange they have never [aux, past, neg] S09

azizwe that (s)he should feel him- or herself [subjunc] S18

azogcina they will eventually [fut] S12

azogcina that/which will eventually [rel Cl. 6] S12

azombulala and (s)he will come and kill her or him [subjunc, venitive] S26

azongisiza they will aid me [fut] S27

azongisiza that/which will aid me [rel Cl. 6] S27

B

b- they [SC Cl. 2] S10

b- it, they [SC Cl. 14] S23

b- of [poss conc Cl. 2; occurs before **e, a, o**] S04

-b- them [OC Cl. 2] S06

-b- [aux indicating past relative tenses; < **-be**] S02

ba- they [SC Cl. 2] S02

ba- of [poss conc Cl. 2] S04

-ba- them [OC Cl. 2] S09

ba- [2nd half of adj conc Cl. 2] S05

-b-a become, be [copula] S01

baba they become [copula, pres, conjoint] S23

baba nezinkinga they have problems or difficulties (lit. they bec with problems) [assoc cop, inch, pres] S23

bababone they see them [subjunc] S13

babaleka they run away (from) [pres, conjoint] S23

babalekela they run away from, they evade [pres, conjoint] S10

babalelwa they are numbered, they are counted [pres, conjoint] S19

babatshela and they told them [narr] S28

babe they should become [copula, subjunc] S19

babe na- ... they should acquire ... (lit. they should bec with) [introduces an assoc cop, inch, subjunc] S28

babe ngabalimi they should bec farmers [ident cop, inch, subjunc] S27

babe ngu-11% they should be 11% [ident cop, inch, subjunc] S19

babe nothando they should want (lit. they should bec with the liking) [assoc cop, inch, sub-junc] S23

babe sebecela they then requested [rem past pres, exclusive] S13

babe yizinkonkoni they should bec homosexuals [ident cop, inch, subjunctive] S23

babe yizisulu they became victims [ident cop, inch, past, conjoint] S10

babebaningi there were many [descr cop, rem past pres] S27

babecindezelekile they had been crushed [rem past past, disjoint] S17

babedinga they were needing [rem past pres] S18

babeka they place, they put [pres, conjoint] S18

babekwenza they were doing it [rem past pres] S23

babemesabisa they used to scare him [rem past pres] S23

babeneminyaka they had years; they were aged [assoc cop, rem past pres] S27

babengafuni they did not want (lit. they were not wanting) [rem past pres, neg] S14

babengahambisani they did not go along [rem past pres, neg] S19

babengaphakathi they were inside (long ago) [loc cop, rem past pres] S17

babengazibekile they had not put themselves [rem past stative, neg] S25

babengazibekile phansi they had not stopped (lit. they had not put themselves down) [v phr] S25

babenomalaleveva they had malaria [assoc cop, rem past pres] S20

babephatha they held [rem past pres] S25

babephephile they had escaped [rem past past, disjoint] S17

babephikisana they were contesting or arguing against [rem past pres] S25

babetholakala they were found [rem past pres] S24

babeyibiza they were calling it [rem past pres] S17

babeyiphila they used to live it, they lived it [rem past pres] S28

babezama they tried, they were trying [rem past pres] S25

babezikhethele they had chosen for themselves, they had made a personal choice [rem past past, disjoint] S25

babezimisele they were determined [rem past stative] S19

babezobaqeqeshela they were going to train them for [rem past fut] S18

babezoqeqeshwa they were going to be trained [rem past fut] S18

babhekana they are looking at, are faced [pres, conjoint] S23

babhekane they will have to face [subjunc] S25

Glossary

babhekene they are facing, they are opposite [stative] S10

babili there are two [descr cop; < **ababili** minus initial vowel] S19

babizwa they are called, they are named as [pres, conjoint] S06

babo their [poss Cl. 14] S23

babone they should see [subjunc] S23

babonele ku- they should copy or imitate [subjunc] S27

baboshwe they should be arrested [subjunc] S10

babulalwa they were killed [rem past] S17

babulawa they are killed [pres, conjoint] S20

babulawa they were killed [rem past] S21

babungaphezu kwamandla it was beyond (lit. above) my strength [loc cop, rem past pres] S23

babusiswe they have been blessed [past, conjoint] S14

babuye they again [aux] S13

babuyela they return to [pres, conjoint] S23

babuyele they will return to [subjunc] S13

bacabanga they think [pres, conjoint] S16

badalulwe they should be divulged [subjunc] S13

badayisa they trade, they offer for sale [pres, conjoint] S17

badla they embezzle; they eat [pres, conjoint] S10

badlula they pass [pres, conjoint] S20

badlula emhlabeni they pass away (lit. they pass from earth) [v phr] S20

badlwenguliwe they have been raped [past, disjoint] S23

badoja they evade, they dodge [pres, conjoint] S10

badutshulwa and they were shot [narrative] S08

badutshulwe they were shot [past, conjoint] S08

bafihla they hide [pres, conjoint] S14

bafile they are dead, they have died [stative] S17

bafisa they desire [pres, conjoint] S12

bafuna they want [pres, conjoint] S05

bafunde they should study or read [subjunc] S14

bafundi students [< **abafundi**] S19

bagcina they end up [pres, conjoint] S20

bagcina they ended up, they eventually [aux, rem past] S25

bagcine they eventually [aux, subjunc] S28

bagila they practice ... (i.e. partake in ...) [pres, conjoint] S23

bagxeka they opposed [narr] S13

bahamba they go, they travel [pres, conjoint] S09

bahambisana they accompany [pres, conjoint] S16

bahlala they stay, they live [pres, conjoint] S19

bahlale they continually [aux] S23

bahlezi they are sitting, they are seated [stative; < -hlal-] S05

bahlukane na- ... they should give up ..., they should part from ..., they should separate from ... [subjunc] S27

bahlukumezeka they are assaulted, attacked [pres, conjoint] S23

bahlukunyezwe they have been assaulted [past, conjoint] S23

bahlukunyezwe they are assaulted, they should be assaulted [subjunc; different tones from item above] S23

bake they sometimes VERB [aux] S14

bake they once VERBed [aux, rem past] S23

bakhala they complain [pres, conjoint] S05

bakhe his, her [poss Cl. 2 & Cl. 14] S14, S27

bakhohlisa they deceive, mislead, cheat [pres, conjoint] S05

bakhokhiswa they are made to pay, they are charged [pres, conjoint] S13

bakholelwa they believe in [pres, conjoint] S23

bakhona they are there [loc cop, pres; may introduce an exist cop] S23

bakhona abantu there are people [exist cop, pres] S23

bakhonze they are keen on, they are passionate about [past, conjoint] S27

bakhubazekile they are disabled or handicapped [stative] S14

bakhulelwe they are pregnant (euph; lit. they have been grown for) [stative] S20

bakugweme they should avoid it [subjunc] S20

bakulendawo of that place [poss Cl. 2] S17

bakwazi they should know, they should be able [subjunc] S14

bakwazile they were able [past, disjoint] S28

bakwezinye from some [poss Cl. 2] S25

-bal-a count, calculate [v.t.] S12

balahlekelwa they lose [pres, conjoint] S20

balahlekelwe they lost [past, conjoint] S08

balale they should sleep [subjunc] S20

balandele they should follow [subjunc] S19

balapha of here, local [poss Cl. 2] S10

-balek-a run away (from), flee [v.i. & t.] S10

-balekel-a run away from or to, evade, flee to [v-appl] S10

-balel-a calculate at [v-appl] S17

-balelw-a be calculated at [v-appl-pass] S17

baleyonkampani of that company [poss Cl. 2] S27

balimala they were injured [rem past] S17

balinganiselwa they are measured at [pres, conjoint] S20

baliqhamukisa they come from [pres, conjoint] S20

balo of this [poss Cl. 2] S11

balokhu they keep on [aux] S05

-balulek-a bec important [v.inch] {Xhosa} S06

balungiselwe they should have sorted out for them [subjunc] S13

balusukumele they must take action about it (lit. they should stand up for it) [subjunc] S21

-balw-a be counted, be included [v-pass] S12

bamabhanoyi of airplanes [poss Cl. 2] S18

-bamb-a hold (back), take hold of, catch [v.t.] S23

-bamb-a undertake, engage in battle [v.t.] S11

bambalwa there are few [descr cop, pres] S18

-bamban-a wrestle, go into battle with, take each other on [v-recip] S11

-bambek-a be held, be tangible [v-neut] S21

-bambel-a take hold of for, catch for; deputize for, take the place of [v-appl] S18

-bambis-a assist in doing, help VERB [v-caus] S10

-bambisan-a cooperate with each other, assist each other in [v-caus-recip] S10

bamdlulisele they transferred or seconded him or her to [subjunc] S14

bamsiza they helped him or her [rem past] S14

banakwe they should be taken notice of [subjunc] S16

banalesifo they have this disease [assoc cop, pres] S20

banawo they have it [assoc cop, pres] S19

banazo they have them [assoc cop, pres] S13

bancane there are few of them, they are small [descr cop, pres] S19

-bandakany-a involve, include [v.t.] S14

bane-AIDS they have AIDS [assoc cop, pres] S20

banecala they are guilty, they are at fault (lit. they have guilt) [assoc cop, pres] S23

bane-HIV they have HIV [assoc cop, pres] S16

-bang-a cause, produce [v.t.] S05

bangaba sethubeni they stand the

chance (lit. they could bec in the chance) [loc cop, inch, pres, potential] S23

bangabi they should not be(come) [copula, subjunc, neg] S19

bangabi nawo ugesi they should not have electricity [assoc cop, inch, subjunc, neg] S19

bangabinakho ukukhululeka and they have no peace of mind [assoc cop, inch, subjunc, neg; < **ba-** SC **-nga-** neg **-b-** become **-i** neg **-na-** with **-kho** it] S23

bangabona they could see [pres, potential] S14

bangaboni they do not see [pres, rel, neg] S14

bangakha they can build [pres, potential] S20

bangakhokhi they do not pay [pres, rel, neg; < **abakhokhi**] S28

bangakunqoba they can overcome or conquer it [pres, potential] S23

bangangeni they should not enter [subjunc, neg] S13

bangangidabukeli they should not pity me [subjunc, neg] S14

bangaphansi they are under [loc cop, pres] S23

bangaphezu kuka-500 million there are more than 500 million [loc cop, pres] S20

bangaphumelela they can, could, would succeed [pres, potential] S19

bangasigwema they can avoid it

[pres, potential] S20

bangathokoza they would be happy [pres, potential] S28

bangawatholi that they do not get [subjunc, neg] S28

bangawatshala they can plant them [pres, potential] S24

bangazenza they can do or make them [pres, potential] S18

bangazimela they can stand for themselves [pres, potential] S27

bangazimela ngokwabo they can stand on their own feet, they can be independent [v phr] S27

bangeke they would never [aux, pres, potential, neg] S23

bangeke bayishaye mkhuba they would never take it seriously [v phr] S23

bangekho esikoleni they are not at school [loc cop, pres, rel, neg] S13

-bangel-a cause for, cause to [v-appl] S13

-bangelw-a be caused for, to or because of [v-appl-pass] S23

bangene they should go into [subjunc] S27

bangenelwe they were attacked unawares [past, conjoint] S08

bangibuze they (should) ask me [subjunc] S14

bangifakela they installed for me [rem past] S27

bangu-158 there are 158 of them [ident cop, pres] S20

bangu-25 there are 25 of them [ident cop, pres] S27

bangu-50 there are fifty of them [ident cop, pres] S24

bangu-300 there are 300 of them [ident cop, pres] S10

bangu-750 000 there are 750,000 of them [ident cop, pres] S20

-bangw-a be caused [v-pass] S05

baningi there are many (lit. they are many) [descr cop, pres] S05

-baniz-a flash (referring to lightning) [v.i.] S17

banobulili they have a gender or sex [assoc cop, pres] S23

banokuzimisela they have determination [assoc cop, pres] S19

banomalaleveva they have or they carry malaria [assoc cop, pres] S20

banothando they are loving, they have a liking [assoc cop, pres] S22

bantu people [< **abantu**] S04

banyakenye of last year [poss Cl. 2] S11

-banzi wide, broad [rel stem] S08

baphathwa they suffer ... [pres, conjoint] S20

baphathwe they should suffer ...; they should be treated, they should be handled [subjunc] S20

baphela they met their end, they came to an end [rem past] S17

baphelele they are well catered for [stative] S06

baphethe they manage, they run, they are in charge of [stative] S21

baphethwe they suffer [stative] S25

baphinde and they repeatedly [aux, subjunc] S23

baphucwe they should be deprived (of), they should have taken away [subjunc] S24

baphula they are breaking [pres, conjoint] S10

baphumelele they should succeed [subjunc] S19

baphumule they should rest [subjunc] S28

baqala they start, they do for the first time [(aux) pres, conjoint] S23

baqala they started [rem past, partic] S13

baqale they (should) begin [subjunc] S28

baqashe they employ [subjunc] S28

baqeqeshelwe they have been trained for [stative] S12

baqeqeshiwe they have been trained [stative] S05

baqhamuka they come from [pres, conjoint] S03

baqhamuke they should come up (lit. they should appear) [subjunc] S09

baqhubeka they carried on, they continued [narr] S13

baqhubeka they carried on, they continued [rem past (differs from the above item in that **ba-** has a long vowel)] S23

baqinisa ikhanda they are obstinate (lit. they make (their) head strong [v phr] S10

Barend (male name) [n Cl. 1a] {Afr} S10

-bas-a make, kindle or light a fire; stir up strife [v.t.] S28

base they already [aux] S17

basebancane there are still few of them, they are still small [descr cop, pres, persistive] S19

basebasha they are still young [descr cop, pres, persistive] S19

basebenzisa they use [pres, conjoint] S18

basebenzise they (should) use [subjunc] S16

baseduze they are nearby, close by [loc cop, pres] S06

basejele of the prison [poss Cl. 2] S23

-basel-a make a fire for, kindle for; stir up strife for; make persistent demands for repayment [v-appl] S28

basemadolobheni they are in towns [poss Cl. 2] S19

basemaphandleni from rural areas [poss Cl. 2] S23

basengcupheni they are in danger [loc cop, pres] S23

basengozini they are in danger [loc cop, pres] S20

baseNingizimu Afrika of South Africa [poss Cl. 2] S07

base-Pretoria West College of Technology they are at the Pretoria ... [loc cop, pres] S19

basethembise they promise (i.e. threaten) us [subjunc] S09

basethimbeni they are in a group of unmarried girls or women [loc cop, pres] S25

basetshenziswa they are used [pres, conjoint] S09

basha they are young [descr cop, pres] S19

bashade they married [past, conjoint] S14

basho they say, they state [pres, conjoint] S06

basilethe and they bring it [subjunc] S20

basithola they get it [pres, conjoint] S20

basitshalile they have planted it [past, disjoint] S27

basiza they assist [pres, conjoint] S27

basizwe they should be helped [subjunc] S23

basuke they just [aux, pres (this item differs from the following one in tone and stress)] S24

basuke they have just [aux, past, conjoint] S16

batelekele they are striking for, they are on strike over [past, conjoint] S13

bathanda 'hey like, love [pres, conjoint] S19

bathembele they believe in [stative] S05

bathenga they buy [pres, conjoint] S28

bathenjiswa and they were promised [narrative] S06

bathi (and) they said [narr] S13

bathola they find [pres, conjoint] S19

bathola they found, they experienced [narr] S23

bathole they should get, they experience [subjunc] S13, S23

bathole they experienced [past, conjoint] S23

bathunjiwe they have been taken hostage, they have been hijacked [stative; < ba- + -thumb- + -w- + -i...e; mb ... -w- > nj ... -w-] S16

bathunjwa they are hijacked or taken hostage [pres, conjoint; < -thumb-w-; mbw > njw] S16

bathwala they carry [pres, conjoint] S20

batshelwa and they were told [narr] S25

bavalelwe they should be shut up in or at [subjunc] S14

bavame they generally VERB [aux, stative] S09

bavela they come from [pres, conjoint] S20

bavezeni bring them out [imper pl] S14

bawaphathe they should treat them [subjunc] S14

bawathathisa okwezitha they take them as enemies [v phr] S09

bawufundele they have studied for it [past, disjoint] S05

bawuguqule they change it [subjunc] S16

bawuqondisisa they understand it thoroughly [pres, conjoint] S18

bawusingathile they supported it [past, disjoint form] S02

bawuthole bona *they* should get it [subjunc] S06

baxoxisana na- ... they had a conversation with ..., they negotiated with ... [v phr, rem past] S13

bayabonga they give thanks [pres, disjoint] S02

bayaboshwa they are arrested [pres, disjoint] S24

bayadlwengulwa they are raped [pres, disjoint] S23

bayafana they are the same, they are similar [pres, disjoint] S23

bayahlukunyezwa they are assaulted [pres, disjoint] S23

bayahluleka they are unable, they are defeated [pres, disjoint] S28

bayahlupheka they suffer, they are troubled, they are afflicted [pres, disjoint] S25

bayakholwa they believe [pres, disjoint] S14

bayakufisa they wish it, they desire it [pres, disjoint] S19

bayakuthanda they like it [pres, disjoint] S20

bayakwazi they can, they are able, they know how to [pres, disjoint] S23

bayaludinga they need it [pres, disjoint] S23

bayamangala they are surprised [pres, disjoint] S18

bayasinukubeza they sexually abuse us [pres, disjoint] S09

bayathinteka they are touched, are affected [pres, disjoint] S08

bayawagqugquzela they nag them, they try to win them over, they persuade them [pres, disjoint] S25

bayawuthola they get it [pres, disjoint] S28

bayaxoxisana they negotiate [pres, disjoint] S16

bayayikhokha they pay it out [pres, disjoint] S28

bayazidayisa they trade them, they offer them for sale [pres, disjoint] S17

bayazikhiqiza they produce them [pres, disjoint] S27

bayazwana are much inclined to [pres, disjoint] S20

baye they should go [subjunc] S18

bayehlulwa they are overcome [pres, disjoint] S23

bayi-ANC they are (the) ANC (African National Congress) [ident cop, pres] S05

bayingcosana there are few, they are a small number [ident cop, pres] S05

bayishaye they should hit it [subjunc] S23

bayishumi there are ten (lit. they are ten) [ident cop, pres] S17

bayizinkonkoni they are homosexuals [ident cop, pres] S23

bayizintatheli they are reporters, journalists [ident cop, pres] S21

bayizivakashi they are visitors [ident cop, pres] S20

bayo its [poss Cl. 2] S05

bazalelwe they have had born to them [stative] S10

bazalelwe yinja endlini they have a huge problem (idiom; lit. they have had a dog born in the house) S10

bazama they try [pres, conjoint] S16

bazame they should try [subjunc] S16

baze until they [aux] S28

bazibandakanye they should involve themselves [subjunc] S24

bazibona they see themselves [pres, conjoint] S23

bazibone they (should) see themselves [subjunc] S23

bazibonela they saw for themselves [rem past] S17

bazidube that they (should) throw or give up [subjunc] S13

bazihlukumeze they should assault them [subjunc] S23

bazihlwaye they should spread them [subjunc] S21

bazikhethela they choose for themselves, they just choose [pres, conjoint] S25

bazikhokhela they pay them to or for [pres, conjoint] S13

bazikhomba they point at themselves [pres, conjoint] S16

bazincisha they deprive them [pres, conjoint] S14

baziphathise okwezinkonkoni they behave like homosexuals [subjunc v phr] S23

baziphilisa they keep themselves alive [pres, conjoint] S20

baziswe they should be informed [subjunc] S25

bazithola they find themselves [pres, conjoint] S23

bazitshalele they have planted for themselves [past, conjoint] S24

bazo their, of them [poss Cl. 2] S09

bazobabiza they will call them [fut] S23

bazobabiza ngezinkonkoni they will call them homosexuals [fut] S23

bazongiphendula they will reply to me [fut] S22

bazonikezela they will present [fut] S11

bazoshusiselwa they will have cases brought against them [fut] S10

bazosika they will cut or mow [fut] S13

bazosizakala they will be assisted [fut] S25

be- they [SC Cl. 2; found in participial] S03

be- of [poss conc Cl. 2 coalesced with i] S05

be (-be, be-) [aux marking relative tenses; followed by partic] S05

be-ANC of the ANC (African National Congress) [poss Cl. 2] S05

bebayengile they have enticed or seduced them [past, partic, disjoint] S28

bebe they PAST [aux, partic; < be- SC + -be aux stem] S19

bebe benawo they had it [assoc cop, past, partic] S19

bebefuna they were wanting [past pres] S13

bebengathandi they were not keen or happy [past pres, neg] S13

bebhekene (they) facing [past stative, partic] S28

beboshelwe they are imprisoned for [past, partic, conjoint] S23

becabanga they think [pres, partic] S23

becashe they have hidden [past, partic, conjoint] S20

becela (they) asking for [pres, partic] S05

becindezelwa they being crushed [pres, partic] S17

bedlulele it (sur)passed, it went beyond [past, conjoint] S23

bedlwenguliwe they have been been raped [past, partic, disjoint] S25

befile (they are) dead [pres, partic] S17

befuna they are on the point of, they are about to; they want [pres, partic] S16

begijima (they) running [pres, partic] S17

behlangabezana they come up against [pres, partic] S16

behleka they (are) laughing [pres, partic] S23

behlukahlukene they differ, they vary [stative] S25

-bek-a put, place; state, add (to what is said), put in or contribute (in a conversation) [v.t.] S05, S23

bekhala (they are) crying [pres, partic] S17

bekhipha (they are) taking out [pres, partic] S17

bekhuza they are (were) calming [pres, partic] S08

bekungaphumi it was not coming from [past pres, neg] S26

bekungumuntu it was a person [ident cop, past pres] S21

bekuthathela they take against

you [pres, partic] S28

-bekw-a be placed, have placed on one [v-pass] S23

-bekw-a icala be found guilty [v phr] S23

belashelwa they are being treated for [pres, conjoint] S20

Belgium [< i-Belgium n Cl. 5] S16

belikhona (s)he was there, (s)he was present [loc cop, past pres; may also introduce an exist cop] S26

belimbuza (s)he questioned him [past pres] S26

belunywe they have been bitten [past, partic, conjoint] S20

benawo they have it [assoc cop, pres, partic] S19

benezinkinga they have problems [assoc cop, pres, partic] S23

bengafunanga they did not want [past, partic] S16

bengayiboni they not seeing it [pres, partic] S27

bengazi without knowing, they not knowing [pres, partic, neg] S10

bengcolile they are dirty [stative, partic] S23

bengekho they not being there, they being absent; there being no ... [loc cop, pres, partic, neg; introduces exist cop, partic, neg] S23

bengekho abesimame in the absence of women [exist cop, pres, partic, neg] S23

beNkatha of Inkatha (Zulu cultural and political organization) [poss Cl. 2] S05

bentela of tax [poss Cl. 2] S10

benukubeze they having sexually abused [past, partic, conjoint] S23

benza they are doing, making [pres, conjoint] S19

benze they should make or do [subjunc] S10

bephoqelelwa they are forced [pres, partic] S09

bephula they break [pres, partic] S10

be-Presbyterian Church of Southern Africa of the Presbyterian ... [poss Cl. 2] S17

beqale they having started [past, partic, conjoint] S10

beqalile they (had) begun [past, partic, disjoint] S17

beqeqeshwa they were (lit. are) hired [pres, partic] S18

beqhubeka they continue [pres, partic] S25

Bergville (place) [n Cl. 9a] S05

besaba they are afraid [pres, conjoint] S23

besabe that they should be afraid [subjunc] S23

bese already (in the past) [aux] S13

bese and then [conjunction; requires a following indicative, non-participial verb] S01

bese bezitholile they had already had or received them [past past, exclusive, disjoint] S13

beselifuna (s)he then wanted [past pres, exclusive] S08

besenkingeni they are in difficulty, they have a problem [loc cop, pres, partic] S23

beshiye they have left [past, partic, conjoint] S20

besifazane female [poss Cl. 2] S08

besikole of the school [poss Cl. 2] S13

besilisa of the masculine gender or sex [poss Cl. 2] S19

besimame female [poss Cl. 2] S14

besimfanele it would have fitted him or her, would have been appropriate for him or her [past past, disjoint] S26

besitholile (they) having contracted it [past, partic, disjoint] S20

besitshelwe (s)he had been told [past past, conjoint] S26

besivande of a garden plot [poss Cl. 14] S27

bethi (they are) saying [pres, partic] S17

bethu our [poss Cl. 2: < ba- + -ithu] S08

bethunjiwe they have been taken hostage, they have been hijacked [stative, partic] S16

beveza they were (lit. are) expressing [pres, partic] S13

bewadubile they having boycotted them [past, partic, disjoint] S13

bezama they try [pres, partic] S25

bezimisele they being prepared [stative, partic] S13

bezimoto of cars [poss Cl. 2] S09

bezimpilo of lives [poss Cl. 2] S17

bezindaba of the news [poss Cl. 2] S09

bezingela they are hunting [pres, partic] S24

bezithola they find themselves [pres, partic] S28

bezitholile they have received them [past, partic, disjoint] S13

bezitshela they tell themselves [pres, partic] S24

bezokwelapha (they) coming to treat [pres, partic, venitive] S23

bezothatha (they) coming to take [pres, participial] S03

bezwe they should feel [subjunc; < **ba-** SC Cl. 2 + **-izw-** feel + **-e**] S23

bhaa be open, be clear, be bare [ideo] S21

-bhak-a bake [v.t.] {Afr *bak*} S01

-bhal-a write, register [v.t.] S12

-bhalel-a write in, write for, write to [v-appl] S13

-bhalis-a cause to register, cause to write, help write [v-caus] S12

-bhalisel-a register for [v-caus-appl] S18

-bhalw-a be written, be registered [v-pass] S18

-bhek-a look (at), watch, keep a watch on, watch over, look after [v.t.] S04

-bhekan-a look at each other, face each other, be opposite [v-recip] S04

-bhekan-a na- ... bec faced with ..., bec opposite ..., deal with ... S04

-bhekel-a look towards, watch for, watch at [v-appl] S17

-bhekelel-a consider definitely [v-perfective] S23

-bhekene na- ... deal with, be facing [< **-bhekan-** + **-i...e**] S24

-bhem-a smoke, sniff (a substance) [v.i. & t.] S09

Bhengu (surname) [n Cl. 1a] S05

-bhikish- protest, fight against [v.t.] S25

-bhubh-a die, suffer annihilation [v.i.] S20

-bhubhis-a wipe out, annihilate, kill, destroy [v-caus] S20

-bi bad [adj stem] S05

-bik-a report, announce [v.t.] S17

-bikel-a report to [v-appl] S23

-bili two [adj stem] S10

-biy-a make a fence, put up a palisade; ward off a blow [v.i.] S27

Biyela (surname) [n Cl. 1a] S24

-biyel-a fence round, enclose in a fence; construct a fence against [v-appl] S27

-biyelw-a be fenced, be protected by enclosure [v-appl-pass] S27

-biz-a call [v.t.] S06

-biz-a cost [v.t.] S28

-biz-a nga- call (by a name, title, etc.; **bambiza ngophulofesa** they call her professor) S06, S23

-biz-a ngokuthi + IDENT COP PREF ... call someone or something ... S23

-bizw-a be called [v-pass] S06

-bizw-a nga- be called (by a name, title, etc.; **ubizwa ngombulali** (s)he is called a murderer) S06

-bizw-a ngokuthi + IDENT COP PREF ... be called ... S20

Bloemfontein (city; capital of Free State Province) {Afr} S15

bo- [quant conc Cl. 2] S02

bo they, them, their [abs pron Cl. 2] S6

bobabili both [quant Cl. 2; < bo- quant conc + **babili** two [adj minus initial vowel]] S23

bobunye of the other, of another [poss Cl. 2] S04

bodwa only, alone [quant Cl. 2] S23

bokuthi of that [poss Cl. 14] S19

-bolek- borrow, lend, loan [v.t.; **-bolek-** + personal noun = lend to, e.g. **ngimboleke usisi imali** I lent my sister money; **-bolek-** + loc pref + personal noun = borrow from, e.g. **ngiboleke imali kusisi** I borrowed money from my sister] S27

bomgunyathi bogus [poss Cl. 2] S05

bomndeni of the family [poss Cl. 2] S23

BOMUNTU OF A PERSON [POSS CL. 14] S23

-bon-a see, witness, understand; be of the opinion [v.t.] S03, S08

bona they, them, their [abs pron Cl. 2 with stabilizer -na] S06

-bonakal-a be visible, be apparent, appear, seem [v-neut] S13

bonakalelwa and who had had destroyed [narr] S17

bonakalelwa nayizimpahla and they also had their goods destroyed (lit. and they were destroyed for even by the goods) [v phr] S17

-bonan-a see each other; **-bonan-a na-** consult [v-recip] S15

bona ngokwabo on their own, of their own will S25

-bonel-a see for [v-appl] S17

-bonel-a ku- copy, imitate [v-appl + loc] S27

-bong-a give thanks, be(come) grateful; recite the praises of [v.i. & t.] S02

Bongani (male name) [n Cl. 1a; imper meaning 'give thanks!' or 'give praise'] S19

-bonis-a show [v-caus] S05

-bonisan-a show one another; exchange views [v-caus-recip] S05

bonke everyone, all [quant Cl. 2] S02

-boph-a arrest, tie (up), bind, make fast [v.t.] S10

-boshelw-a be imprisoned for [v-appl-pass; < **-bophel-w-a**; ph ... -w- > sh ... -w-] S23

-boshw-a be arrested [v-pass; < **-boph-w-a**; phw > shw] S10

Brenda Fassie (name of a South African singer) [n Cl. 1a] S14

bu- it, they [SC Cl. 14] S05

-bu- it [OC Cl. 14] S19

-bucayi unpleasant, uncomfortable [rel stem; < **ubucayi** uncomfortable position, fix, dilemma] S18

bufana it is the same, it resembles, it is like [pres, conjoint] S23

buhlungu painful, sore [rel stem; < **ubuhlungu** pain] S20

-buk-a look (at), watch [v.t.] S05

buka look [imperative] S05

buka nje just look [imper phr] S05

-bukek-a be attractive, remarkable [v-neut] S17

-bukek-a seem, be considered, be regarded (as) [v-neut] S19

-bukel-a watch [v-appl] S18

bukhoma at close range [loc] S08

bukhomba it points [pres, conjoint] S23

bukhona it is there [loc or exist cop, pres] S26

-bulal-a kill [v.t.] S09

-bulalan-a kill one another [v-recip] S09

-bulalw-a be killed [v-pass] S17

-bulaw-a be killed [v-pass; < **-bulal-**; var **-bulalw-a**] S20

bungaphezu it is in addition (lit. it is above) [loc cop, pres] S26

bunobuhlakani it has cleverness [assoc cop, pres] S05

-bus-a enjoy life [v.i.] S02

busha anew, afresh [manner adv; < **ubusha** newness, freshness [n Cl. 14; < **-sha** new, fresh, young [adj stem]] S05

-busis-a bless [v-caus] S02

Busisiwe (female name) [n Cl. 1a; < **-busisiwe** have been blessed] S26

-busisw-a be blessed [v-caus-pass] S14

-buth- gather together, recruit [v.t.] S09

buthule silently [adv; < **bu-** + **-thul-e** < **-thul-a** be silent; this is a very rare form of adverbial derivation] S23

-buy-a return, return from, go back, come back from [v.i.] S09

buyabuthikameza it disturbs or interferes with it, it has a negative impact on it, [pres, disjoint] S23

-buy-e again VERB [aux] S13

-buyel-a return to, go back to [v-appl] S13

buyezwakala it is felt or experienced [pres, disjoint; < **bu-** + **-ya-** + **-izwakal-a**] S23

-buyis-a return, send back [v-caus] S09

-buyisel-a restore to, return to [v-caus-appl] S09

-buyiselw-a be returned to [v-caus-appl-pass] S28

-buz-a ask, question [v.t.] S08

C

-cabang-a think [v.i. & t.] S04

-cac-a bec clear [v.i.] S23

-cacel-a bec clear to [v-appl] S23

cala crime, offence, felony; guilt; wrong, defect; court case; charge [< **icala**] S26

Calalakubo (male name) [n Cl. 1a; < **icala lakubo** the wrong or offence of his family] S06

-canul-a disgust, nauseate [v.t.] S21

-cel-a ask for, request [v.t.] S05

-celel-a plead for, request for [v-appl] S26

-chaz-a explain [v.t.] S07

-chazel-a explain to [v-appl] S07

-chazelek-a get an explanation (lit. get explained to) [v-appl-neut] S13

-chith-a spill, waste, spend [v.t] S09

chwepheshe expert [< **uchwepheshe**] S23

-cindezel-a press down, squeeze, crush; oppress [v.t.] S17

-cindezelek-a get crushed; get injured; get pressurized; get oppressed [v-neut] S17

-cindezelw-a be crushed, be pressed down, be squeezed [v-pass] S17

-cish-e almost VERB, VERB nearly [aux] S17

-cons-a fall (of a drop of liquid), drip, leak [v.i.] S27

-consis-a cause to drip, let fall a drop of liquid [v-caus] S27

-cwaning-a conduct research on, investigate [v.i. & t.] S26

-cwil-a sink, dive [v.i.] S28

D

daba serious matter [< **udaba**] S21

-dabuk-a bec sad, bec sorry, bec contrite, repent [v.inch] S14

-dabukel-a pity, feel sorry for [v-appl] S14

-dak-a intoxicate, make drunk [v.t.] S09

-dakw-a bec intoxicated, get drunk [v-pass, inch] S09

-dal-a create, form, bring into being, cause [v.t.] S14

-dala old [adj stem] S02

-dalel-a create for [v-appl] S23

-dalelw-a be created for [v-appl-pass] S23

-dalul-a expose, divulge [v.t.] S13

-dalulw-a be exposed, be divulged [v-pass] S13

-dalw-a be created, be caused, be formed, be brought into being [v-pass] S14

-damb-a go down (of a swelling), subside, calm down, be allayed [v.i.] S21

-dambis-a cause to subside, assuage, calm down [v-caus] S21

-dayis-a market, offer for sale, auction, trade [v.t.] S12

-dayisel- market to or for, market in or at [v-appl] S24

-dayiselw-a be offered for sale to, be marketed to, be marketed at or in [v-appl-pass] S24

-dayisw-a be marketed, be put up for sale [v-pass] S12

-de tall, long, lengthy [adj stem] S16

-dicilek-a get thrown down, fall flat [v.i.] S17

-dilik-a fall down, collapse [v.i.] S17

-diliz-a pull down, cause to fall down; retrench [v.t.] S03

-dilizw-a be pulled down; be retrenched [v-pass] S03

-din-a weary, tire, sicken [v.t.] S23

-ding-a need, require [v.t.] S14

-dingek-a be necessary, be required, be needed [v-neut] S14

-dinw-a bec sickened, bec wearied, bec troubled, bec bored [v-pass] S23

-divos-a divorce, get divorced [v.i. & t.] {Eng} S22

-dl-a eat, consume [v.t] S11

-dl-a embezzle (lit. eat) [v.t.] S10

-dlal-a play [v.i. & t.] S08

-dlalel-a play at, in, for [v-appl] S08

-dlalw-a be played [v-pass] S11

-dlek- be edible; get expended [v-neut] S12

-dlelan-a be on good terms, be good neighbors (lit. eat for each other) [v-recip] S24

Dlamini (surname) [n Cl. 1a] S16

-dlang-a rage, be overwhelming, be overpowering, take the upper hand [v.i.] S16

-dlondlobal-a get greatly excited, get highly emotional [v.inch] S27

-dlubh-a put on one's best clothes, dress up in (finery) [v.t.] S17

-dlul-a pass, pass by, surpass [v.t.; var **-edlul-a**] S06

-dlul-a emhlabeni pass away (idiom; lit. pass from earth) S20

-dlulel-a pass on to; be extreme for, excel for [v-appl] S20

-dlulis-a pass on, forward [v-caus] S06

-dlulisel-a transfer, second, pass on (to) [v-caus-appl] S14

-dlulw-a be passed (by) [v-pass] S06

-dlwengul-a rape [v.t.] S23

-dlwengulw-a be raped [v-pass] S23

-doj-a evade, avoid, dodge [v.t.] {Eng} S10

-dons-a pull, haul, tug, drag, draw, attract [v.t.] S07

-donsel-a pull (up) for, draw (up) for [v-appl] S14

-dub-a give up, throw up; ignore; boycott, go on strike [v.i. & t.] S13

-dubul-a shoot [v.t.] S08

-dubulek-a get shot [v-neut] S21

Dudu (female name) [n Cl. 1a; abbrev of **uDuduzile**; means 'has consoled'; this name would be given to a girl after her mother has lost one or two other children, or someone in the family has died)] S08

-dudul-a repel an attack [v.t.] S11

-dudulan-a fend off one another's attack [v-recip] S11

-dum-a bec famous, bec renowned; resound, thunder, rumble [v.i.] S07

-dutshulw-a be shot [v-pass; < **-dubul-w-a**; b ... -w- > tsh ... -w-] S08

-dwa only, alone, one (in number) [quant stem] S09

-dwana sole, completely alone [quant stem; < **-dwa** only, alone + **-ana** [dimin suff] (In this instance the diminutive suffix intensifies rather than lessens the meaning of the base stem.)] S04

E

e- he, she [SC Cl. 1; used in participial] S02

e- they [SC Cl. 6; used in participial] S09

e- to, from, in, at, on [loc pref] S02

e- of [poss conc Cl. 6 coalesced with following **i**] S03

e- which, that, who(m) [rel marker used when the SC in the verb concerned has the vowel **i**] S01

e- [form of the pronominalizer **a-** with assimilation to following **i** or **e**] S06

-e [suffix of past, conjoint form; the conjoint form indicates that the verb phrase continues, while the disjoint suffix **-ile** would indicate the end of the v phrase] S01

-e [stative suff found with verbs ending in **el, ol, ul**] S04

-e [subjunctive suff] S01

-e [imperative suffix used when object concord is present] S01

eØ- [adj conc Cl. 9; < **a-** rel marker + **iØ-** NP] S10

e- ... -eni to, from, at, in, on [loc marker] S02

e- ... -ini to, from, at, in, on [loc marker] S01

eba (s)he becoming, (s)he becomes [pres, partic] S18

eba ngumlawuli wokuhamba kwezindiza (s)he became (lit. becomes) an air traffic controller [ident cop, pres, partic] S18

ebaluleke that/which is important [rel Cl. 9] S06

ebalulekile that/which is important [rel Cl. 9] S19

ebandakanya that/which involves [rel Cl. 9] S19

ebangela that causes [rel Cl. 9] S23

ebantwini from people [loc; < **abantu**] S06

ebasela (s)he demands repayment [pres, partic] S28

ebazisa (s)he informs them [pres, partic] S23

ebheka (s)he looks [pres, partic] S27

ebhodweni from, into, in a pot [loc; < **ibhodwe**] S08

ebingenye that/which was one [rel Cl. 9] S11

eBlouberg Hospital at Blouberg Hospital [loc] S14

eBochum to, from, in Bochum [loc] S14

ebuholini in leadership [loc; < **ubuholi**] S05

ebunzimeni through or in hardship [loc; < **ubunzima**] S09

ebusuku at night [loc; < **ubusuku**; one of the exceptions that does not take a locative suffix] S09

ebuzwa (s)he being asked [pres, partic] S26

eCape Flats on the Cape Flats (area of Greater Cape Town to which the former apartheid government relocated Coloreds (people of mixed race), who had been removed by law from their homes which were considered to be in White areas. This area is now infamous for crime, and gang warfare.) [loc] S09

echaza (s)he explains [pres, partic] S18

-edlul-a pass, surpass [v.t.; var -**dlul-a**] S04

edlule last, that has passed [rel Cl. 9 or 4] S08, S24

-edlulel-a pass on to, go past to or for, surpass, go beyond [v-appl] S23

edlwenguliwe who has been raped [rel Cl. 9] S23

edolobheni to, from, in town [loc; < **idolobha**] S17

eduze nearby, close by [loc] S06

eduze kwa- close to, near to [loc noun + link] S20

eduze na- close to, near to [loc phr] S16

e-Europe to, from, in Europe [loc] S16

efana such as, like, that/which resemble [rel Cl. 4] S19

efanayo similar [rel Cl. 9] S16

efanele proper [rel Cl. 9] S09

efile that/which is dead, that/which is broken (down) [rel Cl. 9] S05

efisa (s)he wishes [pres, partic] S23

efuna (s)he is on the point of, (s)he is about to; (s)he wants [pres, partic] S16

efundisa while (s)he is teaching [pres tense, participial aspect] S02

egazini in(to), from blood [loc; < **igazi**] S20

egcekeni in the open ground [loc; < **igceke**] S08

egcotshwe that/which has been spread [rel Cl. 9] S20

egcwele (that/which is) full or complete [rel Cl. 9] S14

eGeorge Maseba Hospital at George Maseba Hospital [loc] S14

eGeorge Town High School at George ... [loc] S13

eGoli to, from, in Johannesburg [loc; < **iGoli**] S14

ehhotela to, from, at, in the hotel [loc; < **ihhotela**; one of the exceptions that does not take a locative suffix] S17

ehhovisini to, from, at, in office [loc; var **ehhovisi**; < **ihhovisi**] S14

-ehl-a descend, come down, go down; take by surprise, befall, happen to [v.i.] S15, S23

-ehlel-a descend to(wards), come or go down to(wards), come down upon, happen to [v-appl] S18

ehlele (s)he should descend [subjunc; < Ø- SC + -ehlel-e] S18

-ehlelw-a be overcome, have happen to one [v-appl-pass] S23

-ehlis-a lower; go down along; reduce [v-caus] S20

-ehlisel-a reduce or lower for [v-caus-appl] S26

-ehliselw-a have reduced for one, have lowered for one [v-caus-appl-pass] S26

ehloniphekile who is respected, respectable [rel Cl. 9] S14

-ehluk-a bec different, differ [v.i.; var **-ahluk-a, -hluk-a**] S10

-ehlukahlukan-a differ in various ways, vary [v-redup; < **-ehlukan-**] S25

-ehlukan-a bec different [v.inch; var **-ahlukan-a, -hlukan-a**] S19

-ehlukanis-a differentiate, distinguish [v-rec-caus; var **-ahlukanis-a, -hlukanis-a**] S19

-ehlul-a defeat, conquer, overcome [v.i.; var **-hlul-a**] S23

-ehlulek-a be beaten, be overcome, be defeated, be conquered; be unable, fail [v-neut; var **-ahlulek-a, -hlulek-a**] S05

-ehlulw-a be overcome, be defeated, be conquered [v-pass; var **-hlulw-a**] S23

ejajini to, from, at the judge [loc;

< ijaji] S26

ejele to, from, in jail or prison [loc; < ijele; one of the exceptions that does not take a locative suffix] S23

-ejwayel-a grow accustomed to, get used to, adjust to [v.t.; var -jwayel-a] S09

-ejwayelek-a bec customary, bec usual, bec normal [v-neut; var -jwayelek-a] S09

ejwayelekile(yo) normal, usual, common [rel Cl. 9] S23

-ek- get VERB-ed, be VERB-able/ -ible [neuter ext] S04

eKapa to, from, in Cape Town [loc; < iKapa] S08

eke that/which once [rel Cl. 4] S26

ekhaya at, to, from, home [loc; < ikhaya; one of the exceptions that does not take a locative suffix] S09

ekhipha while (s)he was passing (lit. bringing out) [pres, partic] S26

ekhishini to, from, in the kitchen [loc; < ikhishi] {Eng} S19

ekhombisa that/which shows [rel Cl. 9] S18

ekhona (s)he is there, there is …, [loc cop, pres, partic; may also introduce an exist cop] S14

ekhululekile (s)he is free [stative, partic] S18

ekhuluma (s)he (is) speaking [pres, partic] S26

ekhungatheke (s)he is over-whelmed, frustrated [past, partic, conjoint] S23

ekhungatheke ngaphezu kwe-nkanuko yezocansi (s)he is more than overwhelmed by sexual desire or lust [v phr] S23

ekilasini to, from, at, in class [loc; < ikilasi] S13

eKing Zwelithini Stadium to, from, at, in the King Zwelithini Stadium [loc] S11

ekolishi to, from, at, in college [loc; < ikolishi; one of the exceptions that does not take a locative suffix] S19

ekubeni in becoming [loc; < ukuba] S19

ekubeni whereas [conj; < ukuba] S23

ekuboshweni in the arrest [loc; < ukuboshwa] S10

ekufeni to, from, in death [loc; < ukufa] S16

ekuhlukumezeni in violence [loc; < ukuhlukumeza] S05

ekukhokheni in paying [loc; < ukukhokha] S10

ekulomsebenzi (s)he being in that job [loc cop, pres, partic] S27

ekulunyweni from, in being bitten [loc; < ukulunywa] S20

ekuphasisweni to, from, at, in the passing [loc; < ukuphasiswa] S25

ekuphikiseni to, from, in, during the debate or dispute [loc; < ukuphikisa] S23

ekuqhubeni in the development [loc; < **ukuqhuba**] S16

ekuseni in the morning [loc; < **ukusa** to dawn] S11

ekushisweni in the burning [loc; < **ukushiswa**] S26

ekutheni that [conj] S19

ekuxazululeni in the settlement (of quarrels, etc.) [loc; < **ukuxazulula**] S09

ekwakheni in the building [loc; < **ukwakha**] S08

ekwenza (s)he doing it [pres, partic] S26

ekwenzeni to, from, in the making [loc; < **ukwenza**] S24

el- which, that, who [rel conc Cl. 5; found before vowels; < **a-** rel marker + **li-** SC] S08, S23

-el- for, on behalf of, with respect to, to the detriment of, in or from the direction of [appl ext] S04

-el- [appl ext; here semantically imprecise] S01

-el- ... -ni? for what reason?, why? [e.g **Bahlekelani?** Why are they laughing?; **Ukhalelani?** What are you crying for?]

elakhe his, hers [poss pron Cl. 5] S27

elakho yours [poss pron Cl. 5] S21

elalihlose that/which it had intended, aimed [rem past past, conjoint] S28

elamaqiniso that of truths [poss pron Cl. 5, agrees with **izwi** word] S08

eLamontville to, from, in Lamontville [loc] S11

elandulela that/which precedes, that/which is the precursor of [rel Cl. 5] S23

-elaph-a heal, cure, treat [v.t.] S19

-elaphel-a treat for [v-appl] S20

elaseMelika that of America [poss pron Cl. 5; agrees with **izwe**] S16

elaseNorthern Province that of the Northern Province [poss pron Cl. 5; agrees with understood **izwe** country, land] S14

elase-South Africa that (country) of South Africa [poss pron Cl. 5; agrees with **izwe**] S20

-elashelw-a be treated for [v-appl-pass; < **-elaphel-** + **-w-**; **ph ... -w- > sh ... -w-**] S20

-elashw-a be treated, be cured [v-pass; < **-elaph-w-a**; **phw > shw**] S20

elazithengela that/which (s)he bought for [ind rel of plain obj rel, Cl. 5] S08

elaziwa that/which is known [rel Cl. 5] S09

eledlule that (day) which has passed [rel Cl. 5] S26

-elel- completely, perfectly [perfective ext] S04

eleMdlwembe Gang that of the Mdlwembe Gang [poss pron Cl. 5] S09

elenza who caused [rel Cl. 5] S21

elenziwa that/which is done or performed [rel Cl. 5] S23

eli- [adj conc Cl. 5; < **a-** rel marker + **ili-** NP] S17

eli- which, that, who [rel conc Cl. 5; < **a-** rel marker + **li-** SC] S01

elibhekele that/which watches [rel Cl. 5] S17

elibhekene na- ... that/which deals with ... [rel phr Cl. 5] S25

elifanele that/which is necessary, which is proper [rel Cl. 5] S05

eligreythiwe (that/which has been) grated [rel Cl. 5] S01

elihle beautiful, nice [adj Cl. 5] S22

elikaGareth Olivier that of Gareth Olivier [poss pron Cl. 5 referring to **igama** name] S27

elikaSnoopy that of Snoopy [poss pron Cl. 5 referring to **igama** name] S09

elikhanyayo that/which is bright, that/which shines [rel Cl. 5] S04

elikhulu great, large, big [adj Cl. 5] S17

elikhulu a hundred [rel Cl. 4] S17

elimnyama black, dark [rel Cl. 5] S02

elingakukhipha that/which can take you out [rel Cl. 5] S28

elingakwazi that/which it is unable [rel Cl. 5] S28

elingakwazi ukuzikhokhela that/

which it is unable to repay [ind rel of plain obj rel, Cl. 5] S28

elinye some, another, a certain, one (i.e. a certain, some) [adj Cl. 5] S17

eliphikelele that/which was headed [rel Cl. 5] S18

eliphikelele kuyo where it was headed [ind rel of plain loc rel, Cl. 5] S18

eliqanjwe that/which was composed [rel Cl. 5] S27

eliqeqeshiwe that/which has been trained [rel Cl. 5] S16

eliseBhambayi that/which is in Bhambayi [rel Cl. 5] S09

eliseduze that/which is near [rel Cl. 5] S16

elisikhiphile that/which (s)he had delivered (lit. brought out) [ind rel of plain obj rel, Cl. 5] S26

elisuke who have just [rel Cl. 5] S23

elithe who said, that/which went [rel Cl. 5] S27

elithe xaxa that/which is better or larger [rel phr Cl. 5] S27

eliyingozi that/which is dangerous [rel Cl. 5] S09

eliyisilima that/which is difficult, which is hard [rel Cl. 5] S23

elizosiza that/which will help [rel Cl. 5] S12

elokhu (s)he kept on [aux, partic] S26

-elulek-a advise, counsel [v.t.] S15

elunywe (s)he has been bitten [past, partic, conjoint] S20

em- [adj conc Cl. 9; occurs with stems starting in **b**; < **a-** rel marker + **im-** NP] S25

emabhange in banks [loc; < **amabhange**; one of the exceptions that does not take a locative suffix] S10

emabhulohweni to, from, on bridges [loc; < **amabhuloho**] S16

emadolobheni to, from, in towns or cities [loc; < **amadolobha**] S09

emadolweni to, from, in, on the knees [loc; < **amadolo**] S28

emafemini to, from, in firms [loc; < **e-** + **amafemu** + **-ini**] S12

emahlombe to, from, in, on the shoulders [loc; < **emahlombe**; one of the exceptions that does not take a locative suffix;] S16

emajele to, from, in jails [loc; < **amajele**; one of the exceptions that does not take a locative suffix] S14

eMakatini [pronounced **eMakathini** at Makatini [loc; < **iMakat(h)ini**] S27

emakhaya at, (to), from home (lit. to, from, at, in homes) [loc; < **amakhaya**; one of the exceptions that does not take a loc suffix] S05

emakhaya in rural areas (lit. where homes are—in former times, the large majority of Black people lived in rural

areas) [loc; < **amakhaya**] S21

emakilasini to, from, at, in classes or classrooms [loc; < **amakilasi**] S13

emali financial, commercial [poss Cl. 6] S10

emalungeni among the members [loc; < **amalunga**] S09

eMandlethu High School at Mandlethu High School [loc; < **iMandlethu** [n Cl. 5]; < **amandla** strength + **ethu** our] S02

emanzini to, from, in, on water [loc; < **amanzi**] S17

emaphandleni to, from, in rural areas [loc; < **amaphandle**] S23

emaphephandabeni to, from, in newspapers [loc; < **amaphephandaba**] S10

emapulazini to, from, on farms [loc; < **amapulazi**] S27

emaqenjini to, from, at, in the teams [loc; < **emaqembwini**; < **e-** + **amaqembu** + **-ini**; mbw > nj] S11

ematheni on the lips (lit. in, from saliva) [loc; < **amathe**] S25

emathinini from, in, into tins [loc; < **amathini**] S01

emaxhophozini to, from, in, at swamps [loc; < **amaxhophozi**] S20

emazweni to, from, in countries [loc; < **amazwe**] S03

emazweni angaphandle to, from, in foreign countries [loc phr] S12

embi bad, naughty, wicked, ugly [adj Cl. 9] S25

emehlweni in, from, into eyes [loc; < **e-** + **amehlo** + **-eni**] S14

eMelika to, from, in America [loc; < **iMelika**] S16

emenywa (s)he is invited [pres, partic] S27

emfuleni to, from, in(to) a river [loc; < **umfula**] S16

eMgungundlovu to, from, in Pietermaritzburg (city; capital of KwaZulu-Natal Province) [loc; < **uMgungundlovu**] S13

emgwaqeni to, from, in, on the street [loc; var **emgwaqweni**; < **umgwaqo**] S17

emgwaqweni to, from, in, on the street [loc; var **emgwaqeni**; < **umgwaqo**] S09

emhlabeni to, from, in, on the world or earth [loc; < **umhlaba**] S02

emi- [adj conc Cl. 4; < **a-** rel marker + **imi-** NP] S05

emide long, lengthy [adj Cl. 4] S20

emigwaqweni to, from, in, on the streets [loc; < **imigwaqo**] S09

emihlanu five [adj Cl. 4] S05

emihle good, pretty [adj Cl. 4] S05

emikhakheni in directions or fields (as of study, knowledge) [loc; < **imikhakha**] S19

emile (s)he is standing up [stative, partic] S20

emine four [adj Cl. 4] S09

emini at midday, at noon; during the day [loc; < **imini**; one of the exceptions that does not take a locative suffix] S14

eminyakeni in years, during years [loc; < **iminyaka**] S09

eminye other, some [adj Cl. 4] S08

emithi that/which is in calf [rel Cl. 9] S21

emithonjeni to, from, in the sources [loc; < **emithombweni**; < **imithombo**; **mbw > nj**] S09

emkhakheni in the field (area) [loc; < **umkhakha**] S19

emkhankasweni to, from, in a scheme or program [loc; < **umkhankaso**] S12

emnyango from or in the doorway [loc; < **umnyango**; one of the exceptions that does not usually take a locative suffix] S17

emnyangweni in the department [loc; < **umnyango**] S12

emotweni to, from, in, on a car [loc; < **imoto**] S17

emoyeni in spirit, in soul, psychologically; to, from, in the air, wind, breath [loc; < **umoya**] S23

eMpangeni to, from, in Empangeni [loc; < **iMpangeni**] S09

emphakathini to, from, in the community [loc; < **umpha-kathi**] S14

empilweni to, from, in life or health [loc; < **impilo**] S17

emsebenzini to, from, in the job [loc; < **umsebenzi**] S19

eMseleni (place) [loc] S18

eMtata [pronounced **eMthatha**] to, from, in Umtata [loc; < **uMtata**] S17

emthethweni to, from, in the law [loc; < **umthetho**] S12

emtholampilo to, from, in, at a clinic [loc; < **umtholampilo** one of the exceptions that does not take a locative suffix] S25

emtholampilo wokuhlelwa kwemindeni to, from, in, at a family planning clinic [loc phr] S25

emuva behind, at the back, after [loc noun] S12

emva (contracted form of **emuva** used when followed by a complement) S12

emva koku- + VERB after VERBing [loc noun + link] S16

emva kokuba after [conj phr; followed by partic] S16

emva kokucwila after sinking [loc phr] S28

emva kokulunywa after being bitten [loc phr] S20

emva kokungaboni ngaso linye na- ... after not having seen eye to eye with ... (lit. after not seeing with one eye with) [loc phr] S27

emva kokuthi after [conj phr; followed by partic] S28

emva kokuzwa after hearing [loc phr] S16

emva kwa- behind, at the back of, after [loc noun + link] S12

emva kwalokho after that, thereafter, then [loc phr] S21

emva kwesikhathi after a time, after a while [loc phr] S17

emzimbeni to, from, in, on a body [loc; < **umzimba**] S20

eMzimkhulu to, from, in Umzimkhulu [loc; < **uMzimkhulu**] S16

emzini to, from, at, in the village [loc; < **umuzi**] S21

eMzumbe to, from, at Umzumbe [loc; < **uMzumbe**] S06

en- [adj conc Cl. 9; < **a-** rel marker + **in-** NP] S02

enabantwana who has children [rel Cl. 9] S27

enake who is concerned about, who is troubled by [past, partic, conjoint] S16

eNanda in Inanda [loc; < **iNanda**] S26

enawo that/which it has [rel Cl. 9] S12

encane small, little [adj Cl. 9] S20

encwadini in, from, on a book or letter [loc; < **incwadi**] S22

endala eldest (old) [adj Cl. 9] S02

endaweni to, from, at, in a place [loc; < **indawo**] S06

endaweni yangakithi to, from, in our area [loc phr] S06

endleleni on the way; to, from, in, on the road [loc; < **indlela**] S23

endlini to, from, at, in the house [loc; < **indlu**] S10

enegunya that/which has the authority [rel Cl. 9] S28

eneminyaka (s)he being aged (lit. (s)he having years) [assoc cop, pres, partic] S09

eneminyaka one who is aged (has years) [rel pron Cl. 9] S16

enenhlonipho (s)he has respect [assoc cop, pres, partic] S22

enepulazi where the farm is (lit. that/which has the farm) [rel Cl. 9] S27

eNewlands East in Newlands East [loc; < **iNewlands East**] S02

engabizi that/which does not cost, that/which does not call [rel Cl. 9] S28

engafuni (s)he does not want [pres, partic] S16

engagcina that/which I in the end (or eventually) [rel 1 p sg] S27

engagcina ngikufundile that/which I had learnt in the end [ind rel of plain obj rel, 1 p sg] S27

engakajwayeleki that/which is not yet customary, normal [rel Cl. 9] S25

engakazalwa unborn, who has not yet been born [rel Cl. 9] S25

engama-Afrika African (lit. who are Africans, i.e. Black Africans) [rel Cl. 9] S18

engamashumi amabili nambili twenty-two (lit. two tens and two) [rel phr Cl. 4] S19

-engam-a lean over, overhang; preside over, administer [v-positional; var **-ongam-a**; **-angam-a**] S23

-engamel-a lean over (for), over-hang; preside over, administer [v-positional-appl; var **-onga-mel-a**; **-angamel-a**] S23

engangabazeki that/which is undoubted [rel Cl. 9] S24

engangena who can get into [rel Cl. 9] S23

engangikulo in which I was [ind rel of plain loc rel, 1 p sg; < **e-** rel pref + **ng-** I + **-a-** rem past + **-ngi-** I + **-ku-** loc pref + **-lo** abs pron Cl. 5] S17

enganginawo that/which I had [ind rel of associative cop rel] S17

engangingaphephela that/which I could take refuge [rel 1 p sg] S18

engangingaphephela kukho in which I could take refuge [ind rel of plain loc rel, 1 p sg] S18

engangingayenza that/which I could do (it) [ind rel of plain obj rel, 1 p sg] S23

engangisithola that/which I experienced (it) [ind rel of plain obj rel, 1 p sg] S09

engangiwuhambele that/which I had attended (it) [ind rel of plain obj rel, 1 p sg] S17

engangizikhethele sona that/ which I had chosen for myself [ind rel of plain obj rel, 1 p sg] S18

engangizimisele that/which I had prepared myself for, which I was determined to [ind rel of plain obj rel, 1 p sg] S18

engangizimisele ngokuyenza that I had prepared myself to do (it) [ind rel of plain adv rel, 1 p sg] S18

-enganyelw-a be presided over, be run, be administered; be over-hung [v-positional-appl-pass; < **-engamel-w-a**; m ... -w- > ny ... -w-]

enganyelwe that/which is run or administered by [rel Cl. 9] S23

engaphansi that/which are under [rel Cl. 4] S20

engaphansi kuka- that/which are under ... [rel phr Cl. 4] S23

engaphuma (s)he were to come out [pres, potential, partic] S26

engazama that/which could try [rel Cl. 9] S26

engazenyezi who does not make him- or herself miserable, allow him- or herself to get despondent [rel Cl. 9] S14

engazicelelanga (s)he did not plead for her- or himself [past, partic, neg] S26

engazicelelanga ukwehliselwa isigwebo (s)he did not plead for a reduced sentence [v phr] S26

engcono better [rel Cl. 9] S14

engcupheni in danger [loc; < **ingcuphe**] S23

engenandaba (s)he not caring, (s)he not bothered (lit. not having a matter) [assoc cop, pres, partic, neg] S16

engenziwa that can be done [rel Cl. 9] S08

engeyinhle that/which is not good [rel Cl. 9; < **ingeyinhle**] S23

-engez-a add to, increase, supplement [v.t.] S16

engihamba I who am walking [rel 1 p sg] S14

engikutholile what I have found (it) [ind rel of plain obj rel, 1 p sg] S23

engilithembile in which I have faith, that/which I trust (it) [ind rel of plain obj rel, 1 p sg] S21

engingalithola that/which I could find (it) [ind rel of plain obj rel, 1 p sg] S23

engiyithola that/which I get (it) [ind rel of plain obj rel, 1 p sg] S24

engizibona that/which I see (them) [ind rel of plain obj rel, 1 p sg] S14

engoLwesine that/which is on Thursday [rel Cl. 9] S11

engompetha who were the finalists [rel Cl. 9] S11

engondlayo who am the bread-winner (lit. who raises, who nourishes) [rel 1 p sg] S24

engozini in danger [loc; < **ingozi**] S20

engqondweni in mind [loc; < **ingqondo**] S18

engu- that/which are; when followed by a number, this indicates 'such-and-such a number of them' [introduces a rel based on ident cop]

engu-10 10 [rel Cl. 4] S09

engu-13 thirteen [rel Cl. 4] S27

engu-21 21 [rel Cl. 4] S19

engu-24 24 [rel Cl. 4] S16

engu-25 25 [rel Cl. 4] S01

engu-506 506 [rel Cl. 4] S26

engu-9 9 [rel Cl. 4] S09

enguSipho who is Sipho [ident cop, pres, partic] S26

engxoxweni in an interview, in a conversation [loc; < **ingxoxo**] S26

enhla higher up, upstairs, upcountry [loc noun] S12

enhlabathini on the soil [loc; < **inhlabathi**] S27

enhlangano of an organization or party [poss Cl. 6] S06

enhlanganweni to, from, in the society or organization [loc; < **inhlangano**] S14

enhle good [adj Cl. 9] S05

enhlobonhlobo of various kinds [poss Cl. 6] S12

enikwe (s)he has been given [past, partic, conjoint] S26

eningi a lot, much [adj Cl. 9] S10

eNingizimu Afrika to, from, in South Africa [loc; < **iNingizimu Afrika**] S07, S09

enjani? what kind of? [rel Cl. 9] S23

enkantini to, from, at, in the cafeteria [loc; < **inkantini**; one of the exceptions that does not take a locative suffix] S14

enkingeni to, from, in(to) a problem [loc; < **inkinga**] S23

enkulu the large one, large, big [adj Cl. 9] S15

eNkume to, from, in Nkume [loc; < **iNkume**] S21

enkundleni in the incident, in the situation [loc; < **inkundla**] S17

enodlame (s)he is violent (lit. (s)he has violence [assoc cop, pres, partic] S16

e-North West in the North West (Province) [loc; < **i-North West**] S20

e-Northern Province to, from, in Northern Province [loc; < **i-Northern Province**] S14

enovalo (s)he having fear [assoc cop, pres, partic] S23

entsheni to, from, among the youth or young people [loc; < **intsha**] S18

eNtuzuma to, from, in Ntuzuma [loc; < **iNtuzuma**] S16

-enu [< **-inu** your [abs pron 2 p pl, used in possessives]] S03

enyakatho to, from, in the north [loc; < **inyakatho**] S18

enyakatho na- ... (to or in the) north of ... [loc phr] S18

enyangeni in, from the month [loc; < **inyanga**] S28

enyanyekayo objectionable, deplorable [rel Cl. 9] S25

enye another, the other, some, one, a certain [adj Cl. 9] S15

enye inhlamvu the other testicle [adj phr Cl. 9] S15

-enyel-a bec dissatisfied, bec displeased, have one's feelings hurt [v.i.] S14

-enyez-a dissatisfy, displease, hurt the feelings of [v-caus; < **-enyel-** + **-Y-**; l + **-Y-** > z] S14

-enyuk-a go up, rise, ascend [v.t.; var **-nyuk-a**] S03

-enz-a make, do, act, perform [v.t.] S01

-enz-a isiqiniseko make sure [v.phr] S18

-enzek-a occur, happen, take place, be feasible [v-neut] S04

enzeke they should happen, occur [subjunc] S04

-enzel-a do for, make for [v-appl] S06

-enzelw-a be made for, be done for [v-pass] S23

-enziw-a be done, be made [v-pass] S05

ephaketheni from, in(to) the pocket [loc; < **iphakethe**] S28

ePhalamende to, from, in, at Parliament [loc; < **iphala-mende**] S25

ePhayindane to, from in Pinetown [loc; < **iPhayindane**] S12

ephepheni to, from, in, on the paper [loc; < **iphepha**] S13

ephephile that/which is safe [rel Cl. 9] S25

ephethwe (s)he suffers from [stative, partic] S20

ephile that/which is in health [rel Cl. 9] S15

ephile kahle that/which is healthy [rel phr Cl. 9] S15

ePhoneficiency College at the Phoneficiency College [loc] S14

-ephul-a break [v.t.; var **-aphul-a, -phul-a**] S10

ephumelele who succeeded [rel Cl. 9] S19

ePietermaritzburg to, from, in Pietermaritzburg [loc] S16

ePM Burg to, from, in Pieter-maritzburg (cf. above) [loc] S13

ePoint Road in Point Road [loc] S09

e-Potgietersrus to, from, in Potgietersrus [loc] S14

epulazini to, from, at, on a farm [loc; < **ipulazi**] S27

-eq-a exceed, jump (across), skip (over); transgress (a law); cross (a boundary) [v.t.] S16

eqala that/which begins [rel Cl. 9] S11

eqhamuka that/which come from [rel Cl. 4] S12

eqhaqhazela (s)he is shivering, trembling [pres, partic] S23

eqhuba that/which continue with, that/which carry on [rel Cl. 4] S25

erenki to, from, at the rank or stand [loc; < **irenki**; one of the exceptions that does not take a locative suffix] S17

-esab-a fear, be afraid (of) [v.i. & t.; var **-sab-a**] S17

esaba (s)he is afraid [pres, partic; two analyses are possible: < Ø-SC Cl. 1 + **-esab-a** verb OR < **e-**SC Cl. 1 + **-sab-a** verb (**-sab-a** and **-esab-a** are variants)] S27

-esabel-a ukuthi be afraid that, fear that S23

-esabis-a scare, make afraid [v-caus; var **-sabis-a**] S23

esadicileka that/which collapsed, got thrown down [rel Cl. 7] S17

esakhula (s)he was (lit. is) still growing up [pres, partic, persistive; < **e-** SC 1 + **-sa-** still + **khula**] S14

esangweni to, from, at the gate [loc; < **isango**] S14

esaseRobben Island that (s)he was on Robben Island (island off Cape Town that has been used as a penitentiary or place for lepers over the centuries. Infamous as a prison for political prisoners during the apartheid era.) [loc cop, pres, partic, persistive] S17

esasidinga that/which required [rel Cl. 7] S27

esasincintisana nabo with whom we were in competition [ind rel of plain adv rel, 1 p pl] S27

esebenza (s)he works [pres, partic] S19

esebenza that/which works [rel Cl. 9] S27

esebenzela (s)he is working for [pres, partic] S21

esedlule that/which has passed [rel Cl. 7; var **esidlule**] S04

ese-Edendale that/which is in Edendale [rel Cl. 9] S13

esegwetshiwe after (s)he had been sentenced [stative, partic, disjoint, exclusive] S26

esegwetshwa as (s)he is being sentenced [pres, partic, exclusive] S26

esejele while (s)he is in jail [loc cop, pres, partic] S26

esejwayelekile usual, customary, normal [rel Cl. 7] S23

-esek-a sponsor, support [v.t.; var **-sek-a**] S11

esekhaya (s)he is at home [loc cop, pres, partic] S14

esememezela (s)he is now announcing [pres, partic, exclusive; < **e-** SC + **-s-** already, now + **-e-** SC + **-memezela**] S18

esemkhankasweni that/which is involved in a scheme or program (lit. that is in a scheme) [loc cop, pres, partic] S12

eseneminyaka (s)he is now ... years old (lit. she now has years) [assoc cop, pres, partic, exclusive] S14

eseneminyaka eyishumi (s)he was ten years old (lit. (s)he already has ten years) [loc cop phr] S14

esengizibalile that/which I have already enumerated [ind rel of plain obj rel, 1 p sg] S18

esenkosi that of a chief [poss pron Cl. 7; refers to **isifunda**] S06

esenyakatho that/which is to the north [rel Cl. 9] S18

esenza that/which makes or causes [rel Cl. 7] S23

eseqhubeka (s)he now continues [pres, exclusive, partic] S13

esesichazela (s)he now explains to us [pres, partic, exclusive] S27

esesikoleni that/which is at or in school [rel Cl. 9] S13

esesuliwe they then being wiped off or removed [past, partic, disjoint, exclusive] S28

esethembisa (s)he now promises [pres, exclusive, partic] S13

esetshenziswayo that/which are used [rel Cl. 4] S20

esewadlala (s)he is playing them [pres, partic, exclusive] S14

eseyibonile (s)he had already seen it [past, partic, disjoint, exclusive] S27

eseyingozi (s)he still being a danger [ident cop, pres, partic, persistive] S26

esezakhiwe that/which have already been built [rel Cl. 8] S24

esezibaliwe that/which have already been enumerated [rel Cl. 10] S20

esezibhubhise that/which have already wiped out [rel Cl. 8] S20

esezidayisela (s)he is already selling for herself [pres, partic, exclusive] S24

esezike zaqoqwa that/which were already once collected [rel phr Cl. 10] S06

eseziqala that/which are already beginning [rel Cl. 8] S08

eshaywe that/which has been beaten [rel Cl. 9] S01

eshisiwe that/which has been burnt [rel Cl. 9] S28

esho (s)he being of the opinion, (s)he states [pres, partic] S05

eshone (s)he died [past tense, participial aspect, conjoint] S02

eShowe to, from, in Eshowe [loc] S21

esi- [adj conc Cl. 7; < **a-** rel marker + **isi-** NP] S04

esi- that, which, who [rel conc Cl. 7; < **a-** rel marker + **si-** SC] S08

esi- that we, which we, whom we [rel conc 1 p pl; < **a-** rel marker + **si-** SC] S13

esibhakabhakeni in, from the sky [loc; < **isibhakabhaka**] S18

esibindini to, from, in liver [loc;

< isibindi] S20

esibizwa that/which is called [rel Cl. 7] S20

esibizwa ngokuthi yi- that/which is called ... [rel phr Cl. 7] S20

esibona that/which we see, that/which we are of the opinion [ind rel of plain obj rel, 1 p pl] S13

esibucayi unpleasant, uncomfortable [rel Cl. 7] S18

esichotho of hail [poss Cl. 6] S17

ESIDE LONG [ADJ CL. 7] S23

esidlule that/which has passed [rel Cl. 7; var esedlule] S18

esifana that/which is like, that/which resembles [rel Cl. 7] S06

esifisa that which we wish [ind rel of plain obj rel, 1 p pl] S21

esifundazweni in the province [loc; < isifundazwe] S24

esifundeni in the province [loc; < isifunda] S09

esihlala that/which keeps on, that/which continually [rel Cl. 7] S20

esihle good [adj Cl. 7] S04

esijwayelekile customary, usual, normal [rel Cl. 7] S13

esikayise that of his father [poss pron Cl. 7] S06

esikhathi of time [poss Cl. 6] S04

esikhathini in (the) time [loc; < isikhathi] S04

esikhulu big, large, great [adj Cl. 7] S11

esikhumulweni port, harbor, depot [loc; < isikhumulo] S18

esikhumulweni sezindiza to, from, at the airport [loc phr] S18

esikhundleni in the place, to, from, in the position [loc; < isikhundla] S03

esikhundleni sa- in place of, instead of [loc phrase] S03

esikoleni to, from, at, in school [loc; < isikole] S13

eSiloam School to, from, at, in Siloam School [loc] S14

esimuncu unpleasant, nasty, unhappy [rel Cl. 7] S28

esimweni to, from, at the status [loc; < isimo status] S13

esinamandla a fierce one [rel Cl. 7] S21

esincane little, small [adj Cl. 7] S23

esingezansi pelvic region (euph; lit. that which is below) [rel Cl. 7, refers to isiqu root, basis, bottom end] S20

esingiphungulele that/which now reduces for me [rel Cl. 9] S27

esingu-60 kuya ku-65km/h of 60 to 65 km/h (lit. that is 60 ...) [rel phr Cl. 7] S17

esinguSipho who is Sipho [rel Cl. 7] S26

esiningi a lot [adj Cl. 7] S16

esinye some, other, certain, one [adj Cl. 7] S16

esinzima difficult, hard, heavy [rel

Cl. 7] S28

esiqinile firm, sturdy [rel Cl. 7] S10

esishaya they hitting us [pres, partic] S09

esisheshayo quick, speedy [rel Cl. 7] S28

esisodwa one [rel Cl. 7] S11

esiteshini to, from, at the station [loc] {Eng *station*} S09

esiteshini samaphoyisa to, from, at, in the police station [loc phr; < isiteshi samaphoyisa] S09

esithi that/which goes, that/which says [rel Cl. 7] S08

esitimeleni to, from, in, in front of a train [loc; < isitimela] S16

esitokisini in a prison cell [loc; < isitokisi] S23

esitolo in the shop [loc; < isitolo; one of the exceptions that does not take a locative suffix] S28

esivela that/which comes from [rel Cl. 7] S14

esivumelwaneni to, from, at, in an agreement [loc; < isivume-lwana] S16

eSiyabonga Crafts Centre to, from, at the Siyabonga Crafts Center [loc] S24

esiyimbangela that/which is the cause [rel Cl. 7] S20

esizama that/which we try [rel 1 p pl] S16

esizama ukuyigwema that/which we try to avoid [ind rel of plain obj rel, 1 p pl] S16

esizweni in, from, the nation, among the people [loc; < isizwe] S25

esobunxele left-hand one [poss pron Cl. 7; refers to isandla hand] S15

esokudla right-hand one [poss pron Cl. 7; refers to isandla hand] S15

e-South Africa to, from, in South Africa [loc] S16

ethandaza (s)he is praying [pres, partic] S23

ethathe it, (s)he took [past, partic, conjoint] S10

eThekwini in Durban (place; large harbor city) [loc; < ethekwini place of the harbor; < itheku harbor] S09

-ethemb-a hope, trust [v.t.; var -themb-a] S09

-ethembis-a promise [v-caus; var -thembis-a] S09

ethi (s)he saying, (s)he says [pres, partic] S13

ethile certain, particular [rel Cl. 4 & 9] S12, S06

ethithiza (s)he is bumbling [pres, partic] S05

ethola (s)he gets, acquires [pres, partic] S27

-ethu [< -ithu our [abs pron 1 p pl, used in possessives]] S03

ethu our [poss Cl. 6] S25

-ethuk-a get a fright [v.i.; var -thuk-a] S17

-ethul-a present (for information) [v.t.] S19

ethumbe (s)he has hijacked [past, partic, conjoint] S16

eThuthukani Outreach Centre to the Thuthukani ... [loc] S09

e-University of South Africa (UNISA) at the University ... [loc] S14

ewakhela (s)he is building for it [pres, partic] S21

exakayo that causes difficulties [rel Cl. 9] S13

-exway-a be on the alert, be cautious, be wary [v.i.; var **-xway-a**] S23

-exwayis-a warn, caution, alert, put on guard [v-caus; var **-xwayis-a**] S23

eyabesilisa [poss pron Cl. 4] S19

eyabonogada that of or for guards [poss pron Cl. 9] S13

eyakho yours [poss pron Cl. 9] S08

eyamabhanoyi that of airplanes [poss pron Cl. 9] S18

eyanele that/which is sufficient, which is enough [rel Cl. 9] S09

eyangenza that/which made me [rel Cl. 9] S27

eyashaqisa that/which shocked [rel Cl. 9] S21

eyayandulele that/which preceded [rel Cl. 9] S17

eyayiphahlwe that/which was surrounded [rel Cl. 9] S17

eyayiphakathi kwakhe that/which was between him or her [rel phr Cl. 9] S27

eyayiphathelene that/which concerned [rel Cl. 9] S27

eyedlule that/which have passed [rel Cl. 4] S09

eyejwayelekile usual, normal, regular, customary [rel Cl. 9] S09

eyindida puzzling, that/which are a puzzle, strange [rel Cl. 4] S14

eyingozi dangerous (lit. which is a danger) [rel Cl. 9] S20

eyiphoyisa who is a policeman [rel Cl. 9] S16

eyi-Principal Telecommunications Operator (s)he being principal ... [ident cop, pres, partic] S14

eyishumi ten (adj) [rel Cl. 4] S14

eyisihlanu five (adj) [rel Cl. 4] S20

eyisipho that/which is a gift [rel Cl. 9] S14

eyisishiyagalombili eight (adj) [rel Cl. 4] S09

eyisithupha six (adj) [rel Cl. 4] S14

eyizinkulungwane ngezinkulungwane thousands upon thousands [rel phr Cl. 9] S10

eyokugibela ibhanoyi that of air travel [poss pron Cl. 9] S18

ez- that, which, who [rel conc Cl. 8 & 10; < **a-** rel marker + **zi-** SC] S17, S08

ezabaMhlophe those of the Whites [poss pron Cl. 10] S16

ezabelweni in the media [loc; < **izabelo**] S21

ezahlukahlukene different, various [rel Cl. 10] S28

ezahlukene various, different [rel Cl. 10] S08

ezakhele who live at or in, who have become resident; which are situated in [rel Cl. 10] S11, S27

ezalwa (s)he was (lit. is) born [pres, partic] S14

ezamabhizinisi business affairs [poss pron Cl. 10] S24

ezamahlathi forestry [poss pron Cl. 10] S11

ezamaholo salary or wage matters [poss pron Cl. 10] S27

ezamanzi water affairs [poss pron Cl. 10] S11

ezansi low, on the coast, down-country, downstairs [loc; < **izansi**] S20

ezase zinesikhathi who already had time [rel phr Cl. 8] S23

ezase zinesikhathi zivalelwe who had already been locked up for some time [rel phr Cl. 8] S23

ezazidlubhe who were smartly dressed, or wearing their best [rel Cl. 8] S17

ezazikubeka that/which put it [rel Cl. 10] S25

ezazingaphansi that/which were under [loc cop, rem past pres] S18

ezaziwela that/which were falling onto, into [rem past pres] S17

ezehlukene different, various [rel Cl. 10] S20

eze-jazz jazz matters [poss pron Cl. 10] S14

ezemfundo educational affairs [poss pron Cl. 10] S13

ezempilo health matters [poss pron Cl. 10] S14

ezengqondo matters of the mind, psychology, psychiatry [poss pron Cl. 10] S26

ezenhlalakahle social welfare [poss pron Cl. 10; < **izindaba zenhlalakahle**] S09

ezenza that/which make [rel Cl. 8 & 10] S28, S09

ezenzekayo that/which occur [rel Cl. 10] S13

ezenziwe that/which have been made [rel Cl. 10] S24

ezepolitiki politics, political matters [poss pron Cl. 10] S25

ezethu ours [poss pron Cl. 10] S08

eze-turner those (studies) of a turner [poss pron Cl. 8] S19

ezi- that, which, who [rel conc Cl. 8 & 10; < **a-** rel marker + **zi-** SC] S08, S04

eziØ- [adj conc Cl. 8 or 10; < **a-** rel marker + **iziØ-** NP] S05, S12

Glossary

ezibangela that/which cause to [rel Cl. 8] S13

ezibeka that/which place [rel Cl. 10] S25

ezibiza who call themselves [rel Cl. 4] S23

ezibiza ngokuthi ng- who call themselves ... [rel phr Cl. 4] S23

ezibulale (s)he has committed suicide [past, partic, conjoint] S16

ezicathulweni to, from, in(to), on shoes [loc; < **izicathulo**] S07

ezifana such as, like, that/which resemble [rel Cl. 10] S19

ezifike that/which immediately [rel Cl. 8] S20

ezifuna that/which want, that/which require [rel Cl. 10] S27

ezifundweni in studies, in lessons [loc; < **izifundo**] S18

ezigcwele that/which abound [rel Cl. 8] S24

ezigebengu of criminals [poss Cl. 6] S09

ezihambayo that/which move [rel Cl. 10] S19

ezihambela that/which are traveling to [rel Cl. 10] S18

ezihambisana that/which go together [rel Cl. 8] S16

ezihlala who live [rel Cl. 10] S09

ezihlotsheni in families [loc; < **ezihlobweni**; < **e-** + **izihlobo** + **-eni**; **bw** > **tsh**] S09

ezikaSiyavuma Mfeka those of Siyavuma Mfeka [poss pron Cl. 8] S11

ezikhethekile particular [rel Cl. 10] S20

ezikhishwe that/which were brought out [rel Cl. 8] S20

ezikhubazekile disabled, handicapped [rel Cl. 10] S14

ezikoleni to, from, at, in schools [loc; < **izikole**] S05

ezikutholayo that/which they get [ind rel of plain obj rel, Cl. 10] S09

ezikweletini from, into debt(s) [loc; < **izikweleti**] S28

eziletha that/which bring [rel Cl. 10] S19

eziluhlaza green [rel Cl. 8] S24

ezim- [adj conc Cl. 10; occurs before stems starting in **b**; < **a-** rel marker + **izim-** NP] S10

ezimakethe in the markets [loc; < **izimakethe**] S19

ezimbalwa a few [rel Cl. 8] S27

ezimbili two [adj Cl. 10] S10

ezimbonini in the factories [loc; < **izimboni**] S03

ezimisele that/which it is ready, that/which it is prepared for [rel Cl. 9] S12

ezimisele ngokuzithatha which they were prepared to take on [ind rel of plain adv rel] S12

ezimnyama black [rel Cl. 10] S17

334

ezimotweni to, from, in, on cars [loc; < **izimoto**] S17

ezimpahla of goods [poss Cl. 6] S03

ezimpahleni in luggage [loc; < **izimpahla**] S20

ezimpilweni from, in, during lives [loc; < **izimpilo**] S08

ezin- [adj conc Cl. 8 or 10; < **a-** rel marker + **izin-** NP] S05, S09

ezinamazinga okushisa that/which have temperatures [rel phr Cl. 10] S20

ezincane small, little [adj Cl. 10] S12

ezindaweni to, from, at, in places [loc; < **izindawo**] S05

ezindizayo flying [rel Cl. 8] S20

ezindlini zangasese to, from, at, in toilets [loc phr; < **izindlu zangasese**] S23

ezindlini zokufundela to, from, in, into, at educational institutions [loc phr; < **izindlu zokufundela**] S13

ezine four [adj Cl. 10] S26

ezinemikhono with sleeves, that/which has sleeves [rel Cl. 10] S20

ezineminyaka who are aged (lit. who have years) [rel Cl. 10] S20

ezineminyaka engaphansi kweyisihlanu those younger than five (lit. those who have years that are under five) [rel phr Cl. 10] S20

ezingafanele that/which are not suitable [rel Cl. 10] S25

ezingagcina that/which could eventually [rel Cl. 8] S24

ezingagcini that/which do not end [rel Cl. 8] S08

ezingakhokheki that/which are unpayable [rel Cl. 8] S28

ezingama-boarding school that/which are boarding schools [rel Cl. 8] S23

ezingaphandle that/which are outside [rel Cl. 10] S20

ezingaphezu kuka-R1mln that/which are above R1m [rel phr Cl. 10] S10

ezingazange that/which they have never [rel Cl. 10] S09

ezingazange zikuthole mutual love that they have never found [ind rel of plain obj rel, Cl. 10] S09

ezingcolile that/which are dirty [rel Cl. 10] S09

ezingenamakhaya homeless (lit. who are not with homes) [rel Cl. 10] S09

ezingenamswakama that/which are not damp (lit. that do not have dampness or moisture) [rel Cl. 10] S20

ezingenayo incoming [rel Cl. 10] S14

ezingeni to, from, at, on a level or degree [loc; < **izinga**] S05

ezingenzeka that/which can happen [rel Cl. 10] S28

ezingutsheni in clothes [loc; < **ezingubweni** < e- + izingubo + -eni; bw > tsh] S09

ezingxenye in parts [loc; < izingxenye; one of the exceptions that does not take a locative suffix] S20

ezinhlanu five [adj Cl. 10] S10

ezinhle good, beautiful, pretty, handsome [adj Cl. 10] S23

eziningana rather many, quite a number [adj Cl. 8] S08

eziningi many, numerous [adj Cl. 8 or 10] S23, S14

ezinjenge-HIV such as HIV (lit. that are like HIV) [rel Cl. 8] S25

ezinkanjini to, from, at, in camps [loc; < **ezinkambwini**; < e- + izinkambu + -ini; mbw > nj] S23

ezinkantolo to, from, at, in the courts [loc; < izinkantolo; one of the exceptions that does not take a locative suffix] S10

ezinkulu large [adj Cl. 8; < ezin- + -khulu; n + kh > nk] S09

ezinkundleni to, from, in the playgrounds oryards [loc; < izinkundla] S13

ezintathu three [adj Cl. 10; < ezin- + -thathu; n + th > nt] S24

ezintweni to, from, in things [loc; < e- + izinto + -eni] S04

ezintweni okufanele uzenze in the things you have to do [loc phr] S04

ezinukayo smelly (lit. that smell) [rel Cl. 10] S09

ezinyathelweni in the steps [loc; < izinyathelo] S19

ezinye other(s), some [adj Cl. 8 or 10] S05, S17

eziphakathi kuka- (that/which are) between [rel phr Cl. 10] S20

eziphathelene that/which concern, that/which relate to, that/which go together with [rel Cl. 8 or 10] S16

eziphinde ziyisebenzisele nokuthiba indlala that/which they repeatedly use also to prevent hunger [ind rel of plain loc rel, Cl. 10] S09

eziphuma that which come(s) from [rel Cl. 10; refers to izindaba news, matters] S08

eziphuma ebhodweni loMhleli zishisa that which comes hot from the editor's pot (comparison of news items to ingredients being added to a pot au feu type stew) [rel phr Cl. 10] S08

eziphumayo outgoing [rel Cl. 10] S14

eziqhamuka that/which come(s) from [rel Cl. 10] S23

eziqhelile that/which are remote [rel Cl. 10] S20

eziqondene na- ... that/which concern ... [rel phr Cl. 10] S25

eziqondile accurate [rel Cl. 8] S25

ezisanda who (or that/which) have just [rel Cl. 10] S20

ezisemadolobheni that/which are in town, urban [rel Cl. 10] S16

ezisemakhaya that/which are in rural areas [rel Cl. 10] S24

ezisetshenziselwa that/which are used or employed for [rel Cl. 10] S19

ezisetshenziswa that/which are used [rel Cl. 10] S23

ezisihluphayo that/which bother us [rel Cl. 10] S09

ezisuke who/which/that happen to VERB, who/which/that just VERB [rel Cl. 8 or 10] S24, S28

ezitaladini to, from, in, on streets [loc; < izitaladi] S09

ezithathelana contagious [rel Cl. 8] S20

ezithathwa that/which are taken [rel Cl. 10] S20

ezithengisa that/which sell, which trade in [rel Cl. 10] S27

ezithengwa that/which are bought [rel Cl. 10] S10

ezithi that/which say, namely [rel Cl. 10] S23

ezithile certain [rel Cl. 10] S20

ezithinta that/which touch, handle, or affect [rel Cl. 8] S08

ezithunyelwa that/which are sent [rel Cl. 10] S28

ezitolo in shops, in stores [loc; < izitolo; one of the exceptions that does not take a locative suffix] S20

ezivalwa that/which are closed (down) [rel Cl. 10] S28

eziyingozi dangerous (ones) [rel Cl. 8 & 10] S20

eziyisibopho that/which are an obligation [rel Cl. 10] S04

eziyisipesheli that/which are special [rel Cl. 10] S10

eziyisithupha six [rel Cl. 10] S20

eziyizinkangala that/which are deserted [rel Cl. 10] S23

ezizenzayo that/which they make [ind rel of plain obj rel] S08

ezizwakala that/which are understandable [rel Cl. 10] S12

ezobambana that/which will take each other on, that/which will go into battle with each other [rel Cl. 9] S11

ezobambana ngezihluthu that/which will go head to head [rel phr Cl. 9] S11

ezobuLungiswa Correctional Services [poss pron Cl. 10; refers to izindaba] S10

ezobunjiniyela (those (studies) of) engineering [poss pron Cl. 8; refers to izifundo] S19

ezocansi sexual matters [poss pron Cl. 10 (refers to izindaba)] S23

ezokubhalela for writing in [poss pron Cl. 10] S13

ezokuhlelwa of planning matters [poss pron Cl. 10] S25

ezokuhlelwa kwemindeni family planning (matters) [poss pron phr Cl. 10] S25

ezokuphatha management or administrative affairs [poss pron Cl. 10] S14

ezokuphepha security matters [poss pron Cl. 10] S21

ezokuvakasha tourism affairs [poss pron Cl. 10] S12

ezokuXhumana noMphakathi Community Relations [poss pron phr Cl. 10] S14

ezokwazisa information affairs [poss pron Cl. 10] S25

ezokwelapha health sciences, those (studies) of healing [poss pron Cl. 8] S19

ezolimo agriculture, farming [poss pron Cl. 10] S27

ezomame things for the ladies, women's matters [poss pron Cl. 10] S08

ezomnotho financial affairs, finance, economy, Economics (as an academic discipline) [poss pron Cl. 10] S07

ezomthetho legal matters, Law (as an academic subject) [poss pron Cl. 10] S07

ezomunye those of another [poss pron Cl. 10] S16

ezotholakala that/which will be obtainable [rel Cl. 4] S12

ezwa (s)he hears [pres, partic] S23

ezweni to, from, in a country [loc; < **izwe**] S09

F

-f-a die; be ill, suffer; break (down) [v.i.] S05, S21

-fak-a place, put in, install [v.t.] S13

-fak-a umuntu amanzi emadolweni threaten or frighten someone (idiom; lit. put water on someone's knees) S28

-fakaz-a bear witness, give evidence, testify [v.i.] S26

-fakel-a place in or on, put in or on, install in, install for [v-appl] S21

-fakelw-a be placed in or on, be put in or on, be installed in [v-appl-pass] S21

-fakw-a be placed, be put in, be installed [v-pass] S10

-fan-a (na-) be similar (to), resemble, be like, be the same (as) [v phr] S06

-fanel-a bec suitable (for), bec fitting, bec appropriate (for, to) [v.inch; v.i. & t.] S19

-fanel-a must, should, ought, have to, be necessary [aux; v.inch] S04

-fel-a die in, die for, die because of [v-appl] S23

-fez-a finish, complete, fulfill, effect, accomplish [v.t.] S03

-fihl-a hide, bury (euph) [v.t.] S02

-fihlw-a be hidden, buried [v-pass] S02

-fik-a arrive (at), reach [v.i.] S03

-fik-e VERB first, VERB immediately [aux; followed by subjunctive] S20

-fikel-a befall, happen to [v-appl] S23

-fikelw-a experience (lit. have arrive to one) [v-appl-pass] S23

-fikis-a cause to arrive, bring [v-caus] S23

-fikisel-a bring to (lit. cause to arrive to) [v-caus-appl] S23

-file(yo) dead, broken (down) [rel stem] S05

-finyelel-a reach (a destination), arrive at [v.i.] S28

-fis-a desire, wish for [v.t.] S12

-fuful-a sweep away, carry off in a rush [v.t.] S22

-fufuz-a act passionately, act impetuously [v-caus; < **-fuful-** + **-Y-**; l + **-Y-** > z] S22

-fun-a want, look for, seek [v.t.] S05

-fun-a be about to, be on the point of [aux; followed by vn] S16

-fund-a learn, study; read [v.t.] S02

-fundel-a study or read in, or at, or for, or towards [v-appl] S05

-fundis-a teach [v-caus] S02

-funel-a look for for, seek out for [v-appl] S14

-fung-a swear, swear by, take an oath [v.i. & t.] S14

futhi again, in addition, also [adv] S03

G

-gad-a guard, be on guard, patrol [v.i. & t.] {Eng *guard*} S13

-gadulisan-a tackle [v-caus-recip] S11

-gang-a bec naughty, bec mischievous [v.inch] S27

-gcin-a keep, preserve, store [v.t.] S12

-gcin-a end, end up VERBing, eventually VERB; last VERB; VERB for the last time [v.i. & t.] S08

-gcizelel-a emphasize, stress [v.i. & t.] S09

-gcob-a grease, smear, rub with oil or ointment, lubricate [v.t.] S01

gcoba rub, smear [imper] S20

-gcobis-a grease [the causative suffix **-is-** is semantically empty here] S01

-gcotshisw-a be greased [v-caus-pass; < **-gcobis-w-a**; b ... **-w-** > tsh ... **-w-**] S01

-gcotshw-a be smeared, be greased, be rubbed with oil [v-pass; < **-gcobw-a**; bw > tshw] S20

-gculis-a satisfy [v.t.] S13

-gculisek-a bec satisfied [v-neut] S13

-gcwal-a bec full, be abundant, abound in [v.i., inch] S03

-gcwele be full (of), abound (in) [stative; < **-gcwal-** + **-i...e**] S05

-gez-a wash; develop (photos) [v.i. & t.] S17

-gibel-a ride, mount (as a horse), board, travel by [v.t.] S18

-gijim-a run [v.i.] S17

-gil-a perform [v.t.] S23

-gil-a umkhuba practice an evil S23

-godl-a hold back, reserve, withhold, suppress [v.t.] S05

-gqam-a be clear, be evident, stand out, be obvious [v.i.] S13

-gqok-a put on (clothes), wear [v.t.] S09

gqoka wear [imper] S20

-gqugquz-a prod, pierce, poke [v.t.] S12

-gqugquzel-a prod, nag, persuade, try to win over; coordinate [v-appl] S12

-gqugquzelw-a be prodded [v-appl-pass] S12

-greyth-a grate [v.t.] {Eng}R01

-greythiwe has been grated [v-pass-stative] S01

-greythw-a be grated [v-pass] S01

Groen (surname) {Afr} S10

-gubh-a celebrate, observe (a festival, occasion) [v.t.] S11

-gunyaz-a promote, force down [v.t.] S25

-guqubal-a bec cloudy or overcast [v.i.] S17

-guquguquk-a be changeable, keep altering, keep turning over [v-redup; < **-guquk-**] S20

-guquk-a change, alter; turn, turn over [v.i.] S20

-gweb-a pass judgment, decide a court case, sentence [v.t.] S26

-gwem-a avoid, evade [v.t.] S04

-gwetshw-a be decided (of a court case),be passed of judgment, be sentenced [v-pass; < **-gwebw-a**; **bw** > **tshw**] S26

-gxil-a stand firm, stand fast, be steadfast [v.i.] S04

H

-halalis-a congratulate, applaud [v.t.] S28

-halalisel-a congratulate, applaud [v-appl; the extension **-el-** is semantically empty here] S28

-hamb-a go, travel [v.i.] S09

-hamb-a ngezinyawo walk, go on foot [v phr] S09

-hambel-a attend, visit, travel towards, travel for [v-appl, inch] S11

-hambis-a cause to go, go with [v-caus] S16

-hambisan-a accompany each other, go with each other [v-caus-recip] S16

-hambisan-a na- ... go together with ..., accompany ..., go along with ... (i.e. agree with); accord with [v phr] S16

-hanjelw-a be attended [v-appl-pass; < **-hambelw-a**; **mb ... -w- > njw**] S11

-hlahl-a divide, distribute [v.t.] S13

-hlal-a sit (down); reside, live, stay [v.i., inch; irregular stative = **-hlezi** or **-hleli**] S05, S09

-hlal-a/-hlal-e continually VERB, keep on VERBing [aux; followed by partic] S20, S09

-hlangabez-a go out to meet or welcome an arrival [v.t.] S16

-hlangabezan-a (na-) come up against, compete, vie with one another, go out to meet one another [v-recip] S16

-hlangan-a meet, join [v.i.] S01

-hlanganis-a bring together, assemble; join, add up [v-caus] S17

-hlanganisw-a be mixed or joined [v-caus-pass] S01

-hlanganyel-a unite against, act together [v.i. & t.] S08

-hlanu five [adj stem] S05

-hlasel-a attack, invade [v.t.] S17

Hlatshwayo (surname) [n Cl. 1a] S19

-hlaz-a disgrace, dishonor, shame [v.t.] S23

-hle good, nice, lovely, pretty, beautiful, handsome [adj stem] S01

-hle beauty [noun stem; < **-hle** good, beautiful [adj stem]] S02

-hlek-a laugh (at) [v.i. & t.] S23

-hlel-a put in order, arrange [v.t.] S04

-hlelel-a arrange for, plan for, put in order for [v-appl] S25

-hlelelw-a be planned for, be arranged for [v-appl-pass] S25

-hlelisis-a put in good order, arrange thoroughly [v-intens] S04

-hlelw-a be arranged, be put in order, be planned [v-pass] S25

-hleng-a escort; assist, help [[v.t.] S17

Hlengiwe (female name) [n Cl. 1a] S26

-hlengw-a be escorted [v-pass]

S17

-hlezi sitting, seated [irregular stative form of **-hlal-a**] S05

hlobo type, sort, kind [< **uhlobo**] S27

-hlol-a examine, test, inspect [v.t.] S15

-hlolw-a be examined, inspected [v-pass] S23

-hlom-a take up arms, arm oneself [v.inch] S27

-hlomul-a reward, give a share (especially the meat of a game animal) [v.t.] S11

-hlomulw-a be rewarded [v-pass] S11

-hloniph-a respect, honor [v.t.; < noun stem **-hloni** shyness, shame + **-ph-** verbalizer] S14

-hloniphek-a bec respected [v-neut] S14

-hlos-a intend, aim at [v.t.] S24

-hlosw-a be intended, be aimed for [v-pass] S24

-hluk-a deviate, separate [v.i.] S07

-hlukan-a part from one another; differ from one another [v-recip; var **-ehlukan-a**, **-ahlukan-a**] S07

-hlukan-a na- part company with; differ from; get away from; give up [v phr] S14

-hlukanis-a separate, make a distinction between [v-recip-caus; **-ahlukanis-a** is a more common variant] S07

-hlukumez-a attack, assault, be violent, violate; shock, jolt, offend, annoy, harass [v.t.] S05

-hlukumezek-a get attacked, assaulted, violated, harassed, shocked, jolted, annoyed, offended [v-neut] S21

-hlukunyezw-a be attacked, assaulted, violated, shocked, jolted [v-pass; < **-hlukumez-w-**; m ... -w- > ny ... -w-] S05

-hlul-a defeat, conquer, overcome [v.t.; var **-ehlul-a**] S05

-hlulek-a be beaten, overcome, defeated, conquered; be unable, fail [v-neut; var **-ahlulek-a**, **-ehlulek-a**] S05

-hlulw-a be overcome, be defeated, be conquered [v-pass; var **-ehlulw-a**] S23

-hluph-a bother, disturb, cause problems or trouble [v.t.] S06

-hluphek-a suffer, be troubled, be afflicted, be in difficulties [v-neut] S25

-hlway-a spread, scatter [v.t.] S21

-hlwayel-a sow by scattering [v-appl; var **-hlwanyel-a**] S27

-hol-a drag, haul, pull along; lead, guide [v.t.] S07

-hol-a draw pay, earn [v.t.] S28

-holel-a drag towards; lead to; be responsible for, cause [v-appl] S26

-hox-a hide, withhold, withdraw [v.i.] S11

-hoxisw-a be withheld, be hidden [v-caus-pass] S21

I

i- it, he, she [SC Cl. 9] S01

i- they [SC Cl.4] S05

i- [enum conc Cl. 9] S05

-i [neg suff] S03

-i [irregular stative suff] S11

-i nominalizing suffix (often corresponds to English -er as in 'farmer, writer') [With few exceptions the nom suff **-i** derives agent nouns, which are generally personal, while the nom suff **-o** forms product or process nouns, always non-personal.] S02

iØ- [NP Cl. 5 & Cl. 9a] S01

-i...e [stative suff used in passive; also occurs with radicals ending in **al, an, am, ath**; coalescence takes place between the **a** and the **i**] S01, S04

i-AIDS [n Cl. 9a] S20

i-Americans the Americans (a gang) [n Cl. 9a] S09

i-ANC the ANC (African National Congress; originally a political organization fighting for the rights of Black South Africans; subsequently it was banned and became an underground liberation movement; it was unbanned in 1990 and won the first fully democratic election in SA in 1994, and is currently still in power.) [n Cl. 9a] S05

i-Annual Tax Return [n Cl. 9a; pl **ama-Annual Tax Returns**] {Eng} S10

ibaluleke it is important [past, conjoint] S06

ibalulekile it is important [past, disjoint] S19

ibamba deputy [n Cl. 5; < **-bamb-** undertake] S25

ibambisene it is cooperating [stative] S10

ibandakanya it involves [pres, conjoint] S19

ibandla assembly of men (for discussion, trial, etc.; these days may include women); congregation, church, denomination [n Cl. 5] S17

iBandla labe-Presbyterian Church of Southern Africa the

Presbyterian Church of ... [n phr Cl. 5] S17

ibanga standard, grade [n Cl. 5] S18

ibangela it causes (for) [pres, conjoint] S23

ibatholele it, (s)he finds for them [subjunc] S14

ibe they should be [copula, subjunc] S05

ibe mihle and they will be good [descr cop, inch, subjunc] S05

ibe mihle imiphumela and the results will be good [v phr] S05

ibe sobala so that it should be out in the open [loc cop, inch, subjunc] S07

ibenzima (that) it should be difficult or hard [descr cop, inch, subjunc] S09

iBhambayi (place) [n Cl. 5] S09

ibhange bank [n Cl. 5] {Afr} S10

ibhanoyi airplane [n Cl. 5] S16

ibhasi bus [n Cl. 5] {Eng} S16

ibhayisikili bicycle [n Cl. 5; var **ibhayisekili**] {Eng} S14

iBhekithemba (name of a football team) [n Cl. 9a; < **bheka** look at + **ithemba** hope] S11

ibhilidi building [n Cl. 5] {Eng} S16

ibhizinisi business, firm [n Cl. 5] {Eng} S10

ibhodlela bottle [n Cl. 5] {Eng/ Afr?} S09

ibhodwe pot [n Cl. 5] {Afr} S08

ibhola ball; football, soccer [n Cl. 5] {Eng} S11

ibhola lezinyawo football, soccer (lit. ball of feet) [n phr Cl. 5] S19

ibhuloho bridge [n Cl. 5] {Afr *brug*} S16

ibhulukwe pair of trousers, pants [n Cl. 5] {Afr *broek*} S20, S22

ibinezigameko it had repeated events [assoc cop, past pres; i-SC + -b- aux + -i- SC + -na- assoc pref+ **izigameko**] S08

ibingenye it was one [ident cop, past pres] S11

ibivame (s)he, they used to, were accustomed to [past past, conjoint] S18

iBochum (place) [n Cl. 5] S14

ibonakale it was visible [past, conjoint] S08

i-Boys U/11 Boys U(nder)/11 [n Cl. 9a] {Eng} S11

ibutho band, troop, regiment [n Cl. 5; < -buth- gather together, recruit] S09

ibuye it, (s)he again [aux] S14

icala crime, offence, felony; guilt, wrong, defect; court case; charge [n Cl. 5] S23

iCape Flats (area of Greater Cape Town to which the former apartheid government relocated Coloreds (people of mixed race), who had been removed by law from their homes which were considered to be in White areas. This area is now infamous for

crime, and gang warfare.) [n Cl. 5] S09

i-castor sugar baker's sugar [n Cl. 9a] S01

iChildline Childline (call center for crisis counseling for or about children) [n Cl. 9a] S09

i-credit card [n Cl. 9a] S28

idlule it has passed [past, disjoint] S08

idlwengule (s)he should rape [subjunc] S23

idlwenguliwe (s)he has been raped [past, disjoint] S23

i-dollar [n Cl. 9a; pl **ama-dollar** Cl. 6] {Eng} S28

idolo knee [n Cl. 5] S07

idolobha town [n Cl. 5] {Afr *dorp*} S17, S09

idudulane will come against (lit. it will mutually fend off an attack) [subjunc] S11

i-Edendale (town) [n Cl. 5] S13

i-electrical engineering [n Cl. 9a] {Eng} S19

i-electronics [n Cl. 9a] {Eng} S19

i-Entuthukweni (name of a football team) [n Cl. 9a] S11

i-Europe Europe [n Cl. 5] {Eng} S16

i-exercise exercise book [n Cl. 9a; pl **ama-exercise**] S13

ifana they resemble, they are like, they are similar [pres, conjoint] S19

ifanele it is proper, it is fitting [stative] S09

ifaqafaqa glue [n Cl. 9a; neutral] S09

ifasitela window [n Cl. 5] {Afr *venster*} S17, S13

ifemu firm [n Cl. 5] {Eng} S12

ifile it or (s)he is dead, it is broken (down) [stative] S05

i-forensic criminologist [n Cl. 9a; pl **ama-forensic criminologist**] S23

i-frosting [n Cl. 9a] {American English (South African English has 'icing')} S01

ifu cloud [n Cl. 5; pl **amafu** Cl. 6] S02

iFunimfundo [n Cl. 5; < -fun- look for, want + imfundo education, learning] [R02

igadulisane it will tackle [subjunc] S11

igama name [n Cl. 5] S05

igazi blood [n Cl. 5] S20

igceke open ground [n Cl. 5] S08

igcine (s)he should end up [subjunc] S18

igciwane particle, bit of dust floating in air; germ, virus, microbe [n Cl. 5] S23

igcotshwe it has been spread, greased, smeared [past, conjoint] S20

igcwele it is full (of), it is complete [stative] S14

i-Germany [n Cl. 5; normally **iJalimani**] {Eng} S16

i-Girls U/14 Boys U(nder)/14 [n Cl. 9a] {Eng} S11

i-glue glue [n Cl. 9a] {Eng} S09

iGoli Johannesburg (largest city in South Africa) [n Cl. 5] S14

igolide gold [n Cl. 5] {Eng} S11

i-gospel music [n Cl. 9a] {Eng} S22

igumbi room [n Cl. 5] S17

igunya authority [n Cl. 5] S28

i-hectare [Cl. 9a; pl **ama-hectare**] S27

ihhotela hotel [n Cl. 5] {Eng or Afr *hotel*} S17

ihhovisi office, bureau [n Cl. 5] {Eng} S14

i-HIV [n Cl. 9a] {Eng} S16

ihlathi forest [n Cl. 5] S11

ihlazo disgrace, dishonor, shame [n Cl. 5; < -hlaz- disgrace, dishonor, shame] S23

ihlo eye [n Cl. 5; var **iso**; p l **amehlo** Cl. 6] S14

ihlombe shoulder [n Cl. 5] S16

ihloniphekile (s)he is respected, (s)he is respectable [stative] S14

ihlulekile it has been unable [stative] S05

iholo wage, salary [n Cl. 5; var **umholo** Cl. 3; < -hol- draw pay, earn] S28

i-icing sugar confectioner's sugar [n Cl. 9a] {Eng} S01

i-IFP IFP (Inkatha Freedom Party [n Cl. 9a] S05

iin- [NP Cl. 10 (common in speech, but less so in writing); var of **izin-**] S11

iinhlobonhlobo various kinds or types [n Cl. 10; reduplicated form of **i(z)inhlobo**] S12

i-instrumentation [n Cl. 9a] {Eng} S19

ijaji judge [n Cl. 5] {Eng} S26

iJalimani Germany [n Cl. 5] {Eng} S07

iJaphani Japan [n Cl. 5] {Eng} S07

i-jazz [n Cl. 9a] {Eng} S14

ijele jail, prison [n Cl. 5] {Eng} S23

ijezi jersey [n Cl. 5] {Eng} S11

ijwayelekile it is normal, usual, common [stative] S23

ikakhulu especially, particularly [adv; < **kakhulu**] S06

ikakhulukazi especially, particularly [adv; alternative to **ikakhulu**] S09

ikamu (military) camp [n Cl. 5] S16

ikamu lamaphoyisa police station [n phr Cl. 5] S16

iKapa Cape Town [n Cl. 5] {Afr *Kaap*}

ike they once VERB [aux, past, conjoint] S26

ikhambi remedy; medicinal herb or concoction used as a remedy [n Cl. 5] S24, S28

ikhanda head [n Cl. 5] S10

ikhasi peel, shell, rind [n Cl. 5] S01

ikhaya home [n Cl. 5] S05

ikheli address [n Cl. 5] {Eng *care of*} S05

ikhemisi pharmacy [n Cl. 5] {Eng *chemist*} S17

ikhishi kitchen [n Cl. 5; back-formation from loc **ekhishini**; < Eng *kitchen*] S19

ikhokho soccer boot [n Cl. 5] S11

ikhombisa it, (s)he shows [pres, conjoint] S18

ikhono skill, dexterity, ability [n Cl. 5] S19

iKhrestu Christian [n Cl. 5; var **umKhrestu** Cl. 1; pl for both singulars **amaKhrestu**] S25

ikhulu hundred (n) [n Cl. 5] S17

ikhwalithi (good) quality [n Cl. 9a] S27

ikhwapha armpit [n Cl. 5] S06

ikilasi class, classroom [n Cl. 5] {Eng *class* or Afr *klas*} S13

ikolishi college [n Cl. 5; var **ikholishi, ikholiji**] S19

ikusasa tomorrow (n), the future [n Cl. 5; < **kusasa** tomorrow [adv]] S04

ikwakhe a home, a place of his or her own [n Cl. 5; < **kwakhe** at his or her place] S22

iKwaShaka the KwaShaka (name of a football team) [n Cl. 9a; < **KwaShaka** the kingdom of Shaka] S11

i-KZN Nature Conservation Service (KZN = KwaZulu-Natal) [n Cl. 9a] S24

ilaka rage [n Cl. 5; **ulaka** Cl. 11 is more usual] S26

iLamontville (place) [n Cl. 5] S11

ilandelana successive (lit. they following one other) [pres, partic] S11

ilanga sun, day [n Cl. 5] S17

-ile [positive past tense suffix for disjoint form] S02

-ile [stative suff, pos & neg] S05

i-Life Line (call center for crisis counseling) [n Cl. 9a] S23

i-lift lift, ride [n Cl. 9a; pl **ama-lift(s)**] {Eng} S23

ilikhulu there are a hundred [ident cop, pres] S17

iliqhamukisa (s)he comes from it [pres, conjoint] S16

ilunga member [n Cl. 5; var **ilungu**] S09

ilungelo right [n Cl. 5; < **-lungel-a** be right for] S14

ilungu member [n Cl. 5; var **ilunga**] S06

im- [NP Cl. 4; occurs before vowels] S10

im- [NP Cl. 9; occurs before stems starting in **b, bh, p, ph, f**] S03

-im-a stand (up); wait; stop [v.i., inch; var of **-m-a** used when preceded by **a**] S17

iMakatini (pronounced **iMaka-thini**; place) [n Cl. 5] S27

imakethe market [n Cl. 9a; pl **izimakethe** Cl. 10a] {Eng} S19

imali money [n Cl. 9a; pl **izimali** Cl. 10a] S09

-imali financial, commercial [poss base; < **imali** money] S10

iManyuswa Manyuswa (name of a football team) [n Cl. 9a] S11

imbangela cause [n Cl. 9; < **-bangel-** cause for] S16

imbewu seed(s) [n Cl. 9; neutral] S27

imboni factory, industry, business [n Cl. 9] S03

imbozwe they are covered [past, conjoint] S09

iMdlwembe Gang Mdlwembe Gang [n Cl. 9a; < **umdlwembe** undisciplined person; wild, uncontrolled animal [n Cl. 1 or 3; pl **imidlwembe**] S09

imehluko differences, distinctions [n Cl. 4; < **-ehluk-** differ; sg **umehluko**] S10

imele so that it can stand for or represent [subjunctive] S05

iMelika America [n Cl. 5] {Eng} S07

imenenja manager [n Cl. 9a; pl **izimenenja** Cl. 10a] {Eng} S24

imenze it has made him or her [past, partic, conjoint] S27

imeya mayor [n Cl. 9a; pl **izimeya** Cl. 10a] {Eng} S11

imfikisela it (the matter) brings him [pres, conjoint] S23

imfiva fever [n Cl. 9] {Eng} S20

imfolomane foreman [n Cl. 9; pl 10a] {Eng *foreman* or Afr *voorman*} S27

imfundo education [n Cl. 9; < **-fund-** study, learn, read] S05

imi- [NP Cl. 4] S01

imi they stand [stative] S11

imibiko reports, announcements [n Cl. 4; sg **u m b i k o**; < **- b i k - a** report] S26

imibuzo questions [n Cl. 4; sg **umbuzo**; < **-buz-** ask] S14

imidlalo games, sports [n Cl. 4; sg **umdlalo**; < **-dlal-** play] S19

imigulukudu hardened criminals, habitual criminals [n Cl. 4; sg **umgulukudu** Cl. 1 or 3] S23

imigwaqo roads, streets [n Cl. 4; sg **umgwaqo**] S09

imikhakha directions, fields [n Cl. 4; sg **umkhakha**] S19

imikhiqizo surpluses, production (normally refers to mass production) [n Cl. 4; sg **umkhiqizo** surplus, produce; < **-khiqiz-** produce in abundance, turn out in large quantities, produce a surplus] S12

imikhono sleeves [n Cl. 4; sg **umkhono**] S20

imiklomelo prizes, awards, rewards [n Cl. 4; sg **umklo-**

melo; < **-klomel-** reward, give a prize or bonus] S11

imingcele borders [n Cl. 4; sg **umngcele**] S10

imini day, daytime [n Cl. 9; no pl] S14

iminyaka years [n Cl. 4; sg **unyaka** Cl. 3a] S05

imiphefumulo lives; breaths [n Cl. 4; sg **u m p h e f u m u l o**; < **-phefumul-** breathe] S08

imiphumela results [n Cl. 4; sg **umphumela**; < **-phumel-** come out for + **-a** nom suff] S05

i m i s e b e n z i jobs [n Cl. 4; sg **umsebenzi** Cl. 3; < **-sebenz-** work **-i** nom suff] S03

imishini machines [n Cl. 4; sg **umshini**] {Eng} S19

imitha meter [n Cl. 5] {Eng} S17

imithandazo prayers [n Cl. 4; sg **u m t h a n d a z o**; < **-t h a n d a z-** pray] S04

imithi medicines [n Cl. 4; sg **umuthi**] S20

imithi it is in calf, it is pregnant [stative; **-i** irregular stative suffix] S21

imitholampilo clinics [n Cl. 4; sg **umtholampilo**] S25

imithombo springs; sources [n Cl. 4; sg **umthombo**] S09

imizamo attempts, efforts, trials [n Cl. 4; sg **umzamo**; < **-zam-** try, attempt] S25

imizimba bodies [n Cl. 4; sg **umzimba**] S09

imizuzu minutes [n Cl. 4; sg **umzuzu**] S01

imizwa feelings, emotions [n Cl. 4; sg **umuzwa**; < **-zw-** feel] S08

iMolopo Molopo River [n Cl. 9a] S20

i-mosquito coil [n Cl. 9a] {Eng} S20

i-mosquito mat [n Cl. 9a] {Eng} S20

i-mosquito net [n Cl. 9a] {Eng} S20

imoto car [n Cl. 9a] {Eng *motor(car)*} S09

impahla goods, property, belongings, luggage [n Cl. 9; < **im-** + **-phahla**; **m** + **ph** > **mp**] S03

iMpangeni Empangeni (place) [n Cl. 5] S09

impela truth [n Cl. 9; < **phela** indeed, really, truly [adv]] S08

impelasonto weekend [n Cl. 9; < **im-** + **-phel-a** end + **isonto** week; **m** + **ph** > **mp**] S08

impendulo answer, response, reply [n Cl. 9; < **-phendul-** answer, reply; **m** + **ph** > **mp**] S06

impesheni welfare grant, pension [n Cl. 9] {Eng} S14

impilo life, health, good health [n Cl. 9; < **-phil-** live, be well, be in good health; **m** + **ph** > **mp**] S04

iMpumalanga east; also an eastern province of South Africa [n Cl. 9; < **im-** + **-phum-a** come out + **ilanga** sun; **m** + **ph** > **mp**] S20

impumelelo success [n Cl. 9; < **-phumelel-** succeed; **m** + **ph** > **mp**] S19

imvelo nature [n Cl. 9; < **-vel-** appear, come into view; come from, originate in] S24

imvula rain [n Cl. 9] S20

in- [NP Cl. 9] S01

inabaholi it has leaders [assoc cop, pres] S05

inabantwana (s)he has children, it has young [assoc cop, pres] S27

inamalungu it has members [assoc cop, pres] S12

iNanda (place) [n Cl. 5] S26

inani number; price [n Cl. 5] S19

inawo it has it [assoc cop, pres] S12

incane it, (s)he is small(er) [descr cop, pres; < **i-** SC Cl. 9 + **-ncane**] S15

incazelo explanation, information, solution [n Cl. 9; < **-chazel-** explain to; **n** + **ch** > **nc**] S14

incwadi letter; book [n Cl. 9a; pl **izincwadi** Cl. 10a] S10

indaba matter, affair, item of news [n Cl. 9] S08

indawo place, locality [n Cl. 9] S06

indawo okudlange kuyo the place where it is rife [n phr Cl. 9] S20

indawo yeziguli ward (lit. place of patients) [n phr Cl. 9] S17

indida puzzle, riddle, confusing thing [n Cl. 9] S14

indima cultivated plot, field; task [n Cl. 9; < -lim- cultivate; n + l > nd] S07

indiva castoff, castaway, worthless thing [n Cl. 9] S05

indiza airplane [n Cl. 7; < -ndiz- fly] S18

indlala hunger [n Cl. 9] S09

indle outside or surroundings of a village or homestead] S03

indleko cost, expense [n Cl. 9; < -dlek- get expended; be edible] S12

indlela path, road, way, method [n Cl. 9; pl **izindlela** Cl. 10] S01

indlela umshayeli ayengabalekela ngayo ukufa a way or road by which a driver could run away from death [n phr Cl. 9] S17

indlovu elephant [n Cl. 9] S22

indlu house [n Cl. 9] S10

indlu yangasese toilet [n phr Cl. 9; pl **izindlu zangasese**] S23

indluzula force, violence [n Cl. 9] S16

indoda man, husband [n Cl. 9; pl **amadoda** Cl. 6] S14

indodakazi daughter [n Cl. 9; pl **amadodakazi** Cl. 6; < **indoda** man + -**kazi** female [feminine suff]] S08

indodana son [n Cl. 9; pl **amadodana** Cl. 6; < **indoda** man + -**ana** little, small, juvenile [diminutive suff]] S02

indoda-thizeni a certain man [n Cl. 9; < **indoda** + -**thizeni** [noun suffix indicating 'a certain']]

indondo medal [n Cl. 9] S11

indondo medals (pronounced: **iindondo**; var of **izindondo**; sg **indondo**) [n Cl. 10] S11

inecala (s)he is guilty (lit. has guilt) [assoc cop, pres, partic] S23

inegunya it, (s)he has the authority [assoc cop, pres] S28

inelungelo it, (s)he has the right [assoc cop, pres] S25

inepulazi it, (s)he has a farm [assoc cop, pres] S27

iNewlands East (place) [n Cl. 5] S02

ingabekwa (s)he, it can be placed, or have placed on her/him/it [pres, potential] S23

ingabekwa icala (s)he can be charged with the offence [v phr] S23

ingabizi it does not cost or call, (s)he does not call [pres, rel, neg; < **ayibizi**] S28

ingakajwayeleki it is not yet customary, normal [pres, rel, exclusive, neg; < **ayikajwayeleki**] S25

ingakazalwa it, (s)he has not yet been born [pres, rel, exclusive, neg] S25

ingakwazi it would be able [pres, potential] S15

ingalo arm [n Cl. 9] S25

ingamashumi amabili nambili there are twenty-two [ident cop, pres] S19

ingane child [n Cl. 9] S05, S17

ingangabazeki it is undoubted [pres, neg, rel; < **ayibabazeki**] S24

ingangena (s)he, it can enter, can get into [pres, potential] S23

ingaphansi they are under [loc cop, pres] S20

ingaphinda it can again [pres, potential] S11

ingazama it, (s)he could try [pres, potential] S26

ingazenyezi (s)he does not make him- or herself miserable, allow him- or herself to get despondent [pres, rel, neg; < **ayizenyezi**]

ingcono it is better [descr cop, pres] S14

ingcosana a small quantity or number, few, a little [n Cl. 9; < **in-** + **-cosana**; **n** + **c** > **ngc**] S05

ingcuphe danger, dangerous position [n Cl. 9; < **in-** + **-cuphe**; **n** + **c** > **ngc**] S23

ingehlanga it has not descended [past, partic] S15

ingekho there is no, it is not present [loc cop, pres, partic, neg; may also introduce an exist cop] S15

ingendoda not being a man at all [ident cop, pres, partic] S23

ingenziwa it can be done, performed, carried out [pres, potential] S08

ingeyinhle [descr cop, pres, rel, neg; < **i-** Cl. 9 pref + **-nge-** neg pref + **-yi-** Cl. 9 pref + **-n-** 2nd half adj conc + **-hle** good] S23

ingoLwesine it is on Thursday [loc cop, pres] S11

ingompetha they are the finalists [ident cop, pres] S11

ingozi danger, accident [n Cl. 9] S09

ingqikithi essence [n Cl. 9] S08

ingqinamba weakness of the knees, nervousness [n Cl. 9] S18

ingqondo mind, intelligence, understanding, common sense; meaning, sense [n Cl. 9; < **-qond-** understand; **n** + **q** > **ngq**] S18

ingu-9 there are 9 of them [ident cop, pres] S09

ingu-10 there are ten of them [ident cop, pres] S09

ingu-13 there are thirteen [ident cop, pres] S27

ingu-25 it is 25 [ident cop, pres] S01

ingubo garment, item of clothing, blanket [n Cl. 9] S08

ingxabano quarrel, dispute [n Cl. 9; < **-xaban-** quarrel; **n + x >** ngx] S27

ingxenye one part, one half [n Cl. 9] S20

ingxoxo conversation, chat, interview; essay [n Cl. 9; < **-xox-** chat, converse; **n + x >** ngx] S26

inhlabathi soil, earth [n Cl. 9] S27

inhlalakahle social welfare [n Cl. 9; < **-hlal-a** live + **kahle** well] S09

inhlalayenza common occurrence, daily event, tendency [n Cl. 9; < **-hlal-a** keep doing + **-yenza** it does; no pl] S08

inhlangano meeting, assembly; association, society, organization [n Cl. 9; < **-hlangan-** meet, assemble] S05

inhlangano yomame women's organization [n phr Cl. 9] S12

inhlanhla good luck, good fortune [n Cl. 9] S04

inhliziyo heart [n Cl. 9; the heart is considered to be the seat of the emotions as well as of nausea] S20

inhliziyo encane nausea; short temper, irritability, irascibility (lit. a small heart; the heart is considered to be the seat of nausea (and emotions)) [n phr Cl. 9] S20

inhlonipho respect, honor [n Cl. 9; < **-hloniph-** respect, honor] S22

inhloso intention, aim [n Cl. 9; < **-hlos-** intend, aim] S16

in hlupheko suffering [n Cl. 9; < **-hluphek-** suffer, be worried, be troubled] S23

ini? what? [enum Cl. 9] S05

i-night club [n Cl. 9a; pl **ama-night club**] {Eng} S23

iningi majority, a large number [n Cl. 5; < **-ningi** many [adj st]] S03

iningi it is plentiful, there are many [descr cop, pres] S05

iNingizimu Afrika South Africa [n Cl. 5] S07

inja dog [n Cl. 9] S10

injongo aim, purpose, resolution [n Cl. 9; < **-jong-** have the mind set on] S28

inkakha skilled person [n Cl. 9] S23

inkambu camp [n Cl. 9] {Afr *kamp*} S23

inkampani company, firm [n Cl. 9] {Eng} S11

inkampani yabangcwabi burial company, company of undertakers [n phr Cl. 9; pl **izinkampani zabangcwabi**] S12

inkangala open, treeless country [n Cl. 9] S23

inkantini cafeteria, canteen [n Cl. 7] {Eng} S14

inkantolo court [n Cl. 9] {Afr *kantoor* office} S10

iNkantolo yoMthethosisekelo the Constitutional Court (South

352

African equivalent to the Supreme Court) [n phr Cl. 9] S25

inkanuko urge, strong desire, lust; jealousy [n Cl. 9; < **-khanuk-** lust, desire strongly; be jealous, be envious; **n + kh > nk**] S23

inkanyamba tornado [n Cl. 9] S17

inkanyezi star [n Cl. 9; < **-khany-** shine; **n + kh > nk**] S04

iNkatha Inkatha (short for Inkatha Freedom Party; < **inkatha** headpad (on which to carry loads), tribal emblem believed to ensure the solidarity and loyalty of members of the tribe) [n Cl. 9; < **in-** + **-khatha**; **n + kh > nk**] S05

inkathi time, period, age, epoch [n Cl. 9; < **in-** + **-khathi** (cf. **isikhathi**); **n + kh > nk**] S13

inkinga problem, puzzle, fix [n Cl. 9] S13

inkolelo belief [n Cl. 9; < **-kholelw-** believe in] S25

inkomishi [n Cl. 9] {Afr *kommetjie* small basin} S11

inkomo head of cattle, "cow," "beast" [n Cl. 9; < **in-** + **-khomo**; **n + kh > nk**] S21

inkonkoni h o m o s e x u a l ; wildebeest [n Cl. 9;] S23

inkosi chief [n Cl. 9; < **in-** + **-khosi**; pl **amakhosi**; **n + kh > nk**] S06

inkosikazi wife, woman (in this sense, considered more polite than **umfazi**); (principal) wife

of chief [n Cl. 9; pl **amakho-sikazi**; **n + kh > nk**; < **inkosi** chief + **-kazi** -ess [feminine suff]] S02

inkululeko freedom, emancipation [n Cl. 9; < **-khululek-** bec free or emancipated, be released; **n + kh > nk**] S25

inkulumo conversation, discussion [n Cl. 9; < **-khulum-** speak; **n + kh > nk**] S25

inkulungwane thousand [n Cl. 9] S10

iNkume (place) [n Cl. 9] S21

inkundla incident, situation [n Cl. 9] S17

inombolo number [n Cl. 9a] {Eng/Afr *nommer*} S04

i-Northern Province [n Cl. 5] S14

i-North West in the North West (Province) [n Cl. 5] S20

inqindi fist [n Cl. 9a] S17

inselelo challenge [n Cl. 9; no pl; var **inselele**] S19

insimbi iron, metal; bell [n Cl. 9] S19

insipho soap [n Cl. 9] {Afr *seep*} S17

insizwa young man, youth [n Cl. 9] S14

intambama afternoon [n Cl. 9; < **-thambam-** slant, decline (of sun in afternoon); **n + th > nt**] S20

intambo rope, string, cord [n Cl. 9; < **in-** + **-thambo**; **n + th > nt**]

S26

intandane orphan [n Cl. 9] S22

intatheli reporter, journalist [n Cl. 9; < -thathel- forage, gather what has been stored; **n + th > nt**] S21

intela tax [n Cl. 9; < -thel- pay tax; **n + th > nt**] S10

into thing, object [n Cl. 9; < -tho (cf. **utho**); **n + th > nt**] S13

intokazi young woman [n Cl. 9] S19

intombazane young girl (up to puberty) [n Cl. 9; pl **amanto-mbazane** Cl. 6] S08

intsha youth, young people [n Cl. 9; < -sha new, young [adj stem]; **n + sh > ntsh**] S18

intuthuko increase, progress, development [n Cl. 9; < -thuthuk- increase, progress; **n + th > nt**] S06

iNtuzuma (place) [n Cl. 5] S16

-inu your [abs pron 2 p pl; used in possessives] S28

inxa origin, cause [n Cl. 9a] S08

inyakatho north [n Cl. 9a] S18

inyama meat, flesh [n Cl. 9a] S23

inyanga month [n Cl. 9a] S10

inyembezi tear (from eye) [n Cl. 9a; pl **izinyembezi**] S23

inzima it is hard, it is difficult [descr cop, pres] S09

inzinhliziyo hearts [n Cl. 9] S23

inzululwane giddiness [n Cl. 9] S20

inzuzo profit, gain [n Cl. 9; < -zuz- earn, acquire, obtain] S27

i-orange juice [n Cl. 9a] {Eng} S01

i-Orange River (The Zulu name is **isAngqu** Cl. 7) [n Cl. 9a] S20

i-patty pan patty pan (equivalent to the American cup cake tin)[n Cl. 9a; pl **ama-patty pans**] {Eng} S01

ipayipi pipe [n Cl. 5] {Eng} S20

i-petrol pump [n Cl. 9a] S27

iphakethe pocket [n Cl. 5] {Eng} S28

iPhalamende Parliament [n Cl. 5] {Eng} S25

iPhayindane Pinetown (town) [n Cl. 5] {Eng} S12

iphepha paper [n Cl. 5] {Eng} S13

iphephandaba newspaper [n Cl. 5; < **iphepha** paper + **indaba** news] S06

iphephile (s)he, it is safe or secure; (s)he it has escaped [stative] S25

iphethelo suburb [n Cl. 5; < -phethel- border on] S11

iphezu kwa- it is in control of, it is heading (lit. is on top of) [loc cop, pres] S12

iphile it is in good health [past, conjoint] S15

iphilisi pill, tablet, capsule [n Cl. 5] {Eng} S16

iphoyisa police officer, policeman, policewoman, cop [n Cl. 5] {Eng} S09

iphumelele (s)he succeeded [stative] S19

iphumelele it succeeds [subjunc] S25

iphupho dream [n Cl. 5; < -phuph- dream] S19

iphutha failing, shortcoming, error, mistake [n Cl. 5] S04

iphuzu point (of discussion) [n Cl. 5] S16

i-Pietermaritzburg (city; capital of KwaZulu-Natal Province; the Zulu name for the city is **uMgungundlovu**) [n Cl. 5] S16

iPoint Road (place; notorious for prostitution and other crime) [n Cl. 5] S09

ipolitiki politics [n Cl. 9a] {Afr *politiek*} S05

i-Potgietersrus (town) [n Cl. 5] S14

i-Presbyterian Church of Southern Africa [n Cl. 9a] {Eng} S17

i-pressure [n Cl. 9] {Eng} S19

ipulazi farm [n Cl. 5] {Afr *plaas*} S27

ipuleti plate [n Cl. 5] {Eng} S09

iqala it begins [pres, conjoint] S11

iqanda egg [n Cl. 5] S01

iqembu small group, band, team [n Cl. 5] S09

iqhamuka they come from [pres, conjoint] S12

iqhuba it continues with, it carries on [pres, conjoint] S25

iqiniso truth [n Cl. 5; < -qinis- strengthen, tighten, make firm] S23

iqolo small of the back [n Cl. 5] S20

i-radar [n Cl. 9a] {Eng} S18

iradio radio [n Cl. 9a; pl **amaradio**] S22

irama margarine [n Cl. 9a] S01

iRama Rama margarine (Rama is a brand name; without the capital letter **irama** is the generic term for margarine) [n Cl. 9a] S01

irandi rand (South African currency unit) [n Cl. 5] S28

i-raspberry raspberry [n Cl. 9a; pl **ama-raspberry** Cl. 6] S27

irenki rank [n Cl. 9a; pl **amarenki** Cl. 6] S17

is- [NP Cl. 7] S06

-is- make VERB, cause to VERB; help VERB [caus ext] S01, S12

-is- + POSS PRON like [The caus ext **-is-** followed by a possessive pronoun translates 'like X,' with X being the base of the pronoun.] S09

isAdtu Sadtu (South African Democratic Teachers Union) [n Cl. 9a] S05

isandla hand [n Cl. 7; pl **izandla** Cl. 8] S06

355

isango gate, gateway; main entrance to cattle-kraal [n Cl. 5] S14

isAngqu Orange River [n Cl. 7] S20

isaphuli-mthetho law-breaker [n Cl. 7; pl **izaphuli-mthetho** Cl. 8; < **-aphul-** break + **umthetho**] S10

i-Saps Commercial Crime Unit SAPS (South African Police Services) ... [n Cl. 9a] S10

isazimisele (s)he is still determined [stative, persistive] S18

isazoba mibi they will still be bad [descr cop, inch, fut] S05

i-scrotum [n Cl. 7; **is-** is interpreted as being the Cl. 7 NP] S15

isebenza it, (s)he works [pres, conjoint] S27

ise-Edendale it is in Edendale [loc cop, pres] S13

isehlo shock, surprising event [n Cl. 7; pl **izehlo**] S23

isekela assistant [n Cl. 5; < **-sekel-** assist, stand in for] S25

i-self-raising flour self-rising flour [n Cl. 9a] {South African English has *self-raising*} S01

isemkhankasweni it is in a scheme or program [loc cop, pres] S12

isenti cent [n Cl. 5] {Eng/Afr} S28

isenyakatho it is in the north [loc cop, pres] S18

isenzo act, action, deed [n Cl. 7; pl **izenzo**; < **-enz-** do, act] S18

isesikoleni it is at or in school [loc cop, pres] S13

isethembiso promise [n Cl. 7; pl **izethembiso**; < **is-** NP + **-ethembis-** promise] S03

isexwayiso warning, caution [n Cl. 7; pl **izexwayiso**; < **-exwayis-** warn; var **isixwayiso**] S27

ishaywe it has been beaten [past, conjoint form] S01

ishisiwe it, (s)he has been burnt [stative, disjoint] S28

iShowe (place) [n Cl. 5] S21

ishumi ten (n) [n Cl. 5] S14

isi- [NP Cl. 7] S03

isibalo number, figure, sum [n Cl. 7; < **-bal-** count] S16

isibazi scar [n Cl. 7] S09

isibhakabhaka sky [n Cl. 7] S18

isibhalisile it had already had registered [past, exclusive, disjoint; < **i-** SC Cl. 9 + **-s-** already [exclusive aspect marker] **-i-** SC Cl. 9 + **-bhalisile**] S12

isibhamu gun [n Cl. 7] S09

isibhedlela hospital [n Cl. 7] {Eng *spital?*} S14

isibili second (ordinal number) [n Cl. 7; < **-bili** two [adj stem]] S11

isibindi courage, bravery; liver (according to Zulu culture, the liver is said to be the seat of bravery) [n Cl. 7] S17

isibonelo example [n Cl. 7; < -bonel- copy, imitate] S23

isibongo clan name, surname [n Cl. 7; < -bong- sing the praises of] S21

isibopho obligation, duty, necessity [n Cl. 7; < -boph- tie (up), bind, make fast] S04

isiboshwa prisoner [n Cl. 7; < -boshw- be arrested] S23

isibuko mirror [n Cl. 7; < -buk- look, watch] S21

isibusiso blessing [n Cl. 7; < -busis- bless] S05

isicabha door [n Cl. 7] S13

isicathulo shoe [n Cl. 7] S07

isicelo request [n Cl. 7; < -cel- ask for, request] S14

isichotho hail [n Cl. 7] S17

isicoco title [n Cl. 7] S11

isidakamizwa drug [n Cl. 7; < -dak-a intoxicate, stupefy + imizwa feelings] S09

isidingo need [n Cl. 7; < -ding- need, require] S06

isidlakela well-built person [n Cl. 7] S17

isidlo meal [n Cl. 7; < -dl- eat] S14

isidlo sasemini lunch (i.e. noon meal) [n phr Cl. 7] S14

isifazane female gender [n Cl. 7]

isifiso desire, wish [n Cl. 7; < -fis- desire, wish for] S04

isifo disease, illness [n Cl. 7; < -f- be ill] S14

isifunda province, district [n Cl. 7] S09

isifundazwe province [n Cl. 7; < isifunda district + izwe country] S18

isifundo lesson, subject (in education), course [n Cl. 7; < -fund-] S08

isigameko repeated incident or statement [n Cl. 7] S08

isigebengu criminal, robber, gangster [n Cl. 7] S09

isigelekeqe criminal [n Cl. 7] S23

isigigaba major event, serious affair [n Cl. 7] S17

isigilamkhuba evil-doer [n Cl. 7; < -gil-a perform + umkhuba bad practice] S23

isiginci guitar [n Cl. 7] S14

isigodi district [n Cl. 7] S06

isiguli patient, sick person [n Cl. 7; < -gul- be sick] S17

isigwebo sentence, judgment [n Cl. 7; < -gweb-a pass judgment, decide a court case, sentence] S26

isigwebo sentambo death sentence (lit. sentence of the rope) [n phr Cl. 7] S26

isigxobo stake, sharpened pole [n Cl. 7] S06

isigxobo sokushaya ucingo telegraph pole [n phr Cl. 7] S06

isihambele (s)he has already visited [past, exclusive, conjoint] S16

isihlahla bush, shrub; among younger speakers, generally used for 'tree' in place of **umuthi** [n Cl. 7] S24

isihlalo chair, seat, stool [n Cl. 7; < -hlal- sit] S14

isihlanu five, a fifth [n Cl. 7] S13, S20

isihlobo relative [n Cl. 7] S09

isihluku cruelty, ill-will [n Cl. 7] S09

isikalo dose [n Cl. 7] {Afr *skaal* scale} S20

isikhala opening, opportunity [n Cl. 7] S05

isikhangiso advertisement [n Cl. 7; < -khangis- advertise] S18

isikhathi time [n Cl. 7] S03

isikhethe (s)he already having chosen [past, exclusive, conjoint; < i- SC + -s- already + -i- SC + -khethe] S16

isikhombise it has already shown [past, exclusive, conjoint] S25

isikhulu person of rank or social standing, important person [n Cl. 7; < -khulu big, important [adj stem]] S06

isikhumba skin, hide; leather [n Cl. 7] S20

isikhumulo place of outspanning or unharnessing [n Cl. 7; < -khumul- outspan, unharness] S18

isikhumulo sezindiza airport [n phr Cl. 7; pl **izikhumulo zezindiza**] S18

isikhundla place, situation [n Cl. 7] S03

isikhungo covered stall [n Cl. 7] S24

isikhwama bag [n Cl. 7] S11

isikibha T-shirt [n Cl. 7] {< Eng. *skipper*} S11

isiko custom, practice [n Cl. 5] S25

isikole school [n Cl. 7] {Afr *skool*} S05

isikwazi (s)he already knows [pres, partic, exclusive] S18

isikweleti debt [n Cl. 7] {Afr *skuld*} S28

isilima deformed person or thing [n Cl. 7] S23

isilisa menfolk, male-kind [n Cl. 7] S19

isiliva silver [n Cl. 7] {Eng} S11

isilwanyazana insect [n Cl. 7; var **isilwanyazane**] S20

isimame womenfolk [n Cl. 7; < **umame** mother] S14

isimanga unbelievable event [n Cl. 7] S21

isimilo nature, character, characteristic [n Cl. 7; < -mil- germinate, grow] S26

isimo standing, status, condition, situation; nature, form, character [n Cl. 7; < -m- stand] S09

isimo sezulu the weather (lit. the state of the weather) [n phr Cl. 7] S17

isimungumungwane measles [n Cl. 7] S14

isinambuzane insect, parasite (lit. small slow-moving person or animal) [n Cl. 7; < **-nambuz-** move lazily; act lethargically] S20

isingili person who is single [n Cl. 5] {Eng} S22

isingiphungulele it has already reduced for me [past, exclusive, conjoint] S27

isinqumo decision, verdict [n Cl. 7; < **-nqum-** decide] S08

isinyathelo step [n Cl. 7; < **-nyathel-** tread, step] S18

isinyathelo engangizikhethele sona the step that I had chosen for myself [n phr Cl. 7] S18

isipesheli special thing [n Cl. 7] {Eng} S10

isiphathimandla person in control; authority, official [n Cl. 7; < **isiphathi** holder + **amandla** power] S21

isiphawu sign [n Cl. 7] S18

isiphepho gale [n Cl. 7; < **-pheph-** blow about] S21

isipho gift, present [n Cl. 7; < **-ph-** give] S14

isipoki ghost [n Cl. 7] {Afr *spook*} S05

isiqalo origin, beginning; initial; prefix [n Cl. 7; < **-qal-** begin] S27

isiqiniseko surety, guarantee, certainty, conviction [n Cl. 7;

< **-qinisek-** be proved true, be fulfilled] S18

isiqiwi game reserve [n Cl. 7] S24

isiqu degree (academic; the plural form of the noun is frequently used with singular meaning) [n Cl. 7] S14

isiqu root, basis, bottom end [n Cl. 7] S20

isiqubulo slogan [n Cl. 7; < **-qubul-** sing loudly in chorus] S11

isiqubulo by a slogan [agent adv; this item differs tonally from the one above] S11

i-siren siren [n Cl. 9a; pl **ama-sirens** Cl. 6] {Eng} S17

-isis- thoroughly, very well, forcefully [intensive ext] S04

isisebenza (s)he now, then or already works [pres, exclusive] S27

isisekelo foundation stone [n Cl. 7; < **-sekel-** prop up, support] S25

isishiyagalombili eight (n) [n Cl. 7; < **-shiy-a** leave + **(izin)galo** fingers + **-mbili** two (In counting on the fingers, 8 is indicated by holding up the right hand with the thumb and first two fingers folded in, leaving two fingers extended.)] S09

isisho saying [n Cl. 7; < **-sh-o** say (so), mean] S08

isisu stomach [n Cl. 7] S20

isisulu victim [n Cl. 7] S10

isitaladi street [n Cl. 7] {Afr *straat*} S09

isiteleka strike; stay-away [n Cl. 7] {Eng} S28

isiteshi station [n Cl. 7] {Eng; back formation from the locative **esiteshini** derived from the English} S09

isiteshi samaphoyisa police station [n phr Cl. 7; pl **iziteshi zamaphoyisa**] S09

isitha enemy [n Cl. 7] S09

isithako ingredient [n Cl. 7; normally found in the plural; < **isi-** NP Cl. 7 + **-thak-** mix, concoct + **-o** nominalizing suffix (henceforth: nom suff. With few exceptions the nom suff **-o** derives product or process nouns, always non-personal, while the nom suff **-i** forms agent nouns, which are generally personal.)] S01

isithelo fruit [n Cl. 7] S27

isitho limb, part of the body [n Cl. 7] S15

isithombe picture, image, photo-graph [n Cl. 7] S18

isithombo seedling [n Cl. 7] S27

isithunzi shadow; moral weight, influence, prestige; personality, soul [n Cl. 7] S23

isithupha thumb; six, sixth (in counting on the fingers, one moves from five on one hand to the thumb of the other for 'six') [n Cl. 7] S14, S21

isithwathwa frost [n Cl. 7] S27

isitifiketi certificate [n Cl. 7] {Eng} S14

isitimela train [n Cl. 7] {Eng *steamer*} S16

isitokisi prison cell [n Cl. 7] {Eng *stocks*} S23

isitolo shop, store [n Cl. 7] {Eng} S20

isitshalo crop [n Cl. 7; < **-tshal-** plant, sow] S24

isivakashi visitor [n Cl. 7; < **-vakash-** visit] S20

isivande garden plot [n Cl. 7] S27

isivinini speed [n Cl. 7] S16

isivumelwana mutual or legal agreement, contract [n Cl. 7; var **isivumelwano**; < **-vumelwan-** be mutually agreed] S16

isivunguvungu gale [n Cl. 7] S21

isivuno harvest, crop [n Cl. 7; < **-vun-** reap, harvest] S27

isixwayiso warning, caution [n Cl. 7; < **-xwayis-** warn; var **isexwayiso**] S27

iSiyabonga Crafts Centre the Siyabonga Crafts Center (**Siyabonga** = We are thankful) [n Cl. 9a] S24

iSiyaphezulu Womens Club yaseNazareth the Siyaphezulu Women's Club of Nazareth [n Cl. 9a; < **siya phezulu** we are going upward] S12

isizathu reason [n Cl. 7] S08

isizwe nation, a people [n Cl. 7] S25

iso eye [n Cl. 5; pl **amehlo** o r **amaso** Cl. 6] S14

i-sodomy [n Cl. 9a] {Eng} S23

isoka bachelor; boyfriend [n Cl. 5]

isokisi sock [n Cl. 5] {back-formation from **amasokisi**; < Eng *socks*} S20

isomiso drought, dry spell [n Cl. 7; pl **izomiso**; < -omis- bec dry (of the weather)] S20

isonto church, week; with capital 's': **iSonto** Sunday [n Cl. 5] {Afr *Sondag* Sunday} SO8, S22

isosha soldier [n Cl. 5] {Eng} S21

i-South Africa [n Cl. 5] {Eng} S16

i-spray spray [n Cl. 7; the **s** of 'spray' is taken as part of the noun prefix **is-**] S20

i-stationery [n Cl. 9a] {Eng} S13

i-stock exchange [n Cl. 9a] {Eng} S28

i-strawberry strawberry [n Cl. 7; pl **ama-strawberry** Cl. 6; **is-** is taken as the Cl. 7 NP] S27

isuke it went from [past, conjoint] S13

isuke it merely [aux] S15

isuke ingehlanga it is merely undescended [v phr] S15

i-supermarket [n Cl. 9a; var **isupamakethe**; pl Cl. 6] {Eng} S27

isusa it removes [pres, conjoint] S17

itekisi taxi, cab [n Cl. 5] {Eng} S17

ithalente talent [n Cl. 5] {Eng} S22

ithathwa it being taken [pres, part] S08

itheku harbor, enclosed bay, lagoon [n Cl. 5] S09

ithemba hope, faith [n Cl. 5; < -themb- hope] S17

ithembakale it should be trustworthy [subjunc] S12

ithimba group (of unmarried girls or women) [n Cl. 9] S16

ithini tin, can [n Cl. 5] {Eng} S01

itholakala they are obtainable [pres, conjoint] S20

itholakale (s)he should be found [subjunc] S23

ithole (s)he received or obtained, (s)he should obtain [subjunc] S27

ithonsi drop [n Cl. 5] S08

-ithu our [abs pron 1 p pl; used in possessives] S03

ithuba opportunity, chance [n Cl. 5] S12, S13

i-track suit [n Cl. 9a] {Eng} S11

i-truck truck, van [n Cl. 5] {Eng} S09

itshelwe it has been told [past, conjoint] S12

i-tunnel [n Cl. 9a; pl Cl. 6] S27

i-turner trade of a turner [n Cl. 9a] S19

iTV TV [n Cl. 9a; pl **amaTV**] {Eng} S22

ivila lazy person [n Cl. 5] S27

-iw- be VERB-ed, be VERB-en [pass ext found after verbs having C or VC structure] S05

i-welding [n Cl. 9a] S19

iWentworth (place) [n Cl. 5] S09

iWeseli the Wesleyan Church [n Cl. 5] {Eng} S02

iwolintshi orange [n Cl. 5] {Eng} S01

ixhophozi swamp [n Cl. 5] S20

iyabudinga they require it [pres, disjoint] S19

iyafana it or (s)he resembles, it or (s)he is like [pres, disjoint] S16

iyamangaza it, (s)he is amazing, is surprising [pres, disjoint] S27

iyangithokozisa it makes me happy [pres, disjoint] S19

iyanyanyeka it is objectionable, deplorable [pres, disjoint] S25

iyasetshenziswa they are used [pres, disjoint] S20

iyaxaka it causes difficulties [pres, disjoint] S13

iyazihlonipha it respects them [pres, disjoint] S25

iye it went [past, conjoint] S13

iyindida they are a puzzle or riddle [ident cop, pres] S14

iyini? it is what? [ident cop, pres] S05

iyiphoyisa (s)he is a policeman [ident cop, pres] S16

iyishumi they are ten [ident cop, pres] S14

iyisihlanu there are five (of them) [ident cop, pres] S20

iyisipho it is a gift [ident cop, pres] S14

iyisithupha there are six of them [ident cop, pres] S14

iyizinkulungwane there are thousands [ident cop, pres] S10

iz- [NP Cl. 8] S03

-iz-a come [variant of **-z-a** found after **a**; then **a + i > e**] S13

izabelo the media [n Cl. 8; < **-abel-** distribute among] S21

izambane potato [n Cl. 5] S27

izansi coastal belt, low country [n Cl. 5] S20

izaphuli-mthetho law-breakers [n Cl. 8; sg **isaphuli-mthetho** Cl. 7; < **-aphul-** break + **umthetho**] S10

ize nothing, a thing of no value; a little, a bit [n Cl. 5] S10, S14

ize (s)he, it should ever [aux, subjunc] S23

izeluleko advice [n Cl. 8; < **-elulek-** advise] S20

izenzele it should just do [subjunc] S11

izethembiso promises [n Cl. 8; sg **isethembiso**; < **is-** NP + **-ethembis-** promise] S03

izi- [NP Cl. 8] S01

iziØ- [NP Cl. 10a] S04

izibazi scars [n Cl. 8; sg **isibazi**] S09

izibhamu guns [n Cl. 8; sg **isibhamu**] S09

izibiza they call themselves [pres, conjoint] S23

izibona (s)he sees him- or herself [pres, conjoint] S23

izibonelo examples [n Cl. 8; sg **isibonelo**] S23

iziboshwa prisoners [n Cl. 8; sg **isiboshwa**; < **-boshw-** be arrested] S23

izibuko spectacles, glasses; mirrors [n Cl. 8; sg **isibuko** mirror; < **-buk-** look, watch] S21

izicabha doors [n Cl. 8; sg **isicabha**] S13

izicathulo shoes [n Cl. 8; sg **isicathulo**] S07

izidakamizwa drugs [n Cl. 8; sg **isidakamizwa**; < **-dak-a** intoxicate, stupefy + **imizwa** feelings] S09

izidingo needs, requirements [n Cl. 8; sg **isidingo** need; < **-ding-** need, require] S06

izidlakela well-built people [n Cl. 8; sg **isidlakela**] S17

izifiso desires, wishes [n Cl. 8; sg **isifiso** Cl. 7; < **-fis-** desire, wish for] S04

izifunda districts, regions, provinces [n Cl. 8; sg **isifunda**] S05

izifundo lessons, studies [n Cl. 8; sg **isifundo**; **-fund-** learn] S18

izigameko repeated incidents [n Cl. 8; sg **isigameko**] S08

izigebengu criminals, robbers, gangsters [n Cl. 8; sg **isigebengu**] S09

izigelekeqe criminals [n Cl. 8; sg **isigelekeqe**] S23

izigilamkhuba evil-doers [n Cl. 8; sg **isigilamkhuba**; < **-gil-a** perform + **umkhuba** bad practice] S23

izigodi districts [n Cl. 8; sg **isigodi**] S06

iziguli patients, sick people [n Cl. 8; sg **isiguli**; < **-gul-** be sick] S17

izihlahla bushes, shrubs; among younger speakers, generally used for 'trees' in place of **umuthi** [n Cl. 8; sg **isihlahla**] S24

izihlobo relatives [n Cl. 8; sg **isihlobo**] S09

izihluthu long mass of hair [n Cl. 8] S11

izikhulu people of rank or social standing, important people [n Cl. 8; sg **isikhulu**; < **-khulu** big, important [adj stem]] S06

izikhungo covered stalls [n Cl. 8; sg **isikhungo**] S24

izikibha T-shirts [n Cl. 8; sg **isikibha**] {< Eng. *skipper*} S11

izikole schools [n Cl. 8; sg **isikole**] S05

izikweleti debts [n Cl. 8; sg **isikweleti**] {Afr *skuld*} S28

izilwandle seas, oceans [n Cl. 10a; sg **ulwandle** Cl. 11; the prefix **izi-** is superimposed on the pref **(u)lw-** of Cl. 11] S18

izilwanyazana insects [n Cl. 8; sg **isilwanyazana**; var **isilwanyazane**] S20

izim- [NP Cl. 10; occurs before stems starting in **b, bh, p, ph, f**] S03

izimakethe markets [n Cl. 10a; sg **imakethe** Cl. 9a] {Eng} S19

izimali monies; bank accounts [n Cl. 10a; sg **imali**] S06, S10

izimanga unbelievable events [n Cl. 8; sg **isimanga**] S21

izimboni factories, industries, businesses [n Cl. 10; sg **imboni**] S03

izimisele it, (s)he is prepared or ready [stative] S12

izimoto cars [n Cl. 10a; sg **imoto**] {Eng *motor(car)*} S09

izimpahla (or **impahla**, Cl. 9) goods, property, belongings, luggage [n Cl. 10; < **izim-** + **-phahla; m + ph > mp**] S03

izimpahla roofs [n Cl. 10; sg **uphahla** Cl. 11; m + ph > mp] S17

izimpawu symptoms, marks, brand-marks, birthmarks [n Cl. 10; sg **uphawu**; var **uphawo** Cl. 11] S20

izin- [NP Cl. 10] S04

izincwadi letters; books [n Cl. 10a; sg **incwadi** Cl. 9a] S10

izincwadi zokuthi baboshwe warrants of arrest (lit. letters that they should be arrested) [n phr Cl. 10a] S10

izindaba affairs, matters, news [n Cl. 10; sg **indaba**] S09

izindaba zenhlalakahle social welfare [n phr Cl. 10] S09

izindawo places [n Cl. 10; sg **indawo**] S05

izindiza airplanes [n Cl. 8; sg **indiza**; < **-ndiz-** fly] S18

izindleko costs, expenses [n Cl. 10; sg **indleko**] S12

izindlu zangasese toilets [n phr Cl. 10; sg **indlu yangasese**] S23

izindlu zokufundela educational institutions (lit. houses for studying in) [n phr Cl. 10] S13

izindondo medals [n Cl. 10; sg **indondo**] S11

izindonga wall [n Cl. 10; sg **udonga** Cl. 11] S17

izinga degree (not academic); elevation between two closely placed grooves, level, standard, rate [n Cl. 5; pl **amazinga**] S01

izinga lemikhiqizo level of production [n phr Cl. 5; pl **amazinga emikhiqizo**] S19

izinga lempilo standard of living [n phr Cl. 5] S28

izinga lokushisa temperature (lit. degree of heat) [n phr Cl. 5; pl **amazinga okushisa**] S20

izingane children, infants [n Cl. 10; sg **ingane**] S05

izingane zabafana boys (lit. children of boys) [n phr Cl. 10]

izingane zamantombazane girls (lit. children of girls) [n phr Cl. 10]

izingozi accidents [n Cl. 10; sg **ingozi**] S08

izingcingo wires; telephones, telegraphs [n Cl. 10; pl **ucingo** Cl. 11; **n + c > ngc**] S06

izingqinamba weakness of the knees, nervousness [n Cl. 10; the sg **ingqinamba** and pl have the same meaning] S18

izingqwembe demonstrations, protests [n Cl. 10] S25

izingubo clothing, clothes [n Cl. 10; sg **ingubo** garment, blanket] S08

izingubo zomfaniswano uniforms (lit. clothing of uniformity) [n phr Cl. 10] S12

izinhlamvu grains, berries, pips, stones (of fruit); testicles (euph) [n Cl. 10; sg **uhlamvu** Cl. 11] S15

izinhlamvu zangasese testicles [n phr Cl. 10; sg **uhlamvu lwangasese**] S15

izinhlamvu zesitho testicles (euph; lit. berries of body part) [n phr Cl. 10; sg **uhlamvu lwesitho**] S15

izinhlamvu zesitho sangasese ezincane small testicles (lit. small berries of the private parts) [n phr Cl. 10] S15

izinhlobo types, sorts, kinds [n Cl. 10; sg **uhlobo** Cl. 11] S10

izinkakha skilled people [n Cl. 10; sg **inkakha**] S23

izinkakha zezigelekeqe master criminals [n phr Cl. 10] S23

izinkampani zokupheka catering companies (lit. companies of cooking) [n phr Cl. 10; sg **inkampani yokupheka**] S12

izinkangala open, treeless country [n Cl. 10; sg **inkangala**] S23

izinkantolo courts [n Cl. 10; sg **inkantolo**] {Afr *kantoor* office} S10

izinkanuko urges, strong desires, lust; jealousies [n Cl. 10; sg **inkanuko**; < **-khanuk-** lust, desire strongly; be jealous, be envious [v.i.] S23

izinkanyezi stars [n Cl. 10; sg **inkanyezi**; < **-khany-** shine; **n + kh > nk**] S04

izinketho elections [n Cl. 10; sg **ukhetho** Cl. 11; < **-kheth-** choose, select, vote] S03

izinkinga problems [n Cl. 10; sg **inkinga**] S09

izinkokheli leaders [n Cl. 10; sg **inkokheli**] S07

izinkolelo beliefs [n Cl. 10; sg **inkolelo**; < **-kholelw-** believe in] S25

izinkonkoni homosexuals; wildebeest [n Cl. 10; sg **inkonkoni**] S23

izinkulumo conversations, discussions [n Cl. 10; sg **inkulumo**; < **-khulum-** speak] S25

izinkulungwane thousands [n Cl. 10; sg **inkulungwane**] S10

izinkundla playgrounds [n Cl. 10; sg **inkundla**] S13

izinombolo numbers [n Cl. 10a; sg **inombolo**] {Eng/Afr?} S04

izinqumo decisions, verdicts, judgments [n Cl. 8; sg **isinqumo** < **-nqum-** decide] S08

izinsimbi metals [n Cl. 10; sg **insimbi** iron, metal; bell] S19

izinsuku days (of 24 hours) [n Cl. 10; sg **usuku** Cl. 11] S04

izintango fence [n Cl. 10; sg **uthango** Cl. 11; **n + th > nt**] S08

izintatheli reporters, journalists [n Cl. 10; sg **intatheli**; < **-thathel-** forage, gather what has been stored; **n + th > nt**] S21

izinto things [n Cl. 10; sg **utho** Cl. 11; **n + th > nt**] S04

izinto ezihambayo moving things [n phr Cl. 10] S19

izinto zocansi sexual objects (lit. things of the sleeping-mat) [n phr Cl. 10] S09

izinyanga months [n Cl. 10a; sg **inyanga**] S20

izinyathelo steps [n Cl. 8; sg **isinyathelo**; < **-nyathel-** tread, step] S08

izinyawo feet [n Cl. 10a; sg **unyawo** Cl. 11] S09

izinyembezi tears [n Cl. 10a; sg **inyembezi**] S23

iziphathimandla the authorities, those in control [n Cl. 8; sg **isiphathimandla**; < **isiphathi** holder + **amandla** power] S21

iziphawu signs [n Cl. 8; sg **isiphawu**] S18

izipoki ghosts (i.e. ghost teachers — non-existent teachers who are on the salary role) [n Cl. 8; sg **isipoki**] {Afr *spook*} S05

iziqalo origins, beginnings; initials; prefixes [n Cl. 8; sg **isiqalo**; < **-qal-** begin] S27

iziqiwi game reserves [n Cl. 8; sg **isiqiwi**] S24

iziqu degree(s) (the plural form of the noun is frequently used with singular meaning) [n Cl. 8; sg **isiqu**] S14

izisulu victims [n Cl. 8; sg **isisulu**] S10

izitaladi streets [n Cl. 8; sg **isitaladi**] {Afr *straat*} S09

iziteleka strikes, stay-aways [n Cl. 8; sg **isiteleka**] {Eng} S28

izitha enemies [n Cl. 8; sg **isitha**] S09

izithako ingredients [n Cl. 8; sg **isithako**; < **isi-** NP Cl. 7 + **-thak-** mix, concoct + **-o** nominalizing suffix (henceforth: nom suff. With few exceptions the nom suff **-o** derives product or process nouns, always non-personal, while the nom suff **-i** forms agent nouns, which are generally personal.)] S01

izithandani lovers [n Cl. 8; < -thandan- love each other; no singular] S08

izithelo fruit(s) [n Cl. 8; sg **isithelo**] S27

izithombe pictures, photographs [n Cl. 8; sg **isithombe**] S16

izithombo seedlings [n Cl. 8; sg **isithombo**] S27

izithupha thumbs [n Cl. 8; sg **isithupha**]

izitolo shops, stores n Cl. 8; sg **isitolo**] {Eng} S20

izitshalo crops, vegetables [n Cl. 8; sg **isitshalo**; < -tshal- plant, sow] S.24, S27

izivakashi visitors [n Cl. 8; sg **isivakashi**; < -vakash- visit] S20

izizathu reasons [n Cl. 8; sg **isizathu**] S05

izobuyela it will return to [fut] S13

izonikwa they will be given (to) [fut] S12

izotholakala they will be obtainable [fut] S12

izotholana it will be in contention with [fut] S11

izulu sky, heaven, weather [n Cl. 5] S17

izulu lingani it is not raining (lit. the sky is not raining) [pres, partic] S20

-izw-a feel, hear, understand [v.t.; var of **-zw-a** found after the vowel **a**] S09

-izwakal-a be audible, comprehensible, understandable, reasonable; be felt, be experienced [v-neut; var **-zwakal-a** found after the vowel **a**] S08, S23

izwakala (they) being heard, being audible [pres, partic] S17

-izwakalis-a make audible, make heard, voice, express [v-neut-caus; var of **-zwakal-a** found after the vowel **a**] S21

-izwan-a hear one another, understand one another, get on together, communicate with one another; be addicted to, be very much inclined to [v-recip; var **-izwan-a** occurs after the vowel **a**] S09

izwane "it will feel each other" [subjunc] S11

izwane amandla it will test (its) strength [v phr] S11

izwe country [n Cl. 5] S03, S07

izwi voice, word [n Cl. 5] S23

J

-jabul-a be or bec happy [v.i.] S23

jaji judge [< **ijaji**] S26

-jik-a turn [v.i.] S17

-jong-a have the mind set on [v.t.] S28

-juluk-a sweat, perspire [v.i.] S20

-jwayel-a get used to, grow accustomed to, adjust to [v.t.; var **-ejwayel-a**] S10

-jwayelek-a bec customary, usual, normal [v-neut] S18

-jwayez-a accustom, make get used to [v-caus; < **-jwayel-** + **-Y-**; l + **-Y-** > z] S28

K

-k- (s)he [SC Cl. 1; found after neg pref **a-** and hort prefixes **(k)a-** and **ma-** when a vowel follows] S26

ka- -ly [adverb formative, prefixed to adj, rel and enum stems] S01, S05

ka- of [poss conc Cl. 1, 3, 4, 6, & 9] S03

-ka- he, she, it [SC Cl. 1; found after neg pref **a-** and hort prefixes **(k)a-** and **ma-**] S02

-ka- they [SC Cl. 6; found after neg pref **a-** and hort prefixes **(k)a-** and **ma-**] S25

-ka- yet [neg exclusive aspect marker] S03

ka-1994 of 1994 [poss Cl. 3] S03

ka-1995 of 1995 [poss Cl. 3] S23

ka-1996 of 1996 [poss Cl. 1] S21

ka-1999 of 1999 [poss Cl. 9] S28

ka-Anton Anton's [poss Cl. 3] S27

kabathembele they do not have faith in, they do not believe in [stative; Note: with different tones, this word could also mean 'let them have faith in' — subjunc with hortative pref] S05

kabi badly, awfully, terribly, very [adv; < **-bi** bad [adj stem]] S15

kabili twice [adv; < **ka-** + **-bili** two [adj stem]] S08

kabusha anew, afresh [manner adv; < **busha** anew, afresh] S05

kade before, and then [conj] S05

kade for a long time [conj; followed here by the partic] S07

Kader (male name) [n Cl. 1a] {Arabic} S11

Kader Asmal (name: former Minister of Water Affairs; now Minister of Education) [n phr Cl. 1a] S11

kahle well, properly [manner adv; < **ka-** -ly [derives adverbs from adj, rel and enum stems] + **-hle** good [adj stem]] S01

kaHlengiwe of Hlengiwe [poss Cl. 1] S26

kakhulu very, a lot, a great deal, highly, too [manner adv; < **ka-** + **-khulu** big, great [adj stem]] S05

kaLionel Richie of Lionel Richie [poss Cl. 3] S14

kalula easily [adv; < **-lula** easy, light [rel stem]] S11

kamfowabo of his or her brother [poss Cl. 3 & 9] S27

kancane a little, somewhat, a bit; slowly [adv; < **-ncane** small, little] S19

kangaka so (much), to this extent [adv; < **-ngaka** of this size, as big as this [rel stem]] S06

kangakanani to what extent?, how much?, to what degree? [adv; < **-ngakanani?** how much? [rel stem]] S25

kangangoba since, inasmuch as, so much so that [conj] S21

kangcono better [manner adv; < **-ngcono** better [rel stem]] S16

kaningi often [adv; < **-ningi** many, much [adj stem]] S23

kanjani? how? [interrogative adv] S04

kanje thus, like this, in this way [adv; < **nje** thus] S11

kanjena thus, in this way, in this fashion [adv; < **njena** thus] S25

kanti after all, whereas, while, but, and [conj] S03

kanti futhi and also [conj phr]

kanye once [adv; < **-nye** o n e [enum stem]] S08

kanye na- ... together with ... [adv phr] S01

kanye nengane together with a child [adv phr] S17

kanye no-30g (30ml) together with 30g (30ml) [adv phr] S01

kanye nojusi together with the juice [adv phr] S01

kanye nomyeni together with my husband [adv phr] S24

kaSipho Sipho's [poss Cl. 1] S26

kaSTD 10 for Std (Standard) 10 (This was formerly the highest level of secondary education) [poss Cl. 4] S05

katiki for three pence, for a tickey (South African word for three pence when it still used sterling) [poss Cl. 1 or 3] S25

-kazi -ess, -lady, -woman, female ... [feminine suff; cf. **indodakazi, inkosikazi, umhlengikazi**] S17

kazwelonke national [poss Cl. 1] S05

ke in order that, so that [conj; followed by subjunctive] S05

-ke- he, she [SC Cl. 1, found in the neg before the Cl. 17 abs pron **kho**] S14

-ke do once, do ever [aux used in formation of the potential, neg; followed by the narrative in the past and the subjunc elsewhere] S06

-ke do sometimes, do occasionally [aux; followed by subjunc] S14

-ke then, so [enclitic attached to last word of phrase] S05

kepha but [conj] S08

Kgopane (surname) [n Cl. 1a] {Sotho/Tswana} S19

-khal-a cry, weep, scream; complain, voice a grievance; request [v.i.] S05

-khalaz-a complain, protest [v.i.] S21

-khalel-a plead for [v-appl] S26

-khaliph-a bec clever, smart, intelligent [v.inch; < **ubukhali** sharpness + **-ph-**] S07

Khambule surname [n Cl. 1a] S09

-**khandl-a** exhaust, tire out, fatigue, weary [v.t.] S27

-**khang-a** be attractive, attract admiration or desire [v.i. & t.]

-**khangis-a** advertise; make attractive, make desirable [v-caus] S18

-**khankas-a** move in a horseshoe formation in order to out-maneuver [v.i.] S10

-**khanuk-** lust, desire strongly; be jealous, be envious [v.i.] S23

-**khany-a** shine, glow, gleam, be bright [v.i.] S04

Khanyile (surname) [n Cl. 1a] S09

-**khathal-a** bec tired [v.inch] S05

-**khathaz-a** tire; worry, disturb, bother, pester [v-caus; < -**kha-thal- + -Y-; l + Y > z**] S05

-**khathazek-a** bec worried, bec disturbed, bec distressed [v-caus-neut] S05

-**khathazekile** worried, disturbed, distressed [v-caus-neut-stative] S05

Khawula (surname) [n Cl. 1a] S06

-**khe** his, her, its [abs pron Cl. 1; used in possessives] S02

-**kheth-a** choose, decide on, opt, select, elect [v.t.] S14

-**khethek-a** be picked out, selected, differentiated, be particular [v-neut] S20

-**khethel-a** choose for, decide on for, select for, elect for [v-appl] S14

-**khiph-a** take out, withdraw, produce (to view) [v.t.] S05

-**khiqiz-a** produce in abundance, turn out in large quantities, produce a surplus [v.t.] S27

-**khishw-a** be taken out, be brought out, be removed, be expelled, have something removed [v-pass; < -**khiph-w-a**; **phw** > **shw**] S05

-**khishw-a isisu** to have diarrhea (lit. to be taken out the stomach) [vn phr Cl. 15]

kho it [abs pron Cl. 15] S05

kho it, there, present [abs pron Cl. 17] S04

-**kho** your [abs pron 2 p sg, used in possessives] S04

-**khohl-a** slip the mind, escape the memory; puzzle, perplex [v.t.] S05

-**khohlis-a** deceive, mislead, cheat [v-caus] S05

-**khokh-a** pay, repay; draw out, withdraw [v.t.] S10

-**khokhek-a** be payable [v-neut] S28

-**khokhel-a** pay to, pay for, pay on behalf of, pay off, repay [v-appl] S13

-**khokhis-a** make pay, charge, fine [v-caus] S13

-**khokhisw-a** be made to pay, be charged [v-caus-pass] S13

-khokhw-a be paid [v-pass] S13

-KHOLELW-A BELIEVE IN [V-APPL-PASS] S23

-kholw-a believe [v.i. & t.] S10

-khomb-a point (at), point out [v.i. & t.] S16

-khombis-a point out, show [v-caus; the caus ext is here used idiomatically] S18

khona it, there, present [abs pron Cl. 17] S04

khona manjalo at that time [conj phr] S17

-khony-a bellow (as a bull), roar (like a lion) [v.i.] S09

-khonz-a bec passionate about, bec keen on; worship; pay respect(s) to [v.t.] S14

-khotham-a bend over, bow; be humble [v.i.] S27

Khoza (surname) [n Cl. 1a] S08

-khubal-a get hurt, damaged, injured, disabled; be disappointed; be ineffective, fail [v.i.] S14

-khubaz-a disable, make ineffective; damage, injure, hurt; intimidate [v-caus; < -khubal- + -Y-; l + -Y- > z] S14

-khubazek-a bec disabled or handicapped, get injured [v-neut] S14

-khukhumal-a swell, expand; rise (of dough) [v.i.] S01

-khul-a grow, grow up; age [v.i.] S14

-khulel-a grow for, grow towards, grow up in [v-appl] S20

-khulelw-a bec pregnant (euph; lit. be grown for) [v-appl-pass] S20

-khulis-a bring up, raise; grow, enlarge [v-caus] S14

-khulisw-a be brought up, be raised; be enlarged [v-caus-pass] S14

-khulu big, large, great, important, adult, grown-up, senior, chief [adj stem] S09

-khulul-a free, release, emancipate [v.t.] S18

-khululek-a bec free or emancipated, be released [v-neut] S18

-khulum-a talk, speak [v.t.] S09

-khulumel-a speak for [v-appl] S13

-khulunyw-a be spoken, be talked [v-pass; < -khulum-w-a; mw > nyw] S10

-khumbul-a remember, miss [v.t.] S17

khumbula remember [imper] S28

-khumbulek-a be memorable [v-neut] S17

-khungath-a frustrate, place in a dilemma, perplex; embarrass, shame [v.t.] S23

-khungathek-a be overwhelmed, bec frustrated, be placed in a dilemma [v-neut] S23

-khuphuk-a rise, go up, ascend [v.i.] S13

-khuphul-a promote; raise, hoist;

expose [v.t.] S27

-khuphulel-a promote to, raise to, expose to [v-appl] S27

-khushulelw-a be promoted to; be raised to [v-appl-pass; < -khuphulel-w-a; ph ... -w- > sh ... -w-] S27

-khuz-a calm, soothe, quieten [v.t.] S08

Khuzwayo (surname) [n Cl. 1a] S25

-khwehlel-a cough [v.i.] S20

ki- to, from, at, on [loc pref; var found before pronouns mi(na), thi(na) and (ni)na] S05

kimina to, from, at, on me [loc] S19

kithi to, from, at, on us; to, from, at our place or country, the place to which I or we belong [loc] S05

kithina to, from, at, on us [loc] S18

-klomel- reward, give a prize or bonus [v.t.] S11

ko- [quant conc Cl. 17] S12

ko- of [< kwa- poss conc Cl. 15 + o] S05

ko- of [< kwa- poss conc Cl. 17 + o] S12

kobasi before the White bosses [loc; < ku- + obasi] S27

kocansi of the sleeping-mat [poss Cl. 17; < kwa- + ucansi] S09

koDlamini the Dlamini clan, the Dlaminis' place [loc] S22

kodwa but [conjunction; < ko- [quant conc Cl. 17] + -dwa only, alone [quant stem]] S03

kokufunda of study [poss Cl. 15; < kwa- + uku...] S13

kokugqugquzelwa of persuasion [poss Cl. 17; < kwa- + uku...] S12

kokuphazamiseka of being disturbed [poss Cl. 17; < kwa- + uku...] S18

kokuqala of beginning [poss Cl. 17; < kwa- + uku...] S23

kokuqeqeshelwa (of) being trained for [poss Cl. 17; < kwa- + uku...] S18

kokuqeqeshwa (of) being trained [poss Cl. 17; < kwa- + uku...] S16

kokuthi of that [poss; < kwa- + ukuthi] S16

kokuthola (of) obtaining, of (receipt) [poss Cl. 17; following emva; < kwa- + uku...] S13

kokuya of going to [poss Cl. 15; < kwa- + uku...] S25

kokuya ocansini of having sex [poss phr Cl. 15] S25

komame from, to the ladies [loc; < ku- + omame] S08

komholo than the salary [loc; < ku- + umholo] S28

komkhankaso of the scheme or program [poss Cl. 17; < kwa- + umkhankaso] S12

koMkhize the Mkhize clan, the Mkhizes' place [loc; < kwa- + oMkhize] S22

komnotho of the economy [poss Cl. 15; < **kwa-** + **umnotho**] S25

komphakathi of the community [poss Cl. 15; < **kwa-** + **umpha-kathi**] S21

koMthembu the Mthembu clan, the Mthembus' place [loc; < **kwa-** + **oMthembu**] S22

komthetho of the law [poss Cl. 15; < **kwa-** + **umthetho**] S25

komuzi of the village, of the household, of the homestead [poss Cl. 15; < **kwa-** + **umuzi**] S26

konke everything, all [quant Cl. 17] S12

konke lokhu all this [quant phr Cl. 17] S12

konyaka of the year [poss Cl. 15; < **kwa-** + **unyaka**] S28

koShozi the Shozi clan, the Shozis' place [loc; < **kwa-** + **oShozi**] S22

kothisha of teachers [poss Cl. 15; < **kwa-** + **othisha**] S05

kowesilisa to, from, at males [loc; < **ku-** + **owesilisa**] S23

ku- it [SC Cl. 15] S04

ku- it, there [indefinite SC, Cl. 17] S01

ku- [NP Cl. 17] S10

ku- [enum conc Cl. 17] S25

ku- to, from, at, in, on [loc pref] S01

-ku- it [OC Cl. 15 & Cl. 17] S01, S05

-ku- [2nd half adj conc, Cl. 17] S08

ku-200 at 200 [loc] S19

ku-23 282 at 23,282 [loc] S20

kuba it becomes [copula, pres, conjoint] S20, S27

kuba khona imali there is money [exist cop, inch, pres] S28

kuba ngumuntu are a person [ident cop, inch, pres, conjoint] S20

kuba yimbangela it becomes a cause [ident cop, inch, pres] S28

kubafowabo from his or her brothers [loc] S27

kubafundi to, from, at, among students [loc] S19

kubakhokhi-ntela towards taxpayers [loc] S10

kubakhubaze it should disable them [subjunc] S17

kubalimi to, from, at farmers [loc] S27

kubaluleke it is important [past, conjoint] S20

kubalulekile it is important [stative] S14

kubalwa there is included, there is counted [pres, conjoint] S13

kubandakanya it involves [pres, conjoint] S23

kubangelwa it is caused [pres, conjoint] S23

kubangwa it is caused [pres, conjoint] S05

kubantu to people [loc] S04

kubashayeli from drivers [loc] S09

kube it becomes; it should be or become [copula, subjunc] S01

kube it was [copula, past, conjoint] S26

kube sekwenza it then caused [past pres] S13

kube yimina it should be me [ident cop, inch, subjunc] S14

kube yizinkinga it should be problems [ident cop, inch, subjunc] S16

kubebuhlungu (or **kube buhlungu**) and there becomes painful, and one has pain [descr cop, inch, subjunc] S20

kubenjalo (or **kube njalo**) it should be so [descr cop, inch, subjunc] S23

kubhake bake it [imperative] S01

Kubheka (surname) [n Cl. 1a] S13

kubo to, from, at, in his, her, their home, place or country [loc] S14

kubona to, from, at, on them [loc] S17

kubonakala to bec apparent [< **ukubonakala**] S10

kubonakale it is apparent, it should be visible [subjunc] S26

kubuhlungu it is painful, it is sad [descr cop, pres] S28

kubukeka it seems [pres, conjoint] S19

kucanula it disgusts, it nauseates [pres, conjoint] S21

kuchaza ... explains ... [pres, conjoint] S10

kudala long ago, a long time [loc n Cl. 17] S10

kudingeke it is necessary [subjunc] S16

kudla food [< **ukudla**] S09

kudlange it is rife [past, conjoint] S20

kudlula there passes [pres, partic] S17

kudokotela from a doctor [loc] S20

kufakwe they should put in, there should be put in [subjunc] S13

kufana it is like, it resembles [pres, conjoint] S27

kufanele it is necessary [aux, stative tense] S04

kufanele ukuba usebenzele phezu kwamaphutha you need to work on the basis of the mistakes [v phr] S04

kufanele uzenze you have to do them [v phr] S04

kufe there died [past, conjoint] S17

kugcina there ending up [aux, pres, partic] S21

kugcina it ends up [pres, conjoint] S28

kugcizelela ... emphasizes ... [pres, conjoint] S09

kugcwala the influx (lit. there becoming full) [pres, partic] S03

kugcwele are full of, it is full (of) [stative; < -gcwal- + -i...e] S05

kugqugquzelwe they should be prodded [subjunc] S24

kugwetshwa judgment is given, sentence is passed [pres, conjoint] S26

kuhamba it is going [pres, partic] S17

kuhhavini in the oven [loc] S01

kuhlala there live [pres, conjoint] S23

kuhlale it continues to be, it remains [aux] S09

kuhlasela there struck (lit. there strikes) [pres, partic] S17

kuhle it is good [descr cop, pres] S08

kuhloswe it is intended [past, conjoint] S24

kuhlukanisa it distinguishes [pres, conjoint] S07

kuhlukunyezwa be assaulted, be attacked, violence [< **uku-hlukunyezwa**] S23

kuhoxe there withdrew [past, partic, conjoint] S11

kuhoxiswe it should be withheld, it should be hidden [subjunc] S21

kuhulumeni to, from, in, with the government [loc] S12

kuka- of [poss conc Cl. 15] S07

kuka- of [poss conc Cl. 17; link between certain locative nouns and a following noun of Cl. 1a] S10

kuka-R1mln of one million rands [poss Cl. 17] S10

kukachwepheshe of an expert [poss Cl. 17] S23

kukaMnuz of Mr. [poss Cl. 15] S07

kukamongameli of the president [poss Cl. 15] S17

kukaMorgan Zama of Morgan [poss Cl. 15] S11

kukaningi it is often [loc cop, pres] S23

kuka-October of October [poss Cl. 17] S20

kukayise of his or her father [poss Cl. 15; < **kuka-** + **uyise**] S10

kuke it sometimes PAST VERB [aux, past, conjoint] S13

kuke kwaba nokuphazamiseka there was sometimes an interruption [assoc cop, inch, rem past, occasional] S13

kukho to, from, at, in, on it [loc] S18

kukhona there is ..., there are ... [loc cop, pres; may also introduce an exist cop] S04

kukhona lapho esho khona there is a place where (s)he states [exist cop, pres] S26

kukhukhumale it rises [subjunc] S01

375

kukhulunywa one speaks (lit. there is spoken) [pres, partic] S10

kulabo to, from, at, among those [loc] S08

kulabobalimi to, from, at, among, with those farmers [loc] S27

kulabobantu to, from, at, among those people [loc] S20

kulahleka there go missing [pres, partic] S08

kulalwa one sleeps, they sleep, there is slept [pres, conjoint] S20

kulalwe there is slept, they have intercourse [subjunc] S23

kulapho it was when [loc cop, pres] S17

kulawo to, from, at, in, on those [loc] S20

kulawomanzi to, from, in, on that water [loc] S20

kulawomazwe to, from, in those countries [loc] S20

kule to, from, at, in, on this (one) [loc] S13

kule to, from, at, in, on these [loc] S19

kuleli to, from, in this (depending on context, **izwe** 'country' is often understood) [loc; short for **kuleli zwe** in this country] S09

kulelikhemisi to, from, at, in this pharmacy [loc] S17

kulelikolishi to, from, at, in this college [loc] S19

kulelipulazi to, from, on this farm

[loc phr] S27

kulelizinga to, from, at this level or stage [loc] S27

kulelizwe to, from, in this country [loc] S25

kuleminyaka during, in these years [loc] S19

kulempilo to, from, in this life [loc] S23

kulendawo (also **kule ndawo**) to, from, at, in this place [loc phr] S06, S09

kulenhlangano to, from, in this organization [loc] S25

kulesi to, from, at, in, on this [loc] S13

kulesi sifunda to, from, in this province [loc] S17

kulesisibhedlela to, from, at, in this hospital [loc] S14

kulesisifundazwe to, from, in this province [loc] S24

kulesisikhungo to, from, at this stall [loc] S24

kulesisivande to, from, in this garden plot [loc] S27

kuleso to, from, at, in, on this (one) [loc] S14

kuleso naleso to, from, at, in this or that [loc phr] S18

kulesosibalo to, from that figure or number [loc] S20

kulesosibhedlela to, from, at, in that hospital [loc] S14

kulesosikalo to, from that dose [loc] S20

kulesosikhangiso to, from, in that advertisement [loc] S18

kulesosikole to, from, at, in that school [loc] S14

kulesosimo from, in that manner [loc] S16

kulethe it has brought [past, conjoint] S25

kuleya to, from, at, in, on that (one) [loc] S06

kuleyo to, from, in, at, on that (one) [loc] S18

kuleyomitholampilo to, from, at, in those clinics [loc] S25

kuleyondawo to, from, at, in that place [loc] S18

kulezo to, from, at, in, on those [loc] S16

kulezozindawo to, from, at, in those places [loc] S16

kulo to, from, at, in this (one) [loc] S13

kulo nyaka this year [loc] S13

kulobo to, from, at, in, on that (one) or those [loc] S28

kulobobunzima to, from, in that difficulty [loc] S28

kulobubi to, from, in this evil [loc] S23

kulokho to, from, at, in that (or this) [loc] S14

kulolu to, from, at, in, on this (one) [loc] S25

kululuphiko to, from, in this section or branch [loc] S25

kulona to, from, at, in, on it [loc] S27

kulowo to, from, at, in, on that (one) [loc] S18

kulowomzila to, from, in that broad track [loc] S18

kulula it is easy [descr cop, pres, partic] S20

kulungiswe they sort out (lit. there should be fixed) [subjunc] S13

kumalaleveva from, against malaria [loc] S20

kuma-patty pans in cupcake tins, in patty pans [locative] S01

kumasipala to, from, in the municipality [loc] S12

kumele it is obligatory, it is requisite; must, should, ought [aux, stative] S08

kumhlonishwa to, from, at the honorable [loc] S21

kumnenge it disgusted him [past, conjoint] S26

ku-mosquito to, from, in, on the mosquito [loc] S20

kumphathi-siteshi to, from, at the station commander [loc] S21

kumuntu to, from, at, on, into a person [loc] S20

kun- compared to, in comparison with, more than [compar adv pref **kuna-** with elision of **a** before **e** and **o**] S15

kuna- compared to, in comparison with, more than [compar adv pref] S05

kuna- there is, there are [though made up of the SC **ku-** and the assoc pref **-na-**, this is conveniently treated as an entity] S06

kunabafundi there are students [assoc cop, pres] S19

kunabangaqeqeshiwe compared with those who are unqualified [comparative adv] S05

kunabantu there are people [assoc cop, pres] S06

kunaleli more than this one [compar adv] S27

kunaleyo (more) than that [compar adv] S28

kunamapayipi there are pipes [assoc cop, pres] S20

kunamaqembu there are groups or gangs [assoc cop, pres] S09

kunciphe there should become less, there should be a decrease (in) [subjunc] S12

kune- there is, there are [< **kuna-** + i] S06

kunenye (more) than the other [compar adv] S15

kunesithwathwa there is frost [assoc cop, pres, partic] S27

kunesomiso there is a drought [assoc cop, pres] S20

kunezibonelo there are examples [assoc cop, pres] S23

kunezigameko there are repeated events [assoc cop, pres] S08

kunezigodi there are districts [assoc cop, pres] S06

kunezindaba there is news, there are matters [assoc cop, pres] S23

kunezinhlelo there are arrangements [assoc cop, pres] S25

kunezinqumo there are decisions [assoc cop, pres] S08

kungaba it could be(come), it would be(come) [copula, pres, potential] S08

kungaba yinselelo it would or could be a challenge [ident cop, inch, pres, potential] S19

kungaba yiqiniso it could be the truth [ident cop, inch, pres, potential] S23

kungaba yisifundo it could be a lesson [ident cop, inch, pres, potential] S08

kungabasiza it can help them [pres, potential] S20

kungahlelelwanga it was not planned for [past, rel, neg; < **akuhlelelwanga**] S25

kungajwayelekile it not being usual [stative, rel, neg] S11

kungalesosikhathi it is at that time [loc cop, pres] S20

kunganginika it could give me [pres, potential] S27

kungani? why? [conj; followed by partic] S26

kunganjani nje? how would it be if?, why not? [followed by subjunc] S08

kungcola to bec corrupt, immoral, dirty [< **ukungcola**] S23

kungcono it is better, it is preferable [descr cop, pres] S08

kungekho ... there is no..., there being no ..., there are no ... [exist cop, pres, partic, neg] S23

kungekho ukungabaza there is no doubt [ident cop, pres, partic] S23

kungekudala before long [loc cop, pres, partic; < **ku-** SC Cl. 17 + **-nge-** neg pref + **kudala**] S10

kungenamigwaqo there are no roads [assoc cop, pres, partic, neg] S18

kungenhla it is above [loc cop, pres] S12

kungenze it has made me [past, conjoint] S14

kungenzeka it could happen, it is possible [pres, potential] S15

kungenziwa without this being done [pres, partic, neg] S05

kungezwakali there not being heard [pres, partic, neg] S21

kungumsebenzi it is a task [ident cop, pres] S16

kuningi there is a lot, there is much, there is a great deal [descr cop, pres] S27

kunjalo it is so, it is like that [descr cop, pres] S08

kunjani? what is it like?, how is it? [descr cop, pres] S23

kuNksz to Miss or Ms [loc] S26

kuNkulunkulu to, from, at God [loc] S14

kuno- there is, there are [< **kuna-** + **u**] S10

kunobufakazi there is evidence [assoc cop, pres] S23

kunokuhlukumezeka there is subjection to violence or assault [assoc cop, pres] S23

kunokwenzeka it could happen, it is possible [assoc cop, pres] S15

kunolwesokudla more than or compared with that of the right [compar adv] S15

kunoma to no matter, to even [loc] S17

kunoma ngubani to no matter whom, to whomever [loc] S17

kunomehluko there is a difference [assoc cop, pres] S10

kunomkhankaso there is a scheme [assoc cop, pres] S24

kunzima it is difficult [descr cop, pres] S09

kuphela only, alone [adv] S08

kuphele there should end [subjunc] S20

kuphephukisa it blew about [pres, conjoint] S17

kuphetha X X finish(es) up, X has/have the last word, X clinch(es) the argument S14

kuphi? which? [enum Cl. 17] S25

kuphikisa it contradicts [pres, conjoint] S23

kuphindaphinde keep repeating it [imper, with OC, Cl. 17] S20

kuphindwe it is repeatedly [aux, subjunc] S23

kupholise cool it [imperative] S01

kuphuma it yields, there comes out [pres, conjoint] S01

kuqala at first, in the beginning [time adv; < **-qal-a** begin] S16

kuqale it began [past, conjoint] S13

kuqalwe there should be begun, one should begin [subjunc] S08

kuqaqambe and there aches or throbs [subjunc] S20

kuqashwe they should employ, there should be employed [subjunc] S13

kuqhathaniswa (it) being compared [pres, partic] S07

kuqhuba it continues [pres, conjoint] S27

kuqhubeke that there should continue [subjunctive] S05

kuqhutshekelwe and one should proceed to, and there should be proceeded to [subjunc] S08

kuqubule it has caused to erupt [past, conjoint] S25

kuqwashiseke they should be put on the look out, they should be alerted [subjunc] S21

ku-R120 to R120 [loc; < **ku-** + **u-R120**] S13

ku-R50 from R50 (R = rand, the unit of South African currency) [loc; < **ku-** + **u-R50**] S13

ku-R90million at R90 million [loc; < **ku-** + **u-R90million**] S17

kusahlukunyezwa there is or are still attacked [pres, persistive] S05

kusahlukunyezwa abayi-ANC those of the ANC are still attacked [v phr] S05

kusasa tomorrow [adv; < **kusasa** it is still dawning [pres, persistive] S04]

kusasetshenziswa it is still used, employed [pres, persistive] S21

kusazothatha it will still take [fut, persistive aspect] S05

kusemithonjeni it is in the sources [loc cop, pres] S09

kusempeleni it is in truth [loc cop; < **ku-** SC 17 + **-se-** loc pref + **impela** truth + **-eni** loc suff] S13

kusemthethweni it is legal, it is in the law [loc cop, pres] S12

kusetshenziswe one should use, there should be used [subjunc] S20

kusewudaba it is now a serious matter [ident cop, pres, exclusive] S25

kushise it is hot [subjunc] S20

kushiwo it is said [subjunc] S06

kusho ... said ... [past, conjoint] S09

kusho that or it means [pres, conjoint] S05

kusho ukuthi that means to say [v phr] S28

kusikwe they should cut, there should be cut [subjunc] S13

kusiphatha it affects us (the 1 p pl OC is used, since the wife is also affected by the problem) S15

kuso to, from, at, in, on it [loc] S14

kusobala it is public, it is in the open [loc cop, pres] S25

kusokhemisi to, from a pharmacist [loc] S20

kusuka it just, it merely [aux, pres, conjoint] S17

kusukela from [conj; < **kusukela** it originates at or in] S08

kuthatha it takes [pres, conjoint] S23

kuthathwe it took (lit. there was taken) [past, conjoint] S05

kuthe lapho just as (in the past) [conj phr] S14

kuthele pour it [imper + obj] S01

kuthi it being so that [conj] S10

kuthi it happens that [pres, conjoint] S20

kuthi it should happen that [subjunc] S16

kuthiwa it is said, they say [pres, conjoint] S12

kuthiwe (then) it's said, (then) 'they' say [subjunc] S08

kutholakale there should be found [subjunc] S08

kutholakale it has been found [past, conjoint] S23

kuthunjwe they have hijacked, there has been a hijacking, they

have held hostage [past, conjoint] S16

kutshalwe there has or have been planted [past, conjoint] S27

ku-Umlazi Soccer Festival at the Umlazi ... [loc] S11

kuvale and the close will be (lit. it will close) [subjunc] S11

kuvame one, it, they normally VERB(S) [aux, past, conjoint] S08

kuvamile it is normal [aux, stative] S15

kuvimbe it prevents [past, conjoint] S19

kuvuvukale and there swells [subjunc] S20

kuvuvuzele sprinkle it [imperative] S01

kuwe(na) to, from, at, on you [loc] S28

kuwo(na) to, from, at, in(to), on, among them [loc] S12, S25

kuwo to, from, at, in(to), on, through it [loc] S27

kuwukuthi it is (the case) that [ident cop, pres; < **ku-** SC 17 + **w-** cop pref + **ukuthi** conj] S13

kuxwayisa there warns [pres, conjoint] S23

kuya it goes [pres, conjoint] S19

kuya it still VERBs [aux] S05

kuya to, up to, as far as [conj; < **kuya** it goes to] S08, S17

kuya kuqhubeka it still continues [v phr] S05

kuyabambeka it is tangible [pres, disjoint] S21

kuyadilizwa they are retrenching (lit. there is being retrenched) [pres, disjoint] S03

kuyafana it is similar, it is the same [pres, disjoint] S23

kuyakukhulula it frees, sets free, releases, emancipates you [pres, disjoint] S23

kuyashaqisa it is amazing [pres, disjoint] S17

kuyasiza it helps [pres, disjoint] S20

kuyaye it sometimes VERBs [aux, pres, disjoint] S16

kuye to, from, at, on him or her [loc] S26

kuyekwe they should stop, there should be stopped [subjunc] S13

kuyenzeka it happens, it occurs, it takes place [pres, disjoint] S16

kuyibona it is them [ident cop, pres] S27

kuyicala it is an offence [ident cop, pres] S23

kuyilapho it is where [ident cop, pres] S16

kuyilowo it is that one [ident cop, pres] S16

kuyilowo nayilowo each and every, individually (lit. it being that one and that one) [ident cop phr] S16

kuyima before [conj; followed by partic; < ident cop; **ku-** + **yi-** + **ma** if, when [conj]] S13

kuyindawo it is a place [ident cop, pres] S18

kuyinkinga it is a problem, it is a puzzle, it is a difficulty [ident cop, pres] S23

kuyinto it is something, it is a thing [ident cop, pres] S06

kuyisikhathi it is time [ident cop, pres] S04

kuyisikhundla it is a position [ident cop, pres] S27

kuyisikole it is a school [ident cop, pres] S14

kuyiwe there should be gone [subjunc] S23

kuyizifundo it is, they are studies [ident cop, pres] S18

kuyo to, from, at, in, on it, him, her [loc] S18

kuyoqashwa they will appoint (lit. there will be appointed) [rem fut] S05

kuza there is going to be (lit. there comes) [pres, conjoint] S05

kuzalwa to be born [< **ukuzalwa**] S20

kuze until it, so that finally, until eventually [aux, subjunctive] S01

kuze kube up to, until [aux phrase] S03

kuze kube yimanje up to now, until now S03

kuze kukhukhumale until it rises [v phr] S01

kuze kuphele until the end of, until after [v phr] S20

k u z e k w a s h a y a uLwesihlanu Friday came (lit. it eventually hit Friday) [v phr] S13

kuzinikeza it hands them [pres, conjoint] S09

kuzo to, from, at, in, on them [loc] S05

kuzo zonke in all these [loc phr] S05

kuzoba it will be [copula, fut] S11

kuzoba yi-track suit it will be a track suit [ident cop, inch, fut] S11

kuzobasiza it will help them [fut] S25

kuzodayiselwa they will market in or at (lit. there will be marketed in or at) [fut] S24

k u z o h l o m u l w a one will be rewarded [fut] S11

kuzokwenza it will make [future] S04

kuzokwenzeka there will happen, it will happen [fut] S11

kuzophelekezelwa it will be accompanied [fut] S11

kuzoyiwa they would go, one would go (lit. there would be gone) [fut] S06

kuzwakala it is understood, there is heard, it is audible [pres, conjoint] S08

kuzwelonke to, from, in the nation [loc] S11

kw- it [SC Cl. 15; found before vowels **a** and **e**] S09

kw- it, there [indefinite SC, Cl. 17; found before vowels **a** and **e**] S03

kw- at the place of [loc pref; form of **kwa-** found before vowels **a** and **e**] S06

kw- to, from, in, at [loc pref; form of **ku-** found before vowels **a, e, i**] S06

-kw- it [OC Cl. 15; found before vowels **a** and **e**] S14

-kw- it [indefinite OC Cl. 17; found before vowels **a** and **e**] S05

-kw- [prefix inserted to separate a vowel from a following **a** or **e** in the future tense] S04

kwa- at the place of [loc pref] S02

kwa- of [poss conc Cl. 15] S04

kwa- of [poss conc Cl. 17; link between certain loc nouns and a following nominal] S04

kwaba (and) it became [copula, narrative] S08

k w a b a it became [copula, rem past] S13

kwaba mnyama and it became black or dark [descr cop, inch, narr] S17

kwaba muncu it became bitter, unpleasant [descr cop, inch, rem past] S21

kwaba ngukunyamalala and then came the disappearance (lit. and then it became the disappearance) [ident cop, inch, narr] S08

kwaba nguyena it was him [ident cop, inch, rem past] S14

kwaba nokuphazamiseka there was interruption (lit. it became with interruption) [assoc cop, inch, narr] S13

kwaba ukuvumelana it became an agreement, it was an agreement [ident cop, inch, rem past] S13

kwabafundi of students [poss Cl. 15] S13

kwabahamba ngezinyawo from pedestrians [loc phr] S09

kwabakwa-Agrilek from the people at Agrilek [loc] S27

kwabantu of people [poss Cl. 15] S17

kwabantwana of children [loc] S08

kwabanye to, from others [loc; < **ku-** + **abanye**] S02

kwabeNkatha to, from those of Inkatha [loc] S05

kwabesilisa to, from, for males [loc] S23

kwabesilisa of males [poss Cl. 15] S23

kwabesimame to, from women [loc] S25

kwabha in the open country, in a bare place; openly, in full view [loc; cf. **bhaa** be open, be clear,

be bare [ideo]] S21

kwabo their [poss Cl. 15] S13

kwabulala and smashed (lit. and killed) [narr] S17

kwabuya there came back [rem past] S18

kwacishe there almost [rem past, partic] S17

KwaDabeka at Dabeka's (place) [loc] S07

kwadalwa it was caused [rem past] S14

kwadingeka it was necessary [rem past] S14

kwadubuleka there was shot [narr] S21

kwa-Eskom to Eskom (national electricity supplier; originally: Electricity Supply Commission) [loc] S06

kwafa and there died [narr] S21

kwakhe his, her, of him, of her [poss Cl. 15 or 17] S14

kwakhe at his or her place [poss Cl. 17] S22

kwakho your [poss Cl. 15] S04

kwakubhalwe there was written [rem past past, conjoint] S18

kwakubukeka it was remarkable, it was attractive [rem past pres] S17

kwakudilika there were collapsing [rem past pres] S17

kwakumi it was standing [rem past stative] S18

kwakumi ngomumo it was in order (idiom; lit. it stood in character) [v phr] S18

kwakundiza there flew [rem past pres] S17

kwakunezinye there were certain [assoc cop, rem past pres] S25

kwakungelikaGareth Olivier it was that, or it used to be that of Gareth Olivier [ident cop, rem past pres] S27

kwakungeyabesilisa they were those for males [ident cop, rem past pres] S19

kwakungezabaMhlophe they were those of Whites [ident cop, rem past pres; < kw- SC Cl. 17 + -a- rem past pref + -ku- SC + -ng- cop pref + ezabaMhlophe] S16

kwakungokamfowabo it was that of his or her brother [ident cop, rem past pres] S27

kwakungokokuqala it was the first (time) [ident cop, rem past pres; kw- SC Cl. 17 + -a- rem past + -ku- SC + -ng- + okoku-qala] S23

kwakungukuba ngummeli it was to become a lawyer [ident cop, rem past pres; < kw- SC + -a- rem past + -ku- it + -ng- is + ukuba to become + ngummeli it is a lawyer] S18

kwakungukuthi it was that [ident cop, rem past pres] S23

kwakungumsebenzi it was a job, it was work [ident cop, rem past pres] S19

kwakuyimigulukudu it was hardened or habitual criminals [ident cop, rem past pres] S23

kwakuzwakala there was audible [rem past pres] S17

kwakwenzeka it used to happen [rem past pres] S23

kwala even though, notwith-standing the fact that [conj] S05

kwalabo of those [poss Cl. 17] S12

kwale of this [poss Cl. 15] S12

kwaleli of this [poss Cl. 15] S26

kwalelo of that [poss Cl. 15] S17

kwalelosonto of that week [poss Cl. 15] S17

kwalesi of this [poss Cl. 15] S20

kwalesisifo of this disease [poss Cl. 15] S20

kwalezi from these, of these [poss Cl. 17] S18

kwalolu of this [poss Cl. 15] S21

kwalomthetho of this law [poss Cl. 15] S25

kwamabhanoyi of airplanes [poss Cl. 15] S18

kwamabhilidi of buildings [poss Cl. 17] S16

kwamabhizinisi of businesses [poss Cl. 15] S12

kwamajele of jails [poss Cl. 17] S23

kwamakhaza of cold [poss Cl. 15] S12

kwamalungu of members [poss Cl. 15] S12

kwamantombazane of girls [poss Cl. 15] S23

kwamanye to, from, at, in, on other [loc] S20

kwamanzi of water [poss Cl. 15] S11

kwamaqembu of the gangs [poss Cl. 15] S09

kwama-strawberry of strawberries [poss Cl. 15] S27

kwami my [poss Cl. 15] S14

kwamnyama and became black or dark [abbreviation of **kwaba mnyama**] S17

kwaMpanza at the Mpanzas' place [loc] S02

KwaMpungose at the place of Mpungose [loc] S21

kwandisa it increases [pres, conjoint] S23

kwaNdlovu at Ndlovu's place [loc] S22

kwangenza it made me [rem past] S19

kwangicacela it became clear to me [rem past] S23

kwangqangqazelisa it caused to tremble, shiver, rattle [rem past] S17

kwanika it gave [rem past] S17

kwanyamalala it disappeared [rem past or narr] S17

kwaphela (and) it ended [narr] S17

kwaphuma (and) there came out [narr] S17

kwaSAA to, from, at SAA (South African Airways) [loc] S18

kwasala there stayed behind [narr] S17

kwasala enkundleni there died (lit. there stayed behind in the incident) [v phr] S17

kwasebenzile to what (s)he has committed (lit. worked) [loc] S26

kwashaya there hit [narr] S13

kwaShezi the Shezi clan, Shezi's place [loc] S22

kwasibanibani at the place of certain people [loc] S06

kwasiza there helped [narr] S21

kwasuka there arose [rem past] S21

kwathi it happened that; then (in the past) [conj] S14

kwathi and they say [narr] S17

kwathunjwa there was a hijacking or a hostage-taking [narr] S16

kwaveza it brought to light, it revealed [rem past] S23

kwavuleka there opened [narr] S17

kwawa (and) there fell [narr] S17

kwayo its, his, her [poss Cl. 15] S08

kwaze until [aux, narr] S21

kwazeke it should bec known [subjunc] S21

kwaziwe it should be known [subjunc] S10

kwazo their [poss Cl. 15] S09

KwaZulu-Natal KwaZulu-Natal (province of South Africa) [loc] S05

KwaZulu Finance and Investment Corporation (KFC) from the KwaZulu ... [loc] S27

kwe- of [poss conc Cl. 15 **kwa-** coalesced with **i**] S12

kwe-Airports Company of South Africa (ACSA) of the Airports Company ...[poss Cl. 17] S18

kwebhange of a bank [poss Cl. 15] S12

kwegazi of blood [poss Cl. 15] S23

kwehla there descended [rem past] S17

kwejwayelekile it is usual, normal, customary [stative] S21

kwekwaShaka High School of the Shaka High School [poss Cl. 15] S11

kwelakho to, from, at, in yours [loc] S21

kwelamaqiniso in true words [loc] S08

kwelaseMelika to, from, in that (country) of America [loc] S16

kwelase-Northern Province to, from, in the Northern Province (lit. in that of in the Northern Province) [loc] S14

kwelase-South Africa to, from, in that (country) of South Africa

[loc] S20

kwelinye to, from, at, in, on one or a certain [loc] S17

kwemali of money [poss Cl. 15] S13

kwemboni of the industry, business, factory [poss Cl. 15 or 17] S18

kwemikhiqizo of surpluses [poss Cl. 15] S12

kwemindeni of families [poss Cl. 15] S25

kwemingcele of the borders [poss Cl. 17] S10

kweminye to, from, in, at, on other [loc] S08

kwemithi of medicines [poss Cl. 15] S20

kwemizwa of feelings [poss Cl. 15] S21

kwemvelo of nature [poss Cl. 15] S24

kwengabizi to one that does not cost [loc; < **ku-** + **engabizi**] S28

kwengxabano of the quarrel [poss Cl. 17] S27

kwenkanuko of sexual desire, of lust [poss Cl. 17] S23

kwenkanyamba of a tornado [poss Cl. 15] S17

kwenswelaboya of the murderer, evil person [poss Cl. 15] S26

kwentela of tax [poss Cl. 15] S10

kwenyuke there has gone up, there has risen [past tense, conjoint] S03

kwenza it makes, it does, it causes [pres, conjoint] S20

kwenzeka it happens [pres, partic] S20

kwenzeka there happened [rem past] S21

kwenzeke it happened [past, conjoint form] S04

kwenzekile it has happened, it has occurred [past, disjoint] S16

kwenziwa it is made, it is done, it is caused [pres, conjoint] S13

kwenziwa it was done, made [rem past] S23

kwenziwa yini ...? what causes ...? S19

kwenziwe it is done [subjunc] S23

kwesenkosi uCalalakubo Khawula in the jurisdiction of Chief Calalakubo Khawula [loc phr] S06

kwesikhathi of time [poss Cl. 15] S18

kwesimilo of nature, of character [poss Cl. 15] S26

kwesimo of condition, status [poss Cl. 17] S18

kwesingezansi in the pelvic region [loc] S20

kwesinye isikhathi sometimes, at other times [loc phr] S16

kwesisu of the stomach [poss Cl. 15] S25

kwesobunxele to, from, on the left [loc] S15

kwexwayisa (there) warns [pres, conjoint] S27

kweyakho to, from, at, in yours [loc] S08

kweyisihlanu to, from five [loc] S20

kwezamabhizinisi to, from, in business affairs [loc] S24

kweze-jazz to, from, in jazz [loc] S14

kwezeMfundo to, from, in Education [loc] S14

kwezethu to, from, at, in, on ours [loc] S08

kweze-turner in those (studies) of a turner [loc] S19

kwezifundo of studies, of lessons [poss Cl. 15] S12

kwezihlahla of bushes, shrubs, trees [poss Cl. 15] S24

kwezikhungo of shelters [poss Cl. 15] S24

kwezincwadi of books [poss Cl. 15 or 17] S13

kwezindiza of airplanes [poss Cl. 15] S18

kwezingane of children [poss Cl. 15] S23

kwezingcingo of calls, of phones [poss Cl. 15] S14

kwezingqinamba of weakness of the knees, of nervousness [poss Cl. 17] S18

kwezingubo of clothing [poss Cl. 15] S12

kwezingubo zomfaniswano of uniforms [poss phr Cl. 15] S12

kwezinhlelo of programs [poss Cl. 15] S12

kwezinkampani of companies [poss Cl. 15] S28

kwezinye in other(s), among other(s) [loc; < **ku-** + **ezinye**] S05

kwezipoki of ghosts [poss Cl. 15] S05

kwezisu of stomachs [poss Cl. 15] S25

kwezokuphatha in management or administration [loc] S14

kwezokuvakasha in tourism [loc] S24

kwezokuxhumana nomphakathi in community relations [loc] S14

kwezolimo in agriculture, in farming [loc] S27

kwezwakala there was audible [rem past] S18

kwi-ANC Women's League in the ANC (African National Congress) Women's League [loc] S25

kwi-Boys U/11 in the Boys U(nder)/11 [loc] S11

kwiChildline at Childline (call center for crisis counseling for or about children) [loc] S09

kwi-Girls Open in the Girls Open [loc] S11

kwi-Girls U/14 in the Girls U(nder)/14 [loc] S11

kwi-IFP to, from, in the IFP (Inkatha Freedom Party) [loc] S25

kwiMolopo at, around the Molopo (River) [loc] S20

kwi-Soccer Festival at the Soccer Festival [loc] S11

kwi-stock exchange to, from, at, in the stock exchange [loc] S28

L

l- it, he, she [SC Cl. 5; found before vowels] S03

l- it is [ident cop pref; used by some speakers before nouns of Cl. 5 and 11] S17

l- of [poss conc Cl. 5; found before vowels **a**, **e** and **o**] S17

la these [1st pos dem Cl. 6] S27

la- these [1st pos dem Cl. 2; in some dialects the abbreviated form **la** is used for the Cl. 2 demonstrative **laba**] S09

la- of [poss conc Cl. 5] S01

laba these [1st pos dem Cl. 2] S05

lababantu these people [dem phr Cl. 2; < **la** + **abantu**] S16

labafanyana these good-for-nothing youths [dem phr Cl. 2; < **la** + **abafanyana**] S09

labaniza and it flashed with lightning [narr] S17

labantu of people [poss Cl. 5] S07

389

labantu these people [dem phr Cl. 2; < la + abantu] S20

labesimame of women [poss Cl. 5] S19

labika it reported [rem past] S17

labo of them, their [poss Cl. 5] S16

labo those (near the addressee, or placed within an utterance) [2nd position dem Cl. 2] S08

labobahlengikazi those nurses [dem phr Cl. 2] S25

labobalimi those farmers [dem phr Cl. 2] S27

labobantu those people [dem phr Cl. 2] S16

lafika it, (s)he arrived [rem past] S23

laguqubala (and) it became cloudy, overcast [narr] S17

-lahl-a throw away [v.t.] S08

-lahlek-a get lost, go missing [v-neut] S08

-lahlekelw-a + AGENTIVE PREFIX lose [v-neut-appl-pass] S08

lakhe his, her [poss Cl. 5] S09

lakho your [poss Cl. 5] S04

lakithi our, of ours [poss Cl. 5] S25

-lal-a (go to) sleep, sleep, go to bed [v.inch] S09

lale of these [poss Cl. 5] S12

-lalel-a listen (to) [v.i. & t.] S05

lalelani-ke listen then [imperative] S07

laligubha it was observing [rem past pres] S17

lalilihle it, (s)he was beautiful [descr cop, rem past pres; < l-SC Cl. 5 + -a- rem past pref + -li- SC + -li- 2nd half adj conc + -hle adj stem] S17

lalowomuntu of that person [poss Cl. 5] S20

-lalw-a be slept [v-pass] S20

lamahhovisi of the offices [poss Cl. 5] S17

lamakhemisi of the pharmacies [poss Cl. 5] S17

lamaphoyisa of the police [poss Cl. 5] S16

lama-strawberry of strawberries [poss Cl. 5] S27

lama-strawberry these strawberries [dem phr Cl. 6] S27

-lamb-a get hungry [v.inch] S09

lambona (s)he saw him or her [rem past] S26

lami my [poss Cl. 5] S05

-land-a relate [v.t.] S18, S23

-landel-a follow [v.t.] S11

-landelan-a follow one another [v-recip] S11

landulela it precedes [pres, conjoint] S23

langempela real, true [poss Cl. 5] S23

lapha here [1st pos dem Cl. 16] S05

lapho there, where [2nd pos dem Cl. 16] S16

lapho when [conj; followed by partic] S10

lapho ... khona where ... [2nd pos dem Cl. 16 + abs pron Cl. 17; frames and ind rel of plain loc rel; see examples below; sometimes **khona** may be omitted as in the second example below] S02

lapho ayeme khona where (s)he was standing [ind rel of plain loc rel] S17

lapho ayephahlwe where (s)he had been surrounded [ind rel of plain loc rel, Cl. 1] S17

lapho bephoqelelwa khona where they are forced [ind rel of plain loc rel] S09

lapho esho khona where (s)he states [ind rel of plain loc rel] S26

lapho iNkatha iningi khona where Inkatha is found in large numbers [ind rel of plain loc rel] S05

lapho kulahleka khona izingane where children go missing [ind rel of plain loc relationship] S08

lapho kuthiwa ubenza khona amacala where it was said (s)he had committed the crimes [ind rel of plain loc rel] S26

lase it already [aux, narr] S17

laseMelika of America [poss Cl. 5] S16

laseMtata of Umtata [poss Cl. 5] S17

lase-Northern Province of the Northern Province [poss Cl. 5] S14

lase-South Africa of South Africa [poss Cl. 5] S16

lasishayela it, (s)he, they beat for it/him/her [rem past] S25

lasishayela elikhulu ihlombe they greatly applauded it [idiom] S25

lavota they, (s)he voted [rem past] S03

lawo those, that (near the person spoken to, or previously referred to) [2nd pos dem Cl. 6] S04

lawomabandla those groups [dem phr Cl. 6] S25

lawomanzi that water [dem phr Cl. 6] S20

lawomaqembu those groups [dem phr Cl. 6] S25

lawomazwe those countries [dem phr Cl. 6] S20

-lawul-a give commands, order; control, regulate [v.t.] S07

lazi it, (s)he should know [subjunc] S21

lazithengela (s)he bought them for [rem past] S08

laziwa it is known [pres, conjoint] S09

lazo of them [poss Cl. 5] S09

le these [1st pos dem Cl. 4 & Cl. 9] S12

le this, these [1st pos dem; in some dialects the abbreviated form **le** is used for all demonstratives that have **i** as 2nd vowel, i.e. Cl. 5, 7, 8, 10] S09, S11

le- of [poss conc Cl. 5 coalesced with following **i**] S01

lebhola of football, of soccer [n Cl. 5] S11

ledlule it has passed [past, disjoint] S26

le-glue of glue [poss Cl. 5] S09

le-glue this glue [dem phr Cl. 9] S09

lehlelwe it is overcome [subjunc] S23

-lekelel-a assist, help, aid [v.t.] S09

-lekelelw-a be assisted, be aided [v-pass] S21

-lele asleep [< -lal- + -i…e] S09

leli this [1st pos dem Cl. 5] S06

lelihlazo this shame, this dishonor [dem phr Cl. 5] S23

lelikhemisi this pharmacy [dem phr Cl. 5] S17

lelikolishi this college [dem phr Cl. 5] S19

lelipulazi this farm [dem phr Cl. 5] S27

lelithimba this team [dem phr Cl. 5] S16

lelizinga this level, this stage, this standard, this degree [dem phr Cl. 5] S27

lelizwe this country [dem phr Cl. 5] S25

lelo that (near the person spoken to, or previously referred to) [2nd pos dem Cl. 5] S17

lelosonto that week [dem phr Cl. 5] S17

lemali this money [dem phr Cl. 9] S24

leMdlwembe Gang of the Mdlwembe Gang [poss Cl. 5] S09

lemikhiqizo of production [poss Cl. 5] S19

leminyaka these years [dem phr Cl. 4] S19

lempilo to (of) life [poss Cl. 5] S14

lempilo this life [dem phr Cl. 9] S23

lendawo (also **le ndawo**) this place [dem phr Cl. 9] S06, S09

lendaba this matter, this affair [dem phr Cl. 9] S23

lendoda this man [dem phr Cl. 9] S27

lengane of the child [poss Cl. 5] S08

lenhlangano this society, this organization [dem phr Cl. 9] S14

lenkanyamba this tornado [dem phr Cl. 9] S17

lenkinga this problem [dem phr Cl. 9] S23

lensizwa this young man [dem phr Cl. 9] S14

lentokazi this young lady [dem phr Cl. 9] S19

lenu your (pl), of you [poss Cl. 5] S28

lenza (s)he, it caused [rem past] S21

lenziwa it is done, made, performed [pres, conjoint] S23

leqembu of the group [poss Cl. 5] S09

lesekela of the assistant [poss Cl. 5] S25

leshumi (of) ten [poss Cl. 5] S18

lesi this [1st pos dem Cl. 7] S04

lesibalo this figure [dem phr Cl. 7; < le + isibalo] S19

lesibhedlela of the hospital [poss Cl. 5] S14

lesifo this disease [dem phr Cl. 7; < le + isifo] S20

lesigameko this repeated incident [dem phr Cl. 7; < le + isigameko] S23

lesihluku this cruelty [dem phr Cl. 7; < le + isihluku] S09

lesinambuzane this parasite, this insect [dem phr Cl. 7; < le + isinambuzane] S20

lesisehlo this shock [dem phr Cl. 7] S23

lesisibhedlela this hospital [dem phr Cl. 7] S14

lesisicelo this request [dem phr Cl. 7] S14

lesisifo this disease [dem phr Cl. 7] S14

lesisifundazwe this province [dem phr Cl. 7] S24

lesisikhathi this time [dem phr Cl. 7] S04

lesisikhungo this stall [dem phr Cl. 7] S24

lesisimo this situation [dem phr Cl. 7] S23

lesisinqumo this decision [dem phr Cl. 7] S25

lesisithelo this fruit [dem phr Cl. 7] S27

lesisivande this garden plot [dem phr Cl. 7] S27

leso that (near the person spoken to, or previously referred to) [2nd pos dem Cl. 7] S14

leso naleso this or that (lit. that or that) [dem phr Cl. 7] S18

lesosenzo that action [dem phr Cl. 7] S18

lesosibalo that figure, that number [dem phr Cl. 7] S20

lesosibhedlela that hospital [dem phr Cl. 7] S14

lesosikalo that dose [dem phr Cl. 7] S20

lesosikhangiso that advertisement [dem phr Cl. 7] S18

lesosikhathi that time [dem phr Cl. 7] S14

lesosikole that school [dem phr Cl. 7] S14

lesosinqumo that decision [dem phr Cl. 7] S25

lesosinyathelo that step [dem phr Cl. 7] S18

lesosithombe that picture, that image [dem phr Cl. 7] S18

lesosizathu that reason [dem phr Cl. 7] S16

le-special task force of a special task force [poss Cl. 5] S16

-leth-a bring [v.t.] S09

lethu our, of us [poss Cl. 5; < la- + -ithu] S03

lewolintshi of an orange [poss Cl. 5] S01

leya that (over there) [3rd pos dem Cl. 9] S06

leyo that (near the person spoken to, previously referred to) [2nd pos dem Cl. 4 & 9] S20, S05

leyomali that money [dem phr Cl. 9] S27

leyomithi those medicines, those oils [dem phr Cl. 4] S20

leyomitholampilo those clinics [dem phr Cl. 4] S25

leyondawo that place [dem phr Cl. 9] S18

leyonhlamvu that testicle [dem phr Cl. 9 S15

leyonkampani that company [dem phr Cl. 9] S27

leyonkinga that problem, that difficulty [dem phr Cl. 9] S16

lezi these [1st pos dem Cl. 8 or 10] S05, S07

lezikhulu of important people [poss Cl. 5] S06

lezilwanyazana these insects [dem phr Cl. 8] S20

lezinambuzane these parasites [dem phr Cl. 8] S20

lezingane these children [dem phr Cl. 10] S09

lezinyawo of feet [poss Cl. 5] S19

lezizigilamkhuba these evil-doers [dem phr Cl. 8] S23

lezizindawo these places [dem phr Cl. 10] S23

lezizinto these things [dem phr Cl. 10] S24

leziziqiwi these reserves [dem phr Cl. 8] S24

lezo those (near the person spoken to, or previously referred to) [2nd pos dem Cl. 8 and 10] S24, S28

lezolimo agricultural [poss Cl. 5] S27

lezozifo those diseases [dem phr Cl. 8] S20

lezozimpahla those goods [dem phr Cl. 10] S28

lezozincwadi those letters, those books [dem phr Cl. 10] S28

lezozindawo those places [dem phr Cl. 10] S16

lezozinjongo those resolutions, aims [dem phr Cl. 10] S28

lezozinto those things [dem phr Cl. 10] S20

li- it, he, she [SC Cl. 5] S01

li- [enum conc Cl. 5] S27

-li- it, him, her [OC Cl. 5] S09

libhekele it, (s)he watches [past, conjoint] S17

libhekene it, (s)he is faced [stative] S28

libhekene na- ... it, (s)he deals with or faces ... [past, conjoint] S25

libona it, (s)he thinks [pres, conjoint] S23

licela it, (s)he is asking for [pres, partic] S09

lidoja it, (s)he evades [pres, conjoint] S10

lifakwe it, (s)he should be put [subjunc] S28

lifanele it is necessary, it is proper [stative] S05

lifike it, (s)he should arrive [subjunc] S18

ligodliwe it has been withheld [past, disjoint] S23

ligreythiwe it has been grated [stative] S01

lijikile it, (s)he has turned [past, disjoint] S17

lika- of [poss conc Cl. 5; occurs before nouns of Cl. 1a] S09

likanobhala of the secretary [poss Cl. 5] S25

lika-R15mln of 15 million rands [poss Cl. 5] S10

likhetha (s)he, it chooses [pres, conjoint] S16

likhona it, (s)he is there [loc cop, pres; may also introduce an exist cop] S28

likhona ikhambi there is a remedy [exist cop, pres] S28

likuthatha they, it, (s)he take it [pres, conjoint] S23

likwazile it, (s)he was able [past, disjoint] S28

-lil-a weep, cry, wail, lament [v.i.] S21

-lim-a cultivate, plough [v.i. & t.] S27

-limal-a bec injured, get hurt, get wounded, get damaged [v.inch] S09

limbuza (s)he asks him [pres, partic] S26

limtshela (s)he tells him [pres, partic] S26

Linda (male or female name) [n Cl. 1a] S09

-lind-a wait (for), expect [v.i. & t.] S08

-ling-a tempt, test, try, attempt [v.t.] S28

lingakukhipha it, (s)he can take you out [pres, potential] S28

lingakunaki it, (s)he does not notice it [pres, partic] S20

lingakwazi it is unable, it cannot [pres, rel, neg; < alikwazi] S28

lingamenza it, (s)he could make him or her [pres, potential] S27

-lingan-a be equal, be the same; bec sufficient [v.i.] S15

lingani it is not raining [pres, partic] S20

-linganis-a measure, weigh, survey, calculate [v-recip-caus] S20

-linganisel-a measure at, weigh at, calculate at [v-recip-caus-appl] S20

-linganiselw-a be measured at or calculated at [v-recip-caus-appl-pass] S20

lingaphezu it, (s)he is greater or higher [loc cop, pres] S28

lingathathi it, (s)he does not take [subjunc, neg] S23

lingu-160°C it is 160°C [ident cop, pres] S01

-lingw-a be tempted, be tested, be tried, be attempted [v-pass] S28

linye one [enum Cl. 5] S27

linyukile it, (s)he has risen, has gone up [past, disjoint] S19

liphikelele it, (s)he is headed [past, conjoint] S18

liqalile it, (s)he began [past, disjoint] S26

liqanjwe it has been named, it has been invented, it has been composed [past, conjoint] S27

liqeqeshiwe it, (s)he has been trained [stative] S16

-li-qhamukis-a come from a place [idiom; The Cl. 5 OC refers to any place mentioned, since place names are generally in Cl. 5. The caus ext is used idiomatically here.] S09

liqhathaniswa it, (s)he is compared [pres, partic] S28

liqonde it, (s)he determined [past, conjoint] S26

lisanda it, (s)he has just VERBed

[aux, pres, conjoint] S19

lisanda kukhipha it, (s)he has just produced [aux v phr] S19

liseBhambayi it, (s)he is in Bhambayi [loc cop, pres] S09

liseduze it, (s)he is near [loc cop, pres] S16

lisekhona it, (s)he is still there [loc cop, pres, persistive; may also introduce an exist cop] S28

lisekhona ithemba there is still hope [exist cop, pres, persistive] S28

lisikhiphile (s)he had brought it out, withdrawn it [past, disjoint] S26

lisuke it, (s)he, they have just [aux] S23

lithe (s)he said [past, conjoint] S26

lithe it went [past, conjoint] S27

lithini? what does (s)he, it say or think? [v phr] S11

liyahambisana it, (s)he agrees with [pres, disjoint] S25

liyakhanya it is bright, it shines [pres, disjoint] S04

liyakungabaza they are, (s)he is uncertain about; they doubt; (s)he doubts [pres, disjoint] S07

liyazisebenzela it, (s)he just works [pres, disjoint] S21

liye it, (s)he sometimes [aux] S23

liyingozi it is danger [ident cop, pres] S09

liyisilima it is a difficult thing, it is a deformity [ident cop, pres] S23

liyixazulule it, (s)he would resolve or settle it [subjunc] S16

lize until it, until (s)he [aux, subjunc] S18

lizibulale (or) they commit suicide; (or) (s)he commits suicide [subjunc] S16

liziphonse (or) they throw themselves; (or) (s)he throws her- or himself [subjunc] S16

lizohamba it, (s)he will travel [fut] S18

lizosiza it, (s)he will help [fut] S12

lo this [1st pos dem Cl. 1 & Cl. 3] S03, S09

lo this, these [1st posi dem, Cl. 11, 14, 15; in some dialects the abbreviated form **lo** is used for all demonstratives that have **u** as 2nd vowel] S23

lo- of [poss conc Cl. 5, **la-**, coalesced with following **u**] S03

lo- of [poss conc Cl. 11, **lwa-**, coalesced with following **u**] S09

lo- [quant conc Cl. 5 & Cl. 11] S19

-lob-a write [v.t.] S26

-lobel-a write for, to [v-appl] S26

lobo that (near the addressee, or placed within an utterance) [2nd pos dem Cl. 14] S23

lobobunzima that difficulty [dem phr Cl. 14] S28

lobubi this evil [dem phr Cl. 14; < **lo + ububi**] S23

lobugebengu of crime [poss Cl. 5; < **la- + ubugebengu**] S03

lobugebengu this crime [dem phr Cl. 14; < **lo- + ubugebengu**] S23

lochwepheshe of an expert [poss Cl. 11] S23

lokho that (near the addressee, or placed within an utterance) [2nd pos dem Cl.15 or 17] S03, S05

lokhu this [1st pos dem Cl. 15 & 17] S23, S05

-lokhu keep on VERBing[aux; followed by the participial; < **lokhu** [1st pos dem Cl. 15] S05

lokhu kubangwa wukuthi this is caused by the fact that (lit. this is caused by that) [v phr] S05

lokhu kungcola this immorality [dem phr Cl. 15] S23

lokuba nekwakhe of having a home [poss Cl. 11] S22

lokudla of food [poss Cl. 5] S09

lokudlwengula of raping [poss Cl. 5] S23

lokudoja of evading [poss Cl. 5] S10

lokugwema for avoiding [poss Cl. 11] S09

lokuhlukumeza of assault [poss Cl. 5] S23

lokukhishwa kwezisu of abortions [poss phr Cl. 11] S25

lokukuphoqa to force or compel you [poss Cl. 5] S28

lokuphila to life, of living [poss Cl. 5] S25

lokuphumela for coming out into [poss Cl. 5] S20

lokuqeda for bringing to and end [poss Cl. 11] S09

lokuthi (of) that [poss Cl. 5 & 11] S23

lokutshala of planting [poss Cl. 5] S27

lokuveza of raising, of bringing out [poss Cl. 5] S13

lokuxoxisana of chatting [poss Cl. 5] S17

lokuya of going [poss Cl. 11] S23

lokuzikhethela to choose for themselves [poss Cl. 7] S25

lolu this [1st pos dem Cl. 11] S06

loludaba this grave matter [dem phr Cl. 11] S25

loluhlobo this way, this type, this sort [dem phr Cl. 11] S27

loluphiko this branch [dem phr Cl. 11] S24

lombutho wamaphoyisa of the police force [poss phr Cl. 5] S16

lomfanyana this little boy [dem phr Cl. 1; < **lo** + **umfanyana**] S09

loMhleli of the editor [poss Cl. 5] S08

lomkhakha this field, this direction [dem phr Cl. 3] S19

lomkhuba this custom, this practice [dem phr Cl. 3] S16

lomlimi this farmer [dem phr Cl. 1] S27

lomnyango this department [dem phr Cl. 3] S25

lo-mosquito of mosquitoes [poss Cl. 5] S20

lomsebenzi this job, this task, this work [dem phr Cl. 3] S16

lomshophi this plague or epidemic [dem phr Cl. 1] S23

lomthetho this law [dem phr Cl. 3] S25

lomuntu of a person [poss Cl. 5] S19

lona it, he, him, she, her [abs pron Cl. 11] S27

lona this [1st pos dem Cl. 1] S17

lonke all, the whole [quant Cl. 5] S19

lonyaka the year, this year [dem phr Cl. 3; var **nonyaka**] S03

lowo that (near the addressee, or placed within an utterance) [2nd pos dem Cl. 1 & 3] S16, S18

lowo-mosquito that mosquito [dem phr Cl. 1] S20

lowomsebenzi that job, work, or task [dem phr Cl. 3] S18

lowomuntu that person [dem phr Cl. 1] S16

lowomzila that broad track [dem phr Cl. 3] S18

lu- it, he, she [SC Cl. 11] S03

-lu- it, him, her [OC Cl. 11] S21

-lu- [2nd half adj conc Cl. 11] S15

lubhekelela it definitely considers [pres, conjoint] S23

lubhekene na- ... it deals with ... [stative] S24

ludalwa it is caused, it is created [pres, conjoint] S20

lufakelwe that it should have placed on it [subjunc] S21

lufakelwe izibuko it should be placed under scrutiny [v phr]

lufanele it is appropriate, it must [stative] S27

-luhlaza green [rel stem] S24

luka- of [poss conc Cl. 11] S20

lukamalaleveva of malaria [poss Cl. 11] S20

lukhule it grew [past, conjoint] S26

lukhulu much, a lot [n Cl. 11, with elision of initial **u**] S12

-lukhuni difficult, hard [rel stem] S27

-lula easy, light [rel stem] S11

-lum-a bite, sting [v.t.] S20

luncane it is small [descr cop, pres] S15

luncane kunolwesokudla it is smaller than the right-hand one [descr cop phr] S15

-lung-a bec in order, bec correct, bec OK [v.i., inch] S13

-lungel-a be ready for, be right for [v-appl] S26

Lungile (female name) [n Cl. 1a; < **-lungile** is OK, is in order] S24

-lungis-a fix, repair, make right, make good, rectify, correct, sort out, arrange, put in order [v-caus] S13

-lungisel-a sort out for, fix for [v-caus-appl] S13

-lungiselw-a have sorted out or fixed for (one) [v-caus-appl-pass] S13

-lunyw-a be bitten, be stung [v-pass; < **-lum-w-a**; **m w** > **nyw**] S20

luphezu komkhankaso it is in control of the scheme [loc cop, pres] S24

luphi? where is it, (s)he? [loc cop, pres] S03

lusaqhubeka it still continues [pres, persistive aspect] S05

lusematheni it is on the lips, it is in the saliva [loc cop, pres] S25

luseyinto it is still something [ident cop, pres, persistive] S25

lusiza it helps [pres, conjoint] S27

lutho something, anything, nothing [< **ulutho**] S05

lutholakala it is available [pres, conjoint] S16

luyashesha it is quick, it hurries [pres, disjoint] S21

luyophela it will come to an end [rem fut] S05

luzokwenza it will produce [fut] S24

luzoyisiza it will help him or her [fut] S16

lw- it, (s)he [SC Cl. 11; found before vowels **a** and **e**] S05

-lw- it [OC Cl. 11] S26

-lw-a fight [v.i.] S09

lwa- of [poss conc Cl. 11] S05

lwabafowabo of his or her brothers [poss Cl. 11] S27

lwabantu of people [poss Cl. 11] S28

lwabazoshushiselwa of those who will have cases against them prosecuted [poss Cl. 11; < **lwa-** poss conc + **abazoshushiselwa**] S10

lwabesimame of women, women's [poss Cl. 11] S25

lwabuye and it again [aux, narr] S24

lwafika it arrived [rem past] S21

lwahlela it arranged [rem past] S24

lwakhe his, her [poss Cl. 11] S27

lwamacala of prosecutions [poss Cl. 11] S10

lwami my [poss Cl. 11] S15

lwangakwesobunxele (of the) left-hand [poss Cl. 11] S15

lwatholela it found for [narr] S24

lwawela it fell onto [rem past] S17

lwazi knowledge [< **ulwazi**] S23

lwe- of [poss conc Cl. 11 coalesced with **i**] S05

lweGospel Music of gospel music [poss Cl. 11] S22

lwemidlalo of the games [poss Cl. 11] S11

lwensipho of soap [poss Cl. 11] S17

lwepolitiki of politics [poss Cl. 11] S05

lwesihlanu fifth [poss Cl. 11] S13

lwesokudla of the right [poss Cl. 11] S15

lwe-South African Police Service's Finance [Department] [poss Cl. 11] S16

lwezindlu of houses [poss Cl. 11] S17

lwezinsuku of days [poss Cl. 11] S24

lwezomthetho of the law [poss Cl. 11] S23

M

-m- him, her, it [OC Cl. 1] S08

-m-a stand (up); wait; stop [v.i., inch] S05

ma if, when [conj; var **uma**] S13

ma- may, let [hortative pref] S02

-ma- [nominal formative; cf. **umabulalephindelela, umasiteshi**] S21, S26

ma-Afrika Africans [< **ama-Afrika**] S16

mabaqine let them be firm [subjunc] S07

mabaqine idolo let them be strong (lit. let them be firm in the knee) S07

Madlala (surname) [n Cl. 1a] S27

maduze nje not too long ago, just recently [adv phr] S28

mahhala for free, free of charge, for nothing, in vain [adv] S16

Mahlatse (name) [n Cl. 1a] {Sotho} S14

Maitsapo (surname) [n Cl. 1a] {Sotho/Tswana} S19

makaphumule may (s)he rest [subjunctive] S02

Makhathini (surname) [n Cl. 1a] S09

mali money [< **imali**] S13

malini? how much money? [n phr Cl. 9; < **imali** money + **ini?** what?] S28

-mandla strong, powerful, mighty [rel stem; < **amandla** strength, power, might [n Cl. 6]] S20

-mangal-a bec surprised, wonder [v.i.] S18

-mangaz-a amaze, surprise [v-caus; < **-mangal-** + -Y-; l + -Y- > z] S27

maningi there are many [descr cop; < **amaningi** adj] S27

manje now [time adv] S03

Manyoni (surname) [n Cl. 1a] S09

Maphanga (surname) [n Cl. 1a] S18

-mash-a march [v.i.] {Eng} S21

Mashilo (surname) [n Cl. 1a] {Sotho} S14

Masiba (surname) [n Cl. 1a] S17

-matasatasa busy, occupied [rel stem; < **amatasatasa** busyness [n Cl. 6]] S17

mayelana na- ... with regard to ..., with respect to ..., concerning ... [conj phr;] S23

-mbalwa few [rel stem] S18

Mbeki (surname; name of South African President) [n Cl. 1a] S07

-mbili two [adj Cl. 9 minus initial vowel] S19

-mboz-a cover (over) [v.t.] S09

-mbozw-a be covered [v-pass] S09

mbulali killer, murderer [< **umbulali**] S26

Mdadane (surname) [n Cl. 1a] S10

-mel-a stand (up) for, represent; manage, look after, oversee, superintend [v-appl] S05

-mel-a bec obligatory [aux, v.inch; followed by subjunc when it has a Cl. 17 SC] S08

-melan-a stand up for or against one another, support one another, defend one another, wait for one another [v-appl-recip] S23, S28

-melan-a na- ... confront ... S28

Memela (surname) [n Cl. 1a] S09

-memez-a shout, call out (to) [v.i. & t.] S18

-memezel-a shout for, announce, proclaim loudly [v-appl] S18

-menyw-a be invited [v-pass; < -mem-w-a; mw > nyw] S27

Mfeka (surname) [n Cl. 1a] S11

mfowabo his, her, their brother [< umfowabo] S27

mfundi student, pupil, scholar [< umfundi] S13

mhlaka the day of [n phr Cl. 3; < umuhla ka-] S04

mhlaka 2 the second (day) [n phr Cl. 3; < umuhla ka-2] S04

mhlawumbe perhaps [conj] S23

mhleli editor [vocative of umhleli] S05

-mhlophe white [rel stem] S16

mi I, me, my [abs pron 1 p sg] S05

-mi- [2nd half of adj conc, Cl. 4] S05

mibi bad [adj minus initial vowel e-] S05

mihle good [adj minus initial vowel e-]

-mil-a germinate, grow (of plants) [v.i.] S26

mina as for me, *I* [abs pron 1 p sg] S14

minyaka years [< iminyaka] S16

minyaka yonke annually, yearly, every year [n phr Cl. 4] S16

misebenzi jobs, tasks [< imisebenzi] S12

-mith-a bec pregnant (used only of animals) [v.i.; var -emith-a] S21

mithi medicines; trees [< imithi] S20

Mjoli (surname) [n Cl. 1a] S26

mkhuba custom, (bad) practice; (bad) habit [< umkhuba] S08

Mndaweni (surname) [n Cl. 1a] S24

Mntomuhle (name) [n Cl. 1a; < umuntu omuhle good person, beautiful person] S06

mnumzane family head; gentleman, mister [< umnumzane] S21

-mnyama black, dark [rel stem] S02

Mnyandu (surname) [n Cl. 1a] S07

mnyango doorway; department [< umnyango] S21

Molokomme (surname) [n Cl. 1a] {Sotho} S14

Moosa (name; this could be an Indian name, or it could be a misspelling of the Sotho male name *Mosa*) [n Cl. 1a] S14

Morgan (male name) [n Cl. 1a] {Eng} S11

mosquito [< u-mosquito] S20

Mpanza (surname) [n Cl. 1a] S02

-mpofu poor [rel stem] S21

Mpumalanga (province of south Africa) [< iMpumalanga] S20

mqhudelwano [< umqhudelwano competition, challenge] S11

msebenzi work, job [< **umsebenzi**] S12

mshophi epidemic [< **umshophi**] S08

mswakama dampness or moisture rising from the ground [< **umswakama**] S20

Mthembu (surname) [n Cl. 1a] S11

mu- [enum conc Cl. 1]

Mufamadi (surname) [n Cl. 1a] {Sotho} S21

-munc-a suck [v.t.; var **-muny-a**] S20

-muncu nasty, unpleasant, unhappy; sour, bitter [rel stem]

muphi? which? [enum Cl. 1] S23

Muzi (male name) [n Cl. 1a; < **umuzi** household] S13

mzila broad track [< **umzila**] S18

Mzizi (surname) [n Cl. 1a] S25

Mzoneli (surname) [n Cl. 1a] S18

N

n- and, with, also, too, even [assoc pref **na-** with vowel elision] S04

n- you [SC 2 p pl] S02

-na [stabilizer (a syllable added to a monosyllabic form to make it disyllabic. Monosyllabic forms are rare in Zulu.)] S04

-n-a rain [v.i.] S20

na- with, and, also, too, even [associative pref] S01

nabahlala and who stay [assoc adv] S20

nabahlengi bezimpilo and, with, even, also life-savers [assoc adv] S17

nabakhwabanisi and frauds [assoc adv] S10

nabamabhizinisi and business-owners [assoc adv] S10

nabangu-300 and 300 [assoc adv] S10

nabantu also people, people too, and people, even people, with people [assoc adv] S14

nabantwana and children [assoc adv] S02

nabanye also other(s) [assoc adv] S19

nabaphathi and or with the warders, authorities, or managers [assoc adv] S23

nabathumbi with hijackers or hostage-takers [assoc adv] S16

nabathunjiwe and who have been taken hostage or hijacked [assoc adv] S16

nabathunjwayo and who are hijacked or taken hostage [assoc adv] S16

nabavela and who come from [assoc adv] S20

nabazali with parents[assoc adv] S09

nabesifazane with women [assoc adv] S23

nabesilisa even males, males too [assoc adv] S23

nabesimame and females [assoc adv] S19

nabo with them, them too, also them, even them [assoc adv]

Naidoo (surname) [n Cl. 1a] {Indian} S24

-nak-a notice, take notice of, be concerned about, be troubled by [v.t.] S16

nakancane in the slightest, in the least, even a little (found after negative verbs) [assoc adv; < **na-** + **kancane** a little] S19

nakanjani most decidedly, no matter what [assoc adv; < **na-** + **kanjani** how] S26

nakhu ... here is ... [presentative dem Cl. 17, 1st pos; var **naku**] S07

nakuba although, even though [conj; followed by participial] S05

nakulezozindawo and to, from, at, in, those places [assoc adv] S23

-nakw-a be noticed, be taken notice of [v-pass] S16

nakwabanye and to others [assoc adv] S02

nakwamanye also in other [assoc adv] S24

nakweminye also to other [assoc adv] S08

nakwezethu also to ours (children) [assoc adv] S08

nakwezinye and in other [assoc adv] S23

nakwiMolopo and around the

Molopo (a river) [assoc adv] S20

nalabo and those, also those, even those [assoc adv] S16

nalawomabandla with those groups [assoc adv] S25

nalesisithelo with this fruit [assoc adv] S27

naleso and that [assoc adv] S18

nalesosinqumo with that decision [assoc adv] S25

nalo with it [assoc adv] S28

nalobo with that [assoc adv] S23

nalokho with that [assoc adv] S19

nalomnyango with this department [assoc adv] S25

nalomsebenzi with this job [assoc adv] S16

nalomthetho with this law [assoc adv] S25

nalonyaka and this year, even this year [assoc adv] S05

nalowo with that one [assoc adv] S16

nama-Annual Tax Returns and Annual ... [assoc adv] S10

namacala with cases [assoc adv] S23

namadoda with men, and men, men too, men also, even men [assoc adv] S14

namahloni with embarrassment [assoc adv] S28

namakhokho and soccer boots [assoc adv] S11

nama-night clubs with, and nightclubs [assoc adv] S23

namanje even now [assoc adv] S05

namaphethelo and suburbs [assoc adv] S11

namaphoyisa and the police [assoc adv] S09

namaqanda and eggs [assoc adv; < **na-** + **amaqanda**] S01

nama-raspberry raspberries as well, also raspberries, and raspberries [assoc adv] S27

namasiko and customs, and culture [assoc adv] S25

namasokisi and socks [assoc adv] S20

nama-trucks and trucks or vans [assoc adv] S09

namatshe also stones [assoc adv] S17

namazambane and potatoes [assoc adv] S27

nambili and two [assoc adv] S19

-nambith-a understand [v.t.] S24

-nambithisis-a understand fully [v-intens] S24

-nambuz-a move lazily; act lethargically [v.i.] S20

namehlo even eyes [assoc adv] S14

nami I too, even I [assoc adv] S18

namuhla today [time adv; < **na-** + **umuhla** day] S09

nangaphandle and without; and, also outside [assoc adv] S18

nangekusasa and about the future, and about tomorrow [assoc adv] S04

nangezwi even by voice [assoc adv] S23

nangobufakazi also about the evidence [assoc adv] S26

nanku ... here is ... [presentative dem Cl. 3, 1st pos; var **nawu**] S06

nansi here is [presentative dem Cl. 9, 1st pos; var **nayi**] S23

nantambama and in the afternoon [assoc adv] S20

nanye and one [assoc adv] S17

nasebephila and who now live [assoc adv] S28

naseFunimfundo and at Funimfundo [assoc adv] S02

nasekushushisweni and in the prosecution [assoc adv] S10

nasemakhemisi and in pharmacies [assoc adv] S20

nasemazweni and to, from, in countries [assoc adv] S16

nasemnyangweni also in the department [assoc adv] S25

nasemoyeni also spiritually, also psychologically [assoc adv] S23

nasezihlotsheni and in families [assoc adv] S09

nasezindlini zangasese and to, from, in toilets [assoc adv]

nasezingxenye and in parts [assoc adv] S20

nasezinkanjini and in camps [assoc adv] S23

naso with it [assoc adv] S25

nawo they too [assoc adv] S09

nawo with it, with them [assoc adv] S19, S23

nawokuzama ukubulala and of attempted murder [assoc adv phr] S26

naye with him, with her [assoc adv] S04

naye (s)he too, (s)he also, even (s)he [assoc adv] S17

nayilowo and it is that one [assoc adv phr] S16

nayizimpahla also (by) the goods, even (by) the goods [assoc adv phr] S17

nayo with it [assoc adv] S12

nazo with them [assoc adv] S04

-ncane small, (a) little, juvenile [adj stem; < **-nci** tiny, minute + **-ane** diminutive suffix] S09

-ncel-a suck [v.t.] S21

-nceng-a beg, plead with [v.i. & t.] S14

-nci tiny, minute [adj stem] S12

-ncint-a excel, be outstanding [v.i.] S27

-ncintisan-a compete [v-caus-recip] S27

-nciph- grow less, diminish [v.i.; < **-nci** tiny, minute + **-ph-** verbalizer] S12

-ncish-a deprive, stint [v.t.] S14

ncwadi letter, book [< **incwadi**] S26

-ne four [adj stem] S02

ne- with, and, also, too, even [assoc pref **na-** coalesced with **i**] S04

neBhekithemba against Bhekithemba (a soccer team) [assoc adv] S11

ne-dollar with the dollar [assoc adv] S28

ne-electronics with, and, also electronics [assoc adv] S19

nejaji with the judge [assoc adv] S26

nekamu lamaphoyisa with a police station [assoc adv] S16

nekhambi and the remedy [assoc adv] S28

nekusasa with a future [assoc adv; < **na-** + **ikusasa**] S04

nelakhe and his or her (own) [assoc adv] S27

neliqanjwe and that was composed [assoc adv] S27

Nelson Mandela (name of former South African President and Nobel Peace Prize winner) [n Cl. 1a] S07

nemali also the money, and money [assoc adv] S27

neMelika and America [assoc adv] S16

nemfiva with, and, also fever [assoc adv] S20

nemindeni and families [assoc adv] S06

nemiphumela with results [assoc adv] S23

nemisebenzi and jobs, even jobs, also jobs [assoc adv] S12

nemishini with, and, even, also machines [assoc adv] S19

nemizamo with attempts [assoc adv] S25

nemizimba and bodies [assoc adv] S09

nemoto and a car [assoc adv] S28

nendlela also a way [assoc adv] S24

neneminyaka and who is one who has years [assoc adv] S16

neneminyaka engu 24 and who is 24 [assoc adv phr] S16

-neng-a disgust, nauseate, offend [v.t.] S26

nengalo with the arm [assoc adv] S25

-nengw-a be disgusted, offended [v-pass] S26

nenhlangano and the association or society [assoc adv] S14

neningi with a great number, with a majority [assoc adv] S25

nenkomo a cow too, also a cow [assoc adv] S21

nenyanyekayo and that is objectionable or deplorable [assoc adv] S25

nenze (may you) do [subjunctive] S02

ne-Orange River and the Orange River [assoc adv] S20

nephuzu also the point [assoc adv] S16

nesenti even a cent [assoc adv] S28

nesibongo and surname [assoc adv] S21

nesifundazwe of the province, and the province [assoc adv] S18

nesifundo and, with the subject [assoc adv] S19

nesihlalo even, also, and a chair [assoc adv] S14

nesimo and, with, also, even a situation [assoc adv] S27

nesingiphungulele and that now reduces for me [assoc adv] S27

nethimba (with) a group [assoc adv] S16

nethuba also an opportunity [assoc adv] S13

ne-Umlazi Comtech (with) Umlazi ... [assoc adv] S11

neVumokuhle with Vumokuhle [assoc adv] S11

neyabonogada also that for guards [assoc adv] S13

neyayiphathelene and which concerned [assoc adv] S27

nezamahlathi and forestry [assoc adv] S11

nezamaholo with salary matters [assoc adv] S27

neze at all, in the slightest [assoc adv; < na- + ize] S10

nezicabha and doors [assoc adv] S13

nezidakamizwa and drugs [assoc adv] S09

nezifiso and desires [assoc adv] S04

nezifundo with studies [assoc adv] S14

nezikaSiyavuma Mfeka with those of Siyavuma Mfeka[assoc adv phr] S11

nezikibha and T-shirts [assoc adv] S11

nezikweleti from debts [assoc adv] S28

nezimoto and cars [assoc adv] S10

nezinambuzane also parasites, also insects [assoc adv] S20

nezindawo and places [assoc adv] S27

nezindiza even airplanes, also airplanes [assoc adv] S18

nezingane zabafana also boys, boys too, even boys [assoc adv phr] S08

nezingenamswakama and which are not damp [assoc adv] S20

nezingqinamba with bouts of nerves [assoc adv] S27

nezingubo and clothes [assoc adv] S20

nezinhlangano and organizations, societies, associations [assoc adv] S09

nezinkakha with skilled people [assoc adv] S23

nezinye also other(s), other(s) too, and other(s) [assoc adv] S23

neziphathelene with those (matters) that concern [assoc adv] S25

neziphawu and signs [assoc adv] S18

neziphumayo and outgoing [assoc adv] S14

neziqu also a degree [assoc adv] S14

nezisuke and that just [assoc adv] S28

nezithelo and fruit [assoc adv] S27

nezithombe and pictures, and photos [assoc adv] S16

neziyisibopho and that are an obligation [assoc adv] S04

nezobunjiniyela and, with, also, even engineering [assoc adv] S19

nezokubhalela and of writing in [assoc adv] S13

nezokuvakasha and of tourism [assoc adv] S12

nezomthetho and of law [assoc adv] S19

nezomunye with or about those (troubles) of another [assoc adv] S16

ng- I [SC 1 p sg; found before vowels] S09

ng- is, are [ident cop pref] S01

ng- by means of, with, through, on account of, about, on, at, in, during, in the vicinity of [instr adv pref with elision of **a**] S04

ng- by [agentive adv pref] S02

-ng- me [OC 1 p sg] S14

-ng- not [neg pref; variant of **-nga-** found before vowels] S05

-ng- can, could, may, might, would, should [potential pref; var of **-nga-** found before vowels] S08

nga- by means of, with, through, on account of, about, on, at, in, during, in the vicinity of, in the direction of, towards [instr adv pref] S01

-nga- not [neg pref; used in participials, relatives and the subjunctive] S04

-nga- can, could, may, might, would, should [potential pref] S06

-nga- like [prefix added to nouns forming a relative stem indicating 'like, as if'] S17

ngabafan' (final **-a** is elided) by boys [agentive adverb] S09

ngabakhwabanisi about frauds [instr adv] S10

ngabakwa-Adidas by people from Adidas [agent adv] S11

ngabakwaLife Line (by) people from Life Line [agent adv] S23

ngabalimi they are, it is farmers [ident cop, pres] S27

ngabantu about people, through people [instr adv] S21

ngabantu by people [agent adv] S10

ngabantwana with (or by) children [agent adv] S14

ngabanye by other [instr adv] S23

ngabaphathi by warders, by managers, by officials [agent adv] S23

ngabatshela I told them [narr] S14

-ngabaz-a be uncertain, doubt, conjecture, imagine [v.i. & t.] S07

-ngabazek-a be doubted [v-neut] S24

ngabe ought, it ought to be (that), it would be, it could be, is it the case that, could it be that [conj] S03

ngabe angikho kulelizinga engikulo I would not be at the stage or level at which I am S27

ngabe asikafiki isikhathi sokuthi ...? isn't it about time that ...? S03

ngabe uyini? what could it be? S20

ngabhalisela I registered for [rem past] S18

ngabhekana I faced, I handled [narr] S23

ngabo about them [instr adv] S14

ngabona I saw [rem past] S17

ngacabanga I thought [rem past] S23

ngadlula I passed [narr] S09

ngafuna and I wanted [narr] S19

ngagcina I eventually, I finally, I ended up [aux, rem past] S27

ngahamba I walked [rem past] S17

ngahlangabezana I came up against [rem past] S27

ngahlangana I met [narr] S17

-ngaka of this size, as big as this [rel stem] S06

-ngakanani? how much? [rel stem] S25

ngake I once [aux, rem past] S23

ngakho by it, through it [instr adv] S05

ngakho ukuvotela by voting for [instr adv phr] S05

ngakho-ke (also spelt **ngakhoke**) therefore, thus, so (lit. through this then) [conj; < instr adv]] S07

ngakithi in the vicinity of our place [instr adv phr] S06

ngakulelikhemisi towards this pharmacy [instr adv phr] S17

ngakwesobunxele on the left [instr adv phr] S15

ngale about this [instr adv] S13

ngaleli about this [instr adv] S26

ngalemali with this money [instr adv phr] S24

ngalesifo with this disease [instr adv phr] S20

ngalesigameko about this repeated incident [instr adv phr] S23

ngalesisikhathi at this time [instr adv phr] S04

ngalesosenzo by that action [instr adv phr] S18

ngalesosikhathi at that time [instr adv phr] S14

ngaleyo through that [instr adv] S05

ngaleyo ndlela (or **ngaleyondlela**) in that way [instr adv phr] S05

ngaleyomali with that money [instr adv phr] S27

ngaleyomithi about those medicines [instr adv phr] S20

ngalezi for these [instr adv] S05

ngaleziziqiwi by, about, concerning these reserves [instr adv phr] S24

ngalo about it, in this [instr adv] S21

ngalokho about that [instr adv] S28

ngalolu into, about, concerning this [instr adv] S21

ngaloludaba about this grave matter [instr adv phr] S25

ngaloluhlobo in this way [instr adv phr] S27

ngalomthetho by, through this law [instr adv phr] S25

ngalonyaka during, in this year [instr adv phr] S28

ngama-28 it is, they are the 28s [ident cop, pres] S23

ngama-Afrika it is, they are Africans [ident cop, pres] S18

ngama-boarding school they are (or it is) boarding schools [ident cop, pres] S23

ngamacala for, about offences [instr adv] S26

ngamakhambi with medicinal herbs [instr adv] S24

ngamalungu they are members [ident cop, pres] S06

ngamamitha it is meters [ident cop, pres] S17

ngamandla by force, strongly, powerfully [instr adv] S23

ngamanye with other, through other [instr adv] S14

ngamaphoyisa by the police [agent adv] S21

ngamaqembu in groups [instr adv] S23

ngamashumi nambili there are twenty-two [ident cop, pres] S19

ngamathuba about opportunities [instr adv] S12

ngambona I saw her or him [rem past] S14

ngamehlo through eyes [instr adv] S17

ngangazi I knew [rem past pres] S19

ngangenza I did, I was doing [rem past pres] S19

ngangidlala I used to play [rem past pres] S19

ngangihlangana I was meeting, I was coming across [rem past pres] S17

ngangihlangene I had met [rem past past] S23

ngangikulo I was in it [loc cop, rem past pres] S17

ngangikuthokozela I was happy about it [rem past pres] S19

nganginawo I had it [assoc cop, rem past pres] S17

ngangingaphephela I could take refuge [rem past pres, potential] S18

ngangingayenza I could do it [rem past pres, potential] S23

ngangingayingeni I had no desire (lit. I was not entering it (referring to **into**)) [rem past pres, neg] S18

ngangingazi I didn't know [rem past pres, neg; < **ng-** SC **-a-** rem past **-ngi-** SC **-ng-** not **-az-i** know] S18

ngangingesiye I was not him or her [ident cop, rem past pres, neg; **ng-** SC + **-a-** rem past + **-ng-** SC + **-nge-** neg partic pref found in copulatives + **-si-** neg pref found in ident copulatives + **ye** abs pron] S23

ngangingesiye nomuntu I was not even a person [ident cop phr, rem past pres, neg] S23

ngangiqhaqhazeliswa I was made to tremble [rem past pres] S23

ngangisematasatasa I was still busy [descr cop, rem past pres, persistive] S17

ngangisithola I experienced (found) it [rem past pres] S09

ngangivame I was accustomed [aux, rem past past, conjoint] S18

ngangiwuhambele I had attended it [rem past past, conjoint] S17

ngangizibuza I used to wonder, I asked myself [rem past pres] S19

ngangizikhethele I had chosen for myself [rem past past, conjoint] S18

ngangizimisele I had prepared myself, I was determined [rem past stative] S18

nganqaba I rejected (that) [rem past] S19

ngaphakathi inside [instr adv] S17

ngaphambi kwa- before [instr adv phr] S08

ngaphambi kokuba before (VERB-ing) [conj phrase; followed by the subjunc] S09

ngaphambi kokuphela before the end [instr adv phr] S28

ngaphambi kokuthatha before taking [instr adv phr] S08

ngaphambi kokuthi before [conj phr; followed by subjunctive] S27

ngaphandle outside [instr adv] S20

ngaphandle kokuhlukumezeka ngokomqondo apart from the emotional (mental) shock [instr adv phr] S23

ngaphandle kosizo without the assistance [instr adv phr] S27

ngaphandle kwa- apart from, except for, without [instr adv phr] S13

ngaphansi under(neath), below, down [instr adv] S16

ngaphansi kophiko in the department or section (lit. under the wing) [instr adv phr] S16

ngaphansi kwa- under [instr adv phr] S16

ngaphansi kwemboni yezindiza within the airline industry [loc] S18

ngaphansi kwesimo under condition(s) [instr adv phr] S18

ngaphezu kuka- above, over, more than [instr adv phr; used with nouns of Cl. 1a] S10

ngaphezu kwa- above, over, more than [instr adv phr] S16

ngaphezu kwalokho in addition to that, more than that [conj phr] S23

ngaphezulu on top [instr adv] S01

ngaphuma I went out [rem past] S17

ngaphumelela that I succeeded [narr] S27

ngaqonda I understood [narr] S17

ngasese privately, secretly [manner adv] S15

ngasinye each [instr adv] S05

ngaso about it, him, her; through it, him her [instr adv] S18

ngaso linye with one eye [instr adv phr] S27

ngasuka I soon [aux, rem past] S17

ngathanda and I liked [narr] S19

ngathola I found [rem past] S17

ngavele I in advance [aux, rem past] S18

ngawo about, with, through it [instr adv] S18

ngawokudlwengula for those (crimes) of rape [instr adv] S26

ngawowonke with all [instr adv phr; < **nga-** instr pref + **wo** abs pron Cl. 6 + **onke** all] S25

ngaye with, by, through him or her [instr adv] S23

ngayo through it [instr adv] S09

ngaze (and) I eventually [aux, rem past] S14

ngazethemba I had faith in myself [narr] S14

ngazibona I saw them [narr] S14

ngazibonela I simply saw [narr] S18

ngazizwa I felt (lit. I felt myself) [rem past] S23

Ngcobo (surname) [n Cl. 1a] S11

-ngcol-a bec dirty [v.inch] S09

Ngcongo (surname) [n Cl. 1a] S12

-ngcono better [rel stem] S08

-ngcwab-a bury [v.t.] S21

nge- by means of, with, through, on account of, about, on, at, in, during, in the vicinity of [instr adv pref **nga-** coalesced with following **i**] S01

-nge- not [neg pref found in copulatives] S09

ngefasitela through the window [instr adv] S17

ngehla and went down [narr] S17

ngeke never [aux; followed by the subjunctive] S06

ngeke bawuthole they could never get it [pres, potential, neg] S06

ngekhasi with rind or zest [instr adv] S01

ngekhono according to ability [instr adv] S19

ngekusasa about the future, about tomorrow [instr adv] S04

ngeledlule yesterday [instr adv] S26

ngeleMdlwembe Gang by that (name) of the Mdlwembe Gang [instr adv phr] S09

ngelikaSnoopy by that (name) of Snoopy [instr adv phr] S09

ngelinye on, by, about a certain [instr adv] S18

ngelinye ilanga some day, one day [instr adv phr] S18

ngemali with money [instr adv] S14

ngemali eshisiwe at great expense, expensively (idiom; lit. with money that has been burnt) [instr adv phr] S28

ngemiklomelo with prizes [instr adv] S11

ngempela indeed, really [instr adv] S08

ngempelasonto during, at the weekend [instr adv] S17

ngempilo about life [instr adv; < **nga-** + **impilo**] S04

-ngen-a enter, come in(to), go in(to) [v.i.] S07

ngendawo about the place [instr adv] S20

ngendlela in a, or the, way [instr adv] S09

-ngenel-a attack unawares [v-appl] S08

-ngenelw-a be attacked unawares [v-appl-pass] S08

ngenhla above [instr adv] S12

ngenhlanhla fortunately, luckily [instr adv] S15

ngenhloso with the intention or aim [instr adv] S16

-ngenis-a bring or put in, insert [v-caus] S24

ngenkathi at the time [instr adv; followed by partic] S13

ngenkomishi with a cup [instr adv] S11

ngenxa ya- because of, on account of, due to, owing to [instr adv phr] S08

ngenxa yokuthi due to the fact that [instr adv phr] S13

ngenyanga during the month, within a month, monthly [instr adv] S10

ngenza I do, I make [pres, conjoint] S27

ngenze I should do or make [subjunc] S19

nge-orange frosting with orange frosting [instr adv] S01

ngesandla with a hand [instr adv] S06

ngesenzo about the incident, about the act [instr adv] S21

ngesigwebo about the sentence [instr adv] S26

ngesikhathi at the time (when), during the time (that), while [instr adv; followed by partic] S09

ngesinye it is one [ident cop, pres] S20

ngesivinini at a speed [instr adv] S16

ngesizathu for the reason [instr adv] S19

ngeyabesilisa they are those for males [ident cop, pres] S19

ngezandla by hand (lit. by hands), about hands, with hands [instr adv] S24

ngezempilo about health matters [instr adv] S14

ngezenzo about actions, deeds [instr adv] S26

ngezibhamu with guns [instr adv] S09

ngezidingo with regard to the needs, as far as the needs are concerned [instr adv] S06

ngezifana na- ... are one's such as ... [ident cop phr, pres] S23

ngezifiso about desires, wishes

[instr adv] S27

ngezimoto by cars, about cars [instr adv] S09

ngezindlela with ways, in ways [instr adv] S12

ngezinga with a level [instr adv] S01

ngezinga elingu-160°C to 160°C [instr adv phr] S01

ngezinhliziyo with desire (lit. with hearts—the seat of emotions, including desire) [instr adv] S23

ngezinkinga about problems [instr adv] S13

ngezinkonkoni (as) homosexuals [instr adv] S23

ngezinkulungwane upon thousands [instr adv] S10

ngezinyawo on foot (lit. by feet) [instr adv] S09

ngezinye by other(s) [agent adv] S17

ngeziqalo with initials [instr adv] S27

ngezitshalo with, by vegetables [instr adv] S27

ngezobunjiniyela about engineering [instr adv phr] S19

ngezolimo about agriculture [instr adv phr] S27

ngezwa I heard [narr; < **nga-** + **-izw-a**] S23

ngezwi by, through voice [instr adv] S23

ngi- I [SC 1 p sg] S05

-ngi- me [OC 1 p sg] S09

ngibancenge that I should plead with them [subjunc] S14

ngibavimbe I should stop them [subjunc] S23

ngibe I should become [copula, subjunc] S19

ngibe ngudokotela I should bec a doctor [ident cop, inch, subjunc] S19

ngibona I am of the opinion [pres, conjoint] S08

ngibonga I am grateful for, I give thanks for [pres, conjoint] S21

ngibonisane in order that I can exchange views [subjunc] S05

ngicela I would like, I request [pres, conjoint] S05

ngifikelwe I have experienced [past, partic, conjoint] S23

ngifisa I wish [pres, conjoint] S14

ngifuna I want [pres, conjoint] S14

ngifunda I read [pres, partic] S18

ngihamba I walk, I go, I travel [pres, conjoint] S14

ngihlangana I met (lit. I (was) meeting) [pres, partic] S14

ngihlukane na- ... I would separate from ..., I would give up ... [subjunc] S14

ngijwayele I should get used to [subjunc] S23

ngikholwa I believe [pres, conjoint] S19

ngikhula I am growing up [pres, partic] S19

ngikufundile I having learnt it [past, partic, disjoint] S27

ngikusho I say it [pres, conjoint] S07

ngikutholile I have found it [past, disjoint] S23

ngilithembile I trust or have faith in it, him, her [past, disjoint] S21

nginabantwana I have children [assoc cop, pres] S24

nginamathalente I am talented (lit. I have talents) [assoc cop, pres] S22

nginawo I have it [assoc cop, pres] S19

ngineqiniso I am sure (lit. I am with truth) [assoc cop, pres] S28

ngingakweluleka I would advise you [pres, potential] S15

ngingalithola I can find or obtain it [pres, potential] S23

ngingathi I believe (that), I am of the opinion (that) [pres, potential, pos] S25

ngingena I went in (lit. I go into) [pres, partic] S17

ngingenazo izibalo I do not have the figures [assoc cop, pres, partic, neg] S25

ngingubufakazi I am witness, I am evidence [ident cop, pres] S19

ngingumakhi I am a builder [ident cop, pres] S22

ngingumfundi I am a reader [ident cop, pres] S06

ngingumuntu I am a person [ident cop, pres] S19

nginichazele so that I can explain to you [subjunc] S07

nginichazele le nto ibe sobala so that I can explain this thing to you openly [v phr] S07

nginonkosikazi I have a wife [assoc cop, pres] S14

ngiphethe I must conclude [subjunc] S21

ngiphezu kwemizamo I am very busy with trials (lit. I am on top of trials) [loc cop, pres] S27

ngiqalaza I look(ed) about [pres, partic] S17

ngisakhula I am still growing up [pres, partic, persistive] S18

ngisaqala I am still beginning [pres, partic, persistive] S27

ngishefa I shave [pres, conjoint] S14

ngisho I mean, I am of the opinion that [pres, conjoint] S06

ngisondela I approached [pres, partic] S17

ngithi I say, I think [pres, conjoint] S05

ngithi-ke I believe then [v phr] S05

ngithokoza I am happy [pres, conjoint] S18

ngiwuthokozele I would enjoy it, I would be glad for it [subjunc] S23

ngixoxa (I am) chatting [pres, partic] S17

ngiyacela I am requesting [pres, disjoint] S08

ngiyawazonda I hate them [pres, disjoint] S09

ngiyazi I know [pres, disjoint] S08

ngiye I went, I should go [subjunc] S09

ngiyithola I get it [pres, conjoint] S24

ngiyobheka (I am) going to look at [pres, partic, andative] S17

ngiyogeza I should go and have developed [subjunc, andative] S17

ngiyohlal' (final -a is elided) I should go and live [subjunc, andative] S09

ngiyondla I bring up, I rear [pres, disjoint] S24

ngiyosebenza I shall work [rem fut] S18

ngizenze I should make them [subjunc] S19

ngizibona I see them [pres, conjoint] S14

ngizikhethele I have chosen for myself [past, conjoint] S14

ngizisole I blamed myself, I regretted [subjunc] S18

ngizithathe I took them, I should take them [subjunc] S19

ngizwakalise let me voice, let me express [subjunc] S21

ngo- by means of, with, through, on account of, about, on, at, in, during, in the vicinity of [instr pref **nga-** coalesced with **u**] S02

ngo-19xx in 19xx (referring to any year [instr adv] S05

ngo-9 at 9 (this structure would be used for any other hour of the day) [instr adv] S11

ngoba because [conj] S16

ngobufakazi about the evidence [instr adv] S26

ngobuhle in beauty [instr adv] S02

ngobulili according to sex or gender [instr adv] S19

ngobuningi in large numbers [instr adv] S11

ngocwaningo about investigation [instr adv] S26

ngo-December 15 on December 15 [instr adv] S17

ngodokotela it is, they are doctors [ident cop, pres] S18

ngo-February 2, 1999 on February 2, 1999 [instr adv phr] S02

ngogesi about, with, by electricity [instr adv] S06

ngohulumeni about the government [instr adv] S05

ngohulumeni kazwelonke about the national government [instr adv phr] S05

ngokocansi sexually, indecently [instr adv phr] S09

ngokokuqala it is the first (time) [ident cop, pres] S23

ngokongiwa about conservation, about preservation [instr adv] S24

ngokuba that [conj; < instr adv pref nga- + ukuba] S19

ngokuba through (that) [instr adv; < nga- + ukuba] S04

ngokuba by becoming [instr adv] S27

ngokuba na- ... by having ... [instr adv phr] S14

ngokuba nezinkinga by having problems [instr adv phr] S14

ngokuba yilungu by becoming a member [instr adv phr] S16

ngokuba yimbangela by becoming a cause [instr adv phr] S28

ngokubafundisa by teaching them [instr adv] S14

ngokubaluleka about the importance [instr adv] S24

ngokubambisana by cooperating, through cooperation [instr adv] S18

ngokucela by requesting [instr adv] S21

ngokudla by eating [instr adv] S20

ngokudlwengulwa about being raped [instr adv] S23

ngokufanayo equally, similarly [instr adv] S23

ngokuhamba through, by, in going; in, through the passage [instr adv] S18

ngokuhamba kwesikhathi in the passage of time [instr adv phr] S18

ngokuhlukunyezwa about the violence, assaults, attacks [instr adv] S21

ngokuka- according to, personally, independently, on one's own [instr adv phr; used before nouns of Cl. 1a; nga- + POSS PRON CL. 17 = according to] S23

ngokukachwepheshe according to an expert [instr adv phr; nga- + POSS PRON CL. 17 = according to] S23

ngokukaNonsikelelo according to Nonsikelelo [instr adv phr] S25

ngokukhiqiza by producing a surplus or an abundance [instr adv] S27

ngokumfunela by seeking out for him or her [instr adv] S14

ngokungaboni about not seeing, about blindness [instr adv] S14

ngokungatholi about not receiving [instr adv] S13

ngokungayi by not going [instr adv] S20

ngokungayiboni by not seeing it [instr adv] S06

ngokunika by providing, by giving [instr adv] S27

ngokunjalo in this way [instr adv phr; < nga- + okunjalo] S08

ngokunqanda by preventing [instr adv] S27

ngokuphangalala by dying [instr adv] S16

ngokuphepha safely, in safety, securely [instr adv] S18

ngokuphuza by drinking [instr adv] S16

ngokuqalwa through the initiation [instr adv] S12

ngokuqhubeka by continuing [instr adv] S18

ngokusabalalisa by furthering [instr adv] S12

ngokusebenza by working [instr adv] S27

ngokusebenzisa by using [instr adv] S20

ngokusemthethweni legally (lit. by what is in the law) [instr adv phr] S12

ngokusetshenziswa about the use [instr adv] S20

ngokushesha hurriedly, quickly [instr adv] S16

ngokusho according to (lit. by the saying so) [instr adv] S11

ngokusho kuka- ... according to ... [instr adv phr; used before a noun of Cl. 1a] S11

ngokusiza in aiding [instr adv] S24

ngokusobala in public, publicly, in the open [instr adv phr] S25

ngokuthi by saying [instr adv] S10

ngokuthi that (lit. about that), so that, about what [instr adv] S09

ngokuthi because [conj] S13

ngokuthinta by affecting, by touching [instr adv] S08

ngokuthola in the finding, by obtaining, by acquiring [instr adv] S12

ngokuthuthukisa by uplifting, by developing [instr adv] S14

ngokuvakashela by visiting [instr adv] S19

ngokuvikela by protecting [instr adv] S27

ngokuvuna by or about reaping, harvesting [instr adv] S27

ngokuwufundisa by teaching them [instr adv] S24

ngokuxoxisana through negotiation [instr adv] S28

ngokuyenza for, about doing it [instr adv] S18

ngokuzidubula by shooting themselves [instr adv] S16

ngokuzikhandla without respite, without let-up (lit. by exhausting oneself) [instr adv] S27

ngokuziphonsa by throwing themselves (himself, herself, oneself, etc.) [instr adv] S16

ngokuziqhenya with pride [instr adv] S27

ngokuzithatha in taking them (on) [instr adv] S12

ngokuzovimbela in order to prevent [instr adv] S20

ngokwa- according to, personally, independently, on one's own [**nga-** + POSS PRON CL. 17 = according to] S13

ngokwabafundi according to the students [instr adv; **nga-** + POSS PRON CL. 17 = according to] S13

ngokwabe-Life Line according to people from Life Line [instr adv] S23

ngokwabo according to them, o n their own, independently [instr adv] S25

ngokwami personally, according to me, in my view, independently [instr adv] S25

ngokwe- according to [< **ngokwa-** + the vowel **i**; **nga-** + POSS PRON = according to ...] S20

ngokwejwayela in adjusting to, in getting used to [instr adv] S23

ngokwenza about doing [instr adv] S19

ngokwenzeka about what happened [instr adv] S21

ngokwenzekayo about what happens [instr adv] S16

ngokwenzeke about what has happened [instr adv] S04

ngokweqile in excess, in overdose [instr adv; < **nga-** + **uku-** + VERB + **-ile**, a formula for deriving adverbs from verbs] S16

ngokwezibalo according to the figures [instr adv; < **okwezibalo** poss pron Cl. 17; **nga-** + POSS PRON = according to ...] S20

ngolisho at the request [instr adv] S22

ngolwazi with knowledge [instr adv] S27

ngoLwesihlanu on Friday [instr adv] S13

ngoLwesine on Thursday [instr adv] S11

ngomkhulu with a huge one, with a with a big one [instr adv] S17

ngompetha it is the finalists [ident cop, pres] S11

ngomsebenzi about work, about a job [instr adv] S14

ngoMsombuluko on Monday [instr adv] S13

ngomumo normally (lit. by state, by characteristic) [instr adv] S18

ngomunye (s)he, it is one [ident cop] S18

ngomusa with or through kindness [instr adv] S21

ngomuthi with medicine, with ointment, with oil [instr adv] S20

ngomuzi with the household [instr adv] S08

ngonqambothi with the entertainment (lit. with the nice flavor, nice smell) [instr adv] S11

ngonyaka in the year, in a year, per year, annually [instr adv] S13

ngosizo with help, with assistance [instr adv] S23

ngothango by a fence [instr adv]

S27

ngoThwala in connection with Thwala [instr adv] S26

ngowokuqala (s)he is the first one [ident cop, pres] S19

ngoYork Road via York Road [instr adv] S17

ngqa be first [ideophone] S11

-ngqangq-a tremble with anger [v.i.] S17

-ngqangqazel-a shiver, tremble, have the shakes [v.i.] S17, S20

-ngqangqazelis-a cause to shiver, tremble, or have the shakes; rattle [v-caus] S17

ngu- it is [ident cop pref; occurs before abs prons **we(na)** and **ye(na)**] S14

ngu- ... by ... (when followed by a name; lit. it is ...)

ngu-11% it is, they are 11% [ident cop, pres] S19

ngu-12 it is twelve [ident cop; pres] S01

ngu-896 it is 896 [ident cop, pres] S10

ngu-anti it is aunt [ident cop, pres] S14

Ngubane (surname) [n Cl. 1a] S13

ngubani? who is it? [ident cop, pres, partic] S08

ngudokotela it, (s)he is a doctor [ident cop, pres] S19

ngu-fitter and turner (s)he is a fitter and turner [ident cop, pres] S19

ngukunyamalala it is disappearance [ident cop, pres] S08

ngukuphela kwendawo is the only place (it is the coming to an end of a place) [ident cop phr, pres] S26

ngukuthi it is that [ident cop, pres; var **wukuthi**] S10

nguUMAFRIKA by *UMAFRIKA* (a newspaper) [agent adv] S26

ngumakhenikha it, (s)he is a mechanic [ident cop, pres] S19

ngumalaleveva by malaria [agent adv] S20

ngumama by mother [agent adv] S14

nguMfundisi by the Reverend [agentive adv] S02

ngumlawuli wokuhamba kwezindiza (s)he, it is an air-traffic controller [ident cop, pres] S18

ngummeli (s)he, it is a lawyer [ident cop, pres] S18

ngumndeni it is, they are a family [ident cop, pres] S09

ngumngani (s)he is a friend [ident cop, pres] S23

ngu-mosquito by a mosquito [agent adv] S20

ngumphakathi by the community [agent adv] S21

ngumqondisi (s)he is a director [ident cop, pres] S09

ngumshayeli (s)he, it is a driver, pilot [ident cop, pres] S18

ngumuntu it is a person [ident cop, pres] S16

ngumuntu by a person [agent adv] S23

ngumxhumanisi (s)he is a public relations officer [ident cop, pres] S19

ngumzali by a parent [agent adv] S23

nguNgqongqoshe wezamanzi nezamahlathi kuzwelonke (Capitalization missing in original) by the National Minister of Water Affairs and Forestry [agent adv] S11

nguNkk by Mrs. (written by) [agent adv] S02

nguNksz by Miss [agent adv] S12

nguSipho by Sipho [agent adv] S26

nguthisha (s)he, it is a teacher [ident cop, pres] S19

nguyena it is him or her [ident cop, pres] S14

nhlangano association, society, organization [< **inhlangano**] S12

nhlobo in any way, at all [adv; < **inhlobo** sort, kind, type] S15

ni- you (plural) [SC 2 p pl] S02

-ni- you (plural) [OC 2 p pl] S02

-ni? what?, what kind?, what sort of?, of what sex? [enum stem] S05

-ni [pluralizing suffix used in imperatives] S07

nifinyelela you (pl) reach [pres, partic] S28

-nik-a give (not as a gift), hand to [v.tt.] S09

-nikel-a give for, hand over to, donate [v-appl] S09

-nikelw-a be donated, be handed over to[v-appl-pass] S11

-nikez-a hand to [v-appl-caus; < -nikel- + -Y-] S09

-nikezel-a present (to) [v-appl-caus-appl] S11

-nikw-a be given (to) [v-pass] S12

ningabafihli you (pl) should not hide them [subjunc, neg] S14

-ningana rather many, quite a number [< -**ningi** + -**ana** dimin suff] S08

-ningi many, a lot of, much, plentiful, numerous [adj stem] S05

nize may you [aux, subjunc] S02

njalo always [adverb] S02

njalo thus, so, like that [adv] S08

njalonjalo etcetera, and so on [adv] S07

njani? how? [interrogative adverb; sometimes interchangeable with **kanjani?**] S04

-njani? what sort or kind of? [rel stem; < interrogative adv] S04

nje just, only, merely, then, so [adv] S05

-nje like this [rel stem] S11

njena just, only, merely, then, so [adv] S25

njenga- like, as, such as [compar adv pref] S08

njengamanje right now, at the moment, at present [adv; < **njenga-** like + **manje** now] S14

njengase-Northern Province such as in Northern Province [compar adv phr] S20

njenge- like, as, such as [compar adv pref coalesced with following **i**] S09

njengebhola lezinyawo such as football, soccer [compar adv phr] S19

njenge-HIV such as, like HIV [compar adv] S25

njengehlazo as a disgrace [compar adv] S23

njengenkampani as a company [compar adv] S12

njengenqindi like a fist [compar adv] S17

njengento as something, like a thing [compar adv] S14

njenge-sodomy as sodomy [compar adv] S23

njenge-switchboard operator as a switchboard operator [compar adv] S14

njengezinto zocansi as sexual objects [compar adv phr] S09

njengezinyanga as months [compar adv] S20

njengeziyingozi as dangerous ones [compar adv phr] S20

njengo- like, as, such as [compar adv pref coalesced with following **u**] S08

njengoba since, just as, seeing that [conj] S04

njengokuthi such as that [conj] S16

njengokuthi nje such as [conj phr] S14

njengokwejwayelekile as usual [compar adv phr] S21

njengomeluleki as advisor, as consultant [compar adv] S27

njengomsizi as assistant [compar adv] S16

njengomuntu as a person, like a person [compar adv] S28

njengomzali as a parent, like a parent [compar adv] S08

njll. etc., and so on [abbreviation of **njalonjalo**] S07

-nke all, every, the whole [quant stem] S02

nkinga problem, puzzle, fix [< **inkinga**] S13

nkulu big, large [adj Cl. 9 minus initial vowel] S27

no- with, and, also, too, even [assoc pref coalesced with **u**] S01

no- [quant conc 2 p pl] S02

-no- [noun formative, often (but not necessarily) used to form feminine nouns; cf. **unobhala, unogada**] S13

no-15ml with 15ml [assoc adv] S01

no-3 and three [assoc adv] S04

no-6 and six [assoc adv] S04

nobaba with, also, even a father; and Mister ... [assoc adv] S19

nobakweletayo with your creditors [assoc adv phr] S28

nobende and spleen [assoc adv] S20

nobhuti with a guy, with a chap (lit. older brother) [assoc adv] S22

nobuhlakani also cleverness [assoc adv] S27

nochwepheshe even experts [assoc adv] S23

nodaba with the serious matter [assoc adv] S25

nodade and my sisters [assoc adv] S21

noDkt with Dr. [assoc adv; abbrev of **noDokotela**] S23

nodokotela with (a/the) doctor [assoc adv] S15

noDudu and Dudu [assoc adv] S11

noGladys to Gladys, with Gladys [assoc adv] S14

noHenry and Henry [assoc adv] S27

nohlelo with a system [assoc adv] S09

noju and honey [assoc adv; < na- + uju] S03

noKhansela ... even Councilor ... [assoc adv] S06

Noko (personal name) [n Cl. 1a] S14

nokongiwa with conservation [assoc adv] S24

nokufunda with studying [assoc adv] S14

nokugwema and to avoid [assoc adv] S25

nokuholele and who was implicated in or responsible for [assoc adv] S26

nokukaMnuz Mandela with that of Mr. Mandela [assoc adv phr] S07

nokuletha and to bring [assoc adv] S09

nokungabantu and people-like things [assoc adv] S17

nokuntuleka and the lack [assoc adv] S20

nokuphazamiseka with interruption [assoc adv] S13

nokupheka and cooking [assoc adv] S22

nokuphoxeka also being mocked, being the butt of jokes too [assoc adv] S23

nokuqashwa and the appointment [assoc adv] S05

nokusindisa with saving [assoc adv] S16

nokuthandana and mutual love [assoc adv] S09

nokuthatha and that that takes [assoc adv] S23

nokuthi and that, also that, even that, with that [assoc adv] S13

nokuthiba also to ward off [assoc adv] S09

nokuthula and peace [assoc adv] S05

nokuwa and the collapse or bankruptcy [assoc adv] S28

nokuyaye and what sometimes [assoc adv phr] S20

nokuyaye kuthi and what sometimes happens [assoc adv phr] S20

nokuyilapho and that is where [assoc adv phr] S16

nokuyinto and which is something [assoc adv phr] S06

nokuyisikhundla and that is a position [assoc adv phr] S27

nokuyizifundo and that were studies [assoc adv phr] S18

nokuzalela also to lay eggs [assoc adv] S20

nokuzisebenza also to work for yourself [assoc adv] S19

nokwangenza and that made me [assoc adv phr] S19

nokwathi and which then [assoc adv] S17

nokwaziyo and who knows [assoc adv phr] S16

nokwenza and to constitute, and to make [assoc adv] S19

nokwesabela also fear of [assoc adv] S23

nolobela with the correspondent for (lit.. with the one who writes for) [assoc adv phr] S26

nolokuqeda and one for bringing to an end [assoc adv phr] S09

noluyindida and which is a con-fusing thing [assoc adv phr] S25

nolwazi and, with, also, even knowledge [assoc adv] S27

noma or; whether; although, as if (in the latter two senses, followed by the participial aspect) [conjunction; < na- and, even + uma if, when] S01, S05, S14

noma ngubani no matter who, anyone (lit. although it is who) S27

noma ngubani omdala any older person, no matter who the older person is S08

noma yimuphi umuntu no matter what person, anyone at all, each and every person (lit. although it is which person) S23

noma yini nonetheless, nevertheless, no matter what, anything at all (even if it is what) S16

noma ... yini whether ... or not S14

no-May and May [assoc adv] S20

nomkhulu and my grandfather [assoc adv] S19

nomndeni also the family [assoc adv] S08

nomnyango and the department [assoc adv] S10

no-mosquito and a mosquito [assoc adv] S20

nomphakathi with, even, and, also the community [assoc adv] S05

nomqashi and the employer [assoc adv] S27

nomsakazo also to the radio [assoc adv] S05

nomsindo also the sound [assoc adv] S17

nomthumbi with a hijacker or hostage-taker [assoc adv] S16

nomuntu even, with, also, a person [assoc adv] S23

nomunye with one, with a certain [assoc adv] S17

nonenhlonipho and who has respect [assoc adv] S22

nongaphuzi and who does not drink [assoc adv phr] S22

nonke you all [quant 2 p pl] S02

noNkk and Mrs. [assoc adv; < na- + uNkk] S02

noNkk Abegail Mpanza and Mrs. Abegail … [assoc adv phr] S02

nonomoya ophansi and who is reserved or gentle [assoc adv phr] S22

Nonsikelelo (female name) [n Cl. 1a] S25

nonyaka this year [time adv] S03

nophiko with the department [assoc adv] S10

noSebata with Sebata [assoc adv] S14

nosethole and who has already received [assoc adv] S24

noshukela and sugar [assoc adv; < na- + ushukela] S01

nosizo further assistance, also assistance [assoc adv] S27

nosokhemisi with the pharmacist, with the chemist [assoc adv] S17

-noth- bec wealthy [v.i.] S07

nothando and love [assoc adv] S22

nothisha and teachers [assoc adv; < na- + othisha] S05

nothisha omkhulu with the principal or head teacher [assoc adv phr] S13

noTshepo and Tshepo [assoc adv] S14

nowawungasetshenziswa and that was not being utilized [assoc adv phr] S27

nowesimame with a lady [assoc adv phr] S17

nowethule and who placed before or laid down [assoc adv phr] S26

noxolo and peace [assoc adv] S05

noyintandane and or even one who is an orphan [assoc adv phr] S22

nozobe ephelekezelwa and who will be accompanied [assoc adv phr] S11

nozwelo and sensitivity [assoc adv] S22

-nqab-a refuse, reject [v.i. & t.] S19

-nqand-a prevent, check, turn away [v.t.] S08

-nqob-a overcome, conquer, defeat [v.t.] S23

-nqum-a decide, give a decision, fix positively [v.t.] S20

-nqumel-a set work for, map out work for, prescribe, assign to, allocate [v-appl] S20

-nqunyelw-a be set, prescribed, allocated [v-appl-pass; < **-nqumel-w-a**; m ... -w- > ny ... -w-] S20

-nqunyelw-a ugwayi katiki be cautioned, given a warning (idiom; lit. to be allocated threepence worth of tobacco or snuff) S25

nsukuzonke daily, every day [adv; < **izinsuku** days + **zonke** all] S09

-nsundu dark brown [rel stem] S01

ntambama in the afternoon [time adv; < **intambama** afternoon; < **-thambam-** slant, decline (of sun in afternoon)] S20

-ntant-a float [v.i.] S17

-nteng-a sway back and forth, oscillate [v.i.] S25

nto thing [< **into**; deletion of init vowel due to preceding dem] S07

Ntshingila (surname) [n Cl. 1a] S16

-ntulek-a be missing, be lacking, be required [v.i.] S20

-nuk-a smell [v.i. & t.] S09

-nukubez-a abuse sexually [v.t.] S09

nya be nothing, be silent (can translate as: completely, utterly, perfectly, absolutely) [ideophone] S14

nyaka year [< **unyaka**] S13

nyakenye last year [adv] S11

-nyamalal-a disappear [v.i.] S08

-nyany-a have an aversion for, dislike strongly [v.t.] S25

-nyanyek-a be objectionable, deplorable [v-neut] S25

-nyathel-a tread (on), step (on) [v.i. & t.] S18

-nye some, certain, other, another, one (in the sense: a certain) [adj stem] S02

-nye one [enum stem] S05

-nyuk-a go up, rise, ascend [v.t.; var **-enyuk-a**] S03

-nzima heavy; hard, difficult [rel stem] S09

-nzulu deep, profound [rel stem] S27

O

o- [NP Cl. 2b] S05

o- of [poss conc Cl. 6 coalesced with following **u**] S01

o- that, which, who(m) [rel marker used when the SC in the verb concerned has the vowel **u**] S01 o- you who, which you, that you, whom you [rel form 2 p sg] S04

o- [form of the pronominalizer a- with assimilation to following u] S07

o- [loc pref used with nouns of Cl. 11] S03

o- [quant conc Cl. 6] S25

o- ... -eni to, from, at, in, on [loc marker; found with nouns of Cl. 11 ending in a, e, i] S03

o- ... -ini to, from, at, in, on [loc marker; found with nouns of Cl. 11 eding in i, u] S10

-o nominalizing suffix [With few exceptions the nom suff -o derives product or process nouns, always non-personal, while the nom suff -i forms agent nouns, which are generally personal.] S01

-o [past, conjunctive, suffix found with the verb -sh-o say (so), mean, believe; differs in tone and length or stress from the default suffix] S09

obakweletayo whom you owe, to whom you are in debt [ind rel of plain obj rel, 2 p sg] S28

obala in the open [loc; < ubala] S07

obamele that/which represents them [rel Cl. 3] S13

obasi White bosses [n Cl. 2b; sg ubasi 1a] {Afr basie young boss. In the apartheid era Black people were expected to call White men baas 'master, boss'

and young White men or even boys basie 'young master'} S27

obevakashele who had visited [rel Cl. 1] S20

obhekele that/which is looking towards [rel Cl. 3] S10

obhekene nakho that/which you are facing (lit. that/which you are looking at each other with it) [ind rel of assoc adverbial relationship, 2 p sg] S04

oboshwayo one who is arrested [rel Cl. 1] S16

obu- [adj conc Cl. 14; < a- rel marker + ubu- NP] S04

obu- which, that [rel form; < a- + bu- by vowel assimilation] S05

obufana that/which is the same [rel Cl. 14] S23

obuhle good [adj Cl. 14] S24

OBUKHOMBA THAT/WHICH POINTS [REL CL. 14] S23

obukhona that/which there was [rel Cl. 14] S26

obukhulu great [adj Cl. 14] S09

obuncane (a) little, small [adj Cl. 14] S23

obungaphezu in addition to, more than [rel Cl. 14] S26

obunobuhlakani intellectual (lit. that/which has cleverness) [rel Cl. 14] S05

obunye other, another [adj Cl. 14] S04

obuzwakalayo that/which is felt or experienced [rel Cl. 14] S23

ocansini to bed, to, from, on a sleeping-mat [loc; < **ucansi**] S23

odade my sisters [n Cl. 2b; sg **udade**] S21

odinga that/which requires, that/which needs [rel Cl. 3] S19

odinga who requires, who needs [rel Cl. 1] S27

odlule last, (that/which has) passed [rel Cl. 3] S13

odlwengulwe who was raped [rel Cl. 1] S26

odume famous, renowned [rel Cl. 1] S17

ofakazi witnesses [n Cl. 2b; sg **ufakazi**] S26

ofana such as, like, that/which resembles [rel Cl. 3] S19

ofuna who wants [rel Cl. 1] S22

ogcina one who ends up [rel Cl. 1] S16

ohamba one who travels [rel Cl. 1] S09

ohlala who resides [rel Cl. 1] S20

ohlala that/which resides [rel Cl. 3] S24

ohlupha that/which is bothering [rel Cl. 3] S06

ohlwini on a/the list [loc; < **o-** + **uhlu** + **-ini**] S10

okamfowabo that of his or her brother [poss pron Cl. 3] S27

okhathazekile one who is worried [rel Cl. 1] S05

okhethweni in the election [loc; < **o-** + **ukhetho** + **-eni**] S03

okhulumela spokesperson for (lit. (s)he who speaks for) [rel Cl. 1] S13

okocansi sexual matters (i.e. (things) of the sleeping-mat; euph) [poss pron Cl. 17] S09

okokuqala first [adv; < poss pron "that of to start"] S11

okokuqala the first (time) [poss pron Cl. 17] S23

oku- [adj conc Cl. 15 or 17; < **a-** rel marker + **uku-** NP] S09, S18

oku- that, which, who [rel conc Cl. 15 & 17; < **a-** rel marker + **ku-** SC] S21, S04

okuba yimbangela that which becomes a cause [rel Cl. 17] S28

okubalekela of evading, of running away from [poss Cl. 6] S10

okubalekela ukukhokha intela for tax evasion [poss phr Cl. 6] S10

okubalulekile what is important [rel Cl. 17] S14

okubalwa to be counted [poss Cl. 6] S12

okubambekayo that which is tangible [rel Cl. 17] S21

okubhaka for baking [poss Cl. 6] S01

okubuhlungu what is sad or painful [rel Cl. 17] S28

okubulala of murder [poss Cl. 6] S26

okucanula what is disgusting [rel Cl. 17] S21

okudayisa to sell (lit. of selling) [poss Cl. 6] S28

okudlange where there is rife [rel Cl. 17] S20

okudlange kuyo the place where it is rife [ind rel of plain loc rel, Cl. 17] S20

okudlange kuzo where it is rife [ind rel of plain loc rel, Cl. 17] S20

okudlwengula of rape [poss Cl. 6] S26

okudlwengulwa of rape (lit. of being raped) [poss Cl. 6] S23

okufanayo that which is similar or the same [rel Cl. 17] S23

okufanele that which is necessary [rel Cl. 17] S20

okufanele akwenze that (s)he should do (it) [ind rel of plain obj rel, Cl. 17] S25

okufanele bakugweme what they must avoid [ind rel of plain obj rel, Cl. 17] S20

okufanele uzenze that/which you have to do [ind rel of plain obj rel, 2 p sg] S04

okugcina of keeping, of preserving [poss Cl. 6] S12

okugcina that ends up [rel Cl. 17] S28

okuguquka of changing [poss Cl. 6] S26

okuhlukanisa that which distinguishes [rel Cl. 17] S07

okukachwepheshe that of an expert [poss pron Cl. 17] S23

okukaMnuz Mandela that of Mr. Mandela [poss pron phr Cl. 15] S07

okukhulu great [adj Cl. 15] S19

okulalwa that/which is slept [rel Cl. 17] S20

okulalwa kuzo in which people sleep (lit. that which there is slept in it) [ind rel of plain loc rel, Cl. 17] S20

okumanje for now [adv; < rel Cl. 17] S12

okumayelana that which concerns [rel Cl. 17] S23

okumele what must [rel Cl. 17] S10

okumnenge what disgusted him [rel Cl. 17] S26

okunabantu where there are people [rel Cl. 17] S06

okuncane little [adj Cl. 15] S09

okungaba yinselelo that/which would be a challenge [rel Cl. 17] S19

okungaba yiqiniso that which could be the truth [rel phr Cl. 17] S23

okungaba yiqiniso it is what could be the truth [ident cop, pres; < Ø- + okungaba] S23

okungabantu things like people, hominoids [rel Cl. 17] S17

okungabasiza something that can

help them [rel Cl. 17] S20

okungahlelelwanga unplanned for [rel Cl. 15] S25

okungajwayelekile something unusual [rel Cl. 17] S11

okungelula that/which is not easy [rel Cl. 17] S20

okungenhla the above, which is above [rel Cl. 17] S12

okuningi much, a lot [adj Cl. 15] S23

okunjalo something like this, or like that [rel Cl. 17] S08

okunye something else, another thing [adj Cl. 15 or 17] S18

okuphikisa that which contradicts [rel Cl. 17] S23

okuphikisa lokhu okungaba yiqi-niso the opposite could be true S23

okuqala of starting (up) [poss Cl. 6] S12

okusasetshenziswa that/which is still used [rel Cl. 15] S21

okusempeleni in truth, indeed (lit. that which is in truth) [rel Cl. 17] S13

okusemthethweni that which is legal [rel Cl. 17] S12

okushaqisayo something amazing [rel Cl. 17] S17

okushisa of heat [poss Cl. 6] S20

okusho that/which is to say, that/which means [rel Cl. 17] S23

okusho ukuthi which means to say [rel phr Cl. 17] S28

okusobala that which is public, that which is out in the open [rel Cl. 17] S25

okuthatha that/which takes [rel Cl. 15] S23

okuthile something [rel Cl. 17] S19

okuthiwa which it is said [rel Cl. 17] S26

okuthiwa uyibhalele which it is said (s)he wrote to [ind rel of plain obj rel, Cl. 17] S26

okuvame where one normally VERBs, where they usually VERB [rel Cl. 17] S08

okuvame ukudlalela khona aba-ntwana where children customarily play [ind rel of plain loc rel, Cl. 17] S08

okuvimbe that which prevents [rel Cl. 17] S19

okuyaye that which sometimes VERBs [rel Cl. 17] S20

okuyibona who are those [rel Cl. 17] S27

okuyilapho that/which is where [rel Cl. 17] S16

okuyindawo that/which is a place [rel Cl. 17] S18

okuyinto that/which is something [rel Cl. 17] S06

okuyisikhundla that/which is a position [rel Cl. 17] S27

okuyisikole that/which is a school [rel Cl. 17] S14

okuyiwona that/which is what [rel Cl. 17] S27

okuyiyona that/which is what, which is the thing [rel Cl. 17] S18

okuyizifundo that/which were (are) studies [rel Cl. 17] S18

okuzama ukubulala of attempted murder [poss phr Cl. 6] S26

okuzodayiselwa kuzo where there will be sold [ind rel of plain loc rel, Cl. 17] S24

okuzokwenza that/which will make [rel Cl. 17] S04

okwa- something like [poss pron pref Cl. 17] S13

okwaba muncu what was nasty (lit. that which became bitter) [rel Cl. 17] S21

okwabafundi that of the students [poss pron Cl. 17] S13

okwakubukeka something remarkable [rel Cl. 17] S17

okwakungelikaGareth Olivier that/which belonged to Gareth Olivier (lit. which was that of Gareth Olivier) [rel Cl. 17] S27

okwakungeyabesilisa that/which were ones for males [rel Cl. 17] S19

okwakungezabaMhlophe that/which were those of Whites [rel Cl. 17] S16

okwakungokamfowabo that/which belonged to his or her brother [rel Cl. 17] S27

okwamaphepha something like papers [poss pron Cl. 17] S17

okwandisa that which increases [rel Cl. 17] S23

okwangenza that which made me [rel Cl. 17] S19

okwangqangqazelisa that/which rattled or made tremble [rel Cl. 15] S17

okwathi that/which then [rel Cl. 17] S17

okwazi(yo) who knows how [rel Cl. 1] S16

okwejwayelekile that which is usual, normal, customary [rel Cl. 17] S21

okwenza that/which makes [rel Cl. 17] S20

okwenzeka(yo) what happens, what occurs, what takes place [rel Cl. 17] S16

okwenzeke that which has happened [rel Cl. 17] S04

okwenziwa that/which was done or made [rel Cl. 15] S23

okwenziwayo that which is being done [rel Cl. 17] S13

okwesithathu third [poss pron Cl. 15] S11

okwezigebengu that of criminals [poss pron Cl. 17] S09

olawula one who controls, regulates, marshals, orders [rel Cl. 1] S18

olawula that which controls, regulates [rel Cl. 3] S07

olawula ukuhamba kwamabhanoyi air-traffic controller (lit. one who controls the traveling of airplanes) [rel phr Cl. 1] S18

olimalayo one who gets hurt or injured [rel Cl. 1] S16

oliqhamukisa who comes from [rel Cl. 1] S09

olobela ... the correspondent for ... (lit. one who writes for) [rel Cl. 1] S26

olokuqeda one for bringing to an end [poss pron Cl. 11] S09

olu- that, which, who [rel conc Cl. 11; < a- rel marker + lu- SC] S16

olubhekene na- ... that/which deals with ... [rel Cl. 11] S24

olufanele appropriate, necessary [rel Cl. 11] S27

olunywe who has been bitten [rel Cl. 1] S20

olunzulu deep, profound [rel Cl. 11] S27

olusematheni that/which is on everyone's lips (lit. which is in the saliva) [rel Cl. 11] S25

olusheshayo quick, speedy [rel Cl. 11] S21

olusiza that/which helps [rel Cl. 11] S27

oluyingozi that/which is dangerous [rel Cl. 11] S20

oluzokwenza that/which will produce [rel Cl. 11] S24

oluzoyisiza that/which would help him or her [rel Cl. 11] S16

olw- that, which, who [rel conc Cl. 11; found before a, e; < a- rel marker + lu- SC] S17

olwawela that/which fell onto [rel Cl. 11] S17

oLwesine Thursday [poss pron Cl. 11; o- pronominalizer + lwa- poss conc Cl. 11 (agreeing with understood **usuku** day) + **isine** fourth] S11

olwesokudla the right-hand one [poss pron Cl. 11] S15

om- [adj conc Cl. 1 & 3] S07, S17

-om-a dry up, bec dry [v.i.] S20

-omis-a bec dry (of the weather); cause to dry; make thirsty [v-caus; inch] S20

omakhelwane neighbors [n Cl. 2b; sg **umakhelwane**] S08

omame mothers, ladies [n Cl. 2b; sg **umame** Cl. 1a] S08

omdala old, elder, the old one [adj Cl. 1] S07

oMkhize the Mkhizes [n Cl. 2b; sg **uMkhize** (surname, clan name)] S22

omkhulu senior [adj Cl. 1] S10

omkhulu large, big [adj Cl. 3] S17

omnyama black, Black person [rel Cl. 1] S18

o-mosquito mosquitoes [n Cl. 2b; sg **u-mosquito**; the Zulu word is **umiyane** Cl. 1a] {Eng} S20

ompetha finalists [n Cl. 2b; sg **umpetha**; < -pheth-a complete, finish; **m + ph > mp**] S11

omphakathi of the community [poss Cl. 6; < **a-** + **umphakathi**] S09

omsebenzi for or of work, for or of employment [poss Cl. 6] S27

oMthembu the Mthembus [n Cl. 2b; sg **uMthembu** surname, clan name] S22

omu- [adj conc Cl. 1 & 3; occurs with monosyllabic stems; < **a-** rel marker + **umu-** NP] S13, S10

omunye a certain, some, one (not in enumeration), another [adj Cl. 1] S13

omusha new [adj Cl. 3] S10

omzimba of the body [poss Cl. 6] S20

-on-a spoil, damage, injure; sin, do wrong; corrupt [v.i. & t.] S17

-onakal-a get spoilt, damaged, injured; bec corrupt, sinful [v-neut] S17

-onakalel-a spoil for, damage for [v-neut-appl] S17

-onakalelw- have sg spoilt or damaged [v-neut-appl-pass] S17

onalesifo who has this disease [rel Cl. 1] S20

onalesinambuzane that/which/who has this parasite [rel Cl. 1] S20

-ondl-a nourish, rear, bring up [v.t.] S24

oneminyaka aged, who has years [rel Cl. 1] S09

onengane who has a child [rel Cl. 1] S22

onengane engenayise a single mother (lit. one with a child who has no father) [rel phr] S22

onenhlonipho who has respect [rel Cl. 1] S22

onepulazi who has a farm [rel Cl. 1] S27

-ong-a save; economize [v.i. & t.] S11

ongahluphi who causes no trouble [rel Cl. 1] S22

-ongam-a lean over, overhang; preside over, administer [v-positional; var **-engam-a**; **-angam-a**] S23

-ongamel-a lean over (for), overhang; preside over, administer [v-positional-appl; var **-engamel-a**; **-angamel-a**] S14

ongaphuzi who does not drink [rel Cl. 1] S22

ongasakwazi that/which you are no longer able [rel 2 p sg] S28

ongasenalo who no longer has it [rel Cl. 1] S28

ongathandi who doesn't like [rel Cl. 1] S06

ongavilaphanga who is not lazy [rel Cl. 1] S27

ongayedwana who is not alone/on his or her own [rel Cl. 1] S04

ongenanembeza who has no conscience [rel Cl. 1] S26

-ongiw-a be saved, conserved, preserved [v-pass] S11

ongowaKwaBester who is from Bester [rel Cl. 1] S26

ongowokuqala who is the first one [rel Cl. 1] S19

onguchwepheshe who is an expert, who is a specialist [rel Cl. 1] S26

onguchwepheshe wezengqondo who is a psychiatrist or psychologist [rel phr Cl.1] S26

ongudadewabo who is his or her or their sister [rel Cl. 1] S26

ongumgqugquzeli who is the coordinator [rel Cl. 1] S11

ongumngani who is a friend [rel Cl. 1] S23

ongumqondisi who is a director [rel Cl. 1] S09

ongumshayi-siginci who is a guitarist [rel Cl. 1] S14

ongumshushisi (s)he who is prosecutor [rel Cl. 1] S10

ongumsizi who is a helper, an assistant [rel Cl. 1] S14

ongumxhumanisi who is a public relations officer [rel Cl. 1] S19

onguSipho namely, Sipho (lit. who is Sipho) [rel Cl. 1] S26

onguzakwabo who is married into the same family [rel Cl. 1] S27

onke all, the whole [quant Cl. 6; var **wonke**] S12

onkosikazi ladies, mesdames [n Cl. 2b; pl **unkosikazi** 1a] S02

ono-40 who is forty (lit. who has 40) [rel Cl. 1] S22

onogada guards, watchmen [n Cl. 2b; sg **unogada** {Eng} S13

onomalaleveva who has malaria [rel Cl. 1] S20

onomoya ophansi who is reserved or gentle (lit. has a spirit that is down) [rel Cl. 1] S22

onqunyelwe sona that/which you have been set, prescribed [ind rel of plain obj rel] S20

onyakeni in the year [loc; < **unyaka**] S28

-oph-a bleed [v.i.] S23

ophinda who also [rel Cl. 1] S09

ophusile solid [rel Cl. 3] S12

osafufuzayo who is still passionate [rel Cl. 1] S22

osebenza who works [rel Cl. 1] S24

osemahlombe that/which is on shoulders [rel Cl. 3] S16

osemnyangweni who is in the department [rel Cl. 1] S25

osendaweni that/which is in a place or locality [rel Cl. 3] S12

osethole who has already received [rel Cl. 1] S24

osewaphuma who already left some time ago [rel Cl. 1] S05

oshayela one who drives [rel Cl. 1] S14

oshisiswe that/which has been heated [rel Cl. 1] S01

oShozi the Shozis [n Cl. 2b; sg uShozi surname, clan name] S22

osibanibani some people or other, certain people [n Cl. 2b; sg usibanibani Cl. 1a] S06

osizini to, from, in sorrow [loc; < usizi] S28

osohlalakahle social workers [n Cl. 2b; sg usohlalakahle] S09

osondelene who is close [rel Cl. 1] S16

osophikweni who is in the league or wing or section [rel Cl. 1] S25

osuke who has just, who has merely [rel Cl. 1] S16

othandayo who likes, who loves [rel Cl. 1] S19

othandweni in love [loc; < o- + uthando + -eni] S04

othisha teachers [n Cl. 2b; sg uthisha Cl. 1a] {Eng} S05

otshale who has planted [rel Cl. 1] S27

ovelele the top (lit. who came to the fore) [rel Cl. 1] S11

owabantu one of people [poss pron Cl. 3] S19

owabulawa who was killed [rel Cl. 1] S21

owadala that/which created [rel Cl. 3] S17

owadivosa a divorcee (lit. one who got divorced) [rel Cl. 1] S22

owake that/which you have once (in the distant past) [rel 2 p sg] S15

owake waba naso that/which you have had [ind rel of assoc adv rel, 2 p sg] S15

owakhula who grew up [rel Cl. 1] S19

owaKwaBester one from Bester's place [poss pron Cl. 1] S26

owakwaNdlovu one of the Ndlovu clan [poss pron Cl. 1] S22

owalahlekelwa who lost (long ago) [rel Cl. 1] S24

owalandela that followed [rel Cl. 3] S18

owangihola who led me [rel Cl. 1] S14

owashonelwa a widow(er) (lit. one who has been died for) [rel Cl. 1] S22

owawukugunyaza that/which promoted it [rel Cl. 3] S25

owawungasetshenziswa one that was not being utilized [rel Cl. 3] S27

owawuzohamba ... on which would travel ... [rel Cl. 3] S18

owayekhala who was crying [rel Cl. 1] S17

owayevame who used (to) [rem past past, conjoint] S18

owayithenga that/which you bought (it) [ind rel of plain obj rel] S28

owazithenga kuso from which you bought them [ind rel of

plain loc rel] S28

oweLamontville High School that (game) of Lamontville High School [poss pron Cl. 3 (agrees with **umdlalo**)] S11

owelapha (one) who treats [rel Cl. 1] S23

owelapha **ngamakhumbi** herbalist [rel phr Cl. 1; pl **abelapaha ngamakhumbi**]

owenza who does, who makes [rel Cl. 1] S19

owesifazane female, (polite term for) woman [poss pron Cl. 1; pl **abesifazane**] S23

owesilisa a male [poss pron Cl. 1; pl **abesilisa**] S23

owesimame lady, woman [poss pron Cl. 1; pl **abesimame**] S17

owethule who placed before or laid down [rel Cl. 1] S26

owezindaba journalist, reporter (lit. (s)he of the news) [poss pron Cl. 1; pl **abezindaba**] S09

owodwa (the) only [rel Cl. 3] S09

owokubanika that of giving them [poss pron Cl. 3] S25

owokubanika is one of giving them [ident cop, pres; Ø- cop pref + **owokubanika**] S25

owokuqala the first one [poss pron Cl. 1] S19

owokuxoxisana that of negotiating, [poss pron Cl. 3] S16

owokuxoxisana is to negotiate [ident cop, pres; < Ø- ident cop pref (realized as breathy voice

on the 1st vowel together with a tonal change) + **owokuxoxisana**] S16

owomdlali that of the player [poss pron Cl. 3] S11

oyibamba who is deputy [rel Cl. 1] S25

oyi-forensic criminologist who is a forensic ... [rel Cl. 1] S23

oyimenenja who is a manager [rel Cl. 1] S24

oyintandane one who is an orphan [rel Cl. 1] S22

oyisingili who is single [rel Cl. 1] S22

oyonginqanda one who will turn me away, who will prevent me [rel Cl. 1] S14

ozalwa who was born [rel Cl. 1] S06

ozihloniphayo self-respecting [rel Cl. 1] S21

ozimele who is independent [rel Cl. 1] S12

ozimisele who is prepared, who is ready [rel Cl. 1] S27

ozithobileyo who is humble [rel Cl. 1] S16

ozobe ephelekezelwa who will be accompanied [rel Cl. 1] S11

ozobe ugubha that/which will be celebrating [rel Cl. 3] S11

ozodlalwa that/which will be played [rel Cl. 3] S11

ozokusabisa who will scare you [rel Cl. 1] S28

ozothandana naye with whom you will share love [ind rel of plain adv rel, 2 p sg] S04

P

-ph- [verbalizer (suffix that changes nouns and adjectives into verbs); cf. **-khaliph-**, **-hloniph-**, **-vilaph-**] S07

-ph-a give (to), donate [v.t.] S02

pha- [NP Cl. 16] S03

-phahl-a surround [v.t.] S17

-phahlw-a be surrounded [v-pass] S17

-phakam-a rise up, mount, bec elevated [v.inch] S17

phakathi inside [loc noun Cl. 16] S17, S08

phakathi kuka- in, inside, between, among [loc noun + link used with nouns of Cl. 1a] S20

phakathi kwa- in, inside, between, among [loc noun + link] S08

phambi kwa- before, ahead of, in front of [loc noun + link] S08

phambi kwakhe ahead of him or her [loc phr] S14

phambili in front, ahead; before, beforehand [loc noun Cl. 16; the final syllable is elided when followed by **kwa-** or **kuka-**, the Cl. 17 poss conc that follows certain loc nouns] S08

phambilini previously, in the past [adv; < **phambili**] S11

phandle outside [loc noun Cl. 16; < **pha-** NP Cl. 16 + **indle** outside or surroundings of a village or homestead] S03

-phangalal-a faint, collapse, die [v.i.] S16

phansi underneath, below, down [loc noun Cl. 16] S16

phansi kwa- under [loc noun + link] S16

-phas-a pass (a test or exam) [v.t.] {Eng} S18

-phasis-a pass (v.t.; a law or student) [v-caus] S25

-phasisw- be passed (a law or student) [v-caus-pass] S25

-phath-a take hold of, handle; affect; treat, manage [v.t.] S12

-phathel-a hold for; treat for, manage for; carry for, bear for [v-appl] S16

-phathelan-a na- ... bec related to ..., bec concerned with ... [v-appl-recip] S16

-phathw-a be handled, be treated, be managed; suffer from [v-pass] S12

-phazam-a be disturbed, be interrupted [v.i.] S13

-phazamis-a interrupt, disturb [v-caus] S13

-phazamisek-a get interrupted, get disturbed [v-caus-neut] S13

-phefumul-a give an opinion [v.i] S13

Phega (surname) [n Cl. 1a] S19

-phek-a cook [v.t.] S12

-phekelez-a accompany [v.t.; var **-phelekez-a**] S11

-phel-a come to an end, cease, get finished [v.i.] S05

phela indeed, truly [adv] S14

-phelekez-a accompany [v.t.; var **-phekelez-a**] S11

-phelekezelw-a be accompanied [v-pass] S11

-phelel-a bec fully satisfied, bec well catered for [v.i.] S06

-phelel-a come to and end for [v-appl] S27

-phelelw-a have come to an end, lose [v-appl-pass] S27

-phendul-a answer, reply [v.i. & t.] S06

-phendulel-a defend (as in a court of law) [v-appl] S26

-pheny-a turn over (a leaf, page); investigate, search [v.t.] S05

-phenyw-a be investigated [v-pass] S05

-pheph-a escape; recover, get well; bec safe, bec secure [v.i., inch] S16

-pheph-a blow about [v.i.] S21

phephandaba newspaper [< **iphephandaba**] S06

-phephel-a take refuge [v-appl] S18

-phephis-a help escape; help recover, cure [v-caus] S16

-phephuk-a get blown away or about [v.i.; cf. **-pheph-a**] S17

-phephukis-a blow about [v-caus] S17

phesheya on the other side, abroad, overseas [loc noun Cl. 16] S16

phesheya kwa- on the other side of, across [loc noun + link] S18

phesheya kwezilwandle overseas (lit. on the other side of seas) [loc phr] S18

-pheth-a complete, conclude, finish, have the last say [v.i. & t.] S10

-phethel- border on [v-appl] S11

phezu kokusebenzisa in spite of the use [loc phr] S20

phezu kokuthi in spite of the fact that [conj phr] S21

phezu kuka- ... above ... [loc noun + link used with nouns of Cl.1a] S10

phezu kwa- above, over, on, on top of; in control of; in addition to; in spite of [loc noun + link] S04, S16

phezu kwemithandazo in spite of prayers (lit. at the top of ...) [loc phr] S23

phezulu (at the) top, above, high [loc n Cl. 16; < **pha-** [NP Cl. 16] + **izulu** sky, heaven; the final syllable is elided when followed by **kwa-** or **kuka-**, the Cl. 17 poss conc that follows certain loc nouns] S01

-phi? where? [interrogative adv] S03

439

-phik-a be obstinate; argue, compete; deny, contradict, repudiate [v.i. & t.] S18

-phikelel-a persist, persevere [v-perfective] S18

-phikis-a dispute, debate, contradict [v-caus] S23

phiko wing, department, section [< **uphiko**] S10

-phil-a live, be alive; be well, be healthy [v.i.; in the speech of some people, this may be v.inch] S20

-philis-a keep alive, keep healthy, make well [v-caus] S20

Philisiwe (female name; means 'has/have been given health or life') [n Cl. 1a] S26

-phind-a repeat, do again; reduplicate; return, go back [v.i. & t.] S20

-phind-a VERB repeatedly, VERB again, VERB also [aux indicating repetition of an action; followed by the subjunc] S04

-phindaphind-a keep repeating [v-redup; < **-phind-**] S20

-phind-e VERB repeatedly, VERB again, VERB also [aux; followed by the subjunc] S09

-phindelel-a repeat again and again, return again and again [v-perfective] S26

-phindis-a send back, return; retaliate, take vengeance [v-caus] S28

-phindisel-a send back to, return to [v-caus-appl] S28

-phindiselw-a be sent back to, be returned to [v-caus-appl-pass] S28

-phindw-e be done repeatedly [aux, pass; followed by the subjunc] S23

-phiq-a force, compel [v.t.] S09

-phol-a bec cool [v.i.] S01

-pholis-a cool [v-caus] S01

-phons-a throw [v.t.; var **-phos-a**] S16

-phoq-a force, compel [v.t.] S09

-phoqelel-a urge continually, pressurize [v-perfective] S09

-phoqelelw-a be continually forced, be compelled, be pressurized [v-perfective-pass] S09

-phos-a throw [v.t.; var **-phons-a**] S16

-phothul-a complete [v.t.] S14

-phox-a make feel stupid, mock, embarrass [v.t.] S23

-phoxek-a be mocked, be the butt of jokes, be made fun of [v-neut] S23

phoyisa policeman [< **iphoyisa**] S21

-phuc-a shave; deprive (of), take away [v.i. & t.] S24

-phucw-a be deprived of, have taken away; be shaved [v-pass] S24

-phul-a break [v.t.; var **-aphul-a** and **-ephul-a**] S10

-phum-a come/go out, come from, emerge, leave, depart [v.i.] S01

-phumel-a come out for, into [v-appl] S20

-phumelel-a succeed [v-perfective] S04

-phumul-a rest [v.i.] S02

-phumulel-a rest for [v-appl] S07

-phungul-a lessen, decrease, reduce, diminish [v.t.] S27

-phungulel-a lessen for, decrease for, reduce for [v-appl] S27

-phunyul-a get loose, escape; let loose, allow to escape [v.i. & t.] S26

-phuph- dream, dream of [v.i. & t.] S19

-phus-a bec solid [v.inch] S12

-phuz-a drink [v.t.] S16

Ponko (name) [n Cl. 1a] S17

Pretorius (surname) [n Cl. 1a] {Afr} S26

Q

-qal-a begin, start, do for the first time [v.i. & t.] S05

-qalaz-a look about, peer around [v.i.] S17

-qalw-a be started, be initiated [v-pass] S08

-qamb-a compose, invent; give a name [v.t.] S27

-qanjw-a be composed, invented, named [v-pass; < **-qamb-w-a**; **mbw > njw**] S27

-qaqamb-a ache, throb [v.i.] S20

-qash-a employ, hire, rent [v.t.] S05

-qashw-a be employed, be hired, be appointed [v-pass] S05

-qed-a bring to an end, finish [v.t.] S05

-qedw-a be ended [v-pass] S05

-qeqesh-a train, coach, instruct [v.t.] S05

-qeqeshel-a train for [v-appl] S12

-qeqeshelw-a be trained for [v-appl-pass] S12

-qeqeshiwe [v-pass-stative; < **-qeqesh- + -w- + -i...e**] S05

-qeqeshw-a be trained, be coached, be instructed [v-pass] S16

-qhamuk-a proceed from, come from, come suddenly into view, appear unexpectedly [v.i.] S03

-qhamukis-a: **-li-qhamukis-a** come from a place [idiom; The Cl. 5 OC refers to any place mentioned. The caus ext is used idiomatically here.] S09

-qhaqhazel-a shiver, tremble [v.i.] S23

-qhath- set to fight, place in opposition to [v.t.] S07

-qhathanis-a compare; place side by side; set to fight each other [v-recip-caus] S07

-qhathanisw-a be compared [v-recip-caus-pass] S07

-qhathw-a be teamed up against, be set up against [v-pass] S11

-qhel-a bec remote [v.i.] S20

-qheny-a show off [v.i.] S14

-qhub-a continue, carry on, proceed, make progress [v.t.] S05

-qhubek-a continue, proceed, carry on [v-neut; the neut ext does not have its usual significance here] S05

-qhubekel-a proceed to [v-appl] S08

-qhutshekelw-a be proceeded towards [v-appl-pass; < **-qhubekel-w-a**; **b** ... **-w-** > **tsh** ... **-w-**] S08

-qikelel-a be on the lookout for, guard against [v.t.] S08

-qin-a bec firm, bec solid, bec tough, bec hard, bec strong [v.inch] S07

-qinis-a strengthen, tighten, make firm [v-caus] S10

-qinis-a ikhanda be obstinate, be stubborn, be headstrong (lit. make the head strong or hard) [v phr] S10

-qinisek- be proved true, be fulfilled [v-neut] S18

-qinisekis-a prove true, show convincingly [v-caus-neut-caus] S26

-qok-a decide, choose [v.t.] S27

-qond-a make straight for, g o directly towards, head straight for; make up one's mind, determine that, decide upon; understand, comprehend, realize [v.t.] S17, S25, S26

-qondan-a be opposite each other, be in line with each other; understand one another [v-recip] S25

-qondan-a na- ... concern ... S25

-qondis-a direct (steer in a direction) [v-caus] S09

-qondisis-a understand thoroughly [v-intens] S18

-qoph-a cut out, notch; peck holes (e.g. a woodpecker) [v.t.] S18

-qoq-a gather (together), collect, tidy up, clear up; put right, reform [v.t.] S06, S26

-qoqw-a be collected, be gathered; be tidied up [v-pass] S06

-qubul-a cause to erupt; scatter at full speed, drive off (as birds); sing loudly in chorus [v.t.] S25

-qwash-a be on the watch [v.i.] S21

-qwashis-a put on the look out, alert to [v-caus] S21

-qwashisek-a be on the look out, be alerted [v-caus-neut] S21

R

Roodepoort (town) S03

S

s- we [SC 1 p pl; found before vowels] S14

s- it, he, she [SC Cl. 7; found before vowels] S04

-s- us [OC 1 p pl; found before vowels] S09

-s- already, now, soon [exclusive aspect marker; found before vowels] S12

-s- dawn [v.i.] S11

sa- of [poss conc Cl. 7] S03

-sa- still; no longer (in negative constructions) [persistive aspect pref] S05, S28

-sab-a be afraid of, fear [v.i. & t.; var **-esab-**] S28

saba it became [copula, rem past]

-sabalal-a spread out [v.i.] S12

-sabalalis-a spread, further [v-caus] S12

sabantu for people, of people [poss Cl. 7] S14

saba sihle it was good (lit. it became good) [descr cop, inch, rem past] S27

-sabis-a scare, make afraid [v-caus; var **-esabis-a**] S28

sabo their, of theirs [poss Cl. 7] S18

sabona we saw [rem past] S17

sadicileka it got thrown down [rem past] S17

sagcina it ended in [rem past] S14

-sakaz-a broadcast, publish, disseminate [v.t.] S10

-sakazek-a get broadcast [v-neut] S26

-sakazw-a be broadcast, be published [v-pass] S10

sakhe his, of his, her, of hers [poss Cl. 7] S13

sakho your [poss Cl. 7] S04

saKwaZulu-Natal of KwaZulu-Natal [poss Cl. 7] S09

-sal-a remain, stay behind [v.i.] S17

salezo of those [poss Cl. 7] S24

salezozifo of those diseases [poss phr Cl. 7] S20

salokho of that, thereof [poss Cl. 7] S03

salokhu for this, of this, hereof [poss Cl. 7] S08

sama-Afrika of Africans [poss Cl. 7] S25

samabhanoyi of airplanes [poss Cl. 7] S18

samaphoyisa of the police [poss Cl. 7] S09

sami my [poss Cl. 7] S27

-sand-a has/have just VERBed [aux; followed by vn; the final **a** is generally omitted] S10

Sandile (male name; cf. **uSandile**) [n Cl. 1a] S09

sangasese private [poss Cl. 7] S15

sangiphiqa it forced me [rem past] S09

sasebusuku of (at) night [poss Cl. 7] S21

sasemini of noon [poss Cl. 7] S14

saseMtata of Umtata [poss Cl. 7] S17

sasidinga it, (s)he required or needed [rem past pres] S27

sasincintisana we competed, were

competing [rem past pres] S27

sasingelula it was not easy [descr cop, rem past pres, neg] S18

sathi and (s)he said [narr] S26

saya (and) we went [narr] S14

sazisa we make known, we advertise [pres, conjoint] S19

se- already, now, soon [exclusive aspect marker] S04

-se- to, from, at, in, on [loc pref] S02

-se- still [persistive pref; var of **-sa-** used in copulatives] S17

-se VERB already, VERB then, VERB now, VERB soon [aux; translation depends on context] S17

-se- ... -ini to, from, at, in, on [loc marker; **-se-** occurs after vowels] S02

se-Afrika to, from, in Africa [loc; < **e-Afrika**] S20

se-AIDS of AIDS [poss Cl. 7] S23

sebebuza they are already asking [pres, exclusive] S08

sebecela they now request [pres, exclusive, partic] S13

sebedlulile they have already passed [past, exclusive, disjoint] S25

sebefakwe [past, exclusive, conjoint] S10

sebefikile they have already arrived [past, exclusive, disjoint] S20

sebehlele they have then arranged

[past, exclusive, conjoint] S28

sebeke they have already once [aux, past, exclusive, conjoint] S23

sebekhetha they now choose, they already choose [pres, exclusive] S16

sebekhethe they have already chosen [past, exclusive, conjoint] S28

sebekhishelwe they have already had taken out against them [past, exclusive, conjoint] S10

sebekhishwe they have already had removed, they have already been removed [past, exclusive, conjoint] S20

sebekhululekile once they have been released [past, exclusive, disjoint] S23

sebengakwazi they are now able [pres, potential, exclusive] S24

sebengakwenza they are now able to do it [pres, potential, exclusive] S25

sebengu-896 there are now 896 [ident cop, pres, exclusive] S10

sebenqunyelwe ugwayi katiki they were cautioned, given a warning (idiom; lit. they were allocated only threepence worth of tobacco or snuff) [past, exclusive, conjoint] S25

-sebenz-a work, operate [v.i.] S04

-sebenzel-a work for, work from, work towards [v-appl] S04

-sebenzis-a use, employ, utilize, make work, put into operation; help work [v-caus] S08

-sebenzisan-a work together, cooperate [v-caus-recip] S12

-sebenzisel-a use for, use in order to [v-caus-appl] S09

sebephethwe they are already infected [stative, exclusive] S20

sebephila they now live, they already live [pres, exclusive] S28

sebeshonile they have already passed away [stative, exclusive] S12

sebesungule they have already initiated [past, exclusive, conjoint] S24

sebethole they have now acquired [past, exclusive, conjoint] S27

sebeya they then go [pres, partic, exclusive] S23

sebusuku at night [loc; < **ebusuku**] S20

sedlule it has passed [stative] S04

seDukuduku to, from, in, at Dukuduku (a forest reserve) [loc; < **eDukuduku**] S24

se-Durban South Central to, from, in, at ... [loc; < **e-Durban South Central**] S11

seduze near, close by [loc; < eduze] S16

seFunimfundo at Funimfundo (school) [loc; < **eFunimfundo**] S02

sefwini under a cloud [loc; < **efwini**] S02

se-Girls Soccer for girls' soccer [poss Cl. 7] S11

sejele to, from, in jail or prison [loc; < **ejele**] S23

sejwayelekile it is usual, customary, normal [stative] S23

-sekel-a prop up, support, assist, stand in for [v.t.] S25

sekhaya to, from, at home [loc; < **ekhaya**] S14

sekufanele it is now necessary [aux, stative, exclusive] S18

sekumele it is now necessary [aux, stative, exclusive] S23

sekunezinye there are now other [assoc cop, pres, exclusive] S28

sekuphele there ended [past, partic, exclusive, conjoint] S27

-sekushushisweni in prosecution [loc; < **ekushushisweni**] S10

sekuyinto it is something [ident cop, pres, exclusive aspect] S09

sekuyisikhathi it is now time, it is high time [ident cop, pres, exclusive] S04

sekuzongena there will soon enter [fut, exclusive] S07

sekwakhe it has already built [past, exclusive, conjoint] S09

sekwenza it now causes [pres, partic, exclusive] S13

sekwenze it has already made or caused [past, exclusive, conjoint] S13

sekwenzeka it is now happening [pres, exclusive] S08

seLamontville to, from, in Lamontville [loc; < eLamontville] S11

selihlala he, she, it already lives [pres, exclusive] S16

selizosuka it, (s)he will soon depart [fut, exclusive] S18

selokhu ever since [conj; followed by partic] S11

seluthathe it has now taken [past, exclusive, conjoint] S24

selwakhe it has already built [past, exclusive, conjoint] S24

selwaphela it ceased a long time ago [remote past, exclusive aspect] S05

semadolobheni to, from, in towns [loc; < emadolobheni] S16

semahlombe to, from, in, on the shoulders [loc; < emahlombe] S16

semajele to, from, in jails [loc; < emajele] S23

semakhemisi to, from, at, in pharmacies [loc; < emakhemisi] S20

semaphandleni to, from, in rural areas [loc; < emaphandleni] S23

sematheni on the lips (lit. in the saliva) [loc; < ematheni] S25

semazweni to, from, in countries [loc; < emazweni] S16

seMelika to, from, in America [loc; < eMelika] S16

semini at midday, at noon; during the day [loc; < emini] S14

semithonjeni to, from, in the sources [loc; < emithombweni < e- + imithombo + -eni; mbw > nj] S09

semkhankasweni to, from, in a scheme or program [loc; < emkhankasweni] S12

semoyeni in spirit, in soul, psychologically; to, from, in the air, wind, breath [loc; < emoyeni] S23

sempilo of life [poss Cl. 7] S16

seMtata to, from, in Umtata [loc; < eMtata] S17

semthethweni to, from, in the law [loc; < emthethweni] S12

sendaweni in a place or locality [loc; < endaweni] S12

sendlini in the house [loc; < endlini] S20

sengathi as if [conj] S17

sengathi if only, would that [conj, followed by potential mood] S08

sengcupheni in danger [loc; < engcupheni] S23

sengibachazela I then explain to them [pres, partic, exclusive] S18

sengifile I am already dead [stative, exclusive] S09

sengifuna I now want [pres, exclusive] S27

sengifunde I have already learnt [past, exclusive, conjoint] S14

sengike I have already [aux, past, exclusive, conjoint] S09

sengikhulile I am already grown up [stative, exclusive] S19

sengikuthokozela I am now happy about it [pres, exclusive] S27

sengixhume I have already linked [past, exclusive, conjoint] S27

sengiyakwazi I am now able, I can now [pres, exclusive, disjoint] S24

sengizibalile I have already enumerated them [past, exclusive, disjoint] S18

sengopha I am already bleeding [pres, partic, exclusive] S23

sengozini in danger [loc; < engozini] S20

seNingizimu Afrika to, from, in South Africa [loc; < eNingizimu Afrika] S07

seNkantolo yoMthethosisekelo of the Constitutional Court [poss Cl. 7] S25

senkosi of chief [poss Cl. 7; < sa- + inkosi] S06

seNkume to, from, in Nkume [loc; < eNkume] S21

se-Northern Province to, from, in Northern Province [loc; < e-Northern Province] S14

sentambo of a rope, of hanging [poss Cl. 7] S26

senyakatho to, from, in the north [loc; < enyakatho] S18

senyangeni in, from the month [loc; < enyangeni] S28

senza it, (s)he makes, causes, does [pres, conjoint] S23

-sesh-a search, pump for information, cross-question [v.t.] {Eng} S04

sesidlo sasemini of or for lunch [poss phr Cl. 7] S14

sesidlulile it has already passed [past, exclusive, disjoint] S27

sesifuna we now want [pres, exclusive] S21

sesifundise we have already taught [past, exclusive, conjoint] S24

sesijwayele we are already accustomed [stative, exclusive] S16

sesikhubaze it already having damaged [past, exclusive, conjoint] S14

sesisenyangeni we are already in the month [loc cop, pres, exclusive] S28

sesithole we have now or already found [past, exclusive, conjoint] S25

sesitholile we have already found [past, exclusive, disjoint] S13

sesiya we were (lit. are) then going [pres, partic, exclusive] S14

sesiyanda it is now increasing [pres, exclusive, disjoint] S20

se-South Africa to, from, in South Africa [loc; < e-South Africa] S20

sethula we present (for information) [pres, partic] S19

-setshenziselw-a be used for, be employed for [v-caus-appl-pass;

< -sebenzisel-w-a; b ... -w- > tsh ... -w-] S19

-setshenzisw-a be used, be utilized, be employed [v-caus-appl; < -sebenzis-w-a; b ... -w- > tsh ... -w-] S09

sewaphuma (s)he already left long ago [rem past, exclusive; < se- + -w- SC Cl. 1 + -a- rem past pref] S05

se-welding of welding [poss Cl. 7] S19

sewuthumela it is already sending [pres, partic, exclusive] S13

sezakhiwe they have already been built [stative, exclusive] S24

sezibaliwe they have already been enumerated [past, exclusive, disjoint] S20

sezibhubhise they have already wiped out [past, exclusive, conjoint] S20

sezihlotsheni in families [loc; < ezihlotsheni < ezihlobweni < e- + izihlobo + -eni; bw > tsh] S09

sezike they already once [aux, past, exclusive] S06

sezike zaqoqwa they were already once collected [past, exclusive, experiential] S06

sezinambuzane of insects, of parasites [poss Cl. 7] S20

sezindiza of airplanes [poss Cl. 7] S18

sezindlini zangasese to, from, at, in toilets [loc phr; < ezindlini zangasese] S23

sezingaphezu once they are higher [loc cop, pres, exclusive] S28

sezingene they have already entered [past, exclusive, conjoint] S20

sezingxenye in parts [loc; < ezingxenye] S20

seziphindiselwe they now having been returned to [past, partic, exclusive, conjoint] S28

seziqala they are already beginning [pres, exclusive] S08

sezizathu of the reasons [poss Cl. 7] S23

sezomnotho of the economy [poss Cl. 7] S28

sezulu of the weather [poss Cl. 7] S17

-sh-a burn, get burnt [v.i.] S01

-sha new, young, fresh [adj stem] S10

-shabalal-a disappear, come to nought, evaporate [v.i.] S17

-shad-a marry, get married, wed [v.i. & t.] S14

-shaq-a bec amazed, astonished, shocked [v.i.] S17

-shaqis-a amaze, astonish, shock [v-caus] S17

-shay-a hit, beat, strike [v.t.] S01

shaya beat! [imperative] S01

-shay-a ihlombe clap rhythmically, applaud [idiom; lit. hit the shoulder] S25

-shay-a indiva dismiss as worthless [idiom] S05

-shay-a mkhuba take seriously [idiom] S23

-shayel-a drive [v.t.] S14, S09

-shayel-a hit for, beat for [v-appl] S25

-shayel-a elikhulu ihlombe applaud (something or someone) greatly [idiom] S25

-shayelel-a drive for, drive to [v-appl] S14

-shayiwe have been beaten [v-pass-stative] S01

-shayw-a be hit, be beaten [v-pass] S01

-shef-a shave [v.i. & t.] {Eng} S14

-shesh-a hurry, rush, be quick, speed [v.i.] S16

Shezi (surname) [n Cl. 1a] S09

-shicilel-a print [v.t.] S21

-shicilelw-a be printed [v-pass] S21

-shintsh-a change [v.t.] S23

-shintshan-a take turns [v-recip] S23

-shintshel-a change to, for [v-appl] S28

-shis-a be hot, burn (t.) [v-caus] S01

-shisel-a forge; burn for [v-caus-appl] S19

-shisis-a heat [v-caus-caus] S01

-shisw-a be burnt down, get burnt [v-caus-pass] S26

-shiw-o be said [v-pass; < -sh-o] S06

-shiy-a leave (behind) [v.t.] S02

-sh-o say, say that, say so, state, mean, be of the opinion that, intend [irregular verb taking the suffix **-o** in all tenses and moods except for the negative of the past tense] S05

-shon-a set (of sun), disappear; die (euph); fail (in an exam); go bankrupt [v.i.] S02

-shonel-a set in the direction of; set, disappear or die to the detriment of; fail because of; go bankrupt because of [v-appl] S02

-shonelw-a have set, disappear or die to one's detriment [v-appl-pass] S02

-shonelw-a y- ... be bereaved of ... S02

-shush-a harass, press [v.t.] S10

-shushis-a prosecute, sue; persecute [v-caus] S10

-shushisel-a prosecute for, sue for [v-caus-appl] S10

-shushiselw-a be sued for, have cases brought against one [v-caus-appl-pass] S10

si- we [SC 1 p pl] S03

si- it, he, she [SC Cl. 7] S03

si- [enum conc Cl. 7] S05

-si- us [OC 1st p pl] S09

-si- it, him, her [OC Cl. 7] S09

-si- [neg cop pref] S19

sibalo figure, number [< **isibalo**] S20

sibatshele we inform them [subjunc] S25

sibe it should be(come) [copula, subjunc] S20

sibhekene we are facing [stative] S25

sibhema we sniff, we smoke [pres, conjoint] S09

Sibisi Msomi (name) refers here to the Sibisi Msomi clan [n Cl. 1a] S22

sibizwa it, (s)he is called [pres, conjoint] S20

sibona we see, we are of the opinion [pres, conjoint] S03

Sibusiso (male name) [n Cl. 1a; < **isibusiso** blessing] S05

sicabanga we think [pres, conjoint] S15

sidinga it needs, it requires [pres, conjoint] S20

sidlange it is rife [past, conjoint] S20

sidlule it has passed [past, disjoint] S18

sidlulele it is extreme for [past, conjoint] S23

sifana it resembles, it is like [pres, conjoint] S06

sifika we reach, we arrive [pres, conjoint] S16

sifisa we wish [pres, conjoint] S21

sifo disease, illness [< **isifo**] S20

sifuna we want [pres, conjoint] S21

siguquguquka it is changeable, it keeps changing [pres, partic] S20

sihamba (it) moving, while it is in motion [pres, partic] S16

sihlala it, (s)he keeps on VERBing; it, (s)he continually VERBs [aux, pres, conjoint] S20

sihlanganyele we should unite in, collaborate in [subjunc] S08

sijwayelekile it is usual, it is customary, it is normal [stative] S13

sika- [poss conc Cl. 7; used before nouns of Cl. 1a] S06

-sik-a cut, mow [v.t.] S13

sikahulumeni of the government [poss Cl. 7] S25

sikamalaleveva of malaria [poss Cl. 7] S20

sikayise of his father [poss Cl. 7] S06

sikhula it grows [pres, conjoint] S16

sikhule it should grow [subjunc] S20

sikhuluma we speak [pres, conjoint] S10

sikhumbuleka it is memorable [pres, partic] S17

sikhumulo sezindiza airport [< **isikhumulo senzindiza**] S18

sikhuphuke it should go up [subjunc] S20

sikole school [< **isikole**] S13

silele we are sleeping [stative, partic] S09

simandla it is strong [descr cop, pres] S20

sinamandla it has strength [assoc cop, pres] S21

-sind-a escape, bec saved [v.i.] S16

-sindis-a save, rescue [v-caus] S16

sinenkinga we have a problem [assoc cop, pres] S13

-singa- something like [prefix deriving nouns; means 'something like'] S09

singabala we can count [pres, potential] S20

singabi muncu it should not bec nasty [descr cop, inch, subjunc] S28

singabukeka it, (s)he can be considered, can be regarded as, may seem [pres, potential] S19

singalambi we should not get hungry [subjunc, neg] S09

singalindi we should not wait [subjunc, neg] S08

singanda it could increase [pres, potential] S23

-singath-a support, hold in the arms [v.t.] S02

singayazi we don't know (it) [pres, partic, neg] S08

singayitholanga we have not got [past, partic, neg] S09

singazitholi that we do not have (lit. get) them [subjunc, neg] S15

singena it enters [pres, conjoint] S20

singenalutho it is empty (lit. it does not have anything) [assoc cop, pres, partic, neg] S15

singesinye it is one [ident cop, pres] S24

singezansi it is lower down, it is downcountry, it is downstairs [loc cop, pres] S20

singomakhelwane we are neighbors [ident cop, pres, partic] S08

sinonkosikazi I am with my wife (lit. we are with a wife) [assoc cop, pres, partic] S15

sinonkosikazi wami when I am (lit. we are) with my wife (the 1 p pl SC is often used in Zulu in place of the singular **ngi-**, when someone associated with the subject is included in the sentence as part of the predicate) S15

sinye one [enum Cl. 7] S05

siphile that it should live [subjunc] S27

Sipho (male name) [n Cl. 1a; < **isipho** gift] S02

siqalaza we look(ed) about [pres, partic] S17

siqhuba we make progress, we proceed [pres, conjoint] S16

siqikelele we should be on the lookout for, guard against [subjunc] S08

siqinile it is firm [stative] S10

sisaxoxa we are still chatting [pres, partic, persistive] S18

sisekhona it is still there, it still exists [loc cop, pres, partic, persistive; may also introduce an exist cop] S26

sisho saying [< **isisho**] S08

sisincane it is small [descr cop, pres, partic] S19

sisiqonda we understand it [pres, conjoint] S16

sister [n Cl. 1a; < **usister**] {Eng} S25

sithanda we like [pres, conjoint] S27

sithembele it relies [stative] S27

sithi (s)he, it goes; (s)he, it says [pres, conjoint, pos] S08

sithola we find [pres, conjoint] S23

sitholakale it is found [subjunc] S20

sivela it, (s)he comes from [pres, conjoint] S14

siwatshele we should tell them [subjunc] S25

sixoxa we mention, we narrate, we discuss, we chat [pres, conjoint] S16

siya we go (to) [pres, partic] S13

siyabahalalisela we congratulate or applaud them [pres, disjoint] S28

siyahamba we travel [pres, disjoint] S16

siyanda it is increasing [pres, disjoint] S16

siyashesha it is quick [pres, disjoint] S28

siyayithokozela we are glad for it [pres, disjoint] S09

siyazi we know [pres, disjoint] S13

siye (and) we go [subjunc] S16

siyimbangela it is the cause [ident cop, pres] S20

siyingxenye it is one (part) [ident cop, pres] S20

siyiphikile (s)he has repudiated or denied it [past, disjoint] S26

siyobe we shall be [aux, rem fut] S05

siyobe sivotela we shall be voting for [rem fut pres] S05

siyohlale it will continue, it will always [aux, rem fut] S17

siyosiza so that we go and help [subjunc, andative] S16

-siz-a help, assist, aid [v.t.] S09

-sizakal-a get help, be assisted, get relief [v-neut] S12

sizalele it should lay eggs [subjunc] S20

sizama we try [pres, conjoint] S16

sizichithela we just spend [pres, conjoint] S09

sizimisele we are determined or prepared [stative] S24

sizisize we should help them [subjunc] S09

sizobuya it will return (i.e. it will be returned) [fut] S22

-sizw-a be helped, assisted, aided [v-pass] S23

sizwa we hear [pres, partic] S17

so- of [poss conc Cl. 7 coalesced with following **u**] S04

so- to, from, at, in, on [loc pref with nouns of Cl. 11; found after vowels] S07

so- [quant conc Cl. 7] S11

so it, its, he, him, his, she, her [abs pron Cl. 7] S14

so eye [< **iso**; pl **amehlo** (var **amaso**); the initial vowel is elided because of the following enumerative] S27

so linye one eye [n phr Cl. 5] S27

sobala in the open [loc; < **obala**] S07

sobunxele of the left [poss Cl. 7] S15

sodwa only, alone [quant Cl. 7] S11

sokongiwa of conservation [poss Cl. 7] S11

sokuba ... for ..., to ..., for becoming [poss Cl. 7] S04, S14

sokucabanga for or of thinking [poss Cl. 7] S04

sokudla of the right, right-hand; for eating (in Zulu custom, it is the right hand that is used for eating) [poss Cl. 7] S15

sokudlwengulwa of being raped [poss Cl. 7] S23

sokuhlasela of striking, attacking, invading [poss Cl. 7] S17

sokuntenga cyclic, volatile [poss Cl. 7] S25

sokuqala first [poss Cl. 7; < **ukuqala** to begin, to start] S27

sokusungula of establishing [poss Cl. 7] S14

sokuthatha for taking [poss Cl. 7] S28

sokuthi (for) that [poss Cl. 7] S03

sokutshalwa for or of being planted [poss Cl. 7] S27

sokwakha of building [poss Cl. 7] S24

sokwenza of doing [poss Cl. 7] S16

-sol-a find fault (with), blame, criticize, grumble, express doubt or dissatisfaction, be suspicious or doubtful [v.i. & t.] S18

-sombuluk- bec unrolled, unraveled [v.i.] S13

sona it, its, he, him, his, she, her [abs pron Cl. 7] S18

-sondel-a approach, come or go near [v.i. & t.] S16

-sondelan-a bec close to one another, approach one another [v-recip] S16

sonke the whole, every [quant Cl. 7] S13

Sono (surname) [n Cl. 1a] S19

sophikweni to, from, on the wing; to, from, in the section, league, division [loc; < **ophikweni**] S25

-suk-a go away, leave (from), set off, originate (at, from), start or arise from some cause [v.i.] S08

-suk-a soon VERB [aux; followed by narr (in past)] S17

-suk-e just VERB, merely VERB, happen to VERB [aux; followed by partic] S14

-sukel-a originate at [v-appl] S08

-sukum-a stand up, get up [v.i.] S21

-sukumel-a stand up for, rise for [v-appl] S21

-sul-a wipe (off) [v.t.] S28

-sulw-a be wiped (off); be removed [v-pass] S28

-sungul-a inaugurate, initiate, establish, found, set up [v.t.] S11

-sungulel-a set up, establish, found, initiate for [v-appl] S27

-sungulw-a be inaugurated, be established [v-pass] S11

-sus-a remove, take away [v-caus; < **-suk-** + **-Y-**; k + **-Y-** > s] S17

-suth-a have enough to eat, bec satiated [v.inch; irregular stative = **-suthi**] S09

-suthis-a satisfy (of food), make full [v-caus] S09

-swakam- bec damp or moist [v.i.] S20

T

-telek-a go on strike [v.i.] S13

-telekel-a strike for, strike over [v-appl] S13

-th-a pour into vessel with narrow aperture [v.t.] S01

Thabo (male name) [n Cl. 1a] {Sotho; < **thabo** happiness} S07

Thabo Mbeki (name of South African President) S07

-thakas-a show kindness, be genial; praise [v.i. & t.] S25

-thakasel-a be kind to, be genial towards; welcome, laud, praise flatteringly; congratulate [v-appl] S25

-thambam-a slant, decline (of sun in afternoon) [v.i.] S20

-thand-a like, love [v.t.] S04

-thandan-a love one another, love each other [v-recip] S08, S09

-thandaz-a pray [v.i.] S23

-thandek-a be lovable, be likable, be popular [v-neut] S04

-thandisis- like greatly, like very much, love passionately [v-intens] S18

-thath-a take, carry away [v.t.] S03

-thathel-a forage, gather what has been stored [v.i. & t.] S21

-thathel-a take for, take against,

take from [v-appl] S28

-thathelan-a contract from one another, be contagious [v-appl-recip] S20

-thathu three [adj stem] S01

-thathw-a be taken [v-pass] S05

-thel-a pour [v-appl] S01

-thel-a pay tax [v.i. & t.] S10

thela pour! [imperative] S01

-thelel-a pour for, pour onto, pour into, scatter for, spread among [v-appl-appl] S20

-themb-a hope, trust, expect [v.t.] S05

Themba (male name) [n Cl. 1a] S16

-thembakal-a be trustworthy, be trustable [v-neut] S12

-thembel-a have faith in, have confidence in, trust, rely on [v-appl, inch] S05

-thembis-a promise, give hope (to) [v-caus] S06

-theng-a buy [v.t.] S08

-thengel-a buy for [v-appl] S08

-thengw-a be bought [v-pass] S10

-thenjisw-a be promised [v-caus-pass; < **-thembis-w-a**; **mb** ... **-w-** > **nj** ... **-w-**] S06

Theresa (female name) [n Cl. 1a] {Eng} S11

-theth-a try a court case, preside over a court; find not guilty, give judgment in favor of; scold, nag [v.t.] S26

-thethw-a be tried (in court), be presided over (in court); be found not guilty, have found in one's favor [v-pass] S26

-th-i say; think (be of the opinion) [irregular verb taking the suffix **-i** in all tenses and moods except for the past tense] S05

-th-i "go" (e.g. it *goes* whiz) [dummy verb that introduces an ideophone] S27

thi we, us [abs pron 1 p pl] S05

-thib-a ward off [v.t.] S09

-thikamez-a disturb, distract, interrupt, have a negative impact on [v.t.] S23

-thile some, (a) certain, particular [rel stem; < **-th-i** say; var **-thize**] S06

thina we, us [abs pron 1 p pl] S16

-thint-a touch, handle, affect [v.t.] S08

-thintek-a be touched, be affected [v-neut] S08

-thithiz-a hesitate, be confused, bumble [v.i.] S05

-thiw-a be said [v-pass] S08

-thize some, (a) certain, particular [rel stem; < **-th-i** say; var **-thile**] S06

-thob-a bend, lower, bow; humble, humiliate [v.t.] S16

-thokoz-a be happy, be glad [v.i.] S09

-thokozel-a be happy about or for, be glad about or for, enjoy [v-appl] S09

-thokozis-a make happy, gladden [v-caus] S19

-thol-a obtain, get, find, receive; experience [v.t.] S03

-tholakal-a get found, be found, be available, be obtainable [v-neut] S03

-tholan-a find each other, get each other; fight, be in contention [v-recip] S11

-tholel-a find for, get for, obtain for [v-appl] S14

-tholis-a provide, secure [v-caus] S15

-thul-a be(c) quiet, be(c) silent, be(c) tranquil [v.i. (normally inch)] S05

Thulani (male name) [n Cl. 1a; < imper **thulani!** settle down! (this name might be given when there is strife within a family)] S09

-thum-a send (a person) [v.tt.] S12

-thumb-a capture, take hostage, hijack, take slyly [v.t.] S16

-thumel-a send to, send (an object), send for; order [v-appl] S12

-thung-a sew [v.t.] S12

-thunjw-a be taken hostage, be hijacked, be taken prisoner [v-pass; < **-thumb-w-a**; **mbw** > **njw**] S16

-thunyelw-a be sent (to) [v-appl-pass; < **-thumel-w-a**; **m** ... **-w-** > **ny** ... **-w-**] S12

Thusi (surname) [n Cl. 1a] S25

-thuth-a move house; transfer; convey, transport [v.i. & t.] S27

-thuthuk-a increase, progress, grow; bec influential [v.i.] S06

-thuthukis-a develop, uplift, enlarge [v-caus] S13

-thuthulek-a increase, grow [v.i.] S20

-thwal-a carry or wear (on the head, in/on the hands, on the feet) [v.t.; inch] S20

Thwala (surname) [n Cl. 1a] S26

-tik-a get the better of, overcome [v.t.] S11

-tshal-a plant, sow [v.t.] S05

-tshalel-a plant for [v-appl] S24

-tshalw-a be planted, be sown [v-pass] S05

-tshel-a tell [v.tt.] S12

-tshelw-a be told [v-pass] S12

U

u- [NP Cl. 1a/3a; = **uØ-**] S01

u- [NP Cl. 11; = **uØ-**] S03

u- [NP Cl. 14; = **uØ-**] S13

u- you [SC 2 p sg] S01

u- he, she, it [SC Cl. 1] S01

u- it [SC Cl. 3] S02

uØ- [NP Cl. 1a/3a] S01

uØ- [NP Cl. 11] S03

uØ- [NP Cl. 14] S13

u-12, u-15ml, u-160°C, U-1994... (all numerals, weights and measures, and years take the Cl. 1a prefix **u-**, which *should* be separated from the numeral by a hyphen (but which often is not) [n Cl. 1a] S01, S03

u-anti aunt [n Cl. 1a] {Eng *auntie*} S14

uAsmal (surname) [n Cl. 1a] {Arabic} S11

u-B.A. B.A. [n Cl. 1a] S14

uba (s)he becomes [copula, pres, conjoint] S20

uba nemfiva (s)he develops a fever (lit. becomes with a fever) [assoc cop, inch, pres] S20

ubaba (my) father; mister [n Cl. 1a] S19

ubala unoccupied, open country [n Cl. 11] S07

ubalelwa it is calculated at [pres, conjoint] S17

ubamele it represents them [stative] S13

ubandakanya it involves [pres, conjoint] S14

ubani? who? (sg) [n Cl. 1a; pl **obani?**] S08

uBarend (male name) [n Cl. 1a] {Afr} S10

ube you should be [copula, subjunc] S04

ube (s)he, it was [aux, indicating relative tense] S13

ube eseqhubeka (s)he then continued [past pres, exclusive] S13

ube nekusasa you should have a future (lit. you should be with a tomorrow) [assoc cop, inch, subjunc] S04

ube ngumuntu you should bec a person [ident cop, inch, subjunc] S16

ube nolwazi it should have (the) knowledge [assoc cop, inch, subjunc] S14

ube sewuthumela it was already sending [past pres, exclusive] S13

ubekuyo (s)he was at or in it [descr cop, past pres] S20

ubelokhu (s)he was constantly, always, continually [aux, past pres] S26

ubende spleen [n Cl. 11; pl **izimbende**] S20

ubengomunye (s)he was one [ident cop, past pres] S26

ubenovalo (s)he was afraid (lit. (s)he had fear) [assoc cop, past pres] S26

ubenza (s)he was committing, doing, making [past pres] S26

ubese umpofu it was already poor [descr cop, past pres, exclusive] S21

ubevakashele (s)he had visited [past past, conjoint] S20

ubezalwa (s)he was born to (lit. (s)he was being given birth to) [past pres] S02

ubhale and (you should) write [subjunc] S28

ubhedu heart fat; prize [n Cl. 11] S11

ubhekele it is looking towards or at [past, conjoint] S10

ubhekene you are facing [stative; < -bhekan- + -i...e] S04

uBhengu (surname) [n Cl. 1a] S05

ubhuti (my) brother [n Cl. 1a] {Afr *boetie* little brother} S22

ubisi milk [n Cl. 11] S03

uBiyela (surname) [n Cl. 1a] S24

ubiyelwe it is fenced [past, conjoint] S27

ubona you see [pres, conjoint] S07

ubonane you should consult [subjunc] S15

ubone and you understand (lit. see) [subjunc] S08

ubone it should see [subjunc] S23

ubonga it thanks [pres, conjoint] S02

uBongani (male name; means 'Give thanks!' or 'Give praise') [n Cl. 1a] S19

ubu- [noun pref Cl. 14] S02

ububi evil, wickedness, ugliness [n Cl. 14; < -bi bad] S23

ubucayi uncomfortable position, fix, dilemma [n Cl. 14] S18

ubudlelwane friendship, good relationship [n Cl. 14; < -dlelan- (with passive ext) be on good terms, be good neighbors (lit. eat for each other)] S24

ubudoda manhood, manliness,

virility; semen [n Cl. 14] S23

ubufakazi evidence, witness, testimony [n Cl. 14; < ufakazi witness] S19

ubugebengu crime, criminality, gangsterism [n Cl. 14] S03

ubuhlakani cunning, craftiness, cleverness [n Cl. 14] S05

ubuhle beauty [n Cl. 14; < -hle beautiful] S02

ubuhlungu pain [n Cl. 14] S23

ubuholi leadership [n Cl. 14] S05

ubukhali sharpness [n Cl. 14] S07

ubukhazikhazi splendor, luxury [n Cl. 14] S28

ubulili gender, sex; sexuality [n Cl. 14] S04

ubuningi large numbers, abundance, plenty [n Cl. 14; < -ningi many] S11

ubunjiniyela engineering [n Cl. 14] {Eng} S19

ubunxele the left [n Cl. 14; var ukunxele Cl. 15] S15

ubunye unity, togetherness [n Cl. 14; < -nye one] S09

ubunzima hardship, difficulty [n Cl. 14; < -nzima hard, difficult [rel stem]] S09

uBusisiwe (female name) [n Cl. 1a; < -busisiwe have been blessed] S26

ubusuku night(s) [n Cl. 14; neutral] S09

ubuye and it also [subjunc] S24

uCalalakubo (male name) [n Cl. 1a; **icala lakubo** the wrong or offence of his family] S06

ucansi sleeping-mat [n Cl. 11; pl **amacansi** Cl. 6] S09

uchwepheshe expert, specialist [n Cl. 1a] S23

u c h w e p h e s h e wezengqondo psychiatrist or psychologist [n phr Cl.1] S26

ucingo wire; telephone, telegraph [n Cl. 11; pl **izingcingo** Cl. 10; n + c > ngc] S06

uClive Wilkes (name) [n phr Cl. 1a] S09

ucwaningo investigation, research [n Cl. 11; < **-cwaning-** conduct research] S26

udaba serious matter [n Cl. 11] S21

udade sister [n Cl. 1a] S26

udadewabo his, her, their sister [n Cl. 1a; < **udade** sister + **wabo** their] S26

udalwa it is caused [pres, conjoint] S20

u-December (December is usually **uDisemba** in Zulu) [n Cl. 1a] {Eng} S17

udinga (s)he requires, needs [pres, conjoint] S27

udinga it requires, it needs [pres, conjoint] S19

uDkt Dr. [n Cl. 1a; abbrev: **uDokotela**] S17

udlame violence [n Cl. 11] S05

udlule it has passed [past, disjoint] S13

udlwengulwe (s)he was raped [past, conjoint] S26

uDoctor Philip Tabane (South African musician) [n phr Cl. 1a] S14

udokotela doctor [n Cl. 1a] {Eng} S15

udonga wall [n Cl. 11] S17

u-Dr Dr. [n Cl. 1a] {Eng} S05

uDudu (female name; abbrev of **u D u d u z i l e**; means 'Has consoled'; this name would be given to a girl after her mother has lost one or two other children, or there has been a death in the family) [n Cl. 1a] S08

udume (s)he is famous, (s)he is well-known [past, conjoint] S07

u-Eskom Eskom (national electricity supplier; originally: Electricity Supply Commission) [n Cl. 1a] S06

ufakazi witness [n Cl. 1a; < **-fakaz-** bear witness, give evidence, testify] S26

u-February (February is usually **uFebhuwari**) [n Cl. 1a] S02

ufikelwa (s)he experiences (lit. (s)he is arrived for) [pres, conjoint] S27

u-fitter and turner [n Cl. 1a] {Eng} S19

ufulawa flour [n Cl. 3a] {Eng} S01

ufuna you want [pres, partic] S16

ufuna (s)he wants [pres, conjoint] S05

ufuna kuqhubeke laba abangazi lutho (s)he wants those who know nothing to continue [v phr] S05

ufunda you read [pres, partic] S05

ufunde (s)he has studied [past, conjoint] S07

ufunde you should learn [subjunc] S18

ufundise (s)he taught [past tense, conjoint] S02

uGareth Olivier (name) [n phr Cl. 1a] S27

ugazi personality, charm [n Cl. 11] S04

ugcina (s)he ends up, (s)he finally [pres, conjoint] S16

ugcine it ended up [aux, past, conjoint] S13

ugesi electricity [n Cl. 3a] {Eng *gas*} S06

ugodle that you should withhold [subjunc] S05

ugogo (my) grandmother [n Cl. 1a] S19

u-Grade 12 (final year of school) [n Cl. 1a] S14

uGroen (surname) [n Cl. 1a] {Afr} S10

ugwayi tobacco, snuff [n Cl. 1a or 3a] S25

ugwebe (s)he sentenced, (s)he

passed judgment [past, conjoint] S26

ugweme you should avoid [subjunc] S28

ugwetshwe (s)he was sentenced [past, conjoint] S26

ugxile you must be firm [subjunc] S04

ugxile (s)he was determined, (s)he stood firm [past, conjoint] S19

uhamba (s)he travels [pres, conjoint] S09

uhambo trip, journey, tour [n Cl. 11; < -hamb- go, travel; pl **izihambo** Cl. 10a or **izinkambo** Cl. 10; n + h > nk] S24

uhhavini oven [n Cl. 1a; pl **ohhavini** Cl. 2b] {Eng} S01

uhhide long line of things, convoy [n Cl. 11; pl **izihhide** Cl. 10a] S17

uhlaba umkhosi (s)he sends out word (lit. sounds the alarm) [v phr] S11

uhlahlo division, distribution [n Cl. 11; < -hlahl- divide, distribute] S13

uhlahlomali budget [n Cl. 11; no pl; < **uhlahlo** division, distribution + **imali** money] S13

uhlala (s)he, it resides [pres, conjoint] S20, S24

uhlale you should continue [aux, subjunc] S19

uhlamvu grain, berry, pip, fruitstone [n Cl. 11] S15

uhlamvu lwesitho testicle (euph; lit. berry of body part) [n phr Cl. 11; pl **izinhlamvu zesitho**] S15

uhlangothi side, section [n Cl. 11] S23

uHlatshwayo (surname) [n Cl. 1a] S19

uhlelo arrangement, system, program [n Cl. 11; < -hlel- put in order, arrange; pl **izinhlelo**] S09

uHlengiwe (female name) [n Cl. 1a] S26

uhlobo type, sort, kind [n Cl. 11] S17

uhlu list, roll [n Cl. 11; pl **izinhlu**] S10

uhlupha it is bothering [pres, conjoint] S06

uhulumeni government [n Cl. 1a; pl **ohulumeni** Cl. 2b] {Afr *goewerment*} S03

uju honey [n Cl. 11] S03

ujusi juice [n Cl. 1a/3a] {Eng} S01

uJustice Justice (judicial title) [n Cl. 1a] {Eng} S26

ujwayele you should get used to [subjunc] S18

uk- [vn pref; NP Cl. 15; found before **o**] S11

uKader (male name) [n Cl. 1a] {Arabic} S11

uKader Asmal (name: former Minister of Water Affairs; now Minister of Education) [n phr Cl. 1a] S11

ukhaliphe (s)he is clever [past, conjoint] S07

ukhaliphe kakhulu kuna-... (s)he is cleverer than ... [v phr] S07

uKhambule (surname) [n Cl. 1a] S09

ukhansela councilor [n Cl. 1a] {Eng} S06

uKhanyile (surname) [n Cl. 1a] S09

ukhathazekile (s)he is worried, disturbed [stative] S05

ukhathazekile it is disturbed, it is distressed [stative] S06

uKhawula (surname) [n Cl. 1a] S06

ukhetho election [n Cl. 11; < -kheth- choose, select, vote; pl **izinketho**; **n + kh > nk**] S03

ukhokhele you should pay off [subjunc] S28

ukholwa (s)he believes [pres, conjoint] S27

ukhonze (s)he is passionate about, is a fan of [past, conjoint] S14

uKhoza (surname) [n Cl. 1a] S08

uKhozi FM (name of radio station) [n Cl. 11] S11

ukhulumela (s)he speaks for [pres, conjoint] S13

ukondla to bring up, to raise, to rear [vn Cl. 15] S24

ukongiwa conservation, preservation, to be conserved, to be saved [vn Cl. 15] S11

uku- to [vn pref; NP Cl. 15] S01

ukuba to become, to be [copula, vn Cl. 15] S08

ukuba (so) that [conj; followed by subjunc] S04

ukuba because, since [conj] S09

ukuba if [conj; var **ukube**] S27

ukuba akungenxa yabo if it were not for them S27

ukuba kuyiwe naye ocansini that (s)he should be the passive partner sexually (lit. that there should be gone with him to bed) S23

ukuba na- ... having ..., to have ... (lit. to be with) [vn form of assoc cop] S04

ukuba nekwakhe to have a home [assoc cop, inch, vn phr Cl. 15] S22

ukuba ngumakhenikha to bec a mechanic [ident cop, inch, vn phr Cl. 15] S19

ukuba ngumlimi to bec a farmer [ident cop, inch, vn phr Cl. 15] S27

ukuba ngumshayeli wamabha-noyi to bec a pilot [ident cop, vn phr Cl. 15] S18

ukuba nogazi kwakho your having charm [assoc cop, vn phr Cl. 15] S04

ukuba sendlini to be in a house [descr cop, inch, vn phr Cl. 15] S20

ukuba wusizo to be of help, to be of assistance [ident cop, inch, vn phr Cl. 15] S27

ukuba yilungu to bec a member [ident cop, inch, vn phr Cl. 15] S16

ukubabeka to put them, putting them [vn Cl. 15] S23

ukubafundisa to teach them [vn Cl. 15] S14

ukubakhona the presence (lit. to be(come) there [loc cop, inch, vn phr Cl. 15] S17

ukubalalela to listen to them [vn Cl. 15] S16

ukubaluleka importance, to bec important [vn Cl. 15] S24

ukubalwa to be counted [vn Cl. 15] S12

ukubamba to hold back, to keep back [vn Cl. 15] S23

ukubanga creating, to create [vn Cl. 15] S09

ukubanika to give to them [vn Cl. 15] S25

ukubathatha to take them [vn Cl. 15] S09

ukube if [conj; more usual var **ukuba**] S26

ukubeka to put [vn Cl. 15] S05

ukubeka imfundo ezingeni eli-fanele to place education on a proper level [vn phr] S05

ukubhaka baking, to bake [vn Cl. 15] {Afr *bak*} S01

ukubhala writing, to write [vn Cl. 15] S22

ukubhalela to write in, to write to, to write for [vn Cl. 15] S13

ukubheka checking, to check, to supervise, supervision, to look (at); to head for [vn Cl. 15] S14

uKubheka (surname) [n Cl. 1a] S13

ukubhikisha to protest, to fight against [vn Cl. 15] S25

ukubika to report [vn Cl. 15] S23

ukubona to see, sight [vn Cl. 15] S08

ukubona kanye wukubona kabili to see once is to see twice (i.e. once bitten twice shy; experience is the best taskmaster) [proverb] S08

ukubonana na- to consult (lit. to see one another with) [vn Cl. 15] S20

ukubonisa to show [vn Cl. 15] S25

ukubopha to arrest [vn Cl. 15] S10

ukuboshwa arrest, to be arrested [vn Cl. 15] S10

ukubukela to watch [vn Cl. 15] S18

ukubulala to kill, to murder [vn Cl. 15] S26

ukubuyisela to restore to, to return to [vn Cl. 15] S09

ukucabanga to think, thinking [vn Cl. 15] S04

ukucasuka contempt (lit. nausea) [vn Cl. 15] S23

ukucela i-lift hitch (a lift, a ride) [vn phr Cl. 15] S23

ukucela to request, to ask for [vn Cl. 15] S21

ukuchazeleka to get an explanation [vn Cl. 15] S13

ukuchema bias, to be prejudiced, to be biased [vn Cl. 15] S16

ukucwila sinking, to sink [vn Cl. 15] S28

ukudambisa to cause to subside, to assuage, to calm down [vn Cl. 15] S21

ukudayisa to market, offer for sale, auction, trade [vn Cl. 15] S27

ukudayiswa to be marketed, offered for sale, sold, traded [vn Cl. 15] S12

ukudinwa to be sickened, to be wearied [vn Cl. 15] S23

ukudinwa to bec bored [vn Cl. 15] S23

ukudla food; to eat, eating; right, right-hand (the right hand is traditionally the one used for eating) [vn Cl. 15] S09, S15

ukudlala to play [vn Cl. 15] S14

ukudlala amabhayisikili to cycle (lit. to ride bicycles) [vn phr Cl. 15] S14

ukudlalela to play at or in [vn Cl. 15] S08

ukudlulisa to pass on [vn Cl. 15] S06

ukudlulisela to pass on, to transfer, to second [vn Cl. 15] S14

ukudlulwa to be passed by, to be bypassed [vn Cl. 15] S06

463

ukudlwengula rape, to rape [vn Cl. 15] S23

ukudlwengulwa to be raped [vn Cl. 15] S23

ukudoja evasion, to evade, to dodge [vn Cl. 15] {Eng} S10

ukuduma thunder, rumbling [vn Cl. 15] S17

ukufa death, to die [vn Cl. 15] S16

ukufela to die in [vn Cl. 15] S23

ukufunda study, to study, to learn, learning. to read, reading [vn Cl. 15] S13

ukufundela to study in, at, for, towards [vn Cl. 15] S13

ukufundela ukuba to study to bec [vn phr Cl. 15] S18

ukufundisa to teach, teaching [vn Cl. 15] S24

ukugcina to keep, to preserve, preservation [vn Cl. 15] S12

ukugcoba you spread it [pres, con-joint] S01

ukugibela to ride, to mount (as a horse), to board, to travel by [vn Cl. 15] S18

ukugqama to be clear, to stand out [vn Cl. 15] S13

ukugqugquzela to persuade, to try to win over, to nag, to prod [vn Cl. 15] S27

ukugqugquzelwa prodding, to prod [vn Cl. 15] S12

ukuguquka to change [v.i.] [vn Cl. 15] S26

ukugwema to avoid [vn Cl. 15] S20

ukugxila to stand firm, to be steadfast [vn Cl. 15] S27

ukuhamba (to) travel, movement, to go, to walk; traffic [vn Cl. 15] S18

ukuhlangana to meet, meeting, coming together [vn Cl. 15] S09

ukuhlanganisa bringing together; completion [vn Cl. 15] S17

ukuhlanganisa iminyaka eli-khulu the centenary (lit. the bringing together or completion of 100 years) [vn phr] S17

ukuhlasela to attack, to invade [vn Cl. 15] S17

ukuhlelwa to be arranged, to be put in order [vn Cl. 15] S25

ukuhlola to carry out an examina-tion; to examine [vn Cl. 15] S15

ukuhlolwa examination, to be examined [vn Cl. 15] S23

ukuhlomula to give a share (especially the meat of a game animal), rewarding [vn Cl. 15] S24

ukuhlukana na- to part company with, to get away from [vn phr] S28

ukuhlukumeza violence, viola-tion, (to) assault, (to) attack, harassment [vn Cl. 15] S05

ukuhlukumezeka assault, attack, violation, to be shocked, jolted, annoyed, offended, violated [vn

Cl. 15] S21

ukuhlukunyezwa be assaulted, be attacked, violence [vn Cl. 15] S21

ukuhola to drag, to haul, to pull along; to lead, to guide [vn Cl. 15] S07

ukuholele (s)he was implicated in or responsible for [past, conjoint] S26

ukukhetha to choose, top select, to elect, to vote [vn Cl. 15] S18

ukukhipha to take out, to withdraw, to produce (to view) [vn Cl. 15] S05

ukukhipha isisu to abort [vn phr Cl. 15] S25

ukukhipha ukudinwa to alleviate boredom [vn phr Cl. 15] S23

ukukhiqiza to produce in abundance, to turn out in large quantities, surplus production [vn Cl. 15] S27

ukukhishwa to be taken out, to be expelled [vn Cl. 15] S20

ukukhishwa isisu to have diarrhea (lit. to be taken out the stomach) [vn phr Cl. 15] S20

ukukhishwa kwesisu abortion (lit. taking out of the stomach) [vn phr Cl. 15; pl **ukukhishwa kwezisu**] S25

ukukhishwa kwezisu abortions (lit. taking out of stomachs) [vn phr Cl. 15; sg **ukukhishwa kwesisu**] S25

ukukhokha paying, to pay [vn Cl. 15] S10

ukukhokhwa payment, to be paid [vn Cl. 15] S13

ukukhombisa to show [vn Cl. 15] S23

ukukhonya power, superiority; influence; turf (lit. bellowing (as a bull), to roar (as a lion)) [vn Cl. 15] S09

ukukhothama to bend down, to bow; to be humble [vn Cl. 15] S27

ukukhubazeka disability, handicap [vn Cl. 15] S14

ukukhula growing, to grow (up) [vn Cl. 15] S20

ukukhulelwa pregnancy, to bec pregnant [vn Cl. 15] S25

ukukhululeka to be freed, to be released, to bec emancipated; relief [vn Cl. 15] S23

ukukhuluma to speak, to talk [vn Cl. 15] S23

ukukhuphuka rise, to rise [vn Cl. 15] S13

ukukuphoqa to force or compel you [vn Cl. 15] S28

ukukuthakasela to welcome it [vn Cl. 15] S25

ukukwazi to know it [vn Cl. 15] S21

ukulahlekelwa to lose (lit. to have something get lost to one's detriment) [vn Cl. 15] S23

ukulahlekelwa yisithunzi loss of self-worth [vn phr Cl. 15] S23

ukulalela to listen (to), listening (to) [vn Cl. 15] S14

ukulawula to give commands, to order; to control, to regulate, to marshal [vn Cl. 15] S18

ukulawulwa to be governed [vn Cl. 15] S08

ukuletha to bring [vn Cl. 15] S09

ukulila weeping, lament [vn Cl. 15] S21

ukulimala to bec injured, hurt, wounded [vn Cl. 15] S09

ukulingwa to be tempted [vn Cl. 15] S28

ukulunywa to be bitten, stung [vn Cl. 15] S20

ukulwa fighting, to fight [vn Cl. 15] S09

ukuma to stand (up), to stop (v.i.) [vn Cl. 15] S16

ukumboza to screen [vn Cl. 15] S20

ukumelana to confront, to stand against [vn Cl. 15] S28

ukumelana na- ... to cope with ... [vn phr Cl. 15] S23

ukumfunela to seek out for him or her [vn Cl. 15] S14

ukumqoqa to reform him [vn Cl. 15] S26

ukumsiza helping him or her, to help him or her [vn Cl. 15] S19

ukunakwa to be noticed, to be taken notice of [vn Cl. 15] S16

ukunengwa to be offended, disgusted annoyed, [vn Cl. 15] S26

ukungabaza doubt, to doubt, to conjecture, to imagine [vn Cl. 15] S23

ukungabi not to become, not being [copula, vn Cl. 15, neg] S13

ukungabi khona absence (lit. not being there) [loc cop, vn phr Cl. 15, neg] S13

ukungaboni not seeing, blindness [vn Cl. 15, neg] S14

ukungafiki non-arrival, not to arrive [vn Cl. 15, neg] S13

ukungagculiseki dissatisfaction, lack of satisfaction, not being satisfied [vn Cl. 15, neg] S13

ukungatholakali non-receipt, non-obtainability [vn Cl. 15, neg] S13

ukungatholi not to receive, non-receipt, not to acquire, not to find [vn Cl. 15, neg] S13

ukungayi not to go, not going [vn Cl. 15, neg] S20

ukungayiboni not to see it, not seeing it [vn Cl. 15, neg] S06

ukungazi not knowing [vn Cl. 15, neg] S09

ukungazikhaleli not pleading for oneself [vn Cl. 15, neg] S26

ukungcola be corrupt, be immoral, be dirty [vn Cl. 15] S23

ukungcwaba burying, to bury [vn Cl. 15] S21

ukungena to enter [vn Cl. 15] S19

ukungenisa to bring in, to put in, to insert [vn Cl. 15] S24

ukungenwa to be entered, to be invaded [vn Cl. 15] S20

ukungibuza to ask me [vn Cl. 15] S14

ukungishaya to beat me [vn Cl. 15] S09

ukunika to give, to hand (to), to provide, provision [vn Cl. 15] S27

ukunqanda preventing, to prevent, checking, to check [vn Cl. 15] S08

ukunqunyelwa to be allocated [vn Cl. 15]

ukunqunyelwa ugwayi katiki to be cautioned, given a warning (idiom; lit. to be allocated threepence worth of tobacco or snuff) S25

ukuntenga to sway back and forth, to oscillate; volatility, oscillation [vn Cl. 15] S25

ukunto thing [n Cl. 15] S05

ukuntuleka lack, to be missing, to be required [vn Cl. 15] S20

ukunyamalala disappearance [vn Cl. 15] S08

ukuphangalala to die, to collapse, to faint [vn Cl. 15] S16

ukuphasiswa to be passed (of a law or student) [vn Cl. 15] S25

ukuphatha handling, to handle, management, to manage, command [vn Cl. 15] S07

ukuphathwa management, to be managed [vn Cl. 15] S12

ukuphathwa to be infected, to be held, to be handled [vn Cl. 15] S20

ukuphathwa kwamakhaza oku-gcina asebeshonile the cold storage of the deceased [vn phr Cl. 15] S12

ukuphazamiseka interruption, to get interrupted, to get disturbed [vn Cl. 15] S13

ukupheka cooking, to cook [vn Cl. 15] S12

ukuphela to come to an end, conclusion, [vn Cl. 15] S26

ukuphepha safety, security [vn Cl. 15] S08

ukuphepha to recover, to get well [vn Cl. 15] S20

ukuphikisa (to) dispute, (to) debate, to contradict [vn Cl. 15] S23

ukuphikisana na- ... to contest ..., to argue against ..., to defy ... [vn phr Cl. 15] S25

ukuphila to live, to be alive, to be well, to be healthy [vn Cl. 15] S25

ukuphila to live, to be well [vn Cl. 15] S28

ukuphoxeka to be mocked, to be the butt of jokes, to be made fun of, embarrassment, shame [vn Cl. 15] S23

ukuphumela to come out for, into [vn Cl. 15] S20

ukuphumelela to succeed [vn Cl. 15] S19

ukuphuza to drink [vn Cl. 15] S16

ukuqala to begin, to start; first, initial [vn Cl. 15] S10

ukuqalwa initiation, to be begun [vn Cl. 15] S12

ukuqasha to employ [vn Cl. 15] S05

ukuqeda to bring to an end, to finish [vn Cl. 15] S09

ukuqedwa removal, to be brought to an end [vn Cl. 15] S05

ukuqeqeshelwa to be trained for [vn Cl. 15] S16

ukuqeqeshwa to be trained [vn Cl. 15] S16

ukuqhuba to progress, to develop [vn Cl. 15] S16

ukuqhubeka to continue, to proceed, to carry on [vn Cl. 15] S18

ukuqinisekisile (s)he showed it convincingly, (s)he proved it [past, disjoint] S26

ukuqoqwa collection, to be collected, to be tidied up; to be put right [vn Cl. 15] S10

ukusa to dawn [vn Cl. 15] S11

ukusabalalisa to further [vn Cl. 15] S12

ukusebenza working, to work, to operate, to function [vn Cl. 15] S14

ukusebenzisa to use, using, to employ (i.e. use), employment [vn Cl. 15] S19

ukusebenzisana to work together, to cooperate [vn Cl. 15] S12

ukusetshenziswa use (n), to be used [vn Cl. 15] S20

ukushada to marry, to get married [vn Cl. 15] S14

ukushaya to hit, to beat, to strike [vn Cl. 15] S06

ukushaya ucingo to phone (lit. to hit the wire) [vn phr Cl. 15] S06

ukushayela to drive, to pilot [vn Cl. 15] S18

ukushaywa beating, to be beaten, corporal punishment [vn Cl. 15] S13

ukushesha to hurry, to rush, to be quick [vn Cl. 15] S16

ukushicelelwa publication, to be printed [vn Cl. 15] S21

ukushisa to be hot, to burn, heat (n) [vn Cl. 15] S20

ukushisela to forge, to burn for [vn Cl. 15] S19

ukushiswa to be burnt down, to get burnt [vn Cl. 15] S26

ukusho saying (so), statement [vn Cl. 15] S11

ukusho (s)he said this [past, conjoint] S26

ukushushiswa prosecution, to be prosecuted [vn Cl. 15] S10

ukusibulala to kill us [vn Cl. 15] S09

ukusidlulisela to pass it on [vn Cl. 15] S27

ukusindisa to save, to rescue [vn Cl. 15] S16

ukusishaya to beat us [vn Cl. 15] S09

ukusiza to help, to assist, to aid [vn Cl. 15] S16

ukusizakala to get helped, assistance, relief, development [vn Cl. 15] S12

ukusungula to establish, establishment, to found, foundation [vn Cl. 15] S14

ukusungulwa foundation, to be founded, establishment, to be established [vn Cl. 15] S12

ukuthandana mutual love, to love or like each other [vn Cl. 15] S09

ukuthatha (s)he takes it [pres, conjoint] S26

ukuthatha taking, to take [vn Cl. 15] S08

ukuthenga to buy, buying [vn Cl. 15] S09

ukuthethwa to be heard (of a court case), hearing [vn Cl. 15] S26

ukuthi saying, to say [vn Cl. 15] S10

ukuthi that [conj; < **ukuthi** to say] S03

ukuthiba to ward off [vn Cl. 15] S09

ukuthola to obtain, to acquire, to get, to find [vn Cl. 15] S13

ukutholisa to provide, to secure [vn Cl. 15] S15

ukuthula to be quiet, quiet, tranquility, peacefulness [vn Cl. 15] S05

ukuthunga sewing, to sew [vn Cl. 15] S12

ukuthunga it is sewing [ident cop, pres: < Ø- + **ukuthunga**] S12

ukuthunyelwa dispatch (n), to be sent [vn Cl. 15] S12

ukuthuthukisa to develop, to uplift [vn Cl. 15] S13

ukuthuthuleka to increase, to grow [vn Cl. 15] S20

ukutshala to plant, to sow [vn Cl. 15] S24

ukutshalwa planting, to be planted or sown [vn Cl. 15] S05

ukutshalwa kabusha renewal, revitalization, rejuvenation, to be planted afresh [vn phr Cl. 15] S05

ukutshele (s)he told it [past, conjoint] S26

ukuvakasha to visit (v.i.) [vn Cl. 15] S12

ukuvakashela to visit (v.t.) [vn Cl. 15] S19

ukuveza to bring out, to produce to view [vn Cl. 15] S13

ukuvikela defence, to defend, protection, to protect [vn Cl. 15] S11

ukuvimbela to prevent, to repel [vn Cl. 15] S08

ukuvotela voting for, to vote for [vn Cl. 15] S05

ukuvula to open (up) [vn Cl. 15]

S27

ukuvumelana mutual agreement, to agree with each other [vn Cl. 15] S13

ukuvumelana it is an agreement [ident cop, pres; < Ø- cop pref + **ukuvumelana**] S13

ukuvuna to reap, to harvest [vn Cl. 15] S27

ukuwa to fall, to collapse, bankruptcy [vn Cl. 15] S28

ukuwabuka to look at them [vn Cl. 15] S18

ukuwabukela to watch them [vn Cl. 15] S18

ukuwasha to wash [vn Cl. 15] S09

ukuwasusa to remove (it) (i.e. standing water not easily drained) [vn Cl. 15] S20

ukuwenza making them, to make them [vn Cl. 15] S01

ukuwenza to do it, doing it [vn Cl. 15] S27

ukuwufundisa to teach it [vn Cl. 15] S24

ukuxazulula settlement, to settle, resolution, to resolve [vn Cl. 15] S09

ukuxhaphaza to exploit, exploitation [vn Cl. 15] S23

ukuxhumana linkage, relations, to link up, to join [vn Cl. 15] S14

ukuxoxela to communicate to [vn Cl. 15] S16

ukuxoxisana to negotiate, negotiation [vn Cl. 15] S16

ukuya going to, to go to [vn Cl. 15] S20

ukuya ocansini to have sex (lit. to go to the sleeping-mat) [vn phr Cl. 15] S23

ukuyenza to do it [vn Cl. 15] S18

ukuyigwema to avoid it [vn Cl. 15] S16

ukuyohlala to go and live [vn Cl. 15, andative] S09

ukuzalela to lay eggs; to give birth to, at [vn Cl. 15] S20

ukuzalwa to be born [vn Cl. 15] S20

ukuzama to attempt, to try [vn Cl. 15] S26

ukuze so that, in order to [conj; followed by subjunctive] S04

ukuze wazi ukuthi so that you should know that S04

ukuzibeka phansi to stop what one is doing (lit. to put oneself down) [idiom; vn phr Cl. 15] S25

ukuzibulala to commit suicide [vn Cl. 15] S16

ukuzidubula to shoot oneself [vn Cl. 15] S16

ukuzifeza to accomplish them [vn Cl. 15] S28

ukuzifikisa to mistreat a newcomer (as bullying a new child at school or when a new member of staff who doesn't know the ropes is given extra work by old staff) [vn Cl. 15] S23

ukuzikhokhela to pay them off, to repay them [vn Cl. 15] S28

ukuzimela to stand up for oneself, to be independent [vn Cl. 15] S14

ukuzimisela determination [vn Cl. 15] S19

ukuziphendulela to defend oneself [vn Cl. 15] S26

ukuziphilisa to earn one's living, to keep oneself alive (lit. to make oneself live) [vn Cl. 15] S14

ukuziqhenya pride, to be proud [vn Cl. 15] S27

ukuzisebenza to work for oneself [vn Cl. 15; var **ukuzisebenzela**] S19

ukuzishayelela to drive for oneself [vn Cl. 15] S14

ukuzisungulela to set up for oneself [vn Cl. 15] S27

ukuzithatha to take them (on) [vn Cl. 15] S12

ukuzithathisa okwezigebengu to take them as criminals [vn phr Cl. 15] S09

ukuzithoba humility, to be humble [vn Cl. 15] S22

ukuzithola to find oneself [vn Cl. 15] S28

ukuzithulela just to keep quiet [vn Cl. 15] S16

ukuzivikela to protect or defend oneself [vn Cl. 15] S20

ukuzovimbela to come and prevent [vn Cl. 15, venitive] S20

ukuzwa to hear, hearing, to feel, to understand [vn Cl. 15] S16

ukuzwana mutual understanding, getting on together [vn Cl. 15] S09

ukw- to VERB, VERBing[prefix of verbal nouns; NP Cl. 15; var of **uku-** found before **a, i, e**] S01

ukwakha to build [vn Cl. 15] S08

ukwazi to know, knowledge [vn Cl. 15] S13

ukwazi you should be able [subjunc] S28

ukwazisa to inform [vn Cl. 15] S09

ukwaziwa renown, fame, reputation [vn Cl. 15] S27

ukwedlula to surpass, more than [vn used to express degree of comparison] S07

ukwehlelwa to be overcome, to have happen to one [vn Cl. 15] S23

ukwehlisa to lower [vn Cl. 15] S20

ukwehliselwa reduction, to have lowered for one [vn Cl. 15] S26

ukwejwayela to adjust to, to get used to, to bec accustomed to [vn Cl. 15] S23

ukwelapha healing, to heal, to cure [vn Cl. 15] S19

ukwelashwa treatment, to be treated, cure, to be cured [vn Cl. 15] S20

ukwengeza to increase [vn Cl. 15] S16

ukwenza doing, to do, making, to make [vn Cl. 15] S01

ukwenza isibonelo to give an example (lit. to make an example) [vn phr Cl. 15] S23

ukwenza isiqiniseko to make sure [vn phr Cl. 15] S18

ukwenze you must do it [subjunc] S20

ukwenzeka to happen, to occur, to take place, to be feasible [vn Cl. 15] S23

ukwesaba fear, to be afraid (of) [vn Cl. 15] S17

ukwesabela fear of, fear that [vn Cl. 15] S23

ukwezokuXhumana noMpha-kathi (s)he is in Community Relations [loc cop, pres] S14

ulaka rage [n Cl. 11; var **ilaka** Cl. 5] S26

ulalela (and) you listen to [pres, partic] S05

ulawula it, (s)he controls, regulates, marshals, orders [pres, conjoint] S07, S18

ulekelelwa it being assisted [pres, partic] S21

uligodle you should withhold it [subjunc] S06

ulimo farming, cultivation [n Cl. 11; < **-lim-** cultivate, plough] S27

uLinda (male or female name) [n Cl. 1a] S09

uLionel Richie (name of an American singer and composer) [n phr Cl. 1a] S14

uliqhamukisa (s)he, it comes from there [pres, conjoint] S09

ulisebenzisa (s)he uses it [pres, conjoint] S27

ulobela (s)he writes for [pres, conjoint] S26

ulokhu ethithiza (s)he keeps on bumbling [v phr] S05

ulu- [NP Cl. 11; var of **uØ-** used by some people before monosyllabic noun stems] S05

ulungile (s)he is OK, fine, in order [stative] S22

uLungile (female name) [n Cl. 1a; < **-lungile** is OK, is in order] S24

ulunywe (s)he has been bitten [past, disjoint] S20

ulutho something, anything, nothing [n Cl. 11] S05

ulw- [NP Cl. 11; occurs before **a** and **e**] S14

ulwandle sea, ocean [n Cl. 11; sg **izilwandle** Cl. 11] S18

ulwazi knowledge [n Cl. 11; < **-az-i** know] S14

ulwenzile (s)he has done it [past, disjoint] S26

uLwesihlanu Friday [n Cl. 1a; < **lwesihlanu** fifth (day); < **lwa-** poss conc Cl. 11 (agreeing with understood **usuku** day) + **isihlanu** fifth] S13

um- [NP Cl. 1 & 3; occurs with polysyllabic stems] S02

uma if, when [conj; followed by the participial aspect; var **ma**] S04

uma kungenzeka if possible S20

uma nje just as long as [conj phr] S22

umabulalephindelela serial killer [n Cl. 1a; < **u-** NP + **-ma-** nominal formative + **-bulal-** kill + **e-** (s)he + **-phindelel-a** repeat again and again] S26

um-Afrika African [n Cl. 1; pl **ama-Afrika** Cl. 6] S18

UMAFRIKA *African* (here the name of a newspaper) [n Cl. 1] S26

uMakhathini (surname) [n Cl. 1a] S09

umakhelwane neighbors [n Cl. 1a; < **-akhelwan-** be built for one another, be lived in close proximity] S08

umakhenikha mechanic [n Cl. 1a] {Eng} S19

umakhi builder [n Cl. 1; pl **abakhi**; < **-akh-** build] S22

umalaleveva malaria [n Cl. 1a] {Eng *malarial fever*} S20

umalume maternal uncle [n Cl. 1a] S23

umama (my) mother [n Cl. 1a; var of **umame**] S09

umame (my) mother [n Cl. 1a] S08

uMandela (surname) [n Cl. 1a] S07

uManyoni (surname) [n Cl. 1a] S09

uMaphanga (surname) [n Cl. 1a] S18

uMasiba (surname) [n Cl. 1a] S17

umasipala municipality [n Cl. 1a] S12

umasiteshi station commander, chief of station [n Cl. 1a; < **-ma-** nominal formative + **isiteshi**] S21

u-May (May is usually **uMeyi** in Zulu) [n Cl. 1a] {Eng} S20

uMbeki (surname) [n Cl. 1a] S07

umbhidlango campaign [n Cl. 3] S10

umbhikishi demonstrator, protestor [n Cl. 1; < **-bhikish-** protest, fight against] S25

umbiko report, announcement [n Cl. 3; < **-bik-a** report] S26

umbono view(point) [n Cl. 3; < **-bon-** see; pl **imibono**] S06

umboshwa prisoner [n Cl. 1; < **-boshw-** be arrested; **isiboshwa** is more usual] S26

umbulali killer, murderer [n Cl. 1a; < **-bulal-** kill] S26

umbutho gathering [n Cl. 3; < **-buth-** gather] S16

umbutho wamaphoyisa police force [n phr Cl. 3] S16

umbuzo question [n Cl. 1; < **-buz-** ask] S17

umculo music [n Cl. 3; < **-cul-sing**] S14

umdabu origin [n Cl. 3] S19

uMdadane (surname) [n Cl. 1a] S10

umdlali player [n Cl. 1; < **-dlal-**play] S11

umdlandla enthusiasm, keenness [n Cl. 3] S19

umdlavuza cancer [n Cl. 3; < **-dlavuz-** tear to pieces, wear away, make ragged] S20

umdlwembe undisciplined person; wild, uncontrolled animal [n Cl. 1 or 3; pl **imidlwembe**] S09

umdoji evader, avoider [n Cl. 1; < **-doj-** dodge, evade] S10

umehluko difference, distinction [n Cl. 4; < **-ehluk-** differ; pl **imehluko**] S10

umeluleki advisor, counsellor, consultant [n Cl. 1; < **elulek-** advise, counsel] S27

uMemela (surname) [n Cl. 1a] S09

umenza it makes him or her [pres, conjoint] S18

umenzi doer, maker, perpetrator [n Cl. 1; < **-enz-** do, make; pl **abenzi**] S23

umeseki sponsor, supporter [n Cl. 1; < **-esek-a** sponsor, support; var **umseki** < **-sek-a**; pl **abeseki**] S11

umfana boy, young man [n Cl. 1; < **umufo** fellow + **-ana** dimin suffix] S23, S08

umfaniswano uniformity [n Cl. 3; < **-faniswan-** be made mutually alike] S12

umfanyana little boy [n Cl. 1; < **umfana** + **-Yana**] S09

uMfeka (surname) [n Cl. 1a] S11

umfokaMadlala Madlala's brother [n Cl. 1a] S27

umfowabo his or her brother [n Cl. 1; < **umufo** fellow, brother + **wabo** their] S27

umfowethu my or our brother [n Cl. 1; pl **abafowethu**; < **umufo** fellow, brother + **wethu** our] S21

umfula river [n Cl. 3] S16

umfundi reader, student, pupil [n Cl. 1; < **-fund-**; pl **abafundi**] S06

umfundisi minister, pastor, priest (**uMfundisi X** the Reverend X) [n Cl. 1; < **um-** NP + **-fundis-** teach + **-i** nom suff; pl **abefundisi** or **abafundisi** Cl. 2; The tones on this noun are HLHLL, which distinguish it from the noun **umfundisi** 'teacher' which carries the tones HLLHL.] S02

umgqugquzeli coordinator [n Cl. 1; < **-gqugquzel-a** persuade, try to win over [v-appl] S11

umgulukudu hardened criminal, habitual criminal [n Cl. 1 or 3; pl Cl. 4] S23

uMgungundlovu Pietermaritzburg (capital of KwaZulu-Natal Province) [n Cl. 3] S09

umgunyathi backdoor methods [n Cl.3] S05

umgwaqo road [n Cl. 3] S08

umhlaba world, earth; land [n Cl. 3] S02

umhleli editor [n Cl. 1; < -hlel- arrange, edit; pl **abahleli** Cl. 2] S05

umhlengi nurse [n Cl. 1; < -hleng- assist, help] S17

umhlengikazi nurse (female) [n Cl. 1; < **umhlengi** + -**kazi** feminine suffix] S17

umhlonishwa respected person, the honorable [n Cl. 1; < -hlonishw- be respected, be honored, be honorable; < -hloniph- respect, honor] S21

umholi leader [n Cl. 1; < -hol- lead] S05

umholo salary, wage [n Cl. 3; var **iholo** Cl. 5; < -hol- draw pay, earn] S28

uMinah (name) [n Cl. 1a] S19

umiyane mosquito [n Cl. 1a] S20

uMjoli (surname) [n Cl. 1a] S26

umkhakha field, direction [n Cl. 3] S19

umkhandlu organization [n Cl. 3] S13

umkhangisi advertiser [n Cl. 1; < -khangis- cause to be desirable, advertise] S28

umkhankaso tactic, scheme (originally a horseshoe move- ment in order to outmaneuver an enemy) [n Cl. 3; < -kha- nkas- move in a horseshoe formation in order to out- maneuver] S10

umkhiqizo surplus, produce, product [n Cl. 3; < -khiqiz- produce in abundance, turn out in large quantities, produce a surplus] S12

uMkhize (surname, clan name) [n Cl. 1a] S22

umkhokhi-ntela taxpayer [n Cl. 1; < -**umkhokhi** payer + **intela** tax] S10

umkhono sleeve [n Cl. 3] S20

umkhosi call of alarm, warning cry [n Cl. 3] S11

umKhrestu Christians [n Cl. 1; var **iKhrestu** Cl. 5; pl **ama- Khrestu** Cl. 6] S25

umkhuba custom, (bad) practice; (bad) habit [n Cl. 3] S08, S16

umkhuhlane cold or cough, normally accompanied by a fever [n Cl. 3] S20

umkhulu (my) grandfather [n Cl. 1a; < -khulu senior] S19

umkhumbi ship [n Cl. 3] S16

umkhwabanisi embezzler, fraud [n Cl. 1; < -khwabanis- embezzle] S10

umklomelo; < -klomel- reward, give a prize or bonus] S11

umlando history [n Cl. 3; < -land- relate] S18

umlawuli marshal, controller [n Cl. 1; < -lawul- control, marshal] S18

umlawuli wamabhanoyi air-traffic controller [n phr Cl. 1; pl **abalawuli bamabhanoyi**] S18

umlawuli wokuhamba kwezindiza air-traffic controller [n phr Cl. 1; pl **abalawuli bokuhamba kwezindiza**] S18

uMlazi (place) [n Cl. 3] S11

umlimi farmer, cultivator, gardener [n Cl. 1; < **-lim-** cultivate, plough] S27

ummbila corn, maize, mealies [n Cl. 3; neutral] S27

ummeli lawyer, representative, spokesperson [n Cl. 1; < **-mel-** stand for, represent] S18

umndeni family [n Cl. 3; **imindeni** Cl. 4] S02

umndeni wakwaMpanza the Mpanza family [n phr Cl. 3] S02

umngani friend [n Cl. 1; var **umngane**] S16

umngcwabi burier, undertaker, mortician [n Cl. 1; < **-ngcwab-a** bury] S12

umnike you have given him or her [past, conjoint] S14

umnotho wealth; economics, finance [n Cl. 3; < **-noth-** bec wealthy] S07

uMntomuhle (given name) [n Cl. 1a; < **umuntu omuhle** good person, beautiful person] S06

umntwana child [n Cl. 1; < **umuntu** person + **-ana** little, small, juvenile [diminutive suff]] S17, S02

umnumzane family head; gentleman, mister [n Cl. 1; pl **abanumzane**] S02

uMnuz Mr. (abbreviation for **uMnumzane**) S02

umnyama (s)he is black [descr cop, pres] S18

uMnyandu (surname) [n Cl. 1a] S07

umnyango doorway [n Cl. 3] S17

umnyango state department [n Cl. 3] S10

uMoiporoti (name) [n Cl. 1a] {Sotho} S14

umonakalo damage, mess [n Cl. 3; < **-onakal-** get spoilt] S17

umongameli president [n Cl. 1; < **-ongamel-** lean over; preside over; pl **abongameli**] S14

umoya spirit, soul, wind, air, breath, personality , nature [n Cl. 3a; pl **imimoya**] S22

uMpanza (surname) [n Cl. 1a] S02

umpetha finalist [n Cl. 1a; < **-pheth-** complete, finish; **m + p > mp**] S11

umphakathi community [n Cl. 3; < **um-** NP + **phakathi** inside; pl **imiphakathi** Cl. 4] S05

umphakathi occupant [n Cl. 1; < **um-** NP + **phakathi** inside] S09

umphathi warden, authority, person in charge, manager, guardian, superintendent [n Cl. 1; < **-phath-** handle] S23

umphathi-siteshi station commander [n Cl. 1; < **umphathi** person in charge + **isiteshi** station] S21

umphefumulo life; breath [n Cl. 3; < **-phefumul-** breathe] S08

umphelela it came to an end for him or her (i.e. (s)he lost his or her job) [pres, partic] S27

umphumela result [Cl. 3; < **-phumel-** come out for + **-a** nom suff] S05

umpofu it is poor [descr cop, pres] S21

uMpungose (name) [n Cl. 1a] S21

umqaphi security officer, guard, warden [n Cl. 1; < - **qaph-** watch intently, be on the lookout] S13

umqashi employer [n Cl. 1; < **-qash-** employ] S27

umqashwa employee [n Cl. 1; < **-qashw-** be employed, hired + **-a** nominalizing suffix found with passive verbs] S10

umqondisi director [n Cl. 1; < **-qondis-** direct] S09

umsakazo radio, broadcast [n Cl. 3; < **-sakaz-** broadcast] S05

umsebenzi worker, laborer [n Cl. 1; the tone on this noun is HLLHL, while the one meaning 'work' is HLLFL; < **-sebenz-** work + **-i** (though the nominal suffix **-i** is generally associated with agent nouns, this is one of the few exceptions)] S27

umsebenzi work, job, task; use [n Cl. 3; the tone on this noun is HLLFL, while the one meaning 'worker' is HLLHL; < **-sebenz-** work] S05

umsebenzi awenzayo the work (s)he does [ind rel of plain obj rel] S18

umshado marriage, wedding [n Cl. 3; < **-shad-** marry] S14

umshayeli driver [n Cl. 1; < **-shayel-** drive] S17, S09

umshayi-siginci guitarist [n Cl. 1a; < **-shay-** hit, play + **isiginci** guitar] S14

umshini machine [n Cl. 3] {Eng} S19

umshophi epidemic, plague [n Cl. 3] S08

umshushisi prosecutor [n Cl. 1; < **-shushis-** persecute, prosecute] S10

umshwalense insurance, assurance [n Cl. 3] S27

umsindo noise; quarrel [n Cl. 3] S08

umsizi helper, assistant [n Cl. 1; < **-siz-** help, assist] S14

uMsombuluko Monday [n Cl. 3; no plural; < **-sombuluk-**bec unrolled, unraveled (the new week unrolls)] S13

uMsomi (surname, clan name) [n Cl. 1a] S22

umswakama dampness or moisture rising from the ground [n Cl. 3; < **-swakam-** bec damp or moist]

umtakuli life-saver [n Cl. 1] S17

uMtata (town) [n Cl. 3; pronounced **uMthatha**] S17

umthandazo prayer [n Cl. 3; < -thandaz- pray] S04

uMthembu (surname, clan name) [n Cl. 1a] S11

umthetho law [n Cl. 3; < -theth- try a court case, preside over a court] S07

umthethosisekelo constitution (legal foundation) [n Cl. 3; < **umthetho** law + **isisekelo** foundation stone] S25

umtholampilo clinic [n Cl. 3; < -thol-a find, get + **impilo** health] S25

umtholampilo wokuhlelwa kwemindeni family planning clinic [n phr Cl. 3] S25

umthombo spring; source [n Cl. 3] S09

umthwalo load, burden [n Cl. 3; -thwal- carry] S27

umu- [NP Cl. 1 & 3; occurs with monosyllabic stems] S04

umufo fellow, brother [n Cl. 1] S08, S21

umuhla day [n Cl. 3; pl **imihla** Cl. 4] S04

umumo state, characteristic [n Cl. 3; < -m- stand] S18

umunca it sucks [pres, conjoint] S20

umuntu person [n Cl. 1] S04

umusa kindness [n Cl. 3] S21

umuthi medicine, (repellent (in context)) [n Cl. 3] S20

umuthi woku(zi)vimbela repellent [n Cl. 3] S20

umuva hind part, rear [n Cl. 3] S12

umuzi household, homestead, village; family [n Cl. 3] S08

uMuzi (male name) [n Cl. 1a; < **umuzi** household] S13

umuzwa feeling, emotion [n Cl. 3; < -zw- feel] S08

umvakashi visitor [n Cl. 1; < -vakash- visit] S20

umvuzo reward [n Cl. 3; < -vuz- reward] S27

umxhumanisi public relations officer [n Cl. 1; < -xhumanis- cause to link up] S19

umyeni husband, bridegroom [n Cl. 1] S24

umzala cousin [n Cl. 1] S23

umzali parent [n Cl. 1; < -zal- give birth (to)] S08

umzamo attempt, effort, trial [n Cl. 3; < -zam- try, attempt] S25

umzila broad track [n Cl. 3] S18

umzimba body [n Cl. 3] S20

uMzimkhulu (place) [n Cl. 3] S16

uMzizi (surname) [n Cl. 1a] S25

uMzoneli (surname) [n Cl. 1a] S18

uMzumbe (place) [n Cl. 3] S06

umzuzu minute [n Cl. 3] S01

uNaidoo (surname) [n Cl. 1a] {Indian} S24

unalesifo (s)he has this disease [assoc cop, pres] S20

unalesinambuzane (s)he, it has this parasite [assoc cop, pres] S20

unamalini? you have how much money? [assoc cop, pres] S28

uNash (male name) [n Cl. 1a] {Eng} S12

unaso it has it [assoc cop, pres] S20

uNdlovu (surname, clan name) [n Cl. 1a; < **indlovu** elephant] S22

unegciwane (s)he has a germ, a virus [assoc cop, pres] S23

uNelson Mandela (name of former South African President) [n phr Cl. 1a] S07

unembeza conscience [n Cl. 1a] S26

uneminyaka (s)he has years, is aged [assoc cop, pres] S09

unengane (s)he has a child [assoc cop, pres] S22

unenhlonipho (s)he has respect [assoc cop, pres] S22

unepulazi (s)he has a farm [assoc cop, pres] S27

unesexwayiso (s)he has a warning [assoc cop, pres] S27

unesifiso (s)he has a wish [assoc cop, pres] S14

uneziqu she has a degree [assoc cop, pres] S14

ungabi you should not become or be [subjunc, neg] S28

ungabi namahloni you should not be ashamed or embarrassed [assoc cop, inch, subjunc, neg] S28

ungabonakalanga it not being visible [past, partic, neg] S13

ungabuza you can ask [pres, potential] S20

ungafunga you would or could swear [pres, potential] S14

ungagwema you can avoid [pres, potential] S28

ungahlomile you are not armed [stative, partic, neg] S27

ungahluphi (s)he does not cause trouble, or disturb [pres, rel, neg; < **akahluphi**] S22

ungakulindi you should not wait for it [subjunc, neg] S28

ungakwazi you would be able [pres, potential] S19

ungama-hectare it is hectares [ident cop, pres] S27

ungaphuzi (s)he does not drink [pres, rel, neg; < **akaphuzi**] S22

ungasakhokhi you no longer pay [pres, partic, persistive, neg] S28

ungasakwazi you are no longer able, you can no longer [pres, persistive, rel, neg; < **awusakwazi**] S28

ungasasikhokheli you no longer pay it off [pres, partic, persistive, neg] S28

ungasebenzi you (are) not working [pres, partic] S19

ungasebenzisa you can use [pres, potential] S20

ungasenalo you no longer have it; (s)he no longer has it [assoc cop, partic, persistive, neg] S28

ungasheshanga if you have not quickly [past, partic] S20

ungasikhokhela you can pay it off [pres, potential] S28

ungasisebenzisa you can use it [pres, potential] S20

ungavilaphanga (s)he is not lazy [past, rel, neg; < **akavila-phanga**] S27

ungawuthola you may find it [pres, potential] S06

ungayidayisa you can sell it [pres, potential] S28

ungaziqeda you can put an end to them [pres, potential] S28

uNgcobo (surname) [n Cl. 1a] S11

uNgcongo (surname) [n Cl. 1a] S12

ungenanembeza who has no con-science [assoc cop, pres, rel, neg; < **akananembeza**] S26

ungeqi you should not exceed [subjunc, neg] S20

ungesinye it is one [ident cop, pres] S20

ungomunye (s)he is one [ident cop, pres] S16

ungowaKwaBester (s)he is one from Bester's place [ident cop, pres] S26

ungowokuqala (s)he is the first one [ident cop, pres] S19

ungqongqoshe minister of state, cabinet minister [n Cl. 1a; pl **ongqongqoshe** Cl. 2b] S05

uNgubane (surname) [n Cl. 1a] S13

unguchwepheshe (s)he is an expert [ident cop, pres] S26

unguchwepheshe wezengqondo (s)he is a psychiatrist [ident cop phr, pres] S26

ungudadewabo she is his, her, their sister [ident cop, pres] S26

ungumbulali you are a killer [ident cop, pres] S26

ungumgqugquzeli (s)he is the coordinator [ident cop, pres] S11

ungumngani (s)he is a friend [ident cop, pres] S23

ungumongameli (s)he is president [ident cop, pres] S14

ungumqondisi (s)he is a director [ident cop, pres] S09

ungumshushisi (s)he is the prosecutor [ident cop, pres] S10

ungumuntu you are a person [ident cop, pres] S04

ungumxhumanisi (s)he is a public relations officer [ident cop, pres] S19

ungunobhala (s)he is a secretary [ident cop, pres] S16

unguSipho (s)he is Sipho [ident

cop, pres] S26

unguzakwabo (s)he is someone married into the same family [ident cop, pres] S27

uNhlanhla (name) [n Cl. 1a; < **inhlanhla** good fortune] S27

uNkk Mrs. (abbreviation for **unkosikazi**) S02

uNkk Constance Lovey Matseng MaMote Mpanza Mrs. Constance ... S02

uNkosazana Miss [n Cl. 1a; < **inkosazana** young lady, princess] S12

unkosikazi lady, missus [n Cl. 1a; pl **onkosikazi** Cl. 2b] S02

uNksz Miss (abbrev of **uNkosazana**) S12

uNkulunkulu God [n Cl. 1a; < **-khulukhulu** very great, very big, very important [reduplicated adj stem; the nasal **n** is presumably a fossilized Cl. 9 prefix] S02

uno-40 (s)he is forty (lit. (s)he has forty [assoc cop, pres] S22

unobhala secretary [n Cl. 1a; < **u-**NP + **-no-** noun formative, often (but not necessarily) used to form feminine nouns) + **-bhal-a** write] S16

unogada guards, watchmen [n Cl. 1a; < **u-** NP + **-no-** noun formative, often (but not necessarily) used to form feminine nouns) + **-gad-** guard {Eng *guard*}] S13

unomalaleveva (s)he has malaria [assoc cop, pres] S20

unomoya ophansi (s)he is reserved or gentle reserved (lit. (s)he has a spirit that is down) [assoc cop phr] S22

unqambothi nice flavor, nice smell [n Cl. 11] S11

unqunyelwe you have been set, you have been prescribed, you have had mapped out [past, disjoint] S20

uNtshingila (surname) [n Cl. 1a] S16

unyaka years [n Cl. 3a; pl **iminyaka** Cl. 4] S05

uNyanga (male name) [n Cl. 1a] S21

unyawo foot [n Cl. 11; pl Cl. **izinyawo** 10a] S09

u-October [n Cl. 1a] {Eng} S20

uphahla roof [n Cl. 11; pl **izimpahla**; **m + ph > mp**] S17

uphahla it is the roof [ident cop; < **Ø-** + **uphahla**] S17

uphansi it is low [loc cop, pres] S28

uphawu symptom, mark, brandmark, birthmark [n Cl. 11; var **uphawo**; pl **izimpawu** Cl. 10; **m + ph > mp**] S20

uPhega (surname) [n Cl. 1a] {Sotho/Tswana} S19

uphenyo investigation, examination [n Cl. 11; pl **izimpenyo**; **m + ph > mp**; < **-pheny-** investigate] S21

uphephe you should escape [subjunc] S20

481

uphephile you being safe [stative, partic] S25

uphephisa (s)he causes to recover, (s)he cures [pres, conjoint] S16

uphephisa ekufeni (s)he treats trauma related to death (lit. (s)he helps to escape death) [v phr] S16

uphethe (s)he concluded [past, conjoint] S10

uphethe (s)he handles, is in charge of, runs, manages [stative; < **-phath- + -i...e**] S25

uphi? where is (s)he? [loc cop, pres] S17

uphiko wing, department, section [n Cl. 11; pl **izimpiko**] S10

uPhilisiwe (female name) [n Cl. 1a; < **philisiwe** has/have been given health or life] S26

uphinda (s)he also VERBs, (s)he again VERBs [aux, pres, conjoint] S09

uphumela you go out to [pres, conjoint] S20

uphumile (s)he has got out [past, disjoint] S26

uphusile it is solid [stative] S12

uPonko (name) [n Cl. 1a] S17

uProf Prof. [n Cl. 1a; pl **oProf** Cl. 2b] {Eng} S05

uqala (when) it began (lit. it begins) [pres, partic] S05

uqale you should begin [subjunc] S16

uqhuba you continue, you proceed (with) [pres, partic] S27

uqhube (s)he continued [past, conjoint] S10

uqhubeke (s)he carried on [past, conjoint] S13

u-R120 (R = rand, South African monetary unit) [n Cl. 1a] S13

u-R15mln 15 million rands [n Cl. 1a] S10

u-R20 000 [n Cl. 1a] S27

u-R50 [n Cl. 1a] S13

u-R90million [n Cl. 1a] S17

uSAA (South African Airways) [n Cl. 1a] S18

usafufuza (s)he is still passionate [pres, persistive] S22

usanda it has just [aux, pres, conjoint] S10

uSandile (male name) [n Cl. 1a; < **sandile** we (the family) have increased in number (the tones on the stem are all LOW; more rarely one finds the name with the tones HIGH LOW LOW which would mean "it (the nation, i.e. **isizwe**) has increased," a name more likely to be given to a prince)] S09

usaqhubeka (s)he is still continuing [pres, persistive] S14

uSebata (male name) [n Cl. 1a] {Sotho: < **sebata** wild beast} S14

usebenza (s)he works [pres, conjoint] S06

usebenza ngesandla esifana nesikayise (s)he acts like his or her father does (lit. (s)he works

482

with a hand that is like that of his or her father) [v phr] S06

usebenzele you should work from [subjunc] S04

usebenzile (s)he has worked [past, disjoint] S26

usefwini it is under a cloud [loc cop, pres, partic] S02

usefwini elimnyama while it was under a black cloud [loc cop phr, pres] S02

usemnyangweni (s)he is in the department [loc cop, pres] S25

usenamasheya (s)he now or already has shares [assoc cop, pres, exclusive] S27

usendaweni it, (s)he is in a place or locality [loc cop, pres] S12

usengumlimi (s)he is now a farmer [ident cop, pres, exclusive] S27

usethole (s)he has already received [past, exclusive, conjoint] S24

usezuze (s)he has already earned or achieved [past, conjoint; < u- (s)he + -s- already + -e- (s)he + -zuz- achieve + -e past] S12

ushade (s)he got married, (s)he married [past, disjoint] S14

uShaka (Zulu king who molded disparate Nguni tribes into the Zulu nation) [n Cl. 1a] S11

ushayela (s)he drives [pres, conjoint] S14

uShezi (surname, clan name) [n Cl. 1a] S09

ushintshele and you should

change to [subjunc] S28

ushisiswe it has been heated [past, conjoint form] S01

ushiye (s)he left [past tense, conjoint] S02

ushone (s)he passed away (euph; lit. set (as of the sun)) [past tense, conjoint form] S02

ushonelwe it has been bereaved [past tense, participial aspect, conjoint] S02

ushonelwe yindodana yawo endala having lost or having been bereaved of its elder son [v phr] S02

ushukela sugar [n Cl. 1a/3a] {Eng} S01

usibanibani somebody or other, a certain person [n Cl. 1a] S06

uSibisi (name) [n Cl. 1a] S22

uSibusiso (male name) [n Cl. 1a; < isibusiso blessing] S05

usingababa father-figure (*not* stepfather) [n Cl. 1a] S09

uSipho (personal name) [n Cl. 1a; < isipho gift] S02

usisi (my) younger sister; young lady, lass [n Cl. 1a] {Afr *sussie* little sister} S22

usithole you should find it [subjunc] S20

usitholile (s)he got it, (s)he acquired it, (s)he obtained it [past, disjoint] S26

usitshalile (s)he has planted it [past, disjoint] S27

usizi distress, misery, mental pain,

sorrow, grief [n Cl. 11] S27

usizo help, aid, assistance [n Cl. 11; < **-siz-** help] S16

usokhemisi pharmacist, chemist [n Cl. 1a; < **u-** NP + **-so-** noun formative, often (but not necessarily) used to form masculine nouns) + **ikhemisi** pharmacy] S17

usondelene (s)he is close [stative; < **-sondelan-** + **-i...e**] S16

uSono (surname) [n Cl. 1a] S19

usophikweni (s)he is in the league, wing or section [loc cop, pres] S25

u-STD 10 Std (Standard) 10 (formerly the highest level of secondary education) [n Cl. 1a] {Eng} S05

usubhekene you are already confronted [stative, exclusive] S16

usubonile you have already seen [past, exclusive, disjoint] S28

usucwile (you) have already sunk [past, partic, exclusive, conjoint] S28

usudlange has gained force, has taken hold [past, exclusive, conjoint; < **u-** SC + **-s-** already + **-u-** SC + **-dlang-** + **-e**] S16

usuke you have just [aux] S14

usuke (s)he has just, (s)he has merely [aux] S16

usuku day (of 24 hours) [n Cl. 11; pl **izinsuku** Cl. 10] S04

usukuqede you have already brought it to an end [past, exclusive, conjoint; < **u-** you + **-s-** already + **-u-** you + **-ku-** it + **-qed-** end + **-e** past] S14

usuluma it then bites [pres, exclusive] S20

usushintshe you have already changed [past, partic, exclusive, conjoint] S28

usuwonke it is already in total [descr cop, pres, exclusive] S17

usuzame you have already tried [past, partic, exclusive, conjoint] S28

uSydney Mufamadi (name; former Minister of Police) [n phr Cl. 1a] S21

uThabo (male name) [n Cl. 1a] {Sotho: **thabo** happiness} S07

uThabo Mbeki (name of South African President) [n phr Cl. 1a] S07

uthanda (s)he likes, (s)he loves [pres, conjoint] S14

uthandeke you should be lovable, likable or popular [subjunc] S04

uthando love [n Cl. 11; < **-thand-** love] S04

uthango fence [n Cl. 11; pl

izintango Cl. 10; **n + th > nt**] S08

uthatha (s)he takes [pres, conjoint] S14

uthathe (and) it takes [subjunc] S20

uthathwe you have to be taken [subjunc] S28

uthe (s)he said [past, conjoint] S10

uThemba (male name) [n Cl. 1a; < **ithemba** hope, faith, trust] S16

uthi (s)he believes, (s)he thinks, (s)he is of the opinion [pres, conjoint] S14

uthi (s)he says [pres, conjoint] S12

uthini? what (s)he thinks, what does (s)he think? S26

uthisha teacher [n Cl. 1a] {Eng} S19

uthishanhloko head teacher, principal [n Cl. 1a; < **uthisha** teacher + **(i)nhloko** head] S16

uthishomkhulu head teacher, principal [n Cl. 1a; < **uthisha + omkhulu**] S13

utho thing [n Cl. 11; pl **izinto** Cl. 10; **n + th > nt**] S04

uthole you should find [subjunc] S04

uThulani (male name) [n Cl. 1a; < imper **thulani!** settle down! (this name might be given when there is strife within a family)] S09

uThusi (surname) [n Cl. 1a] S25

uThwala (surname) [n Cl. 1a] S26

utiki three-penny piece (from a pre-decimal era) [n Cl. 1a] {S.A. English *tickey*} S25

utshale (s)he has planted [past, conjoint] S27

utshani grass, lawn [n Cl. 14] S13

uTshepo (male name) [n Cl. 1a] {Sotho: **tshepo** hope} S14

uvale you should close up [subjunc] S20

uvalo fear, anxiety (lit. diaphragm; Zulus see the diaphragm as the seat of fear) [n Cl. 11; pl **izimvalo**] S09

uvame (s)he normally (does) [stative] S09

uVan Niekerk (surname) [n Cl. 1a] {Afr} S09

uvelele (s)he is outstanding, (s)he is prominent [past, disjoint] S11

uVuma (male name) [n Cl. 1a; < imper **vuma!** agree!, accept!] S23

uwabheka you look at them [pres, partic] S27

uwafake (s)he has placed them [past, conjoint] S27

uwagweme and you should avoid them [subjunc] S04

uwenze you should do it [subjunc] S18

uWeziwe (female name) [n Cl. 1a; < **-weziwe** have been helped out of difficulty] S25

uwuthatha (s)he takes it [pres, conjoint] S14

uxakwe you are embarrassed, are in a fix, are troubled [past, conjoint] S28

uXolani (male name) [n Cl. 1a; < imper **xolani!** forgive! (this name might be given when the mother has done something wrong, e.g. had an illegitimate child)] S09

uxolo peace [n Cl. 11; < -xol- bec peaceful, tranquil, calm] S05

uxoxisana you are negotiating [pres, conjoint] S16

uyabakweleta you owe them [pres, disjoint] S28

uyaboshwa (s)he is arrested [pres, disjoint] S16

uyakuthola (s)he experiences or finds it [pres, disjoint] S23

uyakwamukela it accepts it [pres, disjoint] S23

uyakwazi (s)he is able, (s)he knows how, (s)he can [pres, disjoint; < u- (s)he + -ya- disjoint pref + -kw- OC Cl. 15 (agreeing with any vn) + -azi know] S14

uyalimala (s)he gets hurt, injured [pres, disjoint] S16

uyalwazi (s)he knows it, is familiar with it [pres, disjoint] S27

uyavuma (s)he agrees [pres, disjoint] S23

uyawenza (s)he does it [pres, disjoint] S18

uyayilanda (s)he relates it [pres, disjoint] S23

uyazigangela you are just playing about, you are just being foolish [pres, disjoint] S27

uyazihlonipha (s)he is self-respecting [pres, disjoint] S21

uyaziqhenya (s)he is proud [pres, disjoint] S14

uyazisola (s)he regrets, (s)he is contrite [pres, disjoint] S26

uyexwayisa (s)he focuses attention, alerts [pres, disjoint] S23

uyibamba (s)he is a deputy [ident cop, pres] S25

uyibhalele (s)he wrote it to [past, conjoint] S26

uyi-forensic criminologist (s)he is a forensic ... [ident cop, pres] S23

uyilungu (s)he is a member [ident cop, pres] S09

uyimenenja (s)he is a manager [ident cop, pres] S24

uyindoda he is a man [ident cop, pres] S14

uyintandane (s)he is an orphan [ident cop, pres] S22

uyise his or her father [n Cl. 1a] S06

uyisingili (s)he is single [ident cop, pres] S22

uyonginqanda (s)he will turn me away, will prevent me [rem fut] S14

uyophuma (s)he would come out [rem fut] S26

uzakwabo someone married into the same family as him or her [n Cl. 1a] S27

uzalwa (s)he is born [pres, conjoint] S06

uZama (surname) [n Cl. 1a] S11

uzenze you should do them [subjunc] S04

uzenzele (s)he has made for her- or himself [past, conjoint] S24

uzethembe you should believe in yourself [subjunc] S18

uZethembe (male name) [n Cl. 1a; < imper **zethembe!** believe in yourself!] S16

uzichaze you should describe yourself [subjunc] S22

uzihlelisise you should put them in good order [subjunc] S04

uzijwayeze you should get used to, you should accustom yourself [subjunc] S28

uzimele (s)he is independent [stative] S12

uzimisele (s)he is prepared, (s)he is ready [stative] S27

uziseshe you should ask yourself, you should look into yourself [subjunc] S04

uzithobile (s)he is humble [stative] S16

uzithole you find them [subjunc] S09

uzitholele it should find for itself [subjunc] S24

uzobalungisela (s)he will make things right for them [fut] S13

uzobe ephelekezelwa (s)he will be accompanied [fut pres] S11

uzobe ugubha it will be celebrating [fut pres] S11

uzobe uhanjelwe it will be attended [fut stative] S11

uzobhekana nazo kanjani how you will face them [v phr] S04

uzobikela (s)he will report to [fut] S23

uzodlalwa it will be played [fut] S11

uzokusabisa (s)he will scare you [fut] S28

uzolala (s)he will (go to) sleep, (s)he will go to bed, (s)he will lie down [fut] S09

uzolalaphi (s)he will sleep where [v phr] S09

uzolithola (s)he will get it [fut] S09

uzolitholaphi? where will (s)he get it? [v phr] S09

uzophunyula (s)he will get loose, escape; (s)he will be acquitted [fut] S26

uzothandana naye you and he or she will love each other (lit. you will love each other with her or him) [fut v phr] S04

uzothola you will find [fut] S05

uZulu (surname) [n Cl. 1a] S05

uZwelakhe (male name) [n Cl. 1a; < **izwe lakhe** his country] S11

uZwelithini (male name; name of the present King of the Zulu) [n Cl. 1a; < **izwe lithini?** what does the nation say?] S11

uzwelo sensitivity [n Cl. 11; < **-zwel-** be sensitive] S22

uzwelonke the nation [n Cl. 1a; < **izwe** country + **lonke** the whole [quant]] S05

V

-vakash-a visit (v.i.) [v.i.; may be inchoative in the speech of some people; e.g. **sivakashe lapha** we are visiting here] S12

-vakashel-a visit (v.t.) [v-appl] S19

-val-a close, shut [v.t.] S10

-valel-a shut up in or at [v-appl] S14

-valelw-a be shut up in or at [v-appl-pass] S14

valo fear [< **uvalo**] S26

-valw-a be shut, be closed (down) [v-pass] S28

-vam-a normally VERB, bec accustomed to VERB [aux; followed by vn] S08

-vamis-a VERB generally, usually [aux v-caus] S23

-vel-a come from, originate in; appear, come into view; be prominent, stand out [v.i.] S11, S14

-vel-e VERB in advance, VERB with premeditation, VERB with foresight [aux; followed by subjunc, and in the past by the narrative] S18

-velel-a be prominent, stand out [v-appl] S11

-vez-a bring forth, exhibit, show; disclose, reveal [v-caus; < **-vel-** + **-Y-**] S13

-vik-a ward off, parry [v.t.] S09

-vikel-a stand up for, protect, defend [v-appl] S09

-vikelan-a stand up for one another, protect one another [v-appl-recip] S09

-vilaph-a bec lazy [v.inch; < **ivila** lazy person + **-ph-** verbalizer] S27

-vimb-a block, bar, prevent, hinder, stop [v.t.] S08

-vimbel-a prevent [v-appl] S08

viva [interj] {Portuguese} S05

-vot-a vote [v.i.] {Eng} S03

-votel-a vote for [v-appl] S05

-vul-a open [v.t.] [v.t.] S17

-vulek-a open [v.i.] [v-neut] S17

-vum-a agree, assent, consent, be willing [v.i.] S08

-vumel-a agree to, accept, permit, allow [v-appl] S08

-vumelan-a be in agreement, agree with each other, concur [v-appl-recip] S13

-vun-a reap, harvest [v.t.] S27

-vuvukal-a swell (up) [v.i.] S20

-vuvuzel-a sprinkle (with sugar, powder, ...) [v.t.] S01

-vuz-a reward [v.t.] S27

W

w- you [SC 2 p sg; occurs before vowels] S15

w- he, she, it [SC Cl. 1; occurs before vowels] S02

-w- it [OC Cl. 3; found before vowels] S12

w- of [poss conc Cl. 1 & 3; found before **a, e** and **o**] S23, S10

w- (it) is [ident cop pref; may occur before the vowel **u**] S08

w- by [agentive adv pref; may occur before the vowel **u**] S05

-w- be VERB-ed/-en [pass ext] S01

wa- of [poss conc Cl. 1 & 3] S01, S02

-wa- they, it [SC Cl. 6; found after a vowel] S03

-wa- them [OC Cl. 6] S04

-w-a fall, collapse [v.i.] S17

waba you had [narr] S15

waba (s)he became [rem past] S18

waba naso you had it [assoc cop, inch, narr] S15

waba ngomunye (s)he became one [ident cop, inch, rem past] S18

wabantu of people [poss Cl. 3] S19

wabaqaphi of guards [poss Cl. 1] S17

wabe esethembisa (s)he then promised [rem past pres, exclusive] S13

wabeka (s)he put in, added, contributed [rem past] S23

wabesimame of the women [poss Cl. 1] S24

wabo their, of them [poss Cl. 3 & 1] S14, S26

wabomndeni of the family [poss Cl. 1] S23

wabulawa (s)he was killed [rem past] S21

wabulawa and (s)he was killed [narr] S26

wabuye (s)he again [rem past or narr] S16

wadala it created [rem past] S17

wadivosa (s)he (got) divorced [rem past] S22

wafihlwa and (s)he was buried [narrative aspect] S02

wagcizelela (s)he emphasized, stressed [rem past] S27

wagcizelela and (s)he emphasized, stressed [narr] S16

wake you once [aux, rem past] S15

wake waba naso you have had [assoc cop, inch, rem past, experiential] S15

wakhe his, her [poss Cl. 1 or 3] S14, S13

wakhetha (s)he chose [rem past] S27

wakho your [poss Cl. 3] S21

wakhona local, of or from there [poss Cl. 1 & 3] S21

wakhula (s)he grew up [rem past] S19

wakhushulelwa (s)he was promoted to [rem past] S27

wakithi of our home, of our country [poss Cl. 3] S05

wakubo of his, her, their home or family [poss Cl. 3] S14

wakuleli of this (the noun **izwe** 'country' is understood) [poss Cl. 3] S16

wakulendawo (also **wakule ndawo**) from this place [poss Cl. 3] S06

wakwa-Agrilek from Agrilek [poss Cl. 1] S27

wakwaMpanza of the place of Mpanza [poss Cl. 3] S02

waKwaMpungose of KwaMpungose (Mpungose's place) [poss Cl. 3] S21

wakwaNdlovu of Ndlovu's place [poss Cl. 1] S22

waKwaNgcobo of KwaNgcobo (Ngcobo's place) [poss Cl. 3] S21

wakwaZulu-Natal of KwaZulu-Natal [poss Cl.1] S12

wakwenza (s)he did it [rem past] S26

walabo of those [poss Cl. 1] S25

walabobantu of those people [poss Cl. 1] S16

walahlekelwa (s)he lost [rem past] S24

walandela it followed [rem past] S18

walesi of this [poss Cl. 1] S13

walibuza (s)he asked him or her [rem past] S26

walishiya (s)he left it [rem past] S09

walo of this [poss Cl. 1] S11

walolu of this [poss Cl. 3] S10

wama (s)he stopped [rem past] S17

wamabhanoyi of airplanes [poss Cl. 1] S18

wamaphoyisa of the police [poss Cl. 3] S16

wamasha it marched [narr] S21

wami my [poss Cl. 1 or 3] S09, S16

wangena (and) (s)he went into [narr] S17

wangidonsela (and) (s)he pulled out for me [narr] S14

wangihola (s)he led me [rem past] S14

wangikhulisa (s)he brought me up [rem past] S14

wangithanda (and) she loved me [narr] S14

wangithatha (s)he took me [rem past] S14

wangonyaka of the year (lit. of in the year) [poss Cl. 1a] S13

waphathwa (s)he suffered, (s)he was affected [rem past] S14

waphathwa y- (s)he suffered from measles (lit. was taken hold of by measles) [v phr] S14

waphawula (s)he pointed out, indicated [rem past] S25

waphelelwa (s)he lost [rem past] S27

waphelelwa wumsebenzi his or her job came to an end (lit. (s)he was finished for by job) [v phr] S27

waphendula (s)he answered [rem past] S18

waphothula (s)he completed [rem past] S14

waqala it began [rem past] S14

waqasha that (s)he hired [narr] S27

waqoka (s)he decided [rem past] S27

waqopha (s)he carved out, notched [rem past] S18

waqopha umlando (s)he carved out history [v phr] S18

wasebenza (s)he worked [rem past] S14

wasebenzisa (s)he used [rem past or narr] S27

waseBochum of (in) Bochum (a place) [poss Cl. 3] S14

waseDukuduku of (at) Dukuduku (place) [poss Cl. 1] S24

wase-Inner West Council of (in) Inner … [poss Cl. 1] S12

wasemakhaya of rural areas [poss Cl. 3] S24

washabalala it disappeared, it came to nought [narr] S17

washona and (s)he died [narr] S21

washonelwa (s)he was bereaved [rem past] S22

wasichazela (s)he explained to us [narr] S16

wasikhombisa (s)he showed us

[rem past] S27

wasitshela (s)he told us [rem past] S16

wasixoxela (s)he related to us [rem past] S16

wasuka it was given cause [rem past] S21

wasungulwa since it was inaugurated [rem past, partic] S11

wathatha (s)he took [rem past] S16

wathenga (s)he bought [rem past] S27

wathi (s)he said [rem past] S09

wathi (and) (s)he said [narr] S16

wathola (s)he obtained [rem past] S14

wathola (s)he obtained [narr] S27

wathutha (s)he moved house, (s)he transferred [rem past] S27

wavala and it, (s)he froze (lit. closed) [narr] S10

wawenza (s)he did it [rem past] S14

wawukugunyaza it endorsed it [rem past pres] S25

wawungasetshenziswa it was not being utilized [rem past pres] S27

wawungenayo incazelo it did not have information (long ago) [assoc cop, rem past pres] S14

wawushiya (s)he left it (behind) [rem past] S27

wawushiya phansi (s)he threw it in (lit. (s)he left it down) [v phr]

S27

wawuzizwela you just heard, you heard for yourself [rem past pres] S23

wawuzohamba it would travel, it would give access to travel [rem past fut] S18

waya it went [rem past] S03

waya and (s)he went [narr] S27

wayaphi? where did it go? [v phr] S03

wayebona (s)he saw [rem past pres] S14

wayefuna (s)he wanted [rem past pres] S19

wayefunda (s)he was studying (long ago) [rem past pres] S14

wayekhala (s)he was crying or complaining [rem past pres] S17

wayekholwa (s)he believed [rem past pres] S19

wayelokhu (s)he kept on, (s)he always [aux, rem past pres] S23

wayemlekelela (s)he used to assist him or her [rem past pres] S09

wayengabalekela (s)he could run away from [rem past pres, potential] S17

wayengahambisani (s)he did not go along with [rem past pres, neg] S19

wayengakuthandisisi (s)he did not like it very much [rem past pres, neg] S18

wayengumfana he was a boy [ident cop, rem past pres] S23

wayengumfana wesikole he was a schoolboy [ident cop phr] S23

wayesaba (s)he was afraid [rem past pres] S23

wayesehlengiwe (s)he had already been escorted [rem past past, disjoint; < **w-** SC + **-a-** rem past + **-ye-** SC + **-s-** already + **-e-** SC + **-hleng-** + **-w-** + **-i…e**] S17

wayeselutholile (s)he had already acquired it [rem past past, exclusive, disjoint] S27

wayesenolwazi (s)he already (or then) had the knowledge [assoc cop, rem past pres, exclusive] S27

wayevame (s)he used [aux, rem past past, conjoint] S09

wayewuboleke (s)he had borrowed it (Cl. 3) [rem past past, conjoint] S27

wayeyiboleke (s)he had borrowed it [rem past past, conjoint] S27

wayeyimfolomane he was a foreman [ident cop, rem past pres] S27

wayeyisebenzela (s)he was working for it [rem past pres] S27

wayeyisebenzisa (s)he was using it [rem past pres] S27

wayeziphuzela (s)he passed with ease [rem past pres] S18

wayezovalelwa (s)he would be locked up [rem past fut] S23

wayiswa (and) (s)he was taken [narr] S17

wayithenga you bought it [rem past] S28

wayo his, her, its [poss Cl. 1] S14

wayokhalaza and it went and protested [narr, andative] S21

wazama (s)he tried [rem past] S23

wazi you should know [subjunc] S04

wazibulala (s)he killed him- or herself [rem past] S16

waziphathela they carried by themselves, they bore for themselves [rem past] S21

wazithenga you bought them [rem past] S28

wazo their [poss Cl. 1 or 3] S08

we- [quant conc 2 p sg] S23

we- of [poss conc Cl. 1a/3a coalesced with following **i**] S01, S05, S25

-we- they [SC Cl. 6; found in negative copulatives before **kho**] S26

weBochum After-Care Centre of the Bochum ... [poss Cl. 1] S14

wedwa on your own, (you) alone [quant 2 p sg] S23

wehluleka (s)he was unable [rem past] S05

-wel-a fall into, onto [v-appl] S17

-wel-a cross (a river, path, mountain, ..., go overseas) [v.t.] S25

welapha (s)he treats [pres, conjoint] S23

wemfundo of education [poss Cl. 1] S05

wenyanga monthly, of the month [poss Cl. 3] S28

wenza (s)he is doing, making [pres, conjoint] S14

we-orange juice of orange juice [poss Cl. 1 or 3] S01

weRama of (Rama) margarine [poss Cl. 1] S01

weSantoshi Young Killers of the Santoshi Young Killers [poss Cl. 1] S09

wesibili second [poss Cl. 3] S11

wesifazane female [poss Cl. 1] S20

wesikole of school [poss Cl. 1] S23

wesilisa of the male sex or gender [poss Cl. 1] S23

wethemba (s)he hopes [pres, disjoint] S13

wethembisa (s)he promised [rem past] S21

wethu our [poss Cl. 3] S25

wethukile (s)he got a fright [past, disjoint] S17

wethule (s)he placed before or laid down [past, conjoint] S26

wexwayise (s)he warned [past, conjoint] S26

-wez-a take or transport across (a river, bridge, ...); help out of difficulty [v-caus; < **-wel-** + **-Y-**; l + **-Y-** > **z**] S25

wezamanzi of water affairs [poss Cl. 1] S11

wezemfundo of education [poss Cl. 1] S13

wezengqondo of psychological matters [poss Cl. 1] S26

wezindlu of houses [poss Cl. 1] S22

wezobuLungiswa of Correctional Services (i.e. Prisons) [poss Cl. 3] S10

wezobunjiniyela of engineering [poss Cl. 3] S19

wezocansi of sexual matters [poss Cl. 1] S23

wezokuhlelwa kwemindeni of family planning [poss phr Cl. 3] S25

wezokuPhepha of Security (Minister is understood here) [poss Cl. 1] S21

wezokuvakasha of tourism [poss Cl. 3] S24

wezoKwazisa of Information [poss Cl. 3] S25

wezoMnotho of Finance [poss Cl. 3] S12

wo- of [poss conc Cl. 1 & 3 coalesced with following **u**] S11, S03

wo- [quant conc Cl. 3] S07

wo- [quant conc Cl. 6; var of **o-**] S12

wo it [abs pron Cl. 3] S02

wo they, them, their [abs pron Cl. 6] S09

wobisi of milk [poss Cl. 3] S03

wodwa alone, only [quant Cl. 3] S09

wofakazi of the witnesses [poss Cl. 1] S26

woKhozi FM of Khozi FM [poss Cl. 1] S11

wokuba of being [poss Cl. 3] S19

wokubanika of giving them [poss Cl. 3] S25

wokubopha of arresting [poss Cl. 3] S10

wokubulala for killing [poss Cl. 3] S20

wokufundisa of teaching [poss Cl. 3] S24

wokuhamba of travel, of movement [poss Cl. 1] S18

wokuhlelwa for planning, of being arranged [poss Cl. 3] S25

wokukhala of the crying [poss Cl. 3] S17

wokukhulu by a big one [ident cop, pres] S27

wokulawula of controlling, of regulating [poss Cl. 3] S18

wokuphephisa of helping to recover [poss Cl. 3] S16

wokuqala first [poss Cl. 1 or 3] S18, S11

wokusebenza of working [poss Cl. 3] S27

wokushisela of forging [poss Cl. 3] S19

wokusiza of helping [poss Cl. 3] S17

Glossary

wokusungula of setting up [poss Cl. 3] S12

wokutshalwa for planting [poss Cl. 3] S24

wokuxoxisana of negotiating [poss Cl. 3] S16

womdlali of the player [poss Cl. 3] S11

womuntu of a person [poss Cl. 3] S20

wona them, it [abs pron Cl. 6] S25

wonke the whole, all, every [quant Cl. 3] S07

wonke the whole, all [quant Cl. 6; var **onke**] S12

-wu- it [SC Cl. 3; found after vowels] S05

-wu- it [OC Cl. 3] S02

wudonga by a wall [agent adv] S17

wuhlangothi it is the section [ident cop, pres] S23

wukubona (it) is to see [ident cop, pres] S08

wukudinwa (by) being sickened [agent adv] S23

wukuhlukana it is to get away [ident cop, pres] S28

wukuthi it is that [ident cop, pres; var **ngukuthi**] S14

wukuthi by that, that [agentive adv] S05

wukuthutheleka it is the increase, it is the growth [ident cop, pres] S20

wukwesaba by fear [agent adv] S23

wumkhuhlane it is a cold (and fever) [agent adv] S20

wumsebenzi by work, by a job [agent adv] S24

wusizo it is help, aid, assistance [ident cop, pres] S27

X

-xak-a put into difficulties [v.t.] S13

xaxa bec improved, bec greater [ideophone] S27

-xazulul-a settle or resolve (a quarrel, dispute) [v.t.] S09

-xazululek-a get resolved, get settled [v-neut] S28

-xhaphaz-a exploit [v.t.] S23

-xhum-a join (v.t.), splice, link [v.t.] S14

-xhuman-a join (v.i.), link up [v-recip] S14

-xol- bec peaceful, tranquil, calm [v.inch] S05

Xolani (male name) [n Cl. 1a; < imper **xolani!** forgive! (this name might be given when the mother has done something wrong, e.g. had an illegitimate child)] S09

-xox-a converse, chat; narrate [v.i. & t.] S26

-xoxel-a communicate to, converse for [v-appl] S16

495

-xoxisan-a chat, converse; negotiate [v-caus-recip] S13

-xway-a be on the alert, be cautious, be wary [v.i.] S23

-xwayis-a warn, caution, alert, put on guard [v-caus; var **-exwayis-a**] S23

Y

y- it, he, she [SC Cl. 9] S01

y- they [SC Cl. 4] S09

y- of [poss conc Cl. 9 & 4 found before **a, e** and **o**] S12, S19

y- is, are [ident cop pref used before the vowel **i**] S04

-y- (s)he [partic SC Cl. 1; var of **-ye-** found before vowels] S23

-y- it [OC Cl. 9; found before vowels] S08

-y- [disjoint form marker; variant found before vowels] S09

-Y- cause to [caus ext] S05

ya- of [poss conc Cl. 4 & 9] S06, S01

-ya- [marker of the disjoint form of the present indicative tense, positive; indicates the end of the verb phrase] S02

-y-a go to (direction to a place always implied if not stated) [v.i.] S03

-y-a ocansini have sex (idiom; lit. go to the sleeping-mat) [v phr] S23

-y-a still [aux indicating present continuous action] S05

yaba it, (s)he became [copula, rem past] S23

yabafana of boys [poss Cl. 4] S19

yabakhubazekile of the disabled [poss Cl. 9] S14

yaba nemiphumela it, (s)he had results [assoc cop, inch, rem past] S23

yabangcwabi of buriers, of morticians, of undertakers [poss Cl. 9] S12

yabaqashwa employees' [poss Cl. 9] S10

yabeseki of the sponsors [poss Cl. 9] S11

yabesilisa of males [poss Cl. 4] S19

yabesimame of women [poss Cl. 9] S14

yabezindaba of journalists, or reporters [poss Cl. 4; < **ya-** + **abezindaba**] S09

yabo their [poss Cl. 4 or 9] S06, S23

yabonogada of guards [poss Cl. 9] S13

yagcina (s)he ended up, (s)he eventually [rem past] S16

yahlanganiswa and (it was) mixed [narr] S01

yake it once [rem past] S15

yake yalimala it once got injured [rem past, experiential] S15

yakhe his, her, its [poss Cl. 4 or 9] S23, S02

yakho your [poss Cl. 9] S04

yakhuliswa (s)he was brought up [narr] S14

yakithi of my or our home [poss Cl. 9] S18

yakushaya indiva dismissed it as worthless [v phr, rem past] S05

yakwaSAA of (at) SAA (South African Airways) [poss Cl. 9] S18

yakwaWakefield JHI of Wakefield JHI [poss Cl. 9] S11

-yakwazi be able to, can, know how to [< **-ya-** pres disjoint marker + **-kw-** OC Cl. 15 + **-az-i** know] S14

yalabobantu of those people [poss Cl. 9] S28

yalesisifundazwe of this province [poss Cl. 9] S24

yalesosizathu of, for that reason [poss Cl. 9] S16

yalezozifo of those diseases [poss Cl. 9] S20

yalimala it got injured [narr] S15

yalo of this [poss Cl. 4] S11

yalokho of that [poss Cl. 9] S16

yalokhu of this [poss Cl. 9] S16

yalutho of any use, in any way (lit. of anything) [poss Cl. 9] S23

yamabhanoyi of airplanes [poss Cl. 9] S18

yama-exercise of exercise books [poss Cl. 9] S13

yama-sirens of sirens [poss Cl. 4] S17

yamatekisi of taxis [poss Cl. 9] S17

yami my [poss Cl. 9] S18

-Yana little, small; dear, sweet; wretched, awful, good-for-nothing [dimin suffix; significance depends on context] S09

yanele it is sufficient, it is enough [stative] S09

yangakithi (of) around our area or district [poss Cl. 9] S06

yangenza it made me [rem past] S27

yaphasa (s)he passed [rem past] S18

yasakazeka they got broadcast [narr] S26

yaseDurban South Central of Durban ... [poss Cl. 9] S11

yasejele of in prison [poss Cl. 9] S23

yaseLamontville of Lamontville [poss Cl. 9] S11

yaseMtata of (in) Umtata [poss Cl. 9] S17

yaseNkume of Nkume [poss Cl. 9] S21

yaseThekwini of (in) Durban [poss Cl. 4] S09

yashaqisa it, (s)he shocked [rem past] S21

yashiya it left (behind) [rem past] S17

yasho it said so [remote past, partic] S05

yashona it disappeared [narr] S06

yasitshela (s)he told us [rem past] S16

yaso of it [poss Cl. 9] S20

yawo its [poss Cl. 9] S02

yayandulele it had preceded [rem past past, conjoint; < y- SC + -a- rem past + -y- SC + -andulel- + -e] S17

yayihamba it was traveling [rem past pres] S17

yayingekho it, (s)he was not there [loc cop, rem past pres, neg; may also introduce an exist cop] S17

yayingekho indlela there was no way [exist cop, rem past pres, neg] S17

yayingekho into there was nothing [exist cop, rem past pres, neg] S23

yayingenayo imali (s)he did not have the money [assoc cop, rem past pres, neg; < y- SC -a- rem past -yi- SC -nge- not -na- with -yo it] S18

yayintanta was floating [rem past pres] S17

yayiphahlwe it was surrounded [rem past past, conjoint] S17

yayiphakathi it was between, inside, in the middle [loc cop, rem past pres] S27

yayiphakeme it had risen, it had gone up [rem past stative] S17

yayiphathelene it (argument) concerned [rem past stative] S27

yayizibambela (s)he used to take on, (s)he held or caught for him- or herself [rem past pres] S18

yayizibambela amatoho (s)he took on day jobs [v phr] S18

yazalelwa (s)he was born in [rem past] S14

yazi it knows [pres, partic] S05

yaziwe it is known [past, disjoint] S24

yazo their [poss Cl. 9] S08

ye- [quant conc Cl. 1] S04

ye- of [poss conc Cl. 4 & 9 coalesced with i] S19, S05

-ye- he, she, it [partic SC Cl. 1; found after a vowel] S09

-ye- they, it [partic SC Cl. 6; found after a vowel] S17

ye him, her, it [abs pron Cl. 1] S04

-ye VERB sometimes [aux; followed by subjunc] S16

yedlule they have passed [stative] S09

yedwa alone, on his or her own [quant Cl. 1] S14

yedwana sole, completely alone [quant Cl. 1] S04

ye-IFP of the IFP (Inkatha Freedom Party) [poss Cl. 9] S05

yejwayelekile it is usual [stative] S09

-yek-a let go (of), leave (alone, out), stop VERBing [v.t.] S07

yekani let go (of) [imper] S07

-yekw-a be stopped, be left (alone, out, off) [v-pass] S13

yemali of money [poss Cl. 9] S28

yemindeni of families [poss Cl. 9] S08

yempesheni of the welfare grant [poss Cl. 9] S14

yena he, him, she, her [abs pron Cl. 1] S14

yendaba of the matter [poss Cl. 9] S08

-yeng-a entice, seduce [v.t.] S28

yenganyelwe it is run or administered, it is presided over [past, conjunc]

yenzelwe it was founded in order to [past, conjoint] S23

yesibili second [poss Cl. 9] S28

yesifundazwe of the province [poss Cl. 9] S24

yesimo of the state [poss Cl. 9] S28

yesivuno of the harvest [poss Cl. 9] S27

ye-South African National Council for the Blind of the SANCB [poss Cl. 9] S14

yeziboshwa of prisoners [poss Cl. 9] S23

yeziguli of patients [poss Cl. 9] S17

yezimpahla for goods [poss Cl. 9] S10

yezindiza of aircraft, of planes [poss Cl. 9] S18

yezingane for, of children [poss Cl. 9] S05

yezingozi of accidents [poss Cl. 9] S08

yezinjongo of resolutions [poss Cl. 9] S28

yeziqiwi of game reserves [poss Cl. 9] S24

yezobunjiniyela in (of) engineering [poss Cl. 4] S19

yezocansi sexual [poss Cl. 9] S23

yezokwelapha of healing (i.e. nursing, or medicine) [poss Cl. 4] S19

yezwe of the country [poss Cl. 9] S16

yi- [enum conc Cl. 9] S19

yi- is, are [ident cop pref] S03

yi- by [agent adv pref] S06

yi- (s)he, it is [descr cop pref used with monosyllabic stems in Cl. 9] S23

yi- [stabilizer (a syllable added to a monosyllabic form to make it disyllabic. Monosyllabic forms are unusual in Zulu.)] S20

-yi- it, (s)he [SC Cl. 9] S05

-yi- it [OC Cl. 9] S09

yi-ALHEBROS it is Alhebros [ident cop, pres] S27

yiba become, be [copula, imper] S20

yiba nesiqiniseko make sure, ensure, make certain (lit. bec with certainty) [assoc cop, inch, imper] S20

yibo it is they or them [ident cop, pres] S23

yi-Communicable Disease Control of the Department of Health by the ...[agent adv] S20

yi-credit card by the credit card [agent adv] S28

yi-forensic criminologist (s)he is a forensic ... [ident cop, pres] S23

yi-Hurricane Nelson it is Hurricane Nelson [ident cop, pres] S17

yikhanda from a headache [agent adv] S20

yikho it is that, it is what ... [ident cop, pres] S04

yikuphi it is which [ident cop, pres] S25

yikuphi okufanele akwenze what to do [ident cop phr] S25

yilabo are those [ident cop, pres] S17

yilabo by those [agent adv] S23

yilabobantu it is those people [ident cop, pres] S20

yilapho it is where ... [ident cop, pres] S16

yile-glue by this glue [agent adv] S09

yileli by this [agent adv] S26

yilenkinga by this problem [agent adv] S23

yilesifo by this disease [agent adv] S20

yilesisifo from or by this disease [agent adv] S20

yilomshophi by this plague [agent adv] S23

yilowo it is that one [ident cop, pres] S16

yimanje it is now [ident cop, pres] S03

yimbangela it is the cause [ident cop, pres] S20

yimeya by the mayor [agent adv] S11

yimi(na) it is me, it is I [ident cop, pres] S14

yimiphefumulo by lives [agent adv] S08

yimizwa by feelings, by emotions [agent adv] S08

yimuphi? it is which one? [ident cop, pres] S23

yindida it is a puzzle or riddle [ident cop, pres] S14

yindoda it, he is a man [ident cop, pres] S23

yindoda-thizeni by a certain man [agent adv] S08

yingoba it is because [ident cop, pres] S07

yingozi it is danger [ident cop, pres] S09

yinhle it, (s)he is good, nice, pretty [descr cop, pres] S23

yini? it is what? [ident cop, pres] S08

yini? by what? [agent adv] S19

yini or not [tag] S14

yinja by a dog [agent adv] S10

yinkampani by the company [agent adv] S18

yinkantolo it is a court [ident cop, pres] S28

yinkulu it is large, it is big [descr cop, pres] S27

yinselelo it is a challenge [ident cop, pres] S19

yinto it is something, it is a thing [ident cop, pres] S06

yinye one [enum Cl. 9] S19

yinye there is one [descr cop, pres] S19

yinzululwane by giddiness [agent adv] S20

yiphoyisa (s)he is a policeman [ident cop, pres] S16

yi-Plasmodia falciparum it is *Plasmodia falciparum* [ident cop, pres] S20

yiqiniso it is the truth [ident cop, pres] S23

yiqolo from the small of the back [agent adv] S20

-yis-a take to [v-caus] S09

yishumi there are ten (of them) [ident cop, pres] S14

yisifundo it is a lesson [ident cop, pres] S08

yisihlanu there are five (of them) [ident cop, pres] S20

yisikhathi it is time [ident cop, pres] S04

yisikhathi esihle sokuba uzihlelisise it is a good time to put them in order [ident cop phr] S04

yisikhathi sokucabanga it is time to think [ident cop phr] S04

yisilima it is a difficult thing, it is a deformity [ident cop, pres] S23

yisimo it is the standing, status, state, condition; nature, form, character [ident cop, pres] S20

yisimo sezulu it is the weather [ident cop phr] S20

yisimungumungwane from measles [agent adv] S14

yisinambuzane by a parasite [agent adv] S20

yisipho it is a gift [ident cop, pres] S14

yisishiyagalombili it is eight [ident cop] S09

yisithupha it is six [ident cop, pres] S14

yiso it is the one, it is it, it is him, it is her [ident cop, pres] S17

yisoka by the boyfriend [agent adv] S08

-yisw-a be taken (to) [v-caus-pass] S17

yi-switchboard operator (s)he is a switchboard operator [ident cop, pres] S14

yithemba (by) hope [agent adv] S23

yi-track suit it is a track suit [ident cop, pres] S11

-yiw-a be gone to [v-pass] S06

yiwo it is it [ident cop, pres] S07

yiwo(na) it is them [ident cop, pres] S27

yiwo olawula it is what rules [ident cop phr] S07

yiyona it is it, him, her [ident cop, pres] S18

yiyona inkosi by him the chief [agent adv phr] S06

yize it is to no avail, it is for nothing, it is useless [ident cop, pres] S10

yize it is a little, it is a bit, it is almost [ident cop, pres] S14

yize even though [conj] S18

yize noma even though [conj phr] S18

yizibazi by scars [agent adv] S09

yizifundo it is, they are studies [ident cop, pres] S18

yizikweleti by debts [agent adv] S28

yizimpahla by the goods [agent adv] S17

yizimpilo (by) lives [agent adv] S20

yizindlu by houses [agent adv] S17

yizinkangala they are deserted places [ident cop, pres] S23

yizinkinga it is problems [ident cop] S16

yizinto they are things [ident cop, pres] S09

yizisulu it is victims [ident cop, pres] S10

yiziteleka it is strikes [ident cop, pres] S28

yizivakashi they are visitors [ident cop, pres] S20

yizizathu by reasons [agent adv] S23

yizo by them [agent adv] S25

yizo ezibeka impilo yabo engcupheni by life-threatening situations (lit. by those (things) that put their life in danger) [agent adv phr] S25

yo- of [poss Cl. 4 & 9 coalesced with following **u**] S25, S01

yo- [quant conc Cl. 4 & 9] S05, S13

-yo- will, shall [rem fut marker] S05

-yo- go and, go to [andative marker] S09

yo it, he, him, she, her [abs pron Cl. 9] S05

-yo [rel suff; marks a disjoint form] S04

yobugebengu of gangsterism, of crime [poss Cl. 9] S23

yokuba (of) that [poss Cl. 9] S17

yokubabeka of putting them [poss Cl. 9] S23

yokudlwengulwa of being raped [poss Cl. 9] S23

yokufunda for study [poss Cl. 9] S13

yokugibela of riding, of boarding, of traveling by ... [poss Cl. 9] S18

yokuhola of leading [poss Cl. 9] S07

yokukhipha of taking out [poss Cl. 9] S23

yokungazikhaleli of not entering a plea on his own behalf [poss Cl. 9] S26

yokungenisa of bringing in [poss Cl. 9] S24

yokunqanda of preventing, of checking [poss Cl. 9] S08

yokuphathwa of being infected [poss Cl. 9] S20

yokuphikisana to contest [poss Cl. 4] S25

yokuqala first [poss Cl. 9] S19

yokuqhuba for, of continuing [poss Cl. 9] S18

yokuthenga for buying [poss Cl. 9] S09

yokuthi (of) that [poss Cl. 9] S13

yokuthuthukisa of uplifting [poss Cl. 9] S24

yokutshala for or of planting [poss Cl. 9] S24

yokuvimbela (of) to prevent [poss Cl. 4] S25

yokuwenza for making them [poss Cl. 1] S01

yokuzivikela for protecting one-self [poss Cl. 4] S20

yokwanelisa of satisfying [poss Cl. 9] S23

yokwehlelwa of being overcome [poss Cl. 9] S23

yokwelapha for medical treatment [poss Cl. 4] S24

yokwengeza to increase [poss Cl. 9] S16

yomame of women (lit. of mothers) [poss Cl. 9] S12

yomdabu native, indigenous, aboriginal [poss Cl. 9] S19

yomphakathi of the community [poss Cl. 9] S24

yomshwalense from insurance or assurance [poss Cl. 9] S27

yomthetho of the law [poss Cl. 9] S25

yomthethosisekelo of the constitution [poss Cl. 9] S25

yomuntu of a person [poss Cl. 9] S17

yona it, he, him, she, her [abs pron Cl. 9] S06

yonke every, all, the whole [quant Cl. 4 or 9] S05, S13

yonke indawo everywhere [quant phr Cl. 9] S21

yonke into everything [quant phr Cl. 9] S13

yosizo of the assistance [poss Cl. 9] S27

Young Boys (gang name) S09

Z

z- they [SC Cl. 8 & 10; found before vowels] S17, S06

z- of [poss conc Cl. 10] S09

-z- them [OC Cl. 8 & 10; found before vowels] S08, S04

-z- self (myself, yourself, himself, herself, itself), selves (ourselves, yourselves, themselves) [reflexive pref; found before vowels] S14

-z- ... -el- just, merely [reflexive prefix (before vowels) + appl ext] S11

-z-a come [v.i.] S05

za- of [poss conc Cl. 8 & 10] S01, S04

zabafana of boys [poss Cl. 10] S08

zabafundi of the students [poss Cl. 10] S13

zabaMhlophe of the Whites [poss Cl. 10] S16

zabantu of people [poss Cl. 10] S14

zabesilisa of males [poss Cl. 8] S23

zabo their [poss Cl. 10] S10

zafika they arrived [rem past, partic] S17

zagqama they became clear or obvious [rem past] S27

zahlukahlukene they differ in various ways, they vary [stative] S28

zahlukene they are different [stative; < **-ahlukan-** bec different + **-i...e** stative suff] S08

zajabula they were happy [rem past] S23

zakhe his, her [poss Cl. 8 or Cl. 10] S14, S16

zakhele they live at or in; they are situated in [stative] S11, S27

zakho your [poss Cl. 8 or 10] S04

-zal-a give birth (to) (not considered polite with reference to people) [v.t.] S02

-zalan-a breed prolifically [v-recip] S20

-zalel-a lay eggs; give birth for, at [v-appl] S20

-zalelw-a be born in (lit. be given birth to in) [v-appl-pass] S14

zaleziziqiwi of these reserves [poss Cl. 8] S24

-zalw-a be given birth to, be born [v-pass] S02

Zama (surname) [n Cl. 1a] S11

-zam-a try, attempt [v.i. & t.] S16

zama try [imper] S20

zamabhizinisi of businesses [poss Cl. 10] S24

zamagama of the names [poss Cl. 8] S27

zamahlathi of forests [poss Cl. 10] S11

zamaholo of salaries, wages [poss Cl. 10] S27

zamantombazane of girls [poss Cl. 10] S08

zamaphoyisa of the police [poss Cl. 10] S09

zamasosha of soldiers [poss Cl. 10] S23

zami my [poss Cl. 8 or 10] S19, S24

zande and they multiply [subjunc] S20

zangalonyaka of this year [poss Cl. 10] S28

-z-ang-e never [aux; followed by the subjunc] S09

zaqoqwa (and) they were collected [narrative] S06

zase they already long ago [aux, rem past] S23

zasekhaya domestic, of home [poss Cl. 10] S16

zase zinesikhathi they already had long ago [assoc cop, rem past pres, exclusive] S23

zasho and they said [narr] S23

zaso its, his, her [poss Cl. 10] S20

zayo its, his, her [poss Cl. 9] S18

zazenza they used to make [rem past pres] S24

zazi they should know [subjunc] S08

zaziba they were becoming [copula, rem past pres] S24

zaziba nesiqiniseko they were intent (lit. they were becoming with certainty) [assoc cop, inch, rem past pres] S24

zazidlubhe they were smartly dressed, they were wearing their best [rem past past, conjoint] S17

zazikubeka they put it [rem past pres] S25

zaziyikhwalithi they were (of) quality [ident cop, rem past pres] S27

zazo their, of them [poss Cl. 10] S08

ze- of [poss conc Cl. 8 & 10 coalesced with following **i**] S01, S08

-z-e do ever [aux; followed by subjunc] S09

-z-e until [aux; followed by the subjunctive] S01

ze-electrical engineering of electrical engineering [poss Cl. 8] S19

ze-frosting of frosting [poss Cl. 8] S01

zegolide of gold, golden [poss Cl. 10] S11

zehluke they are different [past, conjoint] S10

zehlukene they are different [stative; < **-ehlukan-** bec different + **-i...e** [stative suff]] S20

ze-instrumentation of instrumentation [poss Cl. 8] S19

zema and they stopped [narr; < **za-** + **-im-a**] S17

zemfundo of education [poss Cl. 10] S13

zempilo of life; of health [poss Cl. 8 & 10] S06, S14

zempumelelo of success [poss Cl. 8] S27

zengqondo of the mind [poss Cl. 10] S26

zenhlanhla lucky, of luck, of good fortune [poss Cl. 10] S04

zenza they make, they do, they perform, they cause [pres, conjoint] S09

zenzani? what are they doing? [v phr] S13

-z-enzel-a make for oneself, do for oneself; do for no apparent reason, just do [v-refl-appl] S21, S24

zenziwe they have been made [past, conjoint] S24

zesifundazwe of the province [poss Cl. 10] S20

zesikole of the school [poss Cl. 10] S13

zesiliva of silver [poss Cl. 10] S11

zesitho of the body (lit. of limbs or body parts) [poss Cl. 10] S15

ze-strawberry of strawberry [poss Cl. 8] S27

zethu our [poss Cl. 8 or 10] S05, S16

zezamabhizinisi for trade [poss Cl. 8] S24

zezaphuli-mthetho of law-breakers [poss Cl. 10; < za- + izaphuli-mthetho] S10

zezenhlalakahle for social welfare [poss Cl. 10; < za- + ezenhlala-kahle] S09

zezepolitiki political [poss Cl. 10] S25

zezigelekeqe of criminals [poss Cl. 10] S23

zezindlu of houses [poss Cl. 10] S17

zezinsizwa of youths [poss Cl. 8] S17

zezokwelapha of health, of healing [poss Cl. 8] S19

zi- they [SC Cl. 8 & 10] S04

-zi- them [OC Cl. 8 & 10] S03, S08

-zi- self (myself, yourself, himself, herself, itself), selves (ourselves, yourselves, themselves) [reflexive pref] S04

-zi- VERB **-el-** VERB for oneself S14

-zi- VERB **-el-** just VERB, merely VERB, VERB for no particular reason S09

ziba they become [copula, pres, conjoint] S09

ziba ngumndeni [ident cop, inch, pres] S09

zibalulekile they are important [stative] S27

zibangela they cause to [pres, conjoint] S13

zibasela they make persistent demands for repayment [pres, conjoint] S28

zibeka they place [pres, conjoint] S25

zibhale write them [imper] S28

-zi-bonel-a see for oneself [v-rel-appl] S17

-zi-bulal-a commit suicide, kill oneself [v-refl] S16

zibulale they kill [subjunc] S09

zibuyiselwe they have to be

returned to [subjunc] S28

-zi-buz-a wonder, ask oneself [v-refl] S19

zidakwe they are intoxicated [past, partic, conjoint] S09

zidayiselwa they are sold to [pres, conjoint] S24

zidlala they play(ing) [pres, partic] S08

zidlula (while) they are passing [pres, partic] S18

zidlulela they pass on to [pres, conjoint] S20

zifana they resemble, they are like [pres, conjoint] S19

zifanele they suit, they fit, they are appropriate to [stative] S19

zifihle they having hidden [past, partic] S09

zifike they immediately [aux, pres, conjoint] S20

-zi-fikis-a mistreat a new-comer (as bullying a new child at school or when a new member of staff who doesn't know the ropes is given extra work by old staff) [v-refl-caus, v.t.] S23

zifiso wishes, desires [< **izifiso**] S12

zifuna they want, they require [pres, conjoint] S27

-zi-gangel-a just play about, just be foolish [v-refl-appl] S27

zigcine they should end up [subjunc] S28

zigcwele they abound, they are full [stative] S24

zigqoka (they) wearing [pres, partic] S09

zihamba they travel, they move about [pres, conjoin t] S09

zihambela they are traveling to [pres, conjoint] S18

zihambisana they go together [pres, conjoint] S16

zihlala they live [pres, conjoint] S09

zihlale they continually VERB, they keep on VERBing [aux] S09

zihlale they should stay [subjunc] S09

-zi-jwayez-a get used to, accustom oneself to [v-refl] S28

zika- of [poss conc Cl. 8; used before nouns of Cl. 1a] S07

zika-BA of BA [poss Cl. 8] S14

zikaMnuz Nelson Mandela of Mr. Nelson Mandela [poss phr Cl. 8] S07

zikhathi times [< **izikhathi**] S20

zikhethekile they are differentiated, picked out, selected [stative] S20

zikhishwe they have been brought out [past, conjoint] S20

zikhubazekile they are disabled, handicapped [stative] S14

zikhulume they should talk [subjunc] S09

zikufaka they put or place you [pres, partic] S28

zikufaka amanzi emadolweni they threaten or frighten you (lit. they put you water on the knees) [v phr] S28

zikukhathaze they should worry, bother or disturb you [subjunc] S28

zikumele they await you, they are standing over you [stative] S28

zikuthola they get it, they obtain it [pres, conjoint] S09

zikuthole they find it, they get it [subjunc] S09

ziletha they bring [pres, conjoint] S19

zilungiswe they must be rectified [subjunc] S13

zilwanyazana insects [< **izilwa-nyazana**] S20

zimbili there are two [descr cop; < **ezimbili** two (adj)] S28

zimbona (when) they saw (lit. see) him or her [pres, partic] S23

-zi-mel-a stand up for one's self, bec independent [v-refl-appl] S12

zimhloniphe they should respect him or her [subjunc] S08

-zi-misel-a get ready for, prepare for, be determined [v-refl-caus-appl; < **-zi-** self + **-m-** stand + **-is-** caus + **-el-** for] S12

zimthathe that they should take him/her [subjunc] S08

zinamazinga okushisa they have temperatures [assoc cop, pres] S20

zincela they suck [pres, conjoint] S21

zincela izithupha they are helpless (idiom; lit. they suck (their) thumbs) S21

zincwadi letters, books [< **izincwadi**] S13

zinemikhono they have sleeves [assoc cop, pres] S20

zineminyaka they are aged (lit. they have years) [assoc cop, pres] S20

zinesikhathi they have time [assoc cop, pres, partic] S23

zingadonsa they can drag on [pres, potential] S20

zingafanele they are not suitable [stative, rel, neg; < **azifanele**] S25

zingagcina they could eventually, they could end up [pres, potential] S24

zingakhokheki they are unpayable [pres, rel, neg; < **azikhokheki**] S28

zingalingani they should not be the same [subjunc, neg] S15

zingama-boarding school they are (or it is) boarding schools [ident cop, pres] S23

zingangeni they should not enter [subjunc, neg] S27

zingaphandle they are outside [loc cop, pres] S20

zingaphezu kuka-R1mln they are above R1m [loc cop, pres] S10

zingaxazululeki they do not get resolved [pres, partic] S28

zingazange they have never [aux, past, rel, neg] S09

zingcolile they are dirty [stative] S09

-zingel-a hunt [v.i. & .t.] S24

zingena they come or go in, they enter [pres, conjoint] S20

zingenamakhaya not having homes [assoc cop, pres, rel, neg] S09

zingenamswakama they are not damp [assoc cop, pres, rel, neg] S20

zingenzeka they can happen, occur, take place [pres, potential] S28

zinhlobo types, sorts, kinds [< izinhlobo] S10

ziningi there are many [descr cop, pres] S13

zinjenge-HIV they are like HIV [descr cop, pres] S25

zinjongo [< izinjongo aims, purposes, resolutions; sg injongo q.v.] S28

zinkokheli leaders [< izinkokheli [n Cl. 10; deletion of init vowel due to preceding dem; sg inkokheli] S07

zinomqondo they having sense [assoc cop, pres, partic] S12

zinyathelo steps [< izinyathelo] S23

ziphakathi kuka- they are between [loc cop, pres] S20

-zi-phath-a behave (lit. carry oneself, hold oneself) [v-refl] S23

ziphathelene they go together, they concern, they relate to [stative] S16

ziphile they (should) live [subjunc] S09

-zi-philis-a keep oneself alive [v-refl-caus] S20

ziphinde they repeatedly VERB, they again VERB [aux] S09

ziphinde ziphile they should again live [v phr] S09

ziphuma they come from, they go out [pres, conjoint] S08

ziphume they should come out [subjunc] S11

ziphumelele they should succeed [subjunc] S04

-zi-phumulel-a rest for oneself, just rest [v-refl-appl] S07

-zi-phuzel-a pass with ease [idiom; v-refl-appl] S18

ziqala they are beginning, they begin [pres, conjoint] S08

ziqhamuka they come from [pres, conjoint] S23

ziqhelile they are remote [stative] S20

-zi-qheny-a be proud [v-refl] S14

ziqhubeke they proceed, they carry on [subjunc] S20

ziqondene na- ... they concern ... [stative] S25

ziqondile they are straight, direct, accurate [stative] S25

zisanda they have just [aux, pres, conjoint] S20

zisebenze they should work [subjunc] S19

zisemadolobheni they are in towns or cities [loc cop, pres] S16

zisemakhaya they are in rural areas [loc cop, pres] S24

zisetshenziselwa they are used or employed for [pres, conjoint] S19

zisetshenziswa they are used [pres, conjoint] S23

zishaye they have hit [past, partic, conjoint] S17

zishaye uhhide backed up, in a traffic jam (lit. having hit a long line) [idiom] S17

zishintshana they taking turns [pres, partic] S23

zishisa they being hot [pres, partic] S08

-zi-sol-a blame oneself, regret, be contrite, show remorse [v-refl] S18

zisuke they happen to, they just [aux] S24

zithandani lovers [< **izithandani**] S08

zithathe they take [subjunc] S09

zithathelana they are contagious [pres, conjoint] S20

zithathwa they are taken [pres, conjoint] S20

zithelele they spread among, the pour for, they scatter for [subjunc] S20

zithengisa they sell, they trade in [pres, conjoint] S27

zithengwa they are bought [pres, conjoint] S10

zithi they say [pres, conjoint] S23

zithinta they touch, handle, affect [pres, conjoint] S08

-zi-thob-a be humble [v-refl] S16

zithole they find [subjunc] S20

zithunyeliwe they have been sent for, they have been ordered [past, disjoint] S13

zithunyelwa they are sent [pres, conjoint] S28

-zi-tik-a overindulge, do in excess [v-refl] S11

zivakashe they visit [past, partic, conjoint] S24

zivalwa they are closed (down) [pres, conjoint] S28

zivalelwe they are imprisoned [stative, partic] S23

zivamise they generally [aux] S23

zivikele protect yourself [imper + OC] S20

zivuke they arose [past, conjoint] S12

ziwusizile they have assisted it [past, partic, disjoint] S24

ziya they go (to) [pres, conjoint] S13

ziyabathinta they influence (lit. touch) them [pres, disjoint] S19

ziyabelana they share among themselves [pres, disjoint] S09

ziyakulandela they follow you

[pres, disjoint] S28

ziyandiza they fly [pres, disjoint] S20

ziyangena they come or go in, they enter [pres, disjoint] S14

ziyanuka they smell [pres, disjoint] S09

ziyaphi? where do they go? [pres, conjoint] S13

ziyaphuma they come or go out, they exit [pres, disjoint] S14

ziyasihlupha they bother us [pres, disjoint] S09

ziyavikelana they stand up for one another, they protect one another [pres, disjoint] S09

ziyazenza they make them [pres, disjoint] S08

ziyenzeka they occur, happen, take place [pres, disjoint] S13

ziyingozi they are dangerous [ident cop, pres] S20

ziyiqembu they being a small group [ident cop, pres, partic] S09

ziyisebenzisele they use it for [subjunc] S09

ziyisibopho they are an obligation [ident cop, pres] S04

ziyisipesheli they are special [ident cop, pres] S10

ziyisithupha there are six of them [ident cop, pres] S20

ziyizinkangala they are deserted places [ident cop, pres] S23

ziza they coming [pres, partic] S17

zizalane they breed prolifically [subjunc] S20

zizathu reasons [< **izizathu**] S05

zizongiyeka they will leave me alone [fut] S23

zizozitika they should come and participate to the fullest [subjunc, venitive] S11

zizulazula roaming about homelessly [pres, partic] S09

zizwakala they are understandable [pres, conjoint] S12

-zi-zwel-a just hear, just feel, hear for yourself [v-refl-appl] S23

zo- [quant conc Cl. 8] S05

-zo- come to, come and [venitive marker] S03

zo- of [poss conc Cl. 8 coalesced with following **u**] S10, S07

zo them, they, their [abs pron Cl. 8 & 10] S05, S04

-zo- will, shall [fut pref] S04

zobunjiniyela of engineering [poss Cl. 8] S19

zocansi sexual [poss Cl. 10] S09

zokubanga of creating [poss Cl. 10] S09

zokubhala for writing [poss Cl. 10] S13

zokubhalela for writing in [poss Cl. 10] S13

zokudayiswa for marketing [poss Cl. 10] S12

zokufunda of reading, of study [poss Cl. 10] S13

zokufundela for studying in [poss Cl. 10] S13

zokuhamba for travel [poss Cl. 10] S20

zokuhlelwa of planning [poss Cl. 10] S25

zokulimala from getting injured [poss Cl. 8] S09

zokungcwaba of burying [poss Cl. 10] S21

zokuphatha of management or administration [poss Cl. 10] S14

zokuphathwa in or for the running, in the management [poss Cl. 8] S12

zokuqala first [poss Cl. 8] S10

zokuqasha of hiring, of employing [poss Cl. 10] S12

zokuthi of to say, of that [poss Cl. 10] S10

zokuvakasha of visiting [poss Cl. 10] S12

zokuyohlal' to go and live (lit. of going to live) [poss Cl. 8] S09

zokuzivikela of protecting oneself [poss Cl. 10] S20

zokwelapha of healing, health [poss Cl. 8] S19

zomfaniswano of uniformity [poss Cl. 10] S12

zomgwaqo of the road [poss Cl. 10] S08

zomsebenzi of jobs [poss Cl. 10] S19

zomshado of a wedding [poss Cl. 8] S17

zomthetho legal, of the law [poss Cl. 8] S28

zomthetho those of law [poss Cl. 10] S07

zomunye [poss Cl. 10] S16

-zond-a hate [v.t] S09

Zondi (surname) [n Cl. 1a] S27

zonke all, every [quant Cl. 8] S05

-zul-a wander, roam homelessly [v.i.] S09

-zulazul-a roam about homelessly [v-redup; < -zul-a] S09

Zulu (surname) [n Cl. 1a] S05

-zuz-a earn, achieve, acquire, obtain [v.t.] S12

-zw-a feel, hear, understand [v.t.; var -izw-a occurs after the vowel a] S09

-zwakal-a be audible, be felt, be experienced; be comprehesible, be understandable, be reasonable [v-neut; var -izwakal-a occurs after the vowel a] S08, S23

-zwakalis-a make audible, make heard, voice, express [v-neut-caus; var -izwakalis-a occurs after the vowel a] S21

-zwan-a hear one another, understand one another, get on together, communicate with one another; be addicted to, be very much inclined to [v-recip; var

-**izwan-a** occurs after the vowel **a**] S09

zwe country [< **izwe**] S25

-**zwel-a** hear for, feel for, feel sorry for, sympathize with [v-appl] S23

Zwelakhe (male name) [n Cl. 1a; < **izwe lakhe** his country] S11

Zwelithini (male name; name of the present King of the Zulu) [n Cl. 1a; < **izwe lithini?** what does the nation say?] S11